THE PREVENTION PRINCIPLE IN INTERNATIONAL ENVIRONMENTAL LAW

Prevention is recognized as a cornerstone of international environmental law, but this principle remains abstract and elusive in terms of exactly what is required of states to prevent environmental harm. In this illuminating work, Leslie-Anne Duvic-Paoli addresses this issue by offering a systematic, comprehensive assessment in which she clarifies the rationale, content and scope of the prevention principle while also placing it in a wider legal context. The book offers a detailed analysis of treaty law, custom codification works and case law before culminating in a conceptualization of prevention based on three definitional traits: (1) its anticipatory rationale, (2) its due-diligence content and (3) its wide spatial scope to protect the environment as a whole. This book should be read by anyone seeking to understand the evolving principle of prevention in international environmental law and how it increasingly shares common ground with reparation in the arena of compliance control.

Leslie-Anne Duvic-Paoli is Lecturer at the Dickson Poon School of Law, King's College London, and a fellow at the Cambridge Centre for Environment, Energy and Natural Resource Governance. Before joining King's College London, she was Philomathia Post-doctoral Research Associate in the Department of Land Economy at the University of Cambridge. Duvic-Paoli is a public international lawyer who researches and teaches in the fields of international environmental law and climate and energy law. She holds master's degrees from Sciences Po Paris and the University of Panthéon-Sorbonne, and a PhD from the Graduate Institute of International and Development Studies in Geneva.

Cambridge Studies on Environment, Energy and Natural Resource Governance

Cambridge Studies on Environment, Energy and Natural Resource Governance publishes foundational monographs of general interest to scholars and practitioners within the broadly defined fields of sustainable development policy, including studies on law, economics, politics, history, and policy. These fields currently attract unprecedented interest due to both the urgency of developing policies to address climate change, the energy transition, food security and water availability and, more generally, to the progressive realization of the impact of humans as a geological driver of the state of the Earth, now called the 'Anthropocene'.

The general editor of the series is Professor Jorge E. Viñuales, the Harold Samuel Chair of Law and Environmental Policy at the University of Cambridge and the Founder and First Director of the Cambridge Centre for Environment, Energy and Natural Resource Governance (C-EENRG).

The Prevention Principle in International Environmental Law

LESLIE-ANNE DUVIC-PAOLI
King's College London

CAMBRIDGE
UNIVERSITY PRESS

CAMBRIDGE
UNIVERSITY PRESS

University Printing House, Cambridge CB2 8BS, United Kingdom

One Liberty Plaza, 20th Floor, New York, NY 10006, USA

477 Williamstown Road, Port Melbourne, VIC 3207, Australia

314–321, 3rd Floor, Plot 3, Splendor Forum, Jasola District Centre, New Delhi – 110025, India

79 Anson Road, #06–04/06, Singapore 079906

Cambridge University Press is part of the University of Cambridge.

It furthers the University's mission by disseminating knowledge in the pursuit of education, learning, and research at the highest international levels of excellence.

www.cambridge.org
Information on this title: www.cambridge.org/9781108429412
DOI: 10.1017/9781108553728

First published 2018

Printed in the United Kingdom by Clays, St Ives plc.

A catalogue record for this publication is available from the British Library.

Library of Congress Cataloging-in-Publication Data
NAMES: Duvic-Paoli, Leslie-Anne, author.
TITLE: The prevention principle in international environmental law / Leslie-Anne Duvic-Paoli, King's College London.
DESCRIPTION: New York, NY : Cambridge University Press, 2018. | Includes bibliographical references.
IDENTIFIERS: LCCN 2017058248 | ISBN 9781108429412
SUBJECTS: LCSH: Environmental law, International. | Environmental policy.
CLASSIFICATION: LCC K3585 .D89 2018 | DDC 344.04/6–dc23
LC record available at https://lccn.loc.gov/2017058248

ISBN 978-1-108-42941-2 Hardback

Contents

Acknowledgements

The community of international lawyers is made up of inspiring scholars and practitioners dedicated to furthering the role of international law in an increasingly complex and unstable world. As I have had the privilege of working with some of them, this 'invisible college' of international lawyers has materialized to make a noticeable difference in my academic journey.

This book finds its origins in a doctoral dissertation written at the Graduate Institute of International and Development Studies in Geneva. I give my warmest thanks to my doctoral supervisor and mentor, Professor Jorge E. Viñuales, for his attentive support. He has always been extremely generous with his time and has given me precious advice regarding the twists and turns of an academic career. His enlightening supervision and insatiable enthusiasm for the topic have been invaluable. I hope this work lives up to the standard of the 'bigger picture' that is dear to his teaching and writings. I also thank Professor Andrea Bianchi, whose critical approach to international law (and life in general), combined with his delightful sense of humour, enlightened my doctoral journey. I must also express my profound appreciation to Professor Laurence Boisson de Chazournes, who spent some of her precious time sharing with me thoughtful advice on life as an academic or, more precisely, as a woman in academia. Finally, I also extend my gratitude to Professor Catherine Redgwell for the detailed feedback she gave on my work and from which this monograph greatly benefitted.

While at the Graduate Institute I had the privilege of working with a number of recognized professors in the field. In particular, I thank Professor Pierre-Marie Dupuy for his generosity – his wisdom and years of experience in the field of international law have been invaluable for an early-career academic such as me; and Professor Eibe Riedel for the many 'cakes and coffee' he shared with me. I hold dear the time spent with Professor Vera Gowlland-

Debbas and will remember her for her sincere kindness and love of teaching. My profound thanks also go to Professor Makane Moïse Mbengue with whom I have had the great pleasure of working at the University of Geneva: I deeply value our fruitful conversations regarding our different but, in reality, often converging perspectives on international law.

The Department of International Law at the Graduate Institute provided excellent working conditions, of which I am extremely appreciative. I have excellent memories of the two years I spent as a research assistant at the Centre on Conflict, Development and Peacebuilding. I am grateful to its staff for welcoming me at the beginning of my stay in Geneva and getting me acquainted with the intricacies of the Institute. I am also indebted to the staff of the Graduate Institute's library for their availability and responsiveness during those four years: it is no overstatement to say that the library is one of the best in the world for an international lawyer.

This book was finalized during the time I spent as a Philomathia Post-doctoral Research Associate in the Department of Land Economy at the University of Cambridge. I am most grateful to the Philomathia Foundation for supporting my research, which gave me what is often a luxury – time to mature my doctoral project and transform it into this study.

My thanks also go to my friends at the Graduate Institute, the University of Geneva, the University of Cambridge and worldwide for their constant support. The 'vie genevoise' would not have been the same without Zuzka, Sandra, Andreas, Emilie and Fabien, with whom I have explored Geneva, and without the daily support of my Villa Barton friends – Jason, Barrie and León.

Similarly, I will keep excellent memories of my time at Cambridge's David Attenborough Building and the time spent with my colleagues at the Cambridge Centre for Environment, Energy and Natural Resource Governance (C-EENRG). I particularly enjoyed working closely with my 'EP06' colleagues Pierre and Pablo. It is a very rewarding and stimulating experience to be surrounded by young and experienced researchers with different origins, experiences and specializations but who all share a passion for environmental issues.

I also extend my heartfelt thanks to several generations of LLM and MPhil students in Geneva and Cambridge with whom I have had the pleasure of sharing my enthusiasm for environmental law. In particular, I am most indebted to the whale-loving Darshika, who has so kindly proofread my work, and to Carlos for his invaluable help in the last stages of my doctoral journey.

It goes without saying that I thank Lucile for her decisive support and unrestrained generosity during the intellectual journey we started together during our Master's degree study in Paris. Between sharing existential doubts and moments of pure laughter, there has never been a dull instant in Geneva thanks to her. Special thanks also go to Michael for his encouragements in writing a 'book', to Raphael for our international law investigations and to Steven for the weekends spent discovering new cities.

Finally, I owe enormous gratitude to my family for their continuous support. It is perhaps no coincidence that I am passionate about maritime affairs and environmental issues when my family nourishes strong links with island life – close or afar. My thanks go to my father, whose knowledge of politics and world issues has undoubtedly spurred my interest in international relations. I am also most grateful to my mother, who has transmitted her curiosity for the unknown and her passion for travelling. To everyone – *un grand merci*.

Abbreviations

AB	Appellate Body
ARSIWA	International Law Commission's Articles on the Responsibility of States for Internationally Wrongful Acts
ASEAN	Association of Southeast Asian Nations
BAT	Best available techniques/technologies
CBD	Convention on Biological Diversity
CBDR(-RC)	Common but differentiated responsibilities (and respective capabilities)
CITES	Convention on International Trade of Endangered Species of Wild Fauna and Flora
CJEU	Court of Justice of the European Union
COP	Conference of the Parties
CSD	Commission on Sustainable Development
CTS	Consolidated Treaty Series
ECHR	European Convention on Human Rights
ECJ	European Court of Justice
ECOSOC	UN Economic and Social Council
EIA	Environmental impact assessment
ECtHR	European Court of Human Rights
EPL	Environmental policy and law
EU	European Union
FAO	Food and Agriculture Organization
FET	Fair and equitable treatment
G22	Group of 22
G77	Group of 77
GATT	General Agreement on Tariffs and Trade
HCB	Hexachlorobenzene
HRC	Human Rights Council

IAEA	International Atomic Energy Agency
ICJ	International Court of Justice
IAmCommHR	Inter-American Commission on Human Rights
IAmCtHR	Inter-American Court on Human Rights
IDI	Institut de droit international
IELMT	International Environmental Legal Materials and Treaties
IELR	International Environmental Law Reports
ILA	International Law Association
ILC	International Law Commission
ILM	International Legal Materials
IMCO	International Maritime Consultative Organization
IMO	International Maritime Organization
IPCC	Intergovernmental Panel on Climate Change
IPE	International Protection of the Environment: Treaties and Related Documents
ISBA	International Seabed Authority
ITLOS	International Tribunal for the Law of the Sea
IUCN	International Union for Conservation of Nature
IWG	Intergovernmental Working Group
LNTS	League of Nations Treaty Series
LRTAP	Convention on Long-Range Transboundary Air Pollution
MEA	Multilateral environmental agreement
MPA	Marine protected area
NAFTA	North American Free Trade Agreement
NCP	Non-compliance procedure
NGO	Non-governmental organization
OECD	Organization for Economic Co-operation and Development
OJ	*Official Journal of the European Union*
ORIL	*Oxford Reports on International Law*
PC	Preparatory Committee
PCA	Permanent Court of Arbitration
PIC	Prior informed consent
POPs	Persistent organic pollutants
RIAA	Reports of International Arbitral Awards
SCS	South China Sea
SPS	Sanitary and phyto-sanitary measures
SRFC	Sub-Regional Fisheries Commission
TFEU	Treaty on the Functioning of the EU

UN	United Nations
UNCC	UN Compensation Commission
UNCCUR	United Nations Conference on the Conservation and Utilization of Resources
UNCED	UN Conference on Environment and Development
UNCLOS	UN Convention on the Law of the Sea
UNECE	UN Economic Commission for Europe
UNEP	UN Environment Programme
UNESCO	UN Educational, Scientific and Cultural Organization
UNFCCC	UN Framework Convention on Climate Change
UNGA	UN General Assembly
UNTS	UN Treaty Series
UNSC	UN Security Council
WCED	World Commission on Environment and Development
WTO	World Trade Organization

Table of Treaties

2013

Minamata Convention on Mercury, Kumamoto, 10 October 2013, in force 16 August 2017, available at: www.mercuryconvention.org/ 209

2015

Paris Agreement to the United Nations Framework Convention on Climate Change, Paris, 12 December 2015, in force 4 November 2016, Doc. FCCC/CP/2015/10/Add.1 190, 195, 291, 331

Table of Cases

Permanent Court of International Justice

International Court of Justice

International Tribunal for the Law of the Sea

Inter-State arbitration

GATT/WTO Dispute Settlement

Investment arbitration tribunals

European Court of Human Rights

Inter-American Court of Human Rights

African Commission on Human and Peoples' Rights

Human Rights Committee

European Court of Justice

Non-compliance procedures

United Nations Compensation Commission

Domestic case-law

Introduction

PREVENTION AS THE CORNERSTONE OF INTERNATIONAL ENVIRONMENTAL LAW

International environmental law is based on the will to avoid causing harm to the environment. It is widely admitted – following the old adagio 'prevention is better than cure' – that the protection of the environment is best ensured by preventing harm from occurring rather than by repairing the damage. The specificity of environmental harm dictates a preventive approach: damage to the environment is often irreversible,[1] and restoration of the situation prevailing prior to harm is often impossible[2] or involves very high costs.[3]

The preventive rationale was first consecrated in international law in the form of a prohibition to cause harm to the territory of another State, as recognized in 1941 by the landmark *Trail Smelter* award.[4] It then consolidated in international law in the form of Principle 21 of the 1972 Stockholm Declaration on the Human Environment (Stockholm Declaration) that formulated the principle in a manner that entailed, at the time, a significant degree of progressive development.

> States have, in accordance with the Charter of the United Nations and the principles of international law, the sovereign right to exploit their own resources pursuant to their own environmental policies, and the responsibility to ensure that activities within their jurisdiction or control do not cause

1 *Gabčíkovo-Nagymaros Project (Hungary/Slovakia)* (Judgment) (1997) ICJ Rep 7, para 140.

2 International Law Commission (ILC), 'Draft Articles on Prevention of Transboundary Harm from Hazardous Activities (with Commentaries)' (2001) *Yearbook of the International Law Commission* (vol II, part 2) 148, Commentaries to the Articles, para 2, at 148.

3 J Strasser, 'Preventing Pollution' (1997) 8 *Fordham Environmental Law Review* 1, at 7.

4 *Trail Smelter (United States v. Canada)* (16 April 1938 and 11 March 1941), (1941) 3 RIAA 1905.

> damage to the environment of other States or of areas beyond the limits of national jurisdiction.[5]

This formulation was eventually admitted, in its entirety, as an expression of customary international law in the 1990s.[6] Despite its customary status, the legal principle of prevention remains abstract and elusive regarding what is required from States, or what they are entitled to, in order to prevent environmental harm.[7]

Until now, prevention has found itself in a paradoxical situation: defined as the 'golden'[8] principle of international environmental law, it is considered to be an axiom in environmental law but tends not to be investigated further. This is surprising because principles generally benefit from a 'high profile' in international environmental law.[9] However, prevention has been sidetracked by discussions – among decision-makers, judges and scholars – on precaution[10] or sustainable development,[11] which are largely considered to

[5] Declaration of the United Nations Conference on the Human Environment (Stockholm, 16 June 1972), (1972) 11 ILM 1416, Principle 21.

[6] *Legality of the Threat or Use of Nuclear Weapons* (Advisory Opinion) (1996) ICJ Rep 226, para 29.

[7] J Vessey, 'The Principle of Prevention in International Law' (1998) 3 *Austrian Review of International and European Law* 181, at 183; J Knox, 'Myth and Reality of Transboundary Environmental Impact Assessment' (2002) 96 *American Journal of International Law* 291, at 292.

[8] N de Sadeleer, *Environmental Principles: From Political Slogans to Legal Rules* (Oxford University Press 2002) 89; A Kiss and J-P Beurier, *Droit international de l'environnement* (4th edn, Pedone 2010) 152; United Nations Environment Programme, *Training Manual on International Environmental Law* (UNEP 2006) 32. Similarly, some authors consider prevention to be the 'cornerstone of international environmental law': A Kiss and D Shelton, *International Environmental Law* (3rd edn, Transnational Publishers 2004) 113; P Sands and J Peel, *Principles of International Environmental Law* (3rd edn, Cambridge University Press 2012) 191.

[9] E Scotford, *Environmental Principles and the Evolution of Environmental Law* (Bloomsbury 2017) 5.

[10] In comparison to the limited number of works on prevention, there is a plethora of publications on precaution: see, among many others, the following books: E Fisher, J Jones and R von Schomberg (eds), *Implementing the Precautionary Principle: Perspectives and Prospects* (Edward Elgar 2006); C Foster, *Science and the Precautionary Principle in International Courts and Tribunals: Expert Evidence, Burden of Proof and Finality* (Cambridge University Press 2011); D Freestone and E Hey, *The Precautionary Principle and International Law: The Challenge of Implementation* (Kluwer 1996); J Peel, *The Precautionary Principle in Practice* (Federation Press 2005); J Peel, *Science and Risk Regulation in International Law* (Cambridge University Press 2010); A Trouwborst, *Evolution and Status of the Precautionary Principle in International Law* (Kluwer 2002); A Trouwborst, *Precautionary Rights and Duties of States* (Martinus Nijhoff 2006).

[11] The literature on sustainable development is similarly well developed; see e.g. and only referencing books, V Barral, *Le développement durable en droit international: Essai sur les*

be more topical norms. Tellingly, on occasion, the prevention principle is sometimes equated with the precautionary approach[12] or included in the concept of sustainable development.[13]

And yet, a better understanding of the prevention principle is essential to clarifying the duties that States (as well as other subjects of international law) have under customary international law[14] and determining the meaning of provisions appearing in environmental, and other, treaties[15] – interpreted in the light of customary law[16] or preambular

incidences juridiques d'une norme évolutive (Bruylant 2016); A Boyle, *International Law and Sustainable Development: Past Achievements and Future Challenges* (Oxford University Press 1999); W Lang, *Sustainable Development and International Law* (Graham & Trotman 1995); N Schrijver, 'The Evolution of Sustainable Development in International Law: Inception, Meaning and Status' (2008) 329 *Collected Courses of the Hague Academy of International Law* 215–370; J Verschuuren, *Principles of Environmental Law: The Ideal of Sustainable Development and the Role of Principles of International, European, and National Environmental Law* (Nomos 2003).

12 On the convergence between precaution and prevention, see e.g. P Birnie, A Boyle and C Redgwell, *International Law and the Environment* (3rd edn, Oxford University Press 2009) 137*ff*, focusing on an obligation of 'prevention of pollution and environmental harm' that includes a precautionary approach; E Louka, *International Environmental Law: Fairness, Effectiveness, and World Order* (Cambridge University Press 2006) 50, considering the 'principles of preventive action and precaution' together. See also M Fitzmaurice, 'International Protection of the Environment' (2001) 293 *Collected Courses of the Hague Academy of International Law* 9–488, chap V, on 'the elements of [the] preventive approach' but starting with an analysis of precaution.

13 P Sands, 'International Law in the Field of Sustainable Development: Emerging Legal Principles', in W Lang (ed), *Sustainable Development and International Law* (Graham & Trotman, Martinus Nijhoff 1995) 53–72, at 62, recognizing Principle 21 and the principle of preventive action as two principles of international law relating to sustainable development; H Trudeau, 'Preventive Action Principle', in J-F Morin and A Orsini A (eds), *Essential Concepts of Global Environmental Governance* (Routledge 2014) 163: 'The principle of preventive action is associated with the concept of sustainable development.' See also the ambiguity in S Palassis, 'Beyond the Global Summits: Reflecting on the Environmental Principles of Sustainable Development' (2011) 22 *Colorado Journal of International Environmental Law and Policy* 41, at 60 and 62, presenting the obligation to prevent as part of the analysis of State practice relative to sustainable development.

14 See *Trail Smelter*, at 1965; *Nuclear Weapons Advisory Opinion*, para 29; *Gabčíkovo-Nagymaros*, para 140; *Pulp Mills on the River Uruguay* (*Argentina v. Uruguay*) (Judgment) (2010) ICJ Rep 14, para 101; *Responsibilities and Obligations of States Sponsoring Persons and Entities with Respect to Activities in the Area*, ITLOS No. 17, Advisory Opinion (1 February 2011); ILC, 'Draft Articles on Prevention of Transboundary Harm', 148.

15 *Gabčíkovo-Nagymaros*, para 140; *Iron Rhine Railway (Belgium v. Netherlands)*, Permanent Court of Arbitration, (2005) 27 RIAA 35, para 59; *Pulp Mills*, para 204; *Indus Waters Kishenganga Arbitration (Pakistan v. India)*, Permanent Court of Arbitration, Partial Award, 18 February 2013, para 452, and Final Award, 20 December 2013, para 111.

16 Vienna Convention on the Law of Treaties, Vienna, 23 May 1969, in force 27 January 1980, 1155 UNTS 331, Article 31(3)(c).

language.[17] Legal commentary has only undertaken such analysis on a fragmented basis, concentrating on the law applicable to one particular environmental medium, such as the atmosphere and the climate,[18] the marine environment[19] or international watercourses.[20] It has, however, remained shy of offering a more comprehensive assessment of prevention under international environmental law as a whole, which is necessary to determine the scope of the general customary duty of prevention and to facilitate a systemic interpretation of treaties.[21] The clarity brought to prevention will also reverberate on other norms of international environmental law, as a sharper understanding of its applicable scope will provide further clarity on the definitional traits of other norms with which it is often intertwined. Significantly, prevention covers a large number of the measures that are often analysed through the lenses of the much more controversial precautionary norm.[22] Also, it has sufficient legal density to translate the sustainable development concept or programme through its substantive and procedural extensions, including the duties to cooperate and to conduct a prior environmental impact assessment (EIA).[23]

More generally, the principle is called to play an increasingly important role at a time when environmental degradation is leading to changes to the Earth's systems that are 'unprecedented in human history'.[24] The warning has become so widely recognized that nowadays it even sounds banal, despite the strong terms used in major reports and publications. As one reads in the latest *Global Environmental Outlook* published by the United Nations, we are currently

17 Marrakesh Agreement Establishing the World Trade Organization, 15 April 1994, 1867 UNTS 154, Preamble; *United States – Import Prohibition of Certain Shrimp and Shrimp Products*, Report of the Appellate Body, 12 October 1998, WT/DS58/AB/R, paras 60, 129 and 131; *Whaling in the Antarctic (Australia v. Japan: New Zealand intervening)* (Judgment) (2014) ICJ Rep 226, paras 56 and 58.

18 P Okowa, *State Responsibility for Transboundary Air Pollution in International Law* (Oxford University Press 2000); R Verheyen, *Climate Change Damage and International Law: Prevention Duties and State Responsibility* (Martinus Nijhoff 2005).

19 B Smith, *State Responsibility and the Marine Environment: The Rules of Decision* (Clarendon Press 1988).

20 O McIntyre, *Environmental Protection of International Watercourses Under International Law* (Ashgate 2007); SC McCaffrey, *The Law of International Watercourses* (2nd edn, Oxford University Press 2007).

21 Vienna Convention on the Law of Treaties, Article 31(3)(c).

22 *Pulp Mills*, separate opinion of Judge Cançado Trindade, para 61, on the close relationship between prevention and precaution.

23 *Pulp Mills*, para 77.

24 UNEP, *Global Environmental Outlook 5: Environment for the Future We Want. Summary for Policy-Makers* (2012), available at www.unep.org/geo/sites/unep.org.geo/files/documents/geo5_spm_english.pdf (last accessed 19 May 2017), at v.

witnessing 'irreversible changes to the life-support functions of the planet ... with significant adverse implications for human well-being'.[25] In this context, more clarity on the applicable scope (material, temporal and spatial) of prevention is essential to understand how the principle can drive international legislative processes and be relied upon in international and national dispute-settlement mechanisms. At the same time, this study will bring to light the existence of intrinsic tensions within the international legal system between, on the one hand, a willingness, grounded in the realization that the international community shares common values and interests, to protect the environment – taking the form of prevention in its most advanced manifestation – and, on the other hand, intrinsic limitations relative to the structure of a system originally designed to facilitate inter-State relations, evidenced by the inability of prevention in its advanced form to express its legal effects fully.

THE TRAJECTORY OF PREVENTION

This study provides a systematic and comprehensive assessment of the state of international law in relation to the prevention of environmental harm.[26] It seeks to clarify the *ratio legis*, scope and content of the prevention principle by placing it in its wider legal context. The project is based on the premise that the specificity of the prevention principle is best understood when it is put in perspective with the traditional route generally taken by international law in the face of harm: reparation. This work demonstrates that while prevention emerged and developed as an alternative to reparation and found a distinct legal expression based on three definitional traits, the preventive and curative approaches increasingly share common grounds in the concept of compliance control.

To do so, the analysis follows a dual approach: a historical perspective that depicts the evolution of the principle to understand how it achieved its current form and how it could develop further and a conceptual perspective that offers a cartography of the current state of the law pertaining to prevention and identifies its definitional traits. The following remarks explain these two contributions in turn, starting with its historical approach.

This study takes the reader on a journey through international environmental law via the lenses of a concept that has significant influence in the field. The choice of an evolutionary perspective rests on the conviction that the best way to understand the specificity of prevention is to look at its

[25] UNEP, *Global Environmental Outlook* 5.
[26] The law stated in this study is as of 15 September 2017.

emergence, evolution and consolidation as a distinct norm. International environmental law, as a relatively new branch of law, is fast moving, and its norms (prevention being no exception) evolve rapidly in light of new technological advances, socio-economic objectives and scientific knowledge. If the approach taken by this study might be coined historical, it is not one that divides the field into precisely dated periods,[27] nor one that seeks to offer a new, radical perspective on the branch.[28] Rather, it concentrates on the paradigm shift in societal values that eventually led to the consecration of an international response unique to environmental damage, taking the form of the principle of prevention.

An evolutionary outlook on prevention leads to a simple, yet important conclusion: the prevention principle in international environmental law has emerged as an alternative, and specialized, norm that operates in contrast with the curative approach that generally drives international law. This comment calls for a brief explanation of what is meant by 'reparation' in this context. Reparation is understood broadly as the expression of an ex post approach to harm. Concretely, reparation can take different forms, made available under the law of State responsibility.[29] However, this analysis conceives of reparation more extensively, not only as specific legal options in the case of an internationally wrongful act but also, more generally, as a reactive response to the occurrence of harm.

Although the study uses reparation to contrast prevention with the rationale against which it emerged, it puts the emphasis on risks, and their anticipation, in opposition to harm and its legal consequences. This is not to say that analysing environmental harm from a curative angle is irrelevant. By contrast, it has actually attracted strong scholarly attention: the large majority of doctrinal works has concentrated on how the law of State responsibility could, or could not, apply to harm to the

[27] For a description of the evolution of international environmental law separated into distinct periods, see e.g. PH Sand, 'The Evolution of International Environmental Law', in D Bodansky, J Brunnée and E Hey (eds), *The Oxford Handbook of International Environmental Law* (Oxford University Press 2007) 29–44, where he divides international environmental law into the three following phases: the traditional era (until 1970), the modern era (1970–92) and the post-modern era (post-Rio). See also E Brown Weiss, 'The Evolution of International Environmental Law' (2011) 54 *Japanese Yearbook of International Law* 1, where she makes the same distinctions.

[28] See e.g. S Humphreys and Y Otomo, 'Theorising International Environmental Law', in A Orford and F Hoffman (eds), *The Oxford Handbook of International Legal Theory* (Oxford University Press 2016) 797–819.

[29] ILC, 'Draft Articles on Responsibility of States for Internationally Wrongful Acts (with Commentaries)' (2001) *Yearbook of the International Law Commission* (vol II, part 2) 31, Article 34.

environment.[30] A certain fascination with the topic is identifiable in the wealth of legal commentary on the *Trail Smelter* arbitration – often considered the backbone of environmental responsibility and the source of prevention.[31] Similarly, the work of the International Law Commission (ILC) on the topic of 'liability for injurious consequences of acts not prohibited by international law' and, more specifically, the difficulties it faced

[30] See e.g. and not mentioning the multitude of articles on the topic, P-M Dupuy, *La Responsabilité internationale des Etats pour les dommages d'origine technologique et industrielle* (Pedone 1977); F Francioni and T Scovazzi (eds), *International Responsibility for Environmental Harm* (Graham & Trotman 1991); R Lefeber, *Transboundary Environmental Interference and the Origin of State Liability* (Kluwer Law International 1996); P Wetterstein and A Rosas (eds), *Harm to the Environment: The Right to Compensation and the Assessment of Damages* (Clarendon Press 1997); M-L Larsson, *The Law of Environmental Damage: Liability and Reparation* (Martinus Nijhoff 1999); P Okowa, *State Responsibility for Transboundary Air Pollution in International Law* (Oxford University Press 2000); E Brans, *Liability for Damage to Public Natural Resources: Standing, Damage and Damage Assessment* (Kluwer Law International 2001); G Cordini and A Postiglione A (eds), *Prevention and Remedying of Environmental Damage: Proceedings of the Workshop on Environmental Law, Ostia Antica, 27 and 28 May 2005* (Bruylant 2005); P Minnerop, C Langenfeld and R Wolfrum (eds), *Environmental Liability in International Law: Towards A Coherent Conception* (Schmidt 2005); M Hinteregger (ed), *Environmental Liability and Ecological Damage in European Law* (Cambridge University Press 2008); H Xue, *Transboundary Damage in International Law* (Cambridge University Press 2009); T Hardman Reis, *Compensation for Environmental Damages Under International Law: The Role of the International Judge* (Kluwer Law International 2011). In relation to the scholarship on prevention, see the following study that analyses it from the perspective of the law of State responsibility: LE Borges, *Les obligations de prévention dans le droit international de l'environnement et ses conséquences dans la responsabilité internationale des Etats* (L'Harmattan 2016), presenting prevention, but from the angle of responsibility and liability.

[31] A Kuhn, 'The *Trail Smelter* Arbitration: United States and Canada' (1941) 35 *American Journal of International Law* 665; JE Read, 'The *Trail Smelter* Dispute' (1963) 1 *Canadian Yearbook of International Law* 213; D Dinwoodie, 'The Politics of International Pollution Control: The *Trail Smelter* Case' (1972) 27 *International Journal* 219; A Rubin, 'Pollution by Analogy: The *Trail Smelter* Arbitration' (1970) 50 *Oregon Law Review* 259; K Michelson, 'Rereading *Trail Smelter*' (1993) 31 *Canadian Yearbook of International Law* 219; J Wirth, *Smelter Smoke in North America: The Politics of Transborder Pollution* (University Press of Kansas 2000); R Bratspies and R Miller (eds), *Transboundary Harm in International Law: Lessons from the 'Trail Smelter' Arbitration* (Cambridge University Press 2006). Commenting on the importance that the dispute has taken in the international legal imaginary, see A Rubin, 'Pollution by Analogy: The *Trail Smelter* Arbitration' (1970) 50 *Oregon Law Review* 259, at 259 noting that '[e]very discussion of the general international law relating to pollution starts, and must end, with a mention of the *Trail Smelter* Arbitration between the United States and Canada'. See also E Brown Weiss et al., *International Environmental Law and Policy* (Aspen 1998) 330, who writes that '[e]verybody loves *Trail Smelter*'; D French, '*Trail Smelter*', in C Miles and E Bjorge (eds), *Landmark Cases in Public International Law* (Hart 2018) 153–88, on the creation of the *Trail Smelter* 'myth'.

in framing the issue have led to a profusion of critical comments.[32] However, this study is not primarily concerned with understanding how prevention operates within a curative framework but rather seeks to identify the essence of prevention that lies in its opposition to ex post approaches to harm. However, it leaves little doubt that the relationship between prevention and responsibility/liability is a close one; it will, indeed, be by comparing and contrasting prevention to the traditional curative approach that the characteristics of prevention will be laid bare.

THE CONCEPTUALIZATION OF PREVENTION

The historical perspective culminates in a conceptualization of prevention that puts in evidence the definitional elements that characterize prevention. Prevention has outgrown the mere conception of no-harm to reach a more advanced form characterized by three distinct features. The specificity of prevention lies in its rationale, content and spatial scope.

1. **Rationale.** Prevention is an anticipatory principle that seeks to avoid foreseeable risks. It operates distinctively from the curative approach that international law traditionally adopts to respond to wrongful acts and seeks to avoid the creation of harm in the first place.
2. **Content.** Prevention requires that States (and other subjects) exercise due diligence in the face of environmental risks. As such, States are not merely expected to exercise restraint vis-à-vis environmental harm but are required to take positive steps to protect the environment.
3. **Spatial Scope.** Prevention seeks to protect the environment irrespective of the location of the occurrence of harm. The principle moved away from the traditional concept of good neighbourliness concerned with

[32] See *inter alia* A Boyle, 'State Responsibility and International Liability for Injurious Consequences of Acts Not Prohibited by International Law: A Necessary Distinction?' (1990) 39 *International and Comparative Law Quarterly* 1; G Handl, 'Liability as an Obligation Established by a Primary Rule of International Law: Some Basic Reflections on the International Law Commission's Work' (1985) 16 *Netherlands Yearbook of International Law* 49; J Barboza, 'International Liability for the Injurious Consequences of Acts Not Prohibited by International Law and Protection of the Environment' (1994) 247 *Collected Courses of the Hague Academy of International Law* 291–406; F Orrego Vicuña, 'Responsibility and Liability for Environmental Damage under International Law: Issues and Trends' (1997) 10 *Georgetown International Environmental Law Review* 279; A Pellet, 'Les Articles de la CDI sur la responsabilité de l'État pour fait internationalement illicite. Suite – et fin?' (2002) 48 *Annuaire français de droit international* 1; J Barboza, *The Environment, Risk and Liability in International Law* (Martinus Nijhoff 2011).

preserving territorial sovereignties to recognize environmental protection as an objective in itself.

The combination of the definitional traits of prevention leads to the conclusion that, in its advanced manifestation, prevention takes the form of a general positive obligation to anticipate risks to protect the environment. This inference warrants three preliminary comments. Firstly, the historical and conceptual map offered to the reader makes explicit the topography of the law applicable in the context of environmental protection. By extracting a legal cartography from a complex web of norms, standards and practices that are all manifestations of the principle of prevention, it necessarily leaves aside some asperities, ambiguities and exceptions that surface when the analysis is undertaken at a more micro level. However, as mentioned previously, an understanding of prevention at a more macro level is essential given the increasing role of the customary form of prevention,[33] as well as the density of international law applicable to the environment that facilitates a systemic interpretation of environmental and other treaties.[34] Similarly, if the study operates on the basis of the dichotomy between prevention and reparation, it will also reveal that the dynamics between the two rationales are more complex than they might first appear. Indeed, this study will show that they interact in a multiplicity of ways, hence building a dialectic between the two that contributes to their concomitant evolution, and that the boundaries between the two rationales are becoming not only more permeable but also are evolving and extending in new ways.

Secondly, a word ought to be said regarding the trajectory of the norm depicted in this study. The objective is to provide a historical and conceptual map to offer an analytical framework that clarifies the rationale and scope of the principle of prevention. This should not tempt the reader to understand that the evolution of the concept has been linear, with a 'clear underlying sense of purpose and direction'.[35] Indeed, the evolution of the principle of prevention has not been sequential.[36] Prevention might have outgrown its initial, more basic expressions as it evolved into its advanced form, but in so

33 See e.g. *Certain Activities Carried out by Nicaragua in the Border Area (Costa Rica v. Nicaragua)* and *Construction of a Road in Costa Rica Along the San Juan River (Nicaragua v. Costa Rica)* (Judgment) (2015) ICJ Rep 665, relying mostly on customary obligations and paying little attention to conventional duties.

34 See e.g. *South China Sea Arbitration (The Republic of the Philippines v. The People's Republic of China)* (Permanent Court of Arbitration), Award on the Merits, 12 July 2016, para 942.

35 B Fassbender and A Peters, 'Introduction', in B Fassbender and A Peters (eds), *The Oxford Handbook of the History of International Law* (Oxford University Press 2012) 2.

36 C Redgwell, 'Transboundary Pollution: Principles, Policy and Practice', in S Jayakumar et al. (eds), *Transboundary Pollution: Evolving Issues of International Law and Policy* (Edward Elgar 2015) 11–35, at 12.

doing it did not deny the relevance of its past expressions; rather, different, and partial, manifestations of the principle of prevention coexist. The complexity of this evolution is evidenced by an intricate question that divides the scholarship, that is, the relationship between prevention and the prohibition to cause transboundary harm. Indeed, some commentators consider that the two are equivalent,[37] while others rely on the assumption that prevention is a broader norm.[38] This analysis will clarify this relationship, demonstrating that because prevention finds its origins in the no-harm rule, it still integrates it to varying degrees. However, it will also show that prevention is characterized by its own rationale and scope and thus has evolved beyond the no-harm rule. It can be deemed to be a more modern, or progressive, norm due to its anticipatory rationale and interest in environmental protection per se, in comparison to no-harm, which, by concentrating on the avoidance of wrongful acts with the view to preserving territorial sovereignties, operates on a more traditional basis. Essentially, prevention, although it includes the no-harm rule, is more than no-harm.

A third, and related, comment pertains to prevention being conceptualized as an anticipatory principle of due diligence that aims to protect the environment. It should not hide the fact that prevention manifests in a multiplicity of forms and that only in its most advanced form does prevention fully meet all these criteria. In addition, even when prevention manifests in its most advanced form, this does not necessarily mean that its definitional traits,

[37] See e.g. U Beyerlin, 'Different Types of Norms in International Environmental Law', in D Bodansky, J Brunnée and E Hey (eds), *The Oxford Handbook of International Environmental Law* (Oxford University Press 2007) 425–48, at 439; G Handl, 'Transboundary Impacts', in D Bodansky, J Brunnée and E Hey (eds), *The Oxford Handbook of International Environmental Law* (Oxford University Press 2007) 531–50, at 539; U Beyerlin and T Marauhn, *International Environmental Law* (Hart 2011) 40–41.

[38] See e.g. Kiss and Shelton, *Guide to International Environmental Law*, 113–14: 'The duty of prevention also clearly emerges from the international responsibility not to cause significant damage to the environment extra-territorially, but the preventive principle seeks to avoid harm irrespective of whether or not there are transboundary impacts'; A Trouwborst, 'Prevention, Precaution, Logic and Law: The Relationship between the Precautionary Principle and the Preventative Principle in International Law and Associated Questions' (2009) 2 *Erasmus Law Review* 105, at 111: 'Specifically, the preventative principle should be told apart from the duty of States to avoid transboundary environmental harm'. See also A Kiss and J-P Beurier, *Droit international de l'environnement* (4th edn, Pedone 2010) 152; L Boisson de Chazournes and S Maljean-Dubois, 'Principes du droit international de l'environnement' (2011) *Jurisclasseur Environnement et Développement Durable* (LexisNexis), paras 11–18 ('principe d'utilisation non dommagable du territoire') and paras 60–63 ('principe de prévention des dommages'); Sands and Peel, *Principles of International Environmental Law*, 200; Louka, *International Environmental Law*, 50; T Koivurova, *Introduction to International Environmental Law* (Routledge 2014) 109; P-M Dupuy and JE Viñuales, *International Environmental Law* (Cambridge University Press 2015) 55.

such as, for instance, its *erga omnes* character[39] or its application in a purely domestic context,[40] are fully able to express their legal consequences or that they do not come with significant legal uncertainties.

TERMINOLOGICAL CLARIFICATIONS

The terminology used in this study and, most specifically, its title ought to be clarified. The reference to 'international environmental law' is used throughout this book as a conceptual help to refer to international law pertaining to the environment: the term is used for convenience to bring under the same heading the questions gravitating around the topic of environmental protection.[41] It should not be understood to refer to a closed legal system but is very much conceived of as being part of international law as a whole.[42] A short additional remark should be made about why prevention is being referred to as a 'principle'. Use of the term could be said to reproduce a general trend in environmental law that generously refers to any type of environmental norm as a 'principle'.[43] However, a more specific analysis of the forms of normativity displayed by prevention will be undertaken towards the end of this study to justify this choice. Generally speaking, this study uses the term 'principle' with the objective to bring to light the flexibility of the norm in fulfilling different roles in the international legal system. It thus distinguishes itself from studies on transboundary harm that understand prevention merely as a primary rule of obligation and perceives of prevention as a principle in the sense of a guiding norm that drives the entire branch of international environmental law.

STRUCTURE OF THIS STUDY

This book is composed of four sections that take on and develop in detail the ideas outlined in this Introduction. Part I concentrates on the emergence of

39 See Section 11.2.3. 40 See Section 8.3.

41 Such is the position of P Weil, 'Le droit international en quête de son identité: cours général de droit international public' (1992) 237 *Collected Courses of the Hague Academy of International Law* 9–370, at 93, in relation to international economic law.

42 A Boyle, 'Relationship between International Environmental Law and Other Branches of International Law', in D Bodansky, J Brunnée and E Hey (eds), *The Oxford Handbook of International Environmental Law* (Oxford University Press 2007) 125–46, at 126–7, noting that international environmental law is a 'convenient label, which helps us locate what we think we are talking about as lawyers'.

43 On the overwhelming presence of principles in international environmental law, see Section 10.1.

prevention by identifying the intellectual origins of prevention in two complementary approaches to environmental harm (Chapter 1) and presenting the contextual factors that led to a paradigm shift in the 1960s in the international law applicable to natural resources and the environment from reparation to prevention, which was eventually crystallized in 1972 in the form of Stockholm Principle 21 (Chapter 2). Part II provides a detailed survey of the manifestations of prevention in treaty law (Chapter 3), custom codification works (Chapter 4) and case law (Chapter 5) since its formulation in the Stockholm Declaration.[44] The historical and normative analysis culminates in proposing a conceptualization of prevention in Part III that identifies its specificities expressed in the form of its rationale, content and spatial scope. Specifically, prevention is characterized by its anticipatory rationale (Chapter 6); its nature as a due-diligence obligation, requiring States to act proactively in the face of environmental risks (Chapter 7); and finally, its concern for the protection of the environment per se, irrespective of the location of the harm (Chapter 8). After having analysed the distinctive characteristics of prevention, Chapter 9 situates prevention in its broader legal context by looking at its relationship with other environmental norms. Finally, Part IV analyses the current trends contributing to the further consolidation of the norm in contemporary international law. To do so, it first presents the consequences of prevention's definitional traits for its role and place in the international legal order (Chapter 10). It ends the study by examining the ways in which prevention is evolving in relation to the rationale against which it originally emerged – reparation – and identifies how the curative approach has, to some extent, been absorbed by the preventive logic in the context of non-compliance procedures (Chapter 11).

[44] Small sections of this and other parts build on already published work: L-A Duvic-Paoli and JE Viñuales, 'Principle 2', in JE Viñuales (ed), *The Rio Declaration on Environment and Development: A Commentary* (Oxford University Press 2015) 107–38' and L-A Duvic-Paoli, 'Prevention and the Anticipation of Risk(s) in International Environmental Law: A Multifaceted Norm', in M Ambrus, R Rayfuse and W Werner (eds), *Conceptions of Risk and the Regulation of Uncertainty in International Law* (Oxford University Press 2017) 141–60.

PART I

FROM REPARATION TO PREVENTION

International Environmental Law through the Lenses of Prevention

This part concentrates on the paradigm shift that resulted in a drastic change of rationale in the law applicable to natural resources and the environment and led to the consecration of prevention as the key norm of international environmental law in the form of Principle 21 of the 1972 Stockholm Declaration on the Human Environment. This study does not desire to rewrite the history of international environmental law; rather, it offers a historical narrative centred on the intellectual origins of prevention that sets the stage to understand the norm in its contemporary form and seeks to understand the factors that led to the adoption of the principle of prevention. It explains how international law put aside its classical curative approach to damage in favour of a specific response to environmental damage in the form of the principle of prevention.

Chapter 1 focuses on the pre-Stockholm developments of the law relative to natural resources and the environment. It identifies the intellectual origins of prevention in two complementary approaches to environmental harm: (1) the law of State responsibility driven by a curative logic that seeks to compensate an injured State in case of infringements upon its territorial sovereignty and (2) the resource management regime concerned with the reasonable utilization of resources. Chapter 2 concentrates on the contextual factors that led to a shift in the 1960s in the international law applicable to natural resources and the environment from reparation to prevention, which was eventually crystallized in 1972 in the form of Stockholm Principle 21.

1

The Foundations of Prevention
Reparation and Resource Management

Traditionally, natural resources had 'no place'[1] in international law; the use of natural resources was considered to be a purely domestic matter that followed the territorial delimitation of sovereignty between States without having external impacts. However, as natural resources became more intensively exploited from the nineteenth century onwards, the need to clarify the rights and obligations of States over their natural resources and to give a legal response to increasingly noticeable external impacts arising from economic activities became acute. This chapter concentrates on how international law responded to this need by following two routes, which constitute the foundations of the prevention principle: a curative approach to damage identified in the application of the classical law of State responsibility for wrongful acts (1.1) and a proactive approach taking the form of a more innovative but less widespread regime of resource management (1.2).

1.1 THE CURATIVE APPROACH: STATE RESPONSIBILITY FOR TRANSBOUNDARY DAMAGE AS THE CLASSICAL REGIME

International law originally responded to environmental harm in the same way as it would for any other kind of injury, through the application of the rules of State responsibility. The prohibition to cause harm to the territory of another State, also known as the 'no-harm rule', provided a legal framework upon which to rely to seek reparation in the event of environmental damage. This section starts by briefly presenting the rationale driving the no-harm rule (1.1.1) before explaining the extent to which it set the stage for the emergence of prevention (1.1.2).

1 I Brownlie, 'Legal Status of Natural Resources in International Law (Some Aspects)' (1979) 16 *Collected Courses of the Hague Academy of International Law* 253.

1.1.1 *Rationale of the No-Harm Rule*

The recognition that sovereignty cannot be absolute is at the heart of the no-harm rule that aims to protect the territorial integrity of other States by prohibiting the creation of transboundary harm. The de facto interdependence existing between States[2] quickly discredited the Harmon doctrine following which a State, by virtue of its sovereignty, is allowed to carry out any activity on its territory, irrespective of its external impacts.[3]

The no-harm rule finds its intellectual origins in classical concepts commonly underpinning legal systems, both municipal and international, including abuse of rights, *sic utere tuo ut alienum non laedas* ('use your own property so as not to harm that of another') and good neighbourliness.[4] These concepts are driven by considerations of fairness and reasonableness[5] which dictate that an entity enjoys the use of its own property in as much as it does not cause injury to its neighbour.[6] Applied in an international law context, they share the common idea that 'the other face of the coin of sovereignty'[7] prohibits exercising the right in a way that 'impedes the enjoyment by other States of their own rights or for an end different from that for which the right was created'.[8] They dictate that a State cannot use its territory in a manner that might cause harm to the territory of

[2] J Andrassy, 'Les relations internationales de voisinage' (1951) 79 *Collected Courses of the Hague Academy of International Law* 77.

[3] 'Opinion by Judson Harmon' (1885) 25 *Official Opinions of the Attorney-Generals of the United States, Advising the President and Heads of Departments in Relation to Their Official Duties* 280–81, in which the United States Attorney-General Harmon declared that, based on the principle of absolute sovereignty, the United States did not have any international obligation towards Mexico regarding the use of the water of the Rio Grande River.

[4] SC McCaffrey, *The Law of International Watercourses* (2nd edn, Oxford University Press 2007) 417.

[5] *State of Georgia v. The Tennessee Copper Company and the Ducktown Sulphur, Copper and Iron Company. Ltd.*, US Supreme Court, 13 May 1907, 206 US 230, at 236, ruling on the basis of equity, finding it 'fair and reasonable' that the air over the territory of Georgia should not be polluted on a great scale.

[6] *Barger v. Barringer*, Supreme Court of North Carolina, 15 December 1909, 151 NC 433, on the origins of *sic utere tuo*: 'The ancient maxim of the common law, Sic utere tuo ut alienum non laedas, is not founded in any human statute, but in that sentiment expressed by Him who taught goodwill toward men, and said, "Love thy neighbor as thyself." Freely translated, it enjoins that every person in the use of his own property should avoid injury to his neighbor as much as possible.'

[7] ILC, 'Preliminary Report of the Special Rapporteur, Mr Robert Quentin-Baxter, on international liability for injurious consequences arising out of acts not prohibited by international law' (1980) UN Doc. A/CN.4/334, para 38.

[8] A Kiss, 'Abuse of Rights', in *Max Planck Encyclopedia of Public International Law* (Oxford University Press 2006), para 1.

another State,[9] while impacts below a certain level should be tolerated.[10] The intellectual origins of no-harm shed light on its rationale – one that seeks to protect territorial sovereignty and facilitate inter-State relations, with little attention given to the specificity of the regulated damage.

1.1.2 *Avoidance of a Tortious Act*

The core objective of prevention, the avoidance of harm, is identifiable in the prohibition to cause transboundary harm. The discussion that follows presents the extent to which no-harm set the stage for the emergence of prevention. On the one hand, it justifies the wide recognition found in the scholarship that prevention has its origins in no-harm; on the other hand, it explains that the two norms cannot be fully assimilated. Indeed, the core rationale of no-harm intrinsically differs from that of prevention in terms of its principal objective and anticipatory outlook.

Let us first examine the objective of the no-harm rule, which is to avoid a tortious act that would infringe upon the territorial sovereignty of a State. The principal object of the regulatory scope of no-harm is, unlike prevention (see Chapter 8), not the environment: this is best exemplified in the fact that the no-harm rule was consecrated by the International Court of Justice (ICJ) in the context of a dispute that did not pertain to natural resources or the environment, the 1949 *Corfu Channel* case. Here the Court confirmed the general dictum of 'every state's obligation not to allow knowingly its territory to be used for acts contrary to the rights of other states',[11] on the basis of which it considered that Albania had failed to take appropriate measures to 'prevent' the mine explosions that had taken place in Albanian waters and for the damage suffered by British warships and the loss of life that had ensued.[12] The dictum has since been constantly referenced as a source of the environmental no-harm rule.[13] This frames no-harm in a specific context: that is to say, one that concentrates on the prohibition of harm as a matter of general international law and not as an ecological rule. As French notes, the practice has had the advantage of 'normalizing and mainstreaming' international

9 On the origins of the no-harm rule, see, in particular, RA Epstein, 'The Harm Principle: And How It Grew' (1995) 45 *University of Toronto Law Journal* 369.

10 I Pop, *Voisinage et bon voisinage en droit international* (Pedone 1980) 180–90.

11 *Corfu Channel (United Kingdom/Albania)* (1949) ICJ Rep 4, at 22.

12 *Corfu Channel*, at 23.

13 P Birnie, A Boyle and C Redgwell, *International Law and the Environment* (3rd edn, Oxford University Press 2009) 144; P Sands and J Peel, *Principles of International Environmental Law* (3rd edn, Cambridge University Press 2012) 197; P-M Dupuy and JE Viñuales, *International Environmental Law* (Cambridge University Press 2015) 55–56.

environmental law by creating the perception that the preventive duty was less an 'esoteric and "green" (invariably viewed as a soft) commitment, and more of a legally binding rule'.[14]

The lack of environmental rationale in the no-harm rule can be seen as an advantage, but it has also restricted the 'environmentalization' of international law. Indeed, no-harm does not conceive environmental harm as intrinsically problematic. The drivers of no-harm, and how they evolved, are best evidenced in international treaties relative to the allocation of rights and responsibilities in shared watercourses. At first, international watercourse treaties were driven by the principle of equality among sovereign States, and environmental preoccupations were completely non-existent. They sought to regulate the changing, and diversifying (beyond boundary delimitation and navigation), usages made of international watercourses to ensure that they would not affect the flow of the watercourse and, thus, harm riparian States.[15] As a result, watercourse treaties adopted at the beginning of the twentieth century integrated a prohibition to cause harm by diverting water[16] or building infrastructures.[17] The no-harm rule subsequently integrated an environmental twist as it extended its scope to cover water quality (in addition to water

[14] D French, '*Trail Smelter*', in E Bjorge and C Miles (eds), *Landmark Cases in Public International Law* (Hart 2018) 153–88, at 178.

[15] See e.g. Treaty between Ethiopia and the United Kingdom Relative to the Frontiers between the Anglo-Egyptian Sudan, Ethiopia and Eritrea, Addis Abeba, 15 May 1902, in force 28 October 1902, in *British and Foreign State Papers, 1901–1902*, vol 95 (London 1905), 467, Article III, on the obligation 'not to construct, or allow to be constructed, any work across the Blue Nile, Lake Tsana, or the Sobat which would arrest the flow of their waters into the Nile'; Institut de droit international, 'International Regulation Regarding the Use of International Watercourses for Purposes Other than Navigation', Session of Madrid, 1911, Article I.

[16] See e.g. Treaty Relating to the Boundary Waters and Questions Arising along the Boundary between the United States and Canada, Washington, DC, 11 January 1909, in force 5 May 1910, 10 IPE 5158, Article III; Agreement between the Government of the Union of South Africa and the Government of the Republic of Portugal Regulating the Use of the Waters of the Kunene River for the Purposes of Generating Hydraulic Power and of Inundation and Irrigation in the Mandated Territory of South West Africa, Cape Town, 1 July 1926, in force 1 July 1926, 70 LNTS 316, para 7; Treaty Relating to the Utilization of the Waters of the Colorado and Tijuana Rivers, and of the Rio Grande (Rio Bravo) from Fort Quitman (Texas) to the Gulf of Mexico, Washington, DC, 3 February 1944, in force 8 November 1945, 3 UNTS 314, Article 9(d)–(f).

[17] See *inter alia* Convention and Protocol between the USSR and Turkey Regarding the Use of Frontier Waters, Kars, 8 January 1927, in force 26 June 1928, *British and Foreign State Papers, 1927*, vol 127 (London 1932), 926, Article 5(1) and Article 6; Convention between Norway and Sweden on Certain Questions Relating to the Law on Watercourses, Stockholm, 11 May 1929, in force 2 August 1930, 120 LNTS 277, Article 12.

quantity).[18] The driver of no-harm moved from being the preservation of territorial sovereignties to the protection of human livelihoods. A prime example of the anthropocentric move of no-harm is found in the 1904 Convention between France and Switzerland for the Regulation of Fishing in Frontier Waters that prohibited industrial plants in the neighbourhood of the Lake of Geneva from discharging waste into the Doubs and Rhône rivers that would be harmful to fish: it explicitly explained that the prohibition aimed to ensure that there were enough fish stocks for human consumption.[19] Similarly, the 1909 Boundary Waters Treaty between the United States and Canada prohibited water pollution that could cause injury to health or property[20]: again, the objective here is to reduce impacts on humans rather than on territorial sovereignty or the environment.

No-harm gives little regard to natural resources and the environment per se, but the closely related good neighbourliness principle can open the door to its environmentalization. It encourages States to cooperate to best accommodate their interests[21] – be it preserving their sovereign rights or, more progressively, achieving common environmental objectives. Its contribution in the context of no-harm was made evident by the Permanent Court of International Justice in the *River Oder* case: not only did it rule that riparian States share equal rights over an international watercourse but also that, as a result, they were forming a "community of interest" in navigation'.[22] This perspective supplements the basic no-harm rationale with an emphasis on commonalities that advocates for a more proactive, and cooperative, approach to harm – elements that eventually became essential in prevention (see Chapter 7).

A second element that defines no-harm relates to its anticipatory outlook, which is significantly more limited than that of prevention (see Chapter 6). No-harm operates on the basis of a dual objective that similarly drives tort law: a compensatory function that provides means for the remediation of harm and a complementary preventive function aimed at potential

18 See e.g. and most notably Institut de droit international, 'International Regulation Regarding the Use of International Watercourses for Purposes Other than Navigation', Session of Madrid, 1911, Article II(2).

19 Convention between France and Switzerland for the Regulation of Fishing in Frontier Waters, Paris, 9 March 1904, in force 4 February 1905, (1904) 195 CTS 108, Articles 6, 17 and 29.

20 Treaty Relating to the Boundary Waters and Questions Arising Along the Boundary between the United States and Canada, Article IV.

21 L Boisson de Chazournes and D Campanelli, 'Neighbour States', in *Max Planck Encyclopedia of Public International Law* (Oxford University Press 2006), para 5.

22 *Territorial Jurisdiction of the International Commission of the River Oder (Czechoslovakia, Denmark, France, Germany, Great Britain, Sweden/Poland)* (1929) PCIJ Series A No. 23, at 27.

tortfeasors.[23] The duality in no-harm is visible in international watercourse treaties that generally provide for both an obligation to avoid harm and, failing that, a duty to repair and compensate – two duties often found in the same provision. A common practice in early watercourse treaties,[24] the approach was reproduced in the Convention on the Law of Non-Navigational Uses of International Watercourses that codifies international watercourse law[25] and whose Article 7 on the obligation not to cause significant harm combines the obligation to avoid harm (para 1) and the obligation to compensate if harm nevertheless occurred (para 2).

No-harm has a strong connection with the reparation approach: following a tort law logic of corrective justice, it strives to repair a wrong by compensating victims (here the State) for the loss suffered due to the tortious act. As a result, it only includes a dose of anticipation in as much as it seeks to dissuade the injuring entity from committing harm that would result in an internationally wrongful act. This is how the no-harm rule was used in the *Trail Smelter* award, one of the main sources of prevention (the award is analysed further in Chapter 5).[26] The tribunal relied on the no-harm rule not to identify a wrongful act (the compromis had recognized Canada's responsibility for the harm caused by the smelter to the United States[27]) but rather to guide the design of a preventive regime applicable to the future management of the smelter. While Canada was allowed to continue operating the smelter, it was ordered to implement regulations controlling the future operation of the smelter in order to avoid the continuation or repetition of

23 M Hinteregger, 'Tort Law as an Instrument for the Prevention and Remediation of Catastrophic Harm', in A Herwig and M Simoncini (eds), *Law and the Management of Disasters: The Challenge of Resilience* (Routledge 2017) 208–23, at 209.

24 See e.g. Declaration of Montevideo Concerning the Industrial and Agricultural Use of International Rivers, 7th Inter-American Conference (fifth plenary session, 24 December 1933), Plenary Sessions, Minutes and Antecedents, Montevideo 1933, 114, paras 2 (on harm avoidance) and 3 (on reparation and compensation); Agreement between the Government of the Republic of Finland and the Government of the USSR concerning the Regime of the Finnish–Soviet State Frontier, Helsinki, 23 June 1960, in force 5 October 1960, 379 UNTS 330, Article 16.

25 Convention on the Law of the Non-Navigational Uses of International Watercourses, New York, 21 May 1997, in force 17 August 2014, (1997) 36 ILM 700.

26 *Trail Smelter (United States v. Canada)* (16 April 1938 and 11 March 1941), (1941) 3 RIAA 1905, at 1965.

27 Convention between the United States of America and the Dominion of Canada Relative to the Establishment of a Tribunal to Decide Questions of Indemnity and Future Regime Arising from the Operation of Smelter at Trail, British Columbia, Ottawa, 15 April 1935, in force 3 August 1935, (1941) 3 RIAA 1907, Article 1, explicitly recognizing the responsibility of Canada for harm which occurred prior to 1932. The questions put to the arbitral tribunal were also assuming Canada's responsibility for harm which happened after 1932.

harm. The tribunal laid down the maximum permissible hourly emissions of sulphur dioxide[28] and determined the type and location of instruments for recording meteorological conditions and sulphur dioxide concentrations.[29] The decision puts in evidence the anticipatory vision of no-harm, but its raison d'être remains to avoid a wrongful act rather than prevent environmental harm per se.

In sum, the no-harm rule influenced the rationale of prevention for its concern over the avoidance of harm, which explains that it was included as one of the three main clauses that structure Stockholm Principle 21 (alongside sovereignty over natural resources and protection of areas beyond national jurisdiction). However, the no-harm rule emerged from the traditional logics driving international law – the avoidance of a tortious act in a world of sovereign States – which did not give prevention its full depth. Hence the origins of prevention can also be identified in another, albeit less common, approach that international law took to natural resources and the environment: resource management.

1.2 THE PROACTIVE APPROACH: RESOURCE MANAGEMENT AS A GROWING CONCERN

Simultaneously to the rise of the no-harm rule, international law created another, alternative framework applicable to natural resources. Resource management treaties were adopted to respond to a particular concern shared by States in the late nineteenth and early twentieth centuries: resource depletion. Movements for the conservation and protection of nature emerged at that time in Europe and North America in reaction to 'two particularly dramatic illustrations of man's power to alter nature': the decimation of the bison in North America and the extinction of the passenger pigeon.[30] Although the protection of nature was primarily regulated at the domestic level, the international dimension of resource management received some attention from the late nineteenth century which culminated in the adoption of a body of international treaties that sought to put an end to unrestrained exploitation.

This section explains how the resource management logic contributed to the emergence of the prevention principle. Compared to no-harm, the resource management approach offered an alternative outlook on the objective of harm avoidance, one concentrated on natural resources and the

[28] *Trail Smelter*, 1976. [29] *Trail Smelter*, 1974–75.

[30] D Bodansky, *The Art and Craft of International Environmental Law* (Harvard University Press 2010) 23.

environment instead of territorial sovereignty and on proactivity instead of restraint. The following section operates in two movements, first concentrating on how resource management treaties announced the subsequent emergence of an environmental rationale dictating proactivity in the face of risks (1.2.1) and then offering a closer examination of how the term 'prevention' itself populated these treaties (1.2.2).

1.2.1 *Premises of an Environmental Rationale*

International treaties adopted at the end of the nineteenth century and the beginning of the twentieth century sought to promote resource management to prevent the extinction of species in order to exploit them in the longer term. Natural resources are envisaged pragmatically for their instrumental value only in as much as they are useful for humans and their survival.[31] A prime example among the first international treaties to regulate resources is the 1885 Treaty Concerning the Regulation of Salmon Fishery in the Rhine River Basin between Switzerland, Germany and the Netherlands: it prohibited certain types of fishing methods if the resulting decrease in salmon stocks was to have significant economic impacts.[32] Another typical example is the 1902 Convention for the Protection of Birds Useful to Agriculture, which sought to protect birds deemed useful for agriculture while allowing for the killing of birds regarded as noxious to hunting, fishing and local agriculture.[33]

Compared to the no-harm rule, the main contribution of resource management treaties to the preventive rationale lies in the fact that by concentrating on the utilization of resources on the domestic soil, they operate outside of an inter-State logic and are hence better suited to take into account the specificity of natural resources. By requiring that States take measures to avoid the extinction of certain species, they move international law away from the traditional regime of State responsibility that demands ex post action to damage: they encourage States to act in anticipation of harm, and in a proactive manner.

[31] A US preparatory document to the UNCCUR provided that '[t]he most important of the many reasons for preserving wildlife is that it may contain the key to the survival of man himself'. *UNCCUR Proceedings*, vol 1: Plenary Meetings' (17 August–6 September 1949, Lake Success, New York), UN Doc. E/CONF.7/7, Final Report (I), at 13.

[32] Treaty concerning the Regulation of Salmon Fishery in the Rhine River Basin, Berlin, 30 June 1885, in force 7 June 1886, available at http://iea.uoregon.edu/pages/view_treaty.php?t=1885-RhineSalmon.FR.txt&par=view_treaty_html (last accessed 19 May 2017).

[33] Convention for the Protection of Birds Useful to Agriculture, Paris, 19 March 1902, in force 20 April 1908, 4 IPE 1615.

Resource management treaties can be considered to integrate an environmental perspective (which then grew into the principle of prevention) because their object of regulation is natural resources.[34] It must, however, be noted that their perspective is inherently limited, not least because of their 'nakedly utilitarian perspective'[35]: they seek to protect 'natural resources', understood as resources worth exploiting, and not the 'environment', conceptualized as a holistic entity worthy of protection per se. Admittedly, modern environmental law is still driven by anthropocentric motivations, but not to the extent found in early resource management treaties that operated on the basis of extremely narrow environmental considerations. They nevertheless started a process encouraging the international community to consider environmental harm as a threat of its own and not uniquely to territorial sovereignty. In addition, a small number of early resource management treaties had a particularly well-developed environmental perspective, as reflected by their objectives to protect some scenic areas from intensive human exploitation. For instance, the 1933 Convention on the Preservation and Conservation of Flora and Fauna in Their Natural State encouraged the creation of national parks on the African continent to avoid 'any act likely to harm or disturb the fauna and flora'.[36] Similarly, the 1940 Convention on Nature Protection and Wildlife Preservation in the Western Hemisphere fostered the creation of national parks and reserves 'to protect and preserve scenery of extraordinary beauty, unusual and striking geologic formations, regions and natural objects of aesthetic, historic or scientific value'.[37] In this sense, resources management provided the foundations for the emergence of a preventive rationale that values resources and the environment irrespective of external considerations.

1.2.2 *Use of the Term 'Prevention'*

Final remarks ought to be made regarding the emergence of the term 'prevention' itself. One will have noted that if the foundations of prevention can be extracted from the no-harm rule and resource management treaties, the very

34 L Caldwell, *International Environmental Policy: Emergence and Dimensions* (2nd edn, Duke University Press 1990) 31, on how resource management treaties represent a new public attitude towards nature and the human environment.

35 P Davies, C Redgwell and M Bowman, *Lyster's International Wildlife Law* (2nd edn, Cambridge University Press 2010) 5.

36 Convention on the Preservation and Conservation of Flora and Fauna in Their Natural State, London, 8 November 1933, in force 14 January 1936, 172 LNTS 241, Article 2(2).

37 Convention on Nature Protection and Wild-Life Preservation in the Western Hemisphere, Washington, DC, 12 October 1940, in force 1 May 1942, 161 UNTS 193, Preamble.

term 'prevention' was barely used before the Stockholm Summit. Even after, one of the specificities of prevention is that it manifests in conventional law in more specific expressions, understood to represent the principle of prevention but without necessarily using the term 'prevention' per se (see Chapter 3). A discrepancy between the widespread recognition of a principle of prevention and the rare occurrence of the term in international legal instruments is noticeable, a particularity that stands out in comparison with the concept of sustainable development, generally mentioned as such in conventional law.[38]

However, some international treaties adopted before the Stockholm Summit contributed to the spread of the term 'prevention' itself. Admittedly, its actual presence in international treaties can be said to have had only an anecdotal impact on the eventual crystallization of the principle of prevention. However, three forms of diffuse impacts can be identified. First, the presence of the very term 'prevention' is indicative of the anticipatory rationale (intrinsic to the concept of prevention) to which international law was opening. Second, it facilitated the transformation of what is originally a policy objective (based on the idea that prevention is better than cure) into an international obligation. Third, it familiarized the international community with the term, hence contributing to its prompt integration in the lexicology of environmental law.

Of relevance to environmental protection are two categories of treaties that relied on the term 'prevention': treaties on plant and animal diseases and resource management treaties. The first category relates to treaties seeking to avoid the transboundary spread of diseases. For instance, the 1949 Agreement for the Establishment of a General Fisheries Council for the Mediterranean used 'prevention' as a verb to describe its goal to 'prevent the spread of occupational disease of fishermen'.[39] Similarly, international treaties referred to prevention to describe their aim to 'prevent the introduction and spread of pests and diseases of plants and plant products'.[40] Evidently, the scope of prevention remained very restricted compared to the legal preventive principle that emerged later. However, its usage as an action verb that describes the

38 V Barral, *Le développement durable en droit international: Essai sur les incidences juridiques d'une norme évolutive* (Bruylant 2016) 124–37.

39 FAO Agreement for the Establishment of a General Fisheries Council for the Mediterranean, Rome, 24 September 1949, in force 3 December 1963, 126 UNTS 237, Article IV(h).

40 FAO International Plant Protection Convention, Rome, 6 December 1951, in force 3 April 1952, 150 UNTS 67, Preamble and Article 1(1). See also FAO Plant Protection Agreement for South-East Asia and the Pacific Region, Rome, 27 February 1956, in force 2 July 1956, 247 UNTS 400, Preamble, describing the goal of the convention as being to 'prevent, through concerted action, the introduction into and spread within the South East Asia and Pacific region of destructive plant diseases and pests'.

objective of a treaty is indicative of the proactive approach to environmental harm that characterizes prevention (see Chapter 7).

The second category of international treaties in which the term 'prevention' can be found relates to the resource management treaties discussed earlier: not only did they provide the premises of the environmental rationale of prevention, but they also contributed to the spread of the term 'prevention' itself. Resource management treaties used the word in relation to the extinction of certain species that they sought to prevent. An early reference in this context can be found in the 1856 Bayonne Boundary Treaty between France and Spain that mentioned the right of the inhabitants of the Bidassoa banks to fish provided that they follow the regulations set up to 'prevent destruction of the fishery'.[41] Similarly, the 1940 Convention on Nature Protection and Wild-Life Preservation in the Western Hemisphere combined the objective of a 'rational utilization of migratory birds' to a duty to 'prevent the threatened extinction of any given species'.[42] Overall, the recognition of the necessity to prevent the extinction of certain species has been instrumental to the development of the principle of prevention and, more specifically, its concern for the protection of natural resources and the environment irrespective of external impacts and its focus on the proactivity to be displayed in the face of harm.

1.3 CONCLUSION

At its roots, the principle of prevention does not come from any particular concern for the environment. Its intellectual heritage can be traced back to (1) the respect of the territorial integrity of neighbouring States and (2) the will to exploit optimally natural resources. The classical approach resulted in the emergence of the no-harm rule aimed at preserving the territorial integrity of States, and the second one brought a new, more original perspective to environmental issues by underscoring the need to protect resources irrespective of sovereignty considerations. Both angles carry with them strong limitations in the context of an objective of environmental protection, as neither values the environment per se. However, premises of the preventive rationale are already visible in both regimes. The combination of the two dimensions explains the rationale of prevention in its modern form, concerned with the avoidance of harm (no-harm

41 Treaty between France and Spain Delimiting the Frontier from the Mouth of the Bidassoa to the Point Where the Department of Basses-Pyrenees Adjoins Aragon and Navarra, Bayonne, 2 December 1856, 1142 UNTS 317, Article 7.

42 Convention on Nature Protection and Wild-Life Preservation in the Western Hemisphere, Article 22.

rationale) irrespective of its location (resource management logic). While the rationale of prevention of environmental harm was already emerging at the beginning of the twentieth century, it transformed into a legal principle when the historical context proved favourable. In the 1960s, the multiplication of new human-made risks of industrial pollution and resource degradation increased environmental awareness and encouraged the crystallization of the preventive rationale in international environmental law.

2

The Paradigm Shift

Prevention as the Cornerstone of International Environmental Law

The chapter presents the paradigm shift, understood as a major change in people's assumptions regarding how the world works,[1] that took place in the late 1960s. As the deteriorating state of the planet started to become highly visible from the 1950s onwards, its protection became a societal issue that greatly mobilized public opinion in the West and beyond and compelled States to take action to avoid environmental damage. Such a novel approach contributed to the radical transformation in how international law had until then dealt with natural resources and the environment. The 1972 Stockholm Conference on the Human Environment gave evidence of the turn that international law was taking in response to environmental harm, away from the law of State responsibility and towards a preventive approach, which was consecrated in the form of Principle 21 of the Stockholm Declaration. The paradigm shift led to a reversal of the original logic (discussed in Chapter 1) driving international law: prevention became the core norm of international environmental law (2.1), while reparation became a residual solution to environmental harm (2.2).

2.1 PREVENTION AS THE CORE NORM OF INTERNATIONAL ENVIRONMENTAL LAW

The 1972 Stockholm Declaration on the Human Environment and, more specifically, its Principle 21 marked the adoption of the principle of prevention

[1] L Caldwell, *International Environmental Policy: Emergence and Dimensions* (2nd edn, Duke University Press 1990) 21. See also MM Mbengue, *Essai sur une théorie du risque en droit international public: l'anticipation du risque environnemental et sanitaire* (Pedone 2009) 2, on epistemic change; J Grinevald, *La Biosphère de l'anthropocène: climat et pétrole, la double menace. Repères Transdisciplinaires (1824–2007)* (Georg 2007) 99, 137, on 1970 as the year of perspective change.

as the core norm of international environmental law. Compared to the traditional no-harm rule that was prevalent before the Stockholm Conference, Principle 21 was reflective of a new societal perspective on environmental matters. The immediate historical context prior to the Stockholm Conference contributed to the shift from reparation to prevention and facilitated the adoption of Principle 21 (2.1.1). This section presents the diplomatic negotiations that led to the adoption of Principle 21 (2.1.2) and analyses the three core components that were eventually included in the provision (2.1.3). The chapter ends its evaluation of Principle 21 by noting that while its wording is undoubtedly a foundational expression of prevention, it does not completely reflect the principle of prevention in its most advanced form (2.1.4).

2.1.1 *The 1960s as the Turning Point: Reasons for Change*

A first event that fostered a new environmental consciousness that eventually led to the holding of the Stockholm Conference was the 1949 United Nations Conference on the Conservation and Utilization of Resources (UNCCUR).[2] Called by the United States and organized by the United Nations Economic and Social Council (ECOSOC), the Conference addressed six issues – minerals, fuels and energy, water, forests, land, and wildlife and fish – and sought to promote resource management and conservation. The UNCCUR was significant for its affirmation of the United Nations as the competent forum to address concerns over natural resources and the environment.[3] The Conference was 'limited to an exchange of experience in the techniques of the conservation and utilisation of resources'.[4] However, by fostering international scientific cooperation, it contributed to the development of scientific knowledge on the causes and effects of environmental degradation,[5]

[2] For an analysis of the UNCCUR and its outputs, see C Goodrich, 'The United Nations Conference on Resources' (1951) 5 *International Organization* 48.

[3] The League of Nations had already discussed some specific environment-related issues, such as oil pollution, but because the United Nations Charter did not list environmental protection among its purposes, the UNCCUR played an important role in positioning the United Nations as the preferred forum to address environmental concerns.

[4] ECOSOC Res. 109 (VI) (11 February 1948).

[5] At the same time, UNESCO and the International Union for the Protection of Nature held a global conference on ecology and education, thereby highlighting the growing importance of environmental issues. For a complete analysis of this conference, see A-K Wöbse, '"The World After All Was One": The International Environmental Network of UNESCO and IUCN, 1945–1950' (2011) 20 *Contemporary European History* 331. International cooperation had already been encouraged by various pre–World War II meetings such as the International Congress for

a precondition to political mobilization.[6] Environmental issues started to be seen not merely as a scientific but also as a political matter in the 1950s, as evidenced by the development of sectoral rules relative to the prevention of pollution and, more specifically, the adoption of major instruments to regulate marine oil pollution[7] and nuclear energy risks.[8] A broader, more holistic approach to the environment followed in the 1960s as a result of an emerging awareness that the international community had a collective responsibility to protect the Earth as a whole.[9] The following section seeks to understand how environmental issues became such a 'hot topic'[10] that eventually led to an international legal paradigm shift. In addition to the gradual developments found in the premises of international environmental law discussed in Chapter 1, five major factors, presented in turn, explain the paradigm shift that led to the adoption of the prevention principle at the Stockholm Conference[11]: (1) a global rise in environmental risks, (2) growing public awareness about the scarcity of natural resources and the need to protect the environment, (3) the mobilization of governments evidenced by the adoption of national environmental legislation, (4) the development of a culture of international cooperation after World War II and in particular during the Détente era, and (5) an evolution in the objectives and structure of general international law.

the Protection of Nature (Paris, 1909), the International Congress on the Protection of Flora, Fauna and Natural Sites and Monuments (Paris, 1923), the International Congress for Study and Protection of Birds (Geneva, 1927), the Second International Congress for the Protection of Nature (Paris, 1931) and the Swiss League for the Protection of Nature Conference (Brunnen, 1947). The International Geophysical Year in 1957 also contributed to scientific exchange in the earth sciences, in particular, in relation to polar studies.

6 R Hahn and K Richards, 'The Internationalization of Environmental Regulation' (1989) 30 *Harvard International Law Journal* 421, at 425.

7 International Convention for the Prevention of Pollution of the Sea by Oil, London, 12 May 1954, in force 26 July 1958, 327 UNTS 3; Convention on the High Seas, Geneva, 29 April 1958, in force 30 September 1962, 450 UNTS 82

8 Grinevald, *La Biosphère de l'anthropocène*, 99, calling the 1950s the 'new nuclear age'. UNGA Res. 912(X) (3 December 1955); UNGA Res. 913(X) (3 December 1955); Treaty Banning Nuclear Weapon Testing in the Atmosphere, in Outer Space and Under Water, Moscow, 5 August 1963, in force 10 October 1963, 480 UNTS 43, Article I.

9 Caldwell, *International Environmental Policy*, 55.

10 A Halvorsen, 'The Origin and Development of International Environmental Law', in S Alam et al. (eds), *Routledge Handbook of International Environmental Law* (Routledge 2013) 29.

11 The first three reasons have been expounded by PH Sand, on the work of whom I rely. See PH Sand, 'The Evolution of International Environmental Law', in D Bodansky, J Brunnée and E Hey (eds), *The Oxford Handbook of International Environmental Law* (Oxford University Press 2007) 29, at 34. I have felt the need to complete his account with two additional reasons of a more general nature.

2.1.1.1 A Global Rise in Environmental Risks

The first factor explaining the paradigm shift consecrated at the Stockholm Conference relates to the multiplication, after World War II, of activities potentially harmful to the environment. Environmental risks were becoming more frequent and widespread, with their impacts extending beyond national borders. The dangers of industrial development became visible when several ecological catastrophes, the first of their kind, hit industrialized countries. Images of the first oil spill in Europe with the *Torrey Canyon* disaster in 1967 put in evidence the fragility of the environment and the disastrous consequences that its exploitation can have for human life. It contributed to the realization that international rules were urgently needed, as States lacked legal tools to act, either preventively or reactively, to such a disaster.[12] The multiplication of catastrophic oil spills, partly explained by the steady increase in world consumption of cheap oil, shocked the public. The statistics are impressive: from 1964 to 1967, ninety-one oil tankers got stranded, 238 were involved in a collision, and of these 329 accidents, thirty-nine resulted in oil spills.[13] Although dramatic, these spillages were not the primary cause of damage to the marine environment – only 20 per cent of the pollutants in the ocean could be attributed to shipping accidents or practices,[14] with most of the pollution coming from routine discharges. However, the spillages helped to show that the marine environment was fragile and should be protected. The advent of nuclear capability at the end of World War II also played an essential role in raising environmental consciousness. As the danger of a nuclear holocaust lessened in the 1960s, concerns about the effects of routine or accidental radiation during energy production and nuclear testing multiplied.[15]

In addition to concerns over the multiplication of potentially harmful activities, consequences of the degradation of the environment started to become more visible. Direct experience of deteriorating environmental conditions considerably raised public awareness. The issue of acid rain killing fish in Scandinavian lakes and destroying forests became recurrent.[16] The smog in

[12] J-P Quéneudec, 'L'incidence de l'affaire du Torrey Canyon sur le droit de la mer' (1968) 14 *Annuaire français de droit international* 701, at 703.

[13] J-Y Morin, 'La pollution des mers au regard du droit international', in A Kiss (ed), *La protection de l'environnement et le droit international: colloque de l'Académie du droit de La Haye* (Martinus Nijhoff 1975) 240, at 258.

[14] D Johnston, 'Environmental Law of the Sea', *IUCN Environmental Law and Policy Paper No. 18* (IUCN 1981) 26.

[15] Johnston, 'Environmental Law of the Sea'.

[16] D Bodansky, *The Art and Craft of International Environmental Law* (Harvard University Press 2010) 19, noting that the link made by Swedish research between sulphur emissions in England

London – due to special weather conditions combined with pollution coming from the coal industry and that claimed between 4,000 and 12,000 lives in 1952[17] – played a significant role in raising public awareness and spurring government action. Ultimately, the global scale of the environmental crisis encouraged the adoption of multilateral agreements driven by an objective of environmental protection, better able to respond to a global crisis than the bilateral or plurilateral texts relative to shared natural resources that were the norm before World War II.

2.1.1.2 Growing Public Consciousness

As environmental issues became more evident, humanity's perception of its environment changed radically. The denomination of the international summits held before Stockholm in relation to natural resources and the environment reflects this evolution.[18] In 1949, the UN Conference on the 'Conservation and Utilisation of Resources' kept discussions within the traditional utilitarian framework that was the norm before World War II. In 1968, the Biosphere Conference focused on the 'impacts of man on the biosphere'[19] and generalized the use of the term 'biosphere', understood as the sum of all ecosystems on Earth.[20] Finally, in 1972, the Stockholm Conference on the Human Environment signalled the consecration of the word 'environment'. Before the 1960s, the term 'environment' was not widely used because its protection had not been conceptualized as a distinct political and physical problem.[21] But the new consciousness that the Earth was a fragile unit[22] – fostered by the first steps of a human on the moon in July 1969, which

and Germany and acid rain in Scandinavia was a 'major impetus' for the Stockholm Conference.

17 M Bell, D Devra and T Fletcher, 'A Retrospective Assessment of Mortality from the London Smog Episode of 1952: The Role of Influenza and Pollution' (2004) 112 *Environmental Health Perspectives* 6.

18 L Caldwell, 'Concepts in Development of International Environmental Policies' (1973) 13 *Natural Resources Journal* 190, on how concepts affect policies and how international environmental policies were affected by the new perspective on the environment.

19 *Use and Conservation of the Biosphere: Proceedings of the Intergovernmental Conference of Experts on the Scientific Basis for Rational Use and Conservation of the Resources of the Biosphere (Paris, 4–13 September 1968)* (UNESCO 1970) 31–47.

20 *Use and Conservation of the Biosphere*, 14–18, on a detailed definition of the biosphere.

21 A Kiss, 'Emergence des principes généraux du droit international et d'une politique internationale de l'environnement', in I Rens (ed), *Le droit international face à l'éthique et à la politique de l'environnement* (Georg 1996) 19–35, at 20, noting that the term was barely used in the French language.

22 Caldwell, *International Environmental Policy*, 23.

contributed to the discovery of the Earth as part of the bigger cosmos[23] – legitimized a more comprehensive approach to the environment.

The emergence of a new public consciousness[24] was influenced by some major studies that had an effect on public opinion, including *The Silent Spring* by Rachel Carson, which aroused public apprehension over new chemicals and pesticides,[25] and the much-cited report of the Club of Rome, *The Limits to Growth*, which made people realize that the Earth's supply of natural resources was limited and at risk due to economic and demographic growth.[26] Thus, concerns over the scarcity and optimal utilization of natural resources contributed to the rise of the environmental movement. The media also contributed to the emergence of environmental awareness by running stories on sensational environmental events and on the rapid deterioration of the Earth that alarmed the public.[27] One striking example of how environmentalism suddenly became a mass movement is the holding of the first 'Earth Day' in the United States in 1970, in which 20 million people participated and which led *Time* magazine to name the environment the 'issue of the year' in 1970.[28] It exemplified the significant change that was occurring in humanity's perception of its planet, one originally centred on understanding the Earth as being created for the exclusive use of human beings to embracing a biosphere for which humankind is a 'temporary residence custodian'.[29]

2.1.1.3 Growth of National Environmental Legislation

As a consequence of deteriorating environmental conditions and in response to public pressure, governments started to take unilateral actions to control pollution via the creation of environmental agencies and the enactment of

23 Grinevald, *La Biosphère de l'anthropocène*, 131.
24 'Final Report', in *Use and Conservation of the Biosphere: Proceedings of the Intergovernmental Conference of Experts on the Scientific Basis for Rational Use and Conservation of the Resources of the Biosphere (Paris, 4–13 September 1968)* (UNESCO 1970) at 235: 'Until this point in history the nations of the world have lacked considered, comprehensive policies for managing the environment. Although changes have been taking place for a long time, they seem to have reached a threshold recently that has made the public aware of them.'
25 R Carson, *The Silent Spring* (Houghton Mifflin 1962).
26 DH Meadows et al., *The Limits to Growth* (Club of Rome 1972).
27 *Time Magazine* published eight articles on environmental issues in the month of January 1970: 'Prosecuting Pollution' (5 January); 'Worried Scientists' (12 January); 'Nixon's 1970 Worries: Economy and Environment' (12 January); 'The Peaceful Atom: Friend or Foe?' (19 January); 'Concern on Campus' (26 January); 'Invisible Killer' (26 January); 'Saving the Everglades' (26 January) and 'Troubled Little Island' (26 January).
28 'Issue of the Year: The Environment', *Time*, 4 January 1971.
29 Caldwell, *International Environmental Policy*, 21.

new laws. By way of example, the United States passed a number of environmental acts in the 1960s, such as the Clean Air Act (1963),[30] the Solid Waste Disposal Act (1965),[31] the Water Quality Act (1965),[32] the Clean Water Restoration Act (1966),[33] the Air Quality Act (1967)[34] and finally the National Environmental Policy Act (1969),[35] considered as the 'environmental Magna Carta' of the United States. In Europe, France voted in a law on water pollution prevention[36] and a law on the creation of a national office in charge of forests in 1964,[37] and the United Kingdom passed Clean Air Acts in 1956[38] and 1968.[39] The European Community adopted its first environmental directive on dangerous substances in 1967[40] and its first environmental action programme in 1973.[41] Environmental issues were first dealt with at local and national levels because they were where the effects of environmental deterioration were directly experienced; however, as explained by Caldwell, these national frameworks made a significant contribution to the development of international environmental law.

> [E]nvironmental policy had to become legitimized at the national level; governments had to be persuaded to take cognizance of environmental issues as regular and official concerns. Nations cannot easily cooperate collectively upon matters with which they have had no experience individually.[42]

As States started to realize that environmental protection would not be achieved through national legislation alone, they engaged in international cooperation. Morrison reflects on the shift from national to international regulation by noting that '[o]ne of the biggest changes was the recognition that environmental harm was a common problem, the magnitude of which was greater than the sum of the individual environmental injuries which were

30 Clean Air Act, 1963, Public Law 88–206, amended October 20, 1965 (Public Law 89–272); October 15, 1966 (Public Law 89–675).

31 Solid Waste Disposal Act, 1965, Public Law 89–272.

32 Water Quality Act, 1965, Public Law 89–234.

33 Clean Water Restoration Act, 1966, Public Law 89–753.

34 Air Quality Act, 1967, Public Law 90–148.

35 National Environmental Policy Act (NEPA), 1 January 1970, Public Law 91–190.

36 Loi relative au régime et à la répartition des eaux et à la lutte contre leur pollution, 16 décembre 1964, Loi no. 64 1245.

37 Loi créant l'Office national des forêts, 23 décembre 1964, Loi no. 64–1278.

38 Clean Air Act, 5 July 1956, HMSO London.

39 Clean Air Act, 1968, HMSO London.

40 Directive 67/548/EEC on the approximation of laws, regulations and administrative provisions relating to the classification, packaging and labelling of dangerous substances (1967) OJ 196, at 234.

41 First Environmental Action Programme (1973) OJ C112/1.

42 Caldwell, *International Environmental Policy*, 21. Caldwell also argues that 'an issue cannot become international until it becomes a matter of national concern', at 13.

its parts'.[43] The global effects of environmental issues forced States to cooperate at the international level in order to take pertinent national decisions.[44] While States were still the main decision-makers in the environmental field, their environmental policies were nevertheless increasingly influenced by multilateral processes, as well as scrutinized internationally.[45]

2.1.1.4 A Culture of International Cooperation

The culture of multilateral cooperation that developed after World War II was also a fundamental factor in the development of the preventive rationale. Contrary to the adversarial regime of State responsibility, prevention requires common anticipatory measures that are most efficient when States coordinate their actions. Admittedly, the UN Charter did not include environmental protection in the mandate of the organization. Nevertheless, the culture of multilateral cooperation that characterizes the United Nations played a decisive role in the recognition of environmental problems as a common global issue. The creation of international institutions relevant to environmental issues, such as the UN Educational, Scientific, and Cultural Organization (UNESCO), the International Atomic Energy Agency (IAEA), the International Maritime Consultative Organization (IMCO) and the Food and Agriculture Organization (FAO), provided forums to coordinate environmental actions, encourage mobilization and follow up on implementation.

Additionally, the political context of the Cold War was instrumental in making environmental issues a subject of international cooperation. The rivalry between the two superpowers, which led to a tense confrontation in Cuba, crises in Berlin and proxy wars in the Third World, transformed during the Détente period (1969–79) into a willingness to promote peaceful coexistence between the two blocs.[46] The new inclination of the two blocs to cooperate translated *inter alia* into a willingness to solve environmental problems that were becoming more evident during that time. As Hünemörder noted, '[t]he new buzzwords *environmental protection* and *environmental crisis* offered governments on both sides of the Iron Curtain

43 F Morrison, 'Changing Approaches to Environmental Law', in F Morrison and R Wolfrum (eds), *International, Regional and National Environmental Law* (Kluwer Law International 2000) 803, at 805.

44 National Environmental Policy Act, Preamble, encouraging international cooperation to 'promote efforts which will prevent or eliminate damage to the environment and biosphere'.

45 R Hahn and K Richards, 'The Internationalization of Environmental Regulation' (1989) 30 *Harvard International Law Journal* 421, at 423.

46 C Daigle, 'The Era of Détente', in A Kalinovsky and C Daigle (eds), *The Routledge Handbook of the Cold War* (Routledge 2014) 195–208.

a unique opportunity to bridge the ideological divide'.[47] The identification of common environmental issues and the shared rhetoric in which it resulted contributed to the normalization of relations between the two blocs. In other words, the realization that there was 'only one Earth' lessened the feeling of divide between them.[48]

Technical and scientific exchange between the two blocs became a key instrument of the renewed cooperation between the two superpowers. The UN Economic Commission for Europe (UNECE) played a significant role in this regard. While first mandated after World War II to rebuild postwar Europe, the UNECE's role changed during the Cold War period as it became the 'only instrument of economic dialogue and cooperation between these two radically different systems'.[49] It worked on questions that were of common interest to the two blocs, among which featured environmental issues. The UNECE therefore had a fundamental role in the promotion of environmental cooperation which culminated in the adoption of the UNECE Long-Rang Transboundary Air Pollution Convention in 1979, an example of the enhanced cooperation between the two blocs that characterized the Détente era.

2.1.1.5 The General International Law Context

Finally, the legal developments relative to environmental protection and, more specifically, to the principle of prevention did not operate in isolation from the rest of international law. Attention must be paid to the directions that general international law were taking at the time. The post–World War II period led to a significant transformation of international law that was famously described by Friedmann as a move from the 'law of co-existence' to the 'law of co-operation'.[50] He noted that the classical model of international law, concentrated on the 'regulation of the conditions of mutual respect for national sovereignty',[51] was being complemented by another model of international regulation based on international cooperation,[52] as epitomized by the adoption of the Declaration on Principles of International Law

47 K Hünemörder, 'Environmental Crisis and Soft Politics: Détente and the Global Environment, 1968–1975', in JR McNeill and C Unger (eds), *Environmental Histories of the Cold War* (Cambridge University Press 2010) 257–276, at 257.

48 Hünemörder, 'Environmental Crisis and Soft Politics', 274.

49 UNECE website: www.unece.org/oes/history/history.html (last accessed 19 May 2017).

50 W Friedmann, *The Changing Structure of International Law* (Stevens & Sons 1964).

51 Friedmann, *The Changing Structure of International Law*, 60.

52 Friedmann, *The Changing Structure of International Law*, 71.

concerning Friendly Relations and Co-operation among States in accordance with the UN Charter.[53] This new cooperation was meant not only to facilitate relations between independent and equally sovereign States but also to protect fundamental universal values, as reflected in the International Court of Justice's (ICJ's) recognition in 1970 that certain international obligations were not reciprocal but rather were owed to the international community as a whole.[54] By opening up to a verticalization of the international system, international law began to accommodate new subject matters, including environmental protection.[55]

The culture of multilateral cooperation, combined with the rise in environmental awareness and the mobilization of the public opinion, acted as a catalyst for change. The tipping point occurred in the 1960s when the scientific evidence regarding the deteriorating state of the environment, the environmental consciousness of the public and the mobilization of political authorities converged to lead to the adoption at the Stockholm Conference on the Human Environment of a new approach to natural resources and the environment.

2.1.2 *The Drafting of the Stockholm Declaration and the Adoption of Principle 21*

The Stockholm Conference on the Human Environment was held in June 1972 and was attended by representatives of 114 member States, various UN bodies and observers from non-governmental organizations (NGOs). Despite the boycott by the socialist bloc, participation was high, and the Conference resulted in the adoption of several key documents: a Declaration on the Human Environment, made of a Preamble and twenty-six principles; an Action Plan with 109 recommendations; and a Resolution on institutional and financial matters.[56] The Conference marked a 'watershed in international relations'[57] because it put the environment at the centre of the international stage. It also was a landmark event in the context of the principle of prevention. This section focuses on the drafting of the Declaration and

53 'Declaration on Principles of International Law Concerning Friendly Relations and Co-operation among States in Accordance with the Charter of the United Nations', UNGA Resolution 2625 (XXV) (24 October 1970).

54 *Barcelona Traction, Light and Power Company Ltd.* (Second Application) *(Belgium v. Spain)* (1970) ICJ Rep 3, para 33.

55 Friedmann, *The Changing Structure of International Law*, 16–19.

56 'Report of the United Nations Conference on the Human Environment, Stockholm' (5–16 June 1972) UN Doc. A/CONF.48/14 and Corr.1, at 2–65.

57 Caldwell, *International Environmental Policy*, 21.

more particularly on the adoption of Principle 21 – a core manifestation of prevention – which, as a reminder, reads as follows:

> States have, in accordance with the Charter of the United Nations and the principles of international law, the sovereign right to exploit their own resources pursuant to their own environmental policies, and the responsibility to ensure that activities within their jurisdiction or control do not cause damage to the environment of other States or of areas beyond the limits of national jurisdiction.[58]

The official initiation of the Stockholm Conference began with a letter in May 1968 from Sweden to the UN Secretary-General 'on the questions of convening an international conference on the problems of human environment'.[59] ECOSOC Resolution 1448[60] and UN General Assembly (UNGA) Resolution 2581 (XXIV),[61] convening the Stockholm Conference, supported the objective of adopting basic principles to guide future actions. These resolutions established a Preparatory Committee (PC) of twenty-seven States[62] to negotiate some key issues prior to the Conference and to draft a declaration on the 'rights and obligations of citizens and Governments with regard to the preservation and improvement of the human environment'.[63] An analysis of the *travaux préparatoires* of the Stockholm Conference[64] reveals that the wording of what eventually became Principle 21[65] finds its origins in the preparatory work undertaken prior to the Conference and, in particular, in proposals made by the UN Secretary-General. The assemblage of the concept of sovereignty over natural resources with the responsibility of the State over

58 Declaration of the United Nations Conference on the Human Environment (Stockholm, 16 June 1972), (1972) 11 ILM 1416, Principle 21.

59 Mentioned in L Sohn, 'The Stockholm Declaration on the Human Environment' (1973) 14 *Harvard International Law Journal* 423, at 425.

60 ECOSOC Res. 1448 (XLVII) (6 August 1969).

61 UNGA Res. 2581 (XXIV) (15 December 1969).

62 The following States were represented in the committee: Argentina, Brazil, Canada, Costa Rica, Cyprus, Czechoslovakia, Egypt, France, Ghana, India, Iran, Italy, Jamaica, Japan, Mexico, Netherlands, Nigeria, Singapore, Sweden, Togo, USSR, United Arab Republic, United Kingdom, United States, Yugoslavia and Zambia. The sessions of the committee were also attended by a variety of observer States and organizations.

63 'Report of the Preparatory Committee on Its Fourth Session' (15 March 1972) UN Doc. A/CONF.48/PC/17, para 16.

64 For a detailed analysis of the Stockholm Declaration on the basis of the *travaux préparatoires*, see Sohn, 'The Stockholm Declaration on the Human Environment', upon which a large number of subsequent works rely, implicitly or explicitly.

65 The numbering, and order, of the principles changed in the different drafts of the declaration. For the sake of simplicity, Principle 21 is always referred to as Principle 21 despite the fact that during the course of the negotiations its numbering might have changed.

environmental damage was the main point of contention in the negotiations that pertained to Principle 21. While the weight to be given to each concept was at the heart of the controversy, there was little disagreement over the necessity to include a reference to the principle of prevention in the Declaration.

2.1.2.1 The Questionnaire Sent by the UN Secretary-General

Prior to starting the drafting of the Declaration, a questionnaire was sent to States to determine their views about the potential format and content of the Declaration.[66] Question 8 of this questionnaire can be identified as having initiated the inclusion of Principle 21 in the Declaration. In this question, the Secretary-General asked whether the Declaration should include 'certain principles which States should recognize as guiding their individual and collective actions affecting the human environment'.[67] A note justifying and explaining the question listed examples of general principles that States could consider for inclusion in the Declaration. Of special interest for Principle 21 are three principles. Firstly, the principle of national sovereignty over natural resources was proposed to mirror the negotiations ongoing at the time at the UNGA over this very concept.[68] Secondly, the Secretary-General referenced the duty of the State to respect the rights of other States when carrying out activities on its territory. It read as follows:

> States should be guided by the principle of co-operation and mutual assistance and should conduct all their activities related to environmental problems with due regard to the corresponding interests of other States, in accordance with international law, including the Charter of the United Nations.

Thirdly, the Secretary-General proposed a principle on the international responsibility of States in case of environmental harm that read as follows:

66 The text of the questionnaire with annexed background notes of 21 December 1970 is available in 'Replies to Questionnaire of 21 December 1970 circulated by the Secretary-General of the Conference in Connexion with the Preparation of a Draft Declaration on the Human Environment' (1 April 1971) UN Doc. A/CONF.48/PC/WG.1/CRP.4.

67 'Replies to Questionnaire'.

68 'Replies to Questionnaire', 3. It is the only principle with a footnote indicating that the principle was recognized by UNGA Resolutions 1803 (XVII) of 14 December 1962 and 2158 (XXI) of 28 November 1966 – the footnote can be understood as a reminder of the state of international law or as a justification of its inclusion in the note.

> States are internationally responsible for harm caused by them or their citizens to environmental resources shared with other States and for ensuring that national activities are carried out in conformity with the principles set forth in the present Declaration.[69]

The inclusion of Principle 21 in the Declaration thus can be traced back to the above-mentioned two suggestions made by the Secretary-General prior to the Conference to include the principle of national sovereignty over natural resources and to recognize the principle of territorial integrity of States and their resulting responsibility in relation to transboundary harm.

In response to the questionnaire, a number of States agreed that the Declaration should include a reference to the principle of national sovereignty over natural resources.[70] Some States also referred to the prohibition to cause transboundary harm either as an independent duty[71] or in the context of international cooperation.[72] Other States did not mention these two concepts but recognized another proposal suggested in the questionnaire: the duty of 'all nations to carefully husband their natural resources',[73] a principle that can be interpreted as a broader obligation to preserve the environment that finds its intellectual origins in resource management treaties.

In relation to Principle 21, one of the most interesting responses to the questionnaire came from Canada, which suggested the inclusion of six principles:

69 'Replies to Questionnaire', 13–14.

70 'Replies to Questionnaire', replies by Colombia (at 26), by the United Arab Republic (at 66), by Guatemala (Add.1, at 5) and by Russia (Add.2, at 6).

71 'Replies to Questionnaire', reply by Denmark, at 29: 'The Declaration should list the most fundamental principles of behaviour in environmental matters, especially in the fields of global and common importance such as the atmosphere, the soil, the ocean, the sea-bed and inland waters. In this connection, mention could be made of the responsibility to avoid unnecessary damage and – learning from earlier mistakes in the history of mankind – to prevent deterioration of environment by including environmental criteria in the planning and location of economic activities at the earliest possible state.' See also 'Replies to Questionnaire', replies by Colombia (at 26) and Switzerland (at 58). Only one State openly voiced its opposition to the inclusion of the principle that States are internationally responsible for harms caused by them: reply by Japan (at 46), arguing that the principle that States are internationally responsible for harms caused by them or their citizens to environmental resources shared with other States is 'too specific' and involves 'various difficult questions'.

72 See e.g. the US reply that proposed the following principle: 'Whenever a proposed activity by any State might cause grave harm to human environment beyond its territory the State or States planning such an activity should undertake appropriate international consultations before proceeding with any such activity' ('Replies to Questionnaire', at 65).

73 'Replies to Questionnaire', reply by Guatemala (Add.1, at 5).

1. Every State has a sovereign and inalienable right to its environment including its land, air and water, and to dispose of its natural resources.
2. Every State has a right to environmental integrity corresponding to its right to territorial integrity.
3. Every State has the right to take all necessary and appropriate measures to protect its environmental integrity.
4. Every State has a duty to conduct its activities with due regard to their effects upon the environment of other States.
5. No State may use or permit the use of its territory in such a manner as to cause damage to the environment of other States or the environment of areas beyond the limits of national jurisdiction.
6. No State may use areas beyond the limits of national jurisdiction in such a manner as to cause damage to the environment of such areas or to the environment of other States.[74]

This proposal already combined a number of elements that were later included in Principle 21: the concept of permanent sovereignty over natural resources (para 1), the prohibition to cause transboundary harm (para 5) and a reference to the protection of areas outside State jurisdiction (para 6). It is thus clear that the questionnaire sent prior to the drafting of the Declaration and the responses received as a result significantly shaped the form in which Principle 21 was eventually adopted.

2.1.2.2 The First Draft of the Intergovernmental Working Group

The draft of the Stockholm Declaration was prepared by an Intergovernmental Working Group (IWG) created by the PC. The replies received from the governments to the questionnaire served as the basis of the work of the IWG.[75] The IWG held an organizational session in New York City in March 1971 and then reconvened in a substantive session during 10–21 May 1971 at which it prepared a preliminary draft of a Preamble and of fundamental principles for the declaration on the human environment for submission to the PC at its third session (13–24 September 1971).

The IWG presented a first document of seventeen principles.[76] In its first draft, the IWG included the following statements as the seventh and eighth paragraphs of the Preamble of the Declaration:

74 'Replies to Questionnaire', reply by Canada (Add.2, at 2–3).

75 As noted in 'Report of the Preparatory Committee, Third Session' (14 June 1971) UN Doc. A/CONF.48/PC.12, at 1.

76 'Report of the Preparatory Committee, Third Session', Annex I.

> Each State has inalienable sovereignty over its natural resources; and
> Each State has the responsibility to exercise its sovereignty over its natural resources in a manner compatible with the need to ensure the preservation and enhancement of the human environment.[77]

In addition, Principle 6 was already very close to what eventually became Principle 21:

> Each State has the responsibility, in accordance with the Charter of the United Nations and consistent with the principles of international law, to conduct its activities so as not to cause damage to the environment of other States, or to the environment of areas beyond the limits of national jurisdiction.[78]

Moreover, the draft included a broad clause providing that '[e]veryone has a responsibility to protect the environment'.[79] It also created an obligation to undertake international consultations before carrying out activities that may cause transboundary damage or damage to areas beyond the limits of national jurisdiction[80] and a right to request consultations if a State believes the activities of another State may damage the environment on its territory or in areas beyond the limits of national jurisdiction.[81]

Many, if not all, of the principles proposed by the IGW were contested during the first substantive session of the IGW.[82] With regard to Principle 21, the inclusion of the concept of sovereignty over natural resources was broadly accepted, but how it translated more specifically in the context of environmental protection was debated. In particular, some delegations felt that the concept should be placed directly in its environmental context by merging the seventh and eighth paragraphs of the Preamble.[83] By contrast, others felt that the exercise of sovereignty could not be 'subject to

77 'Report of the Preparatory Committee, Third Session', seventh and eighth preambular clauses.

78 'Report of the Preparatory Committee, Third Session', 3.

79 'Report of the Preparatory Committee, Third Session', 3, Principle 2.

80 'Report of the Preparatory Committee, Third Session', 3, Principle 6.

81 'Report of the Preparatory Committee, Third Session', 3, Principle 7.

82 'Report of the Rapporteur on Reservations and Observations on the Draft Preamble and Fundamental Principles Expressed by Members of the Intergovernmental Working Group', UN Doc. A/CONF.48/PC.12, Annex II, in particular, paras 3 and 4; 'Report of the Preparatory Committee for the United Nations Conference on the Human Environment, Third Session' (13–24 September 1971) UN Doc. A/CONF.48/PC.13, paras 149–65.

83 'Report of the Preparatory Committee for the United Nations Conference on the Human Environment', PC.13, on the seventh paragraph. While no one questioned the concept of sovereignty over natural resources, some delegations felt that a statement to this effect would be redundant in a declaration on the human environment and that the concept of

qualifications or limitations'[84] and suggested deleting the words 'in a manner compatible with the need to ensure the preservation and enhancement of the human environment'.[85]

There was also support for the inclusion of an additional fundamental principle that would protect the sovereign rights of States over their environment and that would read, 'Each State has a sovereign right to its environment and to dispose of its natural resources and a right to take all necessary and appropriate measures to protect its environmental integrity'.[86] Yet, a number of delegations opposed the linkage made between sovereignty and the environment on the basis that the definition of the 'environment' remained unclear and that, as a result, it could be 'interpreted as implying that each State was left free to define the extent of its environment, and this could not fail to prejudice the established principles of international law'.[87] Given the lack of consensus over the first draft of the Declaration, the PC instructed the IWG to work on a new proposal.

2.1.2.3 The Second Draft of the Intergovernmental Working Group

During the second session of the IGW, a number of States proposed slight changes to the wording of Principle 6 (which subsequently became Principle 21) but in substance agreed to include a reference to the responsibility of the State not to cause transboundary harm. The applicability of the prohibition to cause harm to the territory of another State but also to areas beyond national jurisdiction was found in numerous proposals and was widely accepted.[88]

sovereignty should be placed in its environmental context by merging the seventh and eighth preambular paragraphs (para 16, Annex II). Others strongly felt that the inalienable sovereignty over natural resources was a concept agreed to by a large majority of member States and thus should be clearly stated in the draft declaration. A proposal was also made to add the following words at the end of the paragraph: 'as well as the right to freely exploit such resources' (para 18).

84 'Report of the Preparatory Committee for the United Nations Conference on the Human Environment', para 19.

85 'Report of the Preparatory Committee for the United Nations Conference on the Human Environment', para 19.

86 'Report of the Preparatory Committee for the United Nations Conference on the Human Environment', paras 58 and 63 (some with an additional reference to the exercise of sovereignty in accordance with 'general principles of international law').

87 'Report of the Preparatory Committee for the United Nations Conference on the Human Environment', para 64.

88 See e.g. Brazil, Egypt and Yugoslavia's joint proposal: UN Doc. A/CONF.48/PC/WG.I(II)/CRP.3/Rev.2 (5 January 1972), at 2; Australia's proposal: UN Doc. A/CONF.48/PC/WG.I(II)/CRP.9 (1972), at 2; Sweden's proposal: UN Doc. A/CONF.48/PC/WG.I (II)/CRP.2 (1971), at 4; US statement of interpretation, UN Doc. A/CONF.48/14 (1972), at 118.

Two main amendments were retained. Firstly, the principle was tweaked to include an obligation to 'ensure' that activities within a State's jurisdiction do not cause transboundary harm, hence recognizing that the duty was one of due diligence that called on the State to regulate activities conducted on its territory by private entities.[89] Secondly, the responsibility of the State not to cause damage beyond its boundaries was combined with the concept of sovereign right over natural resources, with proposals either directly merging the two concepts[90] or making references to general principles of international law.[91] The reference to the concept of sovereignty over natural resources in the Preamble was deleted as a result. In retrospect, these two changes have been key to the wording of Principle 21 and its legal effects, clarifying its due-diligence nature and tweaking it to transform it into a norm that balances sovereignty and environmental protection.

Consensus built around a slightly simplified version of the combination between the sovereign right to exploit natural resources and the obligation to avoid harmful effects on the environment was put forward in a joint proposal by Brazil, Egypt and Yugoslavia.[92] It read:

> The sovereign right of each country to exploit its own resources in accordance with its own environmental policies, standards and criteria shall be exercised in consistency with the Charter of the United Nations and the principles of international law, in such a manner as to avoid producing harmful effects on other countries or on areas beyond national jurisdiction.[93]

89 See Sweden's proposal, UN Doc. A/CONF.48/PC/WG.1(II)/CRP.2 (16 December 1971), Principle 14; Canada's proposal, UN Doc. A/CONF.48/PC/WG.1(II)/CRP.4 (5 January 1972), Principle 1.

90 See Brazil's proposal, UN Doc. A/CONF.48/PC/WG.1(II)/CRP.3 (5 January 1972); and Brazil, Egypt and Yugoslavia's joint proposal, UN Doc. A/CONF.48/PC/WG.1(II)/CRP.3/Rev.1 (5 January 1972).

91 Working paper submitted by the Netherlands, UN Doc. A/CONF.48/PC/WG.1(II)/CRP.5 (5 January 1972), Principle 14: 'States have the responsibility, in accordance with the Charter of the United Nations and consistent with the principles of international law, to conduct their activities so as not to produce harmful effects on the environment of other States or of areas beyond the limits of national jurisdiction'; working paper submitted by India, UN Doc. A/CONF.48/PC/WG.1(II)/CRP.6 (5 January 1972), Preamble: 'Recognizing that each State has the responsibility to exercise its inalienable sovereignty over its natural resources in a manner compatible with the need to ensure the preservation and enhancement of the human environment', and Principle 8: 'Each State has the responsibility, in accordance with the Charter of the United Nations and consistent with the principles of international law, whether acting singly or in concert with other States, to conduct its activities so as not to cause damage to the environment of other States or to the environment of areas beyond the limits of national jurisdiction.'

92 Brazil, Egypt and Yugoslavia's joint proposal, UN Doc. A/CONF.48/PC/WG.I(II)/CRP.3/Rev.2, at 2.

93 Brazil, Egypt and Yugoslavia: revised working paper, UN Doc. A/CONF.48/PC/WG.1(II)/CRP.3/Rev.3 (10 January 1972), Principle 6.

The final version of the proposal, sponsored by Brazil, Egypt and Yugoslavia, along with Costa Rica and Zambia, added the phrase that the principle should be exercised in consistency with the UN Charter and the principles of international law.[94] The proposal was eventually accepted (with the exception that the reference to 'environmental policies, standards and criteria' was shortened to 'environmental policies'[95]) and was included in the second draft of the IWG. After its second session, the IWG returned to the PC with a new declaration made of a Preamble and twenty-three principles – including Principle 21 (then numbered Principle 18) in its final form.[96]

2.1.2.4 The Conference Working Group

At its last session (6–17 March 1972), the PC forwarded the draft produced by the IWG[97] – including its Principle 18, later to be Principle 21 – to the Conference without discussing the substance of the text.[98] However, at the Stockholm Conference, several States sought to amend the draft and, given the lack of agreement, a Working Group on the Declaration on the Human Environment, requested by China,[99] was established.

The wording of Principle 21 remained intact during these final negotiations, a reflection of the consensus that had built around it. Only three minor amendments in relation to Principle 21 were proposed,[100] but they were all rejected by the Working Group on the basis that the consensus reached by the

94 Brazil, Costa Rica, Egypt, Yugoslavia and Zambia: revised working paper, UN Doc. A/CONF.48/PC/WG.1(II)/CRP.3/Rev.4 (19 January 1972), Principle 5.

95 Compare UN Doc. A/CONF.48/PC/WG.1(II)/CRP.3/Rev.4 (1972), para 5, at 3, with UN Doc. A/CONF.48/4 (1972), Annex, para 18, at 4.

96 UN Doc. A/CONF.48/PC/16 (1972), Annex III.

97 Second draft of the IWG sent to PC and transmitted directly to the Conference, UN Doc. A/CONF.48/PC.16.

98 UN Doc. A/CONF.48/PC/17 (1972), para 83.

99 Seventh plenary meeting. Establishment of the working group on the Declaration on the Human Environment, Draft resolution proposed by China, no reference, on file with the author.

100 The three proposals were as follows: (1) Brazil: UN Doc. A/CONF.48/WG.1/CRP.6 (9 June 1972), para 5: Delete the 'in accordance with the Charter of the United Nations and the principles of international law' and add 'standards and criteria' after 'own environmental policies'; (2) Holy See: UN Doc. A/CONF.48/WG.1/CRP.7 (10 June 1972), para 5: Place a semicolon after the word 'resources', and replace the words 'pursuant to their own environmental policies, and the responsibility to ensure' by the words: '[t]hey should do so in accordance with a just environmental policy, ensuring in particular that activities within their jurisdiction or control'; (3) Proposal by Algeria, Burundi, Egypt, Guinea, Kenya, Libya, Sudan, United Republic of Tanzania and Zambia: UN Doc. A/CONF.48/WG.1/CRP.22 (12 June 1972): Insert the words 'to control and' between the words 'the sovereign right' and the words 'to exploit'.

Working Group was fragile and ought to be preserved. Similarly, a request by the United States to clarify the text of the principle was rejected by the Working Group.[101]

Negotiations over the Declaration continued until the last day of the Conference. The final text retained twenty-one of the twenty-three committee's principles, notably deleting the principle on the duty of States to inform others of activities within their territories that might have an adverse extraterritorial effect because of an absence of consensus on the obligation,[102] and added four new ones.

2.1.2.5 The Adoption of the Declaration and the Immediate Crystallization of Principle 21

The UNGA adopted the Stockholm Declaration on 15 December 1972 in Resolution 2994 (XXVII).[103] The vote of 112–0 (with ten abstentions from the Soviet bloc and South Africa) illustrates the quasi-universal acceptance of the text. In addition, Resolution 2995 (XXVII), adopted on the same day, reaffirmed the obligation not to cause substantial damage to zones outside the bounds of national jurisdiction[104] and included the principle of information sharing that had been deleted from the final version of the Stockholm Declaration.[105] In response to concerns that the duty to share information

101 'Report of the Working Group on the Declaration on the Human Environment', no reference, para 327, on file with the author. The US comment of interpretation relative to Principle 21 read as follows: 'The United States of America considers it obvious that nothing contained in this principle, or elsewhere in the Declaration, diminishes in any way the obligation of States to prevent environmental damage or gives rise to any right on the part of States to take actions in derogation of the rights of other States or of the community of nations. The statement on the responsibility of States for damage caused to the environment of other States or of areas beyond the limits of national jurisdiction is not in any way a limitation on the above obligation, but an affirmation of existing rules concerning liability in the event of default on the obligation.'

102 The idea can be traced back to the suggestion of the Secretary-General about a principle on 'the right and duty to consult each other if there is reason to believe that any planned activity may cause serious harm to the environment in general or infringe upon the environmental rights of other States' (UN Doc. A/CONF.48/PC/WG.1/CRP.4, at 14). The lack of consensus was particularly due to tensions between Brazil and Argentina, with Argentina wanting to deter Brazil from harming its water supply and wildlife by building more and larger dams on the upper Parana River. See B Garth, 'The Stockholm Conference: A Synopsis and Analysis' (1973) 8 *Stanford Journal of International Studies* 31, at 42.

103 UNGA Res. 2994 (XXVII) (15 December 1972).

104 UNGA Res. 2995 (XXVII) (15 December 1972), para 1.

105 UNGA Res. 2995 (XXVII), para 2: '[C]o-operation between States in the field of the environment, including co-operation towards the implementation of principles 21 and 22 of the

might restrict prevention to an obligation of information sharing, Resolution 2996 (XXVII) clarified that no UNGA resolution adopted at the 27th session could affect Principles 21 and 22,[106] thereby consolidating the status of Principle 21 in international law.

Despite the non-binding character of the Declaration, the text jumpstarted the development of international environmental law. The Stockholm Conference immediately acted as a catalyst for the creation of a new international legal order based on the preventive principle: numerous agreements were signed to translate the new rationale of Principle 21 into legally binding obligations.[107] The legislative dynamism of the post-Stockholm period is evident in the fact that compared to the pre-Stockholm era, the number of multilateral environmental agreements more than doubled between the Stockholm and Rio Conferences.[108] In other words, the Stockholm Conference marked the starting point of an 'environmental revolution',[109] with Principle 21 at its centre.

2.1.3 *The Three Components of Stockholm Principle 21*

While the preceding section presented the diplomatic negotiations relative to the drafting of Principle 21, the analysis in this section explains the legal origins of the three components that form Principle 21: (1) the concept of permanent

Declaration of the United Nations Conference on the Human Environment, will be effectively achieved if official and public knowledge is provided of the technical data relating to the work to be carried out by States within their national jurisdiction, with a view to avoiding significant harm that may occur in the environment of the adjacent area.'

106 UNGA Res. 2996 (XXVII) (15 December 1972).

107 Convention for the Prevention of Marine Pollution by Dumping from Ships and Aircraft, Oslo, 15 February 1972, in force 7 April 1974, (1972) 11 ILM 262; Convention on the Prevention of Marine Pollution by Dumping of Wastes and Other Matter, London, 29 December 1972, in force 30 August 1975, (1972) 11 ILM 1294; Convention for the Conservation of Antarctic Seals, London, 1 June 1972, in force 11 March 1978, (1972) 11 ILM 251; UNESCO Convention for the Protection of the World Cultural and Natural Heritage, Paris, 16 November 1972, in force 17 December 1975, (1972) 11 ILM 1358; Convention on International Trade in Endangered Species of Wild Fauna and Flora, Washington, DC, 3 March 1973, in force 1 July 1975, 993 UNTS 243; International Convention for the Prevention of Pollution from Ships, London, 2 November 1973, in force 2 October 1983, (1973) 12 ILM 1319; Convention on the Conservation of European Wildlife and Natural Habitats, Berne, 19 September 1979, in force 1 June 1982, (1982) UKTS 56 Cmnd 8738; Convention on Long-Range Transboundary Air Pollution, Geneva, 13 November 1979, in force 16 March 1983, (1979) 18 ILM 1442; Convention on the Conservation of Antarctic Marine Living Resources, Canberra, 20 May 1980, in force 7 April 1982, (1980) 19 ILM 841; Convention on the Conservation of Migratory Species of Wild Animals, Bonn, 23 June 1979, in force 1 November 1983, (1980) 19 ILM 15.

108 Sand, 'The Evolution of International Environmental Law', 35.

109 Grinevald, *La biosphère de l'anthropocène*, 137.

sovereignty over natural resources, (2) the obligation to avoid harm to the environment of other States and (3) the duty to avoid harm in areas beyond national jurisdiction.

2.1.3.1 Permanent Sovereignty over Natural Resources

The first element of Principle 21 recognizes the principle of permanent sovereignty over natural resources, a principle that is not driven by an environmental rationale at its core. Indeed, it emerged in the context of the affirmation of the right of peoples under colonial rule to self-determination and the right of newly independent States to economic development. It was adopted to respond to two interrelated claims: one from the peoples under colonial rule that sought to protect and preserve their natural resources from being exploited by the colonial power and another from newly independent States that further affirmed their economic emancipation from foreign companies exploiting their resources.[110] The first legal recognition of the principle can be found in UNGA Resolution 523 (VI), adopted in 1952, that mentioned for the first time the right of States to 'determine freely the use of their natural resources'.[111] Subsequent resolutions brought further clarity to the concept by characterizing it as a 'basic constituent of the right to self-determination'[112] that seeks to protect 'the right of peoples freely to use and exploit their natural wealth and resources'.[113] The work of the UNGA culminated in 1962 with the adoption of Resolution 1803 (XVII),[114] which did not leave the exercise of sovereignty unbridled but specified that it should contribute to national development and to the 'well-being of the people of the state concerned'.[115] The incorporation of the principle in the 1974 Charter of Economic Rights and Duties of States constituted the last step in the elaboration of the concept[116] and re-centred it on the right of the State (in opposition to the right of the peoples) to exercise full permanent sovereignty over their natural resources.[117]

110 G Elian, 'Le principe de la souveraineté sur les ressources nationales et ses incidences juridiques sur le commerce international' (1976) 149 *Collected Courses of the Hague Academy of International Law* 1–85; J Fawcett, 'Trade and Finance in International Law' (1976) 123 *Collected Courses of the Hague Academy of International Law* 215–310.

111 UNGA Res. 523 (VI) (12 January 1952).

112 UNGA Res. 1314 (XIII) (12 December 1958).

113 UNGA Res. 626 (VII) (21 December 1952).

114 UNGA Res. 1803 (XVII) (14 December 1962).

115 UNGA Res. 1803 (XVII), para 1.

116 FX Perrez, *Cooperative Sovereignty: From Independence to Interdependence in the Structure of International Environmental Law* (Kluwer Law International 2000) 85.

117 'Charter of Economic Rights and Duties of States', UNGA Res. 3281 (XXVII) (12 December 1974), Article 2(1).

The concept of permanent sovereignty assigns legal powers over natural resources but is not intended to fulfil environmental objectives. As a result, its inclusion in Stockholm Principle 21 is consequential for the principle of prevention, as it presents it as a pragmatic compromise between a sovereign right to resource use and a duty of environmental protection and not as an absolute principle pertaining to environmental protection. However, this leads to inherent tensions between the different components of Principle 21, which are discussed further in Section 2.1.3.4.

2.1.3.2 Prohibition to Cause Harm to the Environment of Other States

Contrary to the first component of Principle 21, which concentrates on the rights of the sovereign State, its second and third components concentrate on its obligations and, more specifically, on the limitations put on territorial sovereignty. The second clause of Principle 21 recognizes the prohibition to cause harm to the environment of other States. The no-harm rule was described in Chapter 1 as part of the foundations of prevention and will therefore not be analysed further here. Suffice it to say that given its logic of harm avoidance, its inclusion in Principle 21 is no surprise.

2.1.3.3 Prohibition to Cause Harm to Areas beyond the Limits of National Jurisdiction

The third component of Principle 21 prohibits causing damage to the environment beyond national jurisdiction. The progressive nature of Principle 21 lies in this component: no longer concerned with the preservation of territorial sovereignty, it gives prevention its environmental focus. By extending the spatial scope of the principle, the last component changes the principle of prevention from a norm merely justified by considerations of sovereignty to a norm driven by an ultimate objective of environmental protection. Admittedly, the global commons are envisaged by contrast to areas under State sovereignty, which means that the principle still relies on sovereignty as a referential, only to operate in opposition to it. It remains, however, that, as will be discussed in Chapter 8, the third component of Principle 21 has significantly reshaped the rationale underpinning prevention and formed the background to its subsequent evolution as an a-territorial obligation, applicable irrespective of the location of harm.[118]

[118] For further discussion, refer to Chapter 8.4.

2.1.3.4 Tensions within Principle 21

Principle 21 combines three core norms of international law brought together under the umbrella of a single principle. Yet, they have their origins in very different legal conceptualizations of natural resources and the environment. The concept of permanent sovereignty over natural resources recognizes an inalienable link between sovereignty and ownership over natural resources. As for the no-harm rule, it is based on classical legal concepts used to facilitate the coexistence of sovereign States. Finally, the duty to protect the environment beyond national jurisdiction originates from the recognition that the planet is an entity worthy of protection.

Principle 21 treats the three components equally and, given their apparent irreconcilable nature, has been characterized as 'schizophrenic'.[119] Taken separately, the concept of permanent sovereignty over natural resources and the prohibition to cause environmental harm can be read as pretty absolute.[120] Their combination in Principle 21 has been criticized for making the prevention principle inoperative.[121] Some authors note that the concept of sovereignty over natural resources takes precedence over the demands of environmental protection, as exemplified by the fact that States use it to 'resist international pressure to protect their natural resources from overuse and depletion'.[122] Conversely, the inclusion of the sovereignty component in Principle 21 has a reassuring effect on States that are more likely to buy into environmental obligations if they feel that their sovereign rights will be (up to a certain extent) taken into account and preserved. Such is the reason why Stockholm Principle 21 (or its equivalent, Rio Principle 2) is often reiterated in international treaties, generally in the preamble[123] but also possibly in the operative part.[124]

119 T Kuokkanen, *International Law and the Environment: Variations on a Theme* (Kluwer Law International 2002) 350.

120 RD Munro and J Lammers (eds), *Environmental Protection and Sustainable Development: Legal Principles and Recommendations Adopted by the Experts Group on Environmental Law of the World Commission on Environment and Development* (Graham & Trotman 1987) 77.

121 J Knox, 'Myth and Reality of Transboundary Environmental Impact Assessment' (2002) 96 *American Journal of International Law* 291, at 293.

122 Perrez, *Cooperative Sovereignty*, 95.

123 See e.g. United Nations Framework Convention on Climate Change, New York, 9 May 1992, in force 24 March 1994, 1771 UNTS 107, Preamble, which reaffirms Principle 2. See also protocols to the LRTAP Convention, including Protocol to the 1979 Convention on Long Range Transboundary Air Pollution to Abate Acidification, Eutrophication and Ground-Level Ozone, Gothenburg, 30 November 1999, in force 17 May 2005 and amended May 2012, UN Doc. EB/AIR/1999.

124 Convention on Biological Diversity, Nairobi, 22 May 1992, in force 29 December 1993, (1992) 31 ILM 822, Article 3.

The three apparently diverging clauses of Stockholm Principle 21 will tend to be interpreted as being mutually supportive following the tradition in general international law that relies on a 'strong presumption against normative conflict'.[125] This makes sense given that the Stockholm negotiators combined both concepts within one principle to ensure that the two concepts were not read in an absolute manner. The principle of permanent sovereignty over natural resources therefore should be interpreted in light of environmental concerns and not in opposition to those. The discussion that follows presents three interpretive approaches to Stockholm Principle 21 that contribute to moving beyond its apparent tensions.

A RE-CONCEPTUALIZATION OF THE NOTION OF SOVEREIGNTY A first approach to the interpretation of Stockholm Principle 21 consists in defining sovereignty as a rule that is intrinsically limited.[126] As explained in Chapter 1, such is the logic underpinning the no-harm rule, based on the idea that territorial sovereignty involves not only the right of the State to use its own territory as it sees fits but, as a 'corollary',[127] the duty to use its territory so as not to breach the territorial integrity of another State. An extension of this rationale can be applied to Principle 21 more generally by, in the words of the Secretary-General of the Stockholm Conference Maurice Strong, relying on a new understanding of sovereignty 'based not on the surrender of national sovereignties but on better means of exercising them collectively, and with a greater sense of responsibility for the common good'.[128] Similar calls for a renewed interpretation of sovereignty so as to reconcile it with environmental protection are found in the doctrine under the names of 'functional',[129] 'positive'[130] or 'responsible'[131] sovereignty

[125] ILC, 'Fragmentation of International Law: Difficulties Arising from the Diversification and Expansion of International Law. Report of the Study Group of the International Law Commission Finalized by Martti Koskenniemi' (2006) UN Doc. A/CN.4/L.682, para 37.

[126] NS Politis, 'Le problème des limitations de la souveraineté et la théorie de l'abus des droits dans les rapports internationaux' (1925) 5 *Collected Courses of the Hague Academy of International Law* 1–122, at 112; J Andrassy, 'Les relations internationales de voisinage' (1951) 79 *Collected Courses of the Hague Academy of International Law* 73–182, at 95; M Virally, 'Vers un droit international du développement' (1965) *Annuaire français de droit international* 3, at 10.

[127] *Island of Palmas (Netherlands/United States of America)*, (1928) 2 RIAA 829, at 839.

[128] 'Opening statement of the Stockholm Conference on Human Environment by Maurice Strong: Summary of the Debate', para 41(a), on file with the author.

[129] F Francioni, 'The Private Sector and the Challenge of Implementation', in P-M Dupuy and JE Viñuales (eds), *Harnessing Foreign Investment to Promote Environmental Protection: Incentives and Safeguards* (Cambridge University Press 2013) 24–49, at 30, 31.

[130] Perrez, *Cooperative Sovereignty*, 2.

[131] Francioni, 'The Private Sector and the Challenge of Implementation', 34.

exercised 'to the general interest of the world community to respect and protect environmental values'.[132] From this perspective, the principle of sovereignty is not only interpreted as a justification of the no-harm rule but also as enabling environmental protection in a Westphalian international structure.

A RE-CONCEPTUALIZATION OF THE PRINCIPLE OF PERMANENT SOVEREIGNTY OVER NATURAL RESOURCES A second interpretive approach concentrates more specifically on the principle of permanent sovereignty over natural resources and considers that it cannot be understood as being absolute. The limitations put to the exercise of the principle are evident in the wording of Principle 21, which provides that it has to be exercised 'in accordance with the United Nations Charter and the principles of international law'. Although which specific principles are herein referenced remains open for interpretation, it most likely includes the principles of sovereign equality,[133] territorial integrity[134] and good neighbourliness,[135] which all dictate a relative approach to the right to use natural resources. This approach is in line with UNGA resolutions on the principle of permanent sovereignty that provided that it could only be exercised 'in such a manner as to avoid producing harmful effects on other countries'.[136] It was reproduced in the wording of Article 193 of the UN Convention on the Law of the Sea (UNCLOS) – an adaptation of Principle 21 – that the right to exploit natural resources can only be exercised 'in accordance' with the duty to protect the marine environment.[137]

An alternative interpretation of the principle of permanent sovereignty over natural resources contributes to highlighting the intrinsic limits of the principle: it understands the principle as concerned with the well-being of the people and not of the State itself.[138] Such is the position of Abi-Saab, who postulated that permanent sovereignty over natural resources is a people's right to protect themselves from the weaknesses of their own government.[139] Under

132 Francioni, 'The Private Sector and the Challenge of Implementation', 31.

133 Charter of the United Nations, San Francisco, 26 June 1945, in force 24 October 1945, 1 UNTS 980, Article 2(1).

134 Charter of the United Nations, Article 2(4).

135 Charter of the United Nations, Article 1(2).

136 UNGA Res. 2849 (XXVI) (20 December 1971); 'Charter of Economic Rights and Duties of States', UNGA Res. 3281 (XXVII) (12 December 1974).

137 United Nations Convention on the Law of the Sea, Montego Bay, 10 December 1982, in force 16 November 1994, 1833 UNTS 3, Article 193.

138 UNGA Res. 1803 (XVII) (14 December 1962), para 1.

139 G Abi-Saab, 'La souveraineté permanente sur les ressources naturelles', in M Bedjaoui (ed), *Droit international: bilan et perspectives* (vol 2, Pedone 1991) 646: 'La raison d'être juridique de ce principe est donc de protéger l'Etat contre sa propre faiblesse, ou plutôt de protéger sa

this perspective, the principle becomes completely distinct from that of sovereignty itself: it protects the population from governmental abuse of national resources, whereas sovereignty protects the integrity of the State itself.[140] Perhaps counterintuitive at first because a concept including the notion of sovereignty can be expected to relate to the protection of the State itself, this interpretation is nevertheless corroborated by the approach taken at the Stockholm Conference, which was more concerned by what governments should do in relation to their own people rather than by what a State should do in relation to other States[141] and, more broadly, by the fact that the principle of permanent sovereignty over natural resources has been recognized as a right under human rights treaties.[142] On this basis, the concept of permanent sovereignty over natural resources is not only reconciled with but automatically complements the environmental clauses of Principle 21. It forces States to preserve their own domestic environment in order to ensure the well-being of their citizens, thus contributing to the recognition of an obligation to prevent harm operating in a purely domestic context (as discussed in Chapter 9) on the basis of the first clause of Principle 21 itself (and not as a result of the extension of Principle 21 into a more comprehensive obligation of prevention).

A RENEWED INTERPRETATION OF THE PHRASE 'PURSUANT TO THEIR OWN ENVIRONMENTAL [AND DEVELOPMENTAL] POLICIES' A final proposal can be

composante humaine – la population – contre la faiblesse ou les carences de sa composante institutionnelle – le gouvernement.'

140 International Law Association (ILA), Committee on International Law on Sustainable Development, 'Fifth Report of the Committee on International Law on Sustainable Development', Sofia, 75th Session, 2012, at 14, noting that the principle had evolved 'from a merely rights-based into a duties as well as rights-based principle'. See also J Crawford, 'Right of Self-Determination in International Law', in P Alston (ed), *Peoples' Rights* (Oxford University Press 2001) 7, at 22: 'If the people of the State have permanent sovereignty over natural resources, the possibility must be allowed of the people holding their government internationally responsible for its stewardship of those resources'; and N Schrijver, 'Fifty Years Permanent Sovereignty over Natural Resources. The 1962 UN Declaration as the Opinio Iuris Communis', in M Bungenberg and S Hobe (eds), *Permanent Sovereignty over Natural Resources* (Springer 2015) 15–28, at 22, on the 'right holders of permanent sovereignty over natural resources'.

141 Caldwell, *International Environmental Policy*, 65.

142 International Covenant on Civil and Political Rights, 16 December 1966, 999 UNTS 171; International Covenant on Economic and Cultural Rights, 16 December 1966, 993 UNTS 3, joint Article 1(2): 'All peoples may for their own ends, freely dispose of their natural wealth and resources without prejudice to any obligations arising out of international economic co-operation, based upon the principle of mutual benefit and international law. In no case shall a people be deprived of it'; African Charter on Human and Peoples' Rights, Banjul, 27 June 1981, in force 21 October 1986 (1982) 21 ILM 58, Article 21(1): 'All peoples shall freely dispose of their wealth and natural resources.'

made to advance the argument that the right to permanent sovereignty over natural resources operates in association with, and not opposition to, the rest of Principle 21: it consists in reading the first clause of Principle 21 *in light of* the second part of the phrase that clarifies that the right has to be exercised 'pursuant to the State's own environmental policies'. The clause is particularly interesting. While it might give the impression that it concentrates on the right of the State to design its national environmental policies, it in effect limits this prerogative since the State is under the duty to incorporate the international obligations to which it has committed in its national environmental policies. The manner in which international obligations are integrated in the municipal law of a State will evidently depend on the specificities of its domestic system.[143] However, irrespective of such particularities, the right to sovereignty over natural resources is restricted in the context of Principle 21 by the fact that domestic environmental policies have to be compliant with international law; the phrase establishes a minimum threshold of environmental protection below which the State cannot go when exploiting its natural resources. For instance, while a party to UNCLOS would be able to exercise its right to exploit the marine resources under its jurisdiction, it would not be able to design an environmental policy to do so in a manner that would violate its obligation to protect the marine environment under Article 192.

Another level of limitation to the right to permanent sovereignty is found in Principle 2 of the Rio Declaration on Environment and Development (Rio Declaration, discussed further in Chapter 4), which replicates Stockholm Principle 21 but adds the phrase 'and development policies' to the clause on 'pursuant to their own environmental policies'. Under this approach, the imperatives set by prevention direct that developmental policies cannot result in the creation of significant harm to the territory of other States or to areas beyond national jurisdiction. Consequently, the Rio addition has the potential to restrain socio-economic development on the basis that it negatively affects the integrity of the environment. It therefore becomes evident that the right to exploit natural resources cannot be exercised without restraint: the first component operates in complete harmony with the rest of Principle 21.

The three proposed interpretations concerning the first component of Principle 21 leave little doubt about the fact that it cannot be read in an absolute manner. Overall, Principle 21 blends different, contradictory values acting together to find a balance between preserving sovereign rights and protecting the environment.

143 See P-M Dupuy, 'International Law and Domestic (Municipal) Law', in *Max Planck Encyclopedia of Public International Law* (Oxford University Press 2011).

2.1.4 *From Principle 21 to Prevention*

The preceding section having explained the emergence of Principle 21, the relationship between Principle 21 and prevention remains to be clarified. Principle 21 expresses a rationale of prevention: the prohibition of environmental harm undeniably comes from the realization that harm should be avoided rather than repaired. However, prevention has eventually outgrown the three components of Principle 21 to become an independent legal principle. Principle 21 remains a core manifestation of prevention, acknowledged as customary and regularly referred to in treaty and case law. Nevertheless, the evolution of the principle of prevention has not stopped with its inclusion in the Stockholm Declaration (nor the Rio Declaration, for that matter) but has continued to develop to become a more advanced form of prevention that now operates in parallel with Principle 21.

The distinction between the two will become clearer in the course of this study, but, at this stage, two epistemological differences can be put in evidence. The first difference lies in the fact that Principle 21 emphasizes an obligation of restraint (prohibition to cause damage), whereas prevention, its advanced form, is conceptualized as an obligation of proactivity, one that involves 'positive obligations to take active measures to protect and preserve the environment'.[144] The distinction is more one of perspective than of legal requirements because the verb 'ensure' in Principle 21 – added during the Stockholm negotiations – refers to an obligation of conduct, which opens the door to interpreting Principle 21 as a due-diligence obligation. The second difference is perhaps less reconcilable. Principle 21 remains anchored in a territorial perspective, using sovereignty as its referential, whereas prevention in its advanced form promotes the protection of the environment irrespective of location. It operates outside of any reference to sovereignty, as it is concerned with preventing damage to the environment *tout court*. In sum, the expression of prevention in its modern form includes Principle 21 but cannot simply be summarized by it; as this study will demonstrate, it has become a more complex principle in terms of content and spatial scope.

2.2 THE CURATIVE APPROACH AS A SECONDARY REGIME

The first part of this chapter focused on prevention and explained how it became the main norm of international environmental law; the discussion

[144] *South China Sea Arbitration (The Republic of the Philippines v. The People's Republic of China)* (Permanent Court of Arbitration), Award on the Merits, 12 July 2016, para 941.

that now follows concentrates on the rationale that it replaced: reparation. It highlights the reasons why the curative approach was ill suited to respond to environmental degradation (2.2.1) and explains that it was thus relegated to a complementary but not obsolete in specific contexts role (2.2.2).

2.2.1 *Drawbacks to the Reparation Approach*

The preventive approach adopted at the Stockholm Conference provided an alternative to the reparation regime that had revealed itself unable to respond to the specificity of environmental harm due to (1) legal and (2) political constraints.

2.2.1.1 Limitations of the Law of State Responsibility

The law of State responsibility for wrongful acts is ill adapted to cater to the specificity of environmental harm, which explains why the ex post approach to environmental damage was replaced by a preventive logic. The challenges faced by the law of State responsibility in this context are well known and include difficulties in identifying the source of environmental damage, establishing a causal link between a suspected harmful activity and the actual damage and attributing the wrongful act to a State.[145] Additionally, the three types of reparation for harm caused by an internationally wrongful act available under the law of State responsibility – satisfaction, restitution and compensation[146] – are often unsatisfactory from the perspective of an environmental protection objective as they do not respond to the fact that the primary victim is the environment (and not the State) and are no solution to the irreversibility of harm. Compensation for damage also brings its own challenges; irrespective of the fact that it will not restore the status ex ante,[147] it is also faced with intrinsic difficulties related to putting a monetary value on

[145] For a full overview of the limitations of the law of State responsibility, see C Redgwell, 'The Wrong Trousers: State Responsibility and International Environmental Law', in M Evans and P Koutrakos (eds), *The International Responsibility of the European Union: European and International Perspectives* (Hart 2013) 257–74.

[146] ILC, 'Draft Articles on Responsibility of States for Internationally Wrongful Acts (with Commentaries)' (2001) *Yearbook of the International Law Commission* (vol II, part 2) 31, chap 2, in particular, Articles 34–37.

[147] *Dispute Concerning Delimitation of the Maritime Boundary between Ghana and Côte d'Ivoire in the Atlantic Ocean (Ghana/Côte d'Ivoire)* (Provisional Measures) ITLOS No. 23 (25 April 2015), para 90: '[A]ny compensation awarded would never be able to restore the status quo ante in respect of the seabed and subsoil.'

natural resources and the environment,[148] to gathering knowledge of the state of the environment prior to the wrongful act and to establishing a causal link between the wrongful act and the damage.[149] In light of these difficulties, it is clear that the law of State responsibility, which was designed to facilitate inter-State relations, cannot offer an adapted solution to environmental degradation.

2.2.1.2 Political Reluctance towards State Responsibility

The limitations of the law of State responsibility in the context of environmental harm are not only strictly legal but also political, stemming from a general reluctance to apply the principles of State responsibility to environmental harm. This is explained in part by the fact that States are particularly unwilling to accept international responsibility for conduct that is not taken directly by their organs or for harm arising from economic activities in general, which is commonly the case in the context of environmental harm.[150] Such political reluctance is anecdotally evidenced by the famous footnote of the Convention on Long Range Transboundary Air Pollution that specifies that the text 'does not contain a rule on State liability as to damage'.[151] Footnotes are very seldom used in international treaties: this exception reflects strong concerns that the adoption of a preventive treaty could be interpreted as an acknowledgement that its Parties would be liable in case of damage. More generally, the lack of interest of States in further developing international law relative to liability and compensation for environmental damage is evidenced by the fact that the call of Stockholm Principle 22 in this regard had to be reiterated twenty years later in the Rio Declaration because little progress had been made in this context.[152]

148 ILC, 'Draft Articles on Responsibility of States for Internationally Wrongful Acts (with Commentaries)', Commentary to Article 36, para 15, at 101: Damage to environmental values (or non-use values in general) is 'as a matter of principle, no less real and compensable than damage to property, though it may be difficult to quantify'.

149 See e.g. the difficulties faced by the UN Compensation Commission that assessed Iraq's liability for environmental damage and the depletion of natural resources as a result of its invasion of Kuwait in 1991, as discussed in M Huguenin et al., 'Assessment and Valuation of Damage to the Environment', in C Payne and P Sand (eds), *Gulf War Reparations and the UN Compensation Commission: Environmental Liability* (Oxford University Press 2011) 67–94.

150 T Scovazzi, 'State Responsibility for Environmental Harm' (2002) 12 *Yearbook of International Environmental Law* 43, at 56.

151 Convention on Long Range Transboundary Air Pollution, Geneva, 13 November 1979, in force 16 March 1983, (1979) 18 ILM 1442, footnote to Article 8(f).

152 Rio de Janeiro Declaration on Environment and Development (Rio de Janeiro, 3 to 14 June 1992), (1992) 31 ILM 876, Principle 13, calling on States to 'cooperate in *an expeditious and more determined* manner to develop further international law' (emphasis added).

The evident political reluctance towards the law of State responsibility in the context of environmental harm is also reflected in the fact that environmental adjudication is underdeveloped compared to other branches of international law. Historically, States that seemingly had a strong case to bring in front of an international dispute-settlement body[153] have been unwilling to start such proceedings, worried that an international tribunal might set a precedent that would later affect the State's own future conduct or that would put its own environmental practices under the spotlight.[154] The Chernobyl incident provides a striking example. The international responsibility of the Soviet Union to prevent the disaster could have formed the basis of international proceedings, but no State brought a claim against the Soviet Union; on the contrary, preventive measures were immediately agreed internationally to prevent a similar disaster from occurring again.[155] Similarly, and more recently, Ecuador and Colombia preferred to settle the *Aerial Herbicide Spraying* case after having agreed on a preventive framework that would avoid the repetition of harm instead of seeking clarification on their rights and obligations.[156]

As a result, the recognition of a wrongful act has been dissociated from the duty to compensate; while a wrongful act is rarely acknowledged, States accept to pay compensation for environmental harm in order to avoid leaving the victims of the harm uncompensated. A typical example is found in the *Trail Smelter* case, where the arbitral tribunal did not have to rule on the responsibility of Canada as such given that Canada had already accepted responsibility in the compromis[157] but was tasked with identifying the damage caused and the compensation that ought to be provided to the United States.[158] The same dissociation is also visible in relation to a number of major environmental

[153] P Sands and J Peel, *Principles of International Environmental Law* (3rd edn, Cambridge University Press 2012) 938.

[154] A Schwabach, 'The Sandoz Spill: The Failure of International Law to Protect the Rhine from Pollution' (1989) 16 *Ecology Law Quarterly* 443, at 470, on the fact that 'countries may be reluctant to drag the issue of Rhine pollution into court for fear of encountering international criticism of their own pollution'.

[155] See, in particular, Convention on Early Notification of a Nuclear Accident, Vienna, 26 September 1986, in force 27 October 1986, (1986) 25 ILM 1370.

[156] *Aerial Herbicide Spraying (Ecuador v. Colombia)* case, ICJ General List No. 138, Order of 13 September 2013, (2013) ICJ Rep 278, at 279, explaining the preventive measures that have been taken by the two parties to avoid a repetition of the issue (including the establishment of an exclusion zone and the creation of a joint commission).

[157] 'Compromis d'arbitrage' (United States and Canada) (15 April 1935), 3 RIAA 1907–1910, Articles III and XII.

[158] *Trail Smelter (United States v. Canada)* (16 April 1938 and 11 March 1941), (1941) 3 RIAA 1905, questions 1 and 4 in particular.

damage cases for which the responsibility of the State was never explicitly acknowledged. This includes the *Fukuryu Maru* affair involving a Japanese fishing vessel and fishermen caught in the fallout of an American nuclear test in the Pacific in 1954, for which the United States paid the Japanese government *ex gratia* $2 million as compensation,[159] and the 1989 Sandoz chemical spill caused by a fire in the Sandoz storehouse that caused major pollution of the Rhine River and for which the Swiss authorities (alongside Sandoz) did not acknowledge their responsibility.[160] In other words, States tend to be open to compensate for environmental harm but are more reluctant to make it an official recognition of their international responsibility.

In sum, the 'limitations inherent in the very mechanism of reparation' applied in the context of environmental damage[161] and a clear political reluctance to develop a regime of State responsibility adapted to environmental harm explain why the preventive rationale has been favoured over the curative approach. Combined with the contextual factors discussed previously, these actions explain why the alternative principle of prevention proved more attractive politically and consolidated quickly after the Stockholm Conference.

2.2.2 *Nevertheless a Secondary Approach*

As prevention became the primary norm of international environmental law, the curative perspective found in no-harm continued to influence the rationale of international treaties adopted to respond to a particular category of environmental risks related to ultra-hazardous activities. These risks are defined as 'all activities which involve a risk of serious harm on an international scale which cannot be eliminated by the exercise of the utmost care'.[162] Despite the risks these activities carry, they are nevertheless accepted for their social usefulness. The specific nature of these activities calls to a specific legal answer, one that does not seek to avoid risks (that cannot be fully eliminated) but that can repair and compensate in case of harm. It therefore means that ultra-hazardous activities are not regulated by the principle of prevention but by no-harm, which is better suited for its ex post perspective to harm avoidance.

159 Sands and Peel, *Principles of International Environmental Law*, 717.
160 J Kulesza, *Due Diligence in International Law* (Brill/Martinus Nijhoff 2016) 98.
161 *Gabčíkovo-Nagymaros Project (Hungary/Slovakia)* (Judgment) (1997) ICJ Rep 7, para 140.
162 CW Jenks, 'Liability for Ultra-hazardous Activities in International Law' (1966) 117 *Collected Courses of the Hague Academy of International Law* 99–200, at 195.

Civil liability regimes specific to oil pollution[163] and nuclear energy[164] were therefore adopted in the 1960s. They were driven by the rationale of corrective justice that characterizes no-harm: they were not concerned with the wrongful act per se but rather with compensating the victim for the harm experienced.[165] As a result, they only require that the victim puts into evidence a causal link between the accident and the subsequent damage, without having to prove that the operator committed fault. Civil liability regimes integrated the no-harm/tort logic concerned with the compensation of victims. In addition, they provided an alternative to the law of State responsibility by canalizing liability on the economic operator to ensure that the polluter is the one made responsible for the risks that it takes.

The legal regime applicable to ultra-hazardous activities puts into evidence the two paths taken by international environmental law from the 1960s onwards. The most followed route applied a preventive objective to environmental harm, whereas an additional path, concentrating on a curative approach, was designed to respond to the specificity of ultra-hazardous activities. As the preventive rationale was gaining pre-eminence in international environmental law, the reparation approach became a secondary, albeit still relevant, regime in the field.

2.3 CONCLUSION

The Stockholm Conference contributed to a reorientation of the international law framework applicable to natural resources and the environment, moving

163 International Convention on Civil Liability for Oil Pollution Damage, Brussels, 29 November 1969, in force 19 June 1975, 973 UNTS 3; International Convention Relating to the Intervention on the High Seas in Cases of Oil Pollution Casualties, Brussels, 29 November 1969, 970 UNTS 211; International Convention on the Establishment of an International Fund for Compensation for Oil Pollution Damage, Brussels, 18 December 1971, in force 16 October 1978, (1972) 11 ILM 284; Convention on Civil Liability for Oil Pollution Damage Resulting from Exploration for and Exploration of Seabed Mineral Resources, London, 1 May 1977, not in force, (1977) 16 ILM 1450.

164 OECD Convention on Third Party Liability in the Field of Nuclear Energy, Paris, 29 July 1960, in force 1 April 1968, 956 UNTS 251; amended by Additional Protocol to Paris Convention on Third Party Liability in the Field of Nuclear Energy, 28 January 1964, in force 1 April 1968, 956 UNTS 335 and by the Protocol of 16 November 1982, 12 February 2004. See also the 1963 Supplementary Convention to the Paris Convention, Brussels, 31 January 1963, 1041 UNTS 358; Convention on Civil Liability for Nuclear Damage, Vienna, 29 May 1963, in force 12 November 1977, 1063 UNTS 265; Convention on the Liability of Operators of Nuclear Ships, Brussels, 25 May 1962, not in force, (1963) 57 AJIL 268; Convention Relating to Civil Liability in the Field of Maritime Carriage of Nuclear Material, Brussels, 17 December 1971, in force 15 July 1975, 944 UNTS 255.

165 T Berwick, 'Responsibility and Liability for Environmental Damage: A Roadmap for International Environmental Regimes' (1997) 10 *Georgetown International Environmental Law Review* 257.

from the traditional no-harm rule, operating within a classical reactive legal framework, to the prevention principle, concerned with anticipating risks in order to protect the environment. This paradigm shift changed the nature of the reparation and resource-management logics that were at the origins of prevention. In relation to reparation, the no-harm rule followed two different paths: on the one hand, it was integrated into Stockholm Principle 21 in the preventive approach and evolved with a logic of environmental protection; on the other hand, it manifested in civil liability regimes relative to ultra-hazardous activities and developed in a curative context concerned with victim compensation. As for resource management, the preventive approach influenced, in turn, the regime by framing it within a different perspective, one not only based on purely anthropocentric motivations but also valuing resources for their intrinsic worth.

CONCLUSION TO PART I

EMERGENCE OF THE PRINCIPLE OF PREVENTION AND EXISTING TENSIONS

Part I concentrated on the evolution of international environmental law and, more specifically, looked at its premises before World War II and its consecration at the Stockholm Summit through the spectrum of its cornerstone, the principle of prevention. It identified the roots of the principle in the dual response of international law to environmental issues – the general law of State responsibility offering a curative approach to environmental harm and a more specific regime of resource management concerned with reasonable utilization of natural resources for anthropocentric reasons – and identified the contextual factors that make it possible to consecrate the new legal principle in the form of Stockholm Principle 21.

Although the discussion might leave the impression that the trajectory of prevention has been a linear and orderly process, the reality is a complex one, as prevention has built on a diverse intellectual heritage, relying on and going beyond pre-existing concepts but in no way rendering them irrelevant. Similarly, disentangling the different rationales that drive prevention and how they differ from the curative approach can be challenging. The dichotomy between prevention and reparation presented in this part is not always as evident as it might seem, with some close interactions, and sometimes intersections, occurring between the two rationales. As will be seen in Part IV, which goes back to the evolutionary perspective of this study, the dynamic is becoming increasingly complex.

PART II

THE NORMATIVE IMPACTS OF THE PREVENTION PRINCIPLE IN INTERNATIONAL ENVIRONMENTAL LAW

The rationale underpinning prevention – prevention is better than cure – is apparently simple, yet how it translates into a legal norm is complex. As a result, the principle of prevention is not expressed in a uniform, consistent manner. The manifestations of prevention vary depending on the specificity of the harm to be avoided and on the divergent understanding that international negotiators and judges have of the norm. In sum, the widespread use of the preventive approach has resulted in the consolidation of the norm in the field but has also created inconsistencies in its definition and content that make it more difficult to analyse. This second part undertakes a detailed examination of treaty law (Chapter 3), custom codification works (Chapter 4) and case law (Chapter 5) to identify the core manifestations of the principle of prevention in international environmental law.

3

Prevention in Treaty Law

Describing prevention in conventional law presents the initial difficulty that it is a pluriform norm that takes a variety of expressions. International treaties often refer to Stockholm Principle 21 or provide for an explicit obligation to prevent, but the manifestations of prevention can sometimes be more diffuse. Prevention influences the design of environmental treaties in its aim to avoid environmental damage. Generally speaking, the preventive rationale in conventional treaties finds its expressions in norms that make it more specific either in substance or in procedure.[1] Substantive specificity is preferred when the impacts are well known and highly certain and when a consensus is found on the objective to be attained – for instance, prohibiting a dangerous substance or protecting an endangered species. From this perspective, the principle of prevention manifests in techniques such as emissions standards, pollution control methods and the prohibition of substances or activities. Procedural specificity, by contrast, is preferred when only general – if not vague – objectives can be agreed[2] and when environmental impacts can only be assessed on an ad hoc basis. In these circumstances, prevention can take the form of obligations to seek prior authorizations, to undertake an environmental impact assessment or to cooperate with other States or international institutions. In all three cases, the principle of prevention influences treaty design, a process that is discussed further in Chapter 10 on the roles fulfilled by prevention as a 'principle'.

This chapter concentrates on how prevention influences conventional law at a more micro level, that is to say, by driving the formation of the core

[1] N Craik, *The International Law of Environmental Impact Assessment: Process, Substance and Integration* (Cambridge University Press 2008) 123.

[2] Craik, *International Law of Environmental Impact Assessment* 123.

obligation(s) of prevention found in a treaty. The expression of prevention depends on a number of factors that include the type of environmental medium to be protected and its level of tolerance to harm, the kinds of foreseen risks and their impacts, the specific timing of the preventive action, the spatial applicability of the norm and the balance States wish to achieve between preserving their sovereign rights and acting for the common good. Each time, the preventive rationale takes on a different manifestation that best takes into consideration these factors. This chapter offers a typology of the different risks to which prevention seeks to respond and highlights, in keeping with the evolutionary approach of this study, how the material scope of prevention has expanded (3.1). It then reflects on the legal consequences of the multifaceted nature of prevention, which raises fundamental questions about what constitutes the unicity of a norm in a complex legal landscape (3.2). The chapter ends by looking at the other side of the coin, to concentrate on the areas of conventional law where prevention is not present (3.3).

3.1 MANIFESTATIONS OF PREVENTION: A TYPOLOGY

Identifying the expressions of preventive obligations in treaty law is a daunting, if not impossible, task given the sheer number of environmental treaties,[3] which cannot be covered by way of a comprehensive study in the context of this monograph. For the sake of conciseness, this section therefore relies on preventive obligations found in major multilateral environmental agreements, deemed to best represent the most widely accepted expressions of prevention. It presents a typology of preventive obligations commonly found in conventional treaties based on the types of risks they seek to curb. There is, unsurprisingly, a general understanding that prevention under international environmental law aims to curb environmental risks.[4] However, this affirmation would be an oversimplification: despite the fact that prevention emerged as a legal response to multiplying environmental risks, the object of prevention – in other words, its material scope – is not limited to risks to the environment. The ILC Prevention Articles do not refer to the obligation to prevent environmental damage per se but rather seek to

[3] For instance, the International Environmental Agreements Database Project lists over 1,280 multilateral environmental agreements and 2,100 bilateral environmental agreements. Available at https://iea.uoregon.edu/ (last accessed 29 July 2017).

[4] See e.g. G Hafner and I Buffard, 'Obligations of Prevention and the Precautionary Principle', in J Crawford, A Pellet and S Olleson (eds), *The Law of International Responsibility* (Oxford University Press 2010) 521–34, at 525.

avoid the 'physical consequences' of transboundary risks[5] that might harm 'persons, property or the environment'.[6] The broad material scope of prevention can be partly explained by the fact that a consensual definition of what constitutes the 'environment' is lacking.[7] As a result, what qualifies as risks to the environment remain broad and often include other, more tangible risks. Consequently, the manifestations of prevention in international environmental treaties depend on the type of harm that they seek to avoid. The decision to offer a typology of risks falling under the scope of prevention in treaty law is also driven by the fact that it is illustrative of the evolution of prevention and, more specifically, of the extension of its material scope. The first two types of risks that preventive obligations seek to curb will come as no surprise, since they have been presented as having contributed to the emergence of prevention: these are risks to sovereignty (3.1.1) and risks to resource exploitation (3.1.2). While they remain very much at the heart of prevention in its contemporary form, prevention has nevertheless extended to other types of risks, including risks of pollution (3.1.3), risks to human health (3.1.4) and risks to ecosystems (3.1.5).

3.1.1 *Risks to Territorial Sovereignty*

The preventive rationale finds its expression in three fundamental obligations seeking to protect the sovereignty of other States. The first, and most obvious, is the prohibition to cause transboundary harm. Since this form of prevention was discussed in Part I, suffice it to say here that despite being only a basic expression of the preventive rationale that concentrates on wrongfulness instead of anticipation, the prohibition to cause transboundary harm remains an influential – albeit incomplete – expression of the preventive rationale, in particular, given its inclusion in Stockholm Principle 21. In treaty law, the prohibition is most evident in international watercourse conventions, where an obligation to take measures to avoid harmful effects to water flow and quality is commonly found[8] to guarantee the preservation of the sovereign rights of riparian States in the context of shared resource utilization.

5 ILC, 'Draft Articles on Prevention of Transboundary Harm from Hazardous Activities (with Commentaries)' (2001) *Yearbook of the International Law Commission* (vol II, part 2) 148, Article 1.

6 ILC, 'Draft Articles on Prevention of Transboundary Harm', Article 2(b).

7 See Section 6.1.1.

8 Convention on the Protection and Use of Transboundary Watercourses and International Lakes, Helsinki, 17 March 1992, in force 6 October 1996, (1992) 31 ILM 1312, Article 2(1); Convention on the Law of the Non-Navigational Uses of International Watercourses, New York, 21 May 1997, in force 17 August 2014, (1997) 36 ILM 700, Article 7.

A second, and related, expression of prevention is found in the principle of equitable and reasonable utilization.[9] Like the prohibition to cause transboundary harm, the principle of equitable and reasonable utilization finds its origins in the principle of good neighbourliness, which dictates that shared resources should be exploited equitably out of consideration for the rights of neighbouring States, including their right to be free from transboundary harm.[10] The element that distinguished it from the no-harm rule is that the prohibition of transboundary harm is only one element among other considerations in the balancing process operated by the concept of equitable and reasonable utilization. Nevertheless, the obligation of equitable and reasonable utilization cannot be said to dilute the preventive objective.[11] On the contrary, by highlighting the rights of the affected State (instead of focusing uniquely on the obligations of the State of origin), it could lower the threshold that triggers preventive obligations (generally set to 'significant'[12]). A typical scenario is found when several riparian States pollute an international watercourse: the individual harm caused by one State may not reach the significant threshold that renders the harm unlawful, but if several States create minimal harm to the watercourse, the combination of those harms may cause significant harm to a third State. Under these circumstances, the concept of equitable and reasonable utilization, recognizing that harm suffered by the third State is an unjustified infringement of its territorial sovereignty, imposes a duty to avoid harm on each polluting State, even though the required threshold is not met at an individual level.[13]

A third manifestation of the preventive rationale, driven by a willingness to avoid risks to sovereign rights, is the principle of prior informed consent, which prohibits the shipping of a dangerous substance if the receiving State

9 Convention on the Law of the Non-Navigational Uses of International Watercourses, Article 5; Convention on the Protection and Use of Transboundary Watercourses and International Lakes, Article 2(2)(c). For a review of State practice, see ILC, 'Draft Articles on the Law of the Non-Navigational Uses of International Watercourses (with Commentaries)' (1994) *Yearbook of the International Law Commission* (vol II, part 2) 89, at 98.

10 Commission on Sustainable Development, 'Report of the Expert Group Meeting on Identification of Principles of International Law for Sustainable Development', Geneva, Switzerland, 26–28 September 1995, para 197, linking the principle of equitable and reasonable use and the prohibition of harm.

11 ILC, 'Third Report of the Special Rapporteur, Mr Pemmaraju Sreenivasa Rao, on the Prevention of Transboundary Harm from Hazardous Activities' (2000) UN Doc. A/CN.4/510, para 21.

12 See Section 6.1.3.

13 A Nollkaemper, *The Legal Regime for Transboundary Water Pollution: Between Discretion and Constraint* (Martinus Nijhoff/Graham & Trotman 1993) 64–69.

has not agreed to it.[14] This expression of the prevention principle emphasizes the sovereign right of States to be free from environmental harm.[15] It extends prevention to a situation not envisaged in Stockholm Principle 21 in which the source of pollution (as opposed to its impacts) is transferred to an area beyond the jurisdiction of the State of origin[16] – although it could be interpreted to fall under the right to permanent sovereignty over natural resources (understood as a right to give or refuse permission for a potentially dangerous activity).

3.1.2 *Risks to Resource Exploitation*

The preventive rationale also finds its origins in the objective to protect resources in order to better exploit them.[17] This category of risk continues to fall under the scope of the preventive rationale in the form of the more contemporary obligation of 'conservation' that evolved from the notion of 'resource management'. Conservation obligations seek to protect species and their habitats from harm irrespective of the external considerations generally found in prevention. By applying in a domestic context, they extend the spatial scope of prevention beyond its Stockholm Principle 21 expression. At the same time, the rationale is more restrictive. Indeed, conservation can be constrained by an economic outlook on biological resources if interpreted to include a right to use resources.[18] From this perspective, risks falling under a preventive scope are only taken into account because of their potential effects on resource

14 E.g. Convention on the Control of Transboundary Movements of Hazardous Wastes and Their Disposal, Basel, 22 March 1989, in force 24 May 1992, (1989) 28 ILM 657; Convention on the Ban of Import into Africa and the Control of Transboundary Movement and Management of Hazardous Wastes within Africa, Bamako, 29 January 1991, in force 22 April 1998, (1991) 30 ILM 775 ; Protocol on the Prevention of Pollution of the Mediterranean Sea by Transboundary Movement of Hazardous Wastes and Their Disposal to the Barcelona Convention, Izmir, 1 October 1996, in force 19 January 2008, (UNEP) OCA/MED/IG.9/4; Convention on the Prior Informed Consent Procedure for Certain Hazardous Chemicals and Pesticides in International Trade, Rotterdam, 11 September 1998, in force 24 February 2004, (1999) 38 ILM 1; Cartagena Protocol on Biosafety to the Convention on Biological Diversity, Montreal, 29 January 2000, in force 11 September 2003, 39 ILM 1027.

15 K Peiry, 'Prior Informed Consent', in *Max Planck Encyclopedia of Public International Law* (Oxford University Press 2011).

16 K Kummer, *International Management of Hazardous Wastes: The Basel Convention and Related Legal Rules* (Oxford University Press 1995) 13.

17 M Bowman, P Davies and C Redgwell, *Lyster's International Wildlife Law* (2nd edn, Cambridge University Press 2010) 4–6.

18 Some treaties distinguish between the two – see e.g. Convention on Biological Diversity, Nairobi, 22 May 1992, in force 29 December 1993, (1992) 31 ILM 822, Articles 8–10 (the requirements for the conservation of biodiversity are different from those to ensure sustainable use) – while others do not – see e.g. Convention on Wetlands of International Importance Especially as Waterfowl Habitat, Ramsar, 2 February 1971, in force 21 December 1975, 996

exploitation and, eventually, on economic growth. If how conservation relates to resource utilization remains ambiguous, the more recent concept of 'sustainable use' of resources leaves no uncertainty: the principle operates in a context of resource exploitation that it merely seeks to regulate to maintain at a reasonable level.[19] It hence facilitates the utilization of resources as long as the impacts of the exploitation on the environment are also taken into consideration.[20]

3.1.3 *Risks of Pollution*

Designed as a solution to the environmental issues faced in the 1970s, the principle of prevention provided a solution for the main type of risk with which the international community was concerned, mostly because it was the most visible – pollution. This resulted in the inclusion in treaty law of a variety of obligations with the objective to limit pollution to a specific medium (e.g. watercourses[21]) or from a specific source (e.g. vessels[22]), activity (e.g. exploitation of resources in the Area[23]) or substance (e.g. ozone-depleting substances[24]). An area in which the obligation to prevent pollution is particularly well developed is the field of marine protection,[25] which manifests in very detailed obligations to prevent pollution coming from different sources in UNCLOS Articles 207 to

UNTS 245, Article 3(1). See R Rayfuse, 'Biological Resources', in D Bodansky, J Brunnée and E Hey (eds), *The Oxford Handbook of International Environmental Law* (Oxford University Press 2007) 362–94, at 372, defining conservation as 'the maintenance, restoration, sustainable utilization and enhancement of a natural resource or the environment'.

19 Protocol on Integrated Coastal Zone Management in the Mediterranean, Madrid, 21 January 2008, in force 24 March 2011, *OJ*, L 34/19, Article 2(f), describing its objective as being *inter alia* the 'sustainable management and use of coastal zones, taking into account at the same time the *fragility* of coastal ecosystems and landscapes [and] the diversity of *activities and uses*' (emphasis added).

20 For a detailed discussion of the relationship between prevention and sustainable development, see Section 9.2.

21 Convention on the Protection and Use of Transboundary Watercourses and International Lakes, Articles 2(2)(a), 2(3) and 3; Convention on the Law of the Non-Navigational Uses of International Watercourses, Article 21(2).

22 United Nations Convention on the Law of the Sea, Montego Bay, 10 December 1982, in force 16 November 1994, 1833 UNTS 3, Article 211.

23 United Nations Convention on the Law of the Sea, Article 145(a) and 209.

24 Convention for the Protection of the Ozone Layer, Vienna, 22 March 1985, in force 22 September 1988, (1985) 26 ILM 1529.

25 See e.g. D Dzidzornu, 'Four Principles in Marine Environment Protection: A Comparative Analysis' (1998) 29 *Ocean Development & International Law* 91, at 97–98, only discussing the obligation to prevent pollution.

212,[26] reproduced in regional law of the sea treaties[27] and in new treaties or protocols dealing with specific cases of pollution.[28]

Depending on the circumstances, pollution will either be completely prohibited or, most commonly, its level controlled to remain reasonable. Recognition that minimal impacts should be accepted as a result of economic activities is often found in the concept of 'management', particularly present in international treaties relative to dangerous substances that acknowledged the risks represented by such substances and the understanding that these need to be controlled, albeit not necessarily eliminated completely.

Contrary to the other types of risk presented in this section, this category of risk does not concentrate on the consequences of the damage (to State sovereignty or resource exploitation, for instance) but rather on the source of the damage (pollution). As a result, the principle of prevention that manifests in obligations to prevent pollution is not so much driven by a willingness to

26 The United Nations Convention on the Law of the Sea devotes a specific section to the obligation to 'prevent, reduce and control pollution of the marine environment' and addresses six main forms of marine pollution (Part XII, Section 5).

27 Convention on the Protection of the Marine Environment of the Baltic Sea Area, Helsinki, 22 March 1974, in force 3 May 1980, (1974) 13 ILM 546, Articles 7–10; Convention for the Protection of the Mediterranean Sea against Pollution, Barcelona, 16 February 1976, in force 12 February 1978, (1976) 15 ILM 290, Articles 5–9; Kuwait Regional Convention for Co-operation on the Protection of the Marine Environment from Pollution, Kuwait, 24 April 1978, in force 1 July 1979, (1978) 17 ILM 511, Articles IV–IX; Convention for the Protection of the Natural Resources and Environment of the South Pacific Region, Noumea, 25 November 1986, in force 22 August 1990, (1987) 26 ILM 38, Articles 5–13; Framework Convention for the Protection of the Marine Environment of the Caspian Sea, Tehran, 4 November 2003, in force 12 August 2006, available at www.tehranconvention.org/spip.php?article4 (last accessed 19 May 2017), Articles 7–12.

28 Convention on the Prevention of Marine Pollution from Land-Based Sources, Paris, 4 June 1974, in force 6 May 1978, (1974) 13 ILM 352; Protocol for the Protection of the Mediterranean Sea against Pollution from Land-Based Sources and Activities, Athens, 17 May 1980, in force 17 June 1983, (1980) 19 ILM 869; Protocol for the Protection of the South-East Pacific against Pollution from Land-Based Sources, Quito, 22 July 1983, in force 23 September 1986, 983 IELMT 54; Protocol Concerning Specially Protected Areas and Biological Diversity in the Mediterranean Sea by Dumping, Barcelona, 10 June 1995, in force 12 December 1999, available at http://faolex.fao.org/docs/pdf/mul38152.pdf (last accessed 19 May 2017); Protocol for the Protection of the Mediterranean against Pollution from Land-Based Activities, Syracuse, 7 March 1996, in force 11 May 2008, (1996) 7 *Yearbook of International Environmental Law* 678; Protocol for the Protection of the Marine and Coastal Environment of the Western Indian Ocean from Land-Based Sources and Activities, Nairobi, 31 March 2010, not in force, UNEP (DEPI)/EAF/CPP.6/10/Suppl; Protocol on Marine Pollution from Land-Based Sources and Activities in the Caribbean Region, Oranjestad, 6 October 1999, in force 13 August 2010, available at www.cep.unep.org/cartagena-convention/lbs-protocol/protocol-concerning-pollution-from-land-based-sources-and-activities (last accessed 19 May 2017).

protect sovereign interests and integrates a more 'environmental' focus. Such an approach is visible in UNCLOS, which does not merely prohibit causing damage by pollution 'to other States'[29] but also, and more generally, to the 'marine environment'.[30]

The scope of the obligation of pollution prevention necessarily depends on the meaning given to pollution.[31] 'Pollution' can generally be defined as the introduction by humans of substances into the environment that results or is likely to result in deleterious effects.[32] The description is wide enough to cover a large array of sources of environmental harm, which can explain why scholarly interest in the field of environmental protection has concentrated mainly on pollution prevention.[33] Going further in this direction, some authors equate the prevention principle with the principle of pollution prevention, considering the obligation to prevent pollution as the unique expression of the principle of prevention.[34] However, while pollution is the most common type of environmental damage, it has been acknowledged that the obligation to prevent pollution does not cover every type of environmental risk.[35]

29 United Nations Convention on the Law of the Sea, Article 194(2).

30 United Nations Convention on the Law of the Sea, Article 194(1).

31 For the different definitions given to pollution, see, in particular, A Springer, 'Towards a Meaningful Concept of Pollution in International Law' (1977) 26 *International and Comparative Law Quarterly* 531.

32 See e.g. the definition of pollution in United Nations Convention on the Law of the Sea, Article 1(4).

33 See, in particular, the strong interest of the scholarship for 'pollution' in the 1970s and 1980s: C Bramsen, 'Transnational Pollution and International Law' (1972) 42 *Nordisk Tidsskrift for International Ret* 153; V Petaccio, 'Water Pollution and the Future Law of the Sea' (1972) 21 *International and Comparative Law Quarterly* 15; AL Springer, 'Towards a Meaningful Concept of Pollution in International Law' (1977) 26 *International and Comparative Law Quarterly* 531; M Holdgate, *A Perspective of Environmental Pollution* (Cambridge University Press 1979); S Williams, 'Public International Law Governing Transboundary Pollution' (1983) 13 *University of Queensland Law Journal* 112; M Koskenniemi, *International Pollution in the System of International Law* (Suomalainen Lakimiesyhdistys 1984); J Sette-Camara, 'Pollution of International Rivers' (1984) 186 *Collected Courses of the Hague Academy of International Law* 117–217.

34 D Hunter, J Salzman and D Zaelke, *International Environmental Law and Policy* (4th edn, Foundation Press, Thomson/West 2011) 507; T Koivurova, *Introduction to International Environmental Law* (Routledge 2014) 109; and, to a certain extent, E Scotford, *Environmental Principles and the Evolution of Environmental Law* (Bloomsbury 2017) 145.

35 *Chagos Marine Protected Area (The Republic of Mauritius v. United Kingdom of Great Britain and Northern Ireland)*, (Permanent Court of Arbitration), 18 March 2015, paras 320 and 538; *South China Sea Arbitration (Republic of the Philippines v. People's Republic of China)*, (Permanent Court of Arbitration), Award on the Merits, 12 July 2016, para 945.

3.1.4 *Risks to Human Health*

Irrespective of the source of the harm, environmental risks are often framed in relation to their consequences for human health. One difficulty with the argument that the environmental preventive principle integrates risks to human health lies in the fact that it could be argued that these are two separate preventive obligations, one operating under international environmental law and the other under international health law. The existence of preventive obligations in the closely related field of health law is discussed further in Section 3.2.3. However, the argument does not hold when international treaties applicable to the environment merge the obligation to prevent environmental damage and the objective of limiting risks to human health. Such is the focus of this section, which considers the integration of human health risks under the scope of prevention. It is illustrative of the anthropocentric drive underpinning international environmental law, whose objective of risk prevention is often guided by a willingness to protect human livelihoods. If the protection of human health might not be the only motivating factor for the imposition of a preventive duty, it is often an essential driving element. International environmental treaties tend to operate on the basis of more or less explicit anthropocentric concerns: while 'pure' objectives of environmental protection tend to be elusive, more pragmatic drivers are generally more easily visible, including motivations arising from the protection of human health. As a result, the complementarity between environmental and health objectives is sometimes underlined in international treaties that are applicable to both risks to the environment and to human health.[36]

An even closer type of integration is found in treaty provisions that explicitly merge the two types of risks. For instance, the ASEAN Agreement on Transboundary Haze Pollution[37] gives the obligation to prevent harm to human health the same legal basis as the duty to avoid harm to the environment. Indeed, it extends the scope of Stockholm Principle 21 to harm to human health, Article 3 providing that States have the 'responsibility to ensure

36 See e.g. Convention for the Protection of the Ozone Layer, Preamble; Protocol on Water and Health to the 1992 Convention on the Protection and Use of Transboundary Watercourses and International Lakes, London, 11 June 1999, in force 4 October 2005, 2231 UNTS 202, Article 1; Convention on the Prior Informed Consent Procedure, Preamble and Article 1; Convention on Persistent Organic Pollutants, Stockholm, 22 May 2001, in force 17 May 2004, (2001) 40 ILM 532, Preamble; Minamata Convention on Mercury, Kumamoto, 10 October 2013, in force 16 August 2017, available at www.mercuryconvention.org/ (last accessed 19 May 2017), Preamble, Articles 1 and 2.

37 ASEAN Agreement on Transboundary Haze Pollution, Kuala Lumpur, 10 June 2002, in force 25 November 2003, available at http://environment.asean.org/wp-content/uploads/2015/06/ASEANAgreementonTransboundaryHazePollution.pdf (last accessed 19 May 2017).

that activities within their jurisdiction or control do not cause damage to the environment and harm to *human health* of other States or of areas beyond the limits of national jurisdiction'.[38] Similarly, the Protocol on Strategic Environmental Assessment to the Convention on Environmental Impact Assessment in a Transboundary Context[39] operates on the basis that environmental and health risks are intrinsically linked. The prevention principle manifests in the treaty in the form of an ambitious objective to 'provide for a high level of protection of the environment, including health'.[40] A final example of the integration of health risks under the environmental principle of prevention is found in the right to a healthy environment, as acknowledged, for instance, in the Additional Protocol to the American Convention on Human Rights in the Area of Economic, Social and Cultural Rights,[41] which requires States to take preventive measures to protect the environment with a view to limiting the health impacts of environmental risks. These three examples thus illustrate that risks to human health have integrated the material scope of prevention in a way that generally complements, but also drives, its more general objective of environmental protection.

3.1.5 *Risks to Ecosystems*

More recently, the principle of prevention extended its scope to risks of a more 'pure' environmental nature as international treaties adopted an ecosystem-oriented approach to harm.[42] It manifests in obligations to avoid causing harm to ecosystems that can be found in treaties relative to the protection of international watercourses,[43] oceans,[44] biodiversity,[45] fisheries[46] and the

38 ASEAN Agreement on Transboundary Haze Pollution, Article 3.

39 Protocol on Strategic Environmental Assessment to the Espoo Convention, Kiev, 21 May 2003, in force 11 July 2010, UN Doc. ECE/MP/EI/2003/2.

40 Protocol on Strategic Environmental Assessment to the Espoo Convention, Article 1.

41 Additional Protocol to the American Convention on Human Rights in the Area of Economic, Social and Cultural Rights, San Salvador, 16 November 1988, in force 16 November 1999, OAS Treaty Series No. 69, Article 11.

42 O McIntyre, 'The Emergence of an "Ecosystem Approach" to the Protection of International Watercourses under International Law' (2004) 13 *Review of European, Comparative & International Environmental Law* 1, at 2 (in relation to shared water resources).

43 See, *inter alia,* Convention on the Protection and Use of Transboundary Watercourses and International Lakes, Articles 2(2)(d) and 3(1); Convention on the Law of the Non-Navigational Uses of International Watercourses, Article 20.

44 United Nations Convention on the Law of the Sea, Articles 192 and 194(5).

45 Convention on Biological Diversity, Article 2.

46 Agreement for the Implementation of the Provisions of the United Nations Convention on the Law of the Sea of 10 December 1982 Relating to the Conservation and Management of

climate.[47] The obligation to protect ecosystems relies on an understanding of the environment as a fragile interdependent system that highlights the need to avoid disruptions between living and non-living components of the environment.[48] Risk is no longer conceptualized as the danger represented by a specific type of harm but rather as the possibility of affecting an entire, complicated system that relies on a fragile equilibrium which should not be disrupted. From this perspective, the preventive rationale embraces a comprehensive outlook on environmental risks that seeks to protect the environment in an integrated and holistic manner. As a result, obligations pertaining to the protection and preservation of ecosystems tend to operate without reference to the location of harm. Such is the case with Article 192 of UNCLOS, which provides that 'States have the obligation to protect and preserve the marine environment' and Article 20 of the Convention on the Law of the Non-Navigational Uses of International Watercourses, which creates an obligation to 'protect and preserve the ecosystems of international watercourses'.[49]

Obligations to prevent risks to ecosystems have extended the rationale of prevention to focus directly on risks of an environmental nature. However, its extension beyond sovereign concerns is not without challenges relative to the limitations of our scientific understanding of ecosystemic interactions and the obstacles posed by an international legal structure reliant mainly on a Westphalian logic.[50] As a result, it is difficult to ascertain the extent to which the approach legally constrains the behaviour of States.[51]

Straddling Fish Stocks and Highly Migratory Fish Stocks, New York, 4 August 1995, in force 11 December 2001, 2167 UNTS 3, Preamble.

47 United Nations Framework Convention on Climate Change, New York, 9 May 1992, in force 24 March 1994, 1771 UNTS 107, Preamble and Article 2.

48 Convention on Biological Diversity, Article 2, defining 'ecosystems' as 'a dynamic complex of plant, animal and micro-organism communities and their non-living environment interacting as a functional unit'.

49 Convention on the Protection and Use of Transboundary Watercourses and International Lakes, Articles 2(2)(d) and 3(1); Convention on the Law of the Non-Navigational Uses of International Watercourses, Article 20. See also Convention on Co-operation for the Protection and Sustainable Use of the Danube River, Sofia, 29 June 1994, in force 22 October 1998, ECOLEX TRE-001207, Article 2(3); Agreement on Co-operation for Sustainable Development of the Mekong River Basin, Chiang Rai, 5 April 1995, in force 5 April 1995, (1995) 34 ILM 865, Article 3; Convention on the Protection of the Rhine, Rotterdam, 22 January 1998, in force 12 April 1999, OJ L 289 (16 November 2000) 30, Article 2; Nile River Basin Cooperative Framework, open for signature 14 May 2010, available at www.nilebasin.org/index.php/media-center/documents-publications/30-cooperative-framework-agreement/file (last accessed 19 May 2017), Articles 3(7) and 6.

50 D Tarlock, 'Ecosystems', in D Bodansky, J Brunnée and E Hey (eds), *The Oxford Handbook of International Environmental Law* (Oxford University Press 2007) 574–96, at 576.

51 Y Tanaka, *The International Law of the Sea* (2nd edn, Cambridge University Press 2015) 251.

3.1.6 *Combination of Risks*

This brief overview of the main risks covered by the preventive rationale in international environmental treaties shows that the objects that fall under its scope vary significantly. It reveals an evolution in the approach that international environmental law has taken towards risks; although the preventive rationale tends to apply to risks that only give indirect consideration to the protection of the environment, there is a move towards recognizing environmental risks in the strict sense of the word, irrespective of other considerations.

The categorization proposed earlier should not cloud the fact that the five types of risks are not mutually exclusive. Indeed, the different categories may operate in parallel within one treaty regime to ensure that different types of risks are covered. For instance, although the preventive rationale is primarily expressed in relation to risks to human health in treaties relative to hazardous substances, it also takes the form of concerns over risks to the sovereignty of other States and the risk of pollution.[52] In general, contemporary environmental treaties combine both traditional and more progressive approaches to risk; a preventive obligation embodying an ecosystemic approach will usually operate as a supplement to other, older approaches to risk. This is the case in the field of watercourse law, where the preventive rationale finds its expression in the basic obligation not to cause transboundary harm,[53] as well as in the progressive duty to protect ecosystems.[54] Given that each of the categories discussed earlier has its own advantages and limitations, a combination of these different risks ensures that the legal framework covers a diversity of risks that might directly or indirectly affect the environment. More generally, international environmental treaties tend to combine different objectives: driven by anthropocentric motivations of sovereignty preservation and resource management, they can also recognize the value of the planet (and, hence, environmental protection) as such.

[52] See e.g. Convention on the Control of Transboundary Movements of Hazardous Wastes and Their Disposal, Basel, 22 March 1989, in force 24 May 1992, (1989) 28 ILM 657, Article 4(2)(c), on risks to human health; Article 4(2)(d), on transboundary impacts; and Article 4(2)(a), on pollution minimization.

[53] See e.g. Convention on the Law of the Non-Navigational Uses of International Watercourses, Article 7; and Convention on the Protection and Use of Transboundary Watercourses and International Lakes, Article 2(1).

[54] See *inter alia* Convention on the Law of the Non-Navigational Uses of International Watercourses, Article 20; and Convention on the Protection and Use of Transboundary Watercourses and International Lakes, Articles 2(2)(d) and 3(1).

3.2 DEFINING THE BOUNDARIES OF A MULTIFACETED NORM

The multiple manifestations of prevention in international conventional law create a need to circumscribe the boundaries of prevention in order to understand which norms fall under the category of what is being referred to as 'prevention in international environmental law'. The different manifestations of prevention raise the question of whether they are representative of one or multiple norms. This is not purely an academic question regarding the fragmented state of international law; it can have significant practical consequences on the identification, sources, scope and effects of a norm. The following discussion first identifies the environmental principle of prevention in its multiple manifestations (1) in different regimes of international environmental law and (2) in other branches of international law. It then interrogates the relationship that the environmental principle of prevention entertains with other preventive norms in (3) complementary or (4) distinct branches.

3.2.1 *Coexistence: Prevention in International Environmental Law Regimes*

The coexistence of a general preventive norm and its more specific manifestations brings about questions regarding how the norms relate to each other. These difficulties are heightened if these norms are seen to operate within specific international environmental law 'regimes', understood as the collection of rules concerned with the protection of a specific medium. It is generally considered, with slight doctrinal variations, that the international law relative to the environment is structured around the following five functional areas: freshwater law, law of the sea, atmosphere and climate law, biodiversity law and the law relative to hazardous substances and activities.[55] A specific expression of prevention, best suited to the medium to be protected, usually dominates in each of these areas – such as conservation in biodiversity law or mitigation in climate law.

The categorization into functional areas can be viewed as a mere conceptual aid, useful to delimitate a subject of enquiry that does not carry direct legal consequences. However, the argument is sometimes made that these are autonomous, self-contained regimes whose *lex specialis* norms displace the

[55] See e.g. P Sands and J Peel, *Principles of International Environmental Law* (3rd edn, Cambridge University Press 2012), dividing the field into five subfields. See also, combining oceans and freshwater protection in one subfield, P-M Dupuy and JE Viñuales, *International Environmental Law* (Cambridge University Press 2015); and D Bodansky, J Brunnée and E Hey (eds), *The Oxford Handbook of International Environmental Law* (Oxford University Press 2007).

principles of general environmental law. Some authors have argued on this basis that a climate-specific principle of differentiation would take precedence over the general principle of prevention.[56] However, the position is largely unconvincing because States have not 'articulated an intent to classify' the climate regime as a self-contained regime.[57] In addition, it is unlikely that an environmental regime such as the climate regime would operate in direct contradiction to generally accepted environmental principles. Given that environmental regimes tend to be designed with the purpose to avoid harm, it is unconceivable that they would put aside the principle of prevention.

A more difficult question to solve relates to whether the existence of a specific expression of prevention in one regime can necessarily be extended to other regimes. The issue arose in the context of the proposal made by ILC Special Rapporteur Murase to recognize a general obligation to protect the atmosphere replicating the general obligations of prevention found in the law of the sea and the law of watercourses. Identifying the sources of the obligation on the basis that it existed in other environmental regimes was largely unconvincing to some other ILC members.[58] They emphasized that custom can only emerge from practice and *opinio juris* applicable to a specific environmental medium. The disagreement indicated that the general principle of prevention in international environmental law should be distinguished from its manifestations that coexist in more specific regimes. While it cannot be disputed that the general principle of prevention drives the design of these regimes, caution should be exercised when it comes to drawing analogies between the different preventive obligations embodied in these regimes. Indeed, the willingness of States to accept international constraints varies widely depending on the treaty regime and the medium it seeks to protect, and State consent for each specific obligation cannot be non-controversially extended to what is in effect another obligation.

3.2.2 *Integration: The Environmental Preventive Principle in Other Branches of International Law*

Another set of questions emerges from the fact that environmental norms are not merely found in what is generally considered international environmental

[56] A Zahar, 'Methodological Issues in Climate Law' (2015) 5 *Climate Law* 25, 32.

[57] ILA, Committee on Legal Principles Relating to Climate Change, 'First Report', The Hague, 74th Session, 2010, 31.

[58] ILC, 'Third Report of the Special Rapporteur, Mr Shinya Murase, on the protection of the atmosphere, (2016) UN Doc. A/CN.4/692, para 12.

law treaties *stricto sensu*. Indeed, given the crosscutting nature of environmental issues, treaties that are usually considered to fall under the remit of other branches of international law (e.g. international economic law; human rights law) can integrate an objective to prevent environmental harm. As noted previously, the term 'international environmental law' is used in this study to refer to the aggregate of conventional and customary norms, the main objective of which is environmental protection, but should not interpreted to be a self-contained regime. How a norm is classified – in terms of branch of law – matters less than its scope and legal effects.[59] The main variation between prevention in an environmental regime *stricto sensu* (e.g. a multilateral environmental agreement) and prevention in another branch of international law is that, in this context, the principle of prevention manifests differently to accommodate the primary objectives driving these treaties. The discussion that follows illustrates how prevention has integrated other branches of international law.

International treaties that seek to facilitate trade and investment make increasingly frequent references to the fact that environmental considerations should (to varying extents) be considered in the pursuit of economic growth. This provides normative space for the principle of prevention to manifest in international economic law in the context of a balancing act operating between economic and environmental considerations. The most notable example in this context is the WTO's preambular objective to further 'sustainable development' in order to 'protect and preserve the environment'.[60] It introduces a preventive objective that is not per se an independent obligation but that operates alongside economic and social objectives.[61] From this perspective, prevention becomes one of three factors in the balancing act operated by sustainable development. This expresion of prevention is close to Rio Principle 2 that calls for taking economic and developmental strategies into account in the implementation of the preventive norm.[62] Another

59 JE Viñuales, 'A Human Rights Approach to Extraterritorial Environmental Protection? An Assessment', in N Bhuta (ed), *The Frontiers of Human Rights* (Oxford University Press 2016) 177–222, at 187.

60 Marrakesh Agreement Establishing the World Trade Organization, 15 April 1994, 1867 UNTS 154, Preamble.

61 See, in this regard, International Institute for Sustainable Development and UNEP, *Trade and Green Economy: A Handbook* (3rd edn, IISD Geneva 2015), at 10: by listing prevention as one of the principle of international environmental law, it implicitly recognized it to be of relevance for the trade regime.

62 Rio de Janeiro Declaration on Environment and Development (Rio de Janeiro, 3 to 14 June 1992), (1992) 31 ILM 876.

manifestation of prevention in international economic treaties is found in the form of provisions reserving policy space for environmental regulation, including as the rationale justifying exceptions to general trade disciplines,[63] or the right of the State, in an investment context, to regulate in the field of environmental protection.[64]

Conventional law pertaining to human rights finds the principle of prevention expressed in different forms and featuring most prominently in the context of the duty of the State to protect from deprivation (by third parties). It has been elaborated in some detail by human rights bodies in contexts where the environmental damage caused by third parties could have deprived citizens from their right to enjoy their own culture,[65] the right to a private and family life,[66] the right to life,[67] the right to a fair trial[68] and the right to property.[69] Such reinterpretation of existing human rights from an environmental perspective is an implicit application of the principle of prevention. Some human rights treaties also integrate a more direct obligation of prevention by providing specifically for a right to an environment that creates direct obligations on the State to prevent environmental harm that would have negative effects on the life or health of its population.[70] In these cases, prevention is concerned with domestic environmental harm with the view to

63 General Agreement on Trade and Tariffs 1994, Annex 1A of the Marrakesh Agreement, Article XX; Agreement on Sanitary and Phytosanitary Measures, Marrakesh, 15 April 1994, in force 1 January 1995, 1867 UNTS 493, Articles 2(1)–2(2) and 5(1), creating policy space for the implementation of the obligation of prevention by allowing States to take sanitary and phytosanitary measures in case of, *inter alia*, environmental risks and to bypass their general trade obligations. See also provisions on environmental exceptions in regional and bilateral trade agreements in IISD and UNEP, *Trade and Green Economy*, 123.

64 For an overview, see e.g. K Gordon and J Pol, *Environmental Concerns in International Investment Agreements: A Survey* (OECD 2011) 14.

65 International Covenant on Civil and Political Rights, New York, 19 December 1966, in force 3 January 1976, 999 UNTS 171, Article 27.

66 Convention for the Protection of Human Rights and Fundamental Freedoms, Rome, 4 November 1950, in force 3 September 1953, 213 UNTS 221, Article 8.

67 Convention for the Protection of Human Rights, Article 2.

68 Convention for the Protection of Human Rights, Article 6.

69 American Convention on Human Rights, San José, 22 November 1969, in force 18 July 1978, 1144 UNTS 123, Article 21.

70 African Charter on Human and Peoples' Rights, Banjul, 27 June 1981, in force 21 October 1986 (1982) 21 ILM 58, Article 24, on the right to a general satisfactory environment; Additional Protocol to the American Convention on Human Rights in the Area of Economic, Social and Cultural Rights, San Salvador, 16 November 1988, in force 16 November 1999, OAS Treaty Series No. 69, Article 11, on the right to a healthy environment; Association of Southeast Asian Nations, ASEAN Human Rights Declaration, adopted on 18 November 2012, available at www.asean.org/storage/images/ASEAN_RTK_2014/6_AHRD_Booklet.pdf (last accessed 19 May 2017), Article 28(f), on the right to a safe, clean and sustainable environment.

protecting the rights of the individuals and not on transboundary harm with the view to preserving the territorial integrity of a State – a change in perspective that, as discussed later in Chapter 8, is fundamental for the evolution of prevention.

Finally, the principle of prevention also finds major manifestations in the context of humanitarian law, where it holds two fundamental characteristics. Firstly, the obligation of prevention relies on a very high threshold, applying when harm is foreseen to be 'widespread, long-lasting and/or severe'.[71] Secondly, the preventive rationale in humanitarian law seeks to protect the environment as a whole, irrespective of the location of harm[72] – territoriality being itself under challenge in the context of armed conflict. Here the departure from the no-harm rule concerned with the preservation of territorial sovereignty is clear.

The integration of prevention in treaties other than international environmental law treaties confirms the status of prevention as a general principle of international law. As the objective of environmental protection has been integrated in all aspects of societal regulation, the obligation of prevention has pervaded fields other than international environmental law *stricto sensu*. The expression of prevention in non-environmental treaties is necessarily modified by the other norms and concerns of these treaties: economic agreements attempt to find a balance between economic development and environmental protection, whereas human rights treaties focus on harm in a domestic context.

The differences in how prevention manifests raise a tricky question: is the principle of prevention in international environmental treaties (i.e. treaties whose design is driven by environmental concerns) necessarily the same principle as the norm found in other branches of international law? The WTO in *Beef Hormones* had posited that the status of precaution might be different in trade and environmental law, in effect considering that different principles govern the two branches.[73] However, the legal effects of this

[71] Protocol I (Additional to the 1949 Geneva Conventions) Relating to the Protection of Victims of International Armed Conflicts, Geneva, 8 June 1977, in force 7 December 1978, (1977) 16 ILM 1391, Articles 35(3) and 55; Convention on the Prohibition of Military or Other Hostile Use of Environmental Modification Techniques, Geneva, 10 December 1976, in force 18 May 1977, 1108 UNTS 151, Article 1(1).

[72] See e.g. International Committee of the Red Cross, 'Study on Customary International Humanitarian Law', Rule 43 on the application of general principles on the conduct of hostilities to the natural environment. Available at https://ihl-databases.icrc.org/customary-ihl/eng/docs/v1_rul_rule43 (last accessed 29 July 2017).

[73] *European Communities – Measures Concerning Meat and Meat Products (Hormones)*, Appellate Body Report, WT/DS26/AB/R, WT/DS48/AB/R, 13 February 1998, paras 123–25.

position have been minimal. The doctrine largely deemed this position to be 'problematic' because it relies on the premise that each branch can be squarely delimited – a task that appears largely impossible, especially in the context of environmental protection that has large effects outside the restricted branch of environmental law.[74] Subsequent attempts to highlight the convergence between the trade and environmental regimes further weakened the argument.[75] Also, the position of the WTO is not necessarily explained by the fact that it considered environmental and trade law to be completely separate but rather that it considered that norms, such as precaution, that have not consolidated in their branches of origin cannot be considered to be fully applicable in other branches. This does not mean that it would necessarily have drawn the same conclusion in relation to prevention given its recognition as a norm of general international law by the ICJ.[76]

The questions raised here are not so different from the one discussed previously in relation to the different manifestations of prevention in the functional areas of international environmental law. Overall, the legal scholarship at present tends to react to an earlier trend that warned about the risks of fragmentation of international law and portrays international law as a unified legal system,[77] preferring to highlight the commonalities existing between the different branches of international law than their differences.[78] As a result, legal consequences derived from a categorization of international law into separate specialist branches are generally considered to be unhelpful. This categorization does not, however, mean that the risk of norm conflict has been completely neglected, as environmental objectives can sometimes clash with other policy objectives, including those related to economic development. However, scholars tend to underplay such risks on the basis that it is generally

74 ILC, 'Fragmentation of International Law: Difficulties Arising from the Diversification and Expansion of International Law. Report of the Study Group of the International Law Commission Finalized by Martti Koskenniemi' (2006) UN Doc. A/CN.4/L.682, para 55.

75 Ministerial Declaration, adopted at Doha, 14 November 2001, WT/MIN(01)/DEC/1, para 6, on the mutual supportiveness between trade and environmental objectives. See R Pavoni, 'Mutual Supportiveness as a Principle of Interpretation and Law-Making: A Watershed for the "WTO-and-Competing Regimes" Debate?' (2010) 21 *European Journal of International Law* 649.

76 *Legality of the Threat or Use of Nuclear Weapons* (Advisory Opinion) (1996) ICJ Rep 226, para 29.

77 ILC, 'First Report by the Special Rapporteur, Mr Michael Wood, on the formation and evidence of customary international law' (2013) UN Doc. A/CN.4/663, 7–8. See also ILC, 'Fourth Report by the Special Rapporteur, Mr Shinya Murase, on the protection of the atmosphere' (2017) UN Doc. A/CN.4/705, draft guideline 9 on the 'principle of interrelationship'.

78 E Bjorge, *The Evolutionary Interpretation of Treaties* (Oxford University Press 2014) 51.

acknowledged that environmental and other treaties are part of a single international legal system.[79] In this context, the harmonizing potential of treaty interpretation to avoid such norm conflicts is gaining increasing pre-eminence.

3.2.3 *Intersections: Preventive Norms in Related Yet Distinct Branches*

The boundaries of prevention can also be defined by looking at how it intersects with other preventive norms that do not apply to environmental risks per se but are very closely linked.[80] In this context, the fields of health and disaster law can be understood to transpose the environmental obligation of prevention to specific risks and, in the same process, modify it.

Although health and environmental risks are different, they intersect over their mutual concern for the well-being of the individual. As discussed earlier, environmental treaties often merge norms that seek to prevent environmental and health risks, in particular, when the core motivation underpinning the prevention of environmental risks is to limit their consequences for human health.[81] The distinction between the two fields is more clear-cut in international instruments that are concerned with health risks (i.e. not environmental risks *stricto sensu*). However, while the obligations are autonomous, their rationale and content remain very close. This is visible in the context of the international health regulations of the World Health Organization (WHO)[82] that provide a framework for the management of events that might constitute a public health emergency of international concern. As with prevention in the environmental sphere, the rationale is anticipatory,[83] the aim being to curb public health risks, defined on the basis of their magnitude and ability to be foreseen.[84] In addition, the health regulations also interpret prevention as a

79 L Boisson de Chazournes, 'Environmental Treaties in Time' (2009) 6 *Environmental Policy and Law* 293, at 297.

80 T Karimova, 'Sustainable Development and Disasters', in S Breau and K Samuel (eds), *Research Handbook on Disasters and International Law* (Edward Elgar 2016) 177–203, at 202, noting that there is 'convergence in the protections' provided by both obligations.

81 As a result, scholars tend to analyse environmental and health risks together; see e.g. MM Mbengue, *Essai sur une théorie du risque en droit international public: l'anticipation du risque environnemental et sanitaire* (Pedone 2009).

82 World Health Organization (WHO), *International Health Regulations*, 2nd edn, Geneva, 23 May 2005, in force 15 June 2007, available at www.who.int/topics/international_health_regulations/en/ (last accessed 19 May 2017).

83 WHO, *International Health Regulations*, Article 2.

84 WHO, *International Health Regulations*, Article 1, 'a likelihood of an event that may affect adversely the health of human populations, with an emphasis on one which may spread internationally or may present a serious and direct danger'.

positive obligation requiring States to be proactive in light of health risks by fulfilling two major procedural obligations relative to monitoring[85] and notification.[86]

Another field in which the preventive rationale is very close to the environmental principle of prevention is that of disaster relief. The codification work of the ILC in the form of its articles on the protection of persons in the event of disasters could be the premise of a major treaty in the field of disaster law, which has, until now, mostly evolved on the basis of non-legally binding documents. The obligation of prevention under environmental law and disaster law are very close because disaster law has been framed at the international level within the concept of sustainable development.[87] More specifically, the ILC Prevention Articles recognized in Article 16 that States have a 'duty to prevent environmental disasters', whereas, in turn, the ILC Disaster Articles included 'large-scale environmental damage' in their definition of 'disasters'.[88]

Despite a clear convergence between the two fields of law, the obligation of prevention under disaster law is relatively different from the obligation under international environmental law, as the conditions of their application are different. Firstly, disaster law is primarily concerned with 'a primary obligation to prevent harm to one's own population, property and the environment generally'[89] and less with considerations of transboundary harm that underpin the ILC prevention articles.[90] The broadening of the spatial applicability of the obligation to the domestic territory of a State under disaster law brings a new element to prevention, which, as discussed in Chapter 8, could, in turn, influence the environmental obligation by extending its applicability to a purely domestic context. Secondly, the circumstances in which risk is managed are different because risks due to natural disasters cannot be completely eliminated, which means that disaster law prefers to use the term 'risk

85 WHO, *International Health Regulations*, Article 5.

86 WHO, *International Health Regulations*, Article 6.

87 Karimova, 'Sustainable Development and Disasters', at 202. See e.g. United Nations Office for Disaster Risk Reduction, *Living with Risk: A Global Review of Disaster Reduction Initiatives* (2004) at 20, on the relationship between disaster reduction and sustainable development.

88 ILC, 'Draft Articles on the Protection of Persons in the Event of Disasters (with Commentaries)' (2016) *Yearbook of the International Law Commission* (vol II, part 2), Article 3(a).

89 ILC, 'Protection of Persons in the Event of Disasters. Memorandum by the Secretariat' (2007) UN Doc. A/CN.4/590, para 24.

90 ILC, 'Summary Record of the 3178th Meeting' (2013) UN Doc. A/CN.4/SR.3178, ILC member Murphy noting that disasters did not have to be transboundary in nature in order to trigger the application of the draft articles.

reduction' instead of 'prevention'. In light of such an incomplete convergence, relying on the sources of the obligation in international environmental law to justify the customary status of the norm under disaster law is controversial – such was the position of the ILC, in the context of its work on the protection of persons in the event of disasters. Some of its members felt uneasy about deriving legal consequences from the rapporteur's reference to prevention as a unified 'principle of international law' because it put all preventive obligations under the same umbrella.[91] The scholarship remains divided over the extent to which analogies can be drawn between anticipatory rationales found in different branches of international law.[92] The discussion at the ILC on whether it was opportune to rely on the sources of the environmental prevention principle brought to light fundamental questions on how to justify the legal background of a norm that has been influenced by previous norms (i.e. prevention in environmental law) but has necessarily evolved differently from these norms to adapt to the situation to be regulated. The most convincing conceptualization at this stage would be to recognize that prevention is a general principle of international law in the sense that the anticipatory perspective of some norms brings them together and facilitates a process of cross-fertilization between norms sharing a similar rationale. However, one should be cautious to draw analogies when it comes to justifying the origins and content of an obligation to prevent, as States might be more willing to conserve a close control of their preventive duties and to differentiate between them.

More generally, the question of the extent to which the sources of the environmental norm of prevention can be used to justify the existence of a norm prohibiting other types of non-environmental harm, or at least interpret it, is a complex one. There is an overall tendency to rely, perhaps too much, on the *sic utere tuo* rule and *Trail Smelter* precedent to justify the existence of any kind of anticipatory obligation without any discussion of the relevance of such sources. The situation here is slightly different from the two cases discussed earlier in the field of health and disaster law, as the existence of a certain degree of convergence, albeit with its own limitations, between the norms could justify such an approach. However, the sources of the environmental norm of prevention are also sometimes used to justify obligations to avoid transboundary risks of a completely different nature. In this case, how justified is it to transpose the *Trail Smelter* rationale as the source of the obligation to

91 ILC, 'Sixth Report of the Special Rapporteur, Mr Eduardo Valencia-Ospina, on the protection of persons in the event of disasters' (2013) UN Doc. A/CN.4/662, para 41.

92 ILC 'Eighth Report of the Special Rapporteur, Mr Eduardo Valencia-Ospina, on the protection of persons in the event of disasters' (2016) UN Doc. A/CN.4/697, para 193, noting that the analogy drawn with international environmental law and human rights law was criticized.

prevent terrorism when the facts of the case are completely unrelated to terrorism? The question is not easily answered, in particular, because the environmental principle of prevention itself has evolved beyond these traditional sources. The edited volume by Bratspies and Miller entitled, *Transboundary Harm in International Law: Lessons from the Trail Smelter Arbitration*,[93] provided insights on the question: it looked at the extent to which the lessons of *Trail Smelter* could be relevant to a number of issues beyond its original 'environmental' focus, such as terrorism, corporate social responsibility, refugees, the Internet, drug trafficking and human rights. The contributors' assessment of the extent to which the *Trail Smelter* paradigms apply to their respective fields varied greatly, possibly influenced by their different sensibilities towards the award. However, overall, they rejected the argument that the *Trail Smelter* principles had a true doctrinal force, although they recognized that their respective fields of enquiry were drawing 'inspiration from the perspectives and ideas imbedded in the arbitration'.[94] In other words, although the *Trail Smelter* case cannot be considered to be a formal source of non-environmental obligations, it nevertheless acts as a guiding principle and interpretative tool in multiple branches of international law. This study will also take an inclusive position on this question and will, when necessary, make references to related fields, including disaster and health preventive obligations, without, however, loosing track of the inherent limitations of such a method.

3.2.4 *Commonalities: Obligations of Prevention under International Law*

The boundaries of prevention can be delimited following a final method, one that enquires whether a generic obligation to prevent under international law exists, under which the environmental obligation to prevent would fall. The answer of the doctrine is split: some commentators consider different obligations to prevent together on the basis that they share the same rationale,[95] whereas others cautiously note that preventive obligations are too different to fall under the same category.[96] In effect, the question asked here is the

93 R Bratspies and R Miller (eds), *Transboundary Harm in International Law: Lessons from the 'Trail Smelter' Arbitration* (Cambridge University Press 2006).

94 Bratspies and Miller (eds), *Transboundary Harm in International Law*, 9.

95 *Certain Activities Carried out by Nicaragua in the Border Area (Costa Rica v. Nicaragua)* and *Construction of a Road in Costa Rica Along the San Juan River (Nicaragua v. Costa Rica)* (Judgment) (2015) ICJ Rep 665, separate opinion of Judge Cançado Trindade noting that the preventive dimension 'grows in importance in the framework of regimes of protection (such as those e.g. of the human person, and of the environment)'.

96 J Crawford, *State Responsibility: The General Part* (Cambridge University Press 2013) 230.

following: does the obligation to prevent environmental harm share similarities with other obligations to prevent, such as the obligation to prevent genocide, and if so, does it mean that there is a generic obligation to prevent? The answer to these questions will depend on which basis the comparison is made. Intuitively, it is fair to say that the obligations share a common denominator in the form of their anticipatory rationale. The logic arguably influenced the initial work of the ILC on the topic of State responsibility, since it made prevention a specific category of obligation, alongside obligations of result and obligations of conduct.[97] However, the ILC eventually realized that the category was not comparable to the two others because the legal consequences of preventive norms in the context of State responsibility varied, depending on their structure, as obligations of result or conduct.

Commonalities can nevertheless be identified between preventive obligations that are of a due-diligence nature. The character of the environmental principle of prevention as a due-diligence norm will be discussed further in Chapter 7: suffice it here to say that prevention shares commonalities with other norms that concentrate on the conduct of the State in the face of risk and requires it to act proactively. Due diligence has specific expressions in different branches of international law; it nevertheless remains grounded in the same preventive idea,[98] without expressed contradictions between the general standard and its particular expressions.[99] The work of the study group of the International Law Association (ILA) on due diligence has been instrumental in this regard to confirm that due diligence could be considered as a single concept.[100]

To conclude, the multifaceted expressions of prevention in conventional treaty law lead to a complex discussion relative to the unicity of the norm and the coherence of the international legal system. Identifying the specific boundaries of prevention is a difficult undertaking because prevention, shaped by multiple factors, operates differently in numerous treaty regimes. In

97 ILC, 'Draft Articles on State Responsibility with Commentaries Thereto Adopted by the ILC on First Reading' (January 1997) UN Doc. A/CN.4/L.528/Add.3, Articles 20 (conduct), 21 (result) and 23 (prevention).

98 International Law Association, Study Group on Due Diligence in International Law, 'Second Report', Johannesburg, 77th Session, 2016, at 47.

99 ILA, Study Group on Due Diligence in International Law, 'Second Report', at 6. See also T Koivurova, 'Due Diligence', in *Max Planck Encyclopedia of Public International Law* (Oxford University Press 2007), para 2, on the more elaborated rules developed in specific branches of international law.

100 ILA, Study Group on Due Diligence in International Law, 'First Report', Washington, DC, 76th session, 2014, at 1; ILA, Study Group on Due Diligence in International Law, 'Second Report', at 1.

addition, it shares commonalities, and sometimes even intersects, with non-environmental norms in a way that makes it difficult to clearly ascertain its precise boundaries. Overall, what constitutes the unicity of a norm depends on the criteria used for the assessment, with the legal effects of the norm in the context of the law of State responsibility being a pertinent method of categorization.

3.3 IN THE ABSENCE OF PREVENTION

A discussion on the presence of prevention in treaty law should end by looking at the other side coin, that is to say, at areas in which prevention is absent. Although the rationale of prevention is prevalent in international law, not every aspect of environmental damage is the object of a tailored obligation of prevention enshrined in an international environmental treaty. Whether or not this is the case is informative of the type of environmental damage with which the law is concerned. Some environmental risks are neglected by international law either because scientific knowledge is not considered to be sufficiently convincing about the effects of an activity of substance to warrant regulation or because the international community cannot agree on the need to regulate them multilaterally or on how to do so. This applies to a variety of risks, including those pertaining to freshwater resources. Despite the fact that 68.3 per cent of the world's freshwater resources are locked in the form of ice in the polar and other regions,[101] iced freshwater resources have received very limited attention.[102] International law has focused primarily on regulating international watercourses and lakes,[103] which only provide 0.3 per cent of freshwater.[104] Paradoxically, the more a resource can ensure water security, the less its protection is regulated under international law. It is therefore remarkable that conventional law remains largely irresponsive to the fact that global water withdrawals have tripled over the last fifty years and that 80 per cent of today's world population live in areas with high levels of threat to water

[101] World Bank, *World Development Report 2010: Development and Climate Change*, at 139, available at http://siteresources.worldbank.org/INTWDR2010/Resources/5287678-1226014527953/WDR10-Full-Text.pdf (last accessed 19 May 2017).

[102] See in particular JE Viñuales, 'Iced Freshwater Resources: A Legal Exploration' (2009) 20 *Yearbook of International Environmental Law* 188; P-M Dupuy and JE Viñuales, *International Environmental Law* (Cambridge University Press 2015) 113–17.

[103] As exemplified by the fact that there are now *two* universal conventions that regulate watercourse law: the Convention on the Protection and Use of Transboundary Watercourses and International Lakes and the Convention on the Law of the Non-Navigational Uses of International Watercourses.

[104] World Bank, *World Development Report 2010*, at 139.

security.[105] This example underscores the fact that not every environmental risk is regulated by tailored conventional preventive norms. In this light, the customary form of prevention, which some have argued was becoming irrelevant in light of the multiplication of environmental treaties,[106] remains important to fill in regulatory gaps.

The 'absence' of prevention not only brings about questions regarding the political and social construction of risks but also raises legal issues about whether the absence of prevention in international treaties necessarily means that States are under no preventive obligation. The scholarship tends to respond in the negative, on the basis of the principle of evolutionary interpretation that requires that a treaty be interpreted in light of contemporaneous norms.[107] International courts and tribunals have largely relied on the principle to modernize treaties that did not refer explicitly to environmental objectives[108] and, most notably, in *Pulp Mills*, where the ICJ found that the relevant treaty obligations had to be interpreted in accordance with the new customary environmental impact assessment obligation.[109] Caution should nevertheless be exercised as the ICJ was less liberal in the context of the *Certain Activities* judgment.[110] In this case, Nicaragua argued that the 1888 Cleveland Award implied that Nicaragua is free to 'undertake any dredging activity, possibly even if it is harmful to Costa Rica',[111] whereas Costa Rica considered that Nicaragua's rights and obligations under the 1858 treaty and the 1888 award had to be interpreted in light of environmental principles in force today and that they could not override no-harm customary and treaty obligations.[112] The Court did not take a position on this question: it merely restated its recognition of the customary nature of prevention in *Pulp Mills* and the *Advisory Opinion on the Legality of Nuclear Weapons*[113] – implying,

105 United Nations Environment Programme, *Global Environment Outlook 5: Summary for Policy-Makers* (2012), at 10.

106 D Bodansky, 'Customary (and Not So Customary) International Environmental Law' (1995) 3 *Indiana Journal of Global Legal Studies* 105, at 106.

107 Boisson de Chazournes, 'Environmental Treaties in Time', at 296.

108 *Gabčikovo-Nagymaros Project (Hungary/Slovakia)* (Judgment) (1997) ICJ Rep 7, para 140; *Indus Waters Kishenganga Arbitration (Pakistan v. India)*, Permanent Court of Arbitration, Partial Award, 18 February 2013, para 452, and Final Award, 20 December 2013, para 111.

109 *Pulp Mills on the River Uruguay (Argentina v. Uruguay)* (Judgment) (2010) ICJ Rep 14, para 204.

110 For instance, the Court in the *Whaling* case did not follow a similar position on the changing assumptions about whaling; see M Young and S Rioseco Sullivan, 'Evolution through the Duty to Cooperate: Implications of the *Whaling* Case at the International Court of Justice' (2015) 16 *Melbourne Journal of International Law* 311, at 326.

111 *Certain Activities*, para 117.

112 *Certain Activities*, para 117.

113 *Certain Activities*, para 118.

but falling short of affirming, that prevention was a general principle of international law relevant for treaty interpretation. Because Costa Rica had not been able to prove that it had actually suffered significant harm, the Court considered that it did not need to rule on the legality of the harm.[114] The reluctance of the Court to take the opportunity to reaffirm that a principle of evolutionary interpretation was applicable, when it was not indispensable to decide the case, is understandable given that it could be controversially understood to bypass the will of the contracting parties. However, its earlier jurisprudence (subsequently embraced by other international tribunals) leaves little doubt that the principle of prevention should guide the interpretation of international treaties despite the fact that they might not necessarily explicitly refer to it.

3.4 CONCLUSION

The normative impacts of the preventive rationale in conventional law are varied and operate at different levels. Prevention usually influences the overall design of international treaties and translates into more specific duties and regulatory techniques. This chapter concentrated on the substantive preventive obligations most commonly found in treaty law with a view towards determining the material scope of prevention (i.e. the types of risks that prevention in its conventional forms responds to). The multiple manifestations of prevention led to a discussion about whether it should be considered a unique or a plural norm. Definite conclusions are difficult to draw, as the normative impacts of prevention can be differentiated along a number of lines. In addition, the environmental principle of prevention enjoys close proximity with other non environmental preventive norms, which makes it difficult to strictly determine its boundaries.

114 *Certain Activities*, para 118.

4

Prevention in International Customary Law

Prevention is widely acknowledged to be a customary norm.[1] And yet, such a statement is not uncontroversial because of general difficulties relating to the identification of custom under general international law but also because of the multifaceted nature of the preventive norm.

This chapter starts with an examination of the challenges related to the identification of prevention as an international customary norm (4.1). It then offers an analysis of major custom codification works carried out in the field of international environmental law, understood here as non-binding instruments that offer a systematic consolidation of environmental legal rules.[2] The objective is to understand how the principle of prevention has been envisaged in the codification projects of intergovernmental fora (4.2) and non-governmental institutions (4.3). Their analysis reveals that there are as many formulations as the number of bodies that have sought to codify the principle of prevention, although some common elements nevertheless can be extracted.

4.1 ON THE CUSTOMARY STATUS OF PREVENTION

The question of the identification of the customary character of prevention is not easily solved, the two constituent elements of custom – State practice and *opinio juris*[3] – being difficult to review. In particular, undertaking

[1] See *inter alia* P Birnie, A Boyle and C Redgwell, *International Law and the Environment* (3rd edn, Oxford University Press 2009) 137; P Sands and J Peel, *Principles of International Environmental Law* (3rd edn, Cambridge University Press 2012) 203; P-M Dupuy and JE Viñuales, *International Environmental Law* (Cambridge University Press 2015) 44.

[2] T Treves, 'Customary International Law', in *Max Planck Encyclopedia of Public International Law* (Oxford University Press 2006), para 60.

[3] *North Sea Continental Shelf (Federal Republic of Germany/Denmark; Federal Republic of Germany/Netherlands)* (1969) ICJ Rep 3, para 77; ILC, 'Second Report of the Special

a comprehensive survey of State practice can be a difficult, if not impossible, for a lawyer.[4] The *opinio juris* element of custom is generally given priority[5] because it can be more easily assessed. States are regularly given the opportunity to openly endorse the existence of a customary obligation to prevent, as evidenced *inter alia* by proposals to include a reference to the principle of prevention in international legal documents, statements at the UN General Assembly Sixth Committee and reliance on prevention in the context of international judicial proceedings.

The scholarship generally relies on the jurisprudential determination of custom, often citing the *Trail Smelter* award, followed by a reference to the *Corfu Channel* case, which confirmed the prohibition to cause transboundary harm, and to the ICJ's *Advisory Opinion on the Legality of Nuclear Weapons*, recognizing the customary character of Stockholm Principle 21. The approach is based on the belief that international courts and tribunals, and most importantly the ICJ, are best placed to provide an authoritative assessment on the status of a norm. The great weight given by the scholarship – as well as codification bodies[6] – to the general recognition of the preventive rationale in environmental treaties and the international courts and tribunals is in effect a shortcut to a comprehensive assessment of State practice.

Reliance on international jurisprudence to extract the customary character of a norm is not unproblematic because international courts and tribunals tend to be rather 'generous'[7] in their identification of custom. In particular, the

Rapporteur, Mr Michael Wood, on the Identification of Customary International Law' (2014) UN Doc. A/CN.4/672, Draft Conclusion 3, 'Basic approach'.

4 D Bodansky, 'Customary (and Not So Customary) International Environmental Law' (1995) 3 *Indiana Journal of Global Legal Studies* 105, at 113, arguing that 'attempting to induce the rules of customary international law directly from state practice would be a Herculean task' and one for which lawyers are not very well equipped compared to anthropologists or historians. See also P-M Dupuy, 'Formation of Customary International Law and General Principles', in D Bodansky, J Brunnée and E Hey (eds), *The Oxford Handbook of International Environmental Law* (Oxford University Press 2007) 450–65, at 452.

5 P Weil, 'Le droit international en quête de son identité: cours général de droit international public' (1992) 237 *Collected Courses of the Hague Academy of International Law* 9–370, at 173.

6 See e.g. ILC, 'Draft Articles on Prevention of Transboundary Harm from Hazardous Activities (with Commentaries)' (2001) *Yearbook of the International Law Commission* (vol II, part 2) 148, general commentary, para 4 (justifying the 'well-established principle of prevention' on the basis of the *Trail Smelter* case).

7 P-M Dupuy, 'Formation of Customary International Law and General Principles', in D Bodansky, J Brunnée and E Hey (eds), *The Oxford Handbook of International Environmental Law* (Oxford University Press 2008) 450–62, at 452. See also Weil, 'Le droit international en quête de son identité', at 161, on the less and less demanding process of custom identification; Treves, 'Customary International Law', para 5, on the arbitrariness of the ICJ identification of custom.

discrepancy between the insistence of the ICJ on the two constituent elements of custom and its actual practice, which often does not proceed to a detailed assessment of the existence of such elements,[8] is noticeable. This is true in relation to its recognition of the customary character of prevention which the Court offered by way of a mere statement, without further assessments of State practice or *opinio juris*.[9] Because the Court is ill equipped to conduct its own survey of practice,[10] it relies on the 'best and most expedient evidence',[11] which often takes the form of the parties' recognition that the norm is customary or is based on widely accepted international documents.[12] The method is particularly relevant in the case of prevention given that its status is rarely disputed by States and that it is found in a multiplicity of instruments of diverse normative weight. It might give judicial bodies the power to use custom as a cover to create a new norm,[13] but in reality they often merely contribute to filling in the gaps of international normativity.[14]

Although the large majority of the scholarship considers that the customary character of prevention makes little doubt, attention nevertheless should be given to authors who disagree. Some have warned that 'verbal claims and physical behaviour often diverge' in the field of environmental protection and that, as a result, the voluntarist approach taken to custom (which favours *opinio juris* over practice) was inherently flawed.[15] One could convincingly argue that 'transboundary pollution seems much more the rule than the exception in inter-state relations'[16] given that environmental degradation is increasing when, if the preventive obligation were fully respected, it should be diminishing. Knox, for instance, considers that Stockholm Principle 21 is more 'wishful thinking' than evidence of custom.[17] The fact that practice is not in

8 See e.g. S Talmon, 'Determining Customary International Law: The ICJ's Methodology between Induction, Deduction and Assertion' (2015) 26(2) *European Journal of International Law* 417.

9 *Legality of the Threat or Use of Nuclear Weapons* (Advisory Opinion) (1996) ICJ Rep 226, para 29.

10 *Certain Activities Carried out by Nicaragua in the Border Area (Costa Rica v. Nicaragua)* and *Construction of a Road in Costa Rica along the San Juan River (Nicaragua v. Costa Rica)*, (2015) ICJ Rep 665, separate opinion of Judge Donoghue, para 18.

11 P Tomka, 'Custom and the International Court of Justice' (2013) 12(2) *The Law & Practice of International Courts and Tribunals* 195, at 197.

12 N Petersen, 'The International Court of Justice and the Judicial Politics of Identifying Customary International Law' (2017) 28(2) *European Journal of International Law* 357, at 369 and 372.

13 Weil, 'Le droit international en quête de son identité', at 143.

14 Weil, 'Le droit international en quête de son identité', at 142.

15 Bodansky 'Customary (and Not So Customary) International Environmental Law', 115.

16 Bodansky 'Customary (and Not So Customary) International Environmental Law', 110–11.

17 J Knox, 'Myth and Reality of Transboundary Environmental Impact Assessment' (2002) 96 *American Journal of International Law* 291, 319.

perfect conformity with the rule is not per se an issue to the recognition of custom.[18] But the level of inconsistencies is so high that it could cast doubts on the customary character of prevention. However, the discrepancy between declarations and actual practice does not necessarily question the customary status of prevention: it rather highlights the existence of implementation challenges that are common in international environmental law and often related to financial and technological difficulties. In addition, the relative vagueness of prevention, in its conventional as well as customary forms, could be an additional element that explains such discrepancy, as it leaves States uncertain about what their obligations specifically are. Such an approach is corroborated by the fact that in the context of dispute settlement, States present their conduct as legal under their preventive duties, hence revealing their conviction that such an obligation as prevention exists: what is generally disputed is not the existence of the obligation to prevent but rather whether the magnitude of the harm is high enough to engage the responsibility of the State.[19] Another argument put forward by critics of the customary character of prevention relates to the absence of enforcement opportunities.[20] Knox, for instance, considers that 'if Principle 21 is truly part of customary international law, Principle 22 [on the need to develop rules relative to international liability] should be unnecessary' because its violation would simply fall under the rules of State responsibility.[21] Others have argued that the absence of international judicial claims in relation to the Chernobyl accident is explained by the fact that, at the time, there were no customary rules on the basis of which to bring a dispute.[22] The two arguments seem to rely on the assumption that a norm cannot be customary if its violation is not pursued under the rules of State responsibility. However, custom has never been defined, and identified, by how the international legal system responds to its violation: it would be putting too much of a strong emphasis on implementation and enforcement, which is generally international law's weak point. In addition, the argument completely overlooks that prevention has emerged

18 *Military and Paramilitary Activities in and against Nicaragua (Nicaragua v. United States) (Merits)* (1986) ICJ Rep 4, 98, noting that the 'Court does not consider that, for a rule to be established as customary the corresponding practice must be in absolutely rigorous conformity with the rule'.

19 See e.g. *Certain Activities Carried out by Nicaragua in the Border Area (Costa Rica v. Nicaragua)* and *Construction of a Road in Costa Rica along the San Juan River (Nicaragua v. Costa Rica)* (Judgment) (2015) ICJ Rep 665.

20 Knox, 'Myth and Reality of Transboundary Environmental Impact Assessment', 295.

21 Knox, 'Myth and Reality of Transboundary Environmental Impact Assessment', 295.

22 G Lynham, 'The Sic Utere Principle as Customary International Law: A Case of Wishful Thinking?' (1995) 2 *James Cook University Law Review* 172, 187.

as an alternative to the ill-adapted curative approach and as a response to the historical reluctance of States to environmental adjudication.

The near consensus that prevention is a customary norm, despite the limitations discussed earlier, necessarily puts into light the inadequacies of traditional theories on custom. Theories that consider that custom does not necessarily emerge from practice and *opinio juris* but can, on occasion, be the result of the recognition that certain norms should exist as a matter of moral imperative are better able to explain the reality in which prevention operates. They provide a theoretical basis to norms that are widely recognized as custom, even though they did not reach such status from decades of State practice but rather integrated positive law rapidly because they represent common international values.[23] Human rights and humanitarian norms often find their customary status on this basis, 'morally compelling reasons' leading courts to 'rule on the illegality of certain atrocities'.[24] Environmental norms also, albeit to a lesser extent, benefit from such an approach: the legal commentary considers that their customary character is a 'necessity'[25] to protect our planet from degradation and which represent the 'collective ideals of the international community'.[26] René-Jean Dupuy noted that the customary character of the obligation to prevent pollution originated from the role it played as an alarm signal about the threats posed by environmental damage rather than from actual State practice. To explain this discrepancy with traditional theories of custom, he made a distinction between traditional custom, which appears slowly ('coutume sage'), and modern custom, which emerges out of a more disorganized process grounded in morality ('coutume sauvage').[27] If one accepts such an understanding of custom that makes way of actual State practice, then it explains why prevention has been recognized as a customary norm despite discrepancies in State practice.

23 R Pisillo Mazzeschi, 'Closing Keynote Lecture: Coordination of Different Values in International Law', ESIL Annual Conference, 9 September 2017 (on file with the author).

24 NJ Arajärvi, 'The Lines Begin to Blur? Opinio Juris and the Moralisation of Customary International Law' (2011), available at SSRN: https://papers.ssrn.com/sol3/papers.cfm?abstract_id=1823288 (last accessed 5 August 2017). See also Treves, 'Customary International Law', para 13, noting that in the field of human rights custom emerges despite the fact that violations are frequent.

25 B Mayer, 'The Applicability of the Principle of Prevention to Climate Change: A Response to Zahar' (2015) 5 *Climate Law* 1, at 12, arguing that the principle of prevention 'would exist today even without the consent of states, simply out of necessity'.

26 Bodansky 'Customary (and Not So Customary) International Environmental Law', 116.

27 R-J Dupuy, 'Coutume Sage, Coutume Sauvage', in *La communauté internationale: mélanges offerts à Charles Rousseau* (Pedone 1974) 75–87, at 86. See also Weil, 'Le droit international en quête de son identité', 178, on innovative and revolutionary custom that contributes to international change.

The exact scope of the norm under customary law remains, however, to be ascertained. A key challenge arising from this exercise relates to the multifaceted nature of prevention because it means that the different manifestations of prevention carry different normative weight and might therefore not all have the same status. The no-harm rule,[28] Stockholm Principle 21[29] and a general obligation to prevent[30] have all been recognized to have integrated customary international law, as have a number of treaty-specific formulations of prevention.[31] But this might not be the case for other manifestations of prevention. Under such circumstances, can a specific form of prevention that has been recognized as custom be used to justify the customary nature of other preventive obligations with a different material or spatial scope? For instance, is it correct to consider that the *Trail Smelter* recognition of a customary no-harm rule in the context of transboundary air pollution can also be the source of an obligation to avoid radioactive fallout in the high seas[32] or to protect the atmosphere?[33] To what extent can a norm applicable in a transboundary context be extended to apply beyond national jurisdictions? Another issue relates to whether the absence of a single expression of the norm indicates a lack of uniform practice, which, based on traditional theories of sources, would cast doubt on its customary status. It is certain that the different formulations of preventive obligations found in international treaties, as discussed in Chapter 3, raise questions about whether consistent practice exists in relation to harm prevention.[34] However, the multifaceted nature of prevention is justified by the specificity of environmental harm, which calls for a tailored legal response to the diversity of risks falling under the scope of the principle of prevention. Additionally, the concomitant existence of a multiplicity of treaty provisions can facilitate the implementation of the customary obligation that often lacks enough specificity to result in predictable outcomes.[35] In this

28 *Trail Smelter (United States v. Canada)* (16 April 1938 and 11 March 1941), (1941) 3 RIAA 1905.

29 *Legality of the Threat or Use of Nuclear Weapons*, para 29.

30 *Gabčíkovo-Nagymaros Project (Hungary/Slovakia)* (Judgment) (1997) ICJ Rep 7, para 140; *Pulp Mills on the River Uruguay (Argentina v. Uruguay)* (Judgment) (2010) ICJ Rep 14, para 101.

31 Specific formulations of prevention found in multilateral environmental treaties, such as the obligation to protect the marine environment under UNCLOS, are also considered to have reached a customary status.

32 *Nuclear Tests (Australia v. France)* (Judgment) (1974) ICJ Rep 253, Dissenting opinion by Judge de Castro, at 389.

33 ILC, 'Third Report of the Special Rapporteur, Mr Shinya Murase, on the protection of the atmosphere' (2016) UN Doc. A/CN.4/692, para 35.

34 Lynham, 'The Sic Utere Principle as Customary International Law', at 180.

35 *Certain Activities/Construction of a Road*, separate opinion of Judge ad hoc Dugard, para 42, noting that the obligation to formulate and implement their planning so as to promote the

context, the content of the customary obligation of prevention is particularly important when discussing the status of the norm: a customary norm with an unclarified content runs the risk of being an 'empty' obligation.

4.2 CUSTOM CODIFICATION WORKS OF INTERGOVERNMENTAL FORUMS

The preceding section presented some of the difficulties brought about by the identification of prevention as a norm of international customary law. Now we turn to international bodies that have sought to codify customary practices in the field of environmental law. In this section, we analyse the codification works produced by a variety of intergovernmental forums, broadly understood as institutions to which States have given a mandate to codify environmental norms. We look at how prevention has been conceptualized in the work of the International Law Commission (4.2.1), the United Nations Environment Programme (UNEP) Environmental Law Guidelines and Principles on Shared Natural Resources (4.2.2), the World Charter for Nature (4.2.3), the Final Report of the Experts Group on Environmental Law on Legal Principles for Environmental Protection and Sustainable Development (4.2.4), as well as by the United Nations Conference on Environment and Development (4.2.5). Given the difficulties emerging when seeking to identify the specific scope of prevention under customary law, the objective of the analysis is not to provide an overarching assessment of whether the codification works are reflective of international custom but rather to highlight common trends, and as well as innovations, arising from these instruments.

4.2.1 *Prevention in the International Law Commission (1978–2016)*

The ILC spent considerable time on the issue of prevention, at the centre of its work on international liability for injurious consequences arising out of acts not prohibited by international law, which eventually resulted in the adoption of two fundamental documents that have contributed to the consolidation of the prevention principle: the ILC Prevention Articles and the Allocation of Loss Principles (4.2.1.1). In addition, the ILC was also given the opportunity to codify, in a more fragmented manner, specific manifestations of prevention (4.2.1.2).

conservation of the wetlands. Article 3(1) of the Ramsar Convention on formulation and implementation of planning strategies to promote the conservation of wetlands 'enlivens the procedural obligation to conduct an environmental impact assessment under general international law' by giving it a substantive objective: the conservation of the wetlands.

4.2.1.1 International Liability for Injurious Consequences Arising out of Acts Not Prohibited by International Law

Prevention has been at the centre of the work of the ILC on international liability for injurious consequences arising out of acts not prohibited by international law since 1978. After years of hesitation as to the proper angle for the topic, the ILC set two separate tracks, one focusing on the definition of the duty to prevent environmental harm as a duty of States (ILC Prevention Articles,[36] adopted in 2001) and another setting parameters for the allocation of loss in the event harm occurs (ILC Principles on the Allocation of Loss,[37] adopted in 2006). The first reads as an elaboration of the primary norm of prevention, as stated in Principle 21 of the Stockholm Declaration, although with a narrower focus. The second provides guidance on how to organize the consequences of damage to the environment at the national and international levels, much as a civil liability treaty would. The difficulties that the ILC faced to arrive at these two sets of principles relate directly to the core of this study: the conceptualization of the relationship between prevention and reparation. It is through this spectrum that the work of the ILC on prevention that spans three decades will now be briefly summarized.[38]

BRIEF HISTORICAL OVERVIEW OF THE DRAFTING PROCESS The ILC started its work on international liability for injurious consequences arising out of acts not prohibited by international law in 1978. The topic was not initially restricted to environmental harm but was more broadly concerned with transboundary harm caused by lawful activities, which the ILC considered to fall under the regime of 'liability' (in contrast with 'responsibility'). In retrospect, it has been admitted that the ILC's early work on liability was 'fundamentally misconceived'.[39] Indeed, the work of the ILC was built on the premise that liability is a *primary* obligation applicable to non-prohibited activities, whereas responsibility is a secondary rule deploying its effects to sanction a wrongful act. The ILC struggled to conceptualize the relationship between the general regime of State responsibility applicable in case of harm

36 ILC, 'Draft Articles on Prevention of Transboundary Harm'.

37 ILC, 'Draft Principles on the Allocation of Loss in the Case of Transboundary Harm Arising out of Hazardous Activities (with Commentaries)' (2006) UN Doc. A/63/10.

38 For a concise yet detailed assessment of the two sets of articles, see *inter alia* G Hafner and I Buffard, 'The Work of the International Law Commission: From Liability to Damage Prevention', in Y Kerbrat and S Maljean-Dubois (eds), *The Transformation of International Environmental Law* (Hart 2011) 233–51.

39 P Birnie, A Boyle and C Redgwell, *International Law and the Environment* (3rd edn, Oxford University Press 2009) 141.

created by an internationally wrongful act and the specific case of harm arising out of lawful activities. On the one hand, the ILC did not want to 'trespass'[40] on the topic of responsibility (on which it was working in parallel and was also facing considerable difficulties); on the other hand, it also did not want the topic to be assimilated into strict liability, making the State liable for harm arising out of lawful activities on its territory.[41] As a result, the issue of whether activities causing transboundary harm were prohibited under international law remained unclear for a long time. Although the ILC started its work at the time when the rationale of prevention was gaining predominance in international environmental law, it did not recognize that a primary obligation to prevent transboundary harm existed that, if breached, could engage the responsibility of the State.[42]

The angle taken by the ILC to the topic meant that it was focusing on building a reactive framework to the occurrence of harm and therefore did not give proper consideration to the issue of harm anticipation. The rapporteurs did study prevention, but they conceptualized it differently from the form it eventually took in the Prevention Articles. The first rapporteur, Quentin-Baxter, considered that prevention was included inside a primary norm that was 'compound', providing for 'preventing, minimizing and imposing reparation for the occurrence of physical transboundary harm'.[43] Prevention was envisaged ex post, as measures to be adopted after the occurrence of harm to avoid the furtherance or repetition of the wrongful act. It was conceptualized together with the traditional duty to repair, both obligations forming the foundational elements of a reactive regime. The following statement from Rapporteur Quentin-Baxter summarizes his conception of the prevention/reparation dialectic clearly:

> But what is 'prevention' and what is 'reparation'? Reparation has always the purpose of restoring as fully as possible a pre-existing situation; and, in the

40 J Barboza, *The Environment, Risk and Liability in International Law* (Martinus Nijhoff 2011) 78.

41 Barboza, *The Environment, Risk and Liability in International Law* 78.

42 A Boyle, 'Liability for Injurious Consequences of Acts Not Prohibited by International Law', in J Crawford, A Pellet and S Olleson (eds), *The Law of International Responsibility* (Oxford University Press 2010) 95–103, at 96, noting that the ILC 'seemed unable to grasp that international law might, as in Part XII of the 1982 UN Convention on the Law of the Sea, impose obligations of regulation, diligent control, and prevention of harm even on lawful activities without either prohibiting the activity or excluding the possibility of responsibility for breach'.

43 ILC, 'Fourth Report of the Special Rapporteur, Mr Robert Quentin-Baxter, on the Topic of Liability for Injurious Consequences of Acts Not Prohibited by International Law' (1983) UN Doc. A/CN.4/373, para 40.

context of the present topic, it may often amount to prevention after the event.[44]

Quentin-Baxter considered prevention to be part of the obligation to repair because it applies in an ex post context of harm mitigation. However, the ILC eventually took a different route to recognize prevention as an independent anticipatory duty. This study will nevertheless show that the ex post aspect of prevention has not completely disappeared but remains discernible in its temporal scope (see Chapter 6).[45]

The ILC conceptualized prevention in its present form (i.e. as an ex ante obligation) for the first time in the context of the work of its second rapporteur on the topic, Barboza. A new conceptualization of prevention is found in his fourth report that reads as follows: '[s]ource States shall take all reasonable preventive measures to prevent or minimize injury that may result from an activity which presumably involves risk and for which no regime has been established.'[46] In the tenth report, prevention was fully conceptualized as a primary rule of obligation in its own right.[47] A year later, in 1995, the principle was provisionally adopted by the Drafting Committee, which provided that 'States shall take all appropriate measures to prevent or minimise the risk of significant transboundary harm'.[48]

The draft articles proposed in 1996 showed significant progress and included provisions on prevention, cooperation and strict liability.[49] The principle of prevention was expressed in the form of Article 3, which was inspired by Stockholm Principle 21 and that provided that State sovereignty is 'not unlimited' and constrained by an obligation to prevent transboundary harm.[50] It was complemented by Article 4, which presented

44 ILC, 'Fourth Report of the Special Rapporteur, Mr Robert Quentin-Baxter', para 47.

45 See Section 6.2 on the temporal dimensions of risk anticipation.

46 ILC, 'Fourth Report of the Special Rapporteur, Mr Robert Quentin-Baxter', at 34: Article 9 is entitled 'Prevention'.

47 ILC, 'Tenth Report of the Special Rapporteur, Mr Robert Quentin-Baxter, on the Topic of Liability for Injurious Consequences of Acts Not Prohibited by International Law' (1994) UN Doc. A/CN.4/459, para 5.

48 ILC, 'Titles and Texts of Draft Articles on the International Liability for Injurious Consequences Arising out of Acts Not Prohibited by International Law Adopted by the Drafting Committee at Its Forty-Seventh Session' (1995) UN Doc. A/CN.4/L.508, Article C.

49 ILC, 'Report on the Work of Its 48th Session' (1996) UN Doc. A/51/10, chap V, paras 89–101.

50 ILC, 'Report on the Work of Its 48th Session', Article 3, reads as follows: 'The freedom of States to carry on or permit activities in their territory or otherwise under their jurisdiction or control is not unlimited. It is subject to the general obligation to prevent or minimize the risk of causing significant transboundary harm, as well as any specific obligations owed to other States in that regard.'

prevention as an obligation to exercise due diligence.[51] Yet, in 1997, almost twenty years after the start of the work of the ILC, there was still a clear (and worrying) absence of consensus on the overall topic of liability for acts not prohibited by international law. The situation led the ILC to note that 'the scope and content of the topic remained unclear due to such facts as conceptual and theoretical difficulties, appropriateness of the title and the relation of the subject to State responsibility'[52] – a comment that Barboza suitably translated later as being 'almost equivalent to saying that nothing was clear'.[53] As the work on prevention was already at an advanced stage – in opposition to the work on liability – it was recommended that the two issues be treated separately.[54] On this basis, the ILC then rapidly finalized the nineteen articles pertaining to prevention that were adopted in 2001 and completed its work in 2006 with the adoption of a set of principles on the allocation of loss concentrating on the liability of the economic operator in case of harm. The rest of this section focuses on the first instalment, the ILC Prevention Articles, since it is the most directly relevant to the subject matter of this study.

THE ARTICLES TODAY: CONTENT AND RECEPTION The normative contribution of the ILC Prevention Articles can be assessed by concentrating on two main questions, namely, their content and their reception. Regarding the content of the articles, it is noticeable that the ILC carefully circumscribed the scope of its work according to several parameters, which means that their focus is narrower than that of Stockholm Principle 21.[55] The main differences are found in the strictly transboundary scope of the ILC Prevention Articles (thus excluding harm to areas beyond national jurisdiction and harm to the domestic territory without external impacts) and the pragmatic recognition that in some cases harm may be admissible if it is minimized.[56] The risk of significant transboundary harm is defined in a non-limitative manner, as 'includ[ing] risks taking the form of a high probability of causing significant transboundary harm and a low probability of causing disastrous transboundary harm'.[57]

51 ILC, 'Report on the Work of Its 48th Session', Article 4, reads as follows: 'States shall take all appropriate measures to prevent or minimize the risk of significant transboundary harm and, if such harm has occurred, to minimize its effects.'

52 ILC, 'Report on the Work of Its 49th Session' (1997) UN Doc. A/52/10, chap VII, para 165.

53 Barboza, *The Environment, Risk and Liability* 125.

54 ILC, 'Report on the Work of Its 49th Session', paras 162–68.

55 See ILC, 'Draft Articles on Prevention of Transboundary Harm', Commentary to Articles 1 and 2, at 149–53.

56 ILC, 'Draft Articles on Prevention of Transboundary Harm', Commentary to Article 3, para 7, at 154, and to Article 10(b), para 4, at 162.

57 ILC, 'Draft Articles on Prevention of Transboundary Harm', Article 2(a).

Within these bounds, the duty of prevention is characterized by reference to several interrelated obligations that are analysed further in Chapter 7. Inter-State or 'horizontal' obligations include prevention (Article 3), cooperation in prevention and response (Articles 4, 8, 9, 11, 12, 16 and 17) and information and protection due to the public concerned (Articles 13 and 15). Intra-State or 'vertical' obligations include the duty to adopt an appropriate domestic legislation (Article 5) and, more specifically, a system of authorization of potentially harmful activities (Article 6) involving an environmental impact assessment (Article 7). The articles also include a provision on the settlement of disputes (Article 19) and another one on the relations with other rules of international law (Article 18).

The articles have generally been well received by States and have achieved broad support. In light of the difficulties encountered by the ILC in delimiting the topic, the endorsement of the articles, seen as 'authoritative guidance for the conduct of States',[58] is an achievement in itself. Admittedly, the reviews undertaken by the UN of the international case law referring to the articles since their adoption identified only nine cases in which the articles played a role.[59] However, the low number should not lead to the rushed conclusion that the articles are of limited importance. Firstly, it should be kept in mind that the number of environmental cases at the international level is relatively limited; therefore, the ratio between references to the Prevention Articles and the number of environmental cases is not particularly low. Secondly, it is significant in terms of *opinio juris* that even if courts do not often explicitly refer to the articles, States regularly mention them in their pleadings.[60]

58 Sixth Committee, 'Summary Record of the 17th Meeting, Held at Headquarters, New York, on Thursday, 21 October 2010, at 10 a.m.', UN Doc. A/C.6/65/SR.17, New Zealand speaking, para 20.

59 'Consideration of prevention of transboundary harm from hazardous activities and allocation of loss in the case of such harm. Compilation of decisions of international courts, tribunals and other bodies: Report of the Secretary-General' (2013) UN Doc. A/68/94. Of the five cases mentioned, three references to the ILC Prevention Articles were made by judges in their individual opinions, and the report considered that in the *Pulp Mills on the River Uruguay (Argentina v. Uruguay)* case the Court had implicitly relied on the articles. This thus leaves only the ITLOS Advisory Opinion on *Responsibilities and Obligations of States Sponsoring Persons and Entities with Respect to Activities in the Area*, which made an explicit reference to the ILC Prevention Articles (at para 116). Four cases in which the ILC Prevention Articles have been influential were added in the 2016 report: the ICJ *Whaling* and *Certain Activities* cases (in separate opinions) and the PCA *Indus Waters Kishenganga* and *Chagos Marine Protected Area* awards (but only indirectly). See 'Consideration of prevention of transboundary harm from hazardous activities and allocation of loss in the case of such harm: Compilation of decisions of international courts, tribunals and other bodies. Report of the Secretary-General' (2016) UN Doc. A/71/98.

60 See e.g. *Pulp Mills on the River Uruguay (Argentina v. Uruguay)*: Uruguay's memorial, paras 103 and 152, Argentina's counter-memorial, para 21; *Whaling in the Antarctic (Australia v. Japan, New Zealand intervening)*: Japan's memorial, at 425 (on the threshold of harm),

A word should be said here about the extent to which the articles codify existing customary law or contribute to the progressive development of the law. Given the difficulties related to the identification of custom highlighted earlier, the discussion that follows concentrates on how the articles have been perceived by States. Some States consider that the ILC Prevention Articles codify the current state of prevention in international environmental law[61] but are not fully representative of its complete expression[62] given that the geographical scope of prevention is broader than envisaged by the articles.[63] To the contrary, other States consider that they are 'innovative and aspirational'[64] and do not represent current State practice.[65] They also highlight that significant issues remain unresolved by the articles, in particular in relation to the threshold of harm[66] and cooperation duties.[67] The core ILC Articles, and their customary character, are discussed further

New Zealand's memorial, at 59 (on due diligence and the obligation of cooperation) and 61 (procedural obligations); *Certain Activities Carried out by Nicaragua in the Border Area (Costa Rica v. Nicaragua)*: Costa Rica's memorial, para 5.6 (notification), Nicaragua's counter-memorial, para 3.31 and para 3.42 (Article 3 and due diligence), paras 3.36 and 5.133 (Article 8(1) but deemed not applicable in the *cas d'espèce*); *Construction of a Road in Costa Rica along the San Juan River (Nicaragua v. Costa Rica)*: Nicaragua's memorial, para 4.35 (Article 3 on due diligence), para 4.38 (on Articles 8, 9 and 12), para 5.47 (on Article 7). One should note, however, that in the *Aerial Herbicide Spraying (Ecuador v. Colombia)* case, while Ecuador relied extensively on the ILC Prevention Articles, Colombia refused to see them as customary: counter-memorial of Colombia, para 8.27. All the memorials are available at http://www.icj-cij.org/ (last accessed 19 May 2017).

61 Sixth Committee, 'Summary Record 2010', Netherlands speaking, para 16.

62 Sixth Committee, 'Summary Record 2010', Mexico speaking, para 14, on extending the articles to areas beyond the limits of national jurisdiction; and the Netherlands speaking, para 16.

63 Sixth Committee, 'Consideration of Prevention of Transboundary Harm from Hazardous Activities and Allocation of Loss in the Case of Such Harm: Report of the Secretary-General', UN Doc. A/68/170, 22 July 2013, El-Salvador speaking, para 10.

64 Sixth Committee, 'Summary Record 2010', United States speaking (Addendum to the Report of the Secretary-General, UN Doc. A/65/184/Add.1), para 2; Sixth Committee, 'Report of the Secretary-General 2013', US comments, para 31.

65 Sixth Committee, 'Report of the Secretary-General 2013', comments of Colombia, paras 4–9; Sixth Committee, 'Seventy-First Session (2016), 18th and 19th Meetings (AM & PM)' press release, available at www.un.org/press/en/2016/gal3528.doc.htm (last accessed 30 July 2017), Iran speaking, China speaking, Australia speaking, Philippines speaking, Venezuela speaking.

66 Sixth Committee, 'Summary Record 2010', Germany speaking, para 9, on the need to specify the significant threshold; Sixth Committee, 'Summary Record 2010', Malaysia speaking, para 12. This position is opposed by the Russian Federation, which considers that the significant harm threshold should be retained: Sixth Committee, 'Summary Record of the 12th Meeting Held at Headquarters, New York, on Tuesday, 23 October 2007, at 10 a.m.', UN Doc. A/C.6/62/SR.12, para 44.

67 Sixth Committee, 'Summary Record of the meeting, October 2013', available at www.un.org/News/Press/docs/2013/gal3464.doc.htm (last accessed 19 May 2017) 2013', India speaking, Malaysia speaking.

in Chapter 7. Suffice is to say here that the Prevention Articles are both restrictive and progressive in their conceptualization of prevention. On the one hand, their limited application to transboundary harm does not reflect the full spatial reach of prevention. On the other hand, they clarify the standards of care expected, but not made explicit, by Principle 21. The jurisprudence, presented in Chapter 5, has acknowledged that the core system (prevention, cooperation and environmental impact assessment) of this instrument rests on customary law.[68] However, other, peripheral provisions, particularly the detail of the procedures set out in Articles 11 (absence of notification) and 19 (establishment of a fact-finding commission in case of dispute), have not achieved widespread recognition or, like non-discriminatory participation (Article 13), are being gradually integrated into custom.[69]

THE FUTURE OF THE ARTICLES Given the disagreements regarding the customary character of the entire set of articles, their transformation into a general treaty, as recommended by the ILC,[70] remains for now a distant and uncertain prospect. The discussion over the ILC Prevention Articles taking place every three years within the Sixth (Legal) Committee of the UN General Assembly reveals that since their adoption, States have maintained a consistent approach with limited evolution in how they perceive them. Consensus seems to have formed around the idea that the articles should remain in their 'current recommendatory form',[71] while State practice is being assessed[72] and States further implement them by strengthening their domestic framework[73] and adopting further bilateral and regional agreements.[74] The majority of States consider that it would be 'premature'[75] to elaborate an international

68 See Section 7.2.

69 L-A Duvic-Paoli, 'The Status of the Right to Public Participation in International Environmental Law: An Analysis of the Jurisprudence' (2012) 23 *Yearbook of International Environmental Law* 80; J Ebbesson, 'Principle 10: Public Participation', in JE Viñuales (ed), *The Rio Declaration on Environment and Development: A Commentary* (Oxford University Press 2015) 287.

70 ILC, 'Report on the Work of Its 53rd Session' (2001) UN Doc. A/56/10, chap V, para 94.

71 Sixth Committee, 'Summary Record 2013', Israel speaking.

72 Sixth Committee, 'Summary Record 2010', Austria speaking, para 3; Sixth Committee, 'Summary Record 2013', Vietnam speaking, Malaysia speaking; Sixth Committee, 'Summary Record 2016', Malaysia speaking.

73 Sixth Committee, 'Summary Record 2013', Tonga speaking, India speaking. Sixth Committee, 'Summary Record 2016', Iran speaking.

74 Sixth Committee, 'Summary Record 2010', US speaking, Addendum, para 1; Sixth Committee, 'Report of the Secretary-General 2013', comments of Qatar, para 29; Sixth Committee, 'Summary Record 2013', Russia speaking; Sixth Committee, 'Summary Record 2016', Venezuela speaking.

75 Sixth Committee, 'Summary Record 2013', Russia speaking. See also Sixth Committee, 'Summary Record 2016', Philippines speaking. The United States and the United Kingdom are strongly opposed to the elaboration of a global convention on the matter: Sixth

convention now but agree that it could be 'considered for the future'.[76] If this were the case, it seems that States would be willing to adopt a single convention combining the ILC Prevention Articles with the ILC Principles on the Allocation of Loss, since they offer complementary perspectives.[77] The combination of the two sets of provisions would be an interesting development, as the two issues were originally dealt together, only to be separated as a consensus on prevention was reached more quickly than on liability. While the two topics were divided for pragmatic reasons, it appears now that both sets of articles are envisaged by States as a continuum, thereby justifying their merging.[78]

4.2.1.2 Sectoral Approaches

The ILC not only has provided clarity to the general principle of prevention but also has mapped some of its manifestations in specific environmental regimes.

TRANSBOUNDARY AQUIFERS The work of the ILC on the law of transboundary aquifers, which culminated in 2008 with the adoption of the Draft Articles on Transboundary Aquifers (Aquifers Articles),[79] explicitly applied the preventive rationale to aquifers. As in the UN Convention on the Law of the Non-Navigational Uses of International Watercourses that the ILC itself drafted,[80] the prevention principle was translated into several substantive obligations, including an obligation to act diligently to avoid causing significant harm,[81] an obligation to prevent pollution[82] and a duty to protect ecosystems.[83]

Committee, 'Summary Record 2007', US speaking, para 29; Sixth Committee, 'Summary Record 2016', UK speaking.

76 Sixth Committee, 'Summary Record 2013', Russia speaking.

77 Sixth Committee, 'Summary Record 2010', Mexico speaking, paras 12–13, Netherlands speaking, para 18, Portugal speaking, para 32; and Sixth Committee, 'Summary Record 2013', South Africa speaking, Micronesia speaking, Chile speaking; Sixth Committee, 'Report of the Secretary-General 2013', comments of El Salvador, paras 13–14.

78 The continuum is analysed further in Chapter 11.

79 ILC, 'Draft Articles on the Law of Transboundary Aquifers' (2008) *Yearbook of the International Law Commission* (vol II, part 2), Article 3.

80 The ILC also looked at the obligation of prevention in relation to international watercourses, but this was not included here given that it resulted in the adoption of the 1997 Convention on the Law of the Non-Navigational Uses of International Watercourses, analysed as part of Chapter 3 on prevention in conventional law.

81 ILC, 'Draft Articles on the Law of Transboundary Aquifers', Article 6.

82 ILC, 'Draft Articles on the Law of Transboundary Aquifers', Article 12.

83 ILC, 'Draft Articles on the Law of Transboundary Aquifers', Article 10.

The Aquifers Articles explicitly implement the first two components of Stockholm Principle 21. They rely on a geographical scope similar to that of the ILC Prevention Articles by being applicable only to *transboundary* aquifers.[84] In addition, they strongly emphasize that States have sovereignty over the 'the portion of a transboundary aquifer or aquifer system located within its territory'.[85] The provision, presented at the beginning of the set of articles, reaffirms the sovereignty component of Stockholm Principle 21 and highlights the reluctance of States to relinquish their sovereign rights over aquifers.

PROTECTION OF PERSONS IN THE EVENT OF DISASTERS The ILC recognized the relevance of the preventive rationale in the field of disaster law in the context of its work on the protection of persons in the event of disasters that led to adoption of a set of articles in 2016.[86] As mentioned in Chapter 3, although the preventive rationale directed towards environmental and disaster risks is not completely analogous, the two perspectives nevertheless intersect. The ILC followed this approach, justifying the existence of a preventive obligation in disaster law by drawing an analogy with, *inter alia*, prevention in international environmental law.[87]

The ILC Articles on the Protection of Persons in the Event of Disasters provide for an article on 'reduction of the risk of disasters' (Article 9) which reads as follows:

> 1. Each State shall reduce the risk of disasters by taking appropriate measures, including through legislation and regulations, to prevent, mitigate, and prepare for disasters.
> 2. Disaster risk reduction measures include the conduct of risk assessments, the collection and dissemination of risk and past loss information, and the installation and operation of early warning systems.

The provision finds its origins in the acknowledgement of Rapporteur Valencia-Ospina that the law had shifted from a 'primarily response-centric

84 ILC, 'Draft Articles on the Law of Transboundary Aquifers', Article 1(a).
85 ILC, 'Draft Articles on the Law of Transboundary Aquifers', Article 3.
86 The rapporteur recommended to the General Assembly that a convention be elaborated on the basis of the articles; see ILC, 'Eighth Report of the Special Rapporteur, Mr Eduardo Valencia-Ospina, on the Protection of Persons in the Event of Disasters' (2016) UN Doc. A/CN.4/697, para 46.
87 ILC, 'Sixth Report of the Special Rapporteur, Mr Eduardo Valencia-Ospina, on the Protection of Persons in the Event of Disasters' (2013) UN Doc. A/CN.4/662, paras 54–59; and 'Draft Articles on the Protection of Persons in the Event of Disasters (with Commentaries)' (2016) *Yearbook of the International Law Commission* (vol II, part 2), Commentary to Article 9, para 4 (also noting the analogy with human rights principles).

model to one focused largely on prevention and preparedness',[88] which led him to devote an entire report to the notion of prevention in disaster law.[89] Initially, the ILC struggled with drafting the article, as the relationship between the general term 'prevention' and the more specific disaster law term 'risk reduction' appeared blurry. Drawing an explicit distinction between the obligations of States in relation to risk avoidance and harm mitigation also proved challenging. An initial proposal recognized a rather complex obligation to 'prevent the creation of new risk and reduce existing risk and to mitigate and prepare for disasters',[90] which was then streamlined into an obligation to 'reduce the risk of disasters ... to prevent, mitigation, and prepare for disasters'.[91] The ILC clarified the relationship between risk reduction and prevention by considering that risk reduction formed the core obligation (one of conduct), while the general objective is to 'prevent, mitigate, and prepare for disasters'.[92] The decision to identify risk reduction as the principal obligation has been explained by the fact that prevention in disaster law tends to be seen as an operational concept that drives the adoption of 'appropriate' measures[93] and translates into specific sets of international and national mechanisms.[94] Under a context of disaster risk reduction, prevention is not understood as a primary obligation but rather as the rationale that calls upon States to adopt specific implementing measures.

88 ILC, 'Fifth Report of the Special Rapporteur, Mr Eduardo Valencia-Ospina, on the Protection of Persons in the Event of Disasters' (2012) UN Doc. A/CN.4/652, para 114. The integration of the principle of prevention in the context of the articles was not uncontroversial, with a number of States considering that there was no legally binding obligation of prevention. For a brief summary, see ILC, 'Eighth Report of the Special Rapporteur, Mr Eduardo Valencia-Ospina', paras 190 and 193.

89 ILC, 'Sixth Report of the Special Rapporteur, Mr Eduardo Valencia-Ospina'.

90 ILC, 'Eighth Report of the Special Rapporteur, Mr Eduardo Valencia-Ospina', Annex, Article 11(1).

91 ILC, 'Draft Articles on the Protection of Persons in the Event of Disasters', Article 9(1).

92 ILC, 'Draft Articles on the Protection of Persons in the Event of Disasters', Commentary to Article 9, para 10, noting the contemporary view of the international community (e.g. as expressed in the Sendai Framework), which focuses on the 'reduction of the risk of harm caused by a hazard, as distinguished from the prevention and management of disasters themselves'.

93 ILC, 'Draft Articles on the Protection of Persons in the Event of Disasters', Commentary to Article 9, para 15, clarifying that the last clause 'serves to describe the purpose of the "appropriate" measures that States are to take during the pre-disaster phase to address exposure, vulnerability and the characteristics of a hazard, with the ultimate goal of reducing disaster risk'.

94 B Nicoletti, 'The Prevention of Natural and Man-Made Disasters: What Duties for States?', in A de Guttry, M Gestri and G Venturini (eds), *International Disaster Response Law* (Asser Press 2012) 177–98.

PROTECTION OF THE ATMOSPHERE The ILC also consolidated the status of prevention in relation to specific environmental issues. Conscious of the fact that the ILC had not worked on other environment-related topics since its study on prevention and allocation of loss 'at a time when the world was undergoing serious environmental degradation',[95] the ILC put on its agenda two environmental topics in 2013: one on the protection of the atmosphere and the other on the protection of the environment in relation to armed conflicts.

The ILC included the protection of the atmosphere in its work programme in 2013 but, given the political sensibility of the issue at hand, agreed on a restricted mandate.[96] The first report of Special Rapporteur Shinya Murase in 2014 mentioned the principle of prevention in its inventory of the obligations applicable to the protection of the atmosphere. It concluded that on the basis of the *Trail Smelter* award, the *sic utere tuo* rule was customary in relation to transboundary air pollution between adjacent countries.[97] Despite quoting Principle 21,[98] the rapporteur remained considerably more cautious regarding the status of the rule in relation to long-distance air pollution and global atmospheric pollution,[99] putting forward the argument that the determination of custom should be carried out on a 'case-by-case basis'.[100] However, the rapporteur's initial conservative approach was then replaced by a substantially more progressive outlook.[101] In his second report, published in 2015, the rapporteur changed his position with regards to the limited applicability of the *sic utere tuo* rule. While he had initially planned to restrict his analysis to the application of the *sic utere tuo* rule to transboundary air pollution,[102] the second report noted the 'transformation'[103] of the *sic utere tuo* rule that had resulted in an 'extension of its territorial scope to include

95 ILC, 'First Report of the Special Rapporteur, Mr Shinya Murase, on the protection of the atmosphere' (2014) UN Doc. A/CN.4/667, para 10.

96 See the scope of the guidelines, as provisionally adopted in 2015, Draft Guideline 2: ILC, 'Protection of the Atmosphere. Texts and Titles of Draft Conclusions 1, 2 and 5, and Preambular Paragraphs Provisionally Adopted by the Drafting Committee on 13, 18, 19 and 20 May 2015' (2015) UN Doc. A/CN.4/L.851.

97 ILC, 'First Report of the Special Rapporteur, Mr Shinya Murase', para 51.

98 ILC, 'First Report of the Special Rapporteur, Mr Shinya Murase', para 24.

99 ILC, 'First Report of the Special Rapporteur, Mr Shinya Murase', para 24.

100 ILC, 'First Report of the Special Rapporteur, Mr Shinya Murase', para 24.

101 More generally, he was also criticized for interpreting his mandate in a sense that was considered too 'liberal'. See 'Provisional Summary Record of the 3244th Meeting' (2015) UN Doc. A/CN.4/SR.3244, ILC member Park at 6; and 'Provisional Summary Record of the 3246th Meeting' (2015) UN Doc. A/CN.4/SR.3246, ILC member Murphy at 3.

102 ILC, 'First Report of the Special Rapporteur, Mr Shinya Murase', para 92.

103 ILC, 'Second Report of the Special Rapporteur, Mr Shinya Murase, on the Protection of the Atmosphere' (2015) UN Doc. A/CN.4/681, para 51.

addressing the subject of the global commons per se'.[104] As a result, the report embraced a broader approach to prevention and proposed a guideline recognizing that 'States have the obligation to protect the atmosphere'.[105] Presented as a result of the analysis of the *sic utere tuo* concept and its extension in the form of Principle 21, the general obligation to protect the atmosphere was designed after the comprehensive obligation of prevention found in Article 192 of UNCLOS.[106] However, the potential *erga omnes* nature of such an obligation was disputed, and the guideline faced strong opposition from some ILC members and States at the UN General Assembly Sixth Committee.[107]

As a result, the special rapporteur sought to propose an alternative wording in his third report. However, he found it difficult to bring under one single heading the multifaceted dimensions of prevention, to include its customary and conventional sources, its extended temporal scope (prevention and mitigation) and its concern for diverse types of risks (pollution and others).[108] A simplified version of his proposal was eventually provisionally adopted to read as follows: 'States have the obligation to protect the atmosphere by exercising due diligence in taking appropriate measures, in accordance with applicable rules of international law, to prevent, reduce or control atmospheric pollution and atmospheric degradation.'[109] The provision confirms prevention as an obligation to exercise due diligence but, most importantly, contributes to extending its scope to cover the environment in a more comprehensive manner.

THE ENVIRONMENT AND ARMED CONFLICT The ILC also brought clarity to the principle of prevention in the context of armed conflict, pragmatically

[104] ILC, 'Second Report of the Special Rapporteur, Mr Shinya Murase', para 56.

[105] ILC, 'Second Report of the Special Rapporteur, Mr Shinya Murase', Draft Guideline 4.

[106] ILC, 'Second Report of the Special Rapporteur, Mr Shinya Murase', para 41.

[107] As a result, the guideline was not referred to the Drafting Committee.

[108] ILC, 'Third Report of the Special Rapporteur, Mr Shinya Murase, on the Protection of the Atmosphere' (2016) UN Doc. A/CN.4/692, para 40, Draft Guideline 3. It read as follows:

> States have the obligation to protect the atmosphere from atmospheric pollution and atmospheric degradation:
>
> a) Appropriate measures of due diligence shall be taken to prevent atmospheric pollution in accordance with the relevant rules of international law.
>
> b) Appropriate measures shall be taken to minimize the risk of atmospheric degradation in accordance with relevant conventions.

[109] ILC, 'Protection of the Atmosphere: Titles and Texts of Draft Guidelines 3, 4, 5, 6 and 7, Together With a Preambular Paragraph, Provisionally Adopted by the Drafting Committee on 7, 8 and 9 June 2016' (2016) UN Doc. A/CN.4/L.875. Such a wording remains arguably heavy, including in relation to the reference to the due-diligence character of the obligation which could have been specified in the commentaries to the articles.

recognizing the inevitably of environmental harm in such a context but aiming to build a legal framework that would, as much as possible, prevent, minimize and repair such damage. A preventive rationale guides the ILC draft principles on environment and armed conflict, as provisionally adopted in 2015 and 2016. It is evidenced in Draft Principle 2, which presents the objectives of the principles as follows:

> The present draft principles are aimed at enhancing the protection of the environment in relation to armed conflict, including through preventive measures for minimizing damage to the environment during armed conflict and through remedial measures.

The principles, as provisionally adopted, are divided into three parts, each corresponding to a different temporal dimension demanding specific State action: before, during and after the conflict (applicable to armed conflicts of an international character and armed conflicts of a non-international character). The first part, under the heading 'General Principles' (which, notably, the rapporteur had originally called 'Preventive Measures'[110]) brings together principles applicable throughout the three phases. They require *inter alia* that States take measures to 'enhance the protection of the environment in relation to armed conflict'.[111] The first report of Rapporteur Marie Jacobsson, published in 2014, had identified prevention, 'the fundamental tenet on which international environmental law rests with its roots tracing back to the *Trail Smelter* case',[112] and due diligence[113] as norms of international law that are applicable in peacetime and in situations of armed conflict. The second part considers obligations during armed conflict and includes an obligation to 'respect and protect' the natural environment in accordance with applicable international law,[114] the term of 'respect' linking back to the ICJ recognition of

110 ILC, 'Third Report of the Special Rapporteur, Ms Jacobsson, on the Protection of the Environment in Relation to Armed Conflicts' (2016) UN Doc. A/CN.4/700, Annex I.

111 ILC, 'Protection of the Environment in Relation to Armed Conflicts: Text of the Draft Principles Provisionally Adopted during the Present Session by the Drafting Committee' (2016) UN Doc. A/CN.4/L.876, Draft Principle 4.

112 ILC, 'Preliminary Report of the Special Rapporteur, Ms Jacobsson, on the Protection of the Environment in Relation to Armed Conflicts' (2014) UN Doc. A/CN.4/674, para 133. See also UNEP, *Protecting the Environment under Armed Conflict: An Inventory and Analysis of International Law* (2009) 40, implying that the *Trail Smelter* dictum and Principle 21 are applicable norms in the context of armed conflicts.

113 ILC, 'Preliminary Report of the Special Rapporteur, Ms Jacobsson', para 154.

114 ILC, 'Protection of the Environment in Relation to Armed Conflicts: Text of the Draft Principles Provisionally Adopted in 2015 and Technically Revised and Renumbered during the Present Session by the Drafting Committee' (2016) UN Doc. A/CN.4/L.870/Rev.1, Draft Principle 8(1).

the customary character of Stockholm Principle 21 in *Legality of the Threat or Use of Nuclear Weapons*.[115] Finally, the third section recognizes that 'preventive measures and reparative measures are interlinked'[116] and requires that post-conflict measures address the 'restoration and protection of the environment damaged by the conflict'.[117] Overall, the principles require States to (1) take preventive measures prior to the outbreak of the armed conflict, (2) minimize environmental damage during the hostilities and (3) take restorative measures after an armed conflict. They operate in a continuum to find a balance between the realities of armed conflict and the necessities of environmental protection.

4.2.1.3 Concluding Remarks

To conclude on the ILC's contribution to the codification and development of the principle of prevention, it is clear that the process has been met with significant conceptual difficulties. The uncertainties relative to the relationship between State responsibility, reparation and prevention resulted in several misconceptions in the initial project of the ILC on liability for non-prohibited acts. The eventual adoption of the ILC Prevention Articles contributed to clarifying the character of prevention as a primary obligation of due diligence driven by an anticipatory rationale and complemented by a separate curative regime imposing liability on the economic operator.

One of the main weaknesses of the articles as they currently stand is their restricted spatial scope (limited to transboundary harm), which leaves aside the third component of Stockholm Principle 21 – a precedent that could unduly restrict the scope of the future work of the ILC on other topics related to environmental protection and which is sometimes used to argue that prevention does not apply to areas beyond national jurisdiction. By contrast, the core contribution of the ILC, and in particular of the Prevention Articles, has been to clarify the standard of care upon which to determine whether due diligence had been exercised (see Chapter 7). By giving content to the general obligation of prevention and to its different manifestations in specific environmental regimes, the ILC mitigates the criticism commonly made that prevention lacks the specificity necessary to be properly implemented.

115 *Legality of the Threat or Use of Nuclear Weapons*, para 29.

116 ILC, 'Third Report of the Special Rapporteur, Ms Jacobsson', para 98.

117 The ILC provisionally adopted principles on the environment and armed conflicts; see ILC, 'Protection of the Environment in Relation to Armed Conflicts: Text of the Draft Principles Provisionally Adopted', Draft Principle 14(1).

4.2.2 *Prevention in the UNEP 'Principles of Conduct in the Field of the Environment for the Guidance of States in the Conservation and Harmonious Utilisation of Natural Resources Shared by Two or More States' (1978)*

At the same time as the ILC was starting its work on international liability for injurious consequences arising out of acts not prohibited by international law, a UNEP working group of legal experts was drafting environmental law guidelines and principles on shared natural resources. Elaborated upon the request of the UNGA,[118] the principles were an attempt to codify the norms that had emerged in the post-Stockholm years.[119] They had some normative influence in the formulation of subsequent conventions dealing with shared natural resources (including the Convention on Biological Diversity), the UNGA having recommended that they be used as guidelines in such circumstances.[120]

The UNEP principles acknowledge the different types of risks, discussed in Chapter 3, that prevention seeks to curb. Principle 3(3) provides that States should avoid and reduce transboundary harm when using a shared natural resource and highlights three scenarios under which States should pay particular attention to their preventive obligation. The first scenario is concerned with risks of sovereignty and prohibits States from causing harm 'which could have repercussions on the utilization of the resource by another sharing State'.[121] The second scenario, by contrast, concentrates on risks to resources and is a manifestation of prevention in its resource-conservation expression.[122] The third, and final, scenario focuses on health risks: it introduces an extraterritorial human rights perspective to prevention by providing that a State should not allow activities that might affect the health of the population of another State.[123]

The material scope of the preventive norm found in the UNEP principles is necessarily narrower than its generally accepted form because they are only concerned with harm to shared natural resources (and not to the environment in general). The principles seek to establish a balance between the right of a State to exploit its resources and the need to ensure that the rights of the other

118 UNGA Res. 3129 (XIVIII) (13 December 1973).

119 UNEP, 'Principles of Conduct in the Field of the Environment for the Guidance of States in the Conservation and Harmonious Utilisation of Natural Resources Shared by Two or More States' (1978) 17 ILM 1097. Adopted by the UNEP Governing Council, 'Principles on Conservation and Harmonious Utilisation of Natural Resources Shared by Two or More States' (1978) UNEP/IG12/2.

120 'Co-operation in the Field of Environment Concerning Natural Resources Shared by Two or More States', UNGA Res. 34/186 (18 December 1979).

121 UNEP, 'Principles of Conduct in the Field of the Environment', Principle 3(3)(a).

122 UNEP, 'Principles of Conduct in the Field of the Environment', Principle 3(3)(b).

123 UNEP, 'Principles of Conduct in the Field of the Environment', Principle 3(3)(c).

States sharing the same resource are preserved. As a result, prevention in the principles is close to its Stockholm expression, also a legal norm that aims to find an equilibrium between the preservation of sovereign rights and the avoidance of environmental harm.[124]

This said, the UNEP principles are also commendable for their contribution to the progressive development of prevention. They recognize that the objective of harm avoidance is to 'protect the environment'[125] and call on States to consider the effects of their activities 'irrespective of whether the effects occur within or outside their jurisdiction'.[126] In doing so, they extend the spatial scope of prevention: by putting the emphasis on the objective of environmental protection for its own sake (outside of sovereignty considerations), they justify an a-territorial application of prevention. Such a provision is not unique in codification works, as will be shown throughout this chapter, and contributes to a broader trend that recognizes prevention as a duty operating irrespective of the location of harm (see Chapter 8).

4.2.3 *Prevention in the World Charter for Nature (1982)*

The World Charter for Nature, adopted by the UN General Assembly in 1982,[127] is illustrative of a desire to consolidate the international legal framework relative to the protection of the environment. It contains twenty-six principles of conservation, with a focus on the protection of 'nature' that goes beyond the scope of the UNEP principles, which concentrated on 'shared natural resources'.

The preventive rationale is found in the World Charter for Nature in its most comprehensive manifestation – that is to say, it embodies a concern for environmental protection *stricto sensu* irrespective of other considerations. This manifests in Principle 1, which presents the Charter's objectives and expresses a rationale of prevention in its purest form when it provides that '[n]ature shall be respected and its essential processes shall not be impaired'.

124 UNEP, 'Principles of Conduct in the Field of the Environment', Principle 1, which requires States to cooperate to avoid 'adverse environmental effects which may result from the utilization of such resources' and balance the sovereign 'rights and interests' of States. Principle 3(1) confirms this approach by reaffirming Principle 21 of the Stockholm Declaration, which, as discussed in Chapter 2, seeks to find a balance between sovereign considerations and environmental protection.

125 UNEP, 'Principles of Conduct in the Field of the Environment', Principle 3(3).

126 A similar approach was reproduced in the Convention on Biological Diversity, Nairobi, 22 May 1992, in force 29 December 1993, (1992) 31 ILM 822, Article 4(b).

127 'World Charter for Nature', UNGA Res. 37/7 (XXXVII) (28 October 1982).

It also shows in the manner in which the Charter reaffirmed Stockholm Principle 21 while making two consequential modifications. Its Principle 21(d) reads as follows:

> States, and to the extent they are able, other public authorities, international organizations, individuals, groups and corporations shall ensure that activities within their jurisdictions or control do not cause damage to the natural systems located within other States or in the areas beyond the limits of national jurisdiction.[128]

Compared to its Stockholm version, the provision extends the preventive rule to other subjects of international law as a 'soft' obligation ('to the extent they are able' to fulfil it). In addition, it replaces the word 'environment' with 'natural systems', in a modification that favours an ecosystemic approach to harm. Principle 11 confirmed the a-territorial perspective of the Charter by providing that '[a]ctivities which might have an impact on nature shall be controlled', hence operating outside any spatial restrictions. In short, the World Charter for Nature offers a codification of prevention in its more advanced form as a principle that adopts an ecosystemic approach to harm and seeks to avoid harm irrespective of its location.

4.2.4 *Prevention in the 'Final Report of the Experts Group on Environmental Law on Legal Principles for Environmental Protection and Sustainable Development' (World Commission on Environment and Development, 1986)*

The UN World Commission on Environment and Development (WCED), or Brundtland Commission, was established with the view to finding solutions to combine economic prosperity and environmental protection to achieve sustainable development.[129] An Experts Group on Environmental Law on Legal Principles for Environmental Protection and Sustainable Development was established in 1985 to prepare a report on legal principles for environmental protection and sustainable development (WCED Principles Report) that would consolidate existing legal principles and formulate new ones.[130]

[128] 'World Charter for Nature', Principle 21(d).

[129] 'Process of Preparation of the Environmental Perspective to the Year 2000 and Beyond', UNGA Res. 38/161 (19 December 1983), para 8.

[130] RD Munro and J Lammers (eds), *Environmental Protection and Sustainable Development: Legal Principles and Recommendations Adopted by the Experts Group on Environmental Law of the World Commission on Environment and Development* (Graham & Trotman 1987), Chairman's Introduction, 1.

Prevention is explicitly mentioned in the second section of the report devoted to 'transboundary' harm, understood as harm affecting the territory of another State or areas beyond the limits of national jurisdiction.[131] Article 10 codifies the obligation to prevent transboundary harm[132] as a due-diligence obligation, the content of which is specified in subsequent articles pertaining *inter alia* to obligations to cooperate and to undertake environmental impact assessments.[133]

The first section of the report, identifying environmental norms that are applicable irrespective of the location of harm, is perhaps more innovative. Although the obligation to prevent is not explicitly mentioned in this section, some of its provisions can be interpreted as manifestations of prevention, including the obligation to protect ecosystems[134] and the duty to carry out an environmental impact assessment.[135] Their applicability irrespective of any external impacts extends the spatial scope of prevention, including by making it applicable within a purely domestic context, which consecrates the truly environmental perspective of the norm.

The legal principles also tried to conceptualize the relationship between prevention, liability and responsibility and, in this respect, appear to have been heavily influenced by the simultaneous work of the ILC on international liability for injurious consequences arising out of acts not prohibited by international law and on State responsibility for internationally wrongful acts.[136] This is seen in the exceptions to the obligation of prevention found

131 Munro and Lammers (eds), *Legal Principles and Recommendations Adopted by the Experts Group on Environmental Law of the World Commission on Environment and Development*, 'Use of Terms', para (d).

132 Munro and Lammers (eds), *Legal Principles and Recommendations Adopted by the Experts Group on Environmental Law of the World Commission on Environment and Development*, Article 10 provides that States shall 'prevent or abate any transboundary environmental interference or a significant risk thereof which causes substantial harm – i.e. harm which is not minor or insignificant'. The commentaries recognize it as a due-diligence obligation (at 79).

133 Munro and Lammers (eds), *Legal Principles and Recommendations Adopted by the Experts Group on Environmental Law of the World Commission on Environment and Development*, Article 14–18.

134 Munro and Lammers (eds), *Legal Principles and Recommendations Adopted by the Experts Group on Environmental Law of the World Commission on Environment and Development*, Article 3(a).

135 Munro and Lammers (eds), *Legal Principles and Recommendations Adopted by the Experts Group on Environmental Law of the World Commission on Environment and Development*, Article 5.

136 Munro and Lammers (eds), *Legal Principles and Recommendations Adopted by the Experts Group on Environmental Law of the World Commission on Environment and Development*, Articles 11–12 and 21.

in Articles 11 and 12. Article 11, on 'liability for transboundary environmental interferences resulting from lawful activities', acknowledged that in certain cases the costs of adopting a preventive approach might exceed its advantages, such as in the case of ultra-hazardous activities.[137] In these circumstances, Article 11 provides that the duty of prevention does not apply and is replaced by the principle of strict liability of States, which requires them to provide compensation. Article 12, on 'transboundary environmental interferences involving substantial harm far less than cost of prevention', also creates an exception to the duty of prevention in relation to activities that will *definitely* cause substantial transboundary harm (in opposition to creating a potential risk of harm) but for which the foreseen damage is considered less than the cost of prevention. Under these circumstances, the article does not apply the principle of strict liability but requires that the State planning a potentially harmful activity enters into negotiations with the affected State. In other words, it does not make extraterritorial harm unlawful, nor does is make it clearly lawful. The two rules did not crystallize in international law but were displaced by two principles consecrated by the ILC, the obligation to exercise due diligence in the face of foreseeable risks and a principle of strict liability in the case of harm applied to the economic operator.

The legal principles were appended as an annex to the 1987 Brundtland Report, and the WCED recommended that the UN General Assembly prepared a Universal Declaration and later a Convention on Environmental Protection and Sustainable Development.[138] It proposed that a special negotiating group be established to draw up a draft declaration that would serve as the basis for a new convention, but the proposal was never implemented.

4.2.5 *Prevention at the United Nations Conference on Environment and Development and Follow-Up Conferences (1992–2012)*

The work of the Brundtland Commission and its consecration of the concept of sustainable development facilitated the holding of the United Nations Conference on Environment and Development (UNCED), or Rio Conference (3–14 June 1992). The conference played an instrumental role in consolidating Principle 21 of the Stockholm Declaration (4.2.5.1), whereas the follow-up conferences in 2002 and 2012 did not makes substantial

137 Munro and Lammers (eds), *Legal Principles and Recommendations Adopted by the Experts Group on Environmental Law of the World Commission on Environment and Development*, Commentary to Article 11, at 81.

138 World Commission on Environment and Development, 'Our Common Future' (4 August 1987) UN Doc. A/42/427, para 86.

contributions to the preventive rationale (4.2.5.2). However, the Commission on Sustainable Development that was created by the Rio Conference to ensure an effective follow-up of the decisions taken at UNCED had some normative influence (4.1.5.3).

4.2.5.1 Principle 2 of the Rio Declaration: Travaux Préparatoires

In the twenty years following the Stockholm Conference, the prevention principle established itself as the cornerstone of international environmental law. As a result, there was little controversy on the need to include the 'Stockholm principle' in the Rio Declaration on Environment and Development. Negotiations over the wording of the preventive rationale focused on whether to reaffirm or, on the contrary, delete certain components of the principle.

PROPOSALS INCLUDED IN 'L.8' In order to prepare for the Earth Summit, the UN set up a Preparatory Committee (PrepCom) that met four times on substantives issues during 1991–92. At the third meeting of the Preparatory Committee of the Rio Conference (PrepCom III), different formulations of the prevention principle were proposed by delegations and consolidated by the chairman of Working Group III, Dr Bedrich Moldan, into a draft often referred to as 'L.8'.[139] Despite Dr Moldan's efforts, L.8 was not the basis of the negotiations during PrepCom IV that led to the formulation of Principle 2,[140] subsequently adopted without changes at the Rio summit. However, a survey of the proposals included in L.8 provides a useful overview of the range of views expressed by States.

At PrepCom III, the Group of 77 (G77) proposed a text emphasizing the sovereignty clause of Stockholm Principle 21 but not mentioning a corresponding duty.[141] By contrast, Burkina Faso and the Group of 22 (G22) wanted to delete the first part of Principle 21 to concentrate on the two 'environmental' components.[142] Interestingly, Nigeria and the G22 also 'recognized, reaffirmed and defended' the right to sovereignty over natural resources

139 Chairman's consolidated draft entitled, 'Earth Charter: The Rio de Janeiro Declaration on Environment and Development', UN Doc. A/CONF.151/PC/WG.III/L.8/Rev.1 and Add. 1 and 2 ('L.8').

140 'Principles on General Rights and Obligations. Draft principles proposed by the Chairman. Rio Declaration on Environment and Development' (2 April 1992) UN Doc. A/CONF.151/PC/WG.III/L.33/Rev.1 ('L.33'), Principle 2.

141 L.33, para 43. 142 L.33, para 37.

while pushing for the recognition of an obligation to prevent environmental harm in a purely domestic context.[143]

A number of States sought to extend the scope of the principle of prevention. For instance, the proposal made by Canada and Austria created an obligation to protect the planet applicable to States but also to individuals and organizations.

> All individuals, organizations and States shall respect the environment of other individuals, organizations and States, and the Earth's ecosystem; and treat the global commons of the Earth in a manner at least as favourable as their own environment, keeping in mind the interests of human kind as a whole.[144]

The proposal differed from Principle 21 by moving away from the sovereignty referential and using non-traditional concepts such as 'ecosystems', 'global commons' and 'humankind'. By providing that States should treat the global environment no worse than their own environment, it also attempted to renew the relationship between sovereignty and environmental protection. Chile's proposal regarding the prevention principle was equally innovative as it introduced an obligation of prevention for non-State actors such as international organizations, transnational enterprises and individuals.

> National sovereignty of States shall not be an obstacle to the interdependent resolution of the global problems of development and environment by the international community. This will require action in solidarity, *inter alia*, to avoid the degradation of natural resources, infringement of global international security, and to contribute to the eradication of extreme poverty. States, international organizations and transnational corporations shall prevent transfrontier damage and shall protect the global commons.[145]

The European Economic Community (EEC), possibly with the Chernobyl disaster still fresh in its delegates' minds, was more concerned with the procedural aspects of prevention and focused on obligations of information and consultation.[146] The implementation rather than the acceptance of the preventive norm was the main concern of the EEC. Overall, and generally speaking, proposals made by industrialized States tended to favour a progressive development of Principle 21, whereas developing countries were particularly concerned with reaffirming the sovereignty clause of Principle 21.

143 L.33, para 45. 144 L.8, para 38. 145 L.8, paras 39–40.

146 L.8, para 44: 'States shall provide prior and timely notification and relevant information to other concerned States on activities which may have a significant international or transboundary effect and shall consult with those States at an early state and in good faith' (Netherlands/EEC).

THE 'STOCKHOLM PRINCIPLE' IN PREPCOM IV As noted earlier, the negotiations of Working Group III at PrepCom IV were not based on the chairman's consolidated draft or his own 'compromise draft' but took a different course, with several new drafts being submitted by major groups, particularly after the G77 and China decided to submit their new text (L.20).[147] The atmosphere that prevailed during the PrepCom IV negotiations in relation to the prevention principle is well captured by the *Earth Summit Bulletin*, which reported that

> [m]any governments were of the view that [Principle 21 of the Stockholm Declaration] would be best suited for inclusion in the preamble. Some thought it should be restated verbatim, while others argued for greater elaboration which would take into account the important fact that UNCED, unlike Stockholm, is charged with the mandate to consider development as well as environmental problems.[148]

As a result of these diverging views, the prevention principle featured prominently in the different drafts.[149] Some formulations introduced significant variations with respect to the language of the Stockholm principle, such as Japan's proposal that read as follows:

> Each State has the sovereign right to exploit its own resources in accordance with its own environmental policies. However, this right should not be exercised in a manner inconsistent with the goal of integrating development and environmental protection. States have the responsibility to ensure that activities within their jurisdiction or control do not cause damage to the environments of other States.[150]

Japan's proposal blended the prevention principle with the so-called principle of integration, which was eventually consecrated, as a separate principle, in Rio Principle 4.

Other formulations were much closer to the Stockholm principle, including those proposed by the G77 and China, the United States, Australia and the

147 'Rio de Janeiro Charter/Declaration on Environment and Development', UN Doc. A/CONF.151/PC/WG.III/L.20/Rev.1 ('L.20'). See also the drafts presented by the following States: United States, UN Doc. A/CONF.151/PC/WG.III/L.21 ('L.21'); Japan, 'Rights and Obligations', UN Doc. A/CONF.151/PC/WG.III/L.22 ('L.22'); Canada, UN Doc. A/CONF.151/PC/WG.III/L.23 ('L.23'); Australia, UN Doc. A/CONF.151/PC/WG.III/L.24 ('L.24'); EC countries, 'Elements for the Earth Charter', UN Doc. A/CONF.151/PC/WG.III/L.25 ('L.25'); Nordic countries, 'Earth Charter: Elements for Consideration', UN Doc. A/CONF.151/PC/WG.III/L.27 ('L.27').

148 *Earth Summit Bulletin*, vols 1–6, from UNCED-Prep Com IV, 8 March 1992.

149 See L.20, 146, Principle 2; L.21, Principle 5; L.22, Principle 5; L.23, Principle 4; L.24, Principle 5; L.27, Principle 7.

150 L.22, Principle 5.

Nordic countries. The main bone of contention between the formulations of this second category was the 'qualification' of the exercise of sovereignty over natural resources. Whereas Principle 2 of the draft tabled by the G77 and China referred to the sovereign right to exploit natural resources pursuant to their own environmental 'and developmental policies', the US and Nordic drafts omitted any such qualification, including the one appearing in Stockholm Principle 21 ('pursuant to their own environmental policies'). The Australian draft referred, in its Principle 5, to the right to exploit natural resources 'in a sustainable manner'.

Eventually, a compromise was found between the two diverging perspectives. Suggestions to substantially reword Principle 21 were rejected, and the Stockholm formulation was only modified to add that States have the 'sovereign right to exploit their own resources pursuant to their own environmental *and developmental policies*'. This minor change, introduced by the draft of G77 and China, was deemed necessary to integrate a development perspective to environmental protection, as requested by developing countries.

The difference between Stockholm Principle 21 and Rio Principle 2 is subtle but can nevertheless carry important legal consequences. The Rio Declaration did not challenge the consensus that prevention was one of the core norms of international environmental law and consolidated the wording of prevention in the form of Principle 21. As expressed in the Preamble, the Rio Declaration is to be understood as a continuation of the Stockholm Declaration, and the reaffirmation of Principle 21 stresses such continuity. Yet, the new focus on developmental policies can be interpreted as strengthening the right to permanent sovereignty over natural resources over the other environmental clauses. It can be used to justify the design of public policies favouring economic development over environmental protection. Nevertheless, as discussed in Chapter 2, the reference to developmental policies, which should be designed in accordance with the State's obligations under international law, adds an additional layer of restriction to the right to permanent sovereignty over natural resources. As a result, although Principle 2 emphasizes the importance of economic growth, it cannot be said to weaken the preventive obligation.

The plan of action that emerged out of the conference, Agenda 21, did not directly reaffirm Principle 2 but was elaborated 'in full respect of all the principles contained in the Rio Declaration on Environment and Development'[151] with the view to implement the environment-development

[151] 'Agenda 21, Annex II to the Report of the United Nations Conference on Environment and Development (Rio de Janeiro, 3–14 June 1992)' UN Doc. A/CONF.151/26, para 1.6.

nexus of the conference. As a result, the document, aiming to take direct action to limit environmental degradation, can be read as the policy implementation of Rio Principle 2.[152]

4.2.5.2 Post-Rio Conferences

The two fundamental international conferences on the topic of environmental protection that followed the Earth Summit, the 2002 Johannesburg Conference on Sustainable Development and the 2012 Rio + 20 Summit, did not contribute to the normative development of Principle 2.

In 2002, the Johannesburg Declaration on Sustainable Development[153] reaffirmed the commitment of States to the Rio principles[154] but did not specifically mention prevention.[155] Ten years later, the 'Future We Want' outcome document of the Rio + 20 Summit also reaffirmed the Rio principles but only referenced by name one of the Rio principles: the concept of 'common but differentiated responsibilities' (CBDRs).[156] Not only did it not make a reference to the State *obligation* of prevention, but the document, with a strong focus on sustainable development and its derivative concept of 'green economy', also made very scarce references to the *objective* of prevention of environmental harm.[157]

The absence of references to prevention in the post-Rio conferences leads to two conclusions. Firstly, the lack of explicit reaffirmation of prevention might be indicative of the consensual nature of prevention, which therefore does not need to be reaffirmed in a political document. This interpretation explains the reference made in the Rio + 20 outcome document to the concept of CBDRs that remains hotly debated and had to be reaffirmed in a political text. Secondly, the lack of references to prevention also reveals an interesting element regarding the normativity of the principle, or at least how its

152 Agenda 21, 'Annex II to the Report of the United Nations Conference on Environment and Development', see objective 8.31(b), mentioning the objective of prevention of environmental degradation.

153 'Report of the Word Summit on Sustainable Development (Johannesburg, 26 August–4 September 2002)', chap II, UN Doc. A/CONF.199/20.

154 'Report of the Word Summit on Sustainable Development', para 8.

155 Indeed, the Johannesburg Declaration on Sustainable Development does not make a single reference to the terms 'prevention' and 'prevent'.

156 Rio de Janeiro Declaration on Environment and Development (Rio de Janeiro, 3 to 14 June 1992), (1992) 31 ILM 876, Principle 7; 'The Future We Want', UNGA Res. 66/228 (2012), Annex, para 15.

157 'The Future We Want': references to an objective of prevention in an environmental sense relate to the prevention of diseases (paras 112 and 141), marine protection (paras 163, 164, 166 and 170) and waste management (paras 217 and 219).

normativity is conceived: while sustainable development is conceptualized as an 'agenda',[158] decision-makers understand prevention as a legal norm rather than as a policy concept. As a result, and although the post-Rio plans of action actually aim to avoid environmental harm, the concept of 'sustainable development' is the privileged concept on which policy decisions are based.[159]

4.2.5.3 Prevention in the Commission on Sustainable Development (1995)

Despite the lack of explicit reference to the principle of prevention in the UN conferences that followed the Earth Summit, the Commission on Sustainable Development (CSD) that was created in 1992 to ensure the follow-up of the Rio conference (eventually replaced in 2012 by a High Level Political Forum) did examine the preventive norm in the course of its work. In 1995, it convened a meeting of experts to examine the legal principles on sustainable development and issued a report, conceived as a study falling under the framework of the Rio Declaration, the objective of which was to identify the essential principles and concepts of the international law of sustainable development.[160]

The report devotes several paragraphs to what it calls the 'sovereignty over natural resources and responsibility not to cause damage to the environment of other States or to areas beyond',[161] 'the principle of sustainable use of natural resources'[162] and 'prevention of environmental harm'.[163] While these are presented as separate norms, the report depicts them as sharing the same legal foundations and does not operate clear conceptual or legal distinctions between the three principles. As a result, the work of the CSD raised more questions than it resolved. For instance, it fails to explain the distinction between the concept of 'sovereignty over natural resources and responsibility not to cause damage to the environment of other States or to areas beyond' and the principle of 'prevention of environmental harm'. Indeed, the report explains that both norms are grounded in Principle 21/2 but does not justify

158 'The Future We Want', para 18.

159 On how prevention can be considered a policy, see Section 10.1.2.

160 Commission on Sustainable Development, 'Report of the Expert Group Meeting on Identification of Principles of International Law for Sustainable Development' (Geneva, September 1995), EC/N17.1996/BP3.

161 Commission on Sustainable Development, 'Report of the Expert Group Meeting', paras 51–56.

162 Commission on Sustainable Development, 'Report of the Expert Group Meeting', paras 57–63.

163 Commission on Sustainable Development, 'Report of the Expert Group Meeting', paras 64–69.

the choice to list them as two separate norms.[164] It is seemingly based on the assumption that Principle 21 and prevention share commonalities but are nevertheless different – a conceptualization embraced by this study. However, the report neglects to justify this assumption – which this study explains as being the result of the evolution of the norm – and hence fails to provide significant clarity on prevention.

4.3 CUSTOM CODIFICATION WORKS OF NON-GOVERNMENTAL INSTITUTIONS

Non-governmental institutions have also sought to codify prevention; of particular interest is the work of the International Law Association (4.3.1), the Institut de droit international (4.3.2) and the International Union for Conservation of Nature in conjunction with the International Council of Environmental Law (4.3.3). Although such scholarly exercises do not have formal legal authority, they can be considered to be subsidiary elements of practice as the 'teachings of the most highly qualified publicists'[165] and often influence the codification studies of intergovernmental bodies.

4.3.1 *Prevention in the International Law Association (1966–2016)*

The International Law Association (ILA), whose objective is to further the 'study, clarification and development of international law',[166] never analysed prevention as a separate topic of work but worked on different topics that led it to address the preventive norm from different perspectives.

4.3.1.1 Watercourses

Given the partial origins of the no-harm rule in watercourse law, it is unsurprising that the first significant contribution of the ILA to the study of prevention is found in its work on the law of international watercourses. The Helsinki Rules on the uses of the waters of international rivers, adopted by the ILA in 1966,[167] acknowledged the obligation to prevent pollution in a dual form – as

164 Commission on Sustainable Development, 'Report of the Expert Group Meeting', para 67.
165 Treves, 'Customary International Law', para 61.
166 International Law Association, Constitution of the Association, para 3.1, available at www.ila-.hq.org/images/ILA/docs/constitution_english_adopted_johannesburg_2016.pdf (last accessed 19 May 2017).
167 ILA, 'Helsinki Rules on the Uses of the Waters of International Rivers', Helsinki, 52nd Session, 1966.

a duty to prevent new water pollution and as a duty to mitigate existing pollution.[168] This recognition crystallized the obligation to prevent pollution in watercourse law but also contributed to the parallel consolidation of the preventive rationale in general international environmental law. The update of the Helsinki Rules with the 2004 Berlin Rules was also reflective of the latest evolutions of the preventive principle, which was recognized as two separate obligations, applicable to 'all waters', that is to say, all surface waters and groundwater other than marine waters irrespective of whether the waters in question are found in an international drainage basin.[169] The rules reaffirmed a first duty to avoid transboundary harm, this time with an extended material scope not restricted to pollution but including any form of environmental harm,[170] and a second obligation to act with due diligence to avoid or minimize harm, with a strong emphasis on the fact that the duty applies irrespective of the location of harm, including in a purely domestic context.[171]

4.3.1.2 Sustainable Development

The work of the ILA on sustainable development, although not directly addressing prevention as such, contributed to shedding light on the relationship between sustainable development and prevention. Since 1992, the ILA has sought, via three consecutive work committees, to study the law applicable in the context of sustainable development.[172] The main outcome of these initiatives so far has been the adoption, in April 2002, of the New Delhi Declaration of Principles relating to Sustainable Development.[173]

Article 1(1) of the New Delhi Declaration states:

> It is a well-established principle that, in accordance with international law, all States have the sovereign right to manage their own natural resources

168 ILA, 'Helsinki Rules on the Uses of the Waters of International Rivers', Article X, providing that while a State 'must prevent any new form of water pollution or any increase in the degree of existing water pollution', it is only required to 'take all reasonable measures to abate existing water pollution'.

169 ILA, 'Berlin Rules on Water Resources', Berlin, 71st Session, 2004, Article 1, and 'Usage Note' in the commentary, at 4.

170 ILA, 'Berlin Rules on Water Resources', Article 16.

171 ILA, 'Berlin Rules on Water Resources', Article 8 and its commentary.

172 'Legal Aspects of Sustainable Development' (1992–2002); 'International Law on Sustainable Development' (2003–12); and 'Role of International Law in Sustainable Natural Resource Management for Development' (2012–present).

173 ILA, Committee on the Legal Aspects of Sustainable Development, 'New Delhi Declaration of Principles of International Law Relating to Sustainable Development', New Delhi, 70th Session, 2002.

> pursuant to their own environmental and developmental policies, and the responsibility to ensure that activities within their jurisdiction or control do not cause significant damage to the environment of other States or of areas beyond the limits of national jurisdiction.[174]

The wording used is close to that of Rio Principle 2 but qualifies the term 'damage' with the adjective 'significant' and speaks of 'natural' resources. It is noteworthy that this paragraph falls under Article 1, entitled 'The Duty of States to Ensure Sustainable Use of Natural Resources', and is followed by two paragraphs on the duty of States to manage resources 'including natural resources within their own territory or jurisdiction'. The context within which Rio Principle 2 is reasserted depicts prevention in a specific light: by grouping the three paragraphs under the same heading, the ILA links the preventive obligation manifesting in Rio Principle 2 to a duty to protect natural resources within a purely domestic context.

The Sofia Guiding Statements, adopted in 2012 by the ILA to clarify the content of the New Delhi Declaration and foster its use in judicial practice, corroborate this interpretation. The third statement provides that '[a]s a matter of common concern, the sustainable use of all natural resources represents an emerging rule of general customary international law, with particular normative precision identifiable with respect to shared and common natural resources'.[175] The formulation is ambiguous, especially because it derives a rule on the use of 'all' natural resources as a matter of 'common concern' when the latter concept is applicable only in relation to the climatic system and biological diversity. In addition, the reference to 'normative precision' in the law regarding shared and common natural resources leaves the reader guessing about the legal basis of this emerging rule. Indeed, the 2012 report on the topic, which merely mentions that treaty and case law corroborate the emergence of such rule, without giving precise examples, does not clarify the question.[176] Nevertheless, guidance can be found in the commentaries that mention 'the evolution of the principle of sovereignty over natural resources from a merely rights-based into a duties- as well as rights-based principle'.[177] On that basis, it can be assumed that the ILA extracts an obligation to prevent environmental harm within a purely domestic context from the first

[174] ILA, 'New Delhi Declaration', Article 1(1).

[175] ILA, Committee on International Law on Sustainable Development, 'Sofia Guiding Statements on the Judicial Elaboration of the 2002 New Delhi Declaration of Principles of International Law Relating to Sustainable Development', Sofia, 75th Session, 2012, para 3.

[176] ILA, Committee on International Law on Sustainable Development, 'Fifth Report', Sofia, 75th Session, 2012, at 14.

[177] ILA, Committee on International Law on Sustainable Development, 'Fifth Report', at 14.

component of Principle 2. The rule, however, remains very much framed within a 'sustainable development' perspective, the emphasis of the article being on 'natural resources', a term that tends to embrace a perspective focusing strongly on economic exploitability (contrary to the term 'environment', which can be considered worthy of protection independent of other considerations).

Overall, the conceptualization offered by the ILA of the spatial applicability of prevention remains ambiguous. It fails to convince that the law dictates the application of a preventive rationale on the domestic territory, the legal basis and precise rationale of the duty to ensure sustainable use of natural resources remaining unclear. This is not to say that such an obligation does not exist, but, as Chapter 8 shows, a reference to human rights duties could have been a more solid legal basis to an international preventive duty operating in a domestic context.

4.3.1.3 Climate Change

The ILA studied prevention in the context of its work on legal principles relating to climate change. Its first report, however, was cautious in applying the prevention principle to climate change.[178] Understandably, it focused on the principles listed in Article 3 of the UNFCCC – CBDRs, equity, precaution, sustainable development and good faith – and only analysed prevention as part of 'further concepts and principles of relevance to the climate change regime'.[179] The extension of the preventive duty beyond the no-harm rule to protect a 'common concern' of humankind was not considered an obvious development.

The second report gave more weight to prevention by recognizing it as a key principle of the climate change regime[180] on the basis of its inclusion in the Preamble of the UNFCCC and its recognition in the Stockholm Declaration.[181] In a footnote, the report responded to the fact that

> [s]ome might argue that Principle 2 does not apply to climate change given as it does not fit the traditional concept of transboundary pollution. However, neither the decades of ILC debates on the issue of prevention of environmental harm nor international jurisprudence provide evidence that complex

178 ILA, Committee on Legal Principles Relating to Climate Change, 'First Report', The Hague, 74th Session, 2010.
179 ILA, Committee on Legal Principles Relating to Climate Change, 'First Report', 28–29.
180 ILA, Committee on Legal Principles Relating to Climate Change, 'Second Report', Sofia, 75th Session, 2012, 24–26.
181 ILA, Committee on Legal Principles Relating to Climate Change, 'Second Report', 22.

> instances of environmental change are not to be covered by the general duty to prevent harm and minimise the risk thereof.[182]

Recognizing that principles of international environmental law 'assume peculiar characteristics in the context of climate change regulation',[183] the report identified three consequences arising from the application of Rio Principle 2 to the climate change regime: (1) Principle 2 provides a 'normative framework' that justifies the application of prevention in areas beyond national jurisdiction, (2) the principle could play a 'pivotal role' as an obligation on the basis of which to bring claims for climate damage, and (3) prevention is implemented by procedural elements, including an obligation to carry out an environmental impact assessment (EIA) and a duty to cooperate.[184]

The work of the ILA culminated in the 2014 Declaration of Legal Principles Relating to Climate Change (ILA Climate Change Principles).[185] Prevention appears twice in the set of principles. It is found integrated in the provision on 'sustainable development', which reads:

> Where social and economic development plans, programs or projects may result in significant emissions of greenhouse gases or cause serious damage to the environment through climate change, States have a duty to prevent such harm or, at a minimum, to employ due diligence efforts to mitigate climate change impacts.[186]

The commentaries justify the integration of the prevention obligation into the article on sustainable development on the basis that 'the practice of integrated decision-making in the context of sustainable development is tied to the obligation to prevent damage through climate change'.[187] The ILA thus assimilated the duty to prevent into the principle of integration that requires combining economic, social and environmental issues in decision-making processes. Needless to say, sustainable development, whose status under general international law tends to be closer to an approach or a programme than

[182] ILA, Committee on Legal Principles Relating to Climate Change, 'Second Report', 25. Referring to R Verheyen, *Climate Change Damage and International Law: Prevention Duties and State Responsibility* (Martinus Nijhoff 2005) 166–69.

[183] ILA, Committee on Legal Principles Relating to Climate Change, 'Second Report', 45.

[184] ILA, Committee on Legal Principles Relating to Climate Change, 'Second Report', 26.

[185] ILA, Committee on Legal Principles Relating to Climate Change, 'Declaration of Principles Relating to Climate Change', Washington, DC, 76th Session, 2014.

[186] ILA, Committee on Legal Principles Relating to Climate Change, 'Declaration of Principles', Principle 3(5).

[187] ILA, Committee on Legal Principles Relating to Climate Change, 'Third Draft Report', Washington, DC, 76th Session, 2014, 9.

a principle,[188] gains normative weight from being linked to the well-recognized obligation of prevention.

The ILA Climate Change Principles also envisage prevention as an independent obligation in the form of Principle 7. Principle 7 has an original structure, owing to committee members disagreeing over the relationship between prevention and precaution. It is divided into two subparts: Principle 7A is concerned with prevention, and Principle 7B focuses on precaution – a structure that acknowledges the close relationship between the two principles. Principle 7A reasserts Stockholm Principle 21 as an applicable rule in the climate change regime[189] and confirms its nature as a due-diligence obligation.[190] While the first paragraphs of Principle 7B are only applicable to precaution, the rest of the section – on obligations to conduct an EIA[191] and cooperate[192] – apply to both prevention and precaution. It is noticeable that the ILA considers that the two core obligations (EIA and cooperation) upon which due diligence is judged (see Chapter 7) are applicable in a context of scientific certainty and uncertainty.

The contribution of the ILA Climate Change Principles to the codification of prevention is multifocal. They confirmed the move of prevention beyond its no-harm perspective to apply to 'common concerns' of humankind. They also offered a progressive approach to the relationship entertained by prevention to other environmental norms by including prevention under the scope of the sustainable development concept and by conceptualizing prevention and precaution as falling together under the umbrella of due diligence.

4.3.1.4 Due Diligence

Finally, the work of the ILA study group on due diligence in international law is of major importance for prevention, due diligence being 'a key component of the obligation to prevent harm in international environmental law'.[193] The first report of the ILA, published in 2014, provided a summary of the history of due diligence, its development in the context of the rules on State responsibility and

188 See e.g. U Beyerlin and T Marauhn, *International Environmental Law* (Hart 2011) 80–81.

189 ILA, Committee on Legal Principles Relating to Climate Change, 'Declaration of Principles', Article 7A(1).

190 ILA, Committee on Legal Principles Relating to Climate Change, 'Declaration of Principles', Article 7A(2).

191 ILA, Committee on Legal Principles Relating to Climate Change, 'Declaration of Principles', Article 7B(5).

192 ILA, Committee on Legal Principles Relating to Climate Change, 'Declaration of Principles', Article 7B(6).

193 ILA, Committee on Legal Principles Relating to Climate Change, 'Declaration of Principles', 25.

its influence in specific international legal regimes.[194] In this context, the expression of due diligence in international environmental law, where it is particularly well developed, features prominently in the report.[195] The second report of the study group, published in 2016,[196] moved away from the sectoral approach to extract a general standard of due diligence from its manifestations in different fields of international law. Relying on the *Corfu Channel* dictum on the prohibition to cause harm, the report found that the core standard of due diligence under general international law dictates that a sovereign State is obligated to ensure that in its jurisdiction other States' rights and interests are not violated. An additional key contribution of the report lies in its analysis of whether due diligence is a subjective or objective standard (i.e. whether the assessment varies based on certain factors, including, most notably, economic development). The report concludes that an objective standard will apply by default unless a specific treaty provision provides for the possibility of some factors, such as economic development, to enhance the degree of diligence required from States.[197]

4.3.2 *Prevention at the Institut de Droit International (1997)*

The Institut de Droit International (IDI) also had the opportunity to make codification proposals in relation to prevention, first relative to its manifestations in specific environmental regimes (4.3.2.1) and then to the general preventive norm in international environmental law (4.3.2.2).

4.3.2.1 Early Work

The IDI 1911 resolution on the rules relating to the non-navigational use of international watercourses,[198] mentioned in Chapter 1, was an early codification of the no-harm rule.[199] Its subsequent 1961 resolution on the utilization of

194 ILA, Study Group on Due Diligence in International Law, 'First Report', Washington, DC, 76th Session, 2014.

195 ILA, Study Group on Due Diligence, 'First Report', relying heavily on due diligence in international environmental law and the law of the sea (presented as separate branches).

196 ILA, Study Group on Due Diligence in International Law, 'Second Report', Johannesburg, 77th Session, 2016.

197 ILA, Study Group on Due Diligence, 'Second Report', at 13–18.

198 IDI, 'International Regulation Regarding the Use of International Watercourses for Purposes Other than Navigation', Session of Madrid, 1911.

199 IDI, 'International Regulation Regarding the Use of International Watercourses', para 1, provided that when the watercourse forms the border of a State, the use of the watercourse should not be prejudicial to the other State. Paragraph 2 posits *inter alia* that if the

non-maritime international waters recognized that the prohibition to cause harm that would 'seriously affect' the use of the waters by other States[200] was 'one of the basic general principles governing neighborly relations'.[201] The IDI confirmed that the obligation to respect the sovereignty of States results in a duty to avoid any use of the territory likely to cause injury in the territory of another State in its 1979 resolution on the pollution of rivers and lakes and international law.[202] Yet, the IDI did not refer to a threshold, present in its 1961 resolution, specifying the magnitude of harm prohibited by international law.[203] Instead, according to Article II, States are under a duty to 'ensure that their activities or those conducted within their jurisdiction or under their control cause *no* pollution in the waters of international rivers and lakes beyond their boundaries'.[204] The preventive objective hereby expressed can be interpreted to be absolute: States should avoid *any* pollution, even the smallest level of pollution being prohibited. This proposition is in contradiction to the widely accepted understanding that no-harm not only creates a prohibition to cause harm but also a duty to tolerate minimal interferences with territorial sovereignty. It remains, however, uncertain whether the provision should be read in light of the threshold acknowledged by the IDI in its previous resolution, in particular, because the 1987 resolution on transboundary air pollution reaffirmed the duty to avoid harm in terms identical to those found in the 1979 resolution. Article 2 confirmed the anomaly by providing that States should take all appropriate measures to 'ensure that their activities or those conducted within their jurisdiction or under their control cause *no* transboundary air pollution'.[205] By creating an obligation to prevent even minimal transboundary harm, the IDI resolutions proposed a formulation of the preventive duty that is far stricter than generally acknowledged.

By contrast, the IDI resolutions were more progressive in their codification of the spatial scope of prevention. Indeed, both the 1979 and 1987 resolutions provide that they are without prejudice to State obligations to protect individuals from pollution. The statement thus hints to the fact that the IDI assumed that an obligation to prevent environmental harm could exist under human rights law. The 1979 resolution specifies that it is 'without prejudice to the

watercourse is an international watercourse that crosses several States, then any alteration of the water is prohibited.

200 IDI, 'Utilisation of Non-Maritime International Waters (Except for Navigation)', Session of Salzburg, 1961, Article 4.

201 IDI, 'Utilisation of Non-Maritime International Waters', Preamble.

202 IDI, 'The Pollution of Rivers and Lakes and International Law', Session of Athens, 1979.

203 On the threshold of harm applicable to prevention, see Section 6.1.2.

204 IDI, 'The Pollution of Rivers and Lakes' (emphasis added).

205 IDI, 'Transboundary Air Pollution', Session of Cairo, 1987 (emphasis added).

obligations which fundamental human rights impose upon States with regard to pollution occurring in their own territories',[206] whereas the 1987 resolution is less straightforward and provides that it is without prejudice 'to any obligation which a State may have to protect individuals from the effects of air pollution other than transboundary air pollution'.[207] The recognition of an obligation to prevent environmental harm under human rights law is significant because, as this study will discuss later, it makes the obligation of prevention applicable within a purely domestic context. This leads to the conclusion that while the early environmental work of the IDI neglected the important question of the threshold of harm that transforms damage into a wrongful act, it nevertheless was progressive in its recognition of a potential obligation to prevent harm under human rights law.

4.3.2.2 The 1997 Session of Strasbourg

The IDI envisaged environmental protection more broadly (i.e. beyond a sectorial approach) during its 1997 session in Strasbourg. In the three resolutions it adopted, the IDI characterized the duty of prevention[208] and the relevant secondary rules (responsibility and liability)[209] and provided guidance on the process of implementation.[210]

The 1997 resolution, entitled 'Environment', offered a progressive conceptualization of the temporal and spatial scope of prevention.[211] In relation to its temporal scope, Article 6(1) reads as follows:

> Every State, when intervening on the basis of decisions taken in the exercise of its sovereignty in fields of activity where the effects of such decisions on the environment are clear, has the responsibility to ensure that activities within its jurisdiction or under its control do not cause damage which may affect the lives of the present and future generations.

The provision adapts Stockholm Principle 21 by extending it to a prohibition to cause not only present but also future damage. Under this perspective, the temporal outlook of prevention widens to require that States envisage the effects of a risky activity in the short to medium term (i.e. its effects on present

[206] IDI, 'Pollution of Rivers and Lakes', Article IX.
[207] IDI, 'Transboundary Air Pollution', Article 14.
[208] IDI, 'Environment', Session of Strasbourg, 1997.
[209] IDI, 'Responsibility and Liability under International Law for Environmental Damage', Session of Strasbourg, 1997.
[210] IDI, 'Procedures for the Adoption and Implementation of Rules in the Field of Environment', Session of Strasbourg, 1997.
[211] IDI, 'Environment'.

generations) and also over the longer term by including an assessment of its potential effects on future generations.[212] The spatial scope of prevention was also broadened in Article 9(1), which reads:

> States, regional and local governments and juridical or natural persons shall, to the extent possible, ensure that their activities do not cause any damage to the environment that could significantly diminish the enjoyment of the latter by other persons. In this respect, they shall take all necessary care.

Notably, the provision does not define the spatial dimension within which the preventive obligation operates: by contrast, it provides that prevention apply only to the 'environment', without any specific consideration being given to the location of harm.

Additionally, the resolution endorses the approach taken by the World Charter for Nature in extending the preventive obligation to non-State entities: Article 9(1) provides that prevention is not only the duty of States but also of 'regional and local governments and juridical or natural persons'. The resolution also offers a progressive perspective on the beneficiaries of prevention, which Article 9(1) openly identified as human beings ('persons'). The provision recognizes the anthropocentric motivations that drive (in part) the preventive obligation and opens the door to an obligation of prevention under human rights law (a follow-up to its earlier resolutions) on the basis that environmental damage threatens the right to enjoy one's own environment.

One final element of interest in the work of the IDI lies in its elaboration of the due-diligence nature of prevention. The resolution referring to the conduct of an EIA[213] and to cooperation[214] as duties discharging the preventive duty is complemented by the second IDI resolution (on responsibility and liability) that presents due diligence as a test based on 'objective' measurements.[215]

The three elements of prevention just highlighted (temporal and spatial scope of prevention, applicability to non-State actors, and due-diligence nature of prevention) will be analysed further in the course of this study. At this stage, suffice it to say that they reveal that the IDI adopted (what was at the time, in 1997) a progressive approach to prevention and codified it in its most advanced form as a due-diligence obligation that requires States and other international law subjects to take proactive measures to protect the environment.

212 IDI, 'Environment'. The relationship between prevention and intergenerational equity is discussed in Chapter 9.

213 IDI, 'Environment', Article 5.

214 IDI, 'Environment', Articles 6(3) and 7.

215 IDI, 'Responsibility and Liability', Article 3(2).

4.3.3 *Prevention in the Draft International Covenant on Environment and Development of the International Council of Environmental Law and the International Union for Conservation of Nature (1995–2010)*

The Draft International Covenant on Environment and Development is a joint initiative between the International Council of Environmental Law and the IUCN Commission on Environmental Law.[216] Its objective is to combine environmental principles into a document that would form the basis for intergovernmental negotiations on a general treaty on the environment, following the model of the Universal Declaration of Human Rights[217] that was then implemented by the two covenants.[218] The drafters of the Draft Covenant acknowledged that their objective is to codify existing obligations while remaining pragmatic in their progressive development of the law with proposals that could realistically be accepted by decision-makers.[219]

The Draft Covenant was first published in 1995 and contained a Preamble and seventy-two articles arranged topically in eleven parts. Three updates followed, in 2000, 2004 and 2010. The regular update of the Draft Covenant, to reflect the latest developments in the field, is particularly useful in the context of this study, which is concerned with the trajectory of the principle of prevention.

Several articles are of interest for an analysis of prevention. To begin with, Article 6 recognizes prevention as a central principle of international environmental law. It is situated in the section presenting the 'fundamental principles', described as making 'the basis for all the obligations contained in the Draft Covenant' and reflecting 'international consensus'.[220] In its first version, Article 6 read: '[p]rotection of the environment is best achieved by preventing environmental harm rather than by attempting to remedy or compensate for such harm.' The article is an expression of the preventive rationale that underpins the field of international environmental law and, hence, finds its expression 'in nearly every provision of the Draft Covenant'.[221] As in the IDI resolution, prevention in the Draft Covenant is codified in its advanced form,

216 IUCN, 'Covenant on Environment and Development', *IUCN Environmental Policy and Law Paper No. 31* (1st edn, IUCN 1995; 2nd edn, 2000; 3rd edn, 2004; 4th edn, 2010).

217 'Universal Declaration of Human Rights', UNGA Res. 217A(III) (10 December 1948).

218 International Covenant on Civil and Political Rights, New York, 19 December 1966, in force 3 January 1976, 999 UNTS 171; International Covenant on Economic, Social and Cultural Rights, New York, 16 December 1966, in force 3 January 1976, 993 UNTS 3.

219 IUCN, 'Covenant on Environment and Development', Foreword to the First Edition, at xix: 'But we must say that we have not been as "progressive" as we might have liked to be, always bearing in mind that the Draft Covenant should first and foremost be realistic.'

220 IUCN, 'Covenant on Environment and Development', 2nd edn, Commentary, at 32.

221 IUCN, 'Covenant on Environment and Development', 2nd edn, 40.

in relation to its spatial scope (applicable irrespective of the location of harm) and its duty bearers (applicable to 'all actors wherever the consequences of their actions may be felt').[222]

However, Article 6 was drastically modified in the fourth edition of the Covenant to read: '[p]revention of environmental harm is a duty and shall have priority over remedial measures. The costs of pollution prevention, control and reduction measures are to be borne by the originator.' The modifications of the article substantially changed the focus of prevention: it combines the principle with the obligation of the economic operator to bear the costs of prevention. As a result, the article merged two principles (prevention and polluter-pays) with different normative status (prevention is considered to be a customary norm, while the status of the polluter-pays principle remains debated[223]). It transpires that the new version of Article 6 is more concerned with the question of allocation of loss, in continuity with the ILC Allocation of Loss Principles, rather than with the protection of the environment, which was at the centre of the previous version of the article.

The general approach of Article 6 on prevention is complemented by Article 11, which brings more specificity to the preventive duty imposed on States. The first two paragraphs of Article 11, in its first version of 1995, are of particular interest here for their progressive approach to prevention:

> 1. States have, in accordance with the Charter of the United Nations and the principles of international law, the sovereign right to utilize their resources to meet their environmental and sustainable developmental needs, and the obligations:
>   (a) *to protect and preserve the environment within the limits of their national jurisdiction*; and
>   (b) to ensure that activities within their jurisdiction or control do not cause potential or actual harm to the environment of other States or of areas beyond the limits of national jurisdiction.
> 2. States have, in accordance with the Charter of the United Nations and principles of international law, *the right to protect the environment* under their jurisdiction from significant harm caused by activities outside their national jurisdiction. If such harm has occurred, they are entitled to appropriate remedies.[224]

[222] IUCN, 'Covenant on Environment and Development', 2nd edn, 38.

[223] The limitations of the polluter-pays principle are recognized in the commentary: IUCN, 'Covenant on Environment and Development', 4th edn, Commentary, 48–49.

[224] Emphasis added.

Article 11(1) reaffirms Rio Principle 2 with, arguably, a slightly more 'environmental' focus, found in the fact that it mentions 'sustainable development needs' instead of simply referring to 'developmental needs' (which might be unsustainable).[225] Its subparagraph (b), considered by the commentary to be 'declaratory of customary international law',[226] reaffirms Principle 2, while subparagraph (a) creates an obligation to prevent harm within a purely domestic context, a duty not present in Principle 2. The commentary specifies that 'the full scope of subparagraph (a), as such, is without precedent in treaty law' but that 'the essence of it is based on existing international law'.[227] The recognition of such an obligation has important ramifications for international law, and yet, the commentary only justifies the obligation in a footnote by listing a number of instruments applicable within the domestic jurisdiction and control of a State[228] and by arguing that '[a]ll recent developments in international environmental law recognize that the global environment is an integrated whole'.[229] Given the legal consequences deriving from the recognition of a customary obligation for States to prevent harm on their own territory, the justifications given for this new provision is surprisingly limited and rather unconvincing – and this even if the obligation exists under general international law (see Chapter 8). It thus comes as no surprise that the first subparagraph was deleted in the third version of the Draft Covenant.[230]

Additionally, Article 11(2) is also a progressive expression of prevention: it gives States a 'right to protect' the domestic environment from transboundary harm (changed in a later edition to a 'right and duty'[231]) and thus to take lawful action within their jurisdiction to avoid harm (as long as the measures are lawful and proportional). It therefore produces a reversal of Stockholm Principle 21 that envisages prevention from the viewpoint of the harming State and sees prevention from the standpoint of the affected State.

225 The third edition deleted the word 'sustainable' in the expression 'the sovereign right to utilize their resources to meet their environmental and sustainable developmental needs'. This fits with the wording of Rio Principle 2 and also ensures that 'sustainable' is not interpreted as curbing the developmental needs of States.

226 IUCN, 'Covenant on Environment and Development', 2nd edn, Commentary, 48.

227 IUCN, 'Covenant on Environment and Development', 2nd edn, 47.

228 Including the UN Convention on the Law of the Sea and the Convention on Biological Diversity.

229 IUCN, 'Covenant on Environment and Development', 2nd edn, Commentary, 48.

230 Compare to IUCN, 'Covenant on Environment and Development', 3rd edn, Article 11.

231 IUCN, 'Covenant on Environment and Development', 4th edn, Article 13 (former 11) was changed: the 'right and duty to protect the environment' are modified to the 'right and duty to take lawful action to protect the environment'.

In summary, the numerous references to prevention in the Draft Covenant confirmed the importance of the principle in international environmental law.[232] At the same time, the various changes made to the expression of prevention in the different versions of the covenant reveal the difficulties met by the drafting committee to propose a consensual expression of the customary norm of prevention. Surprisingly, while prevention moved over the years closer to the advanced form that the covenant had originally proposed, the different versions of the text became more restrictive and conservative.

4.4 CONCLUSION

To conclude, the different studies presented in this chapter propose a conceptualization of prevention that seeks to represent the norm in its customary form, as well as, sometimes, to contribute to its progressive development. Codification bodies play an important role in the development of a relatively young field the norms of which are under continuous construction. Admittedly, the proposals discussed herein are varied, but irrespective of this diversity, some recurring elements can be identified. Firstly, codification efforts in the field of environmental protection offer varying conceptualizations of the relationship between prevention and other norms of environmental law (most notably the influential concept of sustainable development) depending on what their core mandate is. Secondly, the spatial scope of prevention is envisaged differently in the various codification works: if prevention in areas beyond national jurisdiction is widely acknowledged as customary, some works have preferred to adopt a restrictive, transboundary approach to prevention to avoid difficult questions relative to the actual implementation of such an obligation. In addition, a sense that States are under an international obligation to prevent harm inside their own territory emerges from different codification works, but the legal sources of such an obligation are rarely convincingly presented. Finally, the prevention principle is sometimes made applicable to other subjects of international law, but the inadequacies of international law in this respect are never fully explored. These questions relative to the applicable scope of prevention will be analysed further in Part III.

[232] IUCN, 'Covenant on Environment and Development', 4th edn; see also Article 15 on 'prevention of and response to emergencies'; Article 23 on monitoring obligations for the prevention of harm and Article 50 on the applicability of the State responsibility regime in case of a breach of prevention.

5

Prevention in the Jurisprudence

The challenges facing international environmental law today are not so much related to the absence of dedicated legal norms to respond to environmental degradation but rather to their implementation. Until recently, the original reluctance of States towards the law of State responsibility in situations of environmental damage persisted and restricted the role of international adjudication in environmental protection. However, since the 1990s, judicial decisions pertaining to environmental issues have multiplied.

This chapter offers an analysis of the cases that have referred, directly or indirectly, to prevention as a rationale, a principle or an obligation. For the sake of conciseness, this chapter does not provide a full, detailed analysis of each case: it acts as a preliminary introduction to each case and its contribution to the study of prevention, while additional details will be elaborated further in the course of other chapters. It first offers an analysis of the jurisprudence of international courts and tribunals (5.1) and then turns to the domestic case law that referred to the international principle of prevention (5.2).

5.1 INTERNATIONAL JURISPRUDENCE

The number of international claims with an environmental component remains relatively limited because environmental adjudication only recently started to develop. Yet, the consolidation of prevention owes much to the jurisprudence of international courts and tribunals that have made significant contributions to its crystallization as a core principle of international law, starting with the landmark and much-cited *Trail Smelter* case. Beyond this seminal case, decisions of the ICJ (5.1.1), the International Tribunal on the Law of the Sea (ITLOS) (5.1.3) and inter-State arbitral tribunals (5.1.2) have been instrumental to clarifying its status and content. Other adjudicatory bodies operating in specific branches of international law – relating to human rights (5.1.4), trade (5.1.5), investment (5.1.6) and war compensation (5.1.7) – have also relied on the prevention principle.

5.1.1 *International Court of Justice*

Traces of the prevention logic are found in early cases brought to the World Court (5.1.1.1). However, the ICJ was only given the opportunity to recognize the customary status of Stockholm Principle 21 in its 1996 advisory opinion on the *Legality of the Threat or Use of Nuclear Weapons*[1] (5.1.1.2). The landmark recognition was then followed by judgments on the merits that clarified the content to the obligation of prevention (5.1.1.3) and decisions on provisional measures guided by the principle of prevention (5.1.1.4).

5.1.1.1 The Preventive Rationale in Early Environmental Jurisprudence

The ICJ made its first reference to prevention (in the form of Stockholm Principle 21) in its advisory opinion of 1996 on the *Legality of the Threat or Use of Nuclear Weapons*.[2] However, earlier international proceedings in front of the World Court had acknowledged the premises of prevention. As explained in Chapter 1 and therefore not discussed further here, the *River Oder*[3] and the *Corfu Channel*[4] cases laid the foundations that contributed to the crystallization of the preventive rationale in international environmental law.[5] In addition, after the adoption of Stockholm Principle 21, States started referring to prevention, either implicitly or explicitly, in their pleadings at the ICJ.

The prohibition to cause transboundary harm was relied upon implicitly in Australia and New Zealand's application in the *Nuclear Tests* case, which asked the ICJ to declare that atmospheric nuclear tests in the South Pacific Ocean were in violation of their territorial sovereignty.[6] In retrospect, New Zealand's claims adopted a progressive approach to prevention, as they relied on an understanding that States have an obligation to protect the environment that is owed to the international community. Not only did New

1 *Legality of the Threat or Use of Nuclear Weapons* (Advisory Opinion) (1996) ICJ Rep 226, para 29.

2 *Legality of the Threat or Use of Nuclear Weapons*, para 29.

3 *Territorial Jurisdiction of the International Commission of the River Oder (Czechoslovakia, Denmark, France, Germany, Great Britain, Sweden/Poland)* (1929) PCIJ Series A No. 23.

4 *Corfu Channel (United Kingdom/Albania)* (1949) ICJ Rep 4, at 22.

5 See Section 1.1.

6 *Nuclear Tests (Australia v. France)*, Application instituting proceedings, para 49; *Nuclear Tests (New Zealand v. France)*, Application instituting proceedings, para 28(c)–(e).

Zealand concentrate on the effects of radioactive contamination on the environment (and not only on territorial sovereignty),[7] but it also asked the Court to rule that the French nuclear tests had violated 'the rights of all members of the international community, including New Zealand'.[8] Ruling that nuclear tests had already ceased following French declarations that it would not to continue atmospheric tests, the Court, however, did not pronounce on whether States were under such an *erga omnes* obligation to protect the environment.[9]

Additionally, the first component of Principle 21 – the right to sovereignty over natural resources – was relied upon in a case opposing Nauru to Australia over the rehabilitation of certain phosphate lands worked out before its independence.[10] In the *Certain Phosphate Lands in Nauru* dispute, initiated in 1989, Nauru solely argued that Australia had violated its right to exercise sovereignty over its natural resources (indeed relevant in the context of environmental exploitation by a former colonial power). It is noteworthy that although Principle 21 had been widely accepted for two decades, Nauru did not refer to broader environmental considerations.[11] The ICJ was, however, not even given the opportunity to examine the first clause of Principle 21, as the case was eventually settled.

7 *Nuclear Tests (New Zealand v. France)*, para 28(b), considering that France had breached the rights of the international community to be preserved from 'unjustified artificial radioactive contamination of the terrestrial, maritime and aerial environment and, in particular, of the environment of the region in which the tests are conducted'.

8 *Nuclear Tests (New Zealand v. France)*, para 28(a) and (b). Australia only made a reference to the rights of the international community in its pleadings. See *Nuclear Tests (Australia v. France)*, Australia's memorial on jurisdiction and admissibility, para 459: '[t]he sea is not static; its life systems are complex and closely interrelated. It is evident, therefore, that no one can say that pollution – especially pollution involving radioactivity – in one place cannot eventually have consequences in another. It would, indeed, be quite out of keeping with the function of the Court to protect by judicial means the interests of the international community, if it were to disregard considerations of this character.'

9 *Nuclear Tests (Australia v. France)* (Judgment) (1974) ICJ Rep 253, para 59; *Nuclear Tests (New Zealand v. France)* (Judgment) (1974) ICJ Rep 457, paras 55–57. See, however, dissenting opinion of Judges Ortyeama, Dillard, Jimenez de Arachaga and Sir Humphrey Waldock, (1974) ICJ Rep 312, paras 116–17, acknowledging the fact that that if the Court had ruled on the existence of a general rule of international law prohibiting atmospheric nuclear tests, it would have had also 'to determine what . . . the precise character and content of that rule [is] and, in particular, whether it confers a right on every State individually to prosecute a claim to secure respect for the rule'.

10 *Certain Phosphate Lands in Nauru (Nauru v. Australia)* (1992) (Preliminary Objections) ICJ Rep 240, memorial of the Republic of Nauru, at 155, on the 'breach of the principle of permanent sovereignty and natural wealth and resources'.

11 *Certain Phosphate Lands in Nauru (Nauru v. Australia)*. The memorial does not mention environmental protection.

5.1.1.2 The Status of Prevention

The ICJ examined obligations relating to the protection of the environment for the first time in 1995 in the context of the request for a re-examination of the *Nuclear Tests* case. Although the Court rejected the request, it made clear that the decision was 'without prejudice to the obligations of States to respect and protect the natural environment'[12] and hence left the door open to their subsequent recognition.

Such was the case a year later when the Court, in its advisory opinion on the *Legality of the Threat or Use of Nuclear Weapons* (*Nuclear Weapons Advisory Opinion*), recognized the customary character of the prevention principle in paragraph 29:

> The Court also recognizes that the environment is not an abstraction but represents the living space, the quality of life and the very health of human beings, including generations unborn. The existence of the general obligation of States to ensure that activities within their jurisdiction and control respect the environment of other States or of areas beyond national control is now part of the corpus of international law relating to the environment.[13]

The influence of Stockholm Principle 21 is evident in this paragraph. The World Court slightly reworded Principle 21 by changing the reference to a prohibition to cause damage to an obligation to 'respect' the environment. The difference in the wording of prevention can be seen as significant; indeed, the verb 'respect' (a term which, it should be noted, the Court had already used in 1995 in relation to environmental obligations[14]) leaves more freedom to States to decide on their actions relating to environmental protection. However, the legal consequences of this change remain minimal if it was driven by the Court's reluctance to recognize *ad verbum* the customary character of a provision originating from a non–legally binding document. An additional level of ambiguity remains in this paragraph: the Court did not expressly recognize the customary status of the norm but rather referred to prevention as belonging to 'the corpus of international law relating to the environment'.[15] However, subsequent decisions of the Court confirmed the

[12] *Request for an Examination of the Situation in Accordance with the Court's Judgment of December 1974 in the Nuclear Tests (New Zealand v. France)* (1995) ICJ Rep 288, para 64.

[13] *Legality of the Threat or Use of Nuclear Weapons*, para 29.

[14] *Request for an Examination of the Situation in Accordance with the Court's Judgment of December 1974 in the Nuclear Tests (New Zealand v. France)*, para 64.

[15] JE Viñuales, 'The Contribution of the International Court of Justice: A Contemporary Assessment' (2008) 32 *Fordham International Law Journal* 232, at 246, on the ambiguity of the Court.

customary nature of prevention[16] and put an end to any uncertainty that might have been left regarding its status.

5.1.1.3 The Content of Prevention

Four major environmental disputes brought to the Court contributed to clarifying the content of prevention.

GABČÍKOVO-NAGYMAROS PROJECT CASE The Court recognized prevention for the first time in a contentious case in the 1997 *Gabčíkovo-Nagymaros Project* dispute (*Gabčíkovo-Nagymaros*),[17] pertaining to the construction of dams on the River Danube. In *Gabčíkovo-Nagymaros*, the Court gave special consideration to environmental concerns: it acknowledged that the concerns expressed by Hungary for the environmental state of the Gabčíkovo-Nagymaros region as a result of the construction of dams on the Danube could be qualified as an essential interest, justifying a state of necessity precluding wrongfulness.[18] Paragraph 140 of the judgment is particularly central in the context of prevention: it combines three conclusions that make it a paragraph with rich legal consequences. Firstly, the Court ruled that the 1977 treaty concerning the construction and operation of the Gabčíkovo-Nagymaros system of locks had to be interpreted in light of 'current standards', including preventive obligations 'to maintain the quality of the water of the Danube and to protect nature'. As a result, the Court called on the parties to 'look afresh at the effects on the environment of the operation of the Gabčíkovo power plant'. Secondly, and related, the Court recognized that 'in the field of environmental protection, vigilance and prevention are required on account of the often irreversible character of damage to the environment and of the limitations inherent in the very mechanism of reparation of this type of damage'.[19] It therefore confirmed that the prevalence of the preventive rationale was justified by the shortcomings of the curative approach. Thirdly, the Court specified that a balance had to be achieved between economic development and environmental considerations, thereby depicting the prevention principle as able to constrain, in part,

[16] *Pulp Mills on the River Uruguay (Argentina v. Uruguay)* (Judgment) (2010) ICJ Rep 14, para 101.

[17] *Gabčíkovo-Nagymaros Project* (*Hungary/Slovakia*) (Judgment) (1997) ICJ Rep 7.

[18] *Gabčíkovo-Nagymaros Project* (*Hungary/Slovakia*) (Judgment), para 53 (however, Hungary failed to convince the Court that there was a grave and imminent danger).

[19] *Gabčíkovo-Nagymaros Project* (*Hungary/Slovakia*) (Judgment), para 140. For a detailed analysis of this paragraph, see L-A Duvic-Paoli, 'Vigilance and Prevention', in S Forlati and M Mbengue (eds), *The Gabčíkovo-Nagymaros Judgment and Its Contribution to the Development of International Law* (Cambridge University Press, forthcoming).

economic growth. The reasoning of the Court in paragraph 140, however, is not made fully clear: it superposed three assertions that make fundamental contributions to international environmental law, but transitions linking one idea with another remain missing.

PULP MILLS ON THE RIVER URUGUAY CASE The 2010 *Pulp Mills on the River Uruguay* dispute (*Pulp Mills*),[20] over the construction of a pulp mills on the River Uruguay, consolidated prevention in two ways. Firstly, it explicitly recognized prevention as a customary norm of international law on the basis of paragraph 29 of its *Nuclear Weapons Advisory Opinion*[21] – thereby leaving no uncertainty on the interpretation of the phrase. Secondly, it gave the Court the opportunity to clarify the due-diligence nature of prevention by ruling that prevention has its 'origins in the due diligence that is required of a State in its territory'.[22] As a result, the State is 'obligated to use all the means at its disposal' to avoid environmental harm.[23] In order to assess whether Uruguay had met the level of care expected from it, the Court assessed separately it substantive and procedural obligations of prevention.[24] It concluded that Uruguay had not breached its obligation to prevent pollution, on the basis that it had undertaken an environmental impact assessment (EIA)[25] and had followed international pollution prevention standards.[26] However, it also concluded that Uruguay should have informed Argentina of its plans to authorize the construction of the pulp mills[27] and that, consequently, it was in breach of its obligation to inform, notify and negotiate.[28] The decision of the Court is significant in the context of this study for the content it gave to the due-diligence exercise, ruling that prevention can only be discharged when two customary obligations are fulfilled: the obligation to carry out an EIA[29] and the obligation to cooperate.[30] These will be investigated further in Chapter 7.

20 *Pulp Mills*. 21 *Pulp Mills*, para 101. 22 *Pulp Mills*, para 101.
23 *Pulp Mills*, para 101.
24 For an interesting discussion of the substantive and procedural obligations of prevention as understood by the ICJ, see O McIntyre, 'The Contribution of Procedural Rules to the Environmental Protection of Transboundary Rivers in Light of Recent ICJ Case Law', in L Boisson de Chazournes, C Leb and M Tignino (eds), *International Law and Freshwater: The Multiple Challenges* (Edward Elgar 2013) 239–65.
25 *Pulp Mills*, para 210. 26 *Pulp Mills*, para 214. 27 *Pulp Mills*, paras 104–7.
28 *Pulp Mills*, para 158.
29 *Pulp Mills*, para 204, in which the Court held that the duty of prevention 'would not be considered to have been exercised' if an assessment of the risk of transboundary harm is not carried out.
30 *Pulp Mills*, para 102, in which the Court recognized that cooperation was necessary to 'fulfil the obligation of prevention', and para 77, in which the Court observed that 'it is by co-operating that the States concerned can jointly manage the risks of damage to the

WHALING IN THE ANTARCTIC CASE The next case in relation to environmental protection that reached the Court, the *Whaling in the Antarctic* dispute, brought questions of conservation to the fore.[31] Although the rationale of prevention was at the heart of the proceedings – Australia argued that Japan was in breach of the International Convention for the Regulation of Whaling, of which the objective is to prevent the extinction of whales – the principle itself was of little use. Indeed, while Australia initially claimed that Japan had breached its obligation of prevention under the Convention on Biological Diversity, on the basis of Article 3 (reasserting Stockholm Principle 21),[32] it withdrew this specific claim during the course of the proceedings. This is most likely explained by the fact that Australia considered that a breach of Article 3 was too difficult to convincingly prove, highlighting how prevention can be deemed too vague to bring a claim on its basis in the context of an international dispute. As a result, the parties rarely mentioned prevention in their pleadings[33] – and this is despite the fact that conservation was at the heart of the dispute. The Court itself therefore, as explained by Judge Cançado Trindade, did not see it 'fit to pronounce on the principle of prevention',[34] and the case did not directly further the development of the prevention norm.

CERTAIN ACTIVITIES CARRIED OUT BY NICARAGUA IN THE BORDER AREA AND CONSTRUCTION OF A ROAD IN COSTA RICA ALONG THE SAN JUAN RIVER JOINED CASES Finally, the issue of the prohibition to cause transboundary harm has also been at the centre of the proceedings in the *Certain Activities Carried out by Nicaragua in the Border Area* case, over the dredging activities carried out by Nicaragua in the San Juan River region, an area protected under the Convention on Wetlands of International Importance Especially as Waterfowl Habitat.[35] Contrary to the *Pulp Mills* case, where the Court was limited to an interpretation of the Statute of the River Uruguay,[36] it was, in this case, able to

environment that might be created by the plans initiated by one or other of them, so as to prevent the damage in question'.

31 *Whaling in the Antarctic (Australia v. Japan: New Zealand intervening)* (Judgment) (2014) ICJ Rep 226.

32 *Whaling in the Antarctic*, Application instituting proceedings, filed on 31 May 2010.

33 *Whaling in the Antarctic*, oral pleadings, CR 2013/7, 26 July 2013, at 56–58. Australia nevertheless stressed the importance of conservation under contemporary international environmental law, invoking its 'three main legal pillars', namely, 'intergenerational equity, the principle of prevention and the precautionary approach'.

34 *Whaling in the Antarctic*, separate opinion of Judge of Cançado Trindade, at 70.

35 *Certain Activities Carried out by Nicaragua in the Border Area (Costa Rica v. Nicaragua)* and *Construction of a Road in Costa Rica along the San Juan River (Nicaragua v. Costa Rica)* (Judgment) (2015) ICJ Rep 665.

36 *Pulp Mills*, para 66.

clarify the applicable rules of customary international law in relation to the prevention of transboundary harm. In effect, it paid significantly more attention to the customary obligations of the parties, only briefly examining conventional clauses to conclude that they did not give rise to specific obligations.[37] Both parties recognized the existence of a customary obligation not to cause transboundary harm.[38] At the core of the disagreement between the two parties was whether the threshold of 'significant' damage – which triggers *inter alia* obligations of notification and consultation – has been reached.[39] Similarly, in the related *Construction of a Road in Costa Rica Along the San Juan River* dispute (the two cases having been joined in April 2013[40]), Nicaragua argued that Costa Rica had violated the 'principle of the non-harmful use of the territory'[41] and its 'obligation not to cause significant harm',[42] whereas Costa Rica considered that its construction activities had no adverse impact, or no risk thereof, on the river.[43]

The Court reaffirmed prevention as a duty to exercise due diligence, assessed *inter alia* on the basis of whether an EIA was conducted.[44] It found that the dredging programme carried out by Nicaragua did not give rise to a risk of significant transboundary harm[45] and that, as a result, Nicaragua was not required to carry out an EIA.[46] By contrast, it ruled that Costa Rica had failed to comply with its obligation to carry out an EIA before commencing constructing the road.[47]

37 *Certain Activities/Construction of a Road*, paras 109–11, 218–20, on alleged breaches of treaty obligations.

38 *Certain Activities Carried out by Nicaragua in the Border Area (Costa Rica v. Nicaragua)*, General List No. 150, memorial of Costa Rica, paras 5.29 (referring to paragraph 29 of ICJ's *Nuclear Weapons* advisory opinion) and 5.30 (referring to the *Trail Smelter* award); counter-memorial of Nicaragua, paras 3.28–3.31 (on the due-diligence obligation of prevention), and para 5.138 (on the obligation not to cause transboundary harm).

39 *Certain Activities*, counter-memorial of Nicaragua, para 5.131: 'Nicaragua's very modest dredging program does not begin to approach that threshold. Its effects would be best described as de minimis rather than "significant"'.

40 Joinder of Proceedings, Order of 17 April 2013, (2013) ICJ Rep 166.

41 *Construction of a Road in Costa Rica along the San Juan River (Nicaragua v. Costa Rica)*, General List No. 152, memorial of Nicaragua, paras 141–44.

42 *Construction of a Road*, paras 186–92.

43 *Construction of a Road*, counter-memorial of Costa Rica, paras 47–94.

44 *Construction of a Road*, para 104, clarifying that the obligation to undertake an EIA is not only applicable, as the *Pulp Mills* statement might have suggested, in the context of industrial activities

45 *Construction of a Road*, para 120. The Court found that Nicaragua was responsible for the harm caused by its activities in breach of Costa Rica's territorial sovereignty. The question that remained was whether Nicaragua was responsible for any transboundary harm caused by its dredging activities which took place in areas under Nicaragua's territorial sovereignty, para 113.

46 *Construction of a Road*, para 105.

47 *Construction of a Road*, para 162.

The judgment is rich, and some of the Court's less consensual findings will be analysed further in the course of this study: these include its decision to maintain the distinction previously made in *Pulp Mills* between substantive and procedural duties and to make the obligation to notify and consult dependent on the existence of an EIA duty.[48]

5.1.1.4 Prevention in Provisional Measures

In addition to ruling on prevention at the merits phase of proceedings, the Court also examined the issue of harm avoidance in the context of provisional measures. The rationale of preliminary measures – avoiding irreparable prejudice – is very much linked to that of prevention – avoiding significant environmental damage.[49] Generally speaking, the ICJ has been cautious in deciding provisional measures on the basis of environmental risks, rarely convinced that the party had demonstrated the urgency and existence of 'irreparable damage to the environment'.[50] However, even in cases where the requirements for ordering provisional measures were not met, the Court has nevertheless reaffirmed the 'great significance it attaches to respect for the environment'.[51] For instance, in an order of December 2013, the Court refused to grant provisional measures to Nicaragua, not convinced by the imminence of the environmental damage to the river,[52] but it deemed it necessary to observe that 'Costa Rica acknowledged during the course of the oral proceedings that it has a duty not to cause any significant transboundary harm as a result of the construction works on its territory, and that it would take the measures that it deemed appropriate to prevent such harm'.[53] In sum, it refused to grant provisional measures because it had received assurances that preventive duties would not be breached. Thus, while the rationale of provisional measures is inherently preventive, the threshold for the Court to rule on

48 *Construction of a Road*, paras 108 and 168.

49 *Construction of a Road*, separate opinion of Judge Cançado Trindade, para 18.

50 In this respect, Judge Cançado Trindade criticized the Court's restraint: 'So, only with the worsening of the situation (with the dredging and construction of two new *caños*) in the disputed territory, the Court reconsidered its previous 'self-restrained' approach'. *Certain Activities Carried out by Nicaragua in the Border Area (Costa Rica v. Nicaragua)* (Provisional Measures) Order of 22 November 2013, (2013) ICJ Rep 354, separate opinion of Judge Cançado Trindade, para 58.

51 E.g. *Pulp Mills on the River Uruguay (Argentina v. Uruguay)* (Provisional Measures) Order of 13 July 2006, (2006) ICJ Rep 113, para 72, quoting the *Nuclear Weapons* advisory opinion.

52 *Construction of a Road* (Provisional Measures) Order of 13 December 2013, (2013) ICJ Rep 398, para 34.

53 *Construction of a Road* (Provisional Measures) Order of 13 December 2013, para 37.

the necessity of provisional measures to avoid environmental harm remains high. Nevertheless, orders on provisional measures keep the Court engaged with issues of environmental protection.

5.1.2 *Inter-State Arbitration*

Inter-State arbitrations have also played a key role in the emergence (5.1.2.1) and consolidation (5.1.2.2) of prevention.

5.1.2.1 The Seminal Case: *Trail Smelter*

Prevention, in its early no-harm form, was consecrated in the *Trail Smelter* case, which has since been considered the main source of the principle. The dispute arose in the context of a complaint by the United States that the emissions of sulphur dioxide released by a smelter based in Canadian territory were causing damage to the neighbouring state of Washington. The dispute was submitted to arbitration on the basis of a special agreement[54] and generated two awards in 1938 and 1941. The first decision mainly sought to clarify the facts and decide whether harm had occurred and how to value it. On this matter, the tribunal concluded that harm had occurred between 1932 and 1937 and ordered the payment of an indemnity of $78,000.[55] In its second decision of 11 March 1941, the arbitral tribunal concentrated on how the Trail Smelter should be operated in the future in order to avoid the repetition of harm. On the question of whether the Trail Smelter should refrain from causing future damage to the state of Washington, the tribunal responded in the positive on the basis that under the principles of international law and US law

> no State has the right to use or permit the use of its territory in such a manner as to cause injury by fumes in or to the territory of another or the properties or persons therein, when the case is of serious consequence and the injury is established by clear and convincing evidence.[56]

This paragraph is widely considered to be the foundational basis of the no-harm rule.[57] However, the recognition rested on a 'very narrow basis'[58]

[54] Convention for Settlement of Difficulties Arising from Operation of Smelter at Trail, BC, Ottawa, 15 April 1935, in force 3 August 1935, (1941) 3 RIAA 1905, at 1907.
[55] *Trail Smelter (United States v. Canada)* (16 April 1938 and 11 March 1941), (1941) 3 RIAA 1905, at 1933.
[56] *Trail Smelter*, 1965.
[57] See e.g. R Miller, '*Trail Smelter* Arbitration', in *Max Planck Encyclopedia of Public International Law* (Oxford University Press 2007) on the legacy of the arbitration.
[58] Lammers, *Pollution of International Watercourses*, 525.

because there was no international precedent.[59] It was certainly facilitated by the tribunal's willingness to find a solution balancing the interests of the two parties in application of the principle of good neighbourliness.[60] After having acknowledged the duty to avoid transboundary harm, the tribunal translated it into a very detailed regime of preventive measures regulating the operation of the smelter to avoid the repetition of harm.

Prevention as manifesting in the *Trail Smelter* awards cannot, evidently, be assimilated with prevention in its current form. In particular, the threshold triggering the preventive obligation is now considered to be lower than the one set by the tribunal, which required harm of 'serious consequences'[61] and that the injury be 'established by clear and convincing evidence'.[62] In addition, the tribunal adopted a clear anthropocentric approach to environmental harm by excluding injury to the environment per se (such as animal or plant life) from the range of compensable interests.[63] Finally, the imposition of strict liability on Canada for future harm caused by the smelter, although in line with Canada's 'voluntary assumption of responsibility in the case', is not reflective of the law as it currently stands (i.e. making the State responsible only in case of failure to exercise due diligence).[64]

Questions arise from these limitations, as already mentioned, about whether the *Trail Smelter* precedent can be convincingly referenced as one of the sources of prevention. It is certain that the significance of the *Trail Smelter* case, approaching 'legal veneration',[65] has been facilitated by an apparent simplicity of the stated principles and the paucity of other case law in the field.[66] Overall, it is fair to say that the award articulated 'the kernel of an idea that [was] modified and amplified in future decisions and state practice'.[67] It makes little doubt that it set the stage for the consecration of

59 *Trail Smelter*, 1963–5, noting that '[n]o cases of air pollution dealt with by an international tribunal ha[d] been brought to [its] attention' and hence relying on domestic decisions of the Swiss and US Supreme Courts in relation to air and water pollution.

60 Convention between the United States of America and the Dominion of Canada Relative to the Establishment of a Tribunal to Decide Questions of Indemnity and Future Regime Arising from the Operation of Smelter at Trail, British Columbia, Ottawa, 15 April 1935, in force 3 August 1935, (1941) 3 RIAA 1907, Article IV, presenting the objective of the tribunal as being to reach a 'just' solution.

61 *Trail Smelter*, 1970. 62 *Trail Smelter*, 1964.

63 T Stephens, *International Courts and Environmental Protection* (Cambridge University Press 2009) 135, qualifying it as a 'remarkable' oversight.

64 R Miller, '*Trail Smelter* Arbitration', para 7.

65 D French, '*Trail Smelter*', in C Miles and E Bjorge (eds), *Landmark Cases in Public International Law* (Hart 2018) 153–88, at 153.

66 French, '*Trail Smelter*', at 176.

67 Stephens, *International Courts and Environmental Protection* 124.

prevention as a fundamental principle of international law, but it should also be kept in mind that it reflects a more restricted form of prevention than its contemporary form.

5.1.2.2 Awards under the Permanent Court of Arbitration

The prevention principle also played an important role in recent inter-State arbitrations conducted under the aegis of the Permanent Court of Arbitration (PCA).

IRON RHINE RAILWAY ARBITRATION The 2005 *Iron Rhine Railway* arbitration between Belgium and the Netherlands pertained to the reactivation of a railway passing through Dutch territory. The tribunal considered that economic activities such as these had to be planned so as to prevent environmental damage. It noted, in this context, that the 'duty of prevention' is now a 'principle of general international law' that 'applies not only in autonomous activities but also in activities undertaken in implementation of specific treaties between the Parties'.[68] Relying on the ICJ's *Nuclear Weapons Advisory Opinion*, the arbitral tribunal recognized that

> [t]oday, in international environmental law, a growing emphasis is being put on the duty of prevention. Much of international environmental law has been formulated by reference to the impact that activities in one territory may have on the territory of another.[69]

The tribunal's conception of prevention is instructive on two grounds. Firstly, it broadened the concept of 'transboundary harm' by making the prevention principle applicable 'where a state exercises a right under international law within the territory of another state' – in this case Belgium's right of transit through the Netherlands.[70] In sum, the tribunal considered that in exercising its right of transit, Belgium was expected to protect the environment and to avoid creating environmental damage. Secondly, it must be noted that in referring to prevention, the tribunal did not provide a clear distinction between prevention and sustainable development or, more specifically, the principle of integration. It ruled that because the law of environment and the law of development are mutually reinforcing, there is a duty to prevent harm whenever development might cause environmental harm.[71]

[68] *Iron Rhine Railway (Belgium v. Netherlands)*, Permanent Court of Arbitration, (2005) 27 RIAA 35, para 59.

[69] *Iron Rhine Railway*, para 222.

[70] *Iron Rhine Railway*, para 223.

[71] *Iron Rhine Railway*, para 59.

INDUS WATERS KISHENGANGA ARBITRATION In another PCA arbitration, the *Indus Waters Kishenganga* case, the tribunal also linked the obligation to prevent environmental harm[72] to the need to manage natural resources in a sustainable manner.[73] The case concerned interpretation of the 1960 Indus Waters Treaty[74] and, specifically, the effects of a hydroelectric project pursued by India on the water flowing to Pakistan. The prevention principle was referred to in the partial award as 'a foundational principle of customary international environmental law' to buttress the tribunal's conclusion that 'hydro-electric projects . . . must be planned, built and operated with environmental sustainability in mind'.[75] The tribunal then reaffirmed the customary nature of the 'duty to prevent, or at least mitigate significant harm to the environment when pursuing large-scale construction activities'[76] in the final award. It also set a 'minimum environmental flow' that would prevent harm from occurring to the environment as a result of the hydroelectric project undertaken by India. Although the preventive approach found in the Indus Waters Treaty is closely related to no-harm, the tribunal used customary international law and, more specifically, the duty to prevent harm to determine the 'minimum environmental flow' as the level of water that would satisfy human needs but also the level that would ensure that the watercourse ecosystem was protected.[77] While refusing to go as far as applying a precautionary approach,[78] the tribunal used the customary principle of prevention to interpret the treaty from the perspective of environmental protection (and not purely as a response to explicit anthropogenic impacts).[79]

CHAGOS MARINE PROTECTED AREA ARBITRATION The 2015 award of the arbitral tribunal constituted under Annex VII of UNCLOS under the auspices

72 *Indus Waters Kishenganga Arbitration (Pakistan v. India)*, Permanent Court of Arbitration, Partial Award, 18 February 2013; refers to prevention as formulated in Principle 21 (para 448) and international environment (paras 448–50, on the *Trail Smelter* award and the *Pulp Mills* decision).

73 *Indus Waters Kishenganga Arbitration*, Partial Award, in particular, on the basis of para 140 of *Gabčíkovo-Nagymaros*, at paras 449–50.

74 Indus Waters Treaty concluded between India and Pakistan, Karachi, 19 September 1960, in force 1 April 1960, 419 UNTS 125.

75 *Indus Waters Kishenganga Arbitration*, Partial Award, para 454.

76 *Indus Waters Kishenganga Arbitration*, Final Award, 20 December 2013, para 112.

77 *Indus Waters Kishenganga Arbitration*, Final Award, para 112, where the Court held that a requirement to establish an environmental flow arises from the duty to prevent harm.

78 *Indus Waters Kishenganga Arbitration*, Final Award, para 112.

79 L Boisson de Chazournes, 'The Notion of Environmental Flows and the Law Applicable to International Watercourses' (2014) 108 *Proceedings of the One Hundred Eighth Annual Meeting of the American Society of International Law* 293.

of the PCA over the creation by the United Kingdom of a marine protected area (MPA) in the Chagos Islands offers a different outlook at prevention.[80] The issue at hand pertained not to the existence of transboundary risks but rather challenged a preventive measure taken by the United Kingdom in the context of its UNCLOS Article 194 obligation. In the *cas d'espèce*, the designation by the United Kingdom of a MPA in the Chagos Islands prohibiting all fishing in the area was disputed by Mauritius, which holds fishing rights in the area.

The tribunal ruled that the declaration of the MPA was not in accordance with UNCLOS provisions. Although the decision did not explicitly refer to prevention, it is nevertheless interesting for the purposes of this study. The case highlighted the fact that environmental protection should be carried out in a cooperative spirit. As a result, preventive measures that might affect the rights of third States have to be adopted in full cooperation with those States. The tribunal did not consider that the designation of the MPA was per se unlawful because the infringement of Mauritian fishing rights in the territorial sea can be justified by the preventive objectives found in UNCLOS Article 194(4). However, the procedure that led to its designation made the United Kingdom's decision unlawful because it did not ensure that the decision was taken in close cooperation with Mauritius 'to explain the need for the measure and to explore less restrictive alternatives'.[81] The ruling therefore confirmed the importance of the duty to cooperate in the context of implementation of the preventive duty.

More indirectly, the decision can also be read as a warning that preventive measures should not be taken to disguise ulterior motives. Indeed, Mauritius had claimed that the United Kingdom abused its right by declaring a MPA not in concern for the protection of the environment but was because of the United Kingdom's desire to preclude the Chagossians from returning to the archipelago.[82] The tribunal did not find ulterior motives in the UK designation of the MPA.[83] However, by requiring that the two countries cooperate over the designation of the MPA, it made sure that the reasons underpinning the adoption of preventive measures are transparent and truly grounded in environmental concerns.

80 *Chagos Marine Protected Area (The Republic of Mauritius v. The United Kingdom of Great Britain and Northern Ireland)*, Permanent Court of Arbitration, UNCLOS Annex VII Arbitral Tribunal, 18 March 2015.

81 *Chagos Marine Protected Area*, para 541.

82 *Chagos Marine Protected Area*, Mauritius's memorial, paras 7.81–7.99.

83 *Chagos Marine Protected Area*, para 543.

SOUTH CHINA SEA ARBITRATION Finally, the dispute brought by the Philippines against China in the *South China Sea* case gave the arbitral tribunal constituted under UNCLOS Annex VII the opportunity to consider the application of prevention in a context of disputed sovereignty.[84] The case pertained to the legal basis of maritime rights and entitlements, the status of some geographical features and the lawfulness of actions taken by China in the South China Sea (SCS).

The decision, which relied heavily on the jurisprudence of other courts and tribunals in the field of prevention,[85] clarified the obligation of prevention as found in UNCLOS Article 192. A significant contribution can be found in paragraph 941, which reads as follows:

> Article 192 thus entails the positive obligation to take active measures to protect and preserve the marine environment, and by logical implication, entails the negative obligation not to degrade the marine environment. The corpus of international law relating to the environment, which informs the content of the general obligation in Article 192, requires that States 'ensure that activities within their jurisdiction and control respect the environment of other States or of areas beyond national control'. Thus States have a positive 'duty to prevent, or at least mitigate, significant harm to the environment when pursuing large-scale construction activities'. The Tribunal considers [that] this duty informs the scope of the general obligation in Article 192.[86]

In this paragraph, the tribunal confirmed the origins of Article 192 in Stockholm Principle 21. Most importantly, it made it clear that prevention was not only an obligation to refrain from damaging the environment but also a positive obligation to take proactive steps to protect the environment. In following paragraphs, the tribunal confirmed the due-diligence nature of Article 192.[87] Its interpretation of the content of Articles 192 and 194 in light of other international instruments led it to rely on the definition of ecosystems found in the Convention on Biological Diversity[88] and the protection of certain endangered marine species found in the Convention on International Trade of Endangered Species[89] to assess China's compliance with its preventive obligations. The tribunal concluded that China's failure to prevent the harvesting of endangered species and giant clams was a breach of

84 *South China Sea Arbitration (The Republic of the Philippines v. The People's Republic of China)*, (Permanent Court of Arbitration), Award on the Merits, 12 July 2016.

85 *South China Sea Arbitration*; see e.g. footnotes 1094–95, 1097–102.

86 *South China Sea Arbitration*, para 941.

87 *South China Sea Arbitration*, para 944.

88 *South China Sea Arbitration*, para 945.

89 *South China Sea Arbitration*, paras 847–51, 958.

due-diligence obligations under Articles 192 and 194(5).[90] It also held that China's construction activities at seven reefs in the Spratly Islands were breaching its obligation to protect and preserve the environment under Article 192.[91] In this context, it relied on two core obligations that would have contributed to discharging the duty of care arising from Article 192: the obligations to cooperate[92] and to undertake an EIA,[93] as found in UNCLOS (but interpreted in light of the jurisprudence of the ICJ and the ILC Prevention Articles).[94]

5.1.3 *International Tribunal for the Law of the Sea*

In the field of marine protection, the International Tribunal for the Law of the Sea also clarified the principle of prevention in its orders on provisional measures (5.1.3.1) and advisory opinions (5.1.3.2).

5.1.3.1 Provisional Measures

The tribunal regularly relies on the phrasing 'prudence and caution' to qualify how States are expected to act in the context of protection of the marine environment.[95] Although the tribunal coined this expression, it never explicitly explained how it should be interpreted. As a result, the phrase and its legal consequences remain unclear, especially since the distinction between 'prudence' and 'caution' seems relative, or non-existent. It leaves little doubt, however, that the phrase arises from the preventive logic, an ITLOS Special Chamber having referenced the duty to act with 'prudence and caution' immediately after having quoted paragraph 29 of the ICJ *Nuclear Weapons Advisory Opinion* (on the customary status of Stockholm Principle 21).[96] Uncertainty remains, however, about whether the expression is broader than

90 *South China Sea Arbitration*, para 1203(12). 91 *South China Sea Arbitration*, para 983.

92 *South China Sea Arbitration*, paras 986 and 1203(13).

93 *South China Sea Arbitration*, paras 991 and 1203(13).

94 *South China Sea Arbitration*, footnotes 1182–84.

95 *Southern Bluefin Tuna (New Zealand v. Japan; Australia v. Japan)* (Provisional Measures) ITLOS Nos. 3 and 4 (27 August 1999), para 77; *MOX Plant (Ireland v. United Kingdom)* (Provisional Measures) ITLOS No. 10 (3 December 2001), para 84; *M/V 'Louisa' (Saint Vincent and the Grenadines v. Kingdom of Spain)* (Provisional Measures) ITLOS No. 18 (23 December 2010), para 77; *Responsibilities and Obligations of States Sponsoring Persons and Entities with Respect to Activities in the Area* (Advisory Opinion) ITLOS No. 17 (1 February 2011), para 132.

96 *Dispute Concerning Delimitation of the Maritime Boundary between Ghana and Côte d'Ivoire in the Atlantic Ocean (Ghana/Côte d'Ivoire)* (Provisional Measures) ITLOS No. 23 (25 April 2015), paras 71–72.

prevention and includes a precautionary approach. Indeed, the phrase 'prudence and caution' could be an indirect recognition of the interrelationship between prevention and precaution and an alternative to an explicit endorsement of precaution given its debatable customary status. In addition, the combination of the two principles would be justified on the basis that they can sometimes be difficult to distinguish.[97] This interpretation is corroborated by the fact that the Parties to the ICJ *Whaling in the Antarctic* case resorted to this same expression in their written pleadings,[98] precisely in a case where the preventive and precautionary principles were closely intertwined.[99]

Irrespective of whether the expression of 'prudence and caution' is restricted to foreseeable damage (prevention) or also applies to unforeseeable harm (precaution), the tribunal used the expression several times to refer to the obligation to limit environmental harm and combined it to procedural duties. In *Southern Bluefin Tuna*, the tribunal applied the prevention approach to conservation issues and ruled that 'the parties should in the circumstances act with prudence and caution to ensure that effective conservation measures are taken to prevent serious harm to the stock of southern bluefin tuna'.[100] The tribunal then applied the same expression in the *Land Reclamation* case, directing Singapore not to conduct its land reclamation 'in ways that might cause irreparable prejudice to the right of Malaysia or serious harm to the marine environment'[101] and noticing that

> given the possible implications of land reclamation on the marine environment, prudence and caution require that Malaysia and Singapore establish mechanisms for exchanging information and assessing the risks or effects of land reclamation works and devising ways to deal with them in the areas concerned.[102]

In the *MOX Plant* case, the tribunal further underscored the importance of procedural obligations in discharging the obligation of prevention. It ruled that 'prudence and caution require that Ireland and the United Kingdom cooperate in exchanging information concerning risks or effects of the operation of the MOX plant'[103] and insisted on the fact that 'the duty to cooperate is

[97] On the relationship between prevention and precaution, see Section 9.1.2.

[98] *Whaling in the Antarctic*, memorial of Australia, para 4.90; counter-memorial of Japan, para 9.33: 'Japan does not dispute that it should act with prudence and caution'.

[99] *Whaling in the Antarctic*, separate opinion of Judge Cançado Trindade, para 70.

[100] *Southern Bluefin Tuna*, para 77.

[101] *Land Reclamation by Singapore in and Around the Straits of Johor (Malaysia v. Singapore)*, ITLOS No. 12, Provisional Measures (8 October 2003), para 106(2).

[102] *Land Reclamation by Singapore*, para 99.

[103] *MOX Plant (Ireland v. United Kingdom)*, ITLOS No. 10, Provisional Measures (3 December 2001), para 84.

a fundamental principle in the prevention of pollution of the marine environment under Part XII of the Convention and general international law'.[104] Needless to say that, compared to the ICJ, the ITLOS has, through the route provided by provisional measures, proactively sought to prevent environmental harm, contributing at the same time to clarifying the content to the obligation, in particular, by underlining the importance of impact assessments, cooperation and information exchange.

5.1.3.2 Advisory Opinions

The ITLOS also made important jurisprudential contributions in relation to the application of the prevention principle to the global commons in the context of two advisory opinions.

RESPONSIBILITIES AND OBLIGATIONS OF STATES SPONSORING PERSONS AND ENTITIES WITH RESPECT TO ACTIVITIES IN THE AREA ADVISORY OPINION The 2011 advisory opinion on *Responsibilities and Obligations of States Sponsoring Persons and Entities with Respect to Activities in the Area (ITLOS Advisory Opinion on the Area)* had a fundamental role in shedding light on the application of prevention in areas beyond the limits of national jurisdiction.[105] In this case, the ITLOS Seabed Disputes Chamber was asked to clarify the international obligations of States sponsoring private companies undertaking exploration and exploitation activities in the deep seabed. The Chamber referred to the case law of the ICJ and, more specifically, to paragraph 187 of the ICJ's judgment in the *Pulp Mills* case (on the adoption of a legislative and administrative regime to fulfil the obligation of due diligence) to confirm that sponsoring States had an obligation of due diligence to prevent environmental harm in the Area. It characterized the obligation 'to ensure' arising from Article 139(1) of UNCLOS as an obligation 'of conduct' or 'due diligence'[106] and subsequently assimilated it to the prevention duty stated in Article 194(2) of the UNCLOS.[107] The chamber therefore concluded that if the State has made its best efforts to 'secure compliance with the contractors',[108] then it may be 'absolved' from liability for the occurrence of the damage.[109]

104 *MOX Plant*, para 82.
105 *Responsibilities and Obligations of States Sponsoring Persons and Entities with respect to Activities in the Area*, ITLOS No. 17, Advisory Opinion (1 February 2011).
106 *Responsibilities and Obligations of States*, paras 110–11.
107 *Responsibilities and Obligations of States*, para 113.
108 *Responsibilities and Obligations of States*, para 242.
109 *Responsibilities and Obligations of States*, para 229.

Additionally, the Chamber clarified the level of diligence expected of a State by referencing the so-called direct obligations that discharge the obligation of prevention. It construed due-diligence obligations as encompassing (1) the obligation to adopt appropriate regulatory measures and ensure that they are reasonably enforced,[110] (2) a treaty- and custom-based obligation to conduct an EIA[111] and (3) the obligation to apply the precautionary approach not only as required by the applicable regulations of the International Seabed Authority but also as part of emerging customary international law.[112] More generally, it specified that the degree of care expected from a State in this regard should be proportional to the risk presented by the activity.[113]

SUB-REGIONAL FISHERIES COMMISSION ADVISORY OPINION The second advisory opinion put to the ITLOS by the Sub-Regional Fisheries Commission (SRFC) (*ITLOS Advisory Opinion on the SRFC*), an international organization based in Senegal, also contributed to clarifying the contours of the prevention principle, this time as applied to the obligations of flag States in relation to illegal, unreported or unregulated (IUU) fishing activities.[114] The ITLOS, in its full formation, confirmed the approach taken by its Seabed Chamber in the 2011 advisory opinion. The tribunal reaffirmed the obligation to protect and preserve the marine environment as 'a fundamental principle' of international law.[115] On the basis of the *Advisory Opinion on the Area*[116] and the *Pulp Mills* judgment,[117] it recognized prevention as a due-diligence obligation. As a result, flag States have obligations to ensure that IUU fishing activities are not conducted under their jurisdiction or control.[118] In other words, the same logic applies to States sponsoring the exploration and exploitation of the deep seabed in the Area in relation to the activities of their contractors and to States faced with ships flying their flag and engaged in IUU fishing. In order to exercise their due diligence in this regard,

[110] *Responsibilities and Obligations of States*, paras 115 (referring to the interpretation of the obligation of 'due diligence' provided by the ICJ in the *Pulp Mills* case), 116 (referring to the ILC Prevention Articles) and 117–20 (referring to the more detailed answer given by the chamber in response to the third question put to it).

[111] *Responsibilities and Obligations of States*, para 145.

[112] *Responsibilities and Obligations of States*, paras 125–35, particularly at 131 and 135.

[113] *Responsibilities and Obligations of States*, para 117.

[114] *Sub-Regional Fisheries Commission*, ITLOS No. 21, Advisory Opinion (2 April 2015).

[115] *Sub-Regional Fisheries Commission*, para 216.

[116] *Sub-Regional Fisheries Commission*, paras 126, 128 and 132.

[117] *Sub-Regional Fisheries Commission*, para 131.

[118] *Sub-Regional Fisheries Commission*, para 129.

conventional law requires them to take administrative and legislative measures[119] to ensure that vessels flying their flag comply with UNCLOS Articles 192 and 193[120] and to investigate and remedy situations of IUU fishing.[121] In doing so, the tribunal transposed the conceptualization of due diligence presented in the *Advisory Opinion on the Area* to the case of IUU fishing by requiring States to take active measures to avoid harm without necessarily making them responsible in case of the occurrence of harm.

Overall, ITLOS has established itself as a major international tribunal in the field of environmental protection.[122] It has contributed to recognizing the due-diligence nature of prevention and, most importantly, in clarifying its content, which includes the duties to undertake an EIA and to cooperate, hence making an important contribution to the consolidation of prevention as a primary rule of obligation.

5.1.4 *Human Rights Forums*

Human rights forums have made a significant contribution to an often-neglected aspect of the duty of prevention: the State's obligations to prevent domestic environmental harm when such harm amounts to an impairment of a human right. Human rights adjudicatory bodies have crystallized three manifestations of prevention: a duty to protect individuals from deprivation of their human rights by third parties causing environmental harm (5.1.4.1), an obligation to protect individuals against natural disasters (5.1.4.2) and a potential extraterritorial duty under human rights law not to cause harm to the environment of other States that might result in violating the human rights of their populations (5.1.4.3).

5.1.4.1 Protection from Deprivation

The main contribution of human rights law to the prevention principle lies in its recognition that the State is under an obligation to protect individuals from

119 *Sub-Regional Fisheries Commission*, para 133.

120 *Sub-Regional Fisheries Commission*. These measures include measures to ensure compliance by vessels flying its flag with the laws and regulations adopted by the SRFC Member States (para 134) and measures prohibiting its vessels from fishing in the exclusive economic zones of the SRFC Member States and to ensure that vessels flying its flag comply with the protection and preservation measures pursuant to Articles 192 and 193 of UNCLOS (para 135).

121 *Sub-Regional Fisheries Commission*, para 139.

122 See e.g. C Schwarte, 'Environmental Concerns in the Adjudication of the International Tribunal for the Law of the Sea' (2003) 16 *Georgetown International Environmental Law Review* 421.

deprivation of their human rights by third parties causing environmental harm. The obligation to protect against interference by third parties, which forms the second pillar of the trinity of human rights obligations (alongside 'respecting' and 'fulfilling'), has been understood by human rights courts as a proactive duty to regulate the activities of third parties.[123] The nature of this obligation is similar to that of the preventive duty found in the ILC Prevention Articles: it is a duty of due diligence that requires the State to take all necessary measures to regulate the activities of private parties on its territory. The difference between the two obligations lies in their spatial scope. Whereas prevention under the ILC Prevention Articles requires due diligence to prevent external harm, the positive duty of due diligence arising from human rights dictates that the State regulates activities that might have adverse impacts on its territory. The difference is important because it means that the State has to regulate the activities on its territory that may potentially lead to environmental degradation with ensuing consequences on human rights. Nevertheless, the obligation of prevention in this context remains limited by the fact that the link between environmental harm and its violation, which should be direct and serious,[124] is often difficult to prove. More broadly, it is also restrained in its rationale by the anthropocentric concerns that guide its application and not by a willingness to protect the environment per se.

5.1.4.2 Protection from Natural Disasters

The second contribution also concerns the obligation to protect from deprivation but differs in that, in this case, human rights are impaired by a natural disaster or, more specifically, by the State's failure to provide adequate protection against it. As discussed previously, the obligation to prevent under disaster law is distinct from its manifestation in environmental law; however, both intersect closely, which explains why the obligation is included here.

The ILC draft articles on the protection of persons in the event of disasters adopted on first reading provide for an obligation to take due-diligence measures to prevent, or at least mitigate, disasters. The source of the duty

[123] See *inter alia Tătar v. Romania*, Application No. 67021/01, Judgment, 27 January 2009 (Final 6 July 2009), paras 85–88 (and the overview of similar cases cited therein); *Social and Economic Rights Action Center (SERAC) and Others v. Nigeria*, African Commission Application No. 155/96 (2001–2), paras 52–53; *Indigenous People Kichwa of Sarayaku v. Ecuador*, IAmCtHR Series C No. 245, Judgment of 27 June 2012, paras 145–47 and 159–68.

[124] *Fadeyeva v. Russia*, Application No. 55723/00, Judgment (30 November 2005), paras 68–70.

was identified in part on a jurisprudential basis. A salient example of the recognition of a duty to prevent disasters is found in the *Budayeva v. Russia* case decided by the European Court of Human Rights (ECtHR).[125] It dealt with a claim brought by several Russian citizens alleging a failure by Russian authorities to mitigate the consequences of a mudslide and provide effective domestic remedies.[126] Importantly, the Court considered that, under the circumstances, the duties arising from Article 8 (right to private and family life) in connection with dangerous activities were also applicable in the context of Article 2 (right to life), although the authorities are granted a wide margin of appreciation due to the nature of the threat *in casu*.[127] It recognized that the State had an obligation of due diligence to protect from natural disasters by providing the following:

> In the sphere of emergency relief, where the State is directly involved in the protection of human lives through the mitigation of natural hazards, these considerations should apply in so far as the circumstances of a particular case point to the imminence of a natural hazard that had been clearly identifiable, and especially where it concerned a recurring calamity affecting a distinct area developed for human habitation or use ... The scope of the positive obligations imputable to the State in the particular circumstances would depend on the origin of the threat and the extent to which one or the other risk is susceptible to mitigation.[128]

The Court acknowledged the existence of a positive obligation under Article 2 in what it called its 'substantive aspects' – taking the form of a legislative and administrative framework 'designed to provide effective deterrence against threats to the right to life'[129] – as well as in what it called its 'procedural requirements' – including a duty to provide a judicial response in the event of an alleged violation of Article 2.[130] Applying this standard, the Court concluded that Russia had breached its obligations under Article 2 as a result of its failure to protect the applicants from the disaster in question.

125 The same approach was subsequently confirmed in *Kolyadenko and Others v. Russia*, Application Nos. 17423/05, 20534/05, 20678/05, 23263/05, 24283/05 and 35673/05, Judgment (28 February 2012) (in relation to the absence of measures taken to prevent large-scale flooding due to water release from a water reservoir), paras 185 and 203.

126 *Budayeva and Others v. Russia*, Application Nos. 15339/02, 21166/02, 20058/02, 11673/02 and 15343/02, Judgment (29 September 2008).

127 *Budayeva and Others v. Russia*, paras 128–37.

128 *Budayeva and Others v. Russia*, para 137.

129 *Budayeva and Others v. Russia*, paras 128–37, especially at 129.

130 *Budayeva and Others v. Russia*, paras 138–45.

5.1.4.3 Extraterritorial Protection

The third contribution of human rights jurisprudence to prevention relates to the question of whether a State can be held responsible for breaching its human rights obligations for environmental harm occurring abroad. This perspective creates a diagonal obligation of prevention, which is owed to individuals (vertical obligation) in another State (horizontal obligation). The issue will be discussed further in Chapter 8, but for now, it is noticeable that so far no judicial body has addressed this issue.[131] The argument was nevertheless put forward in the now-settled case between Ecuador and Colombia before the ICJ relating to the aerial spraying of herbicides.[132] In addition, the Inter-American Commission on Human Rights held two hearings in connection with petitions for climate change–related extraterritorial violations of human rights, one brought by the Inuit people[133] and the other by Bolivian farmers.[134] However, both claims were dismissed.[135]

5.1.5 *WTO Dispute-Settlement Body*

The rationale of prevention has been relevant in a number of World Trade Organization (WTO) cases, in particular, as the WTO has interpreted GATT Article XX as justifying exceptions to WTO disciplines in the name of

[131] See, however, the interpretation of the Human Rights Committee of Article 6 in the draft of General Comment 39, para 26, which provides that States have an 'obligation to ensure that all activities taking place in whole or in part within their territory and in other areas subject to their jurisdiction, but having a [direct], significant and foreseeable impact on the right to life of individuals outside their territory, including activities taken by corporate entities, are consistent with article 6'. See Draft General Comment No. 36 on Article 6 of the International Covenant on Civil and Political Rights – Right to Life (July 2017), advance unedited version (no reference, available at www.ohchr.org/EN/HRBodies/CCPR/Pages/GC36-Article6Righttolife.aspx (last accessed 10 September 2017)), para 26, read in conjunction with para 65 on how environmental obligations inform the content of Article 6.

[132] *Aerial Herbicide Spraying (Ecuador v. Colombia)*, removed from the docket list of the ICJ on 13 September 2013.

[133] See Inuit Circumpolar Conference, *Petition to the Inter-American Commission on Human Rights Seeking Relief from Violations Resulting from Global Warming Caused by Acts and Omissions of the United States* (2005), available at www.ciel.org/Publications/ICC_Petition_7Dec05.pdf (last accessed 19 May 2017).

[134] See 'Inter-American Commission on Human Rights hears testimony on freshwater loss due to climate change', 28 March 2011, available at http://earthjustice.org/news/press/2011/inter-american-commission-on-human-rights-hears-testimony-on-freshwater-loss-due-to-climate-change (last accessed 19 May 2017).

[135] See JE Viñuales, 'A Human Rights Approach to Extraterritorial Environmental Protection? An Assessment', in N Bhuta (ed), *The Frontiers of Human Rights* (Oxford University Press 2016) 177–222, explaining the main hurdles that such claims would have to overcome.

environmental protection (i.e. in the name of an objective of prevention). This has been the case in the famous *Shrimp-Turtle* case, where the appellate body (AB) made reference to the Preamble of the Marrakesh Agreement on sustainable development and the protection and preservation of the environment in order to interpret Article XX(g) and specifically the term 'natural resources' as encompassing biological resources[136] and the policies adopted by the United States as 'relating to' a prevention objective.[137] WTO panels and the AB also considered whether different measures taken to avoid environmental degradation could be justified under the exceptions provided for in Article XX(a),[138] (b),[139] (d)[140] and (g).[141]

More specifically, the preventive principle, in the form of Rio Principle 2, has been used by the WTO dispute-settlement body, in part or in full, to interpret Article XX. The principle of sovereignty over natural resources has been used as a norm of general international law to interpret Article XX(g) to advance the argument that resource exploitation is not necessarily in contradiction with a concurrent objective of environmental protection. In *China – Raw Materials*,[142] the panel provided that '[t]he principle of sovereignty over natural resources affords Members the opportunity to use their natural resources to promote their own development while regulating the use of these resources to ensure sustainable development'.[143] This position was confirmed by the panel in *China – Rare Earth*, but this time on the basis of Principle 2 in its entirety. The panel used Principle 2 as an interpretative aid

136 *United States – Import Prohibition of Certain Shrimp and Shrimp Products*, Appellate Body Report, WT/DS58/AB/R (12 October 1998), para 129.

137 *United States – Import Prohibition*, para 135: 'It is well to bear in mind that the policy of protecting and conserving the endangered sea turtles here involved is shared by all participants and third participants in this appeal, indeed, by the vast majority of the nations of the world. None of the parties to this dispute question the genuineness of the commitment of the others to that policy.'

138 See e.g. *European Communities – Measures Prohibiting the Importation and Marketing of Seal Products*, Panel Report, WT/DS400 and WT/DS401 (25 November 2013), paras 7. 625–7.639.

139 See e.g. *United States – Restrictions on Imports of Tuna*, DS21/R-39S/155 (3 September 1991), paras 5.24–5.29; *United States – Measures Concerning the Importation, Marketing and Sale of Tuna and Tuna Products*, DS29/R (16 June 1994), paras 5.28–5.39.

140 *India – Certain Measures Relating to Solar Cells and Solar Modules*, WT/DS456/AB/R (16 September 2016), para 5.3.

141 See e.g. *United States – Standards for Reformulated and Conventional Gasoline*, Panel Report, WT/DS2/R (29 January 1996) at 43–46; *United States – Standards for Reformulated and Conventional Gasoline*, Appellate Body Report, WT/DS2/AB/R (29 April 1996) (appeal limited to the application of Article XX(g)).

142 *China – Measures Related to the Exportation of Various Raw Materials*, Panel Report, WT/DS394/R, WT/DS395/R, WT/DS398/R (5 July 2011).

143 *China – Measures Related to the Exportation of Various Raw Materials*, para 7.381.

for the word 'conservation' in Article XX(g).[144] In this case, China justified its export duties and quotas on rare earth on conservation grounds despite the fact that it was exploiting the resources for domestic use. It argued that the objective of 'conservation' under Article XX(g) was not limited to policies relative to the preservation of exhaustible natural resources but also included policies relative to the use and management of those resources.[145] The complainants, by contrast, refused to define 'conservation' as incorporating sustainable use.[146] The panel sided with China[147] and ruled that

> Resource-endowed WTO Members are entitled to develop conservation policies on the basis of, or taking into account, a full range of policy considerations and goals, including the need to preserve resources in their current state as well as the need to use them in a sustainable manner.[148]

This conclusion was based on a combined interpretation of Rio Principles 2 and 4, quoted in full in the report.[149] Confirming the jurisprudence in *China – Raw Materials*, the panel interpreted the principle of permanent sovereignty over natural resources as the Members' 'right to use their natural resources to promote their own development while also encouraging the regulation of such use to ensure sustainable development' and concluded that 'conservation and economic development are not mutually exclusive policy goals; they can operate in harmony'.[150] The panel did not understand prevention merely as an obligation to avoid environmental harm but rather concentrated on the balance (described in Chapter 2) that Principle 2 seeks to achieve between the right to exploit resources and protection of the environment, an objective corroborated by the Preamble of the Marrakesh Agreement.[151]

144 *China – Measures Related to the Exportation of Rare Earths, Tungsten, and Molybdenum*, Panel Report, WT/DS431/R, WT/DS432/R, WT/DS433/R (26 March 2014) paras 7.252–7.278.

145 *China – Measures Related to the Exportation of Rare Earths*, para 7.252.

146 *China – Measures Related to the Exportation of Rare Earths*, para 7.253.

147 *China – Measures Related to the Exportation of Rare Earths*, para 7.266. The interpretation was not discussed by the appellate body, which noted in a footnote: 'We also note that the Panel's interpretation of the word "conservation" in Article XX(g) is not appealed. Consequently, we neither endorse nor reject the Panel's statements in this regard'. Appellate Body Report, WT/DS431/AB/R, WT/DS432/AB/R, WT/DS433/AB/R (7 August 2014) footnote 544.

148 *China – Measures Related to the Exportation of Rare Earths*, para 7.266.

149 *China – Measures Related to the Exportation of Rare Earths*, para 7.263.

150 *China – Measures Related to the Exportation of Rare Earths*, para 7.265.

151 Marrakesh Agreement Establishing the World Trade Organization, 15 April 1994, 1867 UNTS 154, Preamble.

5.1.6 *Investment Arbitration Tribunals*

There is a significant and growing body of investment awards involving environmental components,[152] which means that the prevention objective is playing a role in investment arbitration. In this field, protection of the environment is analysed from different perspectives, including as a legitimate goal for the exercise of a State's police powers,[153] as a factor capable of justifying different treatment of two projects,[154] as an essential interest capable of being protected by the necessity defence[155] and as a concern that must be taken into account by investors in forming their legitimate expectations[156] or by tribunals in determining compensation.[157] References to the prevention principle, however, are rarely explicit.

The *S. D. Myers v. Canada* case,[158] where the tribunal explicitly relied on the principles of the Rio Declaration to interpret the provisions of Chapter 11 of the North American Free Trade Agreement (NAFTA), is one exception.[159] The case concerned a trade ban imposed by Canada that harmed the operations of a foreign investor active in the waste treatment sector. As part of the relevant context for the interpretation of Article 1102 of the NAFTA, the tribunal referred to

> the various provisions of the NAFTA, its companion agreement the NAAEC and principles that are affirmed by the NAAEC (including those of the Rio declaration). The principles that emerge from that context, to repeat, are as follows ... states have the right to establish high levels of environmental

[152] See JE Viñuales, *Foreign Investment and the Environment in International Law* (Cambridge University Press 2012) 9–23.

[153] *Methanex Corporation v. United States of America*, NAFTA (UNCITRAL), Award (3 August 2005), Part IV, Chap. D, para 7; *Chemtura Corporation (formerly Crompton Corporation) v. Government of Canada*, UNCITRAL, Award (2 August 2010), para 266.

[154] *Parkerings-Compagniet AS v. Republic of Lithuania*, ICSID Case No. ARB/05/8, Award (11 September 2007), para 392.

[155] *Suez, Sociedad General de Aguas de Barcelona S.A. and InterAguas Servicios Integrales del Agua S.A. v. The Argentine Republic*, ICSID Case No. ARB/03/17, Decision on Liability (30 July 2010), para 238; *Suez, Sociedad General de Aguas de Barcelona, S.A. and Vivendi Universal, S.A. v. The Argentine Republic*, ICSID Case No. ARB/03/19, Decision on Liability (30 July 2010), para 260.

[156] *Plama Consortium, Ltd. v. Republic of Bulgaria*, ICSID Case No. ARB/03/24, Award (27 August 2008), paras 219–21; *Chemtura v. Canada*, para 149.

[157] *Southern Pacific Properties (Middle East) Limited (SPP) v. Arab Republic of Egypt*, ICSID Case No. ARB/84/3, Award (20 May 1992), paras 191, 250.

[158] *S. D. Myers, Inc. v. Canada*, NAFTA Arbitration (UNCITRAL Rules), Partial Award (13 November 2000).

[159] North American Free Trade Agreement, Ottawa, Mexico City, Washington, DC, 17 December 1992, in force 1 January 1994, (1993) 32 ILM 296.

> protection. They are not obliged to compromise their standards merely to satisfy the political or economic interests of other states . . . states should avoid creating distortions to trade ... environmental protection and economic development can and should be mutually supportive.[160]

This paragraph references two expressions of the prevention principle. By acknowledging the Rio Principles, the tribunal contextualized the dispute within the Rio legal framework that aimed to reconcile environmental and economic considerations. It indirectly relied on Principle 2, which dictates environmental protection while leaving policy space for economic objectives. In addition, by mentioning the 'right' of States to 'establish high levels of environmental protection', the tribunal acknowledged the preventive rationale in its comprehensive form (turned towards environmental protection) and stressed its importance by recognizing it as a State prerogative (and not only as an obligation). The tribunal eventually concluded that Canada had indeed breached the NAFTA. Nevertheless, its reference to one of the manifestations of the prevention principle illustrates how the latter can be relevant to the settlement of investment disputes.

5.1.7 *UN Compensation Commission*

The UN Compensation Commission (UNCC) was set up as a result of United Nations Security Council (UNSC) Resolution 687 of 3 April 1991 that declared Iraq's liability 'under international law for any direct loss, damage ... or injury to foreign Governments, nationals and corporations, as a result of Iraq's unlawful invasion and occupation of Kuwait'. The objective of the UNCC was to process claims and pay compensation. It refused to be seen as a court *stricto sensu*, considering that its role was that of a 'political organ that performs an essentially fact-finding function'.[161] Nevertheless, its work was close to that of a quasi-judicial body 'examining claims, verifying their validity, evaluating losses, assessing payments and resolving disputed claims',[162] which explains why it is examined in the context of this chapter on jurisprudence.

The UNCC's reports mainly examined the issue of environmental harm from the angle of reparation. However, they merit consideration for the clarifications they bring about the consequences of a breach of the prevention

160 *S. D. Myers v. Canada*, para 247.

161 Secretary-General of the United Nations, 'Report of 2 May 1991 to the Security Council' UN Doc. S/22559, para 20.

162 Secretary-General, 'Report of 2 May 1991'.

obligation.[163] Of particular interest for this study is the work of the F4 Panel tasked with administering claims for 'environmental damage', defined as 'direct environmental damage and the depletion of natural resources'.[164] The panel ruled that a breach in the obligation to prevent environmental harm in times of international armed conflict gave rise to reparations granted on the basis of the *Chorzów Factory* principle (providing that reparation must, as far as possible, wipe out all the consequences of the illegal act).[165] Whenever possible, it favoured compensation for remediation or restoration over compensation for damage to natural resources. On the question of the threshold of harm that makes damage unlawful and triggers a right to reparation, the panel did not follow the general rules of international law, which provide that only damage exceeding the commonly accepted threshold of 'significant' gave rise to compensation.[166] Considering that UNSC Resolution 687 and other decisions of the General Council – which were not referring to a threshold – provided sufficient guidance,[167] it relied on an assessment of the magnitude of the damage but also took into consideration other factors, 'such as the location and nature of the damage and its actual or potential effects on the environment'.[168]

Interestingly, not only did the panel look at Iraq's obligation of prevention, but it also stressed that claimant countries (including Iran, Jordan, Kuwait, Saudi Arabia, Syria and Turkey) had a duty to mitigate and contain environmental damage.[169] As a result, the panel sometimes denied compensation or

163 C Payne and P Sand (eds), *Gulf War Reparations and the UN Compensation Commission: Environmental Liability* (Oxford University Press 2011) xviii; and P Sand, 'Environmental Principles Applied', in Payne and Sand (eds), *Gulf War Reparations* 170–92, claiming that the recommendations of the UNCC represent a 'significant aspect of the work of the United Nations for the prevention of environmental degradation and the preservation of the environment as a whole'.

164 United Nations Compensation Commission, Governing Council Decision 7, S/AC.25/1991/Rev.1 (28 November 1991, as revised 17 March 1992), para 35.

165 United Nations Compensation Commission, Governing Council, 'Report and Recommendations Made by the Panel of Commissioners concerning the First Instalment of "F4" claims', S/AC.26/2005/10 (30 June 2005) ('UNCC Fifth F4 Report'), paras 49 and 80.

166 United Nations Compensation Commission, Governing Council, 'Report and Recommendations Made by the Panel of Commissioners concerning the First Instalment of "F4" claims, S/AC.26/2003/31 (18 December 2003) ('UNCC Third F4 Report'), para 33.

167 'UNCC Third F4 Report', para 35.

168 'UNCC Third F4 Report', para 36. The UNCC panel failed to recognize the malleability of the threshold and as a result decided to refer to the criteria of reasonableness. However, the significant threshold can be interpreted as including considerations over the extent of the damage but also of reasonableness.

169 'UNCC Third F4 Report', paras 42–43; United Nations Compensation Commission, Governing Council, 'Report and Recommendations Made by the Panel of Commissioners concerning the First Instalment of "F4" claims', S/AC.26/2004/17 (9 December 2004)

reduced the amount of compensation when claimants had failed to take measures to prevent aggravation of the environmental damage.[170] It also ruled that claimants had to observe their own obligation of prevention when taking remedial measures to avoid potential negative side effects to their project. In its third report in 2003, the F4 Panel paraphrased the language of the Stockholm and Rio Declarations, stating that 'claimants have the obligation under international law to ensure that the remediation measures that they take do not cause damage to the environment in other States or in areas beyond the limits of national jurisdiction'.[171] The claimants' obligation to consider potential 'transboundary effects' of remediation or compensatory measures was reiterated in the fourth and fifth Panel F4 reports.[172] In addition, the panel rejected claims for remediation projects that themselves posed serious environmental risks, such as the release of genetically modified bacteria to combat marine pollution in Iran.[173] The panel could have endorsed a restrictive approach to the issue of environmental harm given that the circumstances of the case (war compensation) were dictating a curative, inter-State approach to environmental damage. The panel's work was limited by the scope of UNSC Resolution 687 and other decisions of the General Council, but its interpretation of these instruments – in relation to the determination of the threshold of harm and the claimants' duty to prevent harm – revealed a comprehensive and progressive approach to prevention.[174]

('UNCC Fourth F4 Report', part 2), paras 2 and 38; 'UNCC Fifth F4 Report', paras 40–41. See also UNCC, Governing Council Decision, S/AC.26/1992/15 (4 January 1992).

170 See e.g. inadequate management of ordnance sites by Kuwait, United Nations Compensation Commission, Governing Council, 'Report and Recommendations Made by the Panel of Commissioners concerning the First Instalment of "F4" claims', S/AC.26/2004/16 (9 December 2004) ('UNCC Fourth F4 Report', part 1), paras 206 and 216 (amount denied: US$653.8 million).

171 'UNCC Third F4 Report', para 50 and introduction to technical annexes, para 4(g).

172 'UNCC Third F4 Report', para 50 and introduction to technical annexes, para 4(g); 'UNCC Fourth F4 Report', para 2; and 'UNCC Fifth F4 Report'.

173 UNCC, 'Governing Council, Report and Recommendations Made by the Panel of Commissioners concerning the First Instalment of "F4" Claims', S/AC.26/2001/16 (22 June 2001) ('UNCC First F4 Report'), paras 169–77.

174 The panel's progressive approach to prevention is to be put into perspective with the claimant's more conservative approach (in light of the fact that they did not claim reparation for environmental damage beyond national territorial waters). See, in contrast, UNGA Resolutions requesting Israel to assume responsibility for prompt and adequate compensation of the oil spill damage caused by its bombardment of a coastal power state in Lebanon that affected the Mediterranean *marine environmental well beyond Lebanese territorial waters*: including *inter alia* UNGA Res. 61/194 (20 December 2006), para 3; and UNGA Res. 63/211 (19 December 2008), para 4.

5.1.8 *Final Remarks*

The multiplicity, and variety, of international cases that have relied on the principle of prevention is indicative of a new dynamic between prevention and reparation that will be discussed further in Chapter 11. Although it emerged as a complete alternative to reparation, prevention now operates in complementarity with it, as a primary norm of obligation reliant on the law of State responsibility in case of breach. In this context, international courts and tribunals play a fundamental role in putting into light the different normative roles played by prevention in international law and in clarifying the content and scope of preventive obligations.

5.2 DOMESTIC JURISPRUDENCE

In order to complement the overview of the case law relative to prevention, the analysis that follows concentrates on cases in which domestic courts have relied on the international norm of prevention. The approach that domestic courts adopt vis-à-vis an international norm such as prevention will necessarily be constrained by the way international law relates to a specific municipal system and how it is incorporated in domestic law. However, this review does not seek to engage in a comparative analysis of how municipal law relates to international environmental law but rather aims to identify different ways in which domestic courts have relied on the international principle of prevention.[175] Although the number of cases in which a domestic court has referenced the international principle of prevention remains rather small, the inquiry is driven by the fact that references to prevention can be expected to become more common as the boundaries between the national and international levels are becoming increasingly porous.[176]

A few preliminary remarks regarding case selection are necessary. The cases mentioned in this section were selected after a review of the cases referenced in the British Institute of International and Comparative Law's study on international environmental law in national courts,[177] the International

[175] JE Nijman and A Nollkaemper (eds), 'Introduction', in *New Perspectives on the Divide between National and International Law* (Oxford University Press 2007) 6, noting that 'international law scholarship has for a long time, and is arguably still today, engrossed in the monism-dualism dichotomy [which] may well have prevented us from developing new perspectives on the divide between national and international law, and addressing the questions currently at stake'.

[176] P-M Dupuy, 'International Law and Domestic (Municipal) Law', in *Max Planck Encyclopedia of Public International Law* (Oxford University Press 2011) para 134.

[177] M Anderson and P Galizzi (eds), *International Environmental Law in National Courts* (British Institute of International and Comparative Law 2002).

Environmental Law Reports' volume on international environmental law in national courts[178] and, for more recent cases, the Oxford Reports on International Law in Domestic Courts database.[179] A comprehensive coverage of domestic decisions is beyond the scope of this study, but through these three major collections, the core decisions should have been covered. Case selection is not an easy task because domestic courts do not necessarily identify a principle as having its source in international or national law.[180] In addition, when courts rely on international principles, they often fail to engage in a systematic analysis of their legal status, leaving ambiguous or unexplained the basis upon which such reliance occurs.[181] In addition, it is sometimes unclear why courts rely upon international environmental principles: courts tend to use international environmental law not only as an interpretative tool of domestic law but also to rely on its 'persuasive rather than legal power'.[182] In light of such difficulties, two paths were chosen. The first section concentrates on one of the most evident manifestations of prevention and presents instances in which domestic courts have relied upon Stockholm Principle 21 or its equivalent in the form of Rio Principle 2 (5.2.1). The second part focuses on manifestations that are more complex to identify and highlights instances in which domestic courts relied on custom and treaty-based obligations of prevention (5.2.2).

5.2.1 *References to Stockholm Principle 21*

The most obvious circumstances in which domestic courts rely on Stockholm Principle 21 or Rio Principle 2 relate to cases of transboundary damage. One significant example can be found in the *Mines de Potasse* litigation regarding chloride pollution of the Rhine due to mining potassium ore exploitation in France. The French phase of the case confirmed that the prohibition to cause harm was applicable *in casu*, with the administrative tribunal of Strasbourg ruling that authorities must 'determine precisely the effects of these discharges outside the national territory, in accordance with the principles established by international

[178] C Robb and A Palmer (eds), *International Environmental Law in National Courts* (vol 4, Cambridge University Press 2004).

[179] http://opil.ouplaw.com/page/ILDC/oxford-reports-on-international-law-in-domestic-courts (last accessed 9 August 2017) (under the 'international environmental law' section).

[180] Anderson and Galizzi (eds), *International Environmental Law in National Courts* 9.

[181] Anderson and Galizzi (eds), *International Environmental Law in National Courts* 12.

[182] Anderson and Galizzi (eds), *International Environmental Law in National Courts* 20.

law'.[183] The Conseil d'Etat followed the same approach by ruling that the impact statement could not be limited to the environmental consequences felt on French territory but must, as much as is feasible, have a transboundary dimension.[184] The Dutch phase of the litigation also dealt with the international prohibition of transboundary harm but adopted a more unconventional approach. The Tribunal of Rotterdam found that the international principle of *sic utere tuo* – sourced from the *Trail Smelter* case and Stockholm Principle 21 – was regulating not only the relations between two States but also between their citizens.[185] However, the case is an 'anomaly'[186] and was reversed by the Court of Appeal of the Hague, which ruled that it was incorrect to apply 'the unwritten rules of international law, which have no direct effect but which apply exclusively to States as subjects of law, in a dispute between private persons'.[187] As a result, the finding was reversed on the grounds that the international norm of prevention, in its no-harm manifestation, cannot apply directly to private parties.[188]

In the absence of a specific translation in the domestic legal system, Stockholm Principle 21 can be perceived as too vague to be enforceable by a domestic court. Such was the case in *Amlon Metals v. FMC*, where the plaintiffs alleged that the shipping of copper waste residues containing dangerous chemicals from the United States to the United Kingdom amounted to a violation of the customary prevention principle reflected in Stockholm

183 *Société NV PWN et autres v. Etat Ministre de l'Environnement*, Administrative Tribunal of Strasbourg, France, 27 July 1983, in A Palmer and C Robb (eds), *International Environmental Law Reports*, vol 4: *International Environmental Law in National Courts* (Cambridge University Press 2004) ('IELR') 209.

184 *Société 'Les Mines de Potasse d'Alsace' v. Province de la Hollande Septentrionale et autres*, Conseil d'Etat, France, 18 April 1986, in IELR 214–15.

185 *Handelskwekerij G-J Bier B.V. Stichting Reinwater v. Mines de Potasse d'Alsace S.A.*, Rotterdam Court, The Netherlands, 16 December 1983, (1984) 15 NYIL 471–84.

186 Anderson and Galizzi (eds), *International Environmental Law in National Courts* 13.

187 *Mines de Potasse d'Alsace SA v. Onroad Goed Maatschappij Bier BV and Others*, Court of Appeal of the Hague, The Netherlands, 10 September 1986, IELR 343.

188 The applicability of Principle 21 to private actors was also discussed in *Beanal v. Freeport-McMoran*, where a US district court looked at the applicability of Principle 21 only to say that it only applies to States and not corporations as a matter of customary law. *Beanal v. Freeport-McMoran*, US District Court, ED Louisiana, United States, 10 April 1997, 969 F Supp 362. See also *Aguinda v. Texaco*, concerning a claim brought by Ecuadorian plaintiffs for environmental harm caused by Texaco. The district court seemed initially sympathetic to the claim, denying Texaco's motion to dismiss and considering that further discovery had to be ordered to assess whether Texaco had breached customary international law. However, the case was subsequently dismissed on the grounds that Ecuadorian courts were the proper forum. *Aguinda v. Texaco*, US District Court, Southern District of New York, 11 April 1994, 945 F Supp 625.

Principle 21. A US court refused to rely on the Stockholm principles because they 'do not provide any specific prescriptions, but rather refer only in a general sense to the responsibility of nations to ensure that activities within their jurisdiction do not cause damage to the environment beyond their borders'.[189] Similarly, a dissenting opinion to the *Commonwealth of Australia and Another v. State of Tasmania and Others* case noted that Principle 21 was too vague to create an international obligation to preserve the natural heritage and that the State only had a 'sovereign responsibility' to do what it could.[190] However, such a view is not necessarily shared in countries where the domestic legal system remains at its infancy in the field of environmental protection, where the Stockholm and Rio Summits can be seen to have committed States to take environmental action; such was the position of the Supreme Court of Nepal, which ordered the government to 'enact necessary law to prevent noise pollution, the pollution of air and water and to preserve the environment'[191] so as to give effect to the Stockholm and Rio norms.

More broadly, domestic courts generally perceived Principle 21 as symbolizing the commitments taken by the international community towards environmental protection. For instance, in *MC Mehta v. Union of India and Others*, the Supreme Court of India, in a case regarding pollution caused by tanneries, mentioned Stockholm Principles 6 (discharge of toxic substances), 7 (pollution of the seas) and 21 (prevention)[192] as part of a 'few words about the importance of and need for protecting our environment'.[193] In the same vein, in a case of waste disposal endangering the right to life and to a healthy environment, the Supreme Court of Justice of Costa Rica quoted Rio Principle 2 not to extract legal obligations from it but rather to contextualize the dispute within the broader international framework and to identify environmental action as a common, global preoccupation.[194] A similar approach was taken by the Sri Lankan Supreme Court. Although it recognized that the

189 *Amlon Metals, Inc. v. FMC Corp.*, US District Court, Southern District of New York, 13 December 1991, 775 F Supp 671.

190 *Commonwealth of Australia and Another v. State of Tasmania and Others*, High Court of Australia, 1 July 1983, dissenting judgment of Judge Wilson, IELR 33.

191 *Surya Prasad Sharma Dhungel on Behalf of Leaders. Inc. Pvt. Ltd. v. Godavari Marble Industries Pvt. Ltd. and Others* (Writ Petition No 35 of the year 2049(1991)), Full Bench, Supreme Court, Nepal, 14 Kartik 2052 (1994), IELR 326.

192 *M. C. Mehta v. Union of India and Others*, Supreme Court of India, 22 September 1987, IELR 254.

193 *M. C. Mehta v. Union of India and Others*, 253.

194 *Carlos Roberta Mejia Chacón v. Ministry of Health and Municipality of Santa Ana*, Constitutional Chamber, Supreme Court of Justice, San José, Costa Rica, 30 July 1993, IELR 183.

Stockholm principles are non-binding, it nevertheless quoted Principle 21 – complemented by a quotation from Judge Weeramantry's separate opinion in *Gabčíkovo-Nagymaros* on how '[t]he notion of not causing harm to others and hence *sic utere tuo ut alienim non laedas* was a central notion of Buddhism' – to contextualize the need to put economic development 'within the context of our finite environment'.[195] Principle 21 is here understood to reflect a broad rationale of environmental protection irrespective of its initial application to transboundary harm. The court uses the principle to show that its decision is in line with the international consensus.

5.2.2 *References to the International Principle of Prevention*

Outside of a specific reference to Stockholm Principle 21, municipal courts have also referred to the more general principle of prevention either as manifesting in a preventive treaty obligation or as a guiding norm of international environmental law. Such reliance is not common given that international duties will often have been incorporated in municipal law, or if not, their direct effect (should the municipal system provide for such possibility) will be difficult to prove given the generally vague nature of the obligation. However, what is more common is to find references to a general rationale of prevention, either explicitly identified as an internationally recognized norm or merely as a moral requirement, or to treaty- or custom-based preventive obligations used to evaluate State policies.

While the role of national courts in implementing international environmental law has traditionally been limited,[196] they are playing an increasingly important role in holding States accountable for their international obligations. In particular, as evidenced by the recent growth in climate litigation, national courts could be called on to play a central role in holding States accountable for their failure to mitigate climate change.[197] In this context, the international norm of prevention can be used as a support argument to place the dispute within the international legal context and to reinforce the existence and determine the scope of domestic obligations. The first landmark decision in this respect is the case of the Urgenda Foundation (a citizens' platform concerned with the transition to a sustainable society) against the

195 *Bulankulama and Six Others v. Ministry of Industrial Development and Seven Others*, Supreme Court of the Democratic Socialist Republic of Sri Lanka, 2 June 2000, IELR 434.

196 Anderson and Galizzi (eds), *International Environmental Law*, at 9.

197 See P de Vilchez Moragues, 'Broadening the Scope: The Urgenda Case, the Oslo Principles and the Role of National Courts in Advancing Environmental Protection Concerning Climate Change' (2016) 20 *Spanish Yearbook of International Law* 71.

Dutch government.[198] The Hague District Court used the international obligation of prevention as an interpretative tool to rule on the inadequacy of the preventive measures taken by the Netherlands to limit its greenhouse gas emissions. The court recognized that because international norms do not have direct effect in domestic jurisdictions, preventive duties under the UNFCCC and customary international law 'do not have a binding force towards citizens (private individuals and legal persons)' but only involve obligations towards other States.[199] However, it held that the court could nevertheless take these international legal obligations into account to apply and interpret national law standards.[200] It took the same approach in relation to human rights obligations. It considered that Urgenda did not have standing as a victim within the meaning of Article 34 of the European Convention on Human Rights (ECHR) to argue a violation of ECHR Articles 2 and 8 on the basis of its previous case law on the obligation to prevent environmental harm to fulfil its human rights obligations.[201] However, it considered that both articles could nevertheless 'serve as a source of interpretation when detailing and implementing open private-law standards'.[202] In other words, the court used the international principle of prevention as an interpretation tool to assess whether the Netherlands had met the duty of care expected from it pursuant to Article 21 of the Dutch Constitution.[203] On that basis, it ruled that the State had taken insufficient measures to reduce greenhouse gas emissions in the Netherlands in order to 'avert the imminent danger caused by climate change'.

More generally, the principle of prevention (often considered indistinctively in its international and national dimensions) is regularly used when domestic courts are called to strike a balance between environmental and socio-economic interests. In this context, domestic courts tend to integrate the preventive principle into the concept of sustainable development on the basis that forms one of its three core pillars, alongside the economic and social aspects.[204] For instance, in *Vellore Citizens Welfare Forum v. Union of India*

198 *Urgenda Foundation v. The State of the Netherlands (Ministry of the Infrastructure and the Environment)*, Hague District Court, 24 June 2015, available at http://uitspraken.rechtspraak.nl/inziendocument?id=ECLI:NL:RBDHA:2015:7196 (last accessed 19 May 2017).

199 *Urgenda Foundation v. The State of the Netherlands*, para 4.42.

200 *Urgenda Foundation v. The State of the Netherlands*, para 4.43.

201 *Urgenda Foundation v. The State of the Netherlands*, paras 4.45–4.46.

202 *Urgenda Foundation v. The State of the Netherlands*, para 4.46.

203 Article 21 of the Dutch Constitution imposes a duty of care on the State relating to the livability of the country and the protection and improvement of the living environment.

204 *Hellenic Ornithological Society and Others v. Minister of National Economy and Tourism, Minister for the Environment, Land-use Planning and Public Works, Minister of Agriculture, and Minister of Industry, Energy and Technology*, Conseil d'Etat (Chamber E), Greece,

and Others, the Supreme Court of India ruled that the leather industry should not be allowed to cause harm to the environment and health and cannot be permitted to continue its polluting activities.[205] However, the Court did not rule on the basis of Principle 21, as it had done a decade earlier in a similar case,[206] but on the basis of the international concept of sustainable development, which it assumed to include a prevention obligation.[207]

In addition, domestic courts regularly rely on the principle of prevention to interpret a constitutional right to the environment. In *Oposa v. Secretary of the Department of Environment*, the Supreme Court of the Philippines ruled that the right to a healthy environment was imposing a 'correlative duty to refrain from impairing the environment'.[208] Similarly, the Supreme Court of Nepal considered that the right required the adoption of 'regulatory and remedial measures to minimise such an adverse impact on the environment'.[209]

> No one can live a clean and healthy life without a clean and healthy environment. Is not then the clean and healthy environment an integral part of our survival? Indeed, it is in keeping this fact in view that measures have to be adopted to prevent harm to the environment.[210]

9 July 1994, IELR 231; *Narmada Bachao Aandolan v. India, ex parte Narmada Control Authority and ex parte Ministry of Water Resources of India*, Original writ petition, Supreme Court of India, 18 October 2000, ORIL, para 144.

205 *Vellore Citizens Welfare Forum v. Union of India*, Supreme Court of India, 28 August 1996, IELR 270.

206 *M. C. Mehta v. Union of India and Others*.

207 *Vellore Citizens*, 276.

208 *Juan Antonio Oposa and Others v. Secretary of the Department of Environment and Natural Resources and Another* (GR No 101083), Supreme Court, Philippines, 30 July 1993, IELR 388.

209 *Surya Prasad Sharma Dhungel on Behalf of Leaders, Inc. Pvt. Ltd. v. Godavari Marble Industries Pvt. Ltd. and Others* (Writ Petition No 35 of the year 2049(1991)), Full Bench, Supreme Court, Nepal, 14 Kartik 2052 (1994), IELR 326, at 328.

210 *Surya Prasad Sharma Dhungel on Behalf of Leaders*. See also in *Senih Özay v. Ministry of the Environment, Ankara and Eurogold Madencilik AS* (Ref. No. 1996/5477, Ruling No. 1997/2312), Sixth Chamber, Higher Administrative Court, Turkey, 13 May 1997, IELR 450: the Court argued that the fact that gold mining would 'operate at a risk which, if materialised, would certainly directly or indirectly impair human life due to the resulting damage to the environment' would violate the State 'duty to protect the environment, to avoid environmental pollution and to ensure that each individual continues to live in physical and mental health'; *Gbemre (on Behalf of Iwherekan Community, Delta State) v. Shell Petroleum Development Company of Nigeria and Ors*, Federal High Court, Nigeria, 14 November 2005, ORIL online, where the Federal High Court of Nigeria ruled that the failure of the oil companies to carry out an environmental impact assessment concerning the flaring activities contributes to the violation of the fundamental rights to life and dignity of the person.

The Court did not specify whether it was relying on an international or national principle but rather used prevention for its rationale as a general principle of law that supports the existence of a State duty to protect its citizens from environmental degradation. In an approach also commonly used in relation to human rights, domestic courts tend to consider that prevention represents universal values relative to environmental integrity that are common to both the international and national legal orders.[211]

To conclude, domestic courts avoid relying directly on prevention as a rule of decision, preferring (understandably) to ground their decisions in municipal rather than international law. However, they often rely indirectly on prevention as a means of interpretation, in which case they use prevention either as a rationale widely recognized by the international community and in its form as an international treaty obligation that contributes to contextualize and interpret domestic texts.

5.3 CONCLUSION

As a prelude to this conclusion, it is necessary to reiterate that this chapter aimed to introduce the case law that will be analysed in further detail in subsequent chapters. It provided a systematic analysis of the jurisprudence of international and national courts and tribunals to put into light how they conceive, and use, the principle of prevention. The multiplicity of cases that have relied on prevention is evidence of the increasingly important role played by the norm in international law, including in branches that are not strictly driven by an environmental rationale. Since the ICJ's first recognition of the customary nature of Stockholm Principle 21, the role of international courts and tribunals in clarifying the scope of prevention has increased exponentially. The rise of environmental adjudication is evidence of a change in how environmental harm is conceived by States that increasingly consider it to be a matter than can be (and is worth being) adjudicated and by individuals who seek to assert their right to live on a sustainable planet. It gives courts and tribunals the opportunity to bring further clarity to prevention, hence playing a central role in consolidating its three definitional traits that will be presented in Part III.

211 Nijman and Nollkaemper (eds), 'Introduction', 11.

CONCLUSION TO PART II

ON THE SOURCES OF PREVENTION

Prevention is the driving rationale upon which international law in the field of environmental protection has developed. It is hence unsurprising that its normative impacts are widespread and varied. Part II was based on the premise that prevention acts as a legal principle that guides the whole branch of international environmental law and sought to understand how prevention manifests, and is conceptualized, in conventional, customary and case law. It did not provide a systematic analysis of the sources of prevention *stricto sensu* because of the multiple forms taken by prevention that make such assessment challenging. The main difficulty relates to correctly identifying, and distinguishing, the source of prevention in a certain form and not to assimilate together the sources of different manifestations of prevention. Questions raised include: Can the jurisprudential recognition of no-harm in a case of air pollution be used as the source of a more general obligation to prevent? Does the wide recognition of the customary character of the obligation to avoid harm in areas beyond national jurisdiction act as the source of an obligation to protect the atmosphere? Can the sources of prevention in its environmental form be used to justify a preventive norm in a disaster context? A difficult balance needs to be found between a conservative approach that refuses to recognize a source that does not match the exact scope of a specific manifestation of prevention, disregarding the fact that the norm might have evolved on the basis of this very source, and a liberal approach that considers together all the sources of prevention, irrespective of its manifestations, without any distinction.

Beyond the question of how to match the correct sources to the appropriate manifestation of prevention, it is clear that the principle relies heavily on sources that do not necessarily fit well with traditional theories of sources that rely on the sacrosanct Article 38 of the Statute of the ICJ.[1] In particular, one of the major sources of prevention (in addition to conventional law) is found in the formally non–legally binding documents not mentioned in Article 38, commonly referred to as 'soft law'. The central role played by soft law in international environmental law is well documented.[2] Prevention is a prime example of this process, its consecration in the Stockholm Declaration having played a prominent role in building consensus around the norm, so much so that it was in this form that the ICJ recognized its customary character.[3] Soft law plays an important role in relation to prevention not only in the form of political declarations but also as technical documents that set standards that can be relied upon when exercising due diligence.[4] In addition, prevention challenges the traditional understanding associated with the sources of international law found in Article 38. Part II has shown that formal approaches to custom, based on a two-element test, are inadequate to explain the wide recognition that prevention enjoys as a norm of international customary law despite discrepancies in actual practice. Chapter 5 also showed that the decisions of international courts and tribunals do not merely play the 'subsidiary' role assigned by Article 38, as evidenced by constant references to the case law, with a strong dependence on the canonical *Trail Smelter*, to justify the customary status of prevention. In addition, due-diligence duties rely heavily on international courts and tribunals to assess, on a case by case basis, whether the duty of care has been met, giving them a more important role than initially envisaged in Article 38. The difficulties that traditional theories of sources face to systematically explain the normative impacts of prevention are representative of the limitations faced by international law, and its scholarship, to make sense of the specificity of prevention (see Part III) and to provide adapted solutions to ensure that its legal effects are fully expressed (see Part IV).

1 Statute of the International Court of Justice, San Francisco, 26 June 1945, in force 24 October 1945, (1945) 39 AJIL Supp 215.

2 P-M Dupuy, 'Soft Law and the International Law of the Environment' (1990/1991) 12 *Michigan Journal of International Law* 420.

3 *Legality of the Threat or Use of Nuclear Weapons* (Advisory Opinion) (1996) ICJ Rep 226, para 29.

4 J Bendel and J Harrison, 'Determining the Legal Nature and Content of EIAs in International Environmental Law: What Does the ICJ Decision in the Joined *Costa Rica v. Nicaragua/ Nicaragua v. Costa Rica* Cases Tell Us?' (2017) 42 *Questions of International Law Zoom-in* 13, at 19.

PART III

THE THREE DEFINITIONAL DIMENSIONS OF PREVENTION

This part analyses in turn the three definitional elements of prevention in terms of its rationale, content and geographical scope, which characterize it as a positive obligation of anticipation to protect and preserve the environment. To start, Chapter 6 shows that prevention is an anticipatory principle seeking to avoid or, at least, limit risks of foreseeable environmental harm. Secondly, Chapter 7 presents prevention as an obligation of due diligence that requires States to act proactively to avoid environmental harm. Thirdly, Chapter 8 insists on the spatial scope of prevention that underlines its concern for protection of the environment as a whole, irrespective of the location of harm. Finally, Chapter 9 looks at the specificity of prevention from what can be called an 'external perspective': it investigates the relationship between prevention and other key norms of international environmental law in order to better stress the specificity of prevention vis-à-vis other norms.

6

Prevention and Risk Anticipation
The Rationale

The principle of prevention seeks to anticipate risks of environmental damage.[1] The first definitional element of prevention relates to its rationale and explicitly distinguishes it from the traditional law of State responsibility concentrating on the occurrence of harm and its reparation. This chapter presents the anticipatory rationale driving prevention by analysing, firstly, how the principle defines risks and secondly how it conceptualizes anticipation. It identifies the material scope of prevention based on a foreseeability/magnitude matrix (6.1) and its temporal scope applicable to the different stages of the creation of environmental harm (6.2).

6.1 MATERIAL SCOPE

The material scope of prevention has been envisaged in Chapter 3 to define the types of risks that the conventional principle of prevention seeks to curb. This chapter complements the analysis by focusing on the customary form of prevention and the conditions of its application, which are defined as follows: prevention applies when there is a risk of environmental harm (6.1.1) that is foreseeable (6.1.2) and of a certain magnitude (6.1.3).

6.1.1 *Environmental Harm*

Giving a definition of 'environmental harm' in order to delimit the scope of application of prevention is a difficult task given that both terms remain difficult to define.

[1] The etymological origin of the term 'prevention' – from the Latin *praevention*, 'the action of anticipating and forestalling' – is itself evidence of the anticipatory approach of prevention.

6.1.1.1 The Definition of 'Environment'

Trying to define 'environment', 'a term that everyone understands but no one is able to define',[2] is a Sisyphean task. The definition provided by the experts' report of the World Commission on Development and Environment, establishing that 'the environment is where we all live',[3] corroborated by the definition of the *Oxford English Dictionary* that defines the environment as '[t]he set of circumstances or conditions, especially physical conditions, in which a person or community lives, works, develops, etc, or a thing exists or operates'[4] best exemplifies the difficulty that arises when trying to define an element that supports our livelihoods but which fundamentally escapes our understanding. Interestingly, the environment is not defined in the ILC Articles on the Prevention of Transboundary Harm from Hazardous Activities (ILC Prevention Articles) but their corollary, the ILC Principles on the Allocation of Loss in the Case of Transboundary Harm Arising out of Hazardous Activities (ILC Allocation of Loss Principles). The Allocation of Loss Principles adopted a broad definition of the environment, defined as including 'natural resources, both abiotic and biotic, such as air, water, soil, fauna and flora and the interaction between the same factors, and the characteristic aspects of the landscape'.[5] Overall, how the environment is defined is consequential, as it outlines the applicable scope of the principle of prevention. The broader the definition of the environment is, both in terms of its content (i.e. including non-service values) and its spatial scope (i.e. adopting an ecosystemic approach), the more extensive prevention will be.

6.1.1.2 The Definition of 'Harm'

The term 'harm' is often used interchangeably with other concepts and most notably with 'damage'.[6] The ILC attempted to differentiate between the two terms, using the concept of 'harm' to refer to the threat to the legally protected interests of other States and 'damage' as describing their actual

2 L Caldwell, *International Environment Policy: Emergence and Dimensions* (2nd edn, Duke University Press 1990) 170.

3 RD Munro and J Lammers (eds), *Environmental Protection and Sustainable Development: Legal Principles and Recommendations Adopted by the Experts Group on Environmental Law of the World Commission on Environment and Development* (Graham & Trotman 1987) xi.

4 L Brown (ed), *The Shorter Oxford English Dictionary on Historical Principles* (4th edn, Clarendon/Oxford 1993) 832.

5 ILC, 'Draft Principles on the Allocation of Loss in the Case of Transboundary Harm Arising Out of Hazardous Activities (with Commentaries)' (2006) UN Doc. A/63/10, Principle 2(b).

6 ILC, 'Fourth Report of the Special Rapporteur, Mr James Crawford, on State responsibility' (2001) UN Doc. A/CN.4/517 and Add.1, para 30.

infringement.[7] This study has thus followed the same approach, although it recognizes that, in practice, the distinction is not always clear-cut.

The 'environment' is often defined by international law only with the view to identifying the damage that it might suffer; as a result, the environment is generally demarcated in terms of the impacts that a human activity might have on it.[8] In other words, the definition of 'environment' is reliant on the meaning given to 'harm'. The ILC Prevention Articles do not per se define 'harm' but consider it applicable to 'harm caused to persons, property or the environment'.[9] This provision must be read in the light of Article 1, which limits the scope of the preventive duty in the ILC Prevention Articles to 'physical consequences'. It therefore does not cover 'transboundary harm which may be caused by State policies in monetary, socioeconomic or similar fields'.[10] This limitation of the nature of harm is explained in the commentary as an attempt to keep the codification work within manageable bounds,[11] which means that prevention in its customary form is not necessarily equally limited. The distinction has practical implications because it means that other types of harm, such as policies that restrict access to low-carbon technology in other countries, might fall under the remit of prevention.

6.1.2 *Foreseeability*

The principle of prevention is only concerned with risks of environmental harm that meet certain criteria and does not simply address any type of risk. The ILC Prevention Articles provide guidance about the circumstances in which a customary duty of prevention applies. They apply to activities with a 'risk of causing significant transboundary harm'. This is further defined as activities that present a high probability of causing significant transboundary harm or a low probability of causing disastrous transboundary harm.[12] In other

7 ILC, 'Draft Principles on the Allocation of Loss', Commentary to Principle 1, para 11, at 120.

8 Convention on Environmental Impact Assessment in a Transboundary Context, Espoo, 25 February 1991, in force 10 September 1997, (1991) 30 ILM 802, Article 1(vii); Convention on the Law of the Non-Navigational Uses of International Watercourses, New York, 21 May 1997, in force 17 August 2014, (1997) 36 ILM 700, Article 1(2).

9 ILC, 'Draft Articles on Prevention of Transboundary Harm from Hazardous Activities (with Commentaries)' (2001) *Yearbook of the International Law Commission* (vol II, part 2) 148, Article 2(b); confirmed in ILC, 'Draft Principles on the Allocation of Loss', Principle 2(a).

10 ILC, 'Draft Articles on Prevention of Transboundary Harm', Commentary to Article 1, para 16, at 151.

11 ILC, 'Draft Articles on Prevention of Transboundary Harm', Commentary to Article 1, para 16, at 151.

12 ILC, 'Draft Articles on Prevention of Transboundary Harm', Commentary to Article 1, para 16, at 151, Article 2(a) and Commentary to Article 2, para 3, at 152.

words, the significance of the risk is assessed on the basis of two elements, which are usually considered to be definitional of the term 'risk': (1) the probability that the risk will materialize and (2) the magnitude of harm that may be caused.[13] The first element, concentrating on known consequences, distinguishes prevention from precaution, which is applicable when harm is unforeseeable due to scientific uncertainty. The second element makes prevention applicable only in circumstances where harm is foreseen to be 'significant', which is understood as meaning more than 'detectable' but not necessarily serious or substantial.[14] The challenges related to the practice of assessing the foreseeability and magnitude are discussed at further stages of this study (respectively, in Sections 6.1.3 and 9.1.2). Following the matrix, if the likelihood and the impact of the activity are expected to be low, the risk is deemed acceptable; on the contrary, if the likelihood and the impact are expected to be high, the planned activity should not go ahead. The obligation to take preventive measures to avoid or manage risks applies when there is a high likelihood of low impact or a low likelihood of high impact.[15] The ILC Prevention Articles restrict the scope of prevention by apparently leaving out medium-risk situations, for instance, when there is an average probability of medium impacts. Nevertheless, these situations are not necessarily excluded from the scope of prevention: the commentaries only specifically excluded activities with a very low probability of causing significant transboundary harm and made clear that the definition given to the expression 'risk of causing significant transboundary harm' provides a 'spectrum within which the activities under these articles will fall'.[16]

In addition to framing the applicable scope of the customary duty of prevention, the matrix provided by the ILC Prevention Articles facilitates treaty interpretation. One application of the ILC's framework can be found in the 'Integrated Framework and Guidelines for avoiding, mitigating and

[13] ILC, 'Draft Articles on Prevention of Transboundary Harm'; see also Munro and Lammers (eds), *Legal Principles and Recommendations Adopted by the Experts Group on Environmental Law of the World Commission on Environment and Development*, at 78.

[14] ILC, 'Draft Articles on Prevention of Transboundary Harm', Commentary to Article 2, para 4, at 152.

[15] This includes a low probability of creating disastrous harm, such as risks related to nuclear energy production; see Convention on Environmental Impact Assessment in a Transboundary Context, Implementation Committee, 'Findings and Recommendations Further to a Committee Initiative concerning the United Kingdom of Great Britain and Northern Ireland (EIA/IC/CI/5)', in 'Report of the Implementation Committee on Its Thirty–Fifth Session' (2016) ECE/MP.EIA/IC/2016/2, para 51.

[16] ILC, 'Draft Articles on Prevention of Transboundary Harm', Commentary to Article 2, para 4, at 152.

compensating for wetland losses of the Convention on Wetlands of International Importance Especially as Waterfowl Habitat'[17] (adopted as a decision of the Conference of the Parties). In the form of a table, the Integrated Framework and Guidelines explain the circumstances under which the obligation to prevent or mitigate environmental risks to wetlands of international importance is applicable. While not explicitly recognized as such, it mirrors Article 2(a) of the ILC Prevention Articles; it provides that States are under an obligation to avoid or manage risk in cases where risk is low but the impact likely to be high and in cases where risk is high but the impact low. The table also makes clear that there is a need to 'avoid, redirect or significantly modify plans/activities' if the likelihood of harm and the impact are high. By contrast, it also indicates that risk of a low likelihood and impact is acceptable but should mitigated and monitored. This implicit reference to the ILC Prevention Articles illustrates the potential role played by the articles in guiding the interpretation of a treaty that does not specify the circumstances under which the preventive duty would apply.

6.1.3 *Magnitude*

The likelihood/impact matrix found in the ILC Prevention Articles that defines risk and harm together may seem to leave uncertain the issue of whether prevention is concerned with harm or with the risk of harm. The two are closely related, and disentangling them is a challenge. Admittedly, the ultimate objective of prevention is to avoid the occurrence of damage – as presented in the title of the ILC Prevention Articles on the 'prevention of transboundary *harm* from hazardous activities'. However, as discussed further in Chapter 7, the fulfilment of the due-diligence obligation of prevention is solely assessed on the basis of whether the State has taken sufficient action against the *risk* presented by an activity and not on the basis of whether damage has occurred.[18]

The intricate relation between harm and risk is best reflected in the magnitude criteria set by the ILC Prevention Articles, which reveal the close connection between no-harm (and its concern for damage) and prevention (and its focus on risk). The magnitude of harm that is prohibited under customary

17 Convention on Wetlands of International Importance Especially as Waterfowl Habitat, Conference of the Parties, Resolution XI.9, 'An Integrated Framework and Guidelines for avoiding, mitigating and compensating for wetland losses' (2012).

18 ILC, 'Draft Articles on Prevention of Transboundary Harm', Commentary to Article 3, para 7, at 154.

international law is recognized to be that of 'significant' harm.[19] Treaty practice remains rather heterogeneous, with variations in treaty provisions depending on the accepted level of harm, but 'significant' is widely regarded as the threshold which, in the absence of another specified threshold, determines the permissibility of harm.[20] The presence of the significant threshold, which originates from the no-harm rule, in the assessment of risk anchors prevention into a Westphalian rationale. The threshold seeks to preserve the sovereign right of the State to use its resources while ensuring that interference with other sovereign entities is avoided; as a result, not all instances of damage resulting from activities within a State's territory are unlawful, and minimal harm should be tolerated.[21] A realistic criterion in a Westphalian system, it can, however, be ill adapted when it comes to protecting the global commons or assessing cumulative harm.

The threshold operates at two levels: it acts ex post by contributing to the determination of the wrongfulness of damage and ex ante by assessing the level of risk that triggers the obligation of prevention.[22] The assessment of the

[19] ILC, 'Draft Articles on Prevention of Transboundary Harm', Commentary to Article 2, para 3, at 152. See also *Iron Rhine Railway (Belgium v. Netherlands)*, Permanent Court of Arbitration, (2005) 27 RIAA 35, para 222; *Pulp Mills on the River Uruguay* (*Argentina v. Uruguay*) (Judgment) (2010) ICJ Rep 14, para 101; *Indus Waters Kishenganga Arbitration (Pakistan v. India)*, Permanent Court of Arbitration, Partial Award, 18 February 2013, para 451; Final Award, 20 December 2013, para 112; *Construction of a Road in Costa Rica along the San Juan River (Nicaragua v. Costa Rica)* (Judgment) (2015) ICJ Rep 665, para 118, 217. Although there is currently a consensus on the 'significant' threshold, the earlier jurisprudence had dealt with other thresholds; see *Trail Smelter (United States v. Canada)* (16 April 1938 and 11 March 1941), (1941) 3 RIAA 1905 at 1965, on 'serious consequence[s]'; *Lac Lanoux (France v. Spain)*, (1957) 12 RIAA 281, at 293, on the prohibition to 'seriously' prejudice a neighbouring State.

[20] See *inter alia* Convention for the Protection of the Ozone Layer, Vienna, 22 March 1985, in force 22 September 1988, (1985) 26 ILM 1529, Article 1(2); Convention on the Regulation of Antarctic Mineral Resource Activities, Wellington, 2 June 1988, not in force, (1988) 27 ILM 868, Article 4(2); Convention on Environmental Impact Assessment in a Transboundary Context, Espoo, 25 February 1991, in force 10 September 1997, (1991) 30 ILM 802, Article 2(1)–(2); Convention on the Protection and Use of Transboundary Watercourses and International Lakes, Helsinki, 17 March 1992, in force 6 October 1996, (1992) 31 ILM 1312, Article 1(2); United Nations Framework Convention on Climate Change, New York, 9 May 1992, in force 24 March 1994, 1771 UNTS 107, Article 1(1); Convention on Biological Diversity, Nairobi, 22 May 1992, in force 29 December 1993, (1992) 31 ILM 822, Article 14(1)(a); and Convention on the Law of the Non-Navigational Uses of International Watercourses, Article 7.

[21] ILC, 'Draft Articles on Prevention of Transboundary Harm', Commentary to Article 2, paras 4–7, at 152. For a detailed discussion of the threshold applicable to prevention, see K Sachariew, 'The Definition of Thresholds of Tolerance for Transboundary Environmental Injury under International Law: Development and Present Status' (1990) 37 *Netherlands International Law Review* 193.

[22] O McIntyre, *Environmental Protection of International Watercourses under International Law* (Ashgate 2007) 95.

threshold will differ, depending on the context in which it is made, either ex post or ex ante. The threshold will be lower when assessing whether the conditions triggering prevention were met given that the objective is not to determine wrongfulness but rather to anticipate damage. In this context, as explained by Judge ad hoc Dugard in *Certain Activities/Construction of a Road*, it is not 'the high standard for determining whether significant transboundary harm has been caused but the lower standard of risk assessment' that is applicable.[23] However, the Court is yet to develop a specific methodology for such assessment: while in *Certain Activities* it did so on the mere basis of expert evidence, which it considered to be unconvincing in proving the significance of the risk,[24] it undertook a more 'scrupulous' analysis[25] in *Construction of a Road*, where it set out three factors upon which to undertake the assessment of risk (project's nature, magnitude and context).[26]

The variability of the assessment of the threshold depending on whether the perspective is ex post or ex ante is also reflected in preventive obligations that do not reference a threshold at all, such as Article 192 of UNCLOS and Article 20 of the UN Convention on the Law of the Non-Navigational Uses of International Watercourses. The provisions share commonalities with the obligation to adhere to a 'high level of environmental protection' found under EU law[27] that requires States to make their best efforts to protect the environment without explicitly referring to the existence of a threshold.[28] The absence of a threshold appears to imply that the de minimis harm underpinned by a Westphalian logic might not be considered acceptable for environmental purposes: the wording of these obligations reflects a clear move away from no-harm to prevention. However, it would not be appropriate to say that in the case of a dispute between two States, such provisions would not be interpreted in light of the significant threshold when determining the wrongfulness of the action. The interpretation of these provisions is therefore context

23 *Certain Activities/Construction of a Road*, separate opinion of Judge ad hoc Dugard, para 19.

24 *Certain Activities/Construction of a Road*, para 105.

25 *Certain Activities/Construction of a Road*, separate opinion of Judge ad hoc Dugard, paras 20–35.

26 *Certain Activities/Construction of a Road*, para 155.

27 Single European Act, Luxembourg/The Hague, 17 February 1986 and 28 February 1986, in force 1 July 1987, (1987) OJ L 169, Article 100A(3); Treaty on European Union, Maastricht, 7 February 1992, in force 1 November 1993, (1992) OJ C 191, Article 130R(2); Treaty on the Functioning of the European Union, Lisbon, 13 December 2007, in force 1 December 2009, OJ C 83 (30 March 2010), Article 191(2).

28 D Misonne, 'The Importance of Setting a Target: The EU Ambition of a High Level of Protection' (2015) 4 *Transnational Environmental Law* 11; A Epiney, 'Environmental Principles', in R Macrory (ed), *Reflections on 30 Years of EU Environmental Law: A High Level of Protection?* (Europa Law Publishing 2006) 17–39.

dependent. On the one hand, if the provision is interpreted from an ex ante perspective, the lack of threshold should encourage States to achieve the highest level of protection possible irrespective of external impacts. On the other hand, if the provision is interpreted from an ex post perspective, it can be interpreted in light of the significant threshold to ensure that a minimal level of harm remains tolerated.

Determination of the threshold (either ex post or ex ante) can raise considerable difficulties.[29] If the existence of the obligation to prevent harm is rarely contested, the issue of whether the significant threshold that triggers preventive obligations has been met is, on the other hand, often disputed.[30] The practice of international tribunals in determining the magnitude of harm has varied; for instance, while the ICJ has taken a factual approach, relying heavily on expert evidence to assess the level of harm suffered (if any),[31] the *South China Sea* arbitral tribunal favoured a legal interpretation to determine the admissibility of the level of harm, which it assessed on the basis of conventional provisions.[32] Irrespective of the preferred approach, determination of the threshold should pay special attention to several factors. Firstly, the threshold should take into consideration the fragility of the environment, and as such, the interpretation of the 'significant' threshold will be lower if the environment suffering negative impacts is more fragile.[33] The fragility of the environment was a factor in the reasoning of the UNCC panel that considered not only the extent of the damage but also other factors such as 'the location and nature of the damage and its actual or potential effects on the environment'.[34] The UNCC justified its approach as follows:

29 See e.g. J Knox, 'Myth and Reality of Transboundary Environmental Impact Assessment' (2002) 96 *American Journal of International Law* 291, at 294; N Craik, *The International Law of Environmental Impact Assessment: Process, Substance and Integration* (Cambridge University Press 2008) 61.

30 See e.g. *Certain Activities/Construction of a Road*, as presented in Section 5.1.1.

31 *Certain Activities/Construction of a Road, inter alia* paras 119, 203–7.

32 *South China Sea Arbitration (The Republic of the Philippines v. The People's Republic of China)* (Permanent Court of Arbitration), Award on the Merits, 12 July 2016, *inter alia* para 941, interpreting UNCLOS Article 192 in light of previous jurisprudence on the duty to prevent significant harm.

33 Convention on Environmental Impact Assessment in a Transboundary Context, 'Specific Methodologies and Criteria to Determine the Significance of Adverse Transboundary Impact: Report by the Secretariat', CEP/WG.3/R.6 (20 January 1995), Annex III, para 2(iii).

34 United Nations Compensation Commission, Governing Council, 'Report and Recommendations Made by the Panel of Commissioners Concerning the First Instalment of "F4" Claims, Third Report', S/AC.26/2003/31 (18 December 2003), para 36. The UNCC panel failed to recognize the malleability of the threshold and as a result decided to refer to the criteria of reasonableness. However, it can be considered that the significant threshold is not only interested in the extent of the damage but also includes considerations of reasonableness.

> Thus, for example, where damage that might otherwise be characterized as 'insignificant' is caused to an area of special ecological sensitivity, or where the damage, in conjunction with other factors, poses a risk of further or more serious environmental harm, it may not be unreasonable to take remediation measures in order to prevent or minimize potential additional damage.[35]

The ILC concurred with this perspective in relation to its work on aquifers, a particularly fragile environmental medium. The commentaries to the ILC Aquifers Articles noted that the 'significant' threshold is a 'flexible and relative concept. Factual considerations, rather than a legal determination, have to be taken into account in each specific case, in this case also bearing in mind the fragility of aquifers'.[36] Thus, the flexibility of the term 'significant' – deemed adequate to accommodate different circumstances – is fundamental. The evaluation of what constitutes 'significant' harm varies depending on the object that is likely to be harmed. As a result, one would expect that harm to an aquifer would be more easily considered to be 'significant' in light of its fragility compared to harm to a watercourse, for instance. The ICJ, in *Certain Activities/ Construction of a Road*, has been more hesitant to integrate fragility as a factor in its assessment of the significant threshold. In *Construction of a Road*, it recognized that the proximity of Ramsar-protected wetlands near the construed road 'heightens the risk of significant damage because it denotes that the receiving environment is particularly sensitive',[37] but in *Certain Activities*, it paid very little attention to the involvement of a Ramsar advisory mission to report on potential impacts of the dredging programme on the hydrology, taking Nicaragua's word that impacts in the area had been correctly assessed.[38] The difference in treatment between the two situations is perhaps explained by the fact that road construction is considered by the Convention on Environmental Impact Assessment in a Transboundary Context (although not applicable in the cas d'espèce) as an activity automatically triggering an EIA obligation, whereas river dredging is not.[39] The distinction used by the ICJ nevertheless leaves significant uncertainties about whether the fragility of an environmental medium lowers the threshold.

35 UNCC, 'Third Report 2003'.

36 ILC, 'Draft Articles on the Law of Transboundary Aquifers (with Commentaries)' (2008) *Yearbook of the International Law Commission* (vol II, part 2) 27, Commentary to Article 6, para 3, at 47. And confirmed in ILA, Committee on Ground Water Resources, 'Final Report', Rio de Janeiro, 73th Session, 2008, at 12.

37 *Certain Activities/Construction of a Road*, para 155.

38 *Certain Activities/Construction of a Road*, para 103.

39 Convention on Environmental Impact Assessment in a Transboundary Context, Espoo, 25 February 1991, in force 10 September 1997, (1991) 30 ILM 802, Appendix I.

Secondly, the 'significant' threshold is likely to be more easily reached if an activity not only has an impact on the environment but also has negative effects on human beings. Indeed, as mentioned earlier, the ILC Prevention Articles define harm not only as affecting the environment but also 'persons'. Although the articles do not make this explicit, it is likely that harm affecting human beings, their safety and health, and not just the environment will meet the 'significant' threshold more easily. Going further, one way to interpret the permissibility of harm in light of the threshold would be to take into account the effects of harm on present generations and also on future generations, a scenario analysed in Chapter 9.[40]

A final element that could contribute to determining the significance of harm is the environmental standards applicable in the country of origin.[41] This involves the application of a regionally recognized norm (within the OECD), the non-discrimination principle,[42] according to which a State should give equal treatment to the transboundary effects of its activities as it does to the domestic effects. It can be consequential when States have adopted domestic legislative and administrative measures that are more ambitious than what is required under international law. In this context, less than significant transboundary harm could be deemed illegal: if that level of harm is not acceptable in the State of origin, it cannot be imposed on the affected State either. Although the principle remains a regional one, it nevertheless hints to the fact that, more generally, the threshold will be interpreted in light of each country's tolerance for environmental degradation.

Overall, the raison d'être of the threshold should drive its determination. The objective of the threshold is to ensure that minor environmental harm is tolerated, while its vagueness guarantees that different factors are taken into account to determine the acceptability of the damage on a case-by-case basis. What is important is not so much the term used to qualify the threshold than

40 See Section 9.2.3.

41 Convention on Environmental Impact Assessment in a Transboundary Context, 'Specific methodologies and criteria', para 2(i).

42 OECD, 'Recommendation of the Council on Principles concerning Transfrontier Pollution' C(74)224 (14 November 1974); 'Recommendation of the Council for the Implementation of a Regime of Equal Right of Access and Non-Discrimination in Relation to Transfrontier Pollution' C(77)28 (17 May 1977); 'Recommendation of the Council for Strengthening International Co-operation on Environmental Protection in Frontier Regions' C(78)77 (21 September 1978); 'Recommendation on the Assessment of Projects with Significant Impact on the Environment' C(79)116 (8 May 1979). See also Nordic Convention on the Protection of the Environment, Stockholm, 19 February 1974, in force 5 October 1976, (1974) 13 ILM 511, Article 2.

the idea that harm that is beyond reasonable is prohibited. This was the approach followed by the *South China Sea* tribunal: the 'significant' threshold played a minimal role in the interpretation of UNCLOS Article 192. While the tribunal made passing references to the existence of such 'significant' damage based on expert evidence,[43] it did not undertake a factual assessment of whether the threshold was met, nor did it explicitly justify its reference to 'significant', just mentioning in passing previous jurisprudential decisions[44] and existing obligations that include such a reference.[45] The tribunal made sure, on the basis of scientific evidence, that harm was not de minimis but did not engage in a factual assessment of the level of harm. In relation to construction activities, it considered that damage has been done given the 'scale and impact of the island-building activities'[46]; in relation to marine species, it merely took the position that the harvesting of species threatened with extinction 'constitute[s] a harm to the marine environment as such'.[47] The *South China Sea* award therefore put in evidence that the assessment of the significant threshold, which is sometimes seen as an intractable issue, is not necessarily an insurmountable challenge in the context of adjudication.

6.2 TEMPORAL SCOPE

Having presented the material scope of prevention, we now turn to its temporal scope by investigating the legal translation of the notion of 'anticipation', commonly understood as the forestalling of an event.[48] Prevention is applicable in the context of three timeframes[49]: 'imminence', defined as the time when the likelihood of the occurrence of harm can be assessed (6.2.1); 'emergency', concerned with avoiding harm that is almost certain to operate in a very near future (6.2.2); and 'response', operating after the occurrence of harm and concerned with avoiding further harm (6.2.3). Irrespective of the temporal scope within which it operates, prevention remains an obligation of continuous risk anticipation (6.2.4).

43 *South China Sea Arbitration*, paras 903, 923 and 979.

44 *South China Sea Arbitration*, para 941, quoting the *Kishenganga* and *Iron Rhine* disputes.

45 *South China Sea Arbitration*, paras 947 and 961, referencing Article 206 on assessments in the case of 'substantial pollution or of significant and harmful changes'.

46 *South China Sea Arbitration*, para 988.

47 *South China Sea Arbitration*, para 960.

48 Brown, *Shorter Oxford English Dictionary on Historical Principles*, 88.

49 For an in-depth analysis of the different times of anticipation, see MM Mbengue, *Essai sur une théorie du risque en droit international public: l'anticipation du risque environnemental et sanitaire* (Pedone 2009) 29–116.

6.2.1 *Imminence*

The boundaries of the anticipatory rationale of prevention are not defined within an explicit timeframe, but it can be considered that prevention operates in the realm of 'imminence' (not to be confused with 'urgency', discussed in Section 6.2.2). The term is not defined by temporality per se but rather by likelihood or, in other words, by the timeframe in which the likelihood of harm occurrence can be assessed. This was put in evidence by European Directive 2004/35/CE, which considered that when there is a 'sufficient likelihood that environmental damage will occur in the near future', it should be considered an 'imminent' threat.[50] Although the reference to the 'near future' seems to establish temporal restrictions, it is in effect conditional on whether the probability of the occurrence of harm can be assessed. This understanding of the term 'imminent' was also articulated by the ICJ in *Gabčíkovo-Nagymaros*. While the Court was referring to imminence to justify a state of necessity, its reasoning is equally applicable in the context of prevention. In the Court's opinion, 'a "peril" appearing in the long-term might be held to be "imminent" as soon as it is established, at the relevant point in time, that the realization of that peril, however far off it might be, is not thereby any less certain and inevitable'.[51] In sum, the 'imminence' of the threat is linked to the probability of the threat occurring rather than to its closeness, in terms of timing, to the present.

As a result, the preventive rationale can equally be expressed in norms operating within a short- or long-term perspective. This is particularly evident in the Paris Agreement to the UNFCCC (Paris Agreement), where the preventive rationale manifests via two different temporalities: a short-term procedural obligation, which requires States to submit a nationally determined contribution every five years communicating their emissions-reduction targets,[52] and a long-term objective, which calls on States to aim to achieve a carbon-neutral world within the second half of the twenty-first century.[53] The advances in science and modelling in predicting environmental damage over a longer period of time have lengthened the temporal scope of prevention. In the climate regime, the 'near future' spans over the full twenty-first century, the time span covered by climate science and

[50] Directive 2004/35/CE of the European Parliament and of the Council of 21 April 2004 on environmental liability with regard to the prevention and remedying of environmental damage, (2004) OJ L 143, Article 2(9).

[51] *Gabčíkovo-Nagymaros Project (Hungary/Slovakia)* (Judgment) (1997) ICJ Rep 7, para 54.

[52] Paris Agreement to the United Nations Framework Convention on Climate Change, Paris, 12 December 2015, in force 4 November 2016, Doc. FCCC/CP/2015/10/Add.1, Article 4(9).

[53] Paris Agreement, Article 4(1).

modelling.[54] Climate change is thus considered an imminent threat irrespective of the fact that some damage might only materialize in several decades.

6.2.2 *Emergency*

Prevention is concerned not only with risk that is imminent but also with risk that might be urgent. Such a situation might arise in circumstances where the risk was not foreseeable over a longer time period or in the event that preventive measures were not taken or failed to achieve their objective. The principle of prevention hence also includes a specific duty to avoid environmental emergencies, both natural[55] and manmade,[56] and posing threats to the territory of a single State,[57] other States,[58] and areas beyond national jurisdiction.[59]

The principle of prevention in an emergency situation has specificities intrinsic to its temporal scope but nevertheless shares common characteristics with the general principle of prevention. In particular, while the temporal sphere within which prevention operates is more immediate, foreseeability remains one of its core definitional elements. The ILC, in the context of its Prevention Articles, made clear that 'suddenness does not denote that the situation needs to be wholly unexpected'[60] and that, as a result, States were under an obligation to anticipate emergencies by developing contingency plans[61] and operating early warning systems.[62] The preventive principle still

54 Intergovernmental Panel on Climate Change, *Fifth Assessment Report: Summary for Policy-Makers* (2014), see *inter alia* para 2.2: 'Surface temperature is projected to rise over the 21st century under all assessed emission scenarios.'

55 Rio de Janeiro Declaration on Environment and Development (Rio de Janeiro, 3–14 June 1992), (1992) 31 ILM 876, Principle 18.

56 See e.g. Convention on Early Notification of a Nuclear Accident, Vienna, 26 September 1986, in force 27 October 1986, (1986) 25 ILM 1370; Convention on the Transboundary Effects of Industrial Accidents, Helsinki, 17 March 1992, in force 19 April 2000, (1992) 31 ILM 1330.

57 ILC, 'Draft Articles on the Protection of Persons in the Event of Disasters (with Commentaries)' (2016) *Yearbook of the International Law Commission* (vol II, part 2), Article 9.

58 ILC, 'Draft Articles on Prevention of Transboundary Harm', Article 16; Rio Declaration, Principle 18.

59 *Responsibilities and Obligations of States Sponsoring Persons and Entities with respect to Activities in the Area*, ITLOS No. 17, Advisory Opinion (1 February 2011), para 138 (on the basis of the nodules and sulphides regulations).

60 ILC, 'Draft Articles on Prevention of Transboundary Harm', Commentary to Article 17, para 2, at 169.

61 ILC, 'Draft Articles on Prevention of Transboundary Harm', Article 16.

62 Rio Declaration, Principle 18; ILC, 'Draft Articles on Prevention of Transboundary Harm', Article 17; and ILC, 'Draft Articles on the Protection of Persons in the Event of Disasters', Article 9(2).

applies even in situations when there is very limited time to act (ranging from a few days to a few minutes). That said, the timeframe in which to take action to avoid harm is so limited that preventive measures mostly aim to mitigate, and not avoid, harm. This is particularly visible in disaster law, which intersects very closely with emergency prevention given the short temporal scope within which a disaster usually emerges. While the ILC rapporteur on the protection of persons in the event of disasters had proposed an article on the 'duty to prevent'[63] disaster risks, a more pragmatic approach to prevention was preferred: a 'duty to reduce the risk of disasters' was eventually adopted.[64] In the case of a disaster, harm can hardly be avoided all together, but it can nevertheless be reduced. In this sense, the obligation to prevent disasters is opening the door to the third timeframe of prevention: response.

6.2.3 *Response*

When the first two stages of prevention (imminence and urgency) have failed, the principle remains relevant to avoid further harm. It can be counterintuitive, as some authors have not failed to note,[65] to argue that an anticipatory obligation spreads its effects *after* the damage has occurred. However, given ongoing environmental degradation, prevention operates most commonly to minimize further harm (6.2.3.1), as the climate regime best exemplifies (6.2.3.2).

6.2.3.1 The Rationale of Ex Post Anticipation

Conventional law often refers to preventive obligations in the form of obligations to control, eliminate, reduce, minimize or mitigate environmental harm,[66] sometimes combining the different terms. The difference in meaning

63 ILC, 'Sixth Report of the Special Rapporteur, Mr Eduardo Valencia-Ospina, on the protection of persons in the event of disasters' (2013) UN Doc. A/CN.4/662, para 164.

64 ILC, 'Draft Articles on the Protection of Persons in the Event of Disasters', Article 9.

65 N de Sadeeler, 'Les principes comme instruments d'une plus grande cohérence et d'une effectivité accrue du droit de l'environnement', in F Ost and S Gutwirth (eds), *Quel avenir pour le droit de l'environnement?* (Publications des Facultés universitaires Saint-Louis 1996) 239–59, at 245. See also the initial reluctance of the ILC to recognize the existence of a concept of prevention ex post: ILC, 'Twelfth Report of the Special Rapporteur, Mr Julio Barboza, on the Topic of Liability for Injurious Consequences of Acts Not Prohibited by International Law' (1996) UN Doc. A/CN.4/475, para 1.

66 See, e.g., United Nations Convention on the Law of the Sea, Montego Bay, 10 December 1982, in force 16 November 1994, 1833 UNTS 3, Article 194; UNFCCC, Article 3(3); Convention on Environmental Impact Assessment in a Transboundary Context, Article 2(1); Convention on Biological Diversity, Article 14; Convention on the Transboundary Effects of Industrial Accidents, Article 3(1).

between these terms is perhaps less important than the fact that they are more appropriate than a reference to prevention *tout court*, which wrongly implies that the obligation only applies to harm that has not yet materialized. But prevention, driven by its due-diligence character, is more concerned with the risk than with the occurrence of the harmful event per se. In a world where environmental degradation is omnipresent,[67] it is often acknowledged that environmental risks cannot be fully eliminated,[68] and as a result, prevention more often than not enters into play when harm has already occurred.[69]

The anticipatory outlook is nevertheless still present, given that prevention continues to apply as a mechanism for addressing environmental damage subsequent to a harmful event. In keeping with the rules on State responsibility, the obligation to prevent is a continuous one that 'extends over the entire period during which the [harmful] event continues and remains not in conformity with that obligation'.[70] International courts and tribunals have acknowledged this reality by referring to the obligation to prevent environmental damage together with the obligation to mitigate,[71] understood as a duty to stop the continuation of harm already caused and reduce the risk of future damage.

The ex post manifestation of prevention tests the limits of the preventive rationale and its relationship with the curative approach in opposition to which it emerged. Although mitigation (and related concepts) is very close to the boundary that separates the preventive and curative rationales, it falls under the umbrella of prevention and therefore should be distinguished from compensation. A quotation from ILC Special Rapporteur Murase illustrates the complexity of prevention due to its origins (in part in the curative rationale) and its effects (mitigation rather than full prevention):

> As a corollary of the *sic utere tuo* principle, the principle of prevention (obligation of States to take preventive measures) is recognized as a rule of customary international law in the context of transboundary atmospheric pollution. That principle is regarded as consisting of two different

67 UNEP, *Global Environmental Outlook 5: Environment for the Future We Want* (2012), at v.

68 ILC, 'Sixth Report of the Special Rapporteur, Mr Eduardo Valencia-Ospina', para 40.

69 UN International Strategy for Disaster Reduction, *Terminology on Disaster Risk Reduction* (UN 2009) 22, noting that '[v]ery often the complete avoidance of losses is not feasible and the task transforms to that of mitigation. Partly for this reason, the terms prevention and mitigation are sometimes used interchangeably in casual use.'

70 ILC, 'Draft Articles on Responsibility of States for Internationally Wrongful Acts (with Commentaries)' (2001) *Yearbook of the International Law Commission* (vol II, part 2) A/56/10, 31, art 14(3).

71 *Iron Rhine Railway*, para 59; *Indus Waters Kishenganga Arbitration* (Final Award), para 112, both using the same expression: 'to prevent, or at least to mitigate'.

> obligations, one being the obligation to 'prevent' before actual pollution or degradation occurs, and the other the duty to 'eliminate', 'mitigate' and 'compensate' after they have already occurred.[72]

The ghost of the ILC's initial conceptualization of prevention, in the context of its work on liability for injurious consequences of acts not prohibited by international law, is here visible; it had included prevention inside a compound primary norm providing for 'preventing, minimizing and imposing reparation for the occurrence of physical transboundary harm'.[73] It leaves no doubt that prevention is closely related to compensation – especially when considered through the spectrum of the no-harm rule manifesting here via the *sic utere tuo* principle, and in the context of mitigation when harm has already occurred, which means that a right to compensation exists. However, the ILC eventually departed from its conceptualization of prevention as a dual obliga tion, one to prevent and one to compensate, to recognize that despite their closeness, the two rationales operate in two different realms.

6.2.3.2 Temporalities of Prevention in Climate Change Law

The climate change regime offers an interesting case study of the *ratione temporis* of prevention. The study showed that prevention manifests differently depending on the harm to be avoided (see Chapter 3); such is also the case depending on the temporal scope within which it operates. The analysis that follows examines the temporal scope represented by two manifestations of prevention in climate law: mitigation and adaptation.

'Mitigation' is preferred to the term 'prevention' in climate law on the basis that climate change cannot be completely prevented given that changes in the climate are already occurring.[74] However, uncertainties arise when trying to delimit the temporal scope within which mitigation applies. Indeed, the climate regime navigates between an objective to prevent changes in the climate and an objective to avoid their impacts – a distinction that gives a different scope to the preventive rationale. The first objective considers that climate change per se is not be avoided, dictating that measures are taken well in advance to limit the intrinsic causes of the damage, and is based on the assumption that human-induced changes in the climate are

[72] ILC, 'Third Report of the Special Rapporteur, Mr Shinya Murase, on the protection of the atmosphere' (2016) UN Doc. A/CN.4/692, para 15.

[73] ILC, 'Fourth Report of the Special Rapporteur, Mr Robert Quentin-Baxter, on the Topic of Liability for Injurious Consequences of Acts Not Prohibited by International Law' (1983) UN Doc. A/CN.4/373, para 40. See Section 4.2.1 for further analysis.

[74] IPCC, *Fifth Assessment Report*, para 1.1.

detrimental to the planet. The second objective does not consider that climate change per se is problematic but considers that the effects of these changes are harmful: it is more restrictive in terms of the temporal scope and environmental objective of prevention. It is unclear whether mitigation is aimed at the effects or the causes of climate change. Originally, the UNFCCC, by providing that parties should be guided by a willingness to 'anticipate, prevent or minimise the causes of climate change and *mitigate its adverse effects*',[75] defined 'prevention' as an anticipatory obligation concerned with the causes of harm and 'mitigation' as a reactive duty focusing on the effects. However, by contrast, the Intergovernmental Panel on Climate Change (IPCC) defined 'mitigation' as the 'combined action of *preventing* the emission of greenhouse gases and *reducing* them',[76] hence directly aiming to avoid climate change by focusing on its causes. The IPCC definition of mitigation seems to have now earned widespread acceptation, as exemplified by the fact that the Paris Agreement identified climate change per se as the threat.[77]

Another term found in the climate regime also raises fundamental questions about the temporal scope of the preventive rationale in the field: the concept of adaptation. It seems that the mitigation of the effects of climate change referred to in UNFCCC Article 3(3) can now be interpreted as an obligation of what is today called 'adaptation'[78] – a concept not explicitly recognized at the time of the adoption of the convention but fully acknowledged in the Paris Agreement.[79] Adaptation is understood as the 'adjustment in natural or human systems in response to actual or expected climatic stimuli or their effects, which moderates harm or exploits beneficial opportunities'.[80]

75 UNFCCC, Article 3(3) (emphasis added). Article 3(3) reads as follows: 'The Parties should take precautionary measures to anticipate, prevent or minimize the causes of climate change and mitigate its adverse effects.' Although the article concentrates on precautionary measures, it also indirectly represents a manifestation of the prevention rationale.

76 IPCC, Working Group II, *Fourth Assessment Report: Impacts, Adaptation and Vulnerability* (2007), para 18.1.2; IPCC website, glossary, available at www.ipcc.ch/pdf/glossary/ar4-wg3.pdf (last accessed 24 August 2017), which defines 'mitigation' as follows: 'mitigation means implementing policies to reduce GHG [greenhouse gases] emissions and enhance sink'.

77 Paris Agreement to the UNFCCC, Article 2(1), providing that it aims to 'strengthen the global response to the threat of climate change'. See also UNFCCC website, glossary, available at ht tp://unfccc.int/essential_background/glossary/items/3666.php#M (last accessed 24 August 2017).

78 Corroborated by Article 7A(2) of the ILA Climate Change Principles, which reads as follows: States should 'minimise the *adverse effects* of climate change through the adoption of suitable *adaptation* measures' (emphasis added). ILA, Committee on Legal Principles Relating to Climate Change, 'Declaration of Principles Relating to Climate Change', Washington, DC, 76th Session, 2014.

79 Paris Agreement to the UNFCCC, Article 2(b).

80 UNFCCC website, glossary, available at http://unfccc.int/essential_background/glossary/ite ms/3666.php#M (last accessed 24 August 2017).

It can take various forms, ranging from improving infrastructures at the macro level to increasing the height of seawalls at the micro level. The extent to which adaptation embraces a preventive rationale remains unsettled. Adaptation can be seen as a complementary yet opposite obligation to mitigation and prevention. As a reactive measure, it is based on the realization that prevention and mitigation cannot be the sole obligations given the inevitable damage that will result from climate change. However, if one considers that climate change is per se benign unless it has an impact on human well being,[81] then adaptation embraces an anticipatory perspective, with a more restrictive vision of environmental protection nevertheless, since it only seeks to avoid harm to human infrastructures and, potentially, lives but not necessarily to the environment.

6.2.4 *Continuity*

Prevention transposes its legal effects at different stages of the formation of environmental damage. A final question that emerges from such *ratione temporis* relates to whether there is a hierarchy between the different temporal dimensions of prevention.

States are given policy space to decide on when to act to prevent harm. As long as the end result is the avoidance of harm, prevention can be implemented at different stages in the process of harm creation. For instance, in order to protect a watercourse from pollution, preventive measures could either forbid a factory from using certain hazardous products or could require the factory to recycle its polluting substances. In both cases, harm is avoided, but in the first case pollution is avoided altogether, whereas in the second case only pollution to the watercourse is avoided. General international law does not explicitly provide that harm should be avoided as close as possible to the source of creation. This is a source of divergence with EU law, which recognizes a principle of rectification of environmental damage at the source (or principle of proximity),[82] which favours measures that avoid or mitigate harm where created instead of trying to counteract the effects of pollution. By way of example, the design of vehicles that pollute less should be favoured over decisions to restrict traffic when air pollution reaches a certain level. Some international treaties follow this rationale, which is more protective of the environment. For instance, the Convention on the Control of

81 R Verheyen, *Climate Change Damage and International Law: Prevention Duties and State Responsibility* (Martinus Nijhoff 2005) 65 (interpreting Article 2 of the UNFCCC).

82 Treaty on the Functioning of the European Union, Article 191(2).

Transboundary Movements of Hazardous Wastes and Their Disposal aims to prevent transboundary pollution due to hazardous waste but also requires States to reduce the production of waste in the first place.[83] But the principle of prevention at the source cannot be said to have fully integrated international environmental law as it did in EU law, which means that prevention is more often a synonym of 'harm mitigation' than of 'harm avoidance'.

Despite the fact that three distinct temporal dimensions apply to prevention, the core logic that characterizes the principle, based on the concept of due diligence, is continuity. Rare is the damage that has a clear start and end point: environmental harm is often a continuous act, and the complexity of environmental damage calls for a continuous effort of harm prevention, reduction and elimination. As a result, prevention is not 'a one-time effort but requires continuous effort'.[84] The principle of prevention dictates that risks are assessed and monitored at regular intervals to judge whether the criteria of foreseeability and magnitude that trigger prevention are met.[85] The intractable link between prevention and monitoring is found in the call of the ICJ for 'prevention and vigilance' in the face of environmental harm.[86] It may be surprising that the Court put prevention, a customary obligation, on the same level as 'vigilance', which does not have a direct legal translation. However, with this expression, it made clear that prevention, to meet its anticipatory objective, can only be exercised by way of constant monitoring.[87] Monitoring will ensure that States take preventive measures in a 'timely fashion'.[88] It is evident that the sooner

83 Convention on the Control of Transboundary Movements of Hazardous Wastes and Their Disposal, Basel, 22 March 1989, in force 24 May 1992, (1989) 28 ILM 657, Article 4(2)(a). See also Convention on the Ban of Import into Africa and the Control of Transboundary Movement and Management of Hazardous Wastes within Africa, Bamako, 29 January 1991, in force 22 April 1998, (1991) 30 ILM 775, Articles 4(2) and 4(3)(c).

84 ILC, 'Draft Articles on Prevention of Transboundary Harm', Commentary to Article 12, para 2, at 165.

85 R Lefeber, *Transboundary Environmental Interference and the Origin of State Liability* (Kluwer Law International 1996) 34–46, distinguishing three different stages at which monitoring is applicable: (a) the planning phrase of an activity in order to assess the possible impacts of the activity, (b) the operational phrase to prevent the occurrence of significant harm during the course of operation of the activity, and (3) the termination phase, when the activity is terminated and the facilities have to be dismantled.

86 *Gabčíkovo-Nagymaros Project*, para 140; *Pulp Mills*, paras 197 and 204.

87 *Gabčíkovo-Nagymaros Project*, para 112, recognizing that environmental risks have to be assessed 'on a continuous basis'. Already, in the *Trail Smelter* case, the tribunal asked the trail smelter to monitor its activity closely by installing observation stations and equipment necessary to give collect information on emissions and to give regular reports to the tribunal. *Trail Smelter*, at 1974–77.

88 ILC, 'Draft Articles on Prevention of Transboundary Harm', Commentary to Article 3, para 10, at 154.

harm is avoided, the fewer risks it carries of creating further harm, and as a result, the better it is for the environment. The approach is particularly important in the context of ecosystem protection that requires States to act early because 'an ecosystem can be seriously threatened even though harm ... may seem remote'.[89] The possibility of an ex post application of prevention should not be used by States as an excuse to deliberately take action against environmental harm in a belated manner. As a result, timing is a factor in the assessment of the duty of care.

6.3 CONCLUSION

This chapter has shown that the first definitional element of prevention lies in its rationale pertaining to risk anticipation, a specificity that distinguishes it from the traditional reactive framework underpinning classical international law. It operates under a specific set of conditions in relation to the scope, magnitude and temporality of the harm it seeks to avoid. The question that remains is how States are, in practice, expected to implement the principle of prevention. This study hence turns to the second trait of the principle, its due-diligence nature, to identify the content of the principle.

89 SC McCaffrey, *The Law of International Watercourses* (2nd edn, Oxford University Press 2007) 461. See also *South China Sea Arbitration* (Award on the Merits), para 825, recognizing that environmental harm in a specific location can 'affect the health and viability of ecosystems elsewhere in the South China Sea'.

7

Prevention and Proactivity

Content

The second element that characterizes prevention is its due-diligence character. This means that prevention does not make all occurrences of harm unlawful[1] but is concerned with the conduct displayed by the State seeking to avoid harm.[2] The anticipatory rationale of prevention dictates a proactive approach to risk.[3] States are not merely expected to exercise restraint vis-à-vis environmental harm but also to take positive steps to protect the environment.[4] Due diligence generally requires that the State takes 'appropriate measures' to prove that it has made 'reasonable efforts' to prevent environmental harm.[5] Although the margin of interpretation left by this objective is significant, international minimum standards of good governance nevertheless constrain the conduct of the State.[6] This chapter presents prevention as an

1 ILC, 'Draft Articles on Prevention of Transboundary Harm from Hazardous Activities (with Commentaries)' (2001) *Yearbook of the International Law Commission* (vol II, part 2) 148, Commentary to Article 3, para 7, at 154.

2 ILC, 'Draft Articles on Prevention of Transboundary Harm', Commentary to Article 3, para 7, at 154. In the field of international environmental law, the fact that obligations of due diligence and obligations of conduct are connected has been recognized in *Pulp Mills on the River Uruguay (Argentina v. Uruguay)* (Judgment) (2010) ICJ Rep 14, 187; *Responsibilities and Obligations of States Sponsoring Persons and Entities with Respect to Activities in the Area*, ITLOS No. 17, Advisory Opinion (1 February 2011), para 111; *Sub-Regional Fisheries Commission*, ITLOS No. 21, Advisory Opinion (2 April 2015), para 125.

3 L Brown (ed), *Shorter Oxford English Dictionary on Historical Principles* (4th edn, Clarendon/Oxford 1993) 2361, defining 'proactive' as follows: 'creating or controlling a situation by taking the initiative or anticipating events'.

4 *South China Sea Arbitration (The Republic of the Philippines v. The People's Republic of China)* (Permanent Court of Arbitration), Award on the Merits, 12 July 2016, para 941, noting that UNCLOS Article 192 entails the 'positive obligation to take active measures'.

5 ILC, 'Draft Articles on Prevention of Transboundary Harm', Commentary to Article 3, para 10, at 154.

6 ILA, Study Group on Due Diligence in International Law, 'Second Report', Johannesburg, 77th Session, 2016, at 6.

obligation to exercise due diligence (7.1) and then identifies its content (7.2) to better understand how a State is expected to display proactivity in the context of risk anticipation.

7.1 PREVENTION AS AN OBLIGATION TO EXERCISE DUE DILIGENCE: AN INQUIRY

The nature of prevention as a due-diligence obligation raises little controversy, treaty law,[7] codification works,[8] case law[9] and the scholarship[10] all converging in this sense. Due-diligence obligations are becoming increasingly important to regulate the activities of non-State actors in a globalized world; they encourage States to prevent transboundary and global problems in a spirit of good neighbourliness. And yet, if the rationale driving due diligence is uncontroversial, its practical application has brought unresolved questions to the fore. This section starts with an introduction to due diligence in the context of environmental protection (7.1.1) and then presents some intricacies relative to the relationship between prevention and due diligence (7.1.2).

7.1.1 *Due Diligence in the Context of Environmental Protection*

The notion of due diligence in international law emerged in the nineteenth century to clarify the obligations of the State in relation to the activities of private

7 The expression used to express due diligence varies from one treaty to another and includes expressions such as 'take all measures', 'all appropriate measures', 'all necessary measures', 'to ensure'. The term 'due diligence' per se is rarely used in treaty law, often on the basis that the mentioned references are less technical and lead to less confusion regarding what is expected of the State.

8 E.g. ILC, 'Draft Articles on Prevention of Transboundary Harm', Commentary to Article 3, para 7, at 154: 'The obligation of the State of origin to take preventive or minimization measures is one of due diligence.' See also ILA, Study Group on Due Diligence in International Law, 'First Report', Washington, DC, 76th Session, 2014, at 26.

9 E.g., *Pulp Mills; Responsibilities and Obligations of States Sponsoring Persons and Entities*, para 113; *Sub-Regional Fisheries Commission*, para 129; *Certain Activities Carried out by Nicaragua in the Border Area (Costa Rica v. Nicaragua)* and *Construction of a Road in Costa Rica along the San Juan River (Nicaragua v. Costa Rica)* (Judgment) (2015) ICJ Rep 665, paras 104 and 153; *South China Sea Arbitration*, para 944.

10 E.g. H Xue, *Transboundary Damage* (Cambridge University Press 2009) chap 5; T Braz Jardim Oliveira, 'La diligence due dans la prévention des dommages à l'environnement' (2012) 2 *Brazilian Yearbook of International Law* 205; E Hey, *Advanced Introduction to International Environmental Law* (Edward Elgar 2016) 71; J Kulesza, *Due Diligence in International Law* (Brill/Martinus Nijhoff 2016); N Craik, *The International Law of Environmental Impact Assessment: Process, Substance and Integration* (Cambridge University Press 2008) 62–63.

parties. As a large number of foreigners were settling in emerging nations, it became clear that the State could not be held responsible for every private act that infringed the rights of foreigners on its territory and that a standard of protection expected from the State should be determined.[11] Given that private economic actors tend to be the first responsible for environmental harm, the same logic eventually extended to apply in an environmental context. The due-diligence character of prevention can be understood as a pragmatic response to the fact that

> while it is not considered reasonable to make a State liable for each and every violation committed by persons under its jurisdiction, it is not equally considered satisfactory to rely on mere application of the principle that the conduct of private persons or entities is not attributable to the State under international law.[12]

In other words, the due-diligence character creates a balance between two competing realities: most activities harmful to the environment are undertaken by private actors whose actions cannot always engage the responsibility of the State, but environmental harm might be left completely unregulated if the actions of private actors are uncontrolled. The State is therefore required to take proactive measures to ensure that third-party activities do not cause harm to the environment but will not be held responsible for each occurrence of harm.

Variability is a core definitional element of due diligence.[13] Here lies its strength: due diligence gives States significant 'autonomy and flexibility' to discharge their international obligations[14] based on their individual circumstances, policy preferences and the specificity of the risks. What is an advantage can also be deemed to be a fundamental flaw: it may 'not easily be described in precise terms',[15] and as a result, guidance regarding what will be considered 'appropriate' and 'reasonable' remains vague.[16] A general rule is applicable: due diligence requires that the State exercises the 'due care' which would be expected from a 'good government' under the circumstances.[17] The

[11] For a detailed historical overview of the legal regime of due diligence imposed on States in relation to the activities of non-State actors, see RP Barnidge, 'The Due Diligence Principle under International Law' (2006) 8 *International Community Law Review* 81.

[12] *Responsibilities and Obligations of States Sponsoring Persons and Entities*, para 112.

[13] *Responsibilities and Obligations of States Sponsoring Persons and Entities*, para 117. See also *Certain Activities/Construction of a Road*, separate opinion of Judge ad hoc Dugard, para 11, due diligence as an 'open-texture obligation'.

[14] ILA, Study Group on Due Diligence in International Law, 'Second Report', at 2.

[15] *Responsibilities and Obligations of States Sponsoring Persons and Entities*, para 117.

[16] ILA, Study Group on Due Diligence in International Law, 'Second Report', at 8.

[17] ILA, Study Group on Due Diligence in International Law, 'Second Report', at 9–10.

assessment of the due diligence exercised by a State will then vary on the basis of both facts and law. Firstly, it will rely on an evaluation of the nature and magnitude of risks. It is generally admitted that the State has an obligation to 'act in exact proportion to the risks'[18] – as first expressed by the arbitral tribunal in what is generally considered the landmark case in the context of due diligence, the 1872 *Alabama Claims* relative to obligations of neutrality at times of war. The degree of care should be appropriate and proportional to the level of risk that the harm represents: the more hazardous the activity, the higher will be the duty of care.[19] In this context, the assessment will take into account scientific progress, including technological advances that can reduce negative impacts or make them cheaper.[20]

Secondly, due diligence also varies on the basis of the applicable legal framework.[21] Such was the position of the *South China Sea* tribunal that made due diligence a question of law, in contrast to the approach of the ITLOS Seabed Chamber in its *Advisory Opinion on the Area*, which had interpreted the level of due diligence on the basis of factual elements.[22] The *South China Sea* tribunal relied on a systemic approach to treaty interpretation to assess the appropriateness of China's actions based on the rules of UNCLOS read as a whole[23] and in light of general international law[24] – hence, indicating that due-diligence obligations can increase (or in theory decrease) to adapt to changes in customary and treaty law. A fundamental question remains about whether preventive obligations will be interpreted in light of subjective factors such as economic and technological development, a crucial question that will be analysed in further detail in Section 9.2.2. Suffice it to note here that it might actually not be a question relative to the variability of the duty of care: given that 'with fewer resources the same effort will produce lesser outcomes', the different results expected of States at different levels of economic development can be understood to represent not a different level of care but 'differentiated results'.[25]

[18] *Alabama Claims (United States v. Great Britain)*, (1871) 29 RIAA 125, at 129.
[19] *Responsibilities and Obligations of States Sponsoring Persons and Entities*, para 117.
[20] ILA, Study Group on Due Diligence in International Law, 'Second Report', at 20; T Koivurova, 'Due Diligence', in *Max Planck Encyclopedia of Public International Law* (Oxford University Press 2007), para 20.
[21] ILA, Study Group on Due Diligence in International Law, 'Second Report', at 20.
[22] MM Mbengue, 'The South China Sea Arbitration: Innovations in Marine Environmental Fact-Finding and Due Diligence Obligations' (2016) *AJIL Unbound* 285.
[23] *South China Sea Arbitration*, para 942. [24] *South China Sea Arbitration*, para 941.
[25] ILA, Study Group on Due Diligence in International Law, 'Second Report', at 22.

7.1.2 Due Diligence and Its Relationship to Prevention

The nature of prevention as an obligation of due diligence is generally unquestioned, but uncertainties about how prevention and due diligence relate to one another remain important. The relationship between prevention and due diligence tends to be blurred because, given their close proximity, they are often used interchangeably.[26] The ILC Prevention Commentaries, for instance, use the two terms together, mentioning that States have to discharge their 'duty of prevention or due diligence',[27] in an expression that leaves uncertain whether the ILC considers them as synonymous[28] or as two different norms.[29] However, if the two norms are very close, often intertwined, they cannot be understood to be completely synonymous.[30] Mbengue cogently argues that prevention and due diligence do not share either the same nature or the same function. He contends that due diligence is an action that is simultaneous to the risk with the objective to ensure that the risky activity can carry on, whereas prevention is an obligation interested in the risk of harm per se, which it seeks to annihilate.[31] The ICJ saw the relationship between prevention and due diligence as a historical one when it provided that prevention has 'its origins in the due diligence that is required of a state in its territory'.[32] By doing so, it depicted the principle of prevention as one technique used by international law in its attempts at controlling the activities of private actors, hence inserting it within broader legal trends. The Court also characterized prevention as being of a due-diligence nature that dictates that

[26] Koivurova, 'Due Diligence', para 15, noting that the 'no-harm principle' is often referred to as 'the principle of due diligence' because there is consensus that a State can only breach the principle if it fails to act in due diligence. See also P-M Dupuy, *La Responsabilité internationale des Etats pour les dommages d'origine technologique et industrielle* (Pedone 1977) 226, combining the two expressions into a 'preventive diligence'; and Craik, *International Law of Environmental Impact Assessment*, 72, on the proceduralization of no-harm.

[27] ILC, 'Draft Articles on Prevention of Transboundary Harm', General Commentary, para 2, at 148.

[28] ILC, 'Second Report of the Special Rapporteur, Mr Pemmaraju Sreenivasa Rao, on Prevention of Transboundary Harm from Hazardous Activities' (1999) UN Doc. A/CN.4/501, para 18, considering that the duty of prevention, as an obligation of conduct, could be 'summarized' as an obligation of due diligence.

[29] M Fitzmaurice, 'International Protection of the Environment' (2001) 293 *Collected Courses of the Hague Academy of International Law* 9–488, at 289: 'We are not even sure what is the primary and what is the secondary rule in relation between obligations of prevention and that of due diligence.'

[30] The question is not merely an academic one but, as discussed in Chapter 11, can have significant consequences in the context of dispute settlement.

[31] MM Mbengue, *Essai sur une théorie du risque en droit international public: l'anticipation du risque environnemental et sanitaire* (Pedone 2009) 100.

[32] *Pulp Mills*, para 101.

States take measures to assess risk and, if necessary, mitigate it.[33] If this is uncontroversial, the distinction that the Court has made between substance and procedure in the context of prevention gives more scope for criticism because it bears consequences on how the relationship between prevention and due diligence is conceptualized. The discussion that follows concentrates on this core difficulty by first presenting the distinction and then explaining its consequences.

In the context of prevention, a distinction is routinely made between substantive and procedural preventive obligations.[34] Prevention tends to be seen as a framework obligation that translates into more specific subsidiary obligations,[35] most commonly of a procedural nature. It is generally understood that substantive norms relate to the ultimate objective pursued by the legal order (in the case of this study, the prevention of harm), while procedural norms refer to the concrete steps that States are expected to take to achieve this end goal (such as, for instance, undertaking an EIA).[36] The ICJ has until now relied twice on the distinction between substance and procedure in an environmental context, in *Pulp Mills* and *Certain Activities/Construction of a Road*. It has, however, so far failed to clarify the criteria used to assess whether an obligation falls under the substantive or procedural obligations category. In *Pulp Mills*, the distinction was justified by the Court's interpretation of the Statute of the River Uruguay,[37] and the categorization relied mainly on an assessment of how specific the norm is, the Court noting that substantive obligations tend to be broader than procedural ones.[38] In *Certain Activities/Construction of a Road*, the Court did not explicitly justify its choice, despite the fact that the distinction, which had

33 *Certain Activities/Construction of a Road*, paras 104 and 153. See also ILC, 'Draft Articles on Prevention of Transboundary Harm', Commentary to Article 3, para 7, at 154: 'The obligation of the State of origin to take preventive or minimization measures is one of due diligence.'

34 See e.g. U Beyerlin and T Marauhn, *International Environmental Law* (Hart & CH Beck 2011) 44–45; P-M Dupuy and JE Viñuales, *International Environmental Law* (Cambridge University Press 2015) 54; M Koyano, 'The Significance of Procedural Obligations in International Environmental Law: Sovereignty and International Co-operation' (2011) 54 *Japanese Yearbook of International Law* 97, at 112–13; P Okowa, 'Procedural Obligations in International Environmental Agreements' (1996) 67 *British Yearbook of International Law* 275; ILA, Study Group on Due Diligence in International Law, 'First Report', 26–29.

35 LE Borges, *Les obligations de prévention dans le droit international de l'environnement et ses conséquences dans la responsabilité internationale des Etats* (L'Harmattan 2016) 127.

36 J Brunnée, 'International Environmental Law and Community Interests: Procedural Aspects', in E Benvenisti and G Nolte (eds), *Community Interests Across International Law* (Oxford University Press, forthcoming, available on SSRN at https://papers.ssrn.com/sol3/papers.cfm?abstract_id=2784701 (last accessed 28 August 2017)), at 5.

37 *Pulp Mills*, para 78. 38 *Pulp Mills*, para 77.

not been made by the parties in their written and oral pleadings, had significant consequences on the Court's findings.[39] One can only imagine that the Court considered the distinction to be a matter of general international law, especially since the judgment relied heavily on international customary law. It also seems that, implicitly, the Court followed a chronological reasoning that applied procedural obligations in relation to the anticipation of harm, while substantive obligations were applied in the context of ex post consequences, operating only to evaluate whether harm had occurred.

At times, however, the distinction made by the Court seems largely artificial. For instance, in *Pulp Mills*, the ICJ categorized differently two closely related obligations that find their origins in the duty to cooperate, generally considered to be of a procedural nature.[40] The obligation to coordinate measures to avoid changes in the ecological base was classified as a substantive, and independent, norm, while the obligation to notify was deemed procedural.[41] Additionally, the Court looked at the obligation to undertake an EIA under both the procedural and substantive categories in an approach that in effect questions the pertinence of such categories.[42] The main difficulty relates to the fact that the boundaries between the two categories are very permeable.[43] In particular, procedural obligations cannot be merely satisfied by the conduct of a formal process but, in order not to be deprived of practical significance, need to meet substantive requirements.[44] This is not to say that the schematization is not a useful conceptual tool (relied upon, on occasion, in this very study) to refer to the due-diligence content of prevention, but it should nevertheless be used with the full awareness that it tends to oversimplify reality and can be consequential in the context of State responsibility, as discussed further in Chapter 11.

39 As noted in *Certain Activities/Construction of a Road*, separate opinion of Judge Donoghue, para 17.

40 See e.g. Okowa, 'Procedural Obligations in International Environmental Agreements'; I Plakokefalos, 'Prevention Obligations in International Environmental Law' (2012) 23 *Yearbook of International Environmental Law* 3.

41 *Pulp Mills*, para 185. 42 *Pulp Mills*, para 206.

43 Brunnée, 'International Environmental Law and Community Interests', 5: 'Substance typically frames the circumstances in which procedure operates, and the purposes that it is to serve. In turn, procedure has the potential to reinforce and develop, and to give concrete meaning and effect to, substance.'

44 C Leb, *Cooperation in the Law of Transboundary Water Resources* (Cambridge University Press 2013) 109, noting that, in the *North Sea Continental Shelf* cases, the ICJ recognized that 'procedural obligations' under international law are not satisfied by the conduct of a formal process and therefore are not merely 'procedural' but are, in fact, qualified by 'substantive' requirements that must be complied with during their implementation.

stinction made between substance and procedure having been intro- e discussion now turns to explaining how it affects the conceptuali- due diligence. Simply put, it can be consequential when determining whether due diligence is a discrete obligation or an element of prevention. It is true that the terminology referring to due diligence varies widely, including such terms as 'concept',[45] 'duty',[46] 'obligation',[47] 'rule',[48] 'standard'[49] and 'principle'.[50] Among these terms, the distinction between due diligence being the obligation itself or simply a standard of care can have important legal effects. Three different approaches have emerged, brought to light by the diverging ways in which some ICJ judges conceptualized due diligence in their separate opinions to *Certain Activities/Construction of a Road*. The first approach understands due diligence as the primary legal obligation of conduct, with procedural obligations (such as the duty to undertake an EIA and to notify) as possible requirements for its fulfilment. It is visible in the separate opinions of Judges Owada and Donoghue, which considered that the EIA was 'one important constituent element' of the due-diligence process[51] but that it could not be recognized as a separate and customary obligation.[52] The position is only tenable if one refutes the customary character of the duty to undertake an EIA, a position that, as discussed further later (see Section 7.2.2), might be too restrictive and conservative. A second path consists in considering that due diligence guides procedural preventive norms such as the duty to undertake an EIA, which are obligations in their own right. This position, adopted by Judge Cançado Trindade,[53] sees procedural obligations as independent norms of a due-diligence nature. It best explains the distinction made by the Court between substance and procedure

45 Koivurova, 'Due Diligence', para 42

46 ILC, 'Draft Articles on Prevention of Transboundary Harm', Commentary to Article 3, para 7, at 154; Kulesza, *Due Diligence* 254.

47 ILC, 'Draft Articles on Prevention of Transboundary Harm', Commentary to Article 3, para 8, at 154; Koivurova, 'Due Diligence', para 1.

48 ILC, 'Second Report of the Special Rapporteur, Mr. F.V. García-Amador, on International Responsibility' (1957) UN Doc. A/CN.4/106; R Pisillo-Mazzeschi, 'The "Due Diligence" Rule and the Nature of the International Responsibility of States' (1992) *German Yearbook of International Law* 9.

49 ILC, 'Draft Articles on Prevention of Transboundary Harm', Commentary to Article 3, para 11, at 154; ILC, 'Second Report of the Special Rapporteur, Mr. F.V. García-Amador', at 122, 'due diligence as a standard and not a definition'; Koivurova, 'Due Diligence', para 42.

50 Kulesza, *Due Diligence* 269; Barnidge, 'Due Diligence'.

51 *Certain Activities/Construction of a Road*, separate opinion of Judge Owada, paras 14–18.

52 *Certain Activities/Construction of a Road*, separate opinion of Judge Donoghue, para 13.

53 *Certain Activities/Construction of a Road*, separate opinion of Judge Cançado Trindade, para 57.

presented earlier, as it allows a procedural obligation to be breached without breaching a substantive obligation. However, as discussed further in Chapter 11, it can be criticized for being an artificial distinction that fails to let prevention express its full effects. In addition, it was noted that the source of the EIA obligation allows a State to argue that it was not under a duty of due diligence if 'no harm has been proved at the time of the legal proceedings'.[54] The final approach sees due diligence as a standard of conduct that flows from prevention and operates together with independent procedural obligations. Judge ad hoc Dugard considered that 'procedural obligations' are both autonomous primary obligations that can be independently breached and standards that determine the content of due diligence.[55] From this perspective, the EIA is a separate legal obligation,[56] independent of the existence of an obligation to prevent harm[57] but which contributes to ascertaining the risk posed by an activity.[58] This is the most convincing approach because it sees prevention as holistic and gives risk anticipation its full expression, and it recognizes the independent status of other environmental duties, such as the duty to undertake an EIA. It remains that the disagreements relative to the prevention–due-diligence relationship are notable because they bear consequences on the identification of the content of prevention.

7.2 THE DUE-DILIGENCE CONTENT OF PREVENTION

This section presents the measures that a State is expected to take to fulfil its duty of care.[59] Identifying the content of prevention is not an easy task for a multiplicity of reasons that influenced the approach taken by the analysis that follows. The first, and most evident, one is that due diligence will be assessed on a case-by-case basis, which makes any kind of generalization difficult. This should not be understood to mean that the obligation to act in due diligence has 'no content'.[60] However, it complicates the matter because the content of prevention will be found in a mix of measures of a different nature, including international conventional and customary obligations and international standards that, depending on the circumstances, may or not

54 *Certain Activities/Construction of a Road*, separate opinion of Judge ad hoc Dugard, para 10.

55 *Certain Activities/Construction of a Road*, separate opinion of Judge ad hoc Dugard, paras 9–10. See also Plakokefalos, 'Prevention Obligations', 5.

56 *Certain Activities/Construction of a Road*, separate opinion of Judge ad hoc Dugard, para 11.

57 *Certain Activities/Construction of a Road*, separate opinion of Judge ad hoc Dugard, para 9.

58 *Certain Activities/Construction of a Road*, separate opinion of Judge ad hoc Dugard, para 10.

59 ILA, Study Group on Due Diligence in International Law, 'Second Report', at 7; Koivurova, 'Due Diligence', para 42.

60 ILA, Study Group on Due Diligence in International Law, 'Second Report', at 7.

may be applicable.[61] In this section, the content of prevention has been identified on the basis of two main sources: the ILC Prevention Articles, for their status as a custom codification effort and the recognized guidance they provide, explicitly or implicitly, to States and international courts and tribunals, and international jurisprudence, which sheds light on how the level of care is assessed in the context of dispute settlement. A second challenge relates to the fact that the content of prevention will be informed by a combination of customary obligations (often minimal) and treaty norms (more detailed).[62] As a result, this section presents the core measures that a customary obligation of prevention would have to meet and relies on selected examples from conventional law to highlight how this content could be enriched in light of applicable treaty provisions. A final difficulty lies in the fact that the content of prevention is in a flux: it is constantly evolving based on treaty and custom developments, as well as jurisprudential clarifications. As a result, in keeping with the evolutionary perspective of this study, the analysis that follows underlines current trends in international law that hint at how the content of these obligations might evolve.

Firstly, the section presents the obligation to design and implement a national legislative and administrative framework (7.2.1). It then concentrates on the two core elements of due diligence, the obligation to undertake an EIA (7.2.2) and the duty to act in a cooperative manner (7.2.3), before discussing how they interrelate (7.2.4). Finally, it identifies emerging norms on the trend towards integrating the due-diligence content of prevention (7.2.5).

7.2.1 *National Legislative and Administrative Framework*

The first element of the duty of care, which might be 'obvious',[63] relates to the existence of a national legislative and administrative framework that operationalizes international obligations of prevention.[64] While a State is free to

61 IDI, 'Responsibility and Liability under International Law for Environmental Damage', Session of Strasbourg, 1997, Article 3(2).

62 Mbengue, 'The South China Sea Arbitration', 286, noting that the 'normative sophistication or diversification of international environmental law is a source of richness for the standard of due diligence under general international law'.

63 ILC, 'Draft Articles on Prevention of Transboundary Harm', Commentary to Article 5, para 1, at 156.

64 Rio de Janeiro Declaration on Environment and Development (Rio de Janeiro, 3–14 June 1992), (1992) 31 ILM 876, Principle 11; confirmed in ILC, 'Draft Articles on Prevention of Transboundary Harm', Article 5.

decide on how to design its national environmental laws and regulations,[65] it should impose quantitative and qualitative restrictions on private parties undertaking potentially harmful activities under its jurisdiction or control. An appropriate domestic framework is essential to avoid environmental harm, as evidenced in the context of the 1989 Sandoz factory disaster that polluted the Rhine with toxic chemicals: Switzerland might have been able to prevent the disaster if it had set up domestic laws and regulations pursuant to its international obligations[66] to protect the watercourse from the potentially harmful activities of pharmaceutical companies.[67]

The mere adoption of a detailed preventive regime at the domestic level would not be sufficient evidence of due diligence. Domestic laws and regulations should be regularly updated to remain in line with the constant evolution of scientific knowledge pertaining to environmental protection. One way of assessing whether domestic preventive requirements meet international requirements in this respect is to evaluate them against international standards that are known as 'best available techniques/technologies' (BATs)[68] and 'best environmental practices' (BEPs).[69] These standards are 'the most effective' at

65 *Sub-Regional Fisheries Commission*, ITLOS No. 21, Advisory Opinion (2 April 2015), para 138: '[T]he nature of the laws, regulations and measures that are to be adopted by the flag State is left to be determined by each flag State in accordance with its legal system.'

66 Convention on the Protection of the Rhine against Chemical Pollution, Bonn, 3 December 1976, in force 1 February 1979, 1124 UNTS 375, Article 1.

67 See A Schwabach, 'The Sandoz Spill: The Failure of International Law to Protect the Rhine from Pollution' (1989) 16(2) *Ecology Law Quarterly* 443, at 468.

68 E.g. Protocol to the 1979 Convention on Long Range Transboundary Air Pollution on Heavy Metals, Aarhus, 24 June 1998, in force 29 December 2003, available at www.unece.org/env/lrtap/hm_h1.html (last accessed 15 August 2017), Article 3(2)(a) and Annex III; Convention for the Protection of the Marine Environment of the North-East Atlantic, Paris, 22 September 1992, in force 25 March 1998, (1993) 32 ILM 1068, Article 2(3)(b) and Appendix I; Protocol to the 1979 Convention on Long Range Transboundary Air Pollution on Further Reduction of Sulphur Emissions, Oslo, 14 June 1994, in force 5 August 1998, (1998) 33 ILM 1540, Annex IV; Protocol to the 1979 Convention on Long Range Transboundary Air Pollution on Persistent Organic Pollutants, Aarhus, 24 June 1998, in force 23 December 2003, (1998) 37 ILM 505, Articles 3(1) and 3(3) and Annex V (2); Minamata Convention on Mercury, Kumamoto, 10 October 2013, in force 16 August 2017, available at www.mercuryconvention.org/ (last accessed 15 August 2017), Article 2(b).

69 Convention for the Protection of the Marine Environment of the North-East Atlantic, Article 2(3)(b) and Appendix I; Convention on the Protection and Use of Transboundary Watercourses and International Lakes, Helsinki, 17 March 1992, in force 6 October 1996, (1992) 31 ILM 1312, Annex I; Convention on the Protection of the Black Sea against Pollution, Bucharest, 21 April 1992, in force 15 January 1994, (1992) 32 ILM 1110, Article 3(3) and Annex II; Convention on Persistent Organic Pollutants, Stockholm, 22 May 2001, in force 17 May 2004, (2001) 40 ILM 532, Article 5(e) and Annex C.

preventing environmental harm[70] because they act as benchmarks against which to evaluate the degree of care exercised by a State in the context of the technological and scientific knowledge at its disposal. Such was the approach taken by the ICJ in *Pulp Mills*, where the Court observed that the obligation of due diligence required the parties to 'conform to applicable international agreements and to take account of internationally agreed technical standards'.[71] It looked at whether the measures taken by Uruguay were BAT compliant to evaluate whether the substantive obligation of prevention had been breached. The case thus confirmed that the design of domestic preventive frameworks might be left to the discretion of the State but should nevertheless follow international environmental standards.

The quality of the legal framework will also be assessed against its effectiveness. A perfectly designed legal framework that is not implemented properly naturally will not be considered sufficient to fulfil the obligation of due diligence. The international jurisprudence has consistently made clear that the adoption of an appropriate regulatory framework is not sufficient to discharge the duty of care but that vigilance in the observance and enforcement of the adopted measures is necessary.[72]

7.2.2 *Environmental Impact Assessment*

The design and implementation of a national legislative and administrative framework are the first steps in the exercise of the preventive duty of care. Two procedural obligations deal more specifically with the actions that a State should take in light of foreseeable harm in order to discharge its obligation of prevention. The first is the obligation to undertake an EIA. The relationship that the duty to undertake an EIA entertains with due diligence is an evident, and yet complex, one. The discussion that follows goes into a deeper examination of existing uncertainties regarding the status of the EIA in the due-diligence exercise mentioned previously in the context of the discussion of

70 E.g. Minamata Convention on Mercury, Article 2(b), defining 'best available techniques' as 'those *techniques that are the most effective* to prevent and, where that is not practicable, to reduce emissions and releases of mercury to air, water and land and the impact of such emissions and releases on the environment as a whole' (emphasis added).

71 *Pulp Mills*, paras 197 and 225, in which the Court considered that the measures taken by Uruguay seemed BAT compliant.

72 *Gabčíkovo-Nagymaros Project (Hungary/Slovakia)* (Judgment) (1997) ICJ Rep 7, para 185; *Pulp Mills*, para 197; *Sub-Regional Fisheries Commission*, paras 138–39 (considering that the enforcement mechanisms should be complemented by an ex post regime made of a duty to investigate, sanction and remedy cases of IUU fishing activities); *South China Sea Arbitration*, paras 961, 964, and 974.

the prevention–due-diligence relationship. It explains how the EIA qualifies both as an element contributing to discharging the obligation to exercise due diligence to prevent environmental harm (7.2.2.1) and as an independent obligation under international customary law (7.2.2.2). The section then ends by identifying the content of the EIA obligation (7.2.2.3).

7.2.2.1 A Manifestation of Due Diligence

An EIA is generally the 'chief mechanism' by which a State may discharge its obligation of prevention,[73] although it might not always be needed to exercise the correct duty of care. For instance, the existence of a system of adequate regulatory schemes to control pollution could satisfy the due-diligence requirements.[74] The EIA is an anticipatory tool that precedes the conduct of an activity likely to have significant effects[75] to evaluate the impacts of an activity, and their magnitude, on persons, property and the environment.[76] It is thus a central means by which States assess the environmental consequences of potentially risky activities and, if necessary, examine measures to prevent significant harm.[77] As an element of the preventive duty of care, the EIA operationalizes the same likelihood/impact matrix that triggers prevention (see Chapter 6). If the EIA predicts that the risk of harm is low but that the impact is likely to be high or, on the contrary, that the risk is high but that the impact is low, then the State is under an obligation to take measures to prevent the predicted harm. When the EIA indicates a low likelihood and low impact of harm, the State may proceed with the activity but is nevertheless under an obligation to continue monitoring the effects of the activity on the environment. Conversely, if the EIA reveals that both the likelihood of harm and the impact are high, then the State is required to significantly modify its plans.

A fundamental question relates to the circumstances that trigger the obligation to undertake an EIA. The situation is particularly intricate: on the one hand, it is deemed applicable to any proposed activity that might have a

73 N Craik, 'Principle 17: Environmental Impact Assessment', in JE Viñuales (ed), *The Rio Declaration on Environment and Development: A Commentary* (Oxford University Press 2015) 451–70, at 466. See also *Pulp Mills*, para 204; *Certain Activities/Construction of a Road*, paras 104 and 153.

74 Craik, *International Law of Environmental Impact Assessment*, 64.

75 UNEP Governing Council Decision, 'Principles on Conservation and Harmonious Utilisation of Natural Resources Shared by Two or More States', UNEP/IG12/2 (1978), Principle 6; *Certain Activities/Construction of a Road*, para 161.

76 ILC, 'Draft Articles on Prevention of Transboundary Harm', Commentary to Article 7, para 8, at 159.

77 Craik, *International Law of Environmental Impact Assessment*, 466.

significant adverse impact[78]; on the other hand, the very objective of the EIA is to assess whether a risk of significant harm exists. The solution to this circularity problem is not to make the EIA compulsory in all circumstances; regulating activities with minimal impacts would unnecessarily overburden domestic administrations. Two different approaches can offer a solution to this dead end. The first is found in international treaties that include a list of activities that necessarily trigger an EIA obligation because they are presumed to be likely to cause significant transboundary effect.[79] The second possibility has the advantage of not being tied to the existence of conventional provisions: it requires undertaking a preliminary assessment in the form of a screening process that evaluates whether the proposed activity should be subject to an EIA. It is under these circumstances that the difference in the ex post and ex ante significant threshold discussed in Chapter 6 is most visible: the threshold that makes the EIA applicable concentrates on risk and thus will be lower than the threshold that operates once the EIA has been undertaken and which triggers prevention.[80] The legal material,[81] including, most significantly, the ICJ jurisprudence,[82] indicates that a preliminary assessment is consolidating as an element contributing to the assessment of the duty of care. By objectivizing the evaluation of the conditions that make the EIA a compulsory requirement, one limits the risk that a State argues, in hindsight, that the conditions triggering the EIA obligation were not met. The parameters of the initial assessment are, at present, left to the discretion

78 *Pulp Mills*, para 104.

79 See e.g. Convention on Environmental Impact Assessment in a Transboundary Context, Espoo, 25 February 1991, in force 10 September 1997, (1991) 30 ILM 802, Appendix I. Noted in *Certain Activities/Construction of a Road*, separate opinion of Judge Bhandari, para 42.

80 *Certain Activities/Construction of a Road*, separate opinion of Judge ad hoc Dugard, para 19: '[I]n determining the need for an EIA it is necessary to have regard to the risk of harm being caused. (By necessary implication, this rejects that argument that the test is not the risk of transboundary harm but the likelihood or probability of such harm occurring.)'

81 Protocol on Environmental Protection to the Antarctic Treaty, Madrid, 4 October 1991, in force 14 January 1998, (1991) 30 ILM 1461, Annex I, Article 2, on an initial environmental evaluation. See also UNEP Governing Council, 'Goals and Principles of Environmental Impact Assessment', GC Dec. 14/25 (II) (1987), Principle 2(d), on an 'initial environmental evaluation'; Convention on Biological Diversity, Resolution of the Conference of the Parties VIII/28, 'Impact Assessment: Voluntary Guidelines on Biodiversity-inclusive Impact Assessment', UNEP/CBD/COP/8/31, para 5(a); 'Arctic Environment Protection Strategy 1997: Guidelines for Environmental Impact Assessment (EIA) in the Arctic' (Finnish Ministry of the Environment 1997) at 12, on 'screening procedures'. See also *Certain Activities/Construction of a Road*, separate opinion of Judge Bhandari, para 31.

82 *Certain Activities/Construction of a Road*, para 154, recognizing that 'to conduct a preliminary assessment of the risk posed by an activity is one of the ways in which a State can ascertain whether a proposed activity carries a risk of significant transboundary harm'.

of the State.[83] The assessment of the threshold of risk triggering the EIA obligation, however, will be subject to international judicial scrutiny[84] based on factors presented in Chapter 6.

7.2.2.2 An Independent Customary Obligation

The duty to undertake an EIA is not only a manifestation of due diligence but also an independent obligation under international customary law, applicable to transboundary, global and purely domestic risks of harm. In relation to transboundary risks, the customary status of the duty to undertake an EIA seems undisputable in light of its inclusion in the ILC Prevention Articles[85] and the recognition by the ICJ that it was a 'requirement under general international law'.[86] However, not all commentators have understood the *Pulp Mills* statement to mean that the obligation to undertake an EIA is customary law.[87] The controversy emerges out of existing uncertainties regarding whether the term 'general international law' includes customary international law. The majority opinion accepts so,[88] and in the case under scrutiny, the reference to 'practice' and 'acceptance', the two elements of custom, in the same sentence would corroborate the interpretation that the Court was in fact referring to customary international law.[89] A wider interpretation of general international law as referring

83 For a criticism of the absence of international standards with regards to the preliminary assessment, see D Desierto, 'Evidence but Not Empiricism? Environmental Impact Assessments at the International Court of Justice', in *Certain Activities Carried out by Nicaragua in the Border Area (Costa Rica v. Nicaragua) and Construction of a Road in Costa Rica along the San Juan River (Nicaragua v. Costa Rica)* (26 February 2016) *EJIL: Talk!*, available at www.ejiltalk.org/evidence-but-not-empiricism-environmental-impact-assessments-at-the-international-court-of-justice-in-certain-activities-carried-out-by-nicaragua-in-the-border-area-costa-rica-v-nicaragua-and-con/ (last accessed 28 August 2017).

84 See e.g. *Certain Activities/Construction of a Road.*

85 ILC, 'Draft Articles on Prevention of Transboundary Harm', Article 7.

86 *Pulp Mills*, para 204. Confirmed in *Construction of a Road* (Provisional Measures) Order of 13 December 2013, para 19.

87 See e.g. Koyano, 'The Significance of Procedural Obligations in International Environmental Law', 112–13.

88 *Certain Activities/Construction of a Road*, separate opinion of Judge ad hoc Dugard, in relation to the EIA: 'I understand the term "general international law" to denote a rule of customary international law.'

89 *Pulp Mills*, para 204: '[T]he obligation to protect and preserve, under Article 41(a) of the Statute, has to be interpreted in accordance with a *practice*, which in recent years has gained so much *acceptance* among States that it may now be considered a requirement under general international law to undertake an environmental impact assessment' (emphasis added).

both to custom and to treaty law[90] would also be plausible given the widespread inclusion of environmental assessment duties in international treaties.[91] By contrast, some ICJ judges have argued that general international law does not refer to customary law and that the term was chosen to highlight the role of the EIA obligation as a manifestation of due diligence[92] or its status as a general principle of law (in light of its widespread presence in domestic law).[93] Most likely, and given the lack of consistency between the positions of ICJ judges on this matter subsequently revealed in the context of *Certain Activities/Construction of a Road*, the ambiguity of the term was consciously embraced by the Court on the basis that it was vague enough to accommodate different conceptualizations and was leaving the door open for further clarification at a later stage.

This uncertainty has not, however, prevented the obligation to undertake an EIA to extend to the global commons. The ITLOS Seabed Chamber, in its *Advisory Opinion on the Area*, interpreted the ICJ's *Pulp Mills* statement as acknowledging the customary status of the EIA duty, seemingly understanding the term 'general international law' to comprise customary and conventional law.[94] The Chamber's approach to custom can be deemed rather loose on two grounds. Firstly, it used the ICJ's apparent recognition of the customary obligation within a transboundary context as the legal basis to extend the spatial scope of prevention to areas beyond national jurisdiction.[95] Yet, the existence of a customary obligation in a transboundary context does not necessarily mean that the obligation enjoys the same status in areas beyond national jurisdiction. Secondly, not only did the Chamber make the obligation applicable to activities within the Area (the object of the advisory opinion), but it also extended it to all areas beyond national jurisdiction.[96] This might be considered problematic, but the large recognition

[90] G Tunk, 'Is General International Law Customary Law Only?' (1993) 4 *European Journal of International Law* 534, at 541, arguing that general international law includes customary and conventional law.

[91] For an overview of multilateral environmental agreements integrating environmental assessment obligations, see Craik, *International Law of Environmental Impact Assessment* 96–105.

[92] *Certain Activities/Construction of a Road*, separate opinions of Judges Owada and Donoghue.

[93] *Certain Activities/Construction of a Road*, separate opinions of Judges Cançado Trindade and Bhandari.

[94] *Responsibilities and Obligations of States Sponsoring Persons and Entities*, para 145, noting that the obligation to conduct an EIA is an obligation under UNCLOS and under customary international law.

[95] *Responsibilities and Obligations of States Sponsoring Persons and Entities*, paras 145–48, considering that the Court's 'reasoning in a transboundary context may also apply to activities with an impact on the environment in an area beyond the limits of national jurisdiction'.

[96] *Responsibilities and Obligations of States Sponsoring Persons and Entities*, para 148.

of the EIA obligation in treaty law[97] and custom codification works[98] gave the Chamber strong grounds for interpreting the ICJ's statement as recognizing the customary nature of the EIA obligation.

Finally, the obligation to carry out an EIA under international law is also applicable to activities that might harm only the domestic environment. Indeed, treaty obligations do not always restrict the spatial scope of the EIA to a specific location,[99] and codification works have also hinted at the fact that an EIA should be undertaken irrespective of the location of the potential damage.[100] In addition, the need to undertake an EIA to identify harm to the domestic environment has been recognized as an obligation under human rights law. In *Social and Economic Rights Action Center (SERAC) and Others v. Nigeria*, the African Commission on Human and Peoples' Rights considered that the EIA was a necessary duty to discharge the obligations under Articles 16 (right to health) and 24 (right to a satisfactory environment) of the

97 For an overview of multilateral environmental agreements including environmental assessment obligations, see Craik, *International Law of Environmental Impact Assessment*, 96–105.

98 UNEP Governing Council, 'Goals and Principles of Environmental Impact Assessment', Principle 4(g); ILA, Committee on Space Law, Conference Resolution No. 6/2012, Sofia, 75th Session, 2012, Article 7(2); ILA, Committee on Legal Principles relating to Climate Change, 'Declaration of Principles Relating to Climate Change', Washington, DC, 76th Session, 2014, Article 7B (5); ILC, 'Protection of the Atmosphere: Titles and Texts of Draft Guidelines 3, 4, 5, 6 and 7, together with a preambular paragraph, provisionally adopted by the Drafting Committee on 7, 8 and 9 June 2016' (2016) UN Doc. A/CN.4/L.875, guideline 4 on the obligation to undertake an EIA.

99 United Nations Convention on the Law of the Sea, Article 204, on the obligation to assess the risks of pollution to the marine environment (meaning, however, that the material scope of the EIA is limited to pollution); Convention on Biological Diversity, Nairobi, 22 May 1992, in force 29 December 1993, (1992) 31 ILM 822, Article 14 (qualified obligation to conduct EIAs for proposed projects that are likely to have a significant impact on biological diversity); Convention on Biological Diversity, 'Impact Assessment: Voluntary Guidelines'; United Nations Framework Convention on Climate Change, New York, 9 May 1992, in force 24 March 1994, 1771 UNTS 107, Article 4(1)(f).

100 'World Charter for Nature', UNGA Res. 37/7 (XXXVII) (28 October 1982), para 11(b), encouraging assessment activities likely to harm 'nature'; Rio Declaration, Principle 17, which provides for an obligation to carry out an EIA for activities likely to have an impact 'on the environment'; Commission on Sustainable Development, 'Report of the Expert Group Meeting on Identification of Principles of International Law for Sustainable Development', Geneva, Switzerland, 26–28 September 1995, para 134. See also RD Munro and J Lammers (eds), *Environmental Protection and Sustainable Development: Legal Principles and Recommendations Adopted by the Experts Group on Environmental Law of the World Commission on Environment and Development* (Graham & Trotman 1987), Article 5: The obligation to carry out an assessment to activities 'which may significantly affect a natural resources or the environment' is included in the section on 'general principles concerning natural resources and environmental interferences', in opposition to the following section on principles 'specially concerning *transboundary* natural resources and environmental interferences.'

African Charter on Human and Peoples' Rights.[101] A similar obligation was then confirmed at the global level by the Human Rights Council on the basis of the conclusions of the independent expert on human rights and the environment that provided that implementation of the right to a safe, clean, healthy and sustainable environment was facilitated by the assessment of environmental impacts.[102] Admittedly, a majority of States have today adopted national regulations that require the undertaking of an EIA,[103] a situation that could lead to the conclusion that an international obligation to undertake an EIA is of limited added value. However, its parallel existence under international law is consequential for two main reasons. The most obvious reason is that an international obligation to undertake an EIA in a domestic context, once its customary status is ascertained, will force States that have not yet established a regulatory framework relative to environmental assessments applicable in a purely domestic context to do so. The second reason is more progressive: if the EIA obligation is considered to be a manifestation of the obligation to exercise due diligence to prevent harm, its application in a purely domestic context is thus indicative of the existence of an international obligation of prevention operating irrespective of external impacts – a possibility that will be explored further in Chapter 8.

7.2.2.3 Content

Irrespective of whether the EIA is considered an independent norm or merely a factor in the assessment of due diligence, determining its content remains fundamental. The content of the EIA is left to be decided at the national level[104] because it is considered that there is 'no single "correct" approach'[105] to environmental assessments.[106] The highly contextualized obligation should be flexible enough to adapt to the circumstances of each

[101] *Social and Economic Rights Action Center (SERAC) and Others v. Nigeria*, African Commission Application No. 155/96 (2001–2), para 53.

[102] Human Rights Council Resolution, 'Human Rights and the Environment' (15 April 2014) UN Doc. A/HRC/RES/25/21, para 4; 'Report of the Independent Expert on the issue of human rights obligations relating to the enjoyment of a safe, clean, healthy and sustainable environment, John H. Knox: Mapping Report' (30 December 2013) UN Doc. A/HRC/25/53, para 31.

[103] Craik, *International Law of Environmental Impact Assessment*, 23, noting that over a hundred countries have EIA legislation.

[104] *Pulp Mills*, para 205.

[105] *Indus Waters Kishenganga Arbitration (Pakistan v. India)*, Permanent Court of Arbitration, Final Award, 20 December 2013, para 99.

[106] *Certain Activities/Construction of a Road*, para 104.

case. However, leaving the determination of the content of the EIA solely at the domestic level runs the risk of transforming the EIA into an empty obligation that fails to operationalize the preventive principle.[107] While the content of the EIA per se is left to the domestic arena, this does not mean that due diligence will be considered exercised on the mere basis that an EIA has been undertaken; on the contrary, the content of the EIA will be examined by international courts and tribunals to evaluate whether it meets the level of reasonable degree of care expected in light of specific circumstances.[108] An initial examination will consist in assessing whether the State's own legislative standards were enforced when the EIA was undertaken.[109] The assessment of the level of the duty of care exercised will then take a number of factors into account to evaluate whether the duty of care was proportional to the level of risk, paying special attention to the magnitude of the activity, the degree of risk and the complexity of the project.[110] Existing international standards contribute to this assessment, as an indication of what could reasonably be expected from a State.[111] A last essential element in the EIA obligation is that it requires continuous risk

107 See *Certain Activities/Construction of a Road*, separate opinion of Judge Bhandari, para 47: '[T]he current stage of international environmental law is lamentably silent on the exact procedural steps and substantive content that are required when a situation of potential transboundary harm gives rise to the obligation of a nation State to produce an EIA.'

108 Craik, *International Law of Environmental Impact Assessment* 139, on 'skeletal requirements' applicable to the obligation to undertake an EIA; and *Certain Activities/Construction of a Road*, separate opinion of Judge ad hoc Dugard, para 18, noting that there are minimal requirements that should be met to satisfy the due-diligence obligation.

109 *South China Sea Arbitration*, para 990.

110 *Pulp Mills*, para 205. International judicial bodies have considered that a 'comprehensive' EIA is needed for complex projects: *Indus Waters Kishenganga Arbitration* (Final Award), paras 98–99, recognizing that while sometimes 'a simple assessment may indeed be preferred', in the case under scrutiny a comprehensive approach 'attempting to capture complex interactions within the river ecosystem' was better suited given the complexity of the project; *South China Sea Arbitration*, para 990, noting that China's EIA was 'far less comprehensive than EIAs reviewed by other international courts and tribunals'.

111 *Responsibilities and Obligations of States Sponsoring Persons and Entities*, para 149, specifying that the content of an EIA undertaken in the deep seabed can be found in the recommendations and regulations on seabed mining adopted by the International Seabed Authority. See also Convention on Environmental Impact Assessment in a Transboundary Context, referred to as setting international standards; *Certain Activities/Construction of a Road*, separate opinion of Judge Bhandari, para 32, referring to the Convention on Environmental Impact Assessment in a Transboundary Context as setting international standards. International standards could also be derived from Convention on Biological Diversity, 'Impact Assessment: Voluntary Guidelines'; 'Arctic Environment Protection Strategy 1997: Guidelines for Environmental Impact Assessment in the Arctic'.

monitoring[112] during the whole duration of the project[113] to ensure that the actions of the operator comply with the 'terms of the authorization' granted.[114]

7.2.3 *Cooperation*

Cooperation is another 'fundamental'[115] duty in the exercise of due diligence to prevent environmental harm.[116] The close link between prevention and cooperation is made clear in the order in which the ILC Prevention Articles are presented, with the article on cooperation directly following the one on prevention and reading as a procedural obligation in the implementation of the obligation of prevention.[117] The question discussed in relation to the EIA regarding whether it is an independent duty or merely a manifestation of due diligence does not apply in the context of cooperation: it leaves little doubt that cooperation contributes to the duty of care while also being an independent duty. Indeed, whereas the EIA has developed specifically in the context of environmental protection, the obligation to cooperate is much wider and applicable throughout general international law. As a result, the perspective taken by the discussion that follows concentrates on the specificity of cooperation in the context of prevention and presents its three core expressions: a duty to notify (7.2.3.1), to exchange information (7.2.3.2) and to consult and negotiate (7.2.3.3).

7.2.3.1 Notification

The duty to notify is an 'indispensable part of any system designed to prevent harm'.[118] It takes two different forms, a general duty to notify in case of

112 UNEP Governing Council, 'Goals and Principles of Environmental Impact Assessment', Principle 10, talks of 'supervision'; *Pulp Mills*, para 205; *Responsibilities and Obligations of States Sponsoring Persons and Entities*, paras 142–44; Convention on Biological Diversity, 'Impact Assessment: Voluntary Guidelines', para 5(g); ILA, Study Group on Due Diligence in International Law, 'First Report', at 28; *Certain Activities/Construction of a Road*, para 161.

113 *Certain Activities/Construction of a Road*, separate opinion of Judge Bhandari, para 31, identifying three cumulative stages of prevention expressed in the form of a preliminary assessment, an EIA and a post-project assessment.

114 ILC, 'Draft Articles on Prevention of Transboundary Harm', Article 6(2).

115 *MOX Plant (Ireland v. United Kingdom)*, ITLOS No. 10, Provisional Measures (3 December 2001), para 82.

116 *Pulp Mills*, para 77; *South China Sea Arbitration*, para 985.

117 ILC, 'Draft Articles on Prevention of Transboundary Harm', Article 4.

118 ILC, 'Draft Articles on Prevention of Transboundary Harm', Commentary to Article 8, para 2, at 159.

imminent harm, on which this section concentrates, and a more specific duty to notify in case of emergency, envisaged in Chapter 6.[119]

The obligation to notify is a general obligation of international law that has gained pre-eminence in the context of environmental protection.[120] It enables the potentially affected State to make its own evaluation of the situation and, in the case of projected risks, to find an amicable solution with the State of origin.[121] The aim of the notification is to create the 'conditions for successful co-operation'[122] between the State of origin and the State likely to be affected, in particular, by ensuring that the State is able to give due account to the EIA and other information submitted to it.[123]

Like the obligation to undertake an EIA, the details of the notification procedure are left for the State to decide. Admittedly, the ILC Prevention Articles attempted to provide a detailed framework relative to the obligation to notify, including a six-month period during which the State of origin should wait for a response to its notification to the potentially affected State,[124] and the right of the potentially affected State to request that the State of origin exercise its notification duties.[125] However, these provisions are largely considered to go beyond *lex lata*, and the notification procedure will largely vary on a case-by-case basis.

Overall, the fulfilment of the obligation will be judged against a number of criteria, including the nature and seriousness of environmental harm, the importance of the interests likely to be affected and the proximity of a potentially affected State to the proposed project.[126] In particular, the obligation to notify is more strenuous in relation to activities located in border areas in order to ensure that the interests of the potentially affected State are taken into account. If an activity might affect multiple States, and possibly the global commons as well, common practice is to use an international organization that acts as an intermediary, receiving the notification and sharing it with member States.

119 On the obligation to prevent in case of emergency, see Section 6.2.3. For a detailed review, see P Okowa, 'Notification and Assistance in Case of Emergency', in JE Viñuales (ed), *The Rio Declaration on Environment and Development: A Commentary* (Oxford University Press 2015).

120 *Request for an Examination of the Situation in Accordance with the Court's Judgment of December 1974 in the Nuclear Tests (New Zealand v. France)* (1995) ICJ Rep 288, dissenting opinion by Judge Weeramantry, at 361, considering that the *Corfu Channel* case had 'laid down the environmentally important principle' in the form of notification.

121 Okowa, 'Procedural Obligations in International Environmental Agreements', at 291.

122 *Pulp Mills*, para 113. 123 *Pulp Mills*, para 120.

124 ILC, 'Draft Articles on Prevention of Transboundary Harm', Article 8(2).

125 ILC, 'Draft Articles on Prevention of Transboundary Harm', Article 11.

126 Okowa, 'Procedural Obligations in International Environmental Agreements', 290.

A key element in relation to notification relates to who should be notified. The decision will depend on a variety of factors, including the type of risks carried by the activity. In this context, the Compliance Committee of the Espoo Convention considered, in relation to the planned construction of a nuclear power plant in Hinkley Point C, that

> on the basis of the principle of prevention, when considering the affected Parties for the purpose of notification, the Party of origin, *should be exceptionally prospective and inclusive*, in order to ensure that all Parties potentially affected by an accident, however uncertain, are notified.[127]

The inclusiveness of the committee was undoubtedly influenced by the particularly risky nature of the activity under scrutiny and its politically controversial character, but, more generally, it remains that due diligence will be best evidenced by adopting an inclusive approach to cooperation.

7.2.3.2 Exchange of Information

The exchange of information is a routine process in the context of activities that might have a transboundary[128] or global[129] impact. A distinction is usually made between the information exchanged before the activity is undertaken[130] and at the time during which the activity is taking place.[131] The way by which the State of origin transmits the information is left to its discretion, but it cannot expect the interested party to access the information based on its own research or on what was released in the public domain. Overall, the obligation should be carried out in good faith, and the mere exchange of irrelevant or outdated information is insufficient to discharge

127 Convention on Environmental Impact Assessment in a Transboundary Context, Implementation Committee, 'Findings and Recommendations Further to a Committee Initiative concerning the United Kingdom of Great Britain and Northern Ireland (EIA/IC/CI/5)', in 'Report of the Implementation Committee on Its Thirty-Fifth Session' (2016) ECE/MP.EIA/IC/2016/, para 66 (emphasis added).

128 See e.g. UNECE Convention on the Protection and Use of Transboundary Watercourses and International Lakes, Helsinki, 17 March 1992, in force 6 October 1996, (1992) 31 ILM 1312, Article 6; Convention on the Law of the Non-Navigational Uses of International Watercourses, New York, 21 May 1997, in force 17 August 2014, (1997) 36 ILM 700, Article 9.

129 See e.g. Convention for the Protection of the Ozone Layer, Vienna, 22 March 1985, in force 22 September 1988, (1985) 26 ILM 1529, Article 5; United Nations Framework Convention on Climate Change, New York, 9 May 1992, in force 24 March 1994, 1771 UNTS 107, Article 4(1)(h); Agreement to Promote Compliance with International Conservation and Management Measures by Fishing on the High Seas, Rome, 29 November 1993, in force 24 April 2003, FAO Res. 15/93, Article VI.

130 ILC, 'Draft Articles on Prevention of Transboundary Harm', Article 8.

131 ILC, 'Draft Articles on Prevention of Transboundary Harm', Article 12.

the obligation. The content of the information to be shared varies depending on the nature of the activity, the risks involved and the harm it may cause. It can be shared between the concerned States if the scope of the anticipated risks is relatively restrained, but using competent international organizations as intermediaries is advisable if the information could be relevant to a large number of States.[132]

7.2.3.3 Consultations and Negotiations

BILATERAL CONSULTATIONS The duty to cooperate finds its strongest expression in the obligation to consult and negotiate, which enters into play once the State of origin has notified the potentially affected State and shared the necessary information about the identified risks. The goal of the obligation to consult and negotiate is to accommodate the interests of the potentially affected State by discussing the impacts of the proposed activities and, if necessary, by seeking to limit negative impacts.[133] The status of the norm leaves little doubt since the *Lac Lanoux* case, in which the tribunal confirmed that France had an obligation to consult Spain if it wanted to carry out diversion works on the shared watercourse.[134] However, the exact details of its implementation are more controversial.[135]

At the very minimum, consultations have to be carried out 'at an early stage and in good faith'.[136] Certain criteria contribute to evaluating whether this has been the case. The *Lac Lanoux* tribunal provided a useful catalogue of what it deemed unacceptable behaviour during the consultation process, which included 'breaking off discussions without justification, abnormal delays, disregard of the agreed procedures, and systematic refusal to take into consideration adverse proposals or interests'.[137] Importantly, the duty to consult and negotiate is meant to arrive at an equitable and satisfactory solution for all. This means that while consultations are underway, the project should not be

132 ILC, 'Draft Articles on Prevention of Transboundary Harm', Commentary to Article 12, para 4.

133 Okowa, 'Procedural Obligations in International Environmental Agreements', 302.

134 *Lac Lanoux (France v. Spain)*, (1957) 12 RIAA 281, at 310, where the tribunal recognized that while France could carry out diversion works entirely within its own territory, it had an obligation to consult Spain and to safeguard its rights in the watercourse.

135 For a different position, see Plakokefalos, 'Prevention Obligations', 20–25, on consultation and its customary status; and also Koyano, 'The Significance of Procedural Obligations in International Environmental Law', 108, considering that the argument that duties of notification and consultation (outside of the field of watercourse law) are customary is 'not sufficiently convincing'.

136 Rio Declaration, Principle 19. 137 *Lac Lanoux*, 307.

carried out,[138] but it does not grant the potentially affected State a right to veto a project with a risk of significant harm.[139]

The obligation of consultation can be said to be the most controversial provisions of the ILC Prevention Articles.[140] The commission tried to define more precisely the objective of the consultations and how to achieve an equitable and acceptable solution between the State of origin and the potentially affected State.[141] It also dictated that in case the negotiations fail, the State of origin shall nevertheless 'take into account the interests of the State' likely to be affected.[142] Such a 'measure of self-regulation'[143] is more an expression of wishful thinking than the result of practical considerations: if consultations and negotiations fail, it is first and foremost because no balanced agreement could be found between the State of origin and the potentially affected State. It is therefore very unlikely that, despite having failed to reach an agreement, the State of origin would nevertheless take into account the possibly irreconcilable interests of another State. However, under the obligation set up by the ILC, the State of origin would have to take a small step towards the potentially affected State, perhaps by tweaking the project to show that although this change is not satisfactory to the potentially affected State, it nevertheless is a symbol of its willingness to move in the direction of reconciliation.

MULTILATERAL CONSULTATIONS The obligation to consult is particularly difficult to implement when harm can potentially affect a multiplicity of States. In particular, harm to a common interest – such as the preservation of certain species or the protection of the climatic system – requires taking into consideration the diverging interests of various States, which makes consultations a real challenge. These consultations, which form the core of international environmental diplomacy, generally take place within an institutionalized setting, such as meetings of the parties or treaty bodies and,[144] more broadly,

138 Espoo Convention, 'Implementation Committee's findings and recommendations further to a submission by Romania regarding Ukraine' (2008) ECE/MP.EIA/10, Annex I, para 53.

139 *Lac Lanoux*, 306; Okowa, 'Procedural Obligations in International Environmental Agreements', 306.

140 Sixth Committee, 'Summary Record of the 12th Meeting Held at Headquarters, New York, on Tuesday, 23 October 2007, at 10 a.m.', UN Doc. A/C.6/62/SR.12, Russia speaking, paras 48–50;'Summary Record of the 17th Meeting, Held at Headquarters, New York, on Thursday, 21 October 2010, at 10 a.m.', UN Doc. A/C.6/65/SR.17, Malaysia speaking.

141 Article 10. 142 ILC, 'Draft Articles on Prevention of Transboundary Harm', Article 9(3).

143 ILC, 'Draft Articles on Prevention of Transboundary Harm', Commentary to Article 9, para 10, at 161.

144 *Pulp Mills*, para 188, on the 'obligation to co-ordinate, through the Commission, the adoption of the necessary measures, as well as their enforcement and observance'.

international organizations acting in the field of environmental protection.[145] This type of cooperation has led to what can be called an 'institutionalization of prevention' that puts the principle of prevention under the umbrella of multilateral institutions and takes two forms: (1) States can use the institutions as discussion forums to discharge their obligation to cooperate with other potentially affected States and (2) can work with the institutions themselves to receive help in meeting their preventive objectives.

With regards to the first manifestation, international institutions provide a formal forum in which States can discharge their cooperative obligations, in particular, when multiple States are likely to be affected by an activity. In line with the obligation to cooperate under general international law, the consultations should be 'meaningful'.[146] Cooperation is a due-diligence duty that does not impose an obligation to reach a result. However, cooperation should be carried out in good faith; pro forma cooperation with no objective to reach a joint solution[147] will not be considered enough to discharge States from their preventive obligation.

With regards to the second form of institutionalization, the willingness of the State to engage with international institutions will also be evaluated as part of the due-diligence assessment. The ILC Prevention Articles encourage States to 'seek the assistance of one or more competent international organizations in preventing significant transboundary harm or at any event in minimizing the risk thereof'.[148] States may rely on international organizations to help them meet their obligation of prevention either because they do not have the necessary scientific or technological knowledge to avoid environmental harm or because tensions between parties make it necessary to involve a third party. Although merely an encouragement, the ILC provision is becoming an increasingly important standard upon which to judge the due diligence of a State in the prevention of harm.[149] The ICJ, in an order indicating provisional

145 As recognized e.g. in *Pulp Mills*, para 187, noting that due diligence will be exercised 'in acting through the Commission for the necessary measures to preserve the ecological balance of the river'.

146 See, in an environmental context, *Sub-Regional Fisheries Commission*, paras 210–13.

147 On the insistence on result (and not only process), see ILA, 'Declaration of Principles Relating to Climate Change', Article 7B(6), on the obligation to consult States likely to be affected with a 'view to reaching a joint decision'; *Sub-Regional Fisheries Commission*, separate opinion of Judge Paik, paras 34–37, in which he considers that cooperation should be more specifically defined and should include arrangements to jointly determine the total allowable catches for fish stocks.

148 ILC, 'Draft Articles on Prevention of Transboundary Harm', Article 4.

149 In this context, for multilateral environmental agreements with a non-compliance procedure, engagement with the committee to achieve compliance would contribute to proving good faith. See Chapter 11.

measures in the context of the *Certain Activities* dispute, followed a similar logic by imposing on Costa Rica an obligation to consult with the Secretariat of the Ramsar Convention on Wetlands of International Importance to avoid environmental harm in the disputed wetland.[150] The ITLOS also encouraged cooperation with international organizations, which it saw as a manifestation of the duty of care. In its *Advisory Opinion on the Area*, the Seabed Chamber posited that the obligation of States to cooperate with the International Seabed Authority was part of due diligence,[151] and in its *Advisory Opinion on the SFRC*, the tribunal confirmed that the obligation under UNCLOS to ensure the sustainable management of shared stocks is best met by cooperating with competent international organizations.[152] The emphasis put on cooperation with international bodies confirms that under certain circumstances, it can be an important factor in the assessment of the degree of care displayed by a State in the context of harm prevention.

7.2.4 *Sequence of Events*

As is apparent from the preceding discussion, the obligations to conduct an EIA and to cooperate form an ensemble that allows a State to discharge its obligation of due diligence. The two duties are closely linked, with the EIA being a core instrument on the basis of which to notify and consult with the potentially affected State.[153] However, the relationship between the two obligations is not as straightforward as it might seem. In particular, the jurisprudence of the ICJ, in *Certain Activities* and *Construction of a Road*, raised fundamental questions about whether notification and consultation are contingent upon a risk of harm being confirmed by the EIA or whether the two are strictly independent obligations. While State practice leaves little doubt that the EIA must be communicated to potentially affected States,[154] the question of whether notification is solely triggered once the EIA has identified a risk is unsettled. In *Certain Activities*, the Court considered that 'since Nicaragua was not under an international obligation to carry out an environmental

[150] *Certain Activities* (Provisional Measures) Order of 8 March 2011, (2011) ICJ Rep 6, para 80; and Order of 22 November 2013, (2013) ICJ Rep 354, para 54.

[151] *Responsibilities and Obligations of States Sponsoring Persons and Entities*, para 124 (regarding the obligation to assist the Authority) and para 142 (regarding the obligation to cooperate with the Authority regarding EIAs).

[152] *Responsibilities and Obligations of States Sponsoring Persons and Entities*, para 207.

[153] *South China Sea Arbitration*, para 991, on the fact that the obligation to undertake an EIA would not be considered to be met if the results of the assessment had not been communicated.

[154] *South China Sea Arbitration*, paras 987–91.

impact assessment in light of the absence of risk of significant transboundary harm, it was not required to notify, or consult with, Costa Rica'.[155] It reaffirmed the same position in the context of *Construction of a Road*, where it ruled that there was no need to consider whether Costa Rica had a duty to notify or consult because it had not 'complied with its obligation under general international law to perform an environmental impact assessment prior to the construction of the road'.[156]

The Court's approach can be interpreted as an attempt to give more specificity to the EIA process, having faced doctrinal criticisms for having refused in *Pulp Mills* to give the EIA an international minimum content.[157] It is, however, unnecessarily restraining. In particular, it excludes categories of activities that are intrinsically assumed to carry a transboundary risk (as a matter of domestic law or in case of an emergency) from which an obligation to notify emerges. As a result, Judge Donoghue found it necessary to specify in a separate opinion that she was not interpreting the Court's findings restrictively.

> I do not understand the Judgment to mean that a State is obligated to notify a potentially affected State only when an environmental impact assessment finds a risk of significant transboundary environmental harm, nor do I consider that the Court has excluded the possibility that the due diligence obligation of the State of origin would call for notification of different information or consultation regarding topics other than those specified by the Court. The question whether due diligence calls for notification or consultation, as well as the details regarding the timing and content of such notification and consultation, should be evaluated in light of particular circumstances.[158]

The Court's decision can be criticized, but it is certain that general international law offers little guidance about when the notification duty should be undertaken, except for the vague requirement that it should be 'timely'.[159] The lack of clear rules in this regard could explain why the Court did not justify why it made the obligation to notify and consult dependent on the obligation to undertake an EIA. It might be that it simply considered the failure to

155 *Certain Activities/Construction of a Road*, para 108 (see also para 104).

156 *Certain Activities/Construction of a Road*, para 168.

157 *Pulp Mills*, para 205; *Certain Activities/Construction of a Road*, para 104. For a criticism, see e. g. D Anton, 'Case concerning Pulp Mills on the River Uruguay (*Argentina v. Uruguay*)' (2010) 13 *Australian International Law Journal* 213, at 220, considering the ICJ's position somewhat 'disappointing'.

158 *Certain Activities/Construction of a Road*, separate opinion of Judge Donoghue, paras 21–23.

159 ILC, 'Draft Articles on Prevention of Transboundary Harm', Article 8(1).

conduct an EIA had already established a breach of the duty of care. However, it seems more likely that it followed the approach found in the ILC Prevention Articles that set out a similar sequenced approach making notification conditional upon the existence of a risk.[160]

In doing so, the Court conceived the EIA as a purely domestic enterprise. And yet, it is doubtful that risk can reasonably be determined unilaterally. Judge Donoghue raised this concern by noting that in *Construction of a Road*, only Nicaragua was able to take measurements or samples from the San Juan River, which therefore made it difficult to see that 'Costa Rica could conduct a sufficient assessment of the impact on the River without seeking input from its neighbour'.[161] It is evident that the Court's approach is counterproductive in the context of shared resources because it facilitates unilateralism and hence annihilates the effects of the preventive rationale. This is in stark opposition to the triangle of cooperation it created between the parties and the Ramsar Secretariat through the provisional measures it granted in the context of the same dispute.[162] More generally, it is at odds with its recognition in *Pulp Mills* that the duty to notify played an important role in the context of shared resources.[163]

As a matter of good faith and good neighbourliness, notification and consultation should start as early as possible. It would make sense to invite potentially affected States to participate in the EIA once the preliminary assessment has shown that there might be a risk of environmental damage. The assessment of transboundary harm will necessarily gain from the input of the potentially affected States (including its citizens). The Espoo Convention, regularly considered to be an example of best practices, including by ICJ judges,[164] follows this logic – notably contradicting the ILC Prevention Articles: it requires States to notify any party to give the affected State the possibility to take part in the EIA procedure.[165] Unlike the ILC Prevention Articles, which mention the obligation to undertake an EIA before the obligation to notify and consult, the Espoo Convention starts first with the obligation to notify (Article 3) before the EIA (Article 4) and then followed by consultations (Article 5). The importance of the sequence was confirmed by the Espoo Compliance Committee, which rejected the unilateral right to determine the

160 ILC, 'Draft Articles on Prevention of Transboundary Harm', Article 8(1).
161 *Certain Activities/Construction of a Road*, separate opinion of Judge Donoghue, paras 21–23.
162 *Certain Activities/Construction of a Road* (Provisional Measures) Order of 8 March 2011, (2011) ICJ Rep 6, para 80; and Order of 22 November 2013, (2013) ICJ Rep 354, para 54.
163 *Pulp Mills*, para 81.
164 *Certain Activities/Construction of a Road*, separate opinion of Judge Bhandari, para 34; separate opinion of Judge Donoghue, para 21.
165 Convention on Environmental Impact Assessment in a Transboundary Context, Article 3(3).

existence of a risk of significant impact in the context of a procedure concerning the planned construction of a nuclear power plant (NPP) at Hinkley Point C. The committee concluded that the United Kingdom failed to comply with its obligation to notify potentially affected neighbouring States, including Germany and Ireland, about the proposed construction of the two HPC reactors.[166] Despite the low probability of a nuclear accident, the activity was falling within the scope of prevention, and as a result, there was a 'need to enhance international cooperation in assessing environmental impacts', including via notification.[167]

More generally, due diligence calls for a multi-staged process in which notification can take different forms.[168] This means that 'it might be preferable to impose varying levels of data and information requirements at different stages'.[169] The Court followed this approach in *Pulp Mills*, on the basis of the Statute of the River Uruguay.[170] It distinguished between a first stage in which information is shared, without necessarily consisting of a 'full assessment' of the impacts, acknowledging that it 'will often require further time and resources'[171] but with the objective to 'enable the notified party to participate in the process of ensuring that the assessment is complete'[172] and a second stage during which the full EIA is shared. As Rieu-Clarke rightly notes, although such a distinction cannot be considered to reflect custom, the two stages of communication offer useful guidance.[173] Going further, a continuous approach – in opposition to a sequenced one – fits better with the due-diligence rationale, which requires constant monitoring of risks and

166 Espoo Convention, Implementation Committee, 'Findings and recommendations further to a Committee initiative concerning the United Kingdom of Great Britain and Northern Ireland (EIA/IC/CI/5)' in 'Report of the Implementation Committee on Its Thirty-Fifth Session' (2016) UN Doc. ECE/MP.EIA/IC/2016/2.

167 Espoo Convention, Implementation Committee, 'Findings and recommendations further to a Committee initiative concerning the United Kingdom of Great Britain and Northern Ireland (EIA/IC/CI/5)', para 59.

168 *Certain Activities/Construction of a Road*, separate opinion of Judge Donoghue, paras 21–23: '[D]ue diligence may call for notification of a potentially affected State at a different stage in the process.'

169 A Rieu-Clarke, 'Notification and Consultation on Planned Measures concerning International Watercourses: Learning Lessons from the *Pulp Mills* and *Kishenganga* Cases' (2014) 24(1) *Yearbook of International Environmental Law* 102, at 120.

170 Statute on the Navigation and the Exploitation of Natural Resources of the Uruguay River, Salto, 26 February 1975, in force 18 September 1976, 1295 UNTS 340, Article 7, which sets a dual-stage process: firstly, notification of the commission of the plans, which will determine on a preliminary basis whether there is a risk of significant harm, followed, if necessary, by notification of the other party through the commission.

171 *Pulp Mills*, para 105. 172 *Pulp Mills*, para 119.

173 Rieu-Clarke, 'Notification and Consultation', at 119–20.

engagement with potentially affected States. Again, Judge Donoghue favoured this approach in a separate opinion, where she noted that

> there are topics other than measures to prevent or to mitigate the risk of significant transboundary harm as to which consultations could play a role in meeting the State of origin's due diligence obligations, such as the parties' respective views on the sensitivity of the environment in the affected State or the procedural details of an environmental impact assessment process.[174]

The perspective of notification in the context of due diligence therefore calls for a circular approach: cooperation should inform the EIA to ensure that it includes all the available and necessary information; in turn, the EIA will be notified and will lead to further inter-State cooperation.

7.2.5 *Emerging Obligations*

The content of prevention is in constant evolution not only because its two core duties (EIA and cooperation) are becoming increasingly precise but also because additional norms are playing an increasingly important role in the prevention of environmental harm. Such is the case with the two norms that are on a trend towards becoming integral elements of the duty of care: public participation (7.2.5.1) and precaution (7.2.5.2).

7.2.5.1 Public Participation

Effective public participation in decision-making is becoming an element of increasing importance in the exercise of due diligence to prevent environmental harm. Obligations of 'environmental democracy' – right to information, to participate in decision-making and access to justice[175] – are driven by the principle of prevention, in the sense that they are an extension of the logic underpinning the obligation to notify, exchange information and consult with other States applied to individuals and communities. An obligation to share information with the 'public likely to be affected'[176] is found in the ILC Prevention Articles, which acknowledged that public participation is becoming a 'growing right' under international law.[177]

174 *Certain Activities/Construction of a Road*, separate opinion of Judge Donoghue, paras 21–23.
175 Rio Declaration, Principle 10.
176 ILC, 'Draft Articles on Prevention of Transboundary Harm', Article 13.
177 ILC, 'Draft Articles on Prevention of Transboundary Harm', Commentary to Article 13, para 10, at 166, and para 3, at 165; see also ILA, Study Group on Due Diligence in International Law, 'First Report', at 28, recognizing that there may be an obligation to 'consult the public

The customary status of public participation is yet to be fully acknowledged. At present, the emerging status of the principle of public participation tends to be underplayed, possibly explained by the fact that public participation does not operate within the traditional inter-State dynamics of international law.[178] And yet, an increasing number of international tribunals and other bodies have recognized that public participation is part of international customary law,[179] most likely not on the basis of a strict application of the two traditional elements of custom given that practice remains relatively limited but rather on the understanding that public participation is an imperative of social justice.

Admittedly, the ICJ did not recognize the right to public participation as an independent, customary norm in *Pulp Mills*, ruling that 'no legal obligation to consult the affected populations arises for the Parties from the instruments invoked by Argentina'.[180] By considering that the instruments under scrutiny were not creating a duty to involve the public, the Court indirectly ruled out the possibility that the obligation might be part of customary law. However, the refusal of the Court to acknowledge a customary norm relating to public participation should not be overestimated because the Court did not completely close the door to the principle. Indeed, although it refused to recognize the existence of an obligation to engage with the public, the ICJ nevertheless looked at whether consultations with the public had taken place.[181] It thus implicitly took participation into account in its assessment of the level of due diligence exercised by Uruguay. A similar approach has been explicitly followed by human rights bodies that have interpreted access to information[182]

likely to be affected in another State', which was not yet fully integrated into the obligation of due diligence.

178 Craik, *International Law of Environmental Impact Assessment* 146, on the procedural obligations facilitating the 'transnationalization' of international environmental law; P Okowa, 'Procedural Obligations in International Environmental Agreements' (1996) 67 *British Yearbook of International Law* 275, when talking about procedural prevention obligations, mentioning, in the context of procedural obligations, 'new trends in international environmental law'.

179 For an overview, see L-A Duvic-Paoli, 'The Status of the Right to Public Participation in International Environmental Law: An Analysis of the Jurisprudence' (2012) 23 *Yearbook of International Environmental Law* 80.

180 *Pulp Mills*, para 216. 181 *Pulp Mills*, para 219.

182 *Budayeva and Others v. Russia*, ECtHR Application Nos. 15339/02, 21166/02, 20058/02, 11673/02 and 15343/02, Judgment (29 September 2008), para 152, informing the public about inherent risks is one of the 'essential practical measures needed to ensure effective protection of the citizens concerned'; *Kolyadenko and Others v. Russia*, Application Nos. 17423/05, 20534/05, 20678/05, 23263/05, 24283/05 and 35673/05, Judgment (28 February 2012), para 159: in the context of its interpretation of ECHR Article 2, it provided that among the preventive measures set to avoid industrial risks, 'particular emphasis should be placed on

and public participation in decision-making processes[183] as essential elements of the obligation to exercise due diligence to prevent environmental harm in a domestic context. In short, the jurisprudence puts into evidence that public participation could achieve a similar dual status as the EIA duty, as an independent and customary obligation and as a factor in discharging the preventive obligation.

A brief comment should be made about the fact that the general right to public participation should be distinguished from the right to public participation of indigenous communities. This is not only because its status might be different – its integration into international customary law being more evident.[184] The content of the right also varies, in particular, because indigenous communities have a right to veto a project that might have negative consequences on their environment.[185] The obligation to consult with indigenous populations limits the decisional power of the State of origin considerably more than the obligation to consult with another State, given that a potentially affected State is not granted veto power.[186] The possibility given to indigenous peoples to veto a project, if integrated in the assessment of the degree of care, is transformative of the preventive duty: under these circumstances, prevention becomes an absolute norm that prioritizes the voice of indigenous peoples over all other (including economic) considerations.

Public participation could also integrate due diligence via another route, by becoming an element of the obligation to undertake an EIA.[187] In practice, this raises the question of the context in which public participation will be made possible, either as an independent process or under the EIA procedure. The two approaches are not mutually exclusive. There is little doubt that

the public's right to information'. See also ILC, 'Draft Articles on the Protection of Persons in the Event of Disasters (with Commentaries)' (2016) *Yearbook of the International Law Commission* vol. II, part 2), Commentary to Article 9, para 21, noting that 'the prevailing trend focusing on the importance of public access to . . . information'.

183 *Social and Economic Rights Action Center (SERAC) and Others v. Nigeria*, para 53; Human Rights Council Resolution, 'Human Rights and the Environment' (15 April 2014) UN Doc. A/HRC/26/L.22, para 4.

184 *Indigenous People Kichwa of Sarayaku v. Ecuador*, IAmCtHR Series C No. 245, Judgment (27 June 2012), para 165; *Centre for Minority Rights Development (Kenya) and Minority Rights Group International on Behalf of Endorois Welfare Council v. Kenya*, Communication 276/2003, May 2009, para 289.

185 *Saramaka People v. Suriname*, Judgment of 28 November 2007, IAmCtHR Series C No. 172, para 134; *Centre for Minority Rights Development*, para 291.

186 *Lac Lanoux*, 306.

187 S Marsden, 'Public Participation in Transboundary Environmental Impact Assessment: Closing the Gap between International and Public Law?', in B Jessup and K Rubenstein (eds), *Environmental Discourses in Public and International Law* (Cambridge University Press 2012) 238–59.

public participation has a role to play in the EIA, given that the impacts of a projected activity will be best assessed in collaboration with the populations likely to be affected. This logic drives the increasing recognition that public participation is an integral part of the EIA process.[188] As a result, an EIA would not be considered sufficient to discharge the obligation to exercise due diligence to prevent environmental harm if it had not taken into account the impacts of a proposed activity on the community. The advantage of the approach is that it does not rely on the customary status of participation and contributes to giving the EIA duty more content. At the same time, public participation needs to remain an independent duty to cover situations in which an EIA might not be necessary.

7.2.5.2 Precaution

Precaution could also play a fundamental role in the assessment of the obligation to exercise due diligence to prevent environmental harm. The question arises again about whether precaution should be seen as a factor in the due-diligence assessment or an independent duty. The less controversial approach consists in making precaution a factor that proves a high degree of care. From this perspective, the adoption of measures to prevent harm despite the fact that the risk was uncertain is evidence that the State was particularly cautious and went beyond the requirements set by prevention. From this perspective, precaution is one of the factors that can be taken into account to assess the level of care displayed by a State, but not an indispensable one.

A more progressive approach considers precaution to be an independent, customary duty. Such was the position of the ITLOS Seabed Chamber in its *Advisory Opinion on the Area*. Transforming Rio Principle 15 into a binding requirement, it noted that the precautionary approach was on a trend towards becoming customary law[189] and that, like prevention, precaution

188 This recognition was fostered by the UNEP Governing Council, 'Goals and Principles of Environmental Impact Assessment', Principles 7 and 9. See, in particular, *Certain Activities/Construction of a Road*, separate opinion of Judge Owada, para 21, noting that an EIA serves the 'purpose of enabling the public or civil society to participate in the ultimate decision-making process on activities with potentially significant environmental effects'; *Certain Activities/Construction of a Road*, separate opinion of Judge Owada, para 35, noting that the Court refused to recognize a public participation right in *Pulp Mills* but that the Espoo Convention 'places heavy emphasis on the need for public participation of the likely affected population(s)'.

189 *Responsibilities and Obligations of States Sponsoring Persons and Entities*, para 135.

> is also an integral part of the general obligation of due diligence of sponsoring States, which is applicable even outside the scope of the [Nodules] Regulations. The due diligence obligation of the sponsoring States requires them to take all appropriate measures to prevent damage that might result from the activities of contractors that they sponsor. This obligation applies in situations where scientific evidence concerning the scope and potential negative impact of the activity in question is insufficient but where there are plausible indications of potential risks.[190]

The Chamber considered that precaution falls under the due-diligence duty to prevent harm, possibly under customary law. However, this does not mean that precaution itself integrates the obligation of prevention. Prevention and precaution are both due-diligence obligations that, as a result, will share similar content (such as an EIA obligation) and apply in a context of scientific certainty as well as scientific uncertainty.[191] By rendering the distinction between scientific certainty and uncertainty unnecessary, the perspective provides a solution to situations in which the distinction between prevention and precaution is difficult to establish.[192] However, given the contested status of precaution under international law,[193] this remains a progressive approach that might not yet be extended throughout the entire field of international environmental law. It should therefore be concluded that, at this stage, the primary role played by precaution in the context of due diligence is to act as an element in the assessment of the degree of care.

7.3 CONCLUSION

The second definitional trait of prevention relates to its character as a due-diligence obligation that requires that States exercise proactivity (and not only restraint) in the face of risks. This characteristic is not unchallenging for prevention: as a variable concept, it remains an evasive obligation that can be criticized for being an empty shell. Nevertheless, this argument should be mitigated for two reasons. Firstly, international law has determined a core minimum customary content to prevention that is continuously evolving; it is becoming broader by including other obligations (e.g. public participation) and more specific at the same time regarding the implementation of these obligations (e.g. with regard to the content of the obligation to undertake an

190 *Responsibilities and Obligations of States Sponsoring Persons and Entities*, para 131.
191 J-M Arbour and S Lavallée, *Droit international de l'environnement* (Bruylant 2006) 717.
192 This issue is presented in Section 9.1.2.
193 Arbour and Lavallée, *Droit international de l'environnement*.

EIA). Secondly, attention should be given to the rich normative landscape within which the principle of prevention operates, including its multiple manifestations in conventional documents as well as formally non–legally binding instruments that provide more specific guidance on how to exercise sufficient care in the face of environmental risks. By envisaging prevention within its international legal context and building upon its multiple ramifications, the flexibility that characterizes due diligence is not necessarily synonymous with vagueness.

8

Prevention and Protection of the Environment
Spatial Scope

The geographical scope of prevention is the third, and last, definitional element of prevention. This chapter looks at each of the spatial dimensions within which prevention operates in turn to demonstrate that prevention has become an a-territorial principle that aims to protect the environment irrespective of the location of harm. An analysis of the *ratione loci* of prevention necessarily relies on Stockholm Principle 21 because it crystallizes the obligations to avoid transboundary harm (8.1) and to prevent harm to areas beyond the limits of national jurisdiction (8.2). However, over time, the scope of prevention has extended beyond the initial scope of Principle 21: an obligation of prevention applicable on the domestic territory of the State is emerging under general international law (8.3). In light of these legal developments, this chapter concludes that prevention in its advanced form applies irrespective of the location of harm (8.4).

8.1 PREVENTION OF TRANSBOUNDARY HARM

Given its partial origins in the no-harm rule, avoidance of harm in a transboundary context is a core concern of prevention. While first and foremost an inter-State obligation (8.1.1), it might also manifest as a human rights obligation (8.1.2).

8.1.1 An Inter-State Obligation

The ILC 'Draft Articles on Prevention of Transboundary Harm from Hazardous Activities' are the text of reference to analyse the transboundary scope of prevention.[1] The spatial scope of the articles is restricted given that

[1] ILC, 'Draft Articles on Prevention of Transboundary Harm from Hazardous Activities (with Commentaries)' (2001) *Yearbook of the International Law Commission* (vol II, part 2) 148.

they are exclusively applicable to transboundary harm and only to its physical consequences.[2] However, they define what constitutes 'transboundary harm' rather broadly in their identification of both the State of origin and the State likely to be affected. With regards to the later, the articles apply to harm caused to a neighbouring State but also, more generally, to *any* State 'whether or not the States concerned share a common border'.[3] As for the former, the articles apply to activities undertaken on the 'territory of the State' and under its 'jurisdiction or control' that might have a transboundary impact.[4] The term 'jurisdiction' of a State is intended to cover activities over which a State is authorized by international law to exercise its competence and authority (e.g. activities conducted on the high seas),[5] while 'control' covers situations in which a State is exercising de facto jurisdiction (e.g. in the case of occupation).[6] Prevention applies to activities under the jurisdiction or control of a State irrespective of the location of harm as long as a link can be established with the State of origin. This was instrumental in making prevention applicable in the *Iron Rhine Railway* dispute regarding Belgium's right of transit on a railway passing through the Netherlands[7] and in the *South China Sea* case regarding the harmful activities of China, or vessels under its flag, in a disputed maritime area.[8] The articles might also be applicable to harm arising from extraterritorial activities under the jurisdiction of a State, for instance, in relation to overseas greenhouse gas emissions caused by national companies or domestic consumption.[9]

8.1.2 *A Human Rights Obligation*

The transboundary dimension characterizes the no-harm rule, which means that prevention in a transboundary context intersects closely with no-harm.

2 ILC, 'Draft Articles on Prevention of Transboundary Harm', Article 1.

3 ILC, 'Draft Articles on Prevention of Transboundary Harm', Article 2(c).

4 ILC, 'Draft Articles on Prevention of Transboundary Harm', Commentary to Article 1, paras 7 and 8, at 150.

5 ILC, 'Draft Articles on Prevention of Transboundary Harm', Commentary to Article 1, para 10, at 151.

6 ILC, 'Draft Articles on Prevention of Transboundary Harm', Commentary to Article 1, para 12, at 151.

7 *Iron Rhine Railway (Belgium v. Netherlands)*, Permanent Court of Arbitration, (2005) 27 RIAA 35, para 223, on the basis that Belgium was exercising a right under international law within the territory of another State.

8 *South China Sea Arbitration (The Republic of the Philippines v. The People's Republic of China)*, Permanent Court of Arbitration, Award on the Merits, 12 July 2016, para 944.

9 B Mayer, 'State Responsibility and Climate Change Governance: A Light through the Storm' (2014) 13 *Chinese Journal of International Law* 539, at 553–54.

One element of differentiation lies in the fact that, contrary to no-harm, the obligation to prevent transboundary harm can be conceptualized as a human rights obligation.

A 2011 report of the Office of the United Nations High Commissioner for Human Rights acknowledged that '[o]ne country's pollution can become another country's environmental *and human rights* problem'.[10] The statement is significant because it recognizes that transboundary damage not only affects States but also populations. It can evidently be argued that the State is a legal construction representing its citizens, who are the actual victims, and that, as a result, the distinction is minimal. However, this has important legal effects because it gives direct rights to citizens to be protected from environmental harm. From this perspective, prevention becomes a 'diagonal' right, held by individuals or groups against States other than their own.[11]

The extraterritorial obligation to avoid transboundary harm under human rights law is currently in its infancy, with only rare instances found in conventional law. One exception is the ASEAN Agreement on Transboundary Haze Pollution.[12] Article 3 replicates Rio Principle 2 with an interesting twist: it reads that States have the 'responsibility to ensure that activities within their jurisdiction or control do not cause damage to the environment and harm to *human health* of other States or of areas beyond the limits of national jurisdiction'. The wording is progressive but perhaps unfortunate: it adds a reference to 'human health' without mentioning the victims – human beings – in a provision that reads as though States should not harm the human health of other States or of areas beyond national jurisdiction. Yet, it implies that States should not cause damage to the health of the citizens in other States – thereby creating an extraterritorial obligation to protect populations outside the territory of the State of origin from environmental damage.

This conventional law example is anecdotal, and a general extraterritorial obligation of prevention under human rights law has not yet consolidated. There seems, however, to be good support for the obligation both in the

[10] United Nations High Commissioner for Human Rights, 'Analytical Study on the Relationship between Human Rights and the Environment' (16 December 2011) UN Doc. A/HRC/19/34, para 65 (emphasis added).

[11] J Knox, 'Diagonal Environmental Rights', in M Gibney and S Skogly (eds), *Universal Human Rights and Extraterritorial Obligations* (University of Pennsylvania Press 2010) 82–103, at 82.

[12] ASEAN Agreement on Transboundary Haze Pollution, Kuala Lumpur, 10 June 2002, in force 25 November 2003, available at http://environment.asean.org/wp-content/uploads/2015/06/ASEANAgreementonTransboundaryHazePollution.pdf (last accessed 19 May 2017).

scholarship[13] and in practice.[14] In 2002, the ILA had noted that human rights law required States to prevent transboundary risks.[15] More recently, the work of the Independent Expert on Human Rights and the Environment, John Knox (then named Special Rapporteur on the same topic[16]), moved in the same direction when he acknowledged that

> most of the sources reviewed ... do indicate that States have obligations to protect human rights, particularly economic, social and cultural rights, from the extraterritorial environmental effects of actions taken within their territory.[17]

Overall, the extraterritorial obligation to prevent harm relies on relatively weak grounds given that it depends on the interpretation of human rights treaties and corresponding jurisprudence.[18] Practice is embryonic but is nevertheless existent, which led Knox to qualify the 'legal recognition by a State of the rights of individuals who reside outside its territory but who may suffer environmental harm from actions arising within its territory' as 'good practice'.[19] The argument that States have an extraterritorial preventive obligation under human rights law was notably presented to the ICJ in the context of the *Aerial Herbicide Spraying* dispute. It was held that in addition to its obligation to prevent environmental harm towards the State of Ecuador, Colombia has an obligation of prevention towards the Ecuadorian populations. Ecuador claimed that Colombia was bound to prevent harm towards its populations whose health, crops and livestock had suffered on the basis that both countries shared a 'common legal framework' that could not allow for loopholes in the protection of human rights.[20] Colombia refuted the existence

13 See A Boyle, 'Human Rights and the Environment: Where Next?' (2012) 23 *European Journal of International Law* 613, at 640.

14 'Report of the Independent Expert on the issue of human rights obligations relating to the enjoyment of a safe, clean, healthy and sustainable environment, Compilation of Good Practices by John H. Knox' (3 February 2015) UN Doc. A/HRC/28/61, para 85.

15 ILA, 'Transnational Enforcement of Environmental Law: Second Report', New Delhi, 70th Session, 2002, 5.

16 Human Rights Council Resolution, 'Human Rights and the Environment' (26 March 2015) UN Doc. A/HRC/RES/28/11.

17 'Report of the Independent Expert on the issue of human rights obligations relating to the enjoyment of a safe, clean, healthy and sustainable environment, John H. Knox: Mapping Report' (30 December 2013) UN Doc. A/HRC/25/53, para 63.

18 For a full account on the limits of the extraterritorial obligation under human rights law in relation to environmental protection, see JE Viñuales, 'A Human Rights Approach to Extraterritorial Environmental Protection?', in N Bhuta (ed), *The Frontiers of Human Rights* (Oxford University Press 2016) 177–222.

19 'Report of the Independent Expert, Compilation of Good Practices by John H. Knox', para 85.

20 *Aerial Herbicide Spraying (Ecuador v. Colombia)*, reply of Ecuador, 31 January 2011, para 7.28. Ecuador justified the existence of a human rights obligation to prevent transboundary harm on

of such an obligation, refusing to recognize that it had 'obligations to individuals or groups within Ecuador which exceed its obligations to Ecuador itself'.[21] The Court did not get the opportunity to rule on this matter as the case was eventually settled. The dispute nevertheless highlighted that the prohibition to cause transboundary harm can be envisaged as a dual duty to preserve the territorial integrity of a State and the human rights of its populations.

The principles of public participation in decision-making and non-discrimination between citizens on the basis of their State of origin could play a significant role in the consolidation of the right by extending the extraterritorial reach of prevention in its procedural dimensions. Both principles are recognized in the ILC Prevention Articles in the form of an obligation to inform the populations likely to be affected by an activity, irrespective of their location,[22] and a right to access to justice, irrespective of the 'nationality or residence or place where the injury might occur'.[23] The two articles (considered rather progressive) entitle the public to take part in the decision-making processes of another State when there is a risk of transboundary harm. Practice can be found in the context of the UNECE Convention on Access to Information, Public Participation and Decision-Making and Access to Justice in Environmental Matters (Aarhus Convention), which defines the 'public concerned' by environmental decision-making processes broadly.[24] Because the convention does not include location as a criteria for standing, the compliance committee of the convention interpreted it as giving citizens an extraterritorial right to participate in the environmental impact assessment and decision-making procedures.[25] One case of particular interest relates to the confirmation of the committee that in the context of decision-making

the basis of three arguments: (a) Colombia and Ecuador are part of a common legal space at the regional level ('un espace juridique commun') relating to the protection of human rights and indigenous peoples, (b) Colombia and Ecuador are subject to an international public order of human rights that does not allow for loopholes in the effective protection of human rights for any part of their populations, and (c) Colombia is under an obligation not to frustrate the protection of human rights in the regions adjacent to its borders.

21 *Aerial Herbicide Spraying*, counter-memorial of Colombia, 28 April 2009, para 9.13.

22 ILC, 'Draft Articles on Prevention of Transboundary Harm', Commentary to Article 13, at 165, noting that the obligation applies regardless of whether the public is the State's own public or the public of another State.

23 ILC, 'Draft Articles on Prevention of Transboundary Harm', Article 15.

24 Convention on Access to Information, Public Participation and Decision-Making and Access to Justice in Environmental Matters, Aarhus, 25 June 1998, in force 30 October 2001, (1999) 38 ILM 517, Article 2(5).

25 Aarhus Compliance Committee, 'Findings and Recommendations with regard to compliance by Turkmenistan in the case of Act on Public Associations (Communication ACCC/C/2004/05 by Biotica (Republic of Moldova))' (2005) ECE/MP.PP/C.1/2005/2/Add.5 (an NGO in Moldova brought a claim against Turkmenistan regarding its non-compliance relative to non-

processes relative to ultra-hazardous activities (such as nuclear power plants), States are under an obligation to involve the public beyond domestic borders on the basis that harm could affect 'vast areas and regions' and may adversely affect property, health or quality of life.[26] The practice of the Aarhus Convention remains limited to the UNECE region and can only be considered to reflect best practice. However, public participation could play a greater role in the context of an extraterritorial obligation to prevent because its role in the assessment of the level of care exercised in application of prevention is becoming increasingly important (see Chapter 7).

A moderate conclusion regarding the status of a human rights obligation to avoid transboundary harm can be derived from the analysis undertaken in this section. Practice is limited, and as a result, the extraterritorial scope of the prevention principle remains controversial. Yet, at the very least, these anecdotal signs indicate that prevention is moving beyond its original inter-State focus, an extension that is also visible in the other spatial dimensions within which prevention operates (which are presented below).

8.2 PREVENTION IN AREAS BEYOND THE LIMITS OF NATIONAL JURISDICTION

The obligation to prevent environmental harm is also applicable in relation to areas beyond the limits of national jurisdiction, as acknowledged by the third component of Stockholm Principle 21. It modifies significantly the rationale of

discrimination – which the Committee eventually considered to have been violated); Aarhus Compliance Committee, ACCC/C/2009/39 (a Hungarian municipality complaining about the decision of Austrian authorities to permit the construction of a waste incinerator very close to its border – the case was declared inadmissible); Aarhus Compliance Committee, 'Findings and Recommendations with regard to communication ACCC/C/2012/71 concerning compliance by the Czech Republic' (2016) ECE/MP.PP/C.1/2017/3 (referred to the committee by German citizens against the Czech Republic on the basis that members of the public concerned by the construction of a nuclear power plant in the Czech Republic did not have the same possibility to participate as had members of the public concerned in the Czech Republic – the committee declared a violation of Article 6(2) in relation to the inadequacy of the party's legal framework); Aarhus Compliance Committee, 'Findings and recommendations with regard to communication ACCC/C/2013/91 concerning compliance by the United Kingdom' (2017) advanced version (German citizens are alleging non-compliance by the United Kingdom regarding Article 6(2) on the basis that the German public had the right to 'participate in a transboundary environmental impact assessment procedure concerning the proposed construction of two nuclear reactors' – the committee found a violation of Article 6(2)).

26 Aarhus Compliance Committee, 'Findings and recommendations with regard to communication ACCC/C/2012/71', para 75.

prevention by moving beyond its drive to protect the interests of individual States to meet what Judge Weeramantry called the 'greater interests of humanity and planetary welfare'.[27] In other words, prevention in the context of areas beyond national jurisdiction does not seek to avoid external infringements on national sovereignty but rather aims to protect the environment per se. Despite a changed rationale, the norm still operates within a legal framework structured around the concept of sovereignty: it is presented as an exception to the sacrosanct concept, 'areas beyond national jurisdiction' being defined *in opposition* to areas under State jurisdiction.

The third component of Stockholm Principle 21 plays an important role as a legal principle guiding the adoption of international treaties: it has been operationalized in treaty obligations providing for a duty to protect the environment in the 'global commons' (i.e. the outer space,[28] the Antarctic,[29] the high seas[30] and the deep seabed[31] and the atmosphere[32]). These obligations are generally considered to form the backbone of a customary obligation to prevent harm in areas beyond national jurisdiction.[33] However, the affirmation presents two major difficulties relative to the identification of customary law. The first one relates to the extension of the preventive rationale beyond its original transboundary scope, which some scholarly critics refuse to acknowledge, arguing that the principle of permanent sovereignty of natural resources is irreconcilable

27 *Gabčíkovo-Nagymaros Project (Hungary/Slovakia)* (Judgment) (1997) ICJ Rep 7, separate opinion of Judge Weeramantry, at 118.

28 Treaty Banning Nuclear Weapon Testing in the Atmosphere, in Outer Space and Under Water, Moscow, 5 August 1963, in force 10 October 1963, 480 UNTS 43; Agreement Governing the Activities of States on the Moon and Other Celestial Bodies, New York, 5 December 1979, in force 11 July 1984, (1979) 18 ILM 1434, Article 7(1).

29 Protocol on Environmental Protection to the Antarctic Treaty, Madrid, 4 October 1991, in force 14 January 1998, (1991) 30 ILM 1461, Article 2.

30 United Nations Convention on the Law of the Sea, Montego Bay, 10 December 1982, in force 16 November 1994, 1833 UNTS 3, Articles 116–18 (on conservation and management of the living resources of the high seas) and Article 192 (on a general obligation to protect and preserve the marine environment).

31 United Nations Convention on the Law of the Sea, Article 145.

32 The right to take environmental measures to protect the international air space was recognized in *Air Transport Association of America and Others v. Secretary of State for Energy and Climate Change* (Judgment of the Court), C 366/10, Court of Justice of the European Union, Grand Chamber (21 December 2011). See also ILC, 'Titles and Texts of Draft Guidelines 3, 4, 5, 6 and 7, together with a preambular paragraph, provisionally adopted by the Drafting Committee on 7, 8 and 9 June 2016' (2016) UN Doc. A/CN.4/L.875, draft guideline 3, on the protection of the atmosphere.

33 P Birnie, A Boyle and C Redgwell, *International Law and the Environment* (3rd edn, Oxford University Press 2009) 145; P Sands and J Peel, *Principles of International Environmental Law* (3rd edn, Cambridge University Press 2012) 200.

with the concept of 'common natural resources'[34] or that Stockholm Principle 21 does not apply to cumulative harm, a frequent occurrence in the global commons.[35] But, generally, the doctrine presumes that unless otherwise stated, prevention is applicable to 'complex stances of environmental change', even if these were not initially envisaged.[36] The extension of the spatial scope of prevention can only be accepted if prevention is conceptualized in an evolutionary manner as a norm that has moved beyond its originally spatially limited focus. The fact that most judicial decisions pertaining to prevention, including most notably the *Trail Smelter* award, relate to the transboundary application of the norm[37] is not a convincing argument to reject the applicability of prevention to areas beyond national jurisdiction. It mistakenly explains the rarity of environmental adjudication relative to prevention in areas beyond national jurisdiction by the lack of applicable obligations, when it is primarily due to the limitations of the law of State responsibility that do not provide sufficient space to bring a successful claim in this context. The mere fact that the ICJ recognized the customary status of Stockholm Principle 21 should provide enough evidence that prevention has evolved beyond its initial focus.[38]

The second limitation is more intricate and relates to the difficulties arising from the implementation and enforcement of the principle of prevention in areas beyond national jurisdiction. It could be said to be problematic in the context of the identification of custom because State practice is limited, but the argument does not stand if one takes a more 'modern' approach to custom that does not rely so heavily on practice[39] (see Chapter 4). The real challenge lies in effect in the discrepancy that exists between the fact that a general obligation has been recognized as customary (in the form of Stockholm Principle 21) but that it can only be implemented properly when conventional regimes have been set up to operationalize it.

34 A position mentioned in ILA, Committee on the Legal Principles Relating to Climate Change, 'Report', Washington, DC, 2014, Commentary to Article 3, para 4, at 6.

35 A Zahar, 'Methodological Issues in Climate Law' (2015) 5 *Climate Law* 25, at 28.

36 ILA, Committee on Legal Principles Relating to Climate Change, 'Second Report', Sofia, 75th Session, 2012, at 25, noting 'neither the decades of ILC debates on the issue of prevention of environmental harm nor international jurisprudence provide evidence that complex instances of environmental change are not covered by the general duty to prevent harm and minimise the risk thereof'.

37 Zahar, 'Methodological Issues in Climate Law', at 27.

38 *Legality of the Threat or Use of Nuclear Weapons* (Advisory Opinion) (1996) ICJ Rep 226, para 29.

39 B Mayer, 'The Relevance of the No-Harm Principle to Climate Change Law and Politics' (2016) 19 *Asia Pacific Journal of Environmental Law* 79, at 87.

8.3 PREVENTION IN A DOMESTIC CONTEXT

The spatial scope of prevention could also be extended in another direction: the domestic territory. The question that is raised is whether States are required under customary international law to prevent harm to the environment within their territory, jurisdiction or control even when no external impact can be reasonably foreseen. The existence of such an obligation would further demonstrate that prevention is increasingly concerned with environmental protection per se and not merely sovereignty preservation.

Doctrinal discussions on the potential demise of the State and on how the concept of sovereignty is being re-shaped in an interdependent globalized world abound.[40] However, little has been said regarding the potential limitations of the concept of sovereignty over natural resources. The proposition that a State can use its resources as it sees fit is rarely openly challenged.[41] However, signs of the emergence of an international obligation to prevent environmental harm irrespective of external impacts are identifiable. Multiple international treaties create obligations to avoid environmental harm that operate within a purely domestic context, conservation treaties being the most evident example.[42] Also, as mentioned previously, codification works have hinted at the fact that prevention might be applicable within domestic borders as a matter of customary law.[43] The legal scholarship has also alluded to the applicability of the obligation of prevention within domestic borders. For instance, Sands and Peel mention in their textbook that 'under the preventive principle, a State may be under an obligation to prevent ... damage to the

40 See *inter alia* B Badie, *La fin des territoires* (Fayard 1995); J-M Guéhenno, *The End of the Nation-State* (University of Minnesota Press 2000); M Seymour, *Fate of the Nation State* (McGill-Queen's University Press 2004); E Aydinli and J Rosenau, *Globalization, Security, and the Nation State: Paradigms in Transition* (State University of New York Press 2005); G Handl, J Zekoll and P Zumbansen, *Beyond Territoriality: Transnational Legal Authority in an Age of Globalization* (Martinus Nijhoff 2012).

41 F Shuppert, 'Beyond the National Resource Privilege: Towards an International Court of the Environment', (2014) 6 *International Theory* 68, at 69, calling it the 'national resource privilege'.

42 E.g. Convention on Biological Diversity, Nairobi, 22 May 1992, in force 29 December 1993, (1992) 31 ILM 822.

43 UNEP Governing Council Decision, 'Principles on Conservation and Harmonious Utilisation of Natural Resources Shared by Two or More States' (1978) UNEP/IG12/2, Principle 13; RD Munro and J Lammers (eds), *Environmental Protection and Sustainable Development: Legal Principles and Recommendations Adopted by the Experts Group on Environmental Law of the World Commission on Environment and Development* (Graham & Trotman 1987); Covenant on Environment and Development, *IUCN Environmental Policy and Law Paper* No. 31 (1st edn, IUCN 1995), Article 11(a).

environment within its own jurisdiction',[44] while Kiss and Shelton consider that prevention seeks to 'avoid harm irrespective of whether or not there are transboundary impacts'.[45] Others, such as Nollkaemper, take a more theoretical approach to assess the extent to which international law limits a State's power with regard to its own environment.[46] Overall, there is a sense in the doctrine that prevention has evolved to become applicable in a purely domestic context. This intuition is rarely backed by detailed legal investigation but seems to arise from two assumptions: (1) the widespread recognition that prevention is a core principle of environmental law facilitates the extension of its spatial coverage, and (2) the state of the environment gives rise to moral imperatives that dictate that the environment be protected irrespective of the location of harm.

This section identifies an emerging norm of prevention applicable in a domestic context. The task raises, again, fundamental questions about the identification of custom. These, however, did not, constrain Langer when he undertook a similar exercise on the basis of international practice – evidenced, mostly, by multilateral environmental agreements.[47] This study takes a different route and explains how a multiplicity of existing customary (or emerging) norms can be interpreted as obligations of prevention in a domestic context and how together they offer avenues to the emergence of a general obligation to prevent environmental harm applicable irrespective of whether the impacts are felt externally (8.3.4). In this context, international environmental obligations (8.3.1), human rights duties (8.3.2) and investment norms (8.3.3) are examined.

8.3.1 *International Environmental Obligations*

Three different sets of inter-State obligations contribute to making prevention applicable within a purely domestic context: a transposition of the international no-harm rule (8.3.1.1), the emerging obligation of sustainable use of natural resources (8.3.1.2) and a-territorial norms of prevention (8.3.1.3).

[44] Sands and Peel, *Principles of International Environmental Law*, 201.

[45] A Kiss and D Shelton, *Guide to International Environmental Law* (Martinus Nijhoff 2007) 113. See also Birnie, Boyle and Redgwell, *International Law and the Environment*, 128–29.

[46] A Nollkaemper, 'Sovereignty and Environmental Justice in International Law', in J Ebbesson and P Okowa (eds), *Environmental Law and Justice in Context* (Cambridge University Press 2009) 253–69, at 264.

[47] MJ Langer, 'Sovereignty in Trust: Territorial Sovereignty at the Crossroads in International Environmental Law', PhD thesis, Graduate Institute of International and Development Studies, 2016, 405–59.

8.3.1.1 No-Harm Rule by Analogy

The international obligation of no-harm can be applied by analogy to a domestic setting in a situation where an administrative entity in a State (such as a province, a canton or a land) causes environmental harm to the territory of another administrative entity within that same State. The good-neighbourliness logic of the no-harm rule can be transposed to decentralized entities that have been granted 'quite sovereign rights'[48] and whose relations with their neighbours are comparable to State interactions.

In fact, no-harm originated at the municipal level to regulate the relations between administrative units with a certain degree of autonomy. In 1931, in *New Jersey v. New York*, the US Supreme Court held that although 'New York has the physical power of cutting all the water within its jurisdiction . . . the use of this power harming the interests of the downstream States cannot be accepted'.[49] A series of similar Supreme Court decisions was referenced in the *Trail Smelter* award to apply the no-harm rule at an international level.[50] In addition, and most importantly, the international obligation of no-harm has on occasion been directly transposed to the domestic level. This is best seen in the *Provincia de la Pampa v. Provincia de Mendoza* decision taken by the Supreme Court of Argentina in 1987.[51] The Court relied on guidance from a number of international instruments, including the work of the ILC on the law of watercourses,[52] to rule on a case that had a purely domestic scope and to find that the province of Mendoza could only maintain its existing consumption of water as long as it did not prejudice the right of the La Pampa province to use the interprovincial watercourses.

The transposition of the international obligation of no-harm to decide a domestic case creates in effect an obligation to prohibit environmental harm in a purely domestic context but is not without severe limitations. Firstly, it can only operate in States that have a federal system (i.e. in relation to administrative entities that have enough autonomy to act as State-like entities). Secondly, as noted earlier, the rationale of the no-harm rule is more restrictive than prevention in its focus on restraint and limited concern for the environment, which can be consequential. Thirdly, the no-harm rule allows the administrative entity to harm its own territory as long as it does not

48 *Trail Smelter (United States v. Canada)* (16 April 1938 and 11 March 1941), (1941) 3 RIAA 1905, at 1963.

49 *New Jersey v. New York*, US Supreme Court, 4 May 1931, 283 US 336.

50 *Trail Smelter*, at 1964–66.

51 *Provincia de la Pampa v. Provincia de Mendoza*, Supreme Court, Buenos Aires, Argentina, 3 December 1987, IELR 1.

52 *Provincia de la Pampa*, 131–34.

have external impacts: if the administrative entity is large enough for the effects of harm not to be felt outside its borders, the degradation of the domestic territory can still be significant.

8.3.1.2 Duty of Sustainable Use

A second yet still partial proposal can contribute to extending the scope of prevention to the domestic sphere. It relates to the duty found in multiple international treaties to conserve natural resources within the domestic territory[53] and which is now considered to have consolidated into an independent, possibly customary obligation of 'sustainable use of national resources'.[54] The duty of sustainable use merges two norms from which a preventive norm with a domestic scope can be extracted: the principle of permanent sovereignty over natural resources and the concept of sustainable development. The principle of sovereignty over natural resources creates an obligation to avoid harm to domestic natural resources if it is interpreted not merely as the right to freely use natural resources but also as the right to do so in an 'environmentally responsible way'[55] (see Chapter 2). The second concept underlying the obligation of sustainable use is the concept of sustainable development that also integrates a preventive approach, in the form of its environmental pillar.[56] By combining these two norms, the duty to ensure sustainable use of natural resources provides a strong legal basis for a domestic obligation of prevention. The customary status of the norm, however, needs to consolidate further before an obligation to prevent

53 E.g. Convention on Wetlands of International Importance Especially as Waterfowl Habitat, Ramsar, 2 February 1971, in force 21 December 1975, 996 UNTS 245; Convention on International Trade in Endangered Species of Wild Fauna and Flora, Washington, DC, 3 March 1973, in force 1 July 1975, 993 UNTS 243; UNESCO Convention for the Protection of the World Cultural and Natural Heritage, Paris, 16 November 1972, in force 17 December 1975, (1972) 11 ILM 1358; Convention on the Conservation of Migratory Species of Wild Animals, Bonn, 23 June 1979, in force 1 November 1983, (1980) 19 ILM 15; Convention on Biological Diversity, Nairobi, 22 May 1992, in force 29 December 1993, (1992) 31 ILM 822; International Treaty on Plant Genetic Resources for Food and Agriculture, Rome, 4 November 2002, in force 31 March 2004, available at www.fao.org/plant-treaty/en/ (last accessed 24 August 2017).

54 ILA, Committee on International Law on Sustainable Development, 'Fifth Report', Sofia, 75th Session, 2012, at 14.

55 ILA, Committee on Legal Aspects of Sustainable Development, 'Final Report', New Delhi, 70th Session, 2002, at 8.

56 ILA, Committee on Legal Aspects of Sustainable Development, 'Final Report'. See also ILA, Committee on Legal Principles Relating to Climate Change, 'Declaration of Principles Relating to Climate Change', Washington, DC, 76th Session, 2014, Draft Article 3(2), linking sustainable use, prevention and intergenerational equity.

environmental harm within the domestic territory can be derived from it. Another limitation of the duty relates to its rationale. Indeed, the obligation to prevent harm that is extracted from the duty to ensure sustainable use is relative: the later attempts to find a balance between environmental protection and socio-economic development, whereas the former privileges environmental protection.

8.3.1.3 A-territorial Obligations of Prevention

In addition to the two norms just discussed, a number of treaty obligations apply to harm irrespective of its location: their *ratione loci* therefore includes a domestic dimension. The a-territorial scope of such obligations is studied further in Section 8.3.2; only what it means for prevention in a domestic context is discussed here. While multiple treaty provisions create domestic obligations of prevention, three major obligations are highlighted here, chosen for their generality, which provides broad environmental protection, and for their consensual status as customary norms, which makes them widely applicable. These are general obligations to protect the marine environment, international watercourses and the atmosphere.

The domestic marine environment is protected under Article 192 of UNCLOS ('States have the obligation to protect and preserve the marine environment'), whose customary status is undisputed.[57] Tribunals have interpreted the obligation to apply to 'all maritime areas',[58] hence confirming that, as a result, States are under an obligation to prevent harm to the marine environment in their territorial sea and exclusive economic zone irrespective of external impacts. Similarly, international watercourses are protected by Article 20 of the UN Convention on the Law of the Non-Navigational Uses of International Watercourses ('Watercourse States shall, individually or jointly, protect and preserve the ecosystems of international watercourses'), equally of a customary character.[59] This creates an obligation of prevention of harm irrespective of the location of harm, hence including harm in the

[57] Sands and Peel, *Principles of International Environmental Law*, 350 (on the basis of the wide ratification of the convention, its rapid inclusion in other law of the sea treaties and the case-law recognition).

[58] *Sub-Regional Fisheries Commission*, ITLOS No. 21, Advisory Opinion (2 April 2015), para 120. See also *South China Sea Arbitration*, Award on the Merits, para 927; Award on Jurisdiction and Admissibility, 29 October 2015, para 408.

[59] ILC, 'Draft Articles on the Law of the Non-Navigational Uses of International Watercourses (with Commentaries)' (1994) *Yearbook of the International Law Commission* (vol II, part 2), Commentary to Article 20, at 119, para 5.

domestic territory.[60] Finally, one last environmental element could be protected from harm in the domestic context irrespective of external impacts: the atmosphere. Such is the position of the ILC Guidelines on the Protection of the Atmosphere provisionally adopted in 2016, which create a general obligation to protect the atmosphere.[61] However, this last obligation remains a progressive one that has not, contrary to the other two general obligations, achieved customary status.

This section has put in evidence different paths that contribute to the emergence of an obligation of prevention in the domestic territory, albeit in a fragmented manner, since they apply under specific circumstances. The applicability of the no-harm rule in a domestic setting is limited to States that are structured around administrative entities with powerful competences over the control of their territory. The obligation of sustainable use remains attached to economic considerations that put limits to the environmental objectives of prevention. The obligation closest to a domestic duty can be found in general obligations to protect the environment, although they exist only in relation to specific environmental media and thus do not protect the environment as a single entity.

8.3.2 *Human Rights Obligations*

Human rights obligations offer a complementary avenue to the principle of prevention and its manifestation in a domestic context. The World Court recognized that environmental harm can affect human beings by acknowledging that the environment 'represents the living space, the quality of life and the very health of human beings, including generations unborn'.[62] The statement thus recognizes that prevention is driven not only by a willingness to preserve territorial integrity and the environment but also by a need to promote human well-being. The later objective is best met under human rights law,[63] where an obligation to prevent environmental harm in

60 Convention on the Law of the Non-Navigational Uses of International Watercourses, New York, 21 May 1997, in force 17 August 2014, (1997) 36 ILM 70, Article 20, obviously restricted to watercourses meeting the criteria of 'international watercourses'. See also ILA, 'Berlin Rules on Water Resources', Berlin, 71st Session, 2004, Article 8, on the minimization of environmental harm, applicable to 'all waters' (Article 1), irrespective of transboundary impacts and irrespective of the international nature of the watercourse.

61 ILC, 'Second Report of the Special Rapporteur, Mr Shinya Murase, on the Protection of the Atmosphere' (2015) UN Doc. A/CN.4/681, draft guideline 4, at 49.

62 *Legality of the Threat or Use of Nuclear Weapons* (Advisory Opinion) (1996) ICJ Rep 226, para 29.

63 F Francioni, 'International Human Rights in an Environmental Horizon' (2010) 21 *European Journal of International Law* 55, on the complementarities between human rights and environmental law.

a purely domestic context can be identified in the obligation to protect people in the event of disasters (8.3.2.1) and environmental damage (8.3.2.2).

8.3.2.1 Protection of Persons in the Event of Disasters

A specific obligation of prevention in a purely domestic context exists under disaster law in the form of an obligation to protect persons in the event of disasters. It *inter alia* requires States to prevent disasters in their territory irrespective of external impacts, as codified by the ILC draft articles on the topic of protection of persons in the event of disasters.[64] The sixth report of the ILC on the topic noted that 'the principles of prevention and mitigation are among the core principles underpinning contemporary activities in the realm of protection of persons in the event of disasters'.[65] It recognized that States have 'horizontal' rights and obligations 'in relation to one another and the international community' but also 'vertical' obligations towards the population in their territory.[66] The rapporteur justified the existence of an obligation to prevent based on an extensive analysis of State practice[67] but also relied on the environmental principle of prevention to explicate its rationale and due-diligence character.[68]

The obligation can be assimilated to a manifestation of prevention in a purely domestic context but has necessarily a more limited scope given that, as mentioned in Chapter 3, an obligation to prevent disaster is not completely equivalent to an obligation to prevent environmental harm. Although international environmental law and disaster law share a common desire to limit risk, disaster law is concerned with a greater variety of risks (i.e. not only environmental) and focuses on harm of high intensity (that 'seriously disrupt[s] the functioning of society'[69]). As a result, disaster law relies on an obligation to prevent in relation to a specific timeframe (emergency) and with a view to protect the populations (and not necessarily the environment per se).

64 ILC, 'Draft Articles on the Protection of Persons in the Event of Disasters (with Commentaries)' (2016) *Yearbook of the International Law Commission* (vol II, part 2), Article 9.

65 ILC, 'Sixth Report by the Special Rapporteur, Mr Eduardo Valencia-Ospina, on the Protection of Persons in the Event of Disasters' (2013) UN Doc. A/CN.4/662, para 6.

66 ILC, 'Sixth Report by the Special Rapporteur, Mr Eduardo Valencia-Ospina', para 24.

67 ILC, 'Draft Articles on the Protection of Persons in the Event of Disasters', Commentary to Article 9, paras 5–6 (on the basis of multilateral, regional and bilateral instruments as well as national policies and legal frameworks).

68 ILC, 'Sixth Report by the Special Rapporteur, Mr Eduardo Valencia-Ospina', paras 54–69.

69 ILC, 'Draft Articles on the Protection of Persons in the Event of Disasters', Article 3(a).

Although the two obligations might not coincide completely, it is noteworthy that the obligation to prevent under disaster law was partly extracted from, or at least inspired by, the obligation to prevent under international environmental law: its initial application in the context of transboundary harm was not seen as an obstacle to its transposition in a purely domestic context. This reveals that the broadening of the geographical scope of prevention is, at least implicitly, becoming widely accepted, a process facilitated by the concomitant recognition of an obligation to prevent environmental harm under human rights law.

8.3.2.2 Protection of Persons in the Event of Environmental Damage

An obligation to prevent domestic environmental harm is consolidating under human rights law. Concisely stated, human rights judicial bodies recognize that States have an obligation to take preventive measures to ensure that industrial or technological activities do not adversely affect a number of human rights.[70] This obligation is not only a negative one – requiring States to restrain from creating environmental harm that might affect human rights – but also a positive one – dictating that States take proactive measures to avoid environmental harm within their domestic territory.[71] Two fundamental limitations, however, should be highlighted. Most evidently, the obligation is extracted from treaty law, which calls for caution when seeking to derive a general customary obligation. Second, it is grounded in rights that are not purely environmental, such as the right to enjoy one's own culture,[72] the right to property,[73] the right to private and family life,[74] the

[70] See the jurisprudence of human rights bodies discussed in Section 5.1.3.

[71] See *Lopez Ostra v. Spain*, Application no. 16798/90, Judgment, 9 December 1994, (1995) 20 EHRR 277; *Guerra and Others v. Italy*, Application no. 14967/89, Judgment, 19 February 1998, (1998) 26 EHRR 357; *Öneryildiz v. Turkey*, European Convention on Human Rights 2004-XII; *Taskin and Others v. Turkey*, Application no. 46117/99, Judgment, 10 November 2004, Final 30 March 2005, 42 EHRR 50; *Tătar v. Romania*, Application No. 67021/01, Judgment, 27 January 2009 (Final 6 July 2009). See also 'Report of the Independent Expert on the issue of human rights obligations relating to the enjoyment of a safe, clean, healthy and sustainable environment, John H. Knox: Preliminary report' (24 December 2012) UN Doc. A/HRC/22/43, para 50.

[72] Under Article 27 of the International Covenant on Civil and Political Rights, as recognized in *Ilmari Länsman et al. v. Finland*, Communication No. 511/1992, UN Doc. CCPR/C/52/D/511/1992 (1994), paras 9.4–9.5 (although not violated in the *cas d'espèce*).

[73] Under Article 21 of the American Convention on Human Rights, as recognized in *Mayagna (Sumo) Awas Tingni Community v. Nicaragua*, Judgment of 31 August 2001, IAmCtHR Series C No. 79, para 153.

[74] Under Article 8 of the European Convention on Human Rights, as recognized, for instance, in *Lopez Ostra*, para 58.

right to life[75] and the right to a fair trial.[76] As a result, it is dependent upon proving that environmental degradation has led to a violation of these rights.

However, the existence of a customary right to an environment of a certain quality (in addition to its conventional forms[77]) could bypass these two limitations. The large amount of work carried out by the Independent Expert on the topic to identify State practice relative to the right to an environment of a certain quality is contributing to moving the norm towards the realm of custom. The conclusions of the Independent Expert in its 2013 mapping report that identifies substantive and procedural obligations to be fulfilled to 'protect against environmental harm that interferes with the enjoyment of human rights'[78] are of special interest here. Admittedly, the Independent Expert never openly said that his conclusions resulted in acknowledging the existence of an obligation to prevent applicable within a purely domestic context. However, the obligations that the mapping report recognizes as customary are in fact a transposition of the content of prevention identified in Chapter 7. Indeed, the report identifies two substantive obligations in the form of (1) an obligation to adopt and implement legal frameworks to protect against environmental harm that may infringe on enjoyment of human rights and (2) an obligation to regulate private actors to protect against such environmental harm[79] and three procedural obligations as follows: (1) an obligation to assess environmental impacts, (2) an obligation to facilitate public participation in environmental decision-making, and (3) a duty to

[75] Under Article 2 of the European Convention on Human Rights, as recognized *inter alia* in *Öneryildiz*, paras 89–90; under Article 6 of the International Covenant on Civil and Political Rights, as recognized by Draft General Comment No. 36 – Right to Life (July 2017), advance unedited version (no reference, available at www.ohchr.org/EN/HRBodies/CCPR/Pages/GC36-Article6Righttolife.aspx (last accessed 10 September 2017)), para 65; and under Article 4 of the American Convention on Human Rights: see *Request for an Advisory Opinion Presented by the Republic of Colombia, concerning the Interpretation of Article 1(1), 4(1) and 5(1) of the American Convention on Human Rights*, submitted to the Inter-American Court of Human Rights in March 2016, pending.

[76] Under Article 2 of the European Convention on Human Rights, as recognized, for instance, in *Okyay and Others v. Turkey*, Application No. 36220/97, Judgment, 12 July 2005 (Final 12 October 2005), paras 61–69.

[77] Additional Protocol to the American Convention on Human Rights in the Area of Economic, Social and Cultural Rights, San Salvador, 16 November 1988, in force 16 November 1999, OAS Treaty Series No. 69, Article 11; African Charter on Human and Peoples' Rights, Banjul, 27 June 1981, in force 21 October 1986 (1982) 21 ILM 58, Article 24; Association of Southeast Asian Nations, ASEAN Human Rights Declaration, adopted on 18 November 2012, available at www.asean.org/storage/images/ASEAN_RTK_2014/6_AHRD_Booklet.pdf (last accessed 24 August 2017), Article 28(f).

[78] 'Report of the Independent Expert: Mapping Report', paras 79–80.

[79] 'Report of the Independent Expert: Mapping Report', para 46.

provide access to remedies for harm.[80] These obligations were previously presented as constitutive elements in the assessment of the duty of care. In other words, by recognizing the existence of these obligations under human rights law, the Independent Expert transposed the preventive obligation into a human rights context.

It should nevertheless be noted that the obligation to prevent environmental harm under human rights only partly extends prevention to the domestic arena, given that it does not apply to every case of environmental harm but only to cases where human beings are affected. If it is therefore not fully protective of the environment per se, it is, however, indicative of the restrictions put on the sovereign right of States to freely use their natural resources and domestic environment.

8.3.3 *International Investment Law Obligations*

As a complement to inter-State norms and human rights obligations, international investment law could further consolidate the obligation to prevent in a purely domestic setting via the principle of 'fair and equitable treatment' (FET) and, more specifically, the concept of 'legitimate expectations'. Before turning to how an obligation to prevent domestic environmental harm can be derived from investment norms, a few introductory words are in order. Fair and equitable treatment is an investment law standard, considered to have integrated international customary law,[81] that sets a quality requirement separate from domestic law regarding the regulatory and adjudicatory systems of the host State in order to preserve the rights of foreign investors.[82] The FET norm includes the concept of 'legitimate expectations', which refers to the expectations of the foreign investor with regards to the regulatory power of the host State. It is generally admitted that these expectations are based on the presumed stability of the overall legal framework, any representations made explicitly or implicitly by the host State and commitments resulting from the contractual relationship with the host State.[83]

80 'Report of the Independent Expert: Mapping Report', para 29. See also the same obligations applied in the context of climate change in 'Report of the Special Rapporteur on the issue of human rights obligations relating to the enjoyment of a safe, clean, healthy and sustainable environment: climate change and human rights' (2016) UN Doc. A/HRC/31/52, paras 50–64.

81 N Angelet, 'Fair and Equitable Treatment', in *Max Planck Encyclopedia of Public International Law* (Oxford University Press 2011), para 7.

82 Angelet, 'Fair and Equitable Treatment', para 1.

83 R Kläger, *'Fair and Equitable Treatment' in International Investment Law* (Cambridge University Press 2011) 165.

The expectation that the host State has an obligation to prevent environmental harm could form one of these 'legitimate expectations'. Admittedly, the perspective of a foreign investor expecting the host State to fulfil its preventive obligations is an unconventional one. The State is usually the one relying on prevention as part of its regulatory competence to limit investment activities,[84] while foreign investors regularly challenge new environmental regulations on grounds of FET violations.[85] Nevertheless, synergies are growing between the fields of international environmental law and international investment law.[86] FET has been recognized as a 'gateway for the integration of external principles into the investment process',[87] which could, in effect, include prevention. This is particularly important in a context in which investment tribunals are increasingly looking at other fields of international law and their principles to produce decisions coherent with the broader international legal system.[88] More specifically, synergies can be found between FET and prevention as their rationale is driven by their willingness to promote 'good governance', in the form of legal stability for FET and harm avoidance for prevention.[89]

Two scenarios could rely on the FET standard to create or consolidate an obligation to avoid environmental harm within a domestic context in order to fulfil the legitimate expectations of a foreign investor. The first scenario relies on the FET standard to ensure that a State complies with its obligations to prevent environmental harm in a domestic context, most likely treaty-based obligations of conservation. It is established that the non-fulfilment of international obligations by the host State can lead to a breach of FET

84 E.g. *Glamis Gold, Ltd. v. The United States of America*, UNCITRAL, Award, 8 June 2006, where the tribunal determined that the state regulatory measures and decline of the investor's plan of operation, in relation to the cultural and environmental impact of an open-pit gold mine in proximity to sacred Native American sites, were pursuing legitimate objectives. See, similarly, *Parkerings-Compagniet AS v. Republic of Lithuania*, ICSID Case No. ARB/05/8, Award (11 September 2007), para 392, on the refusal of the municipality over the creation of a modern parking system because of international obligations under the UNESCO Convention.

85 E.g. *Plama Consortium Ltd v. Bulgaria*, ICSID Case No. ARB/03/24, Award (27 August 2008), regarding an amendment of the applicable environmental framework which rendered the investor liable for past environmental damages.

86 JE Viñuales, *Foreign Investment and the Environment in International Law* (Cambridge University Press 2013).

87 Viñuales, *Foreign Investment and the Environment in International Law*, 94–97.

88 Viñuales, *Foreign Investment and the Environment in International Law*, 212.

89 On the good governance standard and due diligence in relation to FET, see ILA, Study Group on Due Diligence in International Law, 'First Report', Washington, DC, 76th Session, 2014, at 9.

requirements[90] and thus could be extended to include environmental obligations.[91] This would be conditional upon existing obligations but could act as an important enforcement technique. It offers a solution to the difficulties related to a violation of prevention within domestic borders that is unlikely to be persecuted given the absence of direct injury to another State but that could affect a foreign investor. Such was, in effect, the argument put forward by the investor in *Allard v. Barbardos*,[92] claiming that the host State's failure to take reasonable environmental measures destroyed the value of his ecotourism attraction and was in violation of several investment treaty standards, including FET. The tribunal, however, did not find that the statements relied upon by the claimant could have given rise to legitimate expectations. It therefore did not address the question of whether the environmental treaty obligations of Barbados, arising from the Convention on Biological Diversity and the Ramsar Convention on Wetlands of International Importance, could have confirmed or reinforced the legitimacy of the investor's expectations that Barbados would take steps to protect the nature sanctuary where the investment lay.[93] Overall, although the tribunal did not take a position on the matter, the case has shown that a violation of FET on the basis of an international obligation of prevention operating within a domestic context is conceivable.

The second scenario depends less on a pre-existing obligation of prevention within domestic borders. It relates to a situation in which an investor, influenced by the fact that prevention increasingly manifests in a purely domestic context, legitimately considers that such an obligation exists. This interpretation is evidently conditional on the consolidation of prevention at the domestic level via other routes (inter-State or human rights obligations). But, at the same time, the principle of legitimate expectations remains a subjective concept, an expectation being a belief that something will happen or is likely to. Expectations do not necessarily have to rely on existing legal obligations but can legitimately emerge from the conduct of the State and the

90 See e.g. *Saluka Investments BV v. The Czech Republic*, UNCITRAL, Partial Award (17 March 2006), para 305, where the claimant relied on the EU rules on state aid to demonstrate that the quantum of aid granted by the Czech government to the claimant's competitors to the exclusion of the claimant violated the FET principle.

91 Z Douglas, 'The Enforcement of Environmental Norms in Investment Treaty Arbitration', in P-M Dupuy and JE Viñuales, *Harnessing Foreign Investment to Promote Environmental Protection: Incentives and Safeguards* (Cambridge University Press 2013) 415–55, at 426.

92 *Peter A. Allard v. The Government of Barbados*, PCA Case No. 2012–06, Award (27 June 2016).

93 *Peter A. Allard*, para 208.

general context[94] – which, in this case, relates to a regulatory context concerned with environmental protection and opening up to the applicability of prevention within domestic borders. It could lead the investor to think that the obligation to prevent domestic harm is a State obligation under international law, even if the obligation has not been fully consolidated yet. From this perspective, the foreign investor would have to prove that the failure of the State to act preventively directly affected him, which can be particularly the case if the investment is reliant on a protected environment to succeed, which is common in the tourism industry.

8.3.4 *Overview: A Fragmented Obligation*

Understandably, the extension of the spatial scope of prevention, which goes far beyond the initial rationale of prevention and challenges the traditional structures of international law, does not go uncontested.[95] A general obligation to protect the domestic environment cannot yet be ascertained, but different avenues contribute to extending the international principle of prevention to the domestic context. The most evident manifestation of the principle of prevention in a domestic context relates to its objective to protect human beings from environmental harm. It is best extracted from human rights law, including from the emerging right to an environment of a certain quality, and from disaster law, in cases when environmental harm is of such high intensity that it might severely disrupt the functioning of society. Another core manifestation, with a less evident anthropocentric approach, is found in a general obligation to protect certain elements of the domestic environment. It covers the marine environment, international watercourses and possibly the atmosphere and is complemented by an emerging duty of sustainable use that covers biological resources. Overall, these different manifestations of prevention in a domestic context provide a strong basis for the recognition of an international obligation to protect the domestic environment.

8.4 PREVENTION IRRESPECTIVE OF THE LOCATION OF HARM

The three preceding sections have demonstrated that prevention operates in three contexts: domestic, transboundary and beyond national jurisdictions.

94 I Tudor, *The Fair and Equitable Treatment Standard in the International Law of Foreign Investment* (Oxford University Press 2008) 166.

95 See e.g. ILC, 'Summary Record of the 3178th Meeting' (2013) UN Doc. A/CN.4/SR.3178, ILC member Murphy noting that 'international environmental law was primarily concerned with the prevention of transboundary harm or harm to common areas, such as the seas, and not with harm within national boundaries'.

However, the spatial scope of prevention is more than the sum of the three spatial areas it explicitly covers: prevention has, under certain circumstances, achieved an objective standing that makes it applicable irrespective of the location of harm. Two emerging trends, one regarding the applicability of prevention in disputed areas (8.4.1) and another, albeit less evident, relative to the permissibility of unilateral preventive measures with extraterritorial impacts (8.4.2) justify this proposition.

8.4.1 *Prevention in Disputed Areas*

The objective standing of prevention is visible in the context of obligations of prevention that do not include spatial referentials. Multiple treaty provisions (already mentioned in the context of domestic prevention) refer to the need to protect the environment, or its ecosystems, without any spatial restrictions. The a-territorial aspect of such obligations has been consequential in the context of boundary disputes: international tribunals have considered that the obligation of prevention remained applicable, ensuring that the integrity of the environment does not suffer as a result of sovereignty disputes.

The obligations of prevention under UNCLOS Articles 192 and 193 were deemed applicable by the ITLOS Seabed Chamber in the context of a maritime boundary dispute between Côte d'Ivoire and Ghana.[96] In a request for provisional measures, Côte d'Ivoire asked that Ghana suspend all ongoing oil exploration and exploitation operations in the disputed area and refrain from granting new permits. The provisional measures granted by the Chamber created a dual obligation of prevention in the disputed area: a first obligation was imposed on Ghana, as the country undertaking oil exploitation operations in the disputed area, to 'carry out strict and continuous monitoring' of the activities undertaken to ensure 'the prevention of serious harm to the marine environment', and a second obligation was put on both parties to 'take all necessary steps [including via cooperation] to prevent serious harm to the marine environment'.[97] In doing so, the Chamber provided a pragmatic response to ensure that the delimitation dispute did not put environmental objectives aside: it required the party undertaking the potentially harmful activity to pay special attention to its preventive duties, but

96 *Dispute concerning Delimitation of the Maritime Boundary between Ghana and Côte d'Ivoire in the Atlantic Ocean (Ghana/Côte d'Ivoire)* (Provisional Measures) ITLOS No. 23 (25 April 2015).

97 *Dispute concerning Delimitation of the Maritime Boundary between Ghana and Côte d'Ivoire*, para 108(1)(c) and (d).

at the same time, it also extended the preventive obligation to the other party claiming sovereign rights over the area.

The arbitral tribunal in the *South China Sea* case, asked to interpret environmental obligations under UNCLOS and customary law in the context of disputed sovereignty between China and the Philippines, also deemed that States were not absolved from their preventive obligations in case of territorial disagreements. The tribunal expressly clarified the following:

> [O]bligations in Part XII [of UNCLOS] apply to all States with respect to the marine environment in all maritime areas, both inside the national jurisdiction of States and beyond it. Accordingly, questions of sovereignty are irrelevant to the application of Part XII of the Convention.[98]

The recognition that environmental obligations under UNCLOS were not dependent on which party has sovereignty or related rights over the territory was all the more important because the tribunal, in application of UNCLOS Article 298, lacked jurisdiction over issues pertaining to maritime boundary delimitation or sovereignty.[99] The approach is consequential from the standpoint of the rationale of prevention: applying irrespective of sovereignty considerations, prevention becomes a truly 'environmental' principle operating out of concern for the integrity of the planet per se.

8.4.2 *Right to Take Unilateral Preventive Measures*

The operation of the preventive principle irrespective of the location of harm could have another consequence, that of justifying a right to take unilateral preventive measures to protect common goods, even if they affect the rights of another State. The permissibility of unilateral preventive measures, which allows the objective of environmental protection to prevail over the right of a State to be free from external interferences, would be a strong step towards moving prevention away from its original concerns for the preservation of territorial sovereignties. However, the right to, in the words of Benvenisti, 'legislate for humanity'[100] is not uncontroversial because it potentially

98 *South China Sea Arbitration*, Award on the Merits, paras 940 and 927. See also Award on Jurisdiction and Admissibility, 29 October 2015, para 408.

99 *South China Sea Arbitration*, Award on the Merits, para 892.

100 E Benvenisti, 'Legislating for Humanity: May States Compel Foreigners to Promote Global Welfare?', in R Liivoja and J Petnam (eds), *International Lawmaking: Essays in Honour of Jan Klabbers* (Routledge 2014) 3–16.

infringes on the free exercise of sovereignty and runs counter to the expectation that global issues will be solved cooperatively.[101]

The evidence regarding the acceptability of unilateral preventive action remains scare but is nevertheless existent. Historically, States have occasionally tried to justify unilateral action on environmental grounds but have generally failed to convince judicial bodies that have been unsympathetic to this argument.[102] However, international law does not completely prohibit unilateral action to protect the environment, as exemplified by the balanced approach found in Rio Principle 12, which recognized that unilateral trade measures 'to deal with environmental challenges' outside of a State jurisdiction 'should be avoided'.[103] The absence of a direct prohibition of preventive trade measures with extraterritorial impacts is indicative of the fact that, under specific circumstances, unilateral trade measures might be justified to prevent environmental harm, even if these measures mean restricting the sovereignty of third countries affected by these unilateral measures.[104]

Although practice in relation to the permissibility of unilateral preventive measures with extraterritorial impacts remains limited, it could be called to develop in the context of the regulation of environmental issues where international consensus cannot be met. Such was the approach taken by the European Union when, disconcerted by the lack of progress to mitigate aviation emissions at the International Civil Aviation Organization, it decided to extend the Emissions Trading Directive to aviation, hence requiring companies operating flights departing or landing in EU territory to present carbon allowances for emissions produced beyond EU territory in international air space. The question of the legality of such measures with extraterritorial impacts on the high seas and the territory of third countries was referred to the Court of Justice of the European Union (CJEU) in *Air Transport Association America v. Secretary of State for Energy and Climate*

101 D Bodansky, 'What's So Bad about Unilateral Action to Protect the Environment?' (2000) 11 *European Journal of International Law* 339.

102 *Bering Sea Fur Seals (Great Britain v. United States)* (1893) 1 Moore 755, where the United States argued that the fur seals needed to be brought under State jurisdiction in order to better conserve them and eventually ensure that their long-term exploitation continues (but declined by the arbitral tribunal); *Nuclear Tests (Australia v. France)* (Judgment) (1974) ICJ Rep 253; *Nuclear Tests (New Zealand v. France)* (Judgment) (1974) ICJ Rep 457; *United States – Restrictions on Imports of Tuna*, DS21/R-39S/155 (3 September 1991).

103 Rio de Janeiro Declaration on Environment and Development (Rio de Janeiro, 3–14 June 1992), (1992) 31 ILM 876.

104 *United States – Import Prohibition of Certain Shrimp and Shrimp Products*, Appellate Body Report, 12 October 1998, WT/DS58/AB/R, ruling that a policy requiring the use of turtle excluder devices to meet conservation objectives might have extraterritorial impacts that are not per se prohibited under GATT Article XX.

Change.[105] The Court ruled, on the basis of treaty and customary law,[106] that there was a clear territorial link between the scheme and the airlines because the European Trading Scheme was only applying to airlines that choose to operate to EU airports.[107] In upholding the preventive measure, the Court took a holistic approach to environmental protection: it apprehended environmental protection as an objective for itself, operating irrespective of the location of harm, on the grounds that emissions of greenhouse gases, which contribute to global climate change, have indiscriminate impacts in jurisdictions under and beyond national jurisdiction. Here lies the main advantage of the extension of the scope of prevention: it bypasses the difficult questions of identifying the injured entity and concentrates rather on ensuring that the injuring entity takes preventive measures. The *Air Transport Association* case shows that the objective of environmental protection could, under certain circumstances, gain supremacy over the right of States to be free from external interferences. This operates a complete reversal of the initial aim of Principle 21, which partly emerged to protect States from outside interferences and could now occasionally justify external interferences in the environmental affairs of a sovereign States.

8.5 CONCLUSION

Prevention has been shown to be applicable in three spatial dimensions, each with different rationales and normative weights. Despite the extension of the spatial scope of prevention, it is clear that 'Westphalian territoriality is not dead'.[108] Indeed, the transboundary outlook of no-harm and its concern for territorial integrity are still very much present in the principle of prevention. Yet, this has not stopped prevention from moving – under certain circumstances – beyond the sovereignty paradigm to protect the environment irrespective of the location of harm. By challenging the 'territorial model of international law', it contributes to a 'deterritorialization' of international law,[109] as exemplified by a-spatial preventive norms. This shift of prevention beyond the sovereignty component found in the first element of Stockholm

105 *Air Transport Association*. 106 *Air Transport Association*, para 240(b).

107 *Air Transport Association*, paras 150–55.

108 D-E Kahn, 'Territory and Boundaries', in B Fassbender and A Peters (eds), *The Oxford Handbook of the History of International Law* (Oxford University Press 2012) 225–49, at 248.

109 C Brölmann, 'Deterritorialization in International Law: Moving Away from the Divide between National and International Law', in JE Nijman and A Nollkaemper (eds), *New Perspectives on the Divide between National and International Law* (Oxford University Press 2007) 84–109.

Principle 21 is principally visible in three developments that are currently at a preliminary stage: (1) prevention is becoming applicable to impacts that remain entirely domestic, (2) it could protect individuals in a potentially affected State from transboundary environmental effects, and (3) it has the potential to justify the taking of unilateral measures affecting the rights of a third-party State. It thus transpires that the prevention principle is increasingly concerned with protecting the environment per se instead of concentrating on preserving territorial sovereignties.

9

Prevention and Its Relationship with Other Environmental Norms

The scholarship often tends to present each norm of international environmental law as an independent concept.[1] However, this approach conceptualizes international environmental law as no more than the sum of the different norms that compose the field: it fails to see that the interactions between the norms, and their consequences on law and policy, are as important as the norms taken separately. Accordingly, after having elucidated the internal characteristics of prevention, it is now necessary to discuss how the principle relates to other norms of international environmental law – in other words, to offer an external perspective on prevention.[2] The definition of prevention relies in part on its commonalities and differences with other norms and is also constantly reinvented as a result of its interactions with these norms. Consequently, characterizing prevention in relation to other norms of international environmental law contributes to better determining the contours of the principle.

This chapter looks at the main norms of international environmental law in two blocs, each being characterized by a different rationale. This is based on the understanding that, as cogently proposed by Dupuy and Viñuales, international environmental law is organized around two main pillars[3]: prevention, at the heart of this study, which concentrates on harm avoidance, and balance, which aims 'to regulate access to certain resources or to distribute, among

1 M Virally, 'Le rôle des "principes" dans le développement du droit international', in M Virally, *Le droit international en devenir: essais écrits au fil des ans* (Presses universitaires de France 1990) 195–212, at 205–6, noting that general principles of international law tend to be assessed for their intrinsic value and not for their role in the legal system.

2 The 'external' perspective taken by this chapter means that international environmental norms that form the content of the due-diligence obligation – including the obligation to undertake an EIA and to cooperate, which were presented in Chapter 7 – will not be discussed here.

3 P-M Dupuy and JE Viñuales, *International Environmental Law* (Cambridge University Press 2015) 53–54.

States and among different sectors of human activity, the burden of managing certain environmental problems'.[4] As a result, the question that arises in relation to the prevention principle is the following: how does the prevention principle interact with other norms that share the same preventive rationale and those which are driven by a different logic? Should it be assumed that norms within the same pillar are complementary, while they are in opposition to the norms of the other pillar?

This chapter first considers norms that retain a preventive rationale but nevertheless substantially differ from the prevention principle; these are the polluter-pays principle and the precautionary approach/principle (9.1). It then investigates how norms operating on the basis of a different rationale, one concerned with distributive objectives, interact with prevention; it assesses how the different elements falling under the concept of sustainable development relate to prevention (9.2). Overall, the chapter underlines how prevention continuously redefines its place in international environmental law as other norms emerge and consolidate.

9.1 NORMS WITH A PREVENTIVE RATIONALE

The polluter-pays principle (9.1.1) and the precautionary approach principle[5] (9.1.2) operate within the realm of the preventive pillar of international environmental law but remain nevertheless different from the prevention principle *stricto sensu*. This section underlines the commonalities and differences that exist between prevention and the two norms.

9.1.1 *Prevention and Polluter-Pays*

The polluter-pays principle ensures that the costs of pollution are borne by the person responsible for causing the pollution (often a private operator) and not paid by tax payers. The rationale that drives the polluter-pays principle is complex because of its close interactions with the other rationales driving international environmental law – balance. It undoubtedly shares the same concern as prevention: the avoidance of environmental

4 Dupuy and Viñuales, *International Environmental Law* 54.

5 This chapter does not take a position on whether precaution should be called a 'principle' or an 'approach'. For a discussion of the normativity of precaution, see *inter alia* J Peel, 'Precaution: A Matter of Principle, Approach or Process?' (2004) 5 *Melbourne Journal of International Law* 483; E Hey, 'The Precautionary Concept in Environmental Policy and Law: Institutionalizing Caution' (1991) 4 *Georgetown International Environmental Law Review* 303.

harm.[6] But, despite its preventive outlook, the primary function of the polluter-pays principle is to internalize the social costs borne by public authorities to prevent pollution.[7] It allocates the financial responsibility for taking measures to avoid and repair harm. As a result, the polluter-pays principle operates at the border between the prevention and the balance pillars,[8] furthering an objective of harm avoidance while distributing the responsibility of harm avoidance among various stakeholders.

To further complicate the matter, the polluter-pays principle also interacts closely with the rationale against which prevention emerged – reparation.[9] The polluter-pays principle was originally concerned with the costs of preventive measures. However, the scope of the principle broadened over time: the polluting operator is now financially responsible for both preventive and, when it fails to avoid harm, remedial action. This extension of the scope of the polluter-pays principle finds its origins in the realization that the costs of accidental pollution had to be covered by the operator and not public authorities,[10] which lead to a redesign of the principle to 'include an ex post obligation to pay for harms caused'.[11] The principle was then extended to allocate the general (and not only accidental) costs of damage to the polluting entity,[12] including both preventive and remedial costs. The curative side of the polluter-pays principle does not contradict its preventive rationale but rather

6 Commission on Sustainable Development, 'Report of the Expert Group Meeting on Identification of Principles of International Law for Sustainable Development', Geneva, Switzerland, 26–28 September 1995, at 69, recognizing the connection between the principle of prevention and the polluter-pays principle.

7 OECD, 'Recommendation on Guiding Principles concerning the International Economic Aspects of Environmental Policies', C(72)128 (26 May 1972).

8 Dupuy and Viñuales, *International Environmental Law* 71–72, consider that the polluter-pays principle expresses a rationale of 'balance' because it seeks to allocate the financial burden of pollution. While this chapter does not negate this aspect of the principle, it prefers to envisage the polluter-pays principle in the 'prevention' section to highlight its contribution to the preventive rationale.

9 On the combination between the preventive and curative function of the polluter-pays principle applied to the specific example of the UNECE Water Convention, see L-A Duvic-Paoli and P-M Dupuy, 'The Polluter-Pays Principle', in A Tanzi et al. (eds), *The UNECE Convention on the Protection and Use of Transboundary Watercourses and International Lakes* (Brill/Martinus Nijhoff 2015) 176–95.

10 OECD, 'Recommendation of the Council on the Application of the Polluter-Pays Principle to Accidental Pollution', C(89)88 (7 July 1989).

11 S Gaines, 'The Polluter-Pays Principle: From Economic Equity to Environmental Ethos' (1991) 26 *Texas International Law Journal* 463, at 482–83.

12 OECD, 'Recommendation of the Council on the Use of Economic Instruments in Environmental Policy', C(90)177 (Final) (31 January 1991). See also ILC, 'Draft Principles on the Allocation of Loss in the Case of Transboundary Harm Arising out of Hazardous Activities (with Commentaries)' (2006) UN Doc. A/63/10, Preamble and Principle 3.

complements it. Indeed, the curative logic carries with it a preventive objective: an operator required to pay for the damage caused will try to limit pollution up to the point where the marginal cost of abatement surpasses the compensation avoided. The polluter-pays principle thus seeks to alter the behaviour of polluting entities by having a deterring effect on them: economic operators will see an economic benefit in limiting pollution at the source if they are financially responsible for remedial action. The polluter-pays principle is an example of the rapprochement between the preventive and curative rationales that is ongoing in international environmental law and will be discussed in Chapter 11.

9.1.2 *Prevention and Precaution*

The relationship between prevention and precaution is perhaps the most difficult to articulate at present under international environmental law. There is no doubt that prevention and precaution share the same objective of harm avoidance. They both emerged from the realization that there is a 'pressing need to secure the protection of the environment, given its vulnerability, the risks surrounding everyone, and the harmful consequences of irreparable damages caused to it'.[13] It has therefore been contended that 'far from excluding each other, they serve their purposes together'.[14] The close proximity between the two norms has led a number of scholars to consider that precaution has completely absorbed, or replaced, prevention (9.1.2.1). However, this approach is difficult to justify given that the two concepts relate differently to risks and do not share the same normative status (9.1.2.2). A middle-ground proposal that does not merge the two norms nor completely disassociates them is proposed at the end of this section: it conceptualizes precaution as an advanced form of prevention (9.1.2.3).

9.1.2.1 Approach One: Precaution Replaces Prevention

Academic and policy circles tend to disagree strongly about the status and content of precaution.[15] As a result, the attention given to precaution has overshadowed prevention: the role of the later as the cornerstone of

[13] *Pulp Mills on the River Uruguay (Argentina v. Uruguay)* (Judgment) (2010) ICJ Rep 14, separate opinion of Judge Cançado Trindade, para 52.

[14] *Pulp Mills*, separate opinion of Judge Cançado Trindade, para 98.

[15] For an interesting conceptualization of the debate regarding the status of precaution, refer to O Pedersen, 'From Abundance to Indeterminacy: The Precautionary Principle and Its Two Camps of Custom' (2014) 3 *Transnational Environmental Law* 323.

international environmental law seems to have tamed scholarly interest, possibly on the basis of an assumed consensual nature of the norm. One example of how precaution has gained pre-eminence over prevention in the academic debate can be found in the course given by Fitzmaurice on the international protection of the environment at the Hague Academy of International Law. One chapter is entitled, 'Some General Principles of the Modern Approach to Environmental Protection: The Elements of Preventive Approach'. However, it does not discuss the principle of prevention in the sense in which this study understands it. Although Fitzmaurice presents a number of norms guided by a preventive rationale, she does not mention prevention as an independent norm.[16] Admittedly, Stockholm Principle 21 was presented in an earlier chapter[17] and due diligence is briefly referenced in the chapter under scrutiny.[18] However, the lack of a stand-alone analysis of prevention, especially in a chapter on the preventive approach, is illustrative of a wider trend found in the doctrine that prefers to concentrate on precaution. By starting the chapter with a discussion of the precautionary approach, Fitzmaurice leaves readers to think that the preventive rationale is being first and foremost expressed in precaution. In this context, it is telling that she uses the legal foundation of prevention, Stockholm Principle 21, to shed light on the preventive rationale of precaution.[19] The perspective is indicative of a conception widely found in the legal scholarship that leaves prevention aside because precaution is considered to have replaced prevention and, hence, to be more representative of contemporary environmental law. Overall, the chapter can be read to imply that precaution has become the principal preventive norm of contemporary international environmental law.

This example shows that prevention and precaution tend to be assimilated as a single norm because they share the same objective of harm avoidance. An application of precaution is often considered to be an automatic endorsement of prevention.[20] Some doctrinal works portray precaution as having

16 M Fitzmaurice, 'International Protection of the Environment' (2001) 293 *Collected Courses of the Hague Academy of International Law* 9–488, chap V, at 259–304, analysing the following norms: precaution, environmental impact assessment, polluter-pays, due diligence and liability. Fitzmaurice does not mention prevention as an independent principle/obligation, and the short section on due diligence does not explicitly reference prevention either.

17 Fitzmaurice, 'International Protection of the Environment', chap II, at 106–11.

18 Fitzmaurice, 'International Protection of the Environment', 287–89.

19 Fitzmaurice, 'International Protection of the Environment', 267.

20 L Lucchini, 'Le principe de précaution en droit international de l'environnement: ombres plus que lumières' (1999) 45 *Annuaire français de droit international* 710, at 714, noting that the distinction between both principles is slight and that, as a result, one could be tempted to think that international law could do without prevention.

replaced prevention, often in its role as the cornerstone of international environmental law, simply because it emerged after prevention.[21] It is based on the premise that if the two norms share the same rationale, it is only logical to retain the one that is the most developed in its conception of harm avoidance. This is certainly true in the case of EU law, where precaution has 'absorbed' prevention[22] – its reference before the principle of preventive action in Article 191(2) of the Treaty on the Functioning of the European Union leaves little doubt about its pre-eminence.[23] The consensual status of precaution under EU law makes it possible to consider that prevention falls under the more advanced norm of precaution. However, this reality cannot be transposed to international law, where prevention and precaution are two distinct principles, not least because the status of precaution remains to be consolidated: the separate existence of the prevention principle is therefore not 'superfluous'[24] under international law.

9.1.2.2 Approach Two: Two Distinct Principles

Prevention and precaution share the same objective of harm avoidance, but their approach to anticipation and legal status remain distinct.

A DIFFERENT APPROACH TO ANTICIPATION Despite their similarities, the two norms operate in two distinct spheres.[25] Prevention is concerned with the avoidance of risks that are foreseeable, while precaution regulates risks that are uncertain. Prevention is a legal principle that responds to the notion of 'risk' (i.e. a negative outcome, the probability of which can be assessed). Precaution, by contrast, responds to 'uncertainty'. It is based on the realization that it is not always possible to assess the consequences of some activities in advance and that uncertainty is not an excuse for inaction. Concisely stated, while the two principles deal with anticipation, they do not have the same relationship to foreseeability and predictability. This is aptly summarized by Judge Cançado Trindade

21 A Trouwborst, 'Prevention, Precaution, Logic and Law: The Relationship between the Precautionary Principle and the Preventative Principle in International Law and Associated Questions' (2009) 2 *Erasmus Law Review* 105.

22 Trouwborst, 'Prevention, Precaution, Logic and Law', 126, in relation to prevention under international environmental law.

23 Treaty on the Functioning of the European Union, Lisbon, 13 December 2007, *OJ* C 83 (30 March 2010).

24 Trouwborst, 'Prevention, Precaution, Logic and Law', 107.

25 See JE Viñuales, 'Legal Techniques for Dealing with Scientific Uncertainty in Environmental Law' (2010) 43 *Vanderbilt Journal of Transnational Law* 437, which notes that there is a clear-cut difference between 'risk' as an identifiable adverse outcome (the realm of prevention) and 'uncertainty' (the realm of precaution).

when he notes, '[p]revention envisaged risks, but assumed they were certain. Precaution thus emerged, as an ineluctable principle, to face also uncertain risks, given the uncertainties of life itself, and the intuition of surrounding death'.[26] The emergence of precaution, twenty years after the consecration of prevention,[27] is both an extension of the preventive rationale, pushed further in its relation to scientific knowledge, and also an alternative to the obligation of prevention, whose mandate is limited to foreseeable risks of harm. As a result of their different approaches to anticipation, the two norms operate differently. Prevention applies at a lower level of risk – which ought to be 'significant' and not 'serious' or 'irreversible', as in the case of precaution,[28] and requires a higher level of diligence[29] in comparison to precaution, which only requires States to take 'cost-effective measures'.[30]

A DIFFERENT STATUS Prevention and precaution can be distinguished based on their relationship to risk as well as their status under international law. Indeed, prevention is a well-recognized norm of customary law, while the status of precaution remains disputed. This difference was a key determinant in the *Indus Waters Kishenganga* case, in which the tribunal relied on the customary norm of prevention but refused to expand its powers over precaution, which it considered to be a policy rather than a legal rule.

> As the Court held in its Partial Award, 'States have "a duty to prevent, or at least mitigate" significant harm to the environment when pursuing large-scale construction activities.' In light of this duty, the Court has no difficulty concluding that the requirement of an environmental flow (without prejudice to the level of such flow) is necessary in the application of the Treaty. At the same time, the Court does not consider it appropriate, and certainly not 'necessary', for it to adopt a precautionary approach and assume the role of policymaker in determining the balance between acceptable environmental change and other priorities, or to permit environmental considerations to override the balance of other rights and obligations expressly identified in the Treaty – in particular the entitlement of India to divert the waters of a tributary of the Jhelum. The Court's authority is more limited and extends only to mitigating significant harm.[31]

26 *Pulp Mills*, separate opinion of Judge Cançado Trindade, para 69.
27 Rio de Janeiro Declaration on Environment and Development (Rio de Janeiro, 3–14 June 1992), (1992) 31 ILM 876, Principle 15.
28 Rio Declaration, Principle 15.
29 ILA, Study Group on Due Diligence in International Law, 'Second Report', Johannesburg, 77th Session, 2016, at 2.
30 ILA, Study Group on Due Diligence in International Law, 'Second Report'.
31 *Indus Waters Kishenganga Arbitration (Pakistan v. India)*, Permanent Court of Arbitration, Final Award, 20 December 2013, para 112.

This statement is interesting for the distinction it makes between prevention and precaution. It considers precaution as the expression of the decision of policymakers to favour environmental protection over other considerations and not as a legal rule upon which a tribunal can rule. In other words, it recognizes prevention as an enforceable norm and removes precaution from the decisional realm of tribunals and courts.

The two norms are separated by their different legal statuses. The ILA made this clear in its 2012 report on Legal Principles Relating to Climate Change. It reads as follows:

> In EU environmental law, the prevention principle and the precautionary principle are widely understood as elements of one principle, in that they form part of a continuum. Locating a dispute on the precaution-prevention continuum depends on the extent of scientific uncertainty; only when there is very strong scientific evidence will the prevention principle be engaged … In international law, it appears that the prevention principle and the precautionary principle are regarded as two different principles, having a different legal background, although in some cases working along a continuum.[32]

The difference regarding precaution under EU law and international law lies mainly in what the ILA calls its 'legal background': while both precaution and prevention have entered the realm of EU law, the status of precaution under international law remains unsettled. As a result of this difference in legal status, the ILA confirmed that precaution cannot replace prevention in international law.

REMAINING CONFUSIONS As noted, prevention and precaution can be distinguished based on their rationale and legal status. However, in practice, confusions remain, with regular references being made to precaution when a mere reliance on prevention would have sufficed. This situation is particularly visible in domestic courts, which tend to be heavily influenced by the rise, at the international level, of precaution; as a result, they overlook the fact that applying the principle of prevention would, most of the time, suffice to solve the disputes put to them. The following two examples illustrate perfectly the confusion that reigns in courts with regards to the distinction between prevention and precaution. They both raise fundamental questions about the relationship between international and domestic environmental law that are beyond the scope of this study. Their analysis here will have a more modest

[32] ILA, Committee on Legal Principles Relating to Climate Change, 'Second Report', Sofia, 75th Session, 2012, at 28.

objective: to illustrate how tribunals have made references to precaution even though the existence of a risk had been ascertained.

The first case relates to a decision produced in 1994 by the Colombian Civil Chamber of the Superior Court of Santa Marta in the *Fundepúblico v. Tradenet de Colombia SA and Others* case.[33] This case dealt with a petitioners' request to remove toxic waste from Cartagena Harbour on the basis that it infringed the principle of environmental protection and the right to life and health protected under the country's constitution. In its judgment, the Court relied on precaution when there was no uncertainty regarding the risks represented by the toxic waste. The following reveals the confusion:

> There is no doubt about the advantage of the precautionary principle, adopted by Law No. 99 of 1993, which provides that in the case of danger of grave and irreversible damage, the lack of certainty shall not be used as a reason to delay the adoption of effective measures to avoid environmental degradation. This principle applies to this action for protection, since the risk is obvious.[34]

The Court applied the precautionary principle found in its national legislation, which replicates the international definition of precaution (as expressed in Rio Principle 15). At the same time, the Court presented the risk of harm as 'obvious', which means that there was no uncertainty regarding the risk that the waste represented. The foreseeability of harm was corroborated by a report by the Health Secretariat of the Department of Santa Magdalena that the Court had before it that concluded that the toxic waste could result in a high probability of harm[35] – a threshold that triggers prevention. In short, nowhere is there scientific uncertainty, which calls for a precautionary approach, in this case. Admittedly, the preventive objective as such is not explicitly referred to in Colombia's Law No. 99 of 1993, although its Article 1 lists some environmental principles. However, the Court could have convincingly relied on the Rio Principles referred to in Article 1(1),[36] as well as other principles expressing a preventive rationale acknowledged in the law, including the right to the enjoyment of a healthy environment.[37]

33 *Fundepúblico v. Tradenet de Colombia SA and Others*, Civil Appeal Chamber, Supreme Court of Justice, Colombia, 25 August 1994, IELR 152.

34 *Fundepúblico*, 160. 35 *Fundepúblico*, 159.

36 The Court could have relied on Rio Principle 2 pursuant to Article 1(1) of the law, which provides that the environmental policy of Colombia should be guided by the principles of the Rio Declaration. While Principle 2 operates in an international setting, it has been regularly used by domestic courts to justify preventive measures at the domestic level (see Chapter 5). Law No. 99 of 1993 is available at www.bdlaw.com/assets/htmldocuments/Colombia%20-%20Law%2099–1993.pdf (last accessed 13 May 2017).

37 Law No. 99 of 1993, Article 1(2).

The Court's reliance on precaution instead of prevention can be explained by the fact that it understood precaution as a norm that is applicable when harm has not yet occurred. Indeed, the Court justified its ruling on the basis that 'it would be illogical to wait until health problems appeared, or until the death of one or more people of the area before taking adequate measures to protect the health and life of others'.[38] However, the fact that harm has not yet occurred does not render the obligation of prevention obsolete. Risks that have not yet materialized are not necessarily uncertain. It is precisely when harm is foreseeable but has not yet occurred that the obligation of prevention is most relevant. In this case, the Court mistook the lack of scientific certainty for the lack of actual harm. It is not because harm has not yet occurred that precaution should be necessarily applied: the lack of knowledge initiates precaution, not the lack of harm. Considering the circumstances, a reference to prevention would have sufficed to justify the ruling on the basis that harm was foreseeable and imminent.

A similar case in which a domestic court conflated precaution and prevention can be found in the decision of the Supreme Court of India when it addressed the issue of water pollution due to tanneries in *Vellore Citizens Welfare Forum v. Union of India and Others*.[39] The Supreme Court ruled that the leather industry could not be permitted to continue causing harm to the environment and health. To do so, it relied on, *inter alia*, precaution but did not refer to prevention. Contrary to the case discussed earlier, in this case, harm created by the tanneries, which had been polluting for over a decade, was not only foreseeable but also already a reality. Indeed, the Court recognized that some of the tanneries had been 'polluting the environment for over a decade and in some cases even for a longer period'[40] and described in detail the pollution and its consequences for agriculture and potable water.[41] It is clear that under these circumstances the Court could have relied on prevention to rule against the tanneries.[42] And yet, for reasons that are not entirely clear but probably influenced by the consecration of the precautionary approach at the Rio Summit, the Court felt it necessary to discuss at length

38 *Fundepúblico*, 159.

39 *Vellore Citizens Welfare Forum v. Union of India*, Supreme Court of India, 28 August 1996, IELR 270.

40 *Vellore Citizens Welfare Forum*, 278.

41 *Vellore Citizens Welfare Forum*, 274.

42 The Court could have relied on the Environment Protection Act of 1986, which it mentioned in its ruling and whose Article 3(1) reads as follows: 'Subject to the provisions of this Act, the Central Government, shall have the power to take all such measures as it deems necessary or expedient for the purpose of protecting and improving the quality of the environment and *preventing, controlling and abating environmental pollution*' (emphasis added). This act is available at http://envfor.nic.in/legis/env/env1.html (last accessed 19 May 2017).

the applicability of the precautionary principle in Indian law[43] without explaining its relation to the case under scrutiny. In sum, the Court took this case as an opportunity to consecrate in an *obiter dictum* the existence of an obligation of precaution in its municipal law, but the norm itself was not necessary to rule on the unlawfulness of the tanneries' actions.

A THIN LINE BETWEEN SCIENTIFIC CERTAINTY AND UNCERTAINTY While the confusion found in the decisions of domestic courts sometimes stems from a lack of conceptual precision, prevention and precaution can in practice be difficult to disentangle.[44] Although the distinction between scientific certainty and scientific uncertainty is, in theory, straight-forward, it can, in practice, be difficult to draw a clear line between the two. Disagreements regarding the nature of available scientific knowledge complicate the issue. Indeed, full scientific certainty regarding the potential impacts of an activity on the environment is rarely met – this is exemplified by the work of the IPCC that consolidates the scientific production on climate change and produces conclusions that are evaluated on the basis of a scale presenting the level of scientific certainty ranging from 'virtually certain' (99–100 per cent) to 'extremely unlikely' (0–5 per cent).[45] Indeed, most risks are neither completely certain nor completely uncertain but will be somewhere in between the two extremes. Drawing the line between scientific certainty and scientific uncertainty is challenging because (1) achieving full scientific certainty is almost impossible as there is always a small part of uncertainty in certitude,[46] and, in turn, (2) scientific uncertainty still relies on having a minimum level of scientific knowledge to conclude that science cannot (yet) provide reliable conclusions.[47]

43 *Vellore Citizens Welfare Forum*, 277: It relied on precaution as a result of the interpretation of the Indian Constitution and as a norm of customary international law.

44 ILC, 'Preliminary Report of the Special Rapporteur, Ms Jacobsson, on the protection of the environment in relation to armed conflicts' (2014) UN Doc. A/CN.4/674, para 137, recognizing that in practice 'a separation of the two concepts is difficult to maintain'.

45 Intergovernmental Panel on Climate Change, *Fifth Assessment Report: Summary for Policy-Makers* (2014), at 2.

46 For instance, the IPCC considers that the anthropocentric impacts on climate change are 'extremely likely' but not 'virtually certain'. Intergovernmental Panel on Climate Change, *Fifth Assessment Report*, para 1.2.

47 For an interesting discussion of the 'thin line between ignorance, ambiguity, risk and uncertainty', see M Haritz, *An Inconvenient Deliberation: The Precautionary Principle's Contribution to the Uncertainties Surrounding Climate Change Liability* (Kluwer Law International 2011) 41–49. See also B Wynne, 'Uncertainty and Environmental Learning: Reconceiving Science and Policy in the Preventive Paradigm' (1992) 2 *Global Environmental Change* 111, presenting different 'kinds of uncertainty'.

As a result, it is not clear when (i.e. at which level of probability) 'scientific uncertainty' is turning into 'scientific certainty'. This leads to diverging positions about whether a minimal amount of scientific knowledge should be qualified as scientific uncertainty or certainty. The duty to undertake an environmental impact assessment (EIA), a prime example of the interrelatedness between prevention and precaution, illustrates this difficulty.[48] Epiney postulates that the obligation to undertake an EIA is a 'direct consequence of the precautionary principle'.[49] The affirmation is not uncontroversial since it could also be argued, as presented in Chapter 7, that the principle of prevention is the source of the duty to undertake an EIA. This is not to say that the obligation cannot arise from precaution, a possible scenario when considering precaution as a due-diligence duty; however, the approach remains progressive.[50] It can be assumed that Epiney considers that an EIA is carried out to remediate a situation of scientific uncertainty because it seeks to gain scientific knowledge on the risks that an activity could represent. It makes little doubt that the preliminary studies carried out before the EIA to determine whether the risks are significant enough to justify undertaking a full EIA are based on a precautionary approach because they operate in a context in which scientific evidence is lacking. But whether the obligation to undertake an EIA is the consequence of the preventive or precautionary approach depends on whether the partial knowledge available that triggers an EIA obligation is considered to meet the threshold of 'scientific certainty' or whether it is too limited and should be interpreted as 'scientific uncertainty'. To be sure, the undertaking of an EIA considerably increases the level of scientific knowledge and thus contributes to better scientific certainty. However, the EIA is not carried out as the consequence of complete scientific uncertainty, in which case the significance of the risk could not be measured and therefore the EIA duty as a factor of due diligence would not be triggered. The scientific knowledge necessary to trigger the obligation to carry out an EIA seems high enough to consider that the EIA is a means to

48 *Certain Activities Carried out by Nicaragua in the Border Area (Costa Rica v. Nicaragua)* and *Construction of a Road in Costa Rica along the San Juan River (Nicaragua v. Costa Rica)* (Judgment) (2015) ICJ Rep 665, separate opinion of Judge Cançado Trindade, para 54.

49 A Epiney, 'Environmental Impact Assessment', in *Max Planck Encyclopedia of Public International Law* (Oxford University Press 2009), para 1.

50 *Responsibilities and Obligations of States Sponsoring Persons and Entities with Respect to Activities in the Area*, ITLOS No. 17, Advisory Opinion (1 February 2011), para 132. See Section 7.2.5.

gain more detailed scientific evidence regarding the nature and magnitude of risks that are already foreseeable.

Irrespective of whether a minimal level of knowledge should be categorized as scientific certainty or uncertainty, it can also be difficult to assess whether the knowledge available can be considered as proof of certainty. The question of who is legitimate to assess scientific knowledge, interpret diverging conclusions and rule on whether there is scientific certainty is fundamental yet complex. Tribunals are increasingly relying on the work of bodies such as the IPCC that, by consolidating the scientific knowledge produced worldwide, provide authoritative (albeit not exempt from criticism) assessments on the level of scientific certainty available.[51] However, most environmental issues, either global or local, do not benefit from such authority. Adjudication has shown that parties rely on diverging scientific opinions regarding environmental risks. The *Whaling in the Antarctic* case, where scientific experts disagreed *inter alia* over the necessity to use lethal methods in scientific research on whales,[52] has been a prime example of a situation in which judges were faced with diverging scientific evidence. Scientific uncertainty in this case was not caused by a lack of evidence but rather by divergences in its interpretation. In this context, the difficulty for lawyers is to determine whether scientific evidence can be considered to form 'certainty'. In short, the thin line between scientific certainty and uncertainty results in a complex relation between prevention and precaution, where the threshold that delimits their applicable scopes is itself 'uncertain'.

9.1.2.3 Approach Three: Precaution as an Advanced Form of Prevention

The relationship between prevention and precaution is clearly intricate. This study posits that the best way to conceptualize the relationship is to see precaution as an extension of prevention, in its 'most developed form'.[53] Precaution remains a principle of harm prevention but with a different scope of application. As a result, the two principles can be seen as part of

[51] See e.g. *Urgenda Foundation v. The State of the Netherlands (Ministry of the Infrastructure and the Environment)*, Hague District Court, 24 June 2015, available at http://uitspraken.rechtspraak.nl/inziendocument?id=ECLI:NL:RBDHA:2015:7196 (last accessed 19 May 2017), paras 2.8–2.21.

[52] *Whaling in the Antarctic (Australia v. Japan: New Zealand intervening)* (Judgment) (2014) ICJ Rep 226, para 82.

[53] See also Trouwborst, 'Prevention, Precaution, Logic and Law', 124, as an alternative proposal to his argument that precaution has integrated the prevention principle.

a continuum: they respond to different risks, depending on their magnitude[54] and probability,[55] but are not diametrically different.[56]

NORMATIVE CONTINUUM The continuum that links prevention and precaution reflects the fact that scientific knowledge does not rely on a strict certainty–uncertainty dichotomy. Under these circumstances, the preventive rationale – expressed in the form of prevention and precaution, possibly both as due-diligence obligations[57] – applies irrespective of the level of scientific knowledge. One of the main advantages is that it solves a major difficulty relative to the implementation of prevention, which is to assess whether the level of scientific knowledge is high enough to trigger a preventive obligation.

The continuum also contributes to a better understanding of norms that reflect both a preventive and a precautionary logic: under these circumstances, it is not necessary to arbitrarily distinguish between the two rationales that guide the norm. For instance, the obligation of conservation under biodiversity law is an expression of prevention but can also include a precautionary approach. Australia, in the *Whaling in the Antarctic* case, took this perspective when it argued that conservation had 'three main legal pillars', namely, 'intergenerational equity, the principle of prevention and the precautionary approach'.[58] Judge Cançado Trindade followed the same approach by recognizing in his separate opinion that 'the principles of prevention and precaution appear interrelated' in the case.[59] Although he did not elaborate on why he thought that the two principles were interrelated and what the legal consequences of such relationship would be, his comment stems in all likelihood from the fact that the parties and intervenor pleaded both principles together, in a case which, as discussed above, relied heavily on scientific evidence. The conceptualization of the two norms as operating within a continuum thus becomes an alternative to defining with precision what is meant by scientific certainty and uncertainty.

54 L Lucchini, 'Le principe de précaution en droit international de l'environnement', 715.

55 N de Sadeleer, *Environmental Principles: From Political Slogans to Legal Rules* (Oxford University Press 2002) 75.

56 See e.g. Hungary's argument during the oral proceedings of the *Gabčíkovo-Nagymaros* case, considering that the principle of precaution emerged as the most developed form of the general rule of prevention. *Gabčíkovo-Nagymaros Project (Hungary/Slovakia)*, oral pleadings, CR/1997/2, 3 March 1997, para 23.

57 *Responsibilities and Obligations of States Sponsoring Persons and Entities with Respect to Activities in the Area*, para 113 (on prevention as a due-diligence obligation) and para 132 (on precaution as a due-diligence obligation).

58 *Whaling in the Antarctic*, Oral Pleadings, CR 2013/7, 26 June 2013, paras 50, 55 and 57–58.

59 *Whaling in the Antarctic*, separate opinion of Judge Cançado Trindade, para 70.

TEMPORAL CONTINUUM Understanding prevention and precaution as a continuum also highlights their temporal complementarity. On the one hand, some activities that justified a precautionary approach will move towards prevention as knowledge improves over time.[60] The phenomenon was highlighted in the ILA's Climate Change Principles that put prevention and precaution under the same heading (Article 7). They recognized that the climate regime is shifting from precaution to prevention.

> As new scientific knowledge relating to the causes or effects of climate change becomes available, States must continuously assess their obligation of prevention and the necessity for precautionary measures. Where scientific knowledge about damage from climate change improves sufficiently, protective measures shall be continued by States pursuant to their obligation to prevent environmental damage.[61]

Despite this shift, it is nevertheless important to note that as human beings continue to engage in ever-more hazardous activities, precaution will nevertheless remain relevant, to apply to new human activities.

On the other hand, the opposite move is also possible: the belief previously held that a substance or activity is innocuous can be challenged by new scientific developments highlighting that no definite conclusions can yet be drawn about their harmlessness. This situation was put in evidence by Mbengue based on the example of hexachlorobenzene (HCB), used as a fungicide until 1965 and today classified as a 'possible' carcinogen.[62] He suggests that the interaction between precaution and prevention is circular (and not linear) because not only can precaution be replaced by prevention, but the opposite is also possible.[63] This interesting conceptualization of the relationship between prevention and precaution brings into light the ever-moving nature of scientific knowledge. However, the circularity of the relationship cannot be completely established. Indeed, it is not prevention itself that leads to precaution, but rather it is the lack of applicability of prevention that makes precaution applicable. The HCB scenario moved from a situation in which prevention was not applicable (no probable or foreseeable harm) to

60 L Lucchini, 'Le principe de précaution en droit international de l'environnement', 724, noting that the nature of precaution is by definition to be ephemeral; ILA, Committee on Legal Principles Relating to Climate Change, 'Second Report', Sofia, 75th Session, 2012, at 26.

61 ILA, Committee on Legal Principles Relating to Climate Change, 'Declaration of Principles Relating to Climate Change', Washington, DC, 76th Session, 2014, Article 7B(3).

62 MM Mbengue, *Essai sur une théorie du risque en droit international public: l'anticipation du risque environnemental et sanitaire* (Pedone 2009) 168; and WWF, 'Factsheet: HCB', 2002, available at www.wwf.eu/?4041/Factsheet-HCB (last accessed 19 May 2017).

63 Mbengue, *Essai sur une théorie du risque* 168.

one where precaution became applicable (scientific uncertainty regarding the potential harm of the substance). In other words, the relationship is not properly circular because it is difficult to imagine a situation in which scientific knowledge changed from suggesting that harm was foreseeable to one where harm becomes uncertain – this simply runs counter to the idea of scientific progress. Keeping the relationship between prevention and precaution as a linear interaction is hence preferable.

9.2 NORMS WITH A DISTRIBUTIVE RATIONALE

The fact that prevention still operates within norms such as polluter-pays and precaution as a rationale tends to blur the relationship they entertain with prevention as an independent norm. The discussion now turns to situations in which prevention interacts with norms that operate on the basis of a different rationale, one that does not seek to anticipate harm but rather concentrates on distributing the burdens of environmental management among different actors and sectors of human activity. This rationale, which finds its main expression in the concept of sustainable development,[64] has become such a core element driving environmental action that it is considered to form the second pillar of international environmental law. Sustainable development, as a norm that guides interpretation as an 'element of the process of judicial reasoning',[65] does not have the same international normative status as prevention, a customary duty. It nevertheless has the same considerable influence as prevention in shaping international environmental law. It therefore raises fundamental questions, presented in this section, about how the two norms relate to each other.

Sustainable development is characterized by three key elements that are summarized by Barral as follows: (inter-generational equity + intra-generational equity) × integration.[66] This section examines, in turn, each of the three elements of sustainable development to clarify how they relate to prevention. The first element, and the most influential, as shown in Barral's equation, dictates the integration of economic and environmental concerns (9.2.1). The second component of sustainable development embodies intra-generational equity and favours equity between developed and developing

64 Dupuy and Viñuales, *International Environmental Law* 71.

65 V Lowe, 'Sustainable Development and Unsustainable Arguments', in A Boyle and D Freestone (eds), *International Law and Sustainable Development: Past Achievements and Future Challenges* (Oxford University Press 1999) 19–37, at 31.

66 V Barral, 'Sustainable Development in International Law: Nature and Operation of an Evolutive Legal Norm' (2012) 23 *European Journal of International Law* 377, at 380.

countries (9.2.2). Finally, the last definitional element of sustainable development, inter-generational equity, encourages equity between present and future generations (9.2.3).

9.2.1 *Prevention and Integration*

Sustainable development finds its expression in the objective of 'integration', which was incorporated in Principle 4 of the Rio Declaration and provides that 'environmental protection shall constitute an integral part of the development process and cannot be considered in isolation from it'. The process is particularly interesting for this study because the environmental considerations 'integrated' into the development process are directed by the objective of prevention. This section thus looks at the different forms that this integration can take in international environmental law. It starts with presenting what might be called a 'light' form of integration, where prevention is interpreted considering the normative context within which it operates, one heavily influenced by the concept of sustainable development (9.2.1.1). It then argues that economic and developmental considerations have also directly integrated the obligation of prevention per se, as evidenced by the slight change in the wording of the preventive rationale in Rio Principle 2 (9.2.1.2). Finally, it highlights another form of integration that is currently taking place: it is now the turn of prevention to be included in the norm of sustainable development (9.2.1.3).

9.2.1.1 Approach One: Prevention 'in the Context of Sustainable Development'

The obligation of prevention cannot be interpreted irrespective of the normative legal context within which it operates. As a result, since the Rio Summit, prevention is interpreted in light of another key concept that has established itself as a fundamental norm in the field of international environmental law: sustainable development.

INTERPRETING PREVENTION IN ITS LEGAL CONTEXT The Commentaries to the ILC Prevention Articles explicitly require that prevention be fully incorporated in the framework created at the Rio Summit. They read as follows:

> The prevention of transboundary harm from hazardous activities should also be seen *in the context* of the general principles incorporated in the Rio

> Declaration and other considerations that emphasize the close interrelationship between issues of environment and development.[67]

In this statement, the ILC requires that its articles, driven by an objective of environmental protection, are read while keeping in mind sustainability issues. Admittedly, the 'integration' between the environmental and economic spheres remains light because the ILC Commentary merely requires that prevention be 'seen' (i.e. interpreted) in light of the concerns for development and poverty alleviation that guide the Rio principles. This is, however, consequential: it means that the principle of prevention after Stockholm and Rio might have (almost) the same expression but cannot be understood as being exactly the same because the normative context changed.

The origins of the ILC Commentary are possibly found in the first report of the ILC Rapporteur Rao, which started with a section on 'prevention within the context of sustainable development'.[68] The expression is representative of the normative distinction between prevention and sustainable development mentioned earlier: prevention is understood as an international obligation, whereas sustainable development is seen as a 'contextual' norm that serves as an interpretative aid. The role that sustainable development can play in the interpretation of existing norms is evident in the 2012 ILA Guiding Statements on sustainable development that provided that 'treaties and rules of customary international law should, as far as possible, be interpreted in the light of principles of sustainable development'.[69] Prevention, as a treaty and customary rule, can be understood to fall under the scope of this statement: as a context-sensitive principle adaptable to normative evolutions, it will hence have to be interpreted in light of the concept of sustainable development.

CONFLICTS IN INTERPRETATION In this context, a question that emerges is whether sustainable development should take precedence over prevention in the case of an interpretative conflict. The answer remains unsettled. In this respect, the ILA Guiding Statements on sustainable development suggested that

67 ILC, 'Draft Articles on Prevention of Transboundary Harm from Hazardous Activities (with Commentaries)' (2001) *Yearbook of the International Law Commission* (vol II, part 2) 148, Commentary to the Preamble, para 2, at 149 (emphasis added).

68 ILC, 'First Report of the Special Rapporteur, Mr Pemmaraju Sreenivasa Rao, on the Prevention of Transboundary Harm from Hazardous Activities' (1998) UN Doc. A/CN.4/487, paras 26–31.

69 ILA, Committee on International Law on Sustainable Development, 'Resolution', Sofia, 75th Session, 2012, Statement 2.

> interpretations which might seem to undermine the goal of sustainable development should only take precedence where to do otherwise would be to undermine territorial boundaries and other fundamental aspects of the global legal order, would otherwise infringe the express wording of a treaty or would breach a rule of *jus cogens*.[70]

The consequences of this statement for prevention are uncertain. The reference to norms that might 'undermine the goal of sustainable development' is arguably aimed at norms that would endanger environmental integrity and does not seem designed to apply to prevention. However, sometimes it is not clear whether the objective of an international treaty is to avoid environmental harm *stricto sensu* or to promote the sustainable use of resources, which tends to tilt the balance more towards economic development than environmental protection.[71] In these circumstances, the statement remains ambiguous about whether it would require a tribunal to favour an interpretation promoting sustainable use in (relative) opposition to harm avoidance.

Yet, it is improbable that a question of interpretation would raise a dilemma between prevention and sustainable development that would fall under one of the four scenarios envisaged by the preceding statement. This is especially due to the fact that the norm of sustainable development integrates the environmental objectives of prevention: as a result, the challenge is usually not to solve a direct contradiction between the norms but rather to find a balance between both. Of the four scenarios presented by the ILA, the most relevant one pertains to a situation in which the prevalence of sustainable development over prevention would risk undermining the global legal order. While what constitutes the 'fundamental aspects of the global legal order' remains open to interpretation, ecological integrity could be seen as an integral part in the maintenance of international peace and security[72] that takes precedence over the economic considerations put forward by sustainable development. However, this scenario remains very much hypothetical, especially since it

70 ILA, Committee on International Law on Sustainable Development, 'Resolution', Statement 2.

71 This is the case for the 1946 International Convention for the Regulation of Whaling Convention (Washington, DC, 2 December 1946, in force 10 November 1948, 161 UNTS 361), which the ICJ in *Whaling in the Antarctic* refused to interpret as giving priority to either conservation or sustainable exploitation (paras 57 and 58).

72 See the debates of the UN Security Council on environmental degradation as a threat to international security: Declaration of the Security Council President, S/PRST/2007/22, 25 June 2007; Declaration of the Security Council President, S/PRST/2011/15, 20 July 2011; Security Council, 6982nd Session, 19 June 2013, S/PV.6982.

can also be argued that economic development might itself also be a condition for the maintenance of peace and security.

In sum, the ILA Guiding Statement is relatively unhelpful in solving an interpretative conflict between the objectives of prevention and those of sustainable development. When such conflict arises, it seems that a case-by-case analysis of the situation will be needed to help find a balance among the three pillars of sustainable development. Given that, as will be discussed later, a sustainable development perspective has integrated the principle of prevention and vice versa, at least a minimal amount of consideration should be given to the two other pillars of sustainable development when interpreting preventive norms.

PREVENTION AND THE GREEN ECONOMY It should not be forgotten that sustainable development itself is an evolutive concept; therefore, if prevention is to be understood in the context of sustainable development, it should adapt to its changing definition. Sustainable development as understood in the 1992 Rio context is not the same as sustainable development after the 2012 Rio + 20 Summit, which integrated the concept of 'green economy' into its lexicology.[73] This leads to the following question: how does the evolution of the concept of sustainable development affect the interpretation of prevention?

The question is particularly challenging because it depends on the relationship between sustainable development and the green economy, which lacks an authoritative conceptualization. It might be that a green economy is not intended to 'replace' sustainable development[74] but rather that the implementation of green economy policies should be one of the main approaches available to achieve sustainable development.[75] Yet, it remains that when talking about the green economy, the balance among the three pillars of sustainable development is clearly on the side pursuing economic development. As Viñuales noted, this is an 'economic stimulus package with an environmental dimension, not the other way around'.[76] As a result, the interpretation of prevention in light of sustainable development understood within the Rio + 20 context – that is to say, in light of the green economy concept – facilitates the prevalence of economic considerations over

73 'The Future We Want', UNGA Res. 66/288 (11 September 2012), Section III, paras 56–74.

74 UNEP, *Towards a Green Economy: Pathways to Sustainable Development and Poverty Eradication* (2011), at 17.

75 'The Future We Want', Annex, at paras 56 and 62.

76 JE Viñuales, 'The Rise and Fall of Sustainable Development' (2013) 23 *Review of European, Comparative & International Environmental Law* 3, at 17.

environmental and social concerns. This conclusion, however, should be qualified by the fact that an interpretation of prevention in the context of the green economy contributes to extending the scope of its subjects not in the sense that it directly creates new obligations on non-State actors but by putting the emphasis on the private sector, whose role in the sustainability transition is highlighted by the green economy concept. It strengthens the argument, developed in Chapter 10, that the international legal framework is paying more attention to the accountability of the private sector for environmental harm. It remains, however, that although existing legal (and policy) frameworks influence the interpretation of the principle of prevention, the integration between prevention and sustainable development remains rather superficial at this stage. Deeper levels of integration can be identified, however.

9.2.1.2 Approach Two: Integration of Development Concerns in the Obligation of Prevention

Beyond the interpretation of prevention in light of the legal context within which it operates, prevention has also integrated the economic pillar of sustainable development in the form of the first component of Rio Principle 2.[77] As presented in Chapter 4 and therefore not elaborated further here,[78] the emphasis put by the UN Conference on Environment and Development on sustainable development led to a tweak in the wording of Stockholm Principle 21, reaffirmed in the Rio Declaration with an added reference to the right of States to 'exploit their own resources pursuant to their own environmental and *developmental* policies'.[79] The phrase 'developmental policies' corresponds to the economic pillar of sustainable development, which, in this context, becomes an integral part of the principle of prevention.

The minimal change made to the first component of Rio Principle 2 was consequential in introducing developmental questions to the environmental table, an evolution facilitated by the origins of the concept of permanent sovereignty over natural resources in the claims made by developing countries

77 RKL Panjabi, 'From Stockholm to Rio: A Comparison of the Declaratory Principles of International Environmental Law' (1992) 21 *Denver Journal of International Law and Policy* 215, at 231, noting that the 'addition of "developmental" considerations in the Rio Declaration and its placement in tandem with environmental policies also signalled a new effort at integration of the two concepts'.

78 On prevention at the UN Conference on Environment and Development, see Section 4.2.5.

79 Emphasis added.

for the recognition of their right to economic development.[80] The added reference to 'developmental policies' does not necessarily change the balancing act that operates between the three clauses of Principle 21, as Chapter 2 has already argued.[81] Nevertheless, it facilitates the inclusion of the objective of sustainable development within prevention.[82] It explains why Birnie, Boyle and Redgwell consider that 'like sustainable development, [prevention] requires integration or accommodation of both economic development and environmental protection'.[83] The trend has certainly been confirmed in this chapter. However, saying that prevention at its core is an integrative norm questions whether, under this scenario, it is opportune to keep the concept of sustainable development, or at least its integration element, as an independent norm. It might therefore be preferable to say that Rio Principle 2 is the result of the integration of sustainable development into prevention rather than that prevention is inherently an integrative norm.

But, most importantly, the integration of economic considerations within prevention raises a significant practical question: does it mean that prevention becomes applicable only after a cost-benefit analysis? The answer is not entirely clear. There seems to be a common understanding that prevention leaves a 'margin for socio-economic analysis'.[84] While this might mean that the obligation to prevent harm in cases where the preventive costs would be exceptionally, and perhaps unreasonably, high, it also raises fundamental questions related to whether the preventive obligation differs depending on the level of development of a State, which will be investigated further in the next section.

9.2.1.3 Approach Three: Inclusion of the Obligation of Prevention in the Concept of Sustainable Development

While prevention integrated the rationale of sustainable development within Principle 2 after the Earth Summit, sustainable development, in turn,

80 D Rosenberg, *Le principe de souveraineté des États sur leurs ressources naturelles* (Librairie générale de droit et de jurisprudence 1983) Part III, on permanent sovereignty over natural resources as a principle of international development law.

81 Section 2.1.3.

82 See e.g. N Schrijver, *Sovereignty over Natural Resources: Balancing Rights and Duties* (Cambridge University Press 1997) 394: 'Permanent sovereignty over natural resources is a key principle of both international economic law and international environmental law. As such it can play an important role in the blending of these two fields of law with the aim of promoting sustainable development.'

83 P Birnie, A Boyle and C Redgwell, *International Law and the Environment* (3rd edn, Oxford University Press 2009) 146.

84 N de Sadeleer, *Environmental Principles: From Political Slogans to Legal Rules* (Oxford University Press 2002) 81.

included prevention within its realm. This scenario implements Rio Principle 4 at its best, as it integrates environmental protection (i.e. prevention) with the economic and social considerations at the heart of sustainable development.

PREVENTION AS THE THIRD PILLAR OF SUSTAINABLE DEVELOPMENT The environmental pillar of sustainable development can be interpreted as an expression of the principle of prevention, which hence becomes fully integrated in the concept of sustainable development. In this respect, the first report of ILC Rapporteur Rao had already noted that 'the obligation to avoid causing significant transboundary harm requires an approach which promotes prevention as a duty and as a *concept integral* to the process of development aimed at eradicating poverty'.[85] Rao was therefore promoting the consecration of prevention as an independent obligation but also as a foundational element in the concept of sustainable development. Courts and tribunals have played an important role in ensuring that environmental considerations become an integral part of the design and implementation of developmental policies. National courts often tend to consider that sustainable development automatically includes a duty to prevent environmental harm.[86] However, because national courts often remain vague about the legal sources on which they rely – in particular, on whether they rely on international or national law – to operate this integration, the jurisprudence of international bodies, which follow a similar approach, provides a more telling example. The *Indus Waters Kishenganga* award strikingly integrated the obligation of prevention into the notion of sustainable development. In the partial award, the tribunal associated the norms of sustainable development and prevention so closely that it used the legal background of prevention as the legal basis for sustainable development. While it argued that the existing legal corpus addresses the need to manage natural resources in a sustainable way, the tribunal used the core legal foundations of prevention – the *Trail Smelter* case and Principle 21 of the Stockholm Declaration – to justify the existence of what it called the 'principle of sustainable development'.[87] In addition, the tribunal considered that sustainable development 'translates into' an obligation to carry out an EIA[88] and implied that an obligation to exercise due diligence to prevent environmental harm is required under the 'principle of sustainable development'.[89] The *Indus Waters Kishenganga* tribunal is, in a sense, making the link between prevention and sustainable development that remained missing in the discussion

85 ILC, 'First Report by Rapporteur Rao', para 30 (emphasis added). 86 See Section 5.2.2.

87 *Indus Waters Kishenganga Arbitration (Pakistan v. India)*, Permanent Court of Arbitration, Partial Award, 18 February 2013, paras 449–50.

88 *Indus Waters Kishenganga Arbitration*, Partial Award, para 450.

89 *Indus Waters Kishenganga Arbitration*, Partial Award, para 450.

of the two norms that the ICJ undertook in paragraph 140 of *Gabčíkovo-Nagymaros*.[90] It integrated prevention, its legal background and operative instruments to give normative power to sustainable development. The same type of integration is also found in the work of the ILA, which, as presented in Chapter 4, took this integration further in its New Delhi Declaration of Principles on sustainable development by using the legal basis of prevention to justify the existence of the duty to ensure sustainable use of natural resources.[91] In other words, from this perspective, prevention is not only one pillar of sustainable development but also gives the impression of being its most fundamental, and perhaps only, pillar.

A HIERARCHICAL RELATIONSHIP AMONG THE THREE PILLARS? As the environmental pillar of the concept of sustainable development, prevention is part of a balancing act that sustainable development seeks to achieve among the three pillars.[92] It therefore raises the question of whether a hierarchical relationship exists among the pillars. Generally, sustainable development has been criticized for being 'ill-suited to take clear stances where there are trade-offs between environmental, social and economic considerations'.[93] Moreover, the integration of prevention into sustainable development creates the obvious risk that another pillar takes prevalence and sacrifices environmental protection to economic and social development. Nevertheless, current trends show that the environmental pillar is generally considered to be the fundamental pillar of sustainable development. From this perspective, the integration of prevention into sustainable development does not weaken the obligation of prevention. For instance, in the *Iron Rhine Railway* case, the arbitral tribunal held that the environmental pillar of sustainable development should prevail over its economic pillar.

> Environmental law and the law on development stand not as alternatives but as mutually reinforcing, integral concepts, which require that where development may cause significant harm to the environment there is a duty to prevent, or at least mitigate, such harm.[94]

[90] See Section 5.1.1.

[91] ILA, Committee on the Legal Aspects of Sustainable Development, 'New Delhi Declaration of Principles of International Law Relating to Sustainable Development', New Delhi, 70th Session, 2002, para 1.1.

[92] *Pulp Mills*, para 175, on the balance to be achieved between economic utilization and environmental protection.

[93] Viñuales, 'The Rise and Fall of Sustainable Development'.

[94] *Iron Rhine Railway (Belgium v. Netherlands)*, Permanent Court of Arbitration, (2005) 27 RIAA 35, para 59.

The tribunal, while conceiving the two concepts as complementary, also gave precedence to prevention: development is limited by prevention, and not the other way around. This conclusion should nevertheless be qualified by the fact that the parties to the case were industrialized countries that had already reached a high level of development; it was therefore not developmental considerations per se that were at stake but rather economic ones. Under these circumstances, economic growth would understandably be deemed less important than environmental protection. It is, however, uncertain whether the tribunal's approach would have been the same if the case had involved developing countries.

The ILA 2014 Climate Change Principles adopted the same approach as the *Iron Rhine Railway* tribunal. They made clear that development plans should respect the obligation to prevent

> [w]here social and economic development plans, programs or projects may result in significant emissions of greenhouse gases or cause serious damage to the environment through climate change, States have a duty to prevent such harm or, at a minimum, to employ due diligence efforts to mitigate climate change impacts.[95]

The Commentaries to the principles justified this principle on the basis that 'the practice of integrated decision-making in the context of sustainable development is tied to the obligation to prevent damage through climate change'.[96] The word 'tied' certainly does not completely clarify the relationship between prevention and sustainable development. However, the ILA's statement makes clear that social and economic development should not be undertaken at the expense of the obligation of prevention.

LIMITATIONS AND OPPORTUNITIES The integration of prevention into sustainable development can be seen as a positive legal development because it furthers the two core objectives of international environmental law – the prevention of environmental damage and the distribution of the burdens relative to environmental management. A warning should nevertheless conclude this section. The apparent prevalence of the environmental pillar does not mean that social and economic considerations are being dismissed: it is just indicative of the fact that they should be assessed in light of the environmental harm they are likely to cause, and not the other way around.

95 ILA, Committee on Legal Principles Relating to Climate Change, 'Declaration of Principles Relating to Climate Change', Washington, DC, 76th Session, 2014, Article 3(5).

96 ILA, Committee on Legal Principles Relating to Climate Change, 'Declaration of Principles', Commentary to Article 3, at 9.

In addition, the inclusion of prevention in the concept of sustainable development indicates a better dialogue between the two rationales driving international environmental law but does not mean that they do not operate independently anymore. In particular, the integration of prevention under the scope of sustainable development does not question the status of prevention as an independent obligation. The content of prevention, including the obligation to carry out an EIA, does not derive from a sustainable development logic, as the *Indus Waters Kishenganga* award[97] and legal commentaries have suggested.[98] Surely, the EIA influences the social pillar of sustainable development when assessing the social effects of a potentially harmful activity. It also informs the decisions of policymakers seeking to find a balance between the potential economic benefits and environmental costs of a projected activity. However, the principal objective of the EIA remains to anticipate risks; as a result, it is not a tool that derives directly from the concept of sustainable development.

While the inclusion of prevention into sustainable development runs the risk that important conceptual distinctions will be blurred, the opportunities created by such rapprochement should also be noted. The sustainable development approach (or programme) gains normative density by integrating under its scope an obligation of international customary law. Similarly, prevention can also gain from its integration and, in particular, from being interpreted in light of the social pillar of sustainable development; indeed, it encourages taking future generations into consideration in the assessment of the level of diligence exercised by a State in the prevention of harm, hence contributing to extending the temporal outlook for prevention (see Section 9.2.3).

9.2.2 *Prevention and Differential Treatment*

Alongside integration, intra-generational equity is another foundational element of the concept of sustainable development that refers to its 'development' component. It strives to achieve an equitable 'distribution of the outcomes of

97 *Indus Waters Kishenganga Arbitration*, Partial Award, para 450.

98 See e.g. A Marong, 'From Rio to Johannesburg: Reflections on the Role of International Legal Norms in Sustainable Development' (2003) 16 *Georgetown International Environmental Law Review* 21, at 70–73, considering the EIA as a 'sustainable development principle'. See also ILC, 'Second Report of the Special Rapporteur, Mr Shinya Murase, on the protection of the atmosphere' (2015) UN Doc. A/CN.4/681, considering that the obligation to undertake an EIA falls under the 'principle of sustainable development' but envisaged under the obligation to prevent and mitigate harm in the following report.

development within one generation as much internally (within one national society) as internationally (between developed and developing states)'.[99] This objective is expressed, in part, in the principle of common but differentiated responsibilities (CBDRs).[100] Driven by an aspiration of equity, this principle assigns different obligations to States that take into account their historical contribution to environmental degradation and their financial and technological capabilities to solve the problem.

This section seeks to understand how prevention relates to CBDRs. Unlike precaution, whose application is explicitly made conditional upon domestic capabilities,[101] prevention has not been conceived to take elements of distributive justice into account. And yet, States do not have the same available means to implement their preventive obligations: should prevention therefore be understood as an absolute or variable obligation? Two different scenarios are presented here: the first one looks at conventional examples of differentiated obligations of prevention (9.2.2.1), and the second one concentrates on the more complex situation of due diligence to assess the extent to which it opens the door to differentiation (9.2.2.2). The analysis ends by looking at how the evolution of the concept of differentiation in international environmental law has influenced prevention (9.2.2.3).

9.2.2.1 Differentiated Treaty Obligations

Differentiation is a common feature in multilateral environmental agreements: the CBDR principle is often included in the hope that it will make the regime more equitable and hence encourage States to join.[102] But, under these circumstances, is the principle of prevention displaced by the principle of differentiation? Some authors consider that prevention and differentiation are two completely opposite norms that cannot operate simultaneously. It has been contended that the differentiated treaty obligations render prevention inapplicable. Zahar presented his argument, in the context of climate law, in the following terms:

99 Barral, 'Sustainable Development in International Law', 380.

100 While differential treatment is not the only expression of intra-generational equity, it is the most important for this study. On how differential treatment is directly related to intra-generational equity, see D Shelton, 'Equity', in D Bodansky, J Brunnée and E Hey (eds), *The Oxford Handbook of International Environmental Law* (Oxford University Press 2007) 639–63, at 656.

101 Rio Declaration, Principle 15.

102 P Cullet, *Differential Treatment in International Environmental Law* (Ashgate 2003) 172.

> The no-harm rule is an absolute one. 'States have … the responsibility to ensure that activities within their jurisdiction or control do not cause damage to the environment of other States' … The old rule has no capacity to distinguish between the particular circumstances of states (e.g. the need of some to deal with poverty first) or make a fair assessment of the responsibilities of a given state. Yet, as we know, climate law is all about differentiation. The prevention obligation has no imaginable role to play in climate law.[103]

However, this argument fails to acknowledge the preventive rationale underpinning the climate regime. Differentiation cannot operate in complete opposition to prevention because it applies to obligations that express a preventive rationale; in other words, even if the level of care expected from developed and developing countries differs, the obligations remain driven by prevention.

The true effect of differentiation is not to displace prevention but to transform it into a relative duty, which varies based on the level of developmental and technological advancement. Conventional expressions of this process are found in more stringent obligations of prevention being imposed on developed countries[104] or, in the opposite, developing states benefitting from delays in the implementation of their preventive obligations.[105] The relativity of preventive obligations in this context could be interpreted to weaken the preventive objective. However, differentiation facilitates compliance with prevention by ensuring that States do not disregard it all together on the grounds that the obligation cannot be realistically met or imposes an inequitable burden. In other words, the relationship between differentiation and prevention can be seen to be positive.

9.2.2.2 Differentiation in Due Diligence

Can prevention integrate differentiation in the absence of specific treaty provisions explicitly providing for differentiated duties? The question of

103 A Zahar, 'Methodological Issues in Climate Law' (2015) 5 *Climate Law* 25, at 33.

104 Protocol to the United Nations Framework Convention on Climate Change, Kyoto, 11 December 1997, in force 16 February 2005, (1998) 37 ILM 22, Annex I, imposing quantified emission reductions obligations on industrialized States.

105 Protocol on Substances that Deplete the Ozone Layer, Montreal, 16 September 1987, in force 1 January 1989, (1987) 26 ILM 154, Article 5(1), giving developing States a period of ten years to comply with the general substantive rules of the protocol; Kigali Amendment on HFC Phase-Down, Decision XXVIII/1 Further Amendment of the Montreal Protocol, available at https://treaties.un.org/doc/Treaties/2016/10/20161015%2003–23%20PM/Ch_XXVII-2.f.pdf (last accessed 15 May 2017), creating differentiated obligations between two groups of Article 5 parties and two groups of non-Article 5 parties.

whether the duty of care will be assessed on the basis of economic, financial and technological circumstances remains open.

General international law is clear that the obligation of due diligence integrates considerations of means. An early expression of differential treatment in international law can be found in Max Huber's well-known ruling in the *Spanish Zone of Morocco Claims* arbitral award[106] that the State can only reasonably be expected to exercise the level of vigilance corresponding to its capabilities.[107] The ICJ took the same position in the *United States Diplomatic and Consular Staff in Tehran* case, where it ruled that the Iranian government had failed to exercise due diligence in protecting the US mission against attack by the militants and to prevent the attack,[108] despite the fact that the Iranian authorities 'had the means at their disposal to perform their obligations'.[109]

In the context of international environmental law, the question of how due diligence integrates considerations of capabilities is of special importance. It relates to the difficult balancing act operated by the branch between two 'competing community objectives', one seeking to protect the global commons and the other seeking to avoid putting 'unreasonable normative standards'[110] on historically and economically disadvantaged countries.[111] As a result of this reality, legal commentaries generally acknowledge the need to integrate considerations of means in preventive obligations. For instance, the Report of the Experts Group of the World Commission on Environment and Development supported this view when it noted the following:

> [T]he duty of developing Stats to counteract transboundary environmental interferences may also be somewhat less stringent in that these States are not obliged to take the same sophisticated and expensive measures which developed States must take to prevent or abate transboundary environmental interferences. Support for this view could also be found in the nature of the obligation to counteract transboundary interferences – being a due care or due diligence obligation.[112]

[106] *Affaire des biens britanniques au Maroc espagnol (Espagne v. Royaume-Uni)*, (1925) 2 RIAA 615, at 644.

[107] *Affaire des biens britanniques au Maroc espagnol* 644.

[108] *United States Diplomatic and Consular Staff in Tehran (US v. Iran)* (Judgment) (1980) ICJ Rep 3, paras 61 and 63.

[109] *United States Diplomatic and Consular Staff in Tehran*, para 68(c).

[110] ILA, Study Group on Due Diligence in International Law, 'Second Report', at 3.

[111] ILA, Study Group on Due Diligence in International Law, 'Second Report', at 4.

[112] RD Munro and J Lammers (eds), *Environmental Protection and Sustainable Development: Legal Principles and Recommendations Adopted by the Experts Group on Environmental Law of the World Commission on Environment and Development* (Graham & Trotman 1987) 80.

In the same vein, ILC Rapporteur Rao acknowledged that 'implementation of the principle of prevention and the duty of due diligence is not isolated or divorced from ... consideration of the needs and practices of developing countries or countries in economic transition'.[113] Similarly, the Commentaries of the ILC Prevention Articles recognized that 'the degree of care expected of a State with a well-developed economy and human and material resources and with highly evolved systems and structures of governance is different from States which are not so well placed'.[114]

The *ITLOS Advisory Opinion on the Area*, charged *inter alia* to rule on whether developing States have modulated environmental obligations, provided a welcome opportunity to assess how this would play out in the context of the law of State responsibility. It was the first time the question of differential treatment in the assessment of due diligence was scrutinized in the context of international environmental adjudication. The opinion provided some clarifications but also left a number of uncertainties unresolved. The Seabed Chamber lacked clarity in relation to two issues. First, the Chamber surprisingly did not include a country's level of development when it mentioned the range of factors that might affect the due-diligence obligation.[115] This omission, however, should not necessarily be interpreted as excluding considerations of means in the context of the assessment of due diligence. It is perhaps best explained by the fact that the Chamber had already discussed differential treatment in previous sections of the advisory opinion and wanted to highlight additional factors necessary to assess due diligence, including 'the resources, knowledge and technological capability available'.[116]

A second, and more complex, uncertainty relates to the distinction the Chamber made between the effects of differential treatment on primary and secondary obligations. The Chamber recognized that the direct obligations of the sponsoring State (i.e. obligations of prevention and precaution) 'could provide for differential treatment for developed and developing sponsoring States'.[117] At the same time, it considered that 'general provisions concerning

[113] ILC, 'Third Report of the Special Rapporteur, Mr Pemmaraju Sreenivasa Rao, on the Prevention of Transboundary Harm from Hazardous Activities' (2000) UN Doc. A/CN.4/510, para 23.

[114] ILC, 'Draft Articles on Prevention of Transboundary Harm', Commentary to Article 3, para 17, at 155.

[115] *Responsibilities and Obligations of States Sponsoring Persons and Entities with Respect to Activities in the Area*, para 123.

[116] ILA, Study Group on Due Diligence in International Law, 'Second Report', at 14.

[117] *Responsibilities and Obligations of States Sponsoring Persons and Entities with Respect to Activities in the Area*, para 160 (emphasis added).

the responsibilities and liability of the sponsoring State apply equally to all sponsoring States',[118] as ruling otherwise would favour sponsoring States 'of convenience'[119] chosen for their lower environmental standards. The refusal of the Chamber to apply differential treatment in the context of secondary norms is in line with the ILC Commentaries to the Prevention Articles, which provided that

> the economic level of States was one of the factors to be taken into account in determining whether a State had complied with its obligations of due diligence. However, it is understood that a State's economic level could not be used to discharge a State from its obligation in this regard.[120]

This rationale is convincing; it integrates the logic of due diligence that assesses the level of care on the basis of a variety of factors, including developmental ones, while at the same time it seeks to avoid the use of economic factors as a trump card to justify a breach of prevention. The line between the two, however, is thin; it would only make sense if the statement is understood to mean that a lack of economic capabilities cannot be used as a defence by a State in breach of its obligation of prevention but might nevertheless play a role in a tribunal's assessment of the level of duty of care expected from the State. Along this line, a convincing interpretation has been proposed by the ILA in the context of its study on due diligence: it considered that the distinction operated by the Chamber meant that 'whether or not the degree of diligence required varies between developed and developing States pivots on the applicable primary rules'.[121] It explained that a subjective standard of due diligence – that is to say, a standard integrating considerations of means – will only be applicable if 'provided for in the treaty, binding secondary norms established under the treaty, or in customary law in the relevant, narrow context'.[122] In the negative, an objective international standard would apply.[123] For instance, due-diligence expectations will not vary on the basis of developmental considerations in the context of UNCLOS because its provisions do not explicitly rely on differentiation; it should play a more important role in the context of the climate regime build upon a differentiation logic.

118 *Responsibilities and Obligations of States Sponsoring Persons and Entities with Respect to Activities in the Area*, para 158.
119 *Responsibilities and Obligations of States Sponsoring Persons and Entities with Respect to Activities in the Area*, para 159.
120 ILC, 'Draft Articles on Prevention of Transboundary Harm', Commentary to Article 3, para 13, at 155.
121 ILA, Study Group on Due Diligence in International Law, 'Second Report', at 15.
122 ILA, Study Group on Due Diligence in International Law, 'Second Report', at 15.
123 ILA, Study Group on Due Diligence in International Law, 'Second Report', at 19.

Hence, the integration of differentiation in prevention remains more the exception than the rule. A lighter form of interaction nevertheless can be considered, one that does not relativize prevention but seeks to take into account differences in capabilities to facilitate the fulfilment of objective preventive obligations. It consists in interpreting differential treatment as a principle that requires helping States with lower levels of technological and financial capacities meet their preventive obligations. This perspective was implicitly encouraged by ITLOS in its *Advisory Opinion on the Area*, where, immediately after having refused to apply differentiation in the context of secondary rules, it specified that 'developing States should receive necessary assistance including training'.[124] From this perspective, differential treatment is not viewed as a principle that changes the level of care expected from the State but that reminds States that there is a duty to help States with lesser capabilities meet the international standards of prevention. The approach might raise implementation challenges but has the advantage that it does not lower the level of environmental protection. It is most beneficial for the environment because it is the State that adapts to the obligation of prevention and not the other way around.

9.2.2.3 The Subjects of Differentiation

A central question arising from differential treatment relates to the subjects of the differentiation. Differentiation often operates based on a controversial classification between 'developed' and 'developing' countries, which is more the result of political negotiations than an objective assessment of capabilities; it can thus lead to situations in which the level of preventive actions required of a State does not equitably match its actual capabilities. In response to these difficulties, international environmental law is currently moving away from the developed/developing dichotomy to favour individualized differentiation.

An evident example is found in the climate law principle that emerged in the context of the Paris Agreement: the principle of 'common but differentiated responsibilities and respective capabilities *in light of different national circumstances*'.[125] The qualification of the CBDR principle brings to light the fact that international law environmental law is moving towards increased

[124] *Responsibilities and Obligations of States Sponsoring Persons and Entities with Respect to Activities in the Area*, para 163 (after having refused to apply differentiation in the context of secondary rules).

[125] Emphasis added: Paris Agreement to the United Nations Framework Convention on Climate Change, Paris, 12 December 2015, in force 4 November 2016, Doc. FCCC/CP/2015/10/Add.1, Article 2(2). The expression finds its origins in the 'US-China Joint Announcement on

differentiation.[126] It provides an array of different options to choose from within a common framework underpinned by prevention instead of imposing a pre-set differentiated framework. The logic was pushed to the extreme in the Paris Agreement, which lets each State choose the level of its mitigation actions.[127]

The consequences of individualized differentiation are that due diligence, when integrating differential treatment, is not evaluated based on an arbitrary division but on an individualized assessment. ITLOS took this position in its *Advisory Opinion on the Area* when it looked at whether developing sponsoring States had modulated obligations; it contended that '[w]hat counts in a specific situation is the level of scientific knowledge and technical capability available to a given State in the relevant scientific and technical fields'.[128] The approach does not create arbitrary divisions between States but imposes equitable preventive obligations adapted to their true capabilities.

9.2.3 *Prevention and Inter-Generational Equity*

'Inter-generational equity' refers to the adjective 'sustainable' in the term 'sustainable development'. Greatly influenced by the work of Brown Weiss, the concept posits that States, as 'trustees of the planetary trust',[129] should preserve the environmental capital they hold for the benefit of future generations. Current generations should not restrict the options available to future generations in satisfying their own values ('conservation of options') and should not pass the planet on in a worse condition than the present generation received it ('conservation of quality').[130] This last definitional element of

Climate Change', 11 November 2014, para 2, available at www.whitehouse.gov/the-press-office/2014/11/11/us-china-joint-announcement-climate-change (last accessed 19 May 2017).

126 J Pauwelyn, 'The End of Differential Treatment for Developing Countries? Lessons from the Trade and Climate Change Regimes' (2013) 22 *Review of European, Community & International Environmental Law* 29, at 41. See also D French and L Rajamani, 'Climate Change and International Environmental Law: Musings on a Journey to Somewhere' (2013) 25 *Journal of Environmental Law* 437, at 439–43, 'differentiation in retreat'; C Voigt, 'Equity in the 2015 Climate Agreement. Lessons from Differential Treatment in Multilateral Environmental Agreements' (2014) 4 *Climate Law* 50, at 68–69, on the way forward to 'optioning' and 'self-differentiation'.

127 Paris Agreement, Article 4(2).

128 *Responsibilities and Obligations of States Sponsoring Persons and Entities with Respect to Activities in the Area*, para 162.

129 E Brown Weiss, 'The Planetary Trust: Conservation and Intergenerational Equity' (1984) 11 *Ecology Law Quarterly* 495, at 500–501.

130 Brown Weiss, 'The Planetary Trust', 525.

sustainable development faces fundamental implementation challenges arising mainly from the restricted temporal scope of the law; this means that prevention, as it currently stands, struggles to fully integrate an inter-generational approach. However, integrating considerations of inter-generational equity into prevention is necessary to fully respond to the fact the impacts of environmental degradation are increasingly being felt across generations.[131] Practice is generally lagging; it is notable, however, that the inter-temporal dimension of prevention was recognized by Argentina in the *Pulp Mills* case when it pleaded that '[a]n effective application of the principle of prevention and the precautionary principle by Uruguay would have made it possible to comprehend the risks of grave harm for present and future generations'.[132] Despite the fact that the Court did not discuss the *ratione temporis* of prevention,[133] Argentina's argument nevertheless revealed that some States might be willing to extend the temporal scope of prevention.

The integration of inter-generational equity into prevention could require a different assessment of the risks arising from a potentially harmful activity, generally evaluating the potential impacts of an activity in the near to medium-term future. More specifically, it calls for an EIA that assesses the long-term effects of a proposed activity on future generations.[134] The extension of the temporal scope of the EIA nevertheless raises fundamental challenges. In particular, the interpretation of preventive obligations through an inter-generational lens will be restricted by the fact that science has difficulties assessing the long-term impacts of a potentially harmful activity, especially if the assessment requires taking into account cumulative effects. As a solution, Brown Weiss proposed that '[t]o protect present and future generations, the duty to avoid adverse impacts must include an obligation to engage in the scientific research necessary to discover and

131 On how other principles of international environmental law integrate an inter-generational perspective, see C Redgwell, *Intergenerational Trusts and Environmental Protection* (Manchester University Press 1999) 126–43, discussing the principle of sustainable development, the common heritage of humankind principle, the principle of custodianship or stewardship, the precautionary principle and the principle of common but differentiated responsibilities.

132 *Pulp Mills*, Oral Pleadings, CR 2009/20, 28 September 2009, at 35, para 22.

133 It is noteworthy, however, that the Court had mentioned 'generations unborn' in its advisory opinion on the *Legality of the Threat or Use of Nuclear Weapons* (Advisory Opinion) (1996) ICJ Rep 226, para 29. In addition, the issue of inter-generational equity was discussed by Judge Cançado Trindade in his separate opinion to *Pulp Mills*, paras 114–31.

134 E Brown Weiss, *In Fairness to Future Generations: International Law, Common Patrimony, and Intergenerational Equity* (Transnational Publishers 1989) 63. See also B Jacqmotte, 'Definition and Assessment of the Concept of Harm in a Regime of Transboundary Harm Prevention' (1998) 3 *Austrian Review of International and European Law* 233, at 258.

evaluate threats to the well-being of present and future generations'.[135] Her proposal considers that the duty to prevent would only be discharged if the State has, *inter alia*, fulfilled its obligation to engage in scientific research. Notwithstanding the uncertainty relative to the level of commitment to research that would be necessary to discharge the preventive duty, the suggestion might put a high burden on States with limited means to devote to scientific research. In short, it adds another layer of obligation on developing States that is not unproblematic.

A policy question also arises from the results provided by an impact assessment of long-term risks. It relates to the level of risk that present generations decide to pass to future generations. Indeed, even if the EIA accounts for long-term effects,[136] it does not solve the delicate issue that consists in deciding which level of risk can acceptably be passed to future generations. These difficult moral questions will become more preeminent if, in the future, the inter-generational approach broadens the temporal scope of prevention.

This overview of the relationship between prevention and sustainable development has highlighted how prevention interacts with the three aspects of sustainable development. Prevention does not operate irrespective of other environmental norms that do not share its anticipatory rationale. It clearly participates, in different ways, in the balancing exercise operated by sustainable development between different interests (social, economic and environmental). Its interactions with other distributional objectives, in particular, with regards to different stakeholders (developing and developed States, future generations), are becoming increasingly important but will need to be further clarified.

9.3 CONCLUSION

Lowe claims that the system of international law has reached a 'state of completeness'[137] and that international law is now concerned with the 'regulation of the relationship between existing norms and institutions of international law, rather than in the creation of entirely novel norms and institutions'.[138] This holds particularly true for international environmental

135 Brown Weiss, *In Fairness to Future Generations* 66.

136 These would include uncertain risks as well; it would certainly not fit the concept of inter-generational equity to use scientific uncertainty as a reason for postponing measures to prevent environmental degradation.

137 V Lowe, 'The Politics of Law-Making: Are the Methods and Character of Norm Creation Changing?', in M Byers (ed), *The Role of Law in International Politics: Essay in International Relations and International Law* (Oxford University Press 2000) 207–26, at 209.

138 Lowe, 'The Politics of Law-Making', 212.

law at its current stage of evolution. Indeed, the consolidation of the international environmental legal framework today does not depend on the creation of new norms. Rather, it requires clarifying the specificities of each existing norm to ensure that the relationships between the different norms form a coherent legal framework.

Norms guiding the field of international environmental law are difficult to compare because they rarely operate on the same normative level, which complicates their interactions, and are evolving quickly, which means that their interactions are constantly changing. Charting how the norms interact is also made more difficult by the multiple functions that a norm might fulfil in the international legal system. For instance, it creates confusion in relation to precaution, which shares an *objective* of prevention but should nevertheless be distinguished from the *obligation* of prevention per se. In addition, the subjective aspect related to how these norms are conceptualized should not be underestimated: legal actors tend to understand the rationale and scope of environmental norms differently, which means that they might not always contribute to their logical evolution.

Norms of environmental law operate in a legal system that relies on them, but also their interactions, to meet the two objectives of international environmental law – prevention and balance. As a result, the question of the prevalence of one norm over the other is rarely raised. In this context, the prevention principle contributes to international environmental law by either (1) influencing the rationale of a norm in its avoidance of environmental harm or (2) taking part in the balancing act operating in the law between different considerations and stakeholders. The centrality of prevention in international environmental law does not entitle it to prevail over the other environmental norms but rather requires that it interacts with these norms to ensure the coherence of the field.

CONCLUSION TO PART III

THE CONTOURS OF PREVENTION

The prevention principle in its most advanced form is a positive obligation to anticipate harm to protect and preserve the environment. Intrinsic complexities arise from the three definitional elements of prevention. The anticipatory rationale of prevention is faced with two challenges. First, it has to respond to the fact that the reality of environmental degradation means that it often seeks to minimize harm rather than prevent it altogether. Second, it is reliant on scientific knowledge that is becoming more precise and, also, more complex. Risks of environmental harm are more easily determined thanks to advances in scientific knowledge, and the door to an inter-generational perspective opens as predictions are able to extend over longer periods of time. At the same time, as environmental problems are becoming multidimensional, the science is becoming more complex and demands that the law adapts to be able to evaluate the knowledge at its disposal. The second trait of prevention, relative to its content, is not easily put in practice: it requires that the principle finds an adequate balance between giving States enough policy space in their environmental actions while providing clear international minimum standards upon which to assess due diligence. In addition, requiring States to be proactive in a context of overburdened national bureaucracies is not unchallenging. Finally, prevention faces tensions between its rationale concerned with the protection of the environment and the structural, State-centred conditions within which it evolves and that do not always offer adequate implementation tools. Moreover, it operates within the international legal system that has made environmental protection only one of its many other priorities. It is thus at the centre of a continuous balancing act, operating both at the small scale of a project proposal and a large scale in relation to the design of a country's policy priorities between environmental considerations and economic, social and developmental necessities. As a result, despite being the cornerstone of international environmental law, prevention cannot be seen as an absolute norm but can only be envisaged as part of the international legal system.

PART IV

PREVENTION AS A CONSOLIDATED NORM

Current Trends and Future Prospects

This part closes this study on the current trends that are contributing to the evolution of prevention in its most advanced form. It establishes a parallel with the first two chapters, which sought to understand the conditions of the emergence of prevention. Going back to the evolutionary perspective upon which this analysis relies, it looks at the place of prevention in today's general international law and the directions towards which the norm could develop further. This part relies on the three definitional traits of prevention (anticipation, proactivity and protection of the environment) to shed light on their legal consequences. Chapter 10 shows how the definitional elements frame the role and place of prevention in the international legal order. Chapter 11 ends this study by examining the ways in which prevention is evolving in relation to the rationale against which it originally emerged – reparation – and identifies how the curative approach has, to some extent, been absorbed by the preventive logic in the context of non-compliance procedures.

10

Role and Place of Prevention in the International Legal Order

This chapter concentrates on how prevention operates in the current international legal order and how it could develop its specificities further in light of the structural context. Its objective is not to look at the place of prevention in international law per se, as it would, in effect, mean discussing its conventional and customary manifestations presented in Part II. By relying on the term 'international legal order', this chapter adopts a broader approach to understand the place of prevention in a legal system made of norms and institutions with which it is expected to interact. The international legal order is understood as the 'organization of a system ... made of norms and institutions aiming to apply to the constitutive subjects of a determined community'.[1] On this basis, this chapter aims to test the interactions between prevention and the different subjects and institutions of the broader international community. In short, it is interested not in the norms of international law per se but rather in the relationships that prevention entertains with the various entities that form the order created by international law. It is driven by the understanding that the definitional elements of prevention reflect the fact that the principle operates in an international legal order that can be qualified as 'modern'.[2] It seeks to protect common values, such as environmental integrity, for the benefit of the international community understood broadly as an assemblage of multiple participants. However, the 'traditional' forms of international law continue to drive the branch, which means that prevention has not yet been able to fully develop its specificities.

[1] P-M Dupuy, 'L'unité de l'ordre juridique international. Cours général de droit international public' (2002) *Collected Courses of the Hague Academy of International Law* 9–496, at 66 (my translation).

[2] R Pisillo Mazzeschi, 'Closing Keynote Lecture: Coordination of Different Values in International Law', ESIL Annual Conference, 9 September 2017 (on file with the author), on 'old' and 'new' international law, at 4.

Each of the three definitional elements of prevention has the potential to bring prevention into a new 'corner' of the international legal order. These three corners are admittedly very different, but they all shed light on the current role and place of prevention in the international legal order. Firstly, the nature of the preventive norm is examined to present the different roles, including that of 'principle', that the anticipatory norm plays in the international legal order (10.1). Secondly, an important question arises from the proactivity requirements set by prevention, that is, whether subjects other than States are under an obligation to act diligently in the face of environmental harm (10.2). Finally, the chapter looks at the third trait of prevention, its concern for environmental protection, and at the legal consequences of its operating outside the classical inter-State system (10.3).

10.1 PREVENTION AS A MULTIFACETED NORM TO ANTICIPATE HARM

The rationale of anticipation enriches a primarily reactive international legal system with a new perspective that plays multiple roles. This study, starting with its title, *The Prevention Principle in International Environmental Law*, has until now assumed, without further justification, that the role played by prevention is that of a 'principle'. It is now time to build on the analysis provided in previous chapters to reflect on the normative nature of the norm. Such an examination runs the risk of starting an open-ended debate about how legal systems operate and how different types of norms influence them. This is beyond the scope of this study. This section modestly aims to shed light on the normative depth of prevention, which it presents as a multifaceted norm (10.1.5). It justifies the commonly found denomination of prevention as a 'principle' (10.1.1) and also presents the other roles that prevention plays in the international legal system, as a policy (10.1.2), a rule (10.1.3) and a right (10.1.4).

10.1.1 *Prevention as a Principle*

The following discussion reflects on the nature of prevention as a principle at two levels, firstly by analysing the place of principles under the general theory of law (10.1.1.1) and then, more specifically, under international law (10.1.1.2).

10.1.1.1 Prevention as a Principle of Law

The identification of what constitutes a 'principle' and the roles it plays populates scholarly debates among legal philosophers. Analysing 'principles' under the general theory of law can indeed be a complex matter. For the sake of simplicity, the definition of 'principle' provided by an international arbitral tribunal has been deemed relevant for present purposes. In the *Gentini* award, a principle was described as a 'general truth, which guides our action, serves as a theoretical basis for the various acts of our life, and the application of which to reality produces a given consequence'.[3] It assigns two roles to a principle that the discussion that follows applies to prevention. Firstly, a principle expresses a general truth that frames the theoretical background of our actions, and secondly, by guiding our actions, it contributes to the construction of the legal framework.

Let us first concentrate on the theoretical contribution of principles. They 'pursue an ideal'[4] and point towards an ethically desirable direction.[5] The prevention principle is precisely grounded into two ideals.[6] The first one relates to no-harm's aspirations to facilitate coexistence with the 'other' (an individual or a State),[7] and the second is linked to prevention and its objectives of environmental protection. The moral imperatives driving the principle of prevention have at times been explicitly recognized. For instance, the United Nations General Assembly (UNGA) acknowledged in its resolution 42/186 that the 'safeguarding of species is a moral obligation of humankind'.[8] Another example lies in the famous proposal that was made in the context of the work of the International Law Commission (ILC) on State responsibility to categorize severe pollution as an international crime.[9] While the entire article on international crimes was eventually deleted, the initial inclusion of an environmental crime is instructive: it put environmental protection on a pedestal, signalling it as one of the common values that international law seeks to protect. The origins of prevention in moral aspirations are sometimes used to question its legal character.[10] However, the

3 *Gentini (Italy v. Venezuela)*, (1903) 10 RIAA 551.

4 J Verschuuren, *Principles of Environmental Law: The Ideal of Sustainable Development and the Role of Principles of International, European, and National Environmental Law* (Nomos 2003) 145.

5 Verschuuren, *Principles of Environmental Law* 22. On moral reasoning in the determination of a principle, see also J Waldron, 'The Need for Legal Principles' (1996) 82 *Iowa Law Review* 857.

6 On the definition of ideals, see W Van der Burg, 'The Importance of Ideals' (1997) 31 *Journal of Value Inquiry* 23, at 25.

7 I Pop, *Voisinage et bon voisinage en droit international* (Pedone 1980) 340–41, where he characterizes good neighbourliness as a moral principle.

8 UNGA Res. 42/186 (11 December 1987), para 3(k).

9 ILC, 'Draft Articles on State Responsibility with Commentaries thereto adopted by the ILC on First Reading' (January 1997) UN Doc. A/CN.4/L.528/Add.3, Article 19.

10 G Lynham, 'The *Sic Utere* Principle as Customary International Law: A Case of Wishful Thinking?' (1995) 2 *James Cook University Law Review* 172, at 173, arguing that the '*sic utere* principle remains at best a moral obligation'.

position does not stand because prevention has achieved 'sufficient expression in legal form',[11] not least as a recognized customary norm, for doubts to be put aside.

Now, with regards to the contributions that principles make to a legal framework, prevention guides international law by performing three different functions: (1) an architectural function, (2) an interpretative function, and (3) a decision-making function. Firstly, the preventive rationale is the catalyst behind the adoption of most environmental treaties and drives their contents. Prevention drives the contents of international treaties in multiple ways, depending on the forms in which it manifests (reaffirmation of Stockholm Principle 21, substantive or procedural obligations), and with different normative weight (depending on its place and formulation in the treaty). Secondly, it often guides the interpretation of judges to clarify the meaning of a provision,[12] update its content[13] or conciliate different considerations.[14] Finally, prevention also performs a decision-making function in the determination of the conformity of a given act with what is legally required, prohibited or authorized. The abstractness of principles ensures that they are open to new developments, including new scientific knowledge, and thus can complement more static obligations found in treaty and customary law[15] – although their vagueness can sometimes be seen as weakness because they are generally seen 'not to be law at all'.[16] But, despite its broad formulation, the prevention principle is precise enough to guide judicial bodies in their decisions, as

11 *International Status of South-West Africa* (Advisory Opinion) (1950) ICJ Rep 128, para 49 (on moral obligations that have also achieved a legal character).

12 See e.g. *Responsibilities and Obligations of States Sponsoring Persons and Entities with Respect to Activities in the Area*, ITLOS No. 17, Advisory Opinion (1 February 2011), paras 110–16 (to interpret UNCLOS Article 139(1), Article 153(4)); *South China Sea Arbitration (The Republic of the Philippines v. The People's Republic of China)*, (Permanent Court of Arbitration), Award on the Merits, 12 July 2016, paras 939–49 (to interpret UNCLOS Part XII).

13 See e.g. *Pulp Mills on the River Uruguay (Argentina v. Uruguay)* (Judgment) (2010) ICJ Rep 14, paras 193 and 194; *United States – Import Prohibition of Certain Shrimp and Shrimp Products*, Appellate Body Report, WT/DS58/AB/R, 12 October 1998, paras 129–31, 152 and 153; *Iron Rhine Railway (Belgium v. Netherlands)*, Permanent Court of Arbitration, (2005) 27 RIAA 35, para 58; *Indus Waters Kishenganga Arbitration (Pakistan v. India)*, Permanent Court of Arbitration, Partial Award, 18 February 2013, para 452.

14 See e.g. *S. D. Myers Inc. v. Canada, NAFTA Arbitration* (UNCITRAL Rules), Partial Award (13 November 2000), para 247.

15 R Wolfrum, 'General International Law (Principles, Rules and Standards)', in *Max Planck Encyclopedia of Public International Law* (Oxford University Press 2010), para 60.

16 J Knox, 'Myth and Reality of Transboundary Environmental Impact Assessment' (2002) 96 *American Journal of International Law* 291, at 292 (although the basis of the criticism remains uncertain: does the author mean that Principle 21 is not law because it originates from a non–legally binding document, because it is more a policy than an obligation or because it is not implemented).

illustrated by the classic *Trail Smelter* case, in which the tribunal extracted specific obligations from the no-harm rule regarding the future operation of the smelter.[17] Prevention therefore qualifies as a principle for its dual function: it translates moral imperatives regarding coexistence and environmental protection and guides concrete actions that shape the international legal order.

10.1.1.2 Prevention as a Principle of International Law

There is no doubt that prevention fulfils the role of a principle of law, but such a characterization made in the context of international law raises complex questions about how it fits within the different types of principles populating the field. In this context, three categories should be disentangled: (1) principles of international environmental law, (2) general principles of law pursuant to Article 38 of the ICJ Statute,[18] and finally, (3) general principles of international law. Whether prevention qualifies under one, or several, of these categories will inevitably depend on how the categories are defined. The task is complex. Indeed, there is little consensus on how to interpret these concepts[19] and whether the three categories can convincingly be distinguished.[20] Each category is analysed in turn.

PRINCIPLES OF INTERNATIONAL ENVIRONMENTAL LAW The term 'principle' is often used – and perhaps abused – to qualify norms operating in the field of international environmental law. As illustrated by the title of one of the leading textbooks in the field, *Principles of International Environmental Law*,[21] it is generally considered that international environmental law can be summarized – and understood – via the lens of its principles.[22] The overwhelming

17 *Trail Smelter (United States v. Canada)* (16 April 1938 and 11 March 1941), (1941) 3 RIAA 1905, at 1965. See also *Corfu Channel (United Kingdom/Albania)* (1949) ICJ Rep 4, at 22.

18 Statute of the International Court of Justice, San Francisco, 26 June 1945, in force 24 October 1945, (1945) 39 AJIL Supp. 215.

19 A Gourgourinis, 'General/Particular International Law and Primary/Secondary Rules: Unitary Terminology of a Fragmented System' (2011) 22 *European Journal of International Law* 993, at 1008.

20 In particular, the fact that the ICJ frequently relies on general principles without clarifying the type of principles to which it is referring questions the relevance of the distinction between Article 38 principle and general principles of international law.

21 P Sands and J Peel, *Principles of International Environmental Law* (3rd edn, Cambridge University Press 2012).

22 See also other textbooks that devote a section to the principles of international environmental law e.g. J-M Arbour and S Lavallée, *Droit international de l'environnement* (Bruylant 2006) 43–90 ('concepts et principes généraux'); P-M Dupuy and JE Viñuales, *International Environmental Law* (Cambridge University Press 2015) 51–90 ('the principles of international

presence of principles in international environmental law is partly explained by the fact that the foundational document of international environmental law – the Stockholm Declaration – referred to environmental norms as 'principles'.[23] The term was deemed best suited to reflect the objective of the Stockholm Declaration, which aimed to be 'concise and inspirational, embodying the aspirations of the world's people for a better environment' without including 'specific guidelines for action' or binding commitments.[24] It was able to carry a 'desirable message'[25] that could talk to different audiences – providing guidelines to States but also encouraging self-regulation of other actors (including the general public). Additionally, the term 'principle' tends to benefit from a positive connotation: because they are open textured enough to accommodate diverging positions, principles tend to gather consensus, even if one based on different interpretations of the same norm. The term also gave emerging environmental aspirations a sense of stability and coherence by defining them by a lexicology common to law.

It is not possible, however, to define, in the abstract, what a principle of international environmental law is. There is no universal doctrinal definition of a principle of (international) environmental law.[26] As a result, significant divergences exist in the scholarship about which norms qualify as principles of international environmental law. International environmental law textbooks do not always list the same 'principles' and include concepts as diverse as 'territorial sovereignty of States', 'nuclear power and transportation of hazardous substances' and 'common concerns'.[27] Although the scholarship might not agree on a definite list of principles, it leaves little doubt that prevention is first in line to qualify as a principle of international environmental law.[28] Some authors do not include prevention in their list of

environmental law'); E Hey, *Advanced Introduction to International Environmental Law* (Edward Elgar 2016) 52–86 (on 'principles').

23 Declaration of the United Nations Conference on the Human Environment (Stockholm, 16 June 1972), (1972) 11 ILM 1416.

24 'Report of the Preparatory Committee for the United Nations Conference on the Human Environment, Third Session' (13–24 September 1971) UN Doc. A/CONF.48/PC.13, paras 149–65. For more on why the term 'principles' was chosen in the context of the Stockholm Declaration, see L Sohn, 'The Stockholm Declaration on the Human Environment' (1973) 14 *Harvard International Law Journal* 423, at 424–34.

25 E Scotford, *Environmental Principles and the Evolution of Environmental Law* (Bloomsbury 2017) 87.

26 Scotford, *Environmental Principles*, 45.

27 T Koivurova, *Introduction to International Environmental Law* (Routledge 2014) 104–22.

28 *Pulp Mills*, separate opinion of Judge Cançado Trindade, paras 54–61, on prevention as a principle of international environmental law.

principles,[29] but the omission is most likely explained by the fact that they prefer to concentrate on more controversial, or emerging, norms: it is unlikely that they contest the status of prevention as a principle. Principles emerge in a branch of international law to provide an alternative solution to what 'general law provides for analogous situations'.[30] Given that, as presented in this study, prevention operates as an alternative to the reparative approach favoured in general international law, its status as a principle of international environmental law cannot be contested.

ARTICLE 38 GENERAL PRINCIPLES OF LAW The analysis becomes more complex when one looks at whether prevention would qualify as a 'general principle of law' pursuant to Article 38 of the ICJ Statute. There is no consensus on which norms fall under this category. The scholarship attaches different meanings to the term, which Schachter ordered into a topology offering four different, but not mutually exclusive, perspectives.[31] The approach that understands principles as norms intrinsic to any legal system, either national or international, that contribute to the good administration of justice such as the principle of *res judicata* will immediately be put aside because prevention is not such a norm. But Schachter identified three other meanings that the scholarship gives to Article 38 principles of law. Whether one definition is favoured over another carries few legal consequences: however, they all, in their own way, put certain characteristics of prevention in the spotlight and hence contribute to a better understanding of the norm.

The first scenario understands general principles as basic norms commonly found in various domestic legal systems across the globe[32] and often originating

29 See the following outputs that omit prevention in the list of principles of international environmental law: S Atapattu, *Emerging Principles of International Environmental Law* (Transnational Publishers 2006); S Kravchenko, T Chowdbury and M Bhuiyan, 'Principles of International Environmental Law', in S Alam et al. (eds), *Routledge Handbook of International Environmental Law* (Routledge 2013) 43–60; M Fitzmaurice, *Contemporary Issues in International Environmental Law* (Edward Elgar 2009), discussing precaution, sustainable development, inter-generational equity and human rights; R Saunier and R Meganck, *Dictionary and Introduction to Global Environmental Governance* (Earthscan 2009), which does not have an entry on prevention.

30 ILC, 'Fragmentation of International Law: Difficulties Arising from the Diversification and Expansion of International Law. Report of the Study Group of the International Law Commission Finalized by Martti Koskenniemi' (2006) UN Doc. A/CN.4/L.682, para 129.

31 O Schachter, *International Law in Theory and Practice* (Martinus Nijhoff 1991) 50–55.

32 See e.g. B Cheng, *General Principles of Law as Applied by International Courts and Tribunals* (Stevens and Sons 1953) 25; ChT Kotuby Jr and LA Sobota, *General Principles of Law and International Due Process: Principles and Norms Applicable in Transnational Disputes* (Oxford University Press 2017) 9.

in private law[33]: this perspective does little more than highlight the origins of prevention and in particular the core classical norms on the basis of which it emerged. The second view considers that general principles reflect norms of natural law,[34] such as justice and fairness. This approach is, in sum, in line with Dworkin's well-known thesis that the law not only consists in rules but also in principles deriving their legal validity from a process of moral reasoning.[35] Applied in an international context, it highlights the moral aspirations underpinning prevention and explains that its widespread acceptance might not derive from a strict understanding of custom but rather from the recognition that environmental protection represents a common value shared by the international community as a whole. Finally, prevention enters the Article 38 principle category most easily when general principles are understood to be norms that are 'derived from the specific nature of the international community', such as the principle of territorial sovereignty.[36] This category remains limited to a small number of principles related to the cohabitation role of international law, such as the principle of territorial sovereignty or the obligation of a State 'not to allow knowingly its territory to be used for acts contrary to the rights of other States'.[37] Under each meaning, however, the principle of prevention is only partially taken into account as an Article 38 principle, which is unable to fully characterize prevention in its comprehensive form.

GENERAL PRINCIPLES OF INTERNATIONAL LAW The category of 'general principle of international law' gives a more complete perspective on the role that prevention plays in the international legal order. Some authors do not accept that there is a distinction between general principles of international law and Article 38 principles.[38] However, 'general principles of international law' tend to refer to a separate category of norms: they are generally considered to derive from custom and multilateral treaty law[39] and have become independent of their original sources.[40]

33 Kotuby and Sobota, *General Principles of Law and International Due Process* 13.
34 Cheng, *General Principles of Law* 3.
35 R Dworkin, *Taking Rights Seriously* (Duckworth 1977).
36 Schachter, *International Law in Theory and Practice* 55.
37 *Corfu Channel (United Kingdom/Albania)* (1949) ICJ Rep 4, at 22.
38 E.g. M Biddulph and D Newman, 'A Contextualized Account of General Principles of International Law' (2014) 26 *Pace International Law Review* 286, looking indistinctively at the two categories.
39 P Weil, 'Le droit international en quête de son identité: cours général de droit international public' (1992) 237 *Collected Courses of the Hague Academy of International Law* 9–370, 149; A Cassese, *International Law* (2nd edn, Oxford University Press 2004) 188.
40 Wolfrum, 'General International Law', using the principle of prevention as an example.

A core question relates to whether the uncontested qualification of prevention as a principle of international environmental law makes it a principle of general international law. As discussed previously, the World Trade Organization (WTO) refused to see precaution as more than a principle of international environmental law.[41] However, the decision cannot be generalized to prevention because it pertained to a norm whose status is considerably more uncertain. A more definite answer can therefore be given regarding the extension of prevention as a general principle of international law because its normative (conventional and customary) impacts have permeated international law as a whole. Whether it means that prevention in its other dimensions (i.e. not only in its environmental focus) is a general principle of international law is another issue.[42]

Considering prevention as a general principle of international law is consequential because it guides interpretation and the filling of gaps in existing law.[43] It also contributes to extending the traditionally narrowly construed scope of custom by justifying the general application of a norm that might not fulfil the 'two-elements test' but that is generally recognized by the international community as a whole. It thus offers a complementary perspective on prevention by liberating it from the constraints of custom while recognizing its centrality in the international legal order.

10.1.2 *Prevention as a Policy*

Environmental norms often originate in statements of policy regarding how environmental protection ought to be pursued.[44] Such is the case for prevention, which is based on a rationale – prevention is better than cure – that is closer to a policy choice akin to a favoured option rather than a legal diktat. ILC Special Rapporteur Rao confirmed this in one of his reports by referring to the prevention of environmental harm as the

41 *European Communities – Measures concerning Meat and Meat Products (Hormones)*, Appellate Body Report, WT/DS26/AB/R, WT/DS48/AB/R, 13 February 1998, paras 123–25.

42 For a positive response, see ILC, 'Sixth Report of the Special Rapporteur, Mr Eduardo Valencia-Ospina, on the protection of persons in the event of disasters' (2013) UN Doc. A/CN.4/662, para 41, on prevention as a general principle of international law; Weil, 'Le droit international en quête de son identité', 150, considering the no-harm rule found in the *Corfu Channel* case as a 'general international law principle'.

43 Cassese, *International Law*, 188.

44 E Fisher, B Lange and E Scotford, *Environmental Law: Text, Cases, and Materials* (Oxford University Press 2013) 402, recognizing that 'environmental principles are an amorphous group of policy ideas concerning how environmental protection and sustainable development ought to be pursued'.

'preferred policy'.[45] Interestingly, he did not qualify prevention as a principle or an obligation but contrasted it with ex post approaches. The rapporteur was seemingly not interested in highlighting the role played by prevention in legal reasoning (which distinguishes principles from policies[46]). Rather, by referring to prevention as a policy, he insisted on the choice that prevention expresses regarding 'a goal to be reached'[47]: that is, environmental protection.

Overall, environmental norms navigate freely between the political and the legal. Environmental principles sometimes can have limited legal grounding and be closer to a policy, whereas in other cases environmental policies are directed by principles of a legal nature. The tenuous distinction between policies and principles is reflected in the often-used term 'environmental law and policy', which avoids normative distinctions. Clearly, environmental principles do not have 'pre-programmed legal identities'[48] because, on the contrary, their value lies in their flexibility. This does not mean, however, that they cannot then consolidate into legal norms, as exemplified by the subsequent consolidation of the programmatic statements of the Stockholm Declaration, including Principle 21, in conventional and customary law.

10.1.3 *Prevention as a Rule*

To complicate the matter further, prevention is more than a principle and a policy: it also qualifies as a rule. The challenge that environmental norms pose to the traditional Dworkinian dichotomy between a legal principle and a rule is widely acknowledged.[49] This reality was recognized in the jurisprudence when the *Iron Rhine Railway* arbitral tribunal noted that there is

45 ILC, 'First Report of the Special Rapporteur, Mr Pemmaraju Sreenivasa Rao, on the Prevention of Transboundary Harm from Hazardous Activities' (1998) UN Doc. A/CN.4/487, paras 32–34.

46 On the distinction between principles (legal norms) and policy (non-legal norms), see N MacCormick, *Rhetoric and the Rule of Law: A Theory of Legal Reasoning* (Oxford University Press 2005).

47 Dworkin, *Taking Rights Seriously* 22, defining policies as 'that kind of standard that sets out a goal to be reached, generally an improvement in some economic, political, or social feature of the community'.

48 Scotford, *Environmental Principles* 48.

49 Sands and Peel, *Principles of International Environmental Law* 187, recognizing that 'it is frequently difficult to establish the parameters or the precise international legal status of each general principle or rule'. As a result, the textbook refers to 'general principles and rules' without attempting to establish a distinction.

'considerable debate as to what, within the field of environmental law, constitutes "rules" or "principles"'.[50]

The core theoretical distinction between a rule and a principle relates to their normative precision: a rule is specific enough to trigger concrete behaviour and thus can be violated, whereas a principle plays a guiding role but cannot be breached.[51] While a rule answers the question 'what', a principle concentrates on 'why'.[52] A distinction ought to be made here between no-harm and prevention. There is little doubt that the no-harm rule is itself a rule not only because its name says so but also because the prohibition to cause transboundary harm has been conceived of as a primary rule of obligation that gives the affected State a right to be compensated in the case of harm. Conversely, it could be said that prevention remains a principle because it expresses a policy rationale that only guides the actions of States without necessarily constraining them. However, in practice, prevention falls under the two categories. International courts and tribunals have indeed used prevention for its functions as a guiding principle[53] and also as a primary rule of obligation falling directly under the scope of the law of State responsibility.[54]

10.1.4 *Prevention as a Right*

As a corollary to being an obligation, prevention is also to be understood as a right. This statement can be considered to derive from an apparently simple obligation/right logic. In reality, it is, however, revealing of some of the complexities at play within the principle of prevention. These complexities were discussed in earlier chapters but are briefly recapitulated here for the purpose of our analysis on a rights approach to prevention. To start with, it must be remembered that the origin of prevention in the no-harm rule means

50 *Iron Rhine Railway*, para 58.

51 Dworkin, *Taking Rights Seriously* 24: 'The difference between legal principles and legal rules is a logical distinction. Both sets of norms point to particular decisions about legal obligations in particular circumstances, but they differ in the character of the direction they give. Rules are applicable in an all-or-nothing fashion.'

52 G Fitzmaurice, 'The General Principles of International Law Considered from the Standpoint of the Rule of Law' (1957) 92 *Collected Courses of the Hague Academy of International Law* 1–228, at 7.

53 See e.g. *Gabčíkovo-Nagymaros Project (Hungary/Slovakia)* (Judgment) (1997) ICJ Rep 7, para 140; *Iron Rhine Railway*, para 59; *Indus Waters Kishenganga Arbitration (Pakistan v. India)*, Permanent Court of Arbitration, Partial Award, 18 February 2013, para 452, and Final Award, 20 December 2013, para 111.

54 See e.g. *Pulp Mills*, para 204; *Certain Activities Carried out by Nicaragua in the Border Area (Costa Rica v. Nicaragua)* and *Construction of a Road in Costa Rica Along the San Juan River (Nicaragua v. Costa Rica)* (Judgment) (2015) ICJ Rep 665, paras 113 and 174.

that it initially emerged to protect a right: the right of States to be free from outside interferences. This initial right certainly remains relevant but extends to other contexts and beneficiaries.

Prevention did not extend to a *jus ad bellum* right to self-defence in case of imminent transboundary harm[55] but potentially grants rights to take unilateral preventive measures that might affect third-party States for environmental protection objectives (see Section 8.4.2). From this perspective, prevention is not a duty imposed on States but rather a right that allows States to infringe on the sovereign prerogatives of other States, hence revealing the priority given to environmental protection over sovereign rights.

The extension of the preventive right to other beneficiaries is found under human rights law. As noted earlier, it is widely acknowledged that certain human rights will only be fulfilled if States take measures to prevent environmental harm (see Section 8.3.2), hence granting individuals with an indirect human right to the environment. The full crystallization of a human right to an environment of a certain quality will further the evolution of prevention in this direction, allowing prevention to become an independent right that relies on the existence of another right to gain that status.[56] Additionally, the most advanced scenario under which prevention is recognized as a right relates to the duty of the State to prevent transboundary harm that might affect not only another State but also its population (see Section 8.1.2). From this perspective, the State obligation of prevention is perfectly mirrored in the population's right to be free from environmental harm.

As the obligation of prevention has grown more complex, so has its status as a right. The qualification of prevention as a right (and not only as an obligation) fundamentally reverses the perspective that is traditionally held on prevention. By depicting prevention as the right of a State or an individual to be free from environmental harm, it reminds the bearer of the obligation of the reasons why restrictions are being imposed on it (i.e. to avoid having negative effects on States and human beings). The perspective is particularly

55 Environmental harm, or risk thereof, would not justify the use of self-defence; it would certainly be an aggravating factor if environmental harm is used within a context of an armed attack. In this respect, it is interesting to note the work of the Commission on Sustainable Development, which opens up the possibility of some form of defensive action against 'imminent and significant threats to the environment' but seems to favour trade bans to use of force. 'Report of the Expert Group Meeting on Identification of Principles of International Law for Sustainable Development', Geneva, Switzerland, 26–28 September 1995, para 68.

56 This duality was recognized in relation to self-determination in the *East Timor* case that acknowledged self-determination as a right *erga omnes*: *East Timor (Portugal v. Australia)*, (Judgment) (1995) ICJ Rep 90, para 29.

influential in the current context of increasing environmental degradation: the failure of States to completely fulfil their preventive obligations empowers the victims (be they States or individuals) to claim their rights to be free from environmental harm.

10.1.5 *Prevention as a Multifaceted Norm*

The preceding analysis has shown that prevention plays multiple roles in the international legal order, displaying different degrees of normativity. Prevention is the combination of different functions that it has fulfilled over time, without necessarily negating its previous manifestations. In its most restricted form, prevention is a policy of harm anticipation and a principle that, based on moral aspirations, guides the actions of decision-makers and judges. But prevention has grown into a more complex norm, including an obligation, which, despite sometimes lacking precision, falls under the scope of the law of State responsibility, and a right empowering States and individuals to pursue claims of environmental interference.

In its present form, prevention will perform different functions depending on, *inter alia*, the instrument in which it is inscribed (a policy document or a treaty), on its place in that said document (as an aspirational objective in a preamble or as an obligation in an operative part) and on how the prevention rationale is expressed (either as Principle 21 or as prevention per se). The multifaceted role of prevention in the international legal order is facilitated by the flexibility of the norm itself. In particular, the relationship between the three clauses of Stockholm Principle 21 lends itself to different interpretations depending on the context within which it operates. In addition, prevention is able to manifest differently on the role that it seeks to play in the legal order. For instance, prevention in its Stockholm Principle 21 form is often used as a guiding principle driving the content of an international treaty because it is acknowledged to recognize the rights of States to exercise their sovereign prerogatives while at the same time facilitating the implementation of environmental objectives. Conversely, if the objective is to impose a specific obligation, then preventive norms with more normative precisions, such as 'conservation', will be preferred. Under these circumstances, the term 'principle' is usually used to reflect the wide range of roles played by prevention and to represent its flexible nature. However, if the term is widespread, it should not be understood to negate or detract from the other roles that prevention plays aside from being a fundamental principle of international environmental law.

10.2 PREVENTION AND THE PROACTIVITY OF MULTIPLE SUBJECTS OF INTERNATIONAL LAW

The second characteristic of prevention lies in its insistence on proactivity. The bearer of such duty is most evidently the State. However, given the role that non-State actors play in the degradation, as well as protection, of the environment, the question arises as to whether international law expects other, non-State actors to act in anticipation of harm. This is not a purely academic question: the extension of the principle of prevention to other subjects of international law is acknowledged in the World Charter for Nature, whose Principle 21 (reproducing Stockholm Principle 21) applies to 'States and, to the extent they are able, [to] other public authorities, international organizations, individuals, groups and corporations'.[57] In addition, proposals to extend Stockholm Principle 21 to other entities also were made in the context of the drafting work on the Rio Declaration.[58] Although such proposals were rejected, the question of whether the principle of prevention extends to other subjects of international law remains relevant. A simple answer would be to oppose that there are no subjects of international law other than the State and that, as a result, the obligation of prevention can only be applicable to States.[59] However, such a conservative approach cannot hold in light of the increasing role of non-State actors in today's international legal order. The discussion that follows envisages the influence, when not the legal authority, of the principle of prevention over two categories of, to use Higgins' term, 'participants' that are playing an increasing role in the international legal order[60]: international organizations (10.2.1) and corporations (10.2.2).

10.2.1 *International Organizations*

The legal personality of international organizations provides them with duties and rights.[61] The relevant question in the context of this study is whether this

57 'World Charter for Nature', UNGA Res. 37/7 (XXXVII) (28 October 1982).

58 See e.g. Chile's proposal to reword Stockholm Principle 21 as follows: 'States, international organizations and transnational corporations shall prevent transfrontier damage and shall protect the global commons.' 'Preparatory Committee for the United Nations Conference on Environment and Development, Fourth Session, New York, 2 March–3 April 1992, Working Group III', UN Doc. A/CONF.151/PC/WG.III/L.8/Rev.1, para 40.

59 *Mines de Potasse d'Alsace SA v. Onroad Goed Maatschappij Bier BV and Others*, Court of Appeal of the Hague, the Netherlands, 10 September 1986, IELR 343, recognizing that the no-harm rule cannot be applied in a dispute between private persons.

60 R Higgins, *Problems and Process: International Law and How We Use It* (Oxford University Press 1994) 49–50.

61 *Reparation for Injuries Suffered in the Service of the United Nations* (Advisory Opinion) (1949) ICJ Rep 174, 185.

extends to the duty to prevent environmental harm. Two scenarios should be distinguished here. The first case relates to international organizations that have the capacity to influence the actions of their member States and thus could be under a duty to ensure that member States do not create environmental harm. The second case pertains to whether international organizations themselves have a direct obligation to prevent environmental harm in the context of their operational activities.

The first scenario in which prevention extends to international organizations relates to situations in which they have the capacity to influence the actions of their member States. A typical example is the European Union, which can be held responsible for the actions of its member States when the competencies of the member States have been transferred to it. This very situation was at the heart of one of the questions put to the International Tribunal for the Law of the Sea (ITLOS) in the context of the *Advisory Opinion on the Sub-Regional Fisheries Commission*. The tribunal ruled that the European Union, as a party to United Nations Convention on the Law of the Sea (UNCLOS) and holding exclusive competence on fisheries matters, would be held liable for a breach of its due-diligence obligation if its member States do not respect their obligation in relation to fisheries access agreements to which the European Union is the sole signatory. It clearly stated that

> the liability of an international organization for an internationally wrongful act is linked to its competence . . . it follows that an international organization which in a matter of its competence undertakes an obligation, in respect of which compliance depends on the conduct of its member States, may be held liable if a member State fails to comply with such obligation and the organization did not meet its obligation of 'due diligence'.[62]

The legal relationship created between the international organization and its member States is comparable to the obligation of due diligence that a State has in regulating the activities of private actors; the international organization (acting like a State) has an obligation to ensure that its member States (assimilated to private actors) respect the provisions of the fisheries access agreement in order to prevent harm.

The logic is applicable not only to the specific case of the European Union but also can be extended to international organizations that have an influence on the actions of their member States relative to environmental protection. Former ILC Rapporteur Gaja acknowledged that international organizations have an 'ancillary obligation to prevent the relevant wrongful act of member

62 *Sub-Regional Fisheries Commission*, ITLOS No. 21, Advisory Opinion (2 April 2015), para 168.

States or at least not to contribute to it'[63] and included environmental protection as one such obligation.[64] The obligation will only be triggered if the international organization has the capacity to influence the actions of its member States.[65] An example of an institution that would have such influence is the International Seabed Authority (ISBA). A convincing argument could be made that the ISBA would be in breach of its obligation to ensure that its member States do not harm the marine environment when exploring or exploiting resources in the Area if it were not adopting rules to protect the environment in the Area pursuant to UNCLOS Article 145.[66]

A second, more complex scenario relates to situations in which international organizations are themselves carrying out operational activities that might have environmental impacts. The extent to which an international organization will fall under an obligation of prevention depends on a number of factors, including the type of activity undertaken and the source of its mandate.

The most evident application of prevention relates to situations in which international organizations act as a de facto State (in the case of territorial administration, for instance); they would then be expected to respect and, as far as possible, abide by the international obligations that would be applicable to a State, both under customary and conventional law – even if the international organization is not itself a party to relevant multilateral environmental agreements.[67] Similarly, international organizations engaged in peacekeeping

63 G Gaja, 'The Relations between the European Union and Its Member States from the Perspective of the ILC Articles on Responsibility of International Organizations', *SHARES Research Paper* 25 (2013) 4, available at www.sharesproject.nl/publication/the-relations-between-the-european-union-and-its-member-states-from-the-perspective-of-the-ilc-articles-on-responsibility-of-international-organizations/ (last accessed 13 September 2017).

64 See also K Boon 'International Organizations and the Duty to Prevent', *Opinio Juris* post, 18 June 2013, available at http://opiniojuris.org/2013/06/18/international-organizations-and-the-duty-to-prevent/ (last accessed 12 August 2017): 'I would wager to guess that we can expect to see this duty argued in three cases: the use of force, *conservation of scarce resources*, and situations involving massive human tragedies that trigger the Genocide Convention or other human rights treaties' (emphasis added).

65 The link between the obligation to prevent and the capacity to influence was recognized, in the context of the obligation of a State to prevent genocide, in the *Bosnia v. Serbia* case, where the Court provided that the obligation to prevent depended on the State's 'capacity to influence effectively the action of persons likely to commit, or already committing, genocide'. The same logic is arguably transposable to international organizations. *Application of the Convention on the Prevention and Punishment of the Crime of Genocide (Bosnia and Herzegovina v. Serbia and Montenegro)* (2007) ICJ Rep 43, para 430.

66 United Nations Convention on the Law of the Sea, Montego Bay, 10 December 1982, in force 16 November 1994, 1833 UNTS 3, Article 145.

67 ILA, Study Group on Due Diligence in International Law, 'Second Report', Johannesburg, 77th Session, 2016, at 41–43.

operations are increasingly expected to hold the same due-diligence obligations[68] as the ones carried out by States in similar circumstances.[69]

With regards to activities that are more specific to international organizations, it is also possible that these could cause significant harm to third parties. For instance, a technical assistance project of the Food and Agriculture Organization might use dangerous substances carrying risks of environmental damage,[70] or a financial assistance project of the International Finance Corporation could lead to significant social and environmental damage.[71] In this context, a strong argument can be made that international organizations are bound by the international customary rules applicable to States that are relevant 'to their conduct and functions'.[72] While the scholarship has mainly focused on how human rights obligations apply,[73] the argument is easily extended to environmental obligations. Such was the position taken by the International Law Association (ILA) in the course of its work on the accountability of international organizations that transposed the obligations of the ILC Prevention Articles to international organizations.[74]

Finally, a word should be said about the increasingly common practice among international organizations to adopt environmental policies. This is significant because it does not merely extend existing State obligations to international organizations but rather relies on their own proactivity in devising internal rules and policy standards to limit their environmental impacts. It can be said to develop an 'institutional sense' of commitment to obligations

68 ILA, Study Group on Due Diligence in International Law, 'Second Report', at 18.

69 The ILC Draft Principles, as provisionally adopted in 2016, on the protection of the environment in the context of armed conflicts applied some provisions indiscriminately to States and international organizations, including an obligation to consider the impact of peace operations on the environment; see ILC, 'Protection of the Environment in Relation to Armed Conflicts: Text of the draft principles provisionally adopted during the present session by the Drafting Committee' (2016) UN Doc. A/CN.4/L.876, Draft Principle 8.

70 ILA, Committee of International Organizations, 'Third Report Consolidated, Revised and Enlarged Version of Recommended Rules and Practices', New Delhi Session, 70th Session, 2002, at 11.

71 See e.g. *Jam v. IFC*, US Court of Appeals for the District of Columbia, No. 16–7051, 23 June 2017, in which Indian farmers and fisherman sued the International Finance Corporation for having allowed, and financed, a project of power plant construction even though the plant did not do everything required to limit social and environmental damage.

72 ILA, Study Group on Due Diligence in International Law, 'Second Report', at 41–43.

73 See e.g. the approach taken in ILA, Study Group on Due Diligence in International Law, 'Second Report', that concentrates mainly on human rights obligations.

74 While it transposed the ILC Prevention Articles, it also added an obligation not originally found in the articles: a duty to carry out preventive activities 'in accordance with the precautionary principle': ILA, Committee on Accountability of International Organizations, 'Final Report', Berlin Session, 71st Session, 2004, at 21.

to prevent environmental damage. UN peacekeeping operations are increasingly showing such sense of accountability; it is evidenced by the adoption of environmental policies in the context of peacekeeping operations[75] and reinforced by the UN Security Council first-ever resolution that called on a peacekeeping mission to 'manage' environmental impacts when fulfilling its tasks.[76] Actual practice, as the second element of custom, will need to follow (if one adheres to traditional theories) to consecrate prevention as a rule of 'customary institutional law'.

10.2.2 *Corporations*

The question of how the principle of prevention extends to corporations operates at a different level than the preceding case. Indeed, in this context, the main question is whether corporations qualify as duty holders under international law and less whether prevention would be an applicable duty. A detailed analysis of the subjectivity of corporations under international law is beyond the scope of this study.[77] Suffice it to say here that although corporations, and in particular transnational corporations, are becoming increasingly important participants in the international legal order, the prevailing view is that they do not hold direct obligations under international law (despite being granted rights).[78] Nevertheless, if the principle of international corporate responsibility were to be accepted (either as existing or emerging), it then leaves little doubt that prevention would be part of the normative package applicable to corporations.[79]

75 UNEP, *Greening the Blue Helmets: Environment, Natural Resources and UN Peacekeeping Operations* (UNEP, 2012); UN Department of Field Support, *Environment Strategy: Executive Summary* (UNDFS, April 2017). See also ILC, 'Third Report of the Special Rapporteur, Ms Jacobsson, on the protection of the environment in relation to armed conflicts' (2016) UN Doc. A/CN.4/700, para 169, recognizing that peacekeeping operations have the 'obligation to develop environmental baseline studies and adhere to a number of multilateral environmental agreements'.

76 UN Security Council Resolution 2100 (2013), establishing the UN Multidimensional Integrated Stabilization Mission in Mali, para 32. This is in line with the Rio + 20 outcome document that called on the 'United Nations system to improve the management of facilities and operations, by taking into account sustainable development practices': 'Report of the United Nations Conference on Sustainable Development' (20–22 June 2012) UN Doc. A/CONF.216/16, para 96.

77 See M Karavias, *Corporate Obligations under International Law* (Oxford University Press 2013) 7–16, on corporations as bearers of obligations under international law.

78 E de Brabandere, 'Human Rights and Transnational Corporations: The Limits of Direct Corporate Responsibility' (2010) 4 *Human Rights and International Legal Discourse* 66, at 80; J Crawford, *Brownlie's Principles of Public International Law* (8th edn, Oxford University Press 2012) 122.

79 E Morgera, *Corporate Accountability in International Environmental Law* (Oxford University Press 2009) 185, describing prevention as a 'fundamental component of the emerging concept

Corporate activities that might have negative impacts on the environment fall under the obligation of the State to take due-diligence measures to ensure that the activities conducted under its jurisdiction or control do not cause external environmental harm. However, it remains to be established whether corporations have a direct obligation to prevent environmental harm under international law. Imposing direct preventive obligations on corporations would be, at least theoretically, justified on the basis that they are the 'principal polluters and remediators', not States.[80] In addition, the ineffectiveness of domestic law, related in particular to the multiple ways in which transnational corporations can circumvent State control, calls for a direct international response.[81] This reality applied to climate change (mostly caused by the greenhouse gases produced by a few major transnational corporations[82]) led a group of academics and judges to draft a guiding document entitled, 'Oslo Principles on Global Climate Change Obligations', that made preventive duties applicable to both States and enterprises.[83] But to what extent is a seemingly progressive approach that challenges State-centric conceptions of the international system representative of the law?

At present, a growing body of 'soft law' standards regulates the conduct of corporations in the field of sustainability, both socially[84] and environmentally.[85] However, practice supporting corporate liability for

of corporate environmental accountability' and arguing that 'the emerging international standard on prevention specifically requires private enterprises to avoid damaging the environment outside the borders of the country in which they operate. This would be in addition to the responsibility of the host State to properly monitor and control the activities of the private operators in its territory and would constitute a more specific and result-oriented implication of the prevention standard.'

80 S Ratner, 'Business', in D Bodansky, J Brunnée and E Hey (eds), *The Oxford Handbook of International Environmental Law* (Oxford University Press 2007) 807–26.

81 See SE Pantazopoulos, 'Towards a Coherent Framework of Transnational Corporations' Responsibility in International Environmental Law' (2014) 24(1) *Yearbook of International Environmental Law* 131, at 136–37.

82 R Heede, 'Tracing Anthropogenic Carbon Dioxide and Methane Emissions to Fossil Fuel and Cement Producers, 1854–2010' (2014) 122 *Climatic Change* 229.

83 'Oslo Principles on Global Climate Change Obligations', Expert Group, 1 March 2015, available at http://globaljustice.macmillan.yale.edu/sites/default/files/files/OsloPrinciples.pdf (last accessed 8 August 2017), Principles 6–12.

84 See, in particular, the Ruggie Principles: 'Guiding Principles on Business and Human Rights' (2011) UN Doc. HR/PUB/11/04. For a doctrinal example, see Karavias, *Corporate Obligations*, not referring to environmental duties.

85 For an analysis of soft law environmental standards applicable to transnational corporations, see Pantazopoulos, 'Towards a Coherent Framework', at 154–63. Such standards include the following instruments: UN Global Compact, *Ten Principles* (2000), available at www.unglobalcompact.org/what-is-gc/mission/principles, Principle 7; UN Sub-Commission on

violations of international environmental law is limited,[86] and it is thus difficult to uphold that corporations are under a direct obligation of prevention. Prevention is currently seen as a standard, albeit not a legal rule, that ought to be followed by corporations. Independent Expert Knox on the right to an environment of a certain quality took this position by considering corporate environmental responsibility as 'good practice', requiring that companies take 'due account' of the obligation to avoid environmental harm.[87] In the future, as international law recognises the principle of corporate accountability,[88] the obligation of prevention could have a stronger normative impact on the conduct of corporations.

In conclusion, at this stage, prevention is first and foremost concerned with the proactivity displayed by States in their actions to avoid environmental harm. However, it is becoming increasingly apparent that a multiplicity of entities ought to be involved in the prevention of environmental harm. Although this is challenging traditional conceptions of international law, and in particular its theory of subjects, the international legal regime does not impose full responsibility on these participants. However, 'accountability' is becoming an increasingly popular term[89] to depict the growing expectations that some participants in the international legal system will take on preventive duties and the (incomplete) evolution of international law in this regard.

the Promotion and Protection of Human Rights, 'UN Norms on the Responsibilities of Transnational Corporations and Other Business Enterprises with Regard to Human Rights', UN Doc. E/CN.4/Sub.2/2003/L.11 (2003), para 14; OECD, *Guidelines for Multinational Enterprises* (OECD Publishing, 2011), available at http://mneguidelines.oecd.org/text/ (last accessed 15 June 2015), Part VI; CERES, *21st Century Corporation: The CERES Roadmap to Sustainability* (2010), available at www.ceres.org/ceres-roadmap; ICC, *Business Charter for Sustainable Development* (2015), available at https://iccwbo.org/publication/icc-business-charter-for-sustainable-development-2015/ (all links last accessed 1 September 2017).

86 See the refusal of US courts to hold corporations liable for violating international environmental law under the Alien Tort Statute: *Beanal v. Freeport-McMoran*, US Court of Appeals, 5th Circuit, 29 November 1999, 30 ELR 20231; *Elias Soares Viera et al. v. Eli Lilly and Company et al.*, US District Court for the Southern District of Indiana, 30 September 2010, ILDC 1561 (US 2010).

87 'Report of the Independent Expert on the issue of human rights obligations relating to the enjoyment of a safe, clean, healthy and sustainable environment, Compilation of Good Practices by John H. Knox' (2015) UN Doc. A/HRC/28/61, paras 79 and 80.

88 Human Rights Council Resolution, 'Elaboration of an international legally binding instrument on transnational corporations and other business enterprises with respect to human rights' (14 July 2014) UN Doc. A/HRC/RES/26/9.

89 'Report of the World Summit on Sustainable Development (Johannesburg, 26 August–4 September 2002)', chap II, UN Doc. A/CONF.199/20, para 49.

10.3 PREVENTION AS AN OBLIGATION TO PROTECT THE ENVIRONMENT OWED TO THE INTERNATIONAL COMMUNITY

The third definitional element of prevention lies in its concern for the protection of the environment. This characteristic is consequential in terms of the nature of the obligation. Needless to say, the obligation to protect the environment operates outside the traditional Westphalian structure based on reciprocity. This section shows that as a norm that seeks to protect a common good shared by all, prevention qualifies as an obligation *erga omnes*.

While the term *erga omnes* can be understood in different ways,[90] the discussion here restricts itself to its most common meaning: *erga omnes* will refer to customary obligations owed to the international community as a whole,[91] where 'all States can be held to have a legal interest in their protection'[92] and have legal standing to denounce a violation of the obligation.[93] The rationale of prevention, in its willingness to protect a global good, leaves little doubt about its *erga omnes* character; however, the norm is faced with the common challenges that generally apply in the context of identifying *erga omnes* obligations. International law gives little guidance on how to identify *erga omnes* obligations beyond those which have been explicitly recognized by the International Court of Justice (ICJ). As a result, the scholarship either refuses to identify other obligations than the ones recognized by the ICJ[94] or, if not, is divided on which obligations fall into the *erga omnes* category. Different perspectives on the identification of *erga omnes* obligations exist. Tams' seminal study on the topic distinguished two approaches: either structural, relying on the specific structure of the obligation, or material, based on the central role played by the norm in the international legal system.[95] The two approaches can be identified in the literature pertaining to *erga omnes* obligations in international environmental

90 CJ Tams, *Enforcing Obligations Erga Omnes in International Law* (Cambridge University Press 2010) 99–116, highlighting three different usages made of the term *erga omnes*, including '(i) to justify third party effects of treaties or UN resolutions, (ii) to preclude the territorial restriction of obligations, and (iii) in a descriptive way, as a substitute for "all States"'.

91 *Barcelona Traction, Light and Power Company Ltd.* (Second Application) *(Belgium v. Spain)* (1970) ICJ Rep 3, para 33.

92 *Barcelona Traction*, para 33.

93 ILC, 'Fragmentation of International Law: Difficulties Arising from the Diversification and Expansion of International Law. Report of the Study Group of the International Law Commission Finalized by Martti Koskenniemi' (2006) UN Doc. A/CN.4/L.682, para 380.

94 See e.g. ILC Member Nolte, refusing to extend the *erga omnes* qualification to environmental norms, in ILC, 'Summary Record of the 3246th Meeting' (2016) UN Doc. A/CN.4/SR.3246, at 6.

95 Tams, *Enforcing Obligations Erga Omnes* 128–56.

law. On the one hand, one strand of the literature argues that specific (generally treaty-based) environmental obligations such as prevention of pollution in the high seas are *erga omnes* because they cannot function on the basis of reciprocity.[96] On the other hand, another strand of the literature takes a wider approach by referring to 'environmental protection' *erga omnes* duties, revealing a diffuse sense that all environmental norms would qualify, possibly in light of the fundamental importance of their objective.[97] Both approaches have inherent limitations, the first one being too restrictive given its heavy reliance on treaty provisions without necessarily explaining how they relate to custom[98] and the second one being, on the contrary, overly inclusive, given that not all environmental norm (e.g. sustainable development) would qualify. It is most likely that authors are implicitly thinking about the prevention principle but without naming it. Is prevention the obligation that could provide a middle ground between these two approaches? Admittedly, a major difficulty lies in the multifaceted nature of prevention: considering prevention as *erga omnes* does not tell us which specific form, or forms, of prevention would actually qualify. For the sake of clarity, the discussion here relies on the general obligation to prevent environmental damage as conceptualized in Part III. However, it should not be understood as meaning that sub-obligations, more specific to certain risks, would not qualify as well – a case-by-case study is encouraged but leaves open the question of whether, if a general obligation to prevent has been recognized as *erga omnes*, all its manifestations would necessarily qualify.[99]

A brief analysis of the ways in which prevention fits the criteria of the two approaches put forward by Tams corroborates its *erga omnes* character. Obligations *erga omnes* are non-reciprocal and non-bilateralizable: they are not owed to another State but are performed for the benefit of the international community as a whole. Contrary to no-harm, the obligation of prevention applies irrespective of the actions of other States, the objective

96 I Brownlie, 'A Survey of International Customary Rules of Environmental Protection' (1973) 13(2) *Natural Resources Journal* 179–89, at 183–84, on pollution to atmosphere and high seas, with a broader *locus standi*; P Picone, 'Obblighi reciproci ed obblighi erga omnes' degli Stati nel campo della protezione internazionale dell'ambiente marino dall'inquinamento', in V Starace (ed), *Diritto internazionale e protezione dell'ambiente marino* (Giuff ré 1983) 15, reproduced in P Picone, *Comunità internazionale e obblighi 'erga omnes': Studi critici di diritto internazionale* (3rd edn, Jovene Editore 2013) 1–127.

97 See e.g. E Valencia-Ospina, 'The International Court of Justice and International Environmental Law' (1994) 2 *Asian Yearbook of International Law* 1 (current problems of international environmental law show the 'need for a departure from traditional rules of standing').

98 Tams, *Enforcing Obligations Erga Omnes* 123.

99 See Section 3.2.1.

of environmental protection dictating that a breach of prevention should not justify reciprocal non-performance. Prevention also qualifies as an *erga omnes* obligation with regards to its 'importance', a criterion put forward in the *Barcelona Traction* decision.[100] *Erga omnes* obligations are owed to the international community as a whole precisely because they protect important common values[101] and are deemed to represent a 'value-based international public order based on law'.[102] How to assess what an 'important' value is and which aspects of the obligation ought to be important remain largely undetermined.[103] However, it is undeniable that prevention emerged as a response to a fundamental change in societal values that came to include environmental protection as a core objective[104] and which then acted in the law.[105] At the same time, if *erga omnes* obligations are deemed to represent a 'moral absolute',[106] prevention cannot be considered to be of such a character. Put simply, prevention is no absolute norm. Indeed, environmental protection in and of itself is not always a priority but has to be balanced with socio-economic factors.[107] In this context, the complexity of, and underlying tensions within, prevention emerges in full: it represents a fundamental value (environmental protection) that the international community seeks to protect but remains enshrined in Westphalian considerations of sovereignty. It highlights the existence of conflicting values within the international community, but such complexity does not detract prevention from its *erga omnes* nature, its structure and socio-legal importance providing a strong basis to conclude that the prevention principle is an *erga omnes* obligation.

100 *Barcelona Traction*, para 33: 'In view of the *importance* of the rights involved, all States can be held to have a legal interest of obligation . . . erga omnes' (emphasis added).

101 IDI, 'Obligations and rights *erga omnes* in international law', Session of Krakow, 2005, Article 1.

102 Tams, *Enforcing Obligations Erga Omnes* 3.

103 Tams, *Enforcing Obligations Erga Omnes* 135.

104 As discussed in Part I.

105 Factors put forward in Tams, *Enforcing Obligations Erga Omnes* 136.

106 M Raggazzi, *The Concept of International Obligations Erga Omnes* (Oxford University Press 2000) 183: 'Each of the four obligations *erga omnes* listed by the International Court reflects an exceptionless moral norm (or moral absolute) prohibiting an act which, in moral terms, is intrinsically evil (*malum in se*).'

107 Raggazzi, *The Concept of International Obligations Erga Omnes* 185, noting that compared to genocide, which represented 'an intrinsic evil condemned by all States', the question of the *erga omnes* character of atmospheric testing in the *Nuclear Tests* case represented a 'clash of values and political priorities, namely respect for the environment on the one hand and respect for the sovereign right to national defence on the other, both abstractly worthy of protection'.

10.4 CONCLUSION

This chapter discussed the role and place of prevention in the international legal order from the perspective of three different angles, each linked to one definitional trait of prevention. The normative impacts of prevention are varied, giving it a multifaceted nature and ranging from a policy that guides decision-making to a rule that constrains States. The objective that prevention tries to further – protection of the environment – is a fundamental ethical norm, which explains why the obligation does not operate on the basis of reciprocity but is owed to the international community as a whole. This is followed by two consequences that have not yet fully expressed their legal effects. Firstly, prevention can, as a result, be characterized as an obligation *erga omnes*, although, as discussed in Chapter 11, this qualification is not without limitations. Secondly, international law partially recognizes that the international legal order is also made of other participants that play a role in the degradation and/or protection of the environment. It thus is in the process of extending preventive duties to other actors, including international organizations and transnational corporations, to make them accountable (if not internationally responsible) for the impacts of their actions, or inactions, on the state of the planet. The consolidation of these two processes is likely to significantly influence the future role of prevention in the international legal order.

11

The Frontiers of Prevention?

Reparation and Compliance Control

The crystallization of prevention in its advanced form changes its relationship to reparation, encouraging complementarity instead of opposition between the two rationales. This final chapter confronts prevention with the concept of reparation to understand how it relates to a reactive rationale and to identify where the frontiers of the norm lie, that is to say, the extent to which prevention spreads its rationale until it meets the opposing rationale of reparation.

Current trends reveal that the curative perspective, which had been partly put aside after the consecration of the prevention principle in the 1970s, is gaining pre-eminence in international environmental law. As such, a rapprochement between the preventive and curative approaches is apparent (11.1). If prevention as a 'principle' is interacting more closely with the curative approach, it remains, however, that as an 'obligation' in the context of the law of State responsibility its definitional traits still challenge the way international law, and reparation more specifically, was originally conceived (11.2). However, these limitations can be bypassed under certain circumstances; indeed, the curative approach, to some extent, has been absorbed by the preventive logic in the context of non-compliance procedures (11.3).

11.1 APPARENT RAPPROCHEMENT BETWEEN PREVENTION AND REPARATION

This section starts with a description of a rapprochement between prevention and reparation that started in the 1990s (11.1.1), which contributes to a better understanding of the dynamics currently driving prevention (11.1.2).

11.1.1 *Observable Complementarities*

The curative approach in international environmental law has become increasingly prominent since the 1990s, as illustrated by multiple attempts to consolidate and develop liability regimes for environmental harm and by the growth of international environmental adjudication. The call of the Rio Declaration to develop further international law in the field of environmental liability and compensation[1] (a reiteration from the Stockholm Declaration) translated into different initiatives that sought to consolidate and develop liability regimes from the 1990s onwards. The update of a number of pre-existing civil liability regimes, in the fields of nuclear energy[2] and oil pollution,[3] complemented by new liability conventions on transportation,[4] confirmed the supremacy of the curative approach in the field of ultra-hazardous activities. But the relationship between prevention and reparation was most fundamentally renewed by the adoption of several international documents treating prevention and reparation as complementary approaches. The inclusion of liability provisions in prevention-based treaties reveals this new outlook. While international treaties had tended to focus on either the preventive or the curative approach, the inclusion of delegation clauses in preventive multilateral environmental agreements

1 Rio de Janeiro Declaration on Environment and Development (Rio de Janeiro, 3 to 14 June 1992), (1992) 31 ILM 876, Principle 13.

2 Protocol to Amend the Vienna Convention on Civil Liability for Nuclear Damage, Vienna, 12 September 1997, in force 4 October 2003, (1997) 36 ILM 1454. It had also been modified by the Joint Protocol Relating to the Application of the Vienna Convention and the Paris Convention, Vienna, 21 September 1988, in force 27 April 1992, (1988) 42 *Nuclear Law Bulletin* 56; Convention on Supplementary Compensation for Nuclear Damage, Vienna, 12 September 1997, not in force, (1997) 36 ILM 1473.

3 International Convention on Civil Liability for Oil Pollution Damage, Brussels, 29 November 1969, in force 19 June 1975, 973 UNTS 3; International Convention on Civil Liability for Oil Pollution Damage, Brussels, 27 November 1992, in force 30 May 1996, IMO Doc. LEG/CONF.9.15; Protocol to Amend the 1971 Oil Pollution Fund Convention, London, 27 November 1992, in force 30 May 1996, 21 BNA 1751; Protocol to the International Convention on the Establishment of an International Fund for Compensation for Oil Pollution Damage, London, 16 May 2003, in force 3 May 2005, 92 FUND/A.8/4, Annex I; IMO Convention on Civil Liability for Bunker Oil Pollution Damage, London, 27 March 2001, in force 21 November 2008, (2001) 40 ILM 1493.

4 Convention on Civil Liability for Damage Caused During Carriage of Dangerous Goods by Road, Rail and Inland Navigation Vessels, Geneva, 10 October 1989, not in force, UN Doc. ECE.TRANS/79; International Convention on Liability and Compensation for Damage in Connection with the Carriage of Hazardous and Noxious Substances by Sea, London, 3 May 1996, not in force, (1996) 25 ILM 1406; Protocol of 2010 to the International Convention on Liability and Compensation for Damage in Connection with the Carriage of Hazardous and Noxious Substances by Sea, London, 30 April 2010, not in force, IMO Doc. LEG/CONF.17/10.

committing parties to develop liability protocols lessened the divide between the two rationales.[5] The re-balancing between the curative and preventive pillars is also visible in attempts to create general liability rules presented as a complementary approach to the preventive rationale. The Council of Europe's 1993 Convention on Civil Liability for Damage Resulting from Activities Dangerous to the Environment (Lugano Convention)[6] proposed a general regime of liability with the view to contribute to the prevention of harm and to ensure adequate compensation for damage.[7] Similarly, the International Law Commission (ILC) Principles on the Allocation of Loss in the Case of Transboundary Harm Arising Out of Hazardous Activities, adopted in 2006, complemented the ILC Prevention Articles by looking at the other side of the coin (reparation) and setting up a general liability regime.[8]

The adoption of a curative approach, which had been partly put aside in the 1970s, is indicative of a willingness to achieve a better balance between the preventive and curative rationales. The reluctance that States have historically demonstrated towards liability rules in the context of environmental harm might have lessened but cannot, however, be said to have completely disappeared. The denomination chosen for the norms codified by the ILC work on loss allocation is one illustration: the choice of the ILC to refer to 'principles' – in opposition to the more common reference to 'articles' – is indicative of a recognition that the adoption of strict compensation rules might not be welcomed by States. In practice, the apparent willingness to negotiate liability regimes complementing preventive treaties is limited by an absence of consensus on how these regimes should be designed.[9] Similarly, provisions encouraging the elaboration of a complementary liability regime in the context of a multilateral environmental agreement (MEA) have often remained empty promises[10] or have resulted in the elaboration of restricted liability

5 For a detailed analysis, see A Daniel, 'Civil Liability Regimes as a Complement to Multilateral Environmental Agreements: Sound International Policy or False Comfort?' (2003) 12 *Review of European Community & International Environmental Law* 225.

6 Convention on Civil Liability for Damage Resulting from Activities Dangerous to the Environment, Lugano, 21 June 1993, not in force, (1993) 32 ILM 1228.

7 Convention on Civil Liability for Damage Resulting from Activities Dangerous to the Environment, Article 1.

8 See also IDI, 'Responsibility and Liability under International Law for Environmental Damage', Session of Strasbourg, 1997, which links State responsibility and civil liability to establish a coherent system.

9 The failure of the Lugano Convention to gather the mere three ratifications it needed to enter into force is primarily explained by the fact that the text provides for unlimited liability.

10 See e.g. the work of the Convention on Persistent Organic Pollutants that never translated into a liability protocol: 'Liability and Redress concerning the Use and Intentional Introduction

regimes.[11] Protocols to MEAs on civil liability struggle to gather enough ratifications to enter into force,[12] with the exception of the Nagoya-Kuala Lumpur Supplementary Protocol on Liability and Redress to the Cartagena Protocol on Biosafety.[13] In short, the legislative attempts made to complement preventive treaties with a curative approach are not matched with a real commitment to follow up on their implementation. Despite a willingness to treat prevention and reparation as two equally necessary approaches, practice does not always follow. The comeback of the curative rationale cannot therefore be interpreted to indicate that the outlook of States on reparation in the context of environmental harm has completely changed.

A similar balanced assessment can be made in relation to the recent growth of international environmental adjudication, which represents the meeting point of the preventive rationale, in its form as a primary rule of obligation, and the curative rationale, expressed in dispute-settlement mechanisms. Given the historical reluctance towards adjudication in the context of environmental damage, the main jurisprudential sources of prevention were limited before 1996, mostly reliant on the *Trail Smelter* and *Corfu Channel* cases. However, since the 1990s, an unprecedented number of environmental cases has reached international bodies, a trend that some coined the 'spring' of international environmental adjudication.[14] Chapter 5 on international jurisprudence illustrated how cases pertaining to environmental protection have multiplied at the International Court of Justice (ICJ) and how forums called to take into consideration environmental objectives have multiplied.[15] Some international courts and tribunals, expecting this trend to become more pre-

into the Environment of Persistent Organic Pollutants: Final Report' (19–21 September 2002), no reference, available at http://enb.iisd.org/crs/scwlr/ (last accessed 15 August 2017).

11 Annex VI to the Protocol on Environmental Protection to the Antarctic Treaty: Liability Arising from Environmental Emergencies, Stockholm, adopted 17 June 2005, not in force, (2006) 45 ILM 5.

12 See e.g. Protocol on Liability and Compensation for Damage Resulting from Transboundary Movements of Hazardous Wastes and Their Disposal, ratified as of 12 August 2017 by eleven parties out of the twenty needed; UNECE Protocol on Civil Liability and Compensation for Damage Caused by Transboundary Effects of Industrial Accidents on Transboundary Waters that has until now (12 August 2017) acquired only one ratification out the sixteen necessary.

13 Nagoya-Kuala Lumpur Supplementary Protocol on Liability and Redress to the Cartagena Protocol on Biosafety, Nagoya, 15 October 2010, in force 5 March 2018, BS VI-11.

14 D French, 'Environmental Dispute Settlement: The First (Hesitant) Signs of Spring?' (2006) 19 *Hague Yearbook of International Law* 3; T Stephens, *International Courts and Environmental Protection* (Cambridge University Press 2009) 345, on 'the flourishing of international environmental litigation'.

15 See Section 5.1.

eminent, even tried (albeit with limited success[16]) to adapt to environmental cases that they saw as peculiar – such was the rationale that drove the creation of a Chamber for Environmental Matters at the ICJ in 1993[17] and the adoption of Optional Rules for Conciliation and Arbitration relating to natural resources and/or the environment by the Permanent Court of Arbitration.[18] While a number of attempts made at bringing environmental cases to courts that were eventually not followed through,[19] generally due to the limitations of the law of State responsibility, they nevertheless highlight the fact that international adjudication is increasingly seen as a viable solution to pursue violations of the obligation of prevention.

11.1.2 *Understanding the Rapprochement*

The rapprochement between the two concepts underpinned by different rationales can be explained by two seemingly contradictory realities that characterize prevention: its consolidation as a primary rule of international law, on the one hand, and its inability to provide a solution to large-scale environmental degradation, on the other. The rapprochement is illustrative of the maturation of prevention as a primary obligation of international law; in addition to being a 'principle', prevention has also become an 'obligation' whose breach is assimilated to an internationally wrongful act – hence explaining the growth of international environmental adjudication. The two

16 Not reconstituted since 2006. Mentioned on the ICJ website: www.icj-cij.org/en/chambers-and-committees (last accessed 12 August 2017).

17 Pursuant to Article 26(1) of its statute.

18 Optional Rules for the Arbitration of Disputes Relating to Natural Resources and/or the Environment (effective 2001), Permanent Court of Arbitration; Optional Rules for the Conciliation of Disputes Relating to Natural Resources and/or the Environment (effective 2002), Permanent Court of Arbitration.

19 See petitions filed to the Inter-American Commission of Human Rights over responsibility for climate change: Inuit Circumpolar Conference, *Petition to the Inter-American Commission on Human Rights Seeking Relief from Violations Resulting from Global Warming Caused by Acts and Omissions of the United States* (2005), available at www.ciel.org/Publications/ICC_Petition_7Dec05.pdf (last accessed 19 May 2017); 'Inter-American Commission on Human Rights hears testimony on freshwater loss due to climate change', 28 March 2011, available at http://earthjustice.org/news/press/2011/inter-american-commission-on-human-rights-hears-testimony-on-freshwater-loss-due-to-climate-change (last accessed 19 May 2017). See also discussions on putting a request to the ICJ for an advisory opinion on whether countries have a legal responsibility to ensure that activities in their territory that emit greenhouse gases do not harm other countries were eventually not followed through: Johnson Toribiong, President, Republic of Palau, 'Statement to the 66th Regular Session of the United Nations General Assembly' (22 September 2011), available at http://gadebate.un.org/sites/default/files/gastatements/66/PW_en.pdf (last accessed 2 September 2017).

rationales used to operate in an 'either/or' scenario – either a preventive treaty or a civil liability treaty. They are now understood as an ensemble, as exemplified by the willingness of States to combine the ILC Prevention Articles and the ILC Allocation of Loss Principles into one single treaty (if they were to be transformed into conventional law).[20] The rapprochement is, in effect, beneficial for prevention because a reparation regime not only sanctions harm, but its very existence also can have a deterrent effect that induces compliance.[21] Put simply, the renewed interest in applying a curative approach to environmental harm reinforces the preventive objective.

At the same time, the rapprochement is also symptomatic of the failure of prevention to fully achieve its goal of environmental protection. This coincided with the realization that despite the efforts undertaken since the Stockholm Summit, environmental degradation remains omnipresent: prevention, more often than not, merely seeks to avoid further harm. This reality brings the preventive and curative rationales closer but also blurs the distinction between them. A salient example is found in the fact that liability instruments also include preventive measures, such as the ILC Allocation of Loss Principles that define 'response measures'[22] as indiscriminately applying to cases in which there is a risk of harm or in which harm has already occurred,[23] or liability treaties that use the term 'preventive measures' to refer to mitigation measures taken after an incident has occurred to prevent or minimize further damage.[24]

The climate change regime is perhaps the most evident illustration of the failure of a preventive regime to avoid environmental damage. As discussed earlier, the UN Framework Convention on Climate Change (UNFCCC)

20 The possibility of an assemblage between the two ILC sets of articles is presented in Section 4.1.

21 IDI, 'Responsibility and Liability under International Law for Environmental Damage', Session of Strasbourg, 1997, Preamble, highlights the preventive nature of responsibility and liability: 'Both responsibility and liability have in addition to the traditional role of ensuring restoration and compensation that of enhancing prevention of environmental damage.' See also MG Faure and A Nollkaemper, 'International Liability as an Instrument to Prevent and Compensate for Climate Change' (2007) 26 *Stanford Environmental Law Journal* 123, at 139.

22 ILC, 'Allocation of Loss Principles', Principle 5(c).

23 ILC, 'Allocation of Loss Principles', Commentaries to Principle 5, paras 4 and 5.

24 Convention on Civil Liability for Damage Resulting from Activities Dangerous to the Environment, Articles 2(7)(d) and 2(9); International Convention on Civil Liability for Oil Pollution Damage, Brussels, 29 November 1969, in force 19 June 1975, 973 UNTS 3, Article 1(7); Convention on the Regulation of Antarctic Mineral Resource Activities, Wellington, 2 June 1988, not in force, (1988) 27 ILM 868, Article 8(2)(d); Protocol to Amend the Vienna Convention on Civil Liability for Nuclear Damage, Vienna, 12 September 1997, in force 4 October 2003, (1997) 36 ILM 1454, Article 10(1)(n).

regime, initially concerned with the mitigation of harm, was called to evolve as science brought to light the potential irreversibility of the changes in the Earth's systems occurring as a result of climate change.[25] The Paris Agreement therefore recognized the need to adapt to the impacts of climate change[26] and included a tailored form of reparation manifesting in the concept of 'loss and damage'.[27] The concept of 'loss and damage', which emerged in the 1990s, encourages industrialized nations that have contributed to the creation of the problem to bear the associated costs by providing financial and technological assistance to countries facing the adverse effects of climate change. Although it has been made clear that the concept is not a recognition of liability,[28] it can, however, be read as an indirect manifestation of the principle of State liability for climate harm – and, therefore, as a recognition of the curative rationale in a preventive treaty.

More broadly, the surge of international environmental adjudication reflects the consolidation of the obligation of prevention as a primary norm of international law that makes it easier to claim a violation, but it also finds its sources in the fact that as the preventive rationale shows its limits, States and individuals do not hesitate to resort to adjudication to avoid the continuance of harm and seek reparation for the harm suffered. In sum, the re-emergence of the curative approach in international environmental law leads to a balanced assessment. On the one hand, it has been driven by the failure of prevention to avoid large-scale environmental degradation; on the other hand, it shows that international law attempts to respond to this failure via an ex post framework.

11.2 REMAINING DIVERGENCES: THE RELATIVE MISFIT BETWEEN PREVENTION AND STATE RESPONSIBILITY

The consolidation of the curative approach to environmental harm is evident, and yet, as presented earlier, it is also met with practical difficulties, the reluctance of States to fully embrace the legal consequences of such approach remaining strong. After having analysed the intersections between the curative and preventive 'rationales', this section offers a more detailed look at

[25] Intergovernmental Panel on Climate Change, *Fifth Assessment Report: Summary for Policy-Makers* (2014), para 2.4.

[26] Paris Agreement to the United Nations Framework Convention on Climate Change, Paris, 12 December 2015, in force 4 November 2016, Doc. FCCC/CP/2015/10/Add.1, Article 7.

[27] Paris Agreement, Article 8.

[28] COP Decision 1/CP.21, 'Adoption of the Paris Agreement', 12 December 2015, FCCC/CP/2015/10/Add.1, para 51, stating that Article 8 does not 'involve or provide a basis for any liability or compensation'.

prevention in its manifestation as an 'obligation' to assess its operation in the context of the curative regime par excellence, the law of State responsibility for internationally wrongful act. Some of the intrinsic difficulties encountered by the international law regime when dealing with a breach of the no-harm rule were presented at the start of this study to explain the emergence of prevention.[29] With prevention having evolved into a more advanced and comprehensive form, it is now necessary to highlight the specific issues that a breach of prevention presents to international law. The three characteristics of prevention – risk anticipation (11.2.1), due-diligence obligation (11.2.2) and protection of the environment (11.2.3) – challenge the rationale and structure of the law of State responsibility that is only able to partly respond to violations of the obligation.

11.2.1 *An Ex Post Framework for an Anticipatory Obligation*

The construction of prevention as an alternative to the general regime of State responsibility is in part explained by the fact that, by definition, the curative approach lacked the anticipatory perspective that defines prevention. The adoption, the same year, of the ILC Articles on State Responsibility and of the ILC Prevention Articles is evidence of two different routes. Yet, they do not operate in strictly separate realms: the rules on State responsibility apply, when necessary, to prevention in its form as a primary rule of obligation.[30] The apparent dichotomy between the two approaches can, at times, become blurred. Indeed, it has been noted that the due-diligence character of prevention gives States limited possibilities to ascertain 'clearly, and in advance' that they are meeting their obligations of conduct.[31] As a result, the duty of care is generally assessed ex post facto, after a harmful event that should have been avoided occurred.[32] In addition, the reactive rationale of the law of State responsibility is not absolute and can sometimes include an element of anticipation. The most obvious example is found in the provisional measures granted by dispute-settlement bodies that seek to avoid the occurrence of further ham and are thus inherently future oriented. Decisions on the merits

29 Section 2.2.

30 IDI, 'Responsibility and Liability Under International Law for Environmental Damage', Session of Strasbourg, 1997, Article 3.

31 ILA, Study Group on Due Diligence in International Law, 'Second Report', Johannesburg, 77th Session, 2016, at 7.

32 C Dominicé, 'Obligation de prévention et droit international de l'environnement', in P Borba Casella (ed), *Dimensão internacional do direito: estudos em homenagem a G.E. do Nascimento e Silva* (LTr 2000) 187–99, at 199.

can also embrace a preventive approach in their concern over the avoidance of harm repetition, as evidenced by the regime designed by the *Trail Smelter* arbitral tribunal to avoid future harm from the smelter[33] and, more indirectly, by the ICJ's reminder to parties of their preventive duties for any future activities they might wish to undertake.[34]

11.2.2 *Identifying a Breach of a Due-Diligence Obligation*

The complexity of the application of the law of State responsibility to prevention relates in part in its due-diligence character. Indeed, significant uncertainties regarding the relationship between prevention and due diligence remain. As a result, different positions exist regarding the extent to which a breach of prevention differs from a breach of due diligence (11.2.2.1). Another (but related) issue pertains to whether a distinction should be made between prevention in its substantive and procedural forms (11.2.2.2).

11.2.2.1 Breach of Prevention or Breach of Due Diligence

One core ambiguity relates to whether a breach of prevention is similar to or different from a breach of due diligence. Two different routes are usually followed. The first approach adopts the position taken by the ILC in its codification of the rules on State responsibility, which considered that an obligation of prevention is not breached unless the event happens,[35] whereas the obligation of due diligence can be breached by a failure to exercise care, even if harm has not (yet) materialized.[36] This position was particularly evident in the ILC's Articles on the Responsibility of States for Internationally Wrongful Acts (ARSIWA) Draft Article 23, which specifically created an independent category for preventive obligations.[37] The provision

33 *Trail Smelter (United States v. Canada)* (16 April 1938 and 11 March 1941), (1941) 3 RIAA 1905, questions 2 and 3.

34 *Certain Activities Carried out by Nicaragua in the Border Area (Costa Rica v. Nicaragua)* and *Construction of a Road in Costa Rica along the San Juan River (Nicaragua v. Costa Rica)* (Judgment) (2015) ICJ Rep 665, para 112 (taking note of Nicaragua's assurances to carry out a new environmental impact study before any substantial expansion of its current dredging programme) and 173 (noting that Costa Rica remained under an obligation to undertake an EIA and consult with Nicaragua for any further works on the road or in the area adjoining the San Juan River).

35 J Crawford, *State Responsibility: The General Part* (Cambridge University Press 2013) 227.

36 ILA, Study Group on Due Diligence in International Law, 'First Report', Washington, DC, 76th Session, 2014, at 27.

37 ILC, 'Draft Articles on State Responsibility with Commentaries thereto adopted by the ILC on First Reading' (January 1997) UN Doc. A/CN.4/L.528/Add.3, Draft Article 23, on a 'breach

was eventually deleted in the final version of the articles because it became apparent that there was no need to create a new category of obligations on top of the distinction already made between obligations of result and conduct. The final version of the articles, however, acknowledges, in the form of Article 14(3), that some (but not all) obligations of prevention have a specific temporal dimension, in which case a 'breach of an international obligation requiring a State to prevent a given event occurs when the event occurs'.[38]

The ICJ confirmed the distinction made by the ILC in the context of the prevention of acts of genocide in the *Application of the Convention on the Prevention and Punishment of the Crime of Genocide* case.[39] It ruled that States are under no obligation to 'succeed, whatever the circumstances, in preventing the commission of genocide' because the obligation to prevent genocide is an obligation of conduct.[40] Responsibility is only incurred 'if the State manifestly failed to take all measures to prevent genocide which were within its power, and which might have contributed to preventing the genocide' and thus failed to show due diligence.[41] The Court employed a distinction between the consequences of a violation of the obligation of due diligence and the obligation to prevent, aptly summarized by Crawford as follows:

> [D]ue diligence is an important factor in discharging the obligation of prevention, the latter cannot be categorized as an obligation of due diligence per se, because such an obligation would be breached by a state party's failure to take action, regardless of whether the prohibited event in fact took place. The obligation to prevent genocide requires both a failure to take steps and the occurrence of genocide before responsibility is triggered.[42]

of an international obligation to prevent a given event' read as follows: 'When the result required of a State by an international obligation is the prevention, by means of its own choice, of the occurrence of a given event, there is a breach of that obligation only if, by the conduct adopted, the State does not achieve that result.'

38 ILC, 'Draft Articles on Responsibility of States for Internationally Wrongful Acts (with Commentaries)' (2001) *Yearbook of the International Law Commission* (vol II, part 2) 31, Article 14(3) and Commentary to Article 14, para 14, at 62.

39 *Application of the Convention on the Prevention and Punishment of the Crime of Genocide (Bosnia and Herzegovina v. Serbia and Montenegro)* (2007) ICJ Rep 43, para 430.

40 *Application of the Convention on the Prevention and Punishment of the Crime of Genocide*, para 430.

41 *Application of the Convention on the Prevention and Punishment of the Crime of Genocide*, para 430.

42 Crawford, *State Responsibility: The General Part* 231–32.

In line with the recognition that ARSIWA Article 14(3) does not apply to all obligations of prevention,[43] the Court made clear that its conclusions were only applicable to the case at hand and were not to be generalized to all obligations of prevention.[44] The question that follows is whether the conclusion could be extended to the obligation to prevent environmental harm. The situation is rather blurry. On the one hand, the ARSIWA Commentaries give the example of the obligation to prevent transboundary damage caused by air pollution contained in the *Trail Smelter* case as a relevant example of an Article 14(3) preventive duty.[45] On the other hand, it was also used as a pertinent example in the context of activities not prohibited by international law, where it is recognized as an obligation of conduct.[46] This therefore leads to the conclusion that the two regimes intersect: under Article 14(3), the obligation of prevention will only be breached if and when the event occurs, but the obligation of due diligence will also be breached in the absence of any damage to the environment.

The approach followed by the ICJ in the *Pulp Mills* and *Certain Activities/ Construction of a Road* cases can be interpreted to have employed a similar categorization, although the Court did not explicitly differentiate between a breach of prevention and a breach of due diligence. Violations of the substantive obligation not to cause transboundary harm were assessed on the basis of the occurrence of damage, whereas violations of procedural obligations relied on the existence of a risk of damage. The two decisions reveal, albeit implicitly, that the Court understands the principle of prevention as being divided into the no-harm rule, breached only on evidence of material damage, and procedural preventive obligations, breached when the required level of diligence was not met. This categorization, however, raises significant uncertainties, as the next section will show.

An alternative route consists in concentrating on the breach to exercise due diligence to prevent environmental harm without making a sharp distinction

43 G Hafner and I Buffard, 'Obligations of Prevention and the Precautionary Principle', in J Crawford, A Pellet and S Olleson (eds), *The Law of International Responsibility* (Oxford University Press 2010) 521–34, at 523, highlighting that obligations to prevent under diplomatic law do not correspond to the preventive obligations falling under Article 14(3) because the obligation exists even if the event to be prevented has not yet occurred.

44 *Application of the Convention on the Prevention and Punishment of the Crime of Genocide*, para 429.

45 ILC, 'Draft Articles on Responsibility of States for Internationally Wrongful Acts, Commentaries to Article 14, para 14, at 62.

46 ILC, 'Draft Articles on Prevention of Transboundary Harm from Hazardous Activities (with Commentaries)' (2001) *Yearbook of the International Law Commission* (vol II, part 2) 148, General Commentary, para 4, at 148.

between due diligence and prevention. From this perspective, prevention is the primary norm breached irrespective of the presence of material damage,[47] and due diligence is the standard of care that, if not met, leads to a violation of the obligation to prevent.[48] The approach is justified on the basis that prevention is an obligation of conduct. Dupuy thus argues that prevention cannot be 'left, even implicitly, on the side of obligations of result'[49] because 'what is important is the content of the duty to prevent, not the consequences'.[50] This was, in effect, the approach taken in the *South China Sea* award, where the tribunal did not concentrate on the existence of harm, or risk of harm, but rather focused on whether the conduct of the State had breached its obligation to exercise due diligence in the prevention of environmental harm. The only difference arising from the existence of material damage is that it will have to be taken into account in the context of the assessment of the reparations due to the affected State.[51]

In sum, the two approaches do not refute that due diligence will be breached without material damage, but they do not agree on whether, under these circumstances, the obligation that is violated in this case is the obligation to prevent or the obligation of due diligence. At present, the jurisprudence on violations of the preventive obligation is too limited, in particular, because it relies on different sources of law and refers to different factual circumstances (in relation to the existence of risk and material damage) to identify a general trend regarding how international courts and tribunals deal with the intricate relationship between prevention and due diligence. The ICJ seems to be following the first route, relying on the distinction that it made twice between substantive and procedural preventive obligations, whereas the other tribunals did not followed suit and adopted the second route. This distinction between substantive and procedural obligations made by the ICJ is analysed further in the following section.

11.2.2.2 Breach of Substantive or Procedural Obligations

A second uncertainty currently existing in the context of environmental dispute settlement lies in whether a violation of a procedural obligation of

47 *Certain Activities/Construction of a Road*, separate opinion of Judge ad hoc Dugard, para 9.

48 *Certain Activities/Construction of a Road*, separate opinion of Judge ad hoc Dugard, para 9.

49 P-M Dupuy, 'Reviewing the Difficulties of Codification: On Ago's Classification of Obligations of Means and Obligations of Result in Relation to State Responsibility' (1999) 10 *European Journal of International Law* 371, at 380.

50 Dupuy, 'Reviewing the Difficulties of Codification'.

51 *Certain Activities/Construction of a Road*, separate opinion of Judge ad hoc Dugard, para 9.

prevention, which operationalizes the duty of due diligence, automatically brings about a breach of the substantive obligation of prevention. The ICJ, in both the *Pulp Mills* and *Certain Activities/Construction of a Road* cases, responded in the negative, ruling that substantive obligations were met even though procedural obligations had been breached.[52] The Court drew a distinction between the duty to take diligent steps to prevent significant transboundary harm, which it looked at under the rubric of separate procedural obligations, and the duty to take diligent steps not to cause harm, which it considers cannot be violated simply by a failure to act diligently. It considered that the absence of harm did not exonerate the State from its procedural duties,[53] but it did not wish to consider that a violation of a procedural obligation automatically brings about a breach of the obligation to exercise due diligence to prevent harm.

The approach is justifiable, on theoretical grounds, on the basis that procedural obligations can work in isolation from the substantive duty of prevention and can therefore be breached separately. However, the distinction between breaches of the substantive obligation and breaches of the procedural obligations is not unproblematic.[54] Indeed, if prevention, as an obligation of due diligence, can only be fulfilled when a number of other procedural obligations are met, it is difficult to understand how a breach of a procedural obligation does not automatically lead to a breach of prevention. The two are inextricably linked. Conceptually speaking, a failure to fulfil a procedural obligation defeats the objective and purpose of a treaty aiming at the prevention of harm. For instance, even if the breach of the environmental impact assessment (EIA) requirement did not lead to environmental damage, the duty of care arising from the due-diligence obligation of prevention cannot be considered to have been met. This was the approach taken by Judges Al-Khasawneh and Simma in their dissenting opinion to the *Pulp Mills* decision. They argued that given the generality of the substantive principles in international environmental law, 'respect for procedural obligations . . . comes to the forefront as being an essential indicator of whether, in a concrete case, substantive obligations were or were not breached'.[55] The Court's distinction seems conceptually flawed but, most importantly, is consequential in the

[52] *Pulp Mills*, para 282; *Certain Activities/Construction of a Road*.

[53] *Certain Activities/Construction of a Road*, separate opinion of Judge ad hoc Dugard, para 19.

[54] J Brunnée, 'Procedure and Substance in International Environmental Law: Confused at a Higher Level?' (2016) 5(6) *ESIL Reflections*; K Brent, 'The *Certain Activities* Case: What Implications of the No-harm Rule?' (2017) 20 *Asia Pacific Journal of Environmental Law* 28, at 55–56.

[55] *Pulp Mills*, joint dissenting opinion by Judges Al-Khasawneh and Simma, para 26.

context of State responsibility. The affected State will face difficulties proving the existence of harm in cases where the State of origin has not met its procedural obligations, which means that the affected State has not been given proper access to the necessary information or decision-making processes. Such was, in effect, the case in both *Pulp Mills* and *Certain Activities*, where the affected States convinced the Court that the State of origin had violated its procedural obligations but failed to prove a breach of substantive obligations.

It can be reasonably assumed that the Court favours this distinction because a violation of a procedural obligation tends to be more easily established than that of a substantive duty.[56] By concentrating on less controversial questions relative to decision-making processes, the Court manages to escape dwelling into 'controversial inquiries as to the content of substantives rules'.[57] In addition, by doing so, the Court is able to deliver a balanced judgment that holds the harming party accountable for its violations of the procedure but does not impose excessive reparations. For instance, in the *Pulp Mills* case, had the Court ruled that Uruguay had violated its substantive obligation, it would possibly have had to order that the factory be dismantled.[58]

However, tensions are visible in the position of the Court, which navigates rather uneasily between no-harm and prevention, between a traditional approach to damage and an awareness of the specificities of the environmental principle of prevention. The uneasiness of the Court is visible in its *Certain Activities/Construction of a Road* judgment that goes back and forth between references to harm and risk. For instance, while it noted that with regards to alleged harm to water quality and the aquatic ecosystem that 'Nicaragua's case shifted from its prior claim of actual harm to the river's ecosystem to a claim based on the risk of harm', the Court did not act on this and continued to look at evidence of actual harm.[59] A disconnect exists between the Court's repeated recognition of the anticipatory nature of prevention and its treatment of the obligation in the context of State responsibility; in other words, it fails to draw

56 Brunnée, 'Procedure and Substance', at 6, taking the example of the climate regime where procedural duties would avoid falling in the difficult obligation to try to establish causality between greenhouse gas emissions and climate damage.

57 ILA, Study Group on Due Diligence in International Law, 'Second Report', at 5.

58 Y Kerbat, 'Obligations procédurales et obligations substantielle en droit international des dommages transfrontières', oral presentation given at a workshop organized by the University of Paris I Panthéon-Sorbonne 'Procédure et substance en droit international: Dialectiques et influences croisées', 12 December 2016, noting that the Court's conclusions would have been the same even without the substance/procedure distinction because the harm was not important enough to justify the dismantling of the factory.

59 *Certain Activities/Construction of a Road*, para 211.

legal consequences from the anticipatory perspective of prevention, hence highlighting again the uneasy link between prevention and the law of State responsibility. The Court concentrates on risks only to assess whether procedural obligations have been met and relies on the substantive preventive obligation to evaluate actual harm. It does not consider that procedural obligations operationalize the substantive principle of prevention and therefore does not see them as a means to assess the duty of care.[60] Hence, the Court failed to adopt a holistic approach to the principle of prevention, contrary to the arbitral tribunal in the *South China Sea* case, which relied on the multiple manifestations of prevention, in its substantive[61] and procedural[62] forms, and in conventional,[63] customary[64] and case law,[65] to interpret the obligations of China and assess its degree of diligence. Such is the core advantage of the multifaceted nature of prevention.

11.2.3 A *Non-Reciprocal Obligation to Protect the Environment*

A final major problem arising from a breach of prevention lies in its character as an *erga omnes* obligation that operates outside a reciprocal framework ill suited to protect a global common (the environment). Indeed, significant uncertainties exist, partly explained by limited practice. The *erga omnes* qualification of prevention tends to be used to refer to the moral underpinnings of the principle and not necessarily to derive legal consequences from its character.[66] This seems to have been the approach of the UN Compensation Commission F4 Panel when it recognized, twice in its reports, the existence of a 'common concern for the protection and conservation of the environment'

60 *Pulp Mills*, para 78, noting that compliance with substantive obligations does not automatically mean that procedural obligations were complied with.

61 *South China Sea Arbitration (The Republic of the Philippines v. The People's Republic of China)* (Permanent Court of Arbitration), Award on the Merits, 12 July 2016, para 941 (on UNCLOS Article 192).

62 *South China Sea Arbitration*, para 946 (on cooperation pursuant to UNCLOS Articles 123 and 197) and para 948 (on environmental assessment on the basis of UNCLOS Article 206).

63 *South China Sea Arbitration*, para 945 (using CBD Article 2 to interpret UNCLOS Article 194(5)) and para 956 (relying on CITES to inform UNCLOS Article 192 and 194(5)).

64 *South China Sea Arbitration*, para 941 (relying on the customary character of prevention as recognized by the ICJ *Nuclear Weapons* advisory opinion).

65 *South China Sea Arbitration*, paras 941 and 944 (interpreting Article 192 on the basis of the jurisprudence of the ICJ, ITLOS and arbitral awards).

66 P Weil, 'Le droit international en quête de son identité: cours général de droit international public' (1992) 237 *Collected Courses of the Hague Academy of International Law* 9–370, 290, noting that lawyers tend to dwell on the theory behind the *erga omnes* concept but are more hesitant when it comes to extracting practical consequences from it.

that 'entails obligations towards the international community and future generations'.[67] The reference to 'obligations towards the international community' hints to the fact that the commission considered prevention as an *erga omnes* obligation. However, it did not derive any direct legal consequences from this recognition. Rather, the panel used the *erga omnes* character to examine the obligations of the claimants to prevent and mitigate environmental damage in the context of Iraq's invasion of Kuwait[68] and to extend the scope of its investigation to environmental damage that occurred in neighbouring territories.[69] In effect, the commission did not use the *erga omnes* qualification to extend standing but rather relied on the qualification to justify the extended coverage of its analysis in terms of duty bearers and spatial scope.

Similarly, in the context of the ILC's work on the protection of the atmosphere, Special Rapporteur Murase included a general obligation to protect the atmosphere that he qualified as *erga omnes*.[70] However, the qualification in the context of atmospheric pollution led to strong disagreements from members of the ILC[71]. The special rapporteur responded to the controversy by arguing that an *erga omnes* qualification does not necessarily give rise to procedural obligations.

> In the absence of any multilateral convention on the protection of the atmosphere, draft guideline 4 merely recognized the existence of the obligation *erga omnes* in substantive law without intending to give standing to any State in procedural law. It was important to recognize, albeit in an abstract fashion, the general obligation of every State to protect the atmosphere.[72]

67 United Nations Compensation Commission, Governing Council, 'Report and Recommendations Made by the Panel of Commissioners concerning the First Instalment of "F4" claims', S/AC.26/2003/31 (18 December 2003), paras 42 and 43; United Nations Compensation Commission, Governing Council, 'Report and Recommendations Made by the Panel of Commissioners concerning the First Instalment of "F4" claims', S/AC.26/2004/17 (9 December 2004), para 38; United Nations Compensation Commission, Governing Council, 'Report and Recommendations Made by the Panel of Commissioners concerning the First Instalment of "F4" claims', S/AC.26/2005/10 (30 June 2005), para 40.

68 United Nations Compensation Commission, Governing Council, 'Report and Recommendations Made by the Panel of Commissioners concerning the First Instalment of "F4" claims', S/AC.26/2005/10 (30 June 2005), para 41.

69 United Nations Compensation Commission, Governing Council, 'Report and Recommendations Made by the Panel of Commissioners concerning the First Instalment of "F4" claims', S/AC.26/2001/16 (22 June 2001), para 53 (i.e. Iran, Jordan, Saudi Arabia, Syria and Turkey).

70 ILC, 'Second Report of the Special Rapporteur, Mr Shinya Murase, on the protection of the atmosphere' (2015) UN Doc. A/CN.4/681, para 41.

71 ILC, 'Third Report of the Special Rapporteur, Mr Shinya Murase, on the protection of the atmosphere' (2016) UN Doc. A/CN.4/692, footnotes 35 and 36, summarizing the critical views expressed by different members of the commission.

72 ILC, 'Provisional Summary of the 3244th Meeting' (18 December 2015) UN Doc. A/CN.4/SR.3244, at 5–6

The special rapporteur's argument raises several issues, including whether an obligation *erga omnes* can exist in substantive law without necessarily having procedural consequences and what would be the added value of a characterization that carries no legal consequences. The rapporteur's position departs from the ICJ's position in *Barcelona Traction*, which was primarily concerned with describing the 'specific features of the secondary rules governing the invocation of responsibility for violations of obligations called *erga omnes*'.[73] Its position is symptomatic of the fact that the legal community is ill at ease with the *erga omnes* qualification[74] but nevertheless uses it strategically to refer to some common values shared by the international community. By arguing that it is 'important to recognize, albeit in an abstract fashion' the *erga omnes* nature of the obligation, the special rapporteur emphasizes the symbolic nature of the qualification, which is important to highlight the fundamental values represented by the principle[75] while, in effect, also acknowledging the limitations of the international legal system in protecting these values.

The main legal consequence arising from an *erga omnes* qualification is that it extends standing, allowing States that are not directly injured to invoke the responsibility of another State for a breach of such obligation.[76] Recognized in the famous *Barcelona Traction* case, such a possibility was crystallized in Article 48 of ARSIWA.[77] The right of a non-injured State to invoke the responsibility of another State under an Article 48(1)(a) scenario – in the context of an obligation owed to a group of States including that State and protecting a collective interest – is generally accepted.[78] However, the situation becomes more complex when it comes to apply Article 48(2)(b),

[73] CJ Tams, *Enforcing Obligations Erga Omnes in International Law* (Cambridge University Press 2010) 102.

[74] Weil, 'Le droit international en quête de son identité', 288, considers that the inclusion of environmental norms as *erga omnes* is 'politically correct' but 'practically unlikely'.

[75] ILC, 'Provisional Summary of the 3244th Meeting', at 5–6, based in particular on paragraph 29 of the ICJ's *Nuclear Weapons* advisory opinion.

[76] IDI, 'Obligations and rights *erga omnes* in international law', Session of Krakow, 2005, Article 1, recognized that *erga omnes* obligations are in part characterized by a common concern of the international community for compliance with the obligation.

[77] ILC, 'Draft Articles on Responsibility of States for Internationally Wrongful Acts'.

[78] In the *Whaling in the Antarctic* case, there was an implicit understanding, by the parties and the Court, that Australia, while not directly injured by Japan's whaling activities, had standing under a situation similar to that of Article 48(1)(a), Japan's obligations under the International Convention for the Regulation of Whaling being interpreted as *erga omnes partes* obligations. P Urs, 'Are States Injured by Whaling in the Antarctic?', *Opinio Juris* post, 14 August 2014, available at http://opiniojuris.org/2014/08/14/guest-post-states-injured-whaling-antarctic/ (last accessed 14 August 2017).

which grants a non-injured State the possibility to invoke the responsibility of another State violating obligations owed to the international community as a whole. When it comes to prevention, courts and tribunals have traditionally been weary of accepting claims by parties that were acting as representatives of the international community but had not been directly affected by environmental harm.[79] It remains that the *Barcelona Traction* jurisprudence, combined with ARSIWA Article 48(1)(b), gives, at least theoretically, legal standing to all States to react to a breach of preventive obligations.[80] However, this is largely untested. It is, however, noteworthy that the ITLOS Seabed Chamber considered that the International Seabed Authority, acting on behalf of mankind and UNCLOS parties, could be entitled, pursuant to ARSIWA Article 48, to bring a claim in the case of environmental harm in the Area.[81] By doing so, it confirmed the standing of non-injured States under ARSIWA Article 48 but also highlighted the role of international institutions in acting as environmental trustees.

A corollary question relates to whether a non-injured State would be able to seek reparation. In line with the ARSIWA, which provide that a non-injured State can demand reparation 'in the interest of the injured State or of the beneficiaries of the obligation breached',[82] the ITLOS Seabed Chamber responded in the positive.[83] Two questions emerge from such possibility, acknowledged by the ARSIWA Commentaries as involving a 'measure of progressive development'.[84] Firstly, the notion of 'beneficiaries' remains unresolved – who benefits from environmental protection and, more specifically, from preventive actions? The environment is the ultimate beneficiary, but the international community, broadly understood as comprising States, individuals and communities, also benefits from harm avoidance.[85] The Institut de

79 *Bering Sea Fur Seals (Great Britain v. United States)* (1893) 1 Moore 755; *Nuclear Tests (Australia v. France)* (Judgment) (1974) ICJ Rep 253; *Nuclear Tests (New Zealand v. France)* (Judgment) (1974) ICJ Rep 457.

80 IDI, 'Obligations and rights *erga omnes* in international law', Session of Krakow, 2005: The resolution attempted to ensure that States to which the obligation is owed have standing in front of international judicial institutions to bring a claim (Article 3) or to participate in proceedings (Article 4).

81 *Responsibilities and Obligations of States Sponsoring Persons and Entities with respect to Activities in the Area*, ITLOS No. 17, Advisory Opinion (1 February 2011), para 180.

82 *Responsibilities and Obligations of States Sponsoring Persons and Entities with respect to Activities in the Area*, para 180.

83 ILC, 'Draft Articles on Responsibility of States for Internationally Wrongful Acts', Article 48(2)(b).

84 ILC, 'Draft Articles on Responsibility of States for Internationally Wrongful Acts', Commentary to Article 48, para 12, at 127.

85 On the beneficiaries of the principle of prevention, see L-A Duvic-Paoli, 'Prevention and the Anticipation of Risk(s) in International Environmental Law: A Multifaceted Norm', in

droit international suggested the creation of a High Commissioner for the Environment that would act 'on behalf or in the interests of the international community',[86] but the proposal had limited resonance. The second question relates to the kind of reparation that a non-injured State would be able to claim: it is likely that it would demand cessation of the act but not seek compensation.[87] Although often difficult to undertake, restoration should be the preferred option, as it is in effect the most beneficial to the injured entity that is the environment. Such was the approach taken by the Czech Republic, which, following a submission by the Federated States of Micronesia, recognized the effects on climate change of a project to expand a coal power plant and required the owner of the plant to provide a compensation plan that would offset 5 million tons of carbon dioxide to mitigate the climate impact of the project.[88]

To conclude, the rapprochement between the preventive and curative approaches is visible in the context of the relationship between prevention and the law of State responsibility. The ILC Articles on State Responsibility are commendable for their consideration of breaches of non-reciprocal obligations, a fundamental element to accommodate the traditional outlook of curative rationale to some of the specificities of prevention. However, significant divergences remain, the two logics operating in two separate – albeit sometimes intersecting – realms. Nevertheless, current trends discussed in the next section reveal that the frontier between prevention and reparation is, to a certain extent, being redrawn.

11.3 FRONTIERS OF PREVENTION: COMPLIANCE CONTROL

The curative perspective, which had been partly put aside after the consecration of the prevention principle in the 1970s, has, to some extent and under specific circumstances, been absorbed by the preventive logic. Mechanisms that would normally serve a traditional post-breach enforcement purpose are falling under a preventive approach; these are non-compliance procedures

M Ambrus, R Rayfuse and W Werner (eds), *Conceptions of Risk and the Regulation of Uncertainty in International Law* (Oxford University Press 2017) 141–60, at 154.

86 IDI, 'Responsibility and Liability under International Law for Environmental Damage', Session of Strasbourg, 1997, Article 28.

87 For instance, *Whaling in the Antarctic (Australia v. Japan: New Zealand intervening)* (Judgment) (2014) ICJ Rep 226, para 25(5)(b).

88 Greenpeace International, 'Threatened Pacific Island Nation Makes Legal History by Challenging European Carbon Emitter' (23 May 2011), available at www.greenpeace.org/international/en/press/releases/2011/Threatened-Pacific-Island-Nation-makes-legal-history-by-challenging-European-carbon-emitter/ (last accessed 1 September 2017).

(NCPs). NCPs have multiplied since the 1990s, as evidenced by the number of MEAs that have established[89] – or strive to establish[90] – such a mechanism.

[89] See Protocol on Substances that Deplete the Ozone Layer (Montreal Protocol), Annex V of the Report of the Fourth Meeting of the Parties, 'Indicative list of measures that might be taken by a meeting of the Parties in respect of non-compliance with the Protocol' UNEP/OzL. Pro.4/15 (1992); Convention on Long Range Transboundary Air Pollution on Further Reduction of Sulphur Emissions, and its Protocols (LRTAP Convention), Decision 1997/2 (1997) and Decision 2012/25 (2012); Convention on the Control of Transboundary Movements of Hazardous Wastes and their Disposal (Basel Convention), COP Decision V/16, 'Mechanism for Promoting Implementation and Compliance of the Basel Convention', UNEP/CH.5/29 (10 December 1999); Convention on Environmental Impact Assessment in a Transboundary Context (Espoo Convention), Decision II/4, on the establishment of the Implementation Committee (2001), and Decision III/2, 'Structure and Functions of the Implementation Committee and Procedures for Review of Compliance', Annex II (2002); Convention on Access to Information, Public Participation in Decision making and Access to Justice in Environmental Matters (Aarhus Convention), Meeting of the Parties Decision I/7, Annex 'Structure and Functions of the Compliance Committee and Procedures for the Review of Compliance', ECE/MP.PP/2/Add.8 (2 April 2004); Alpine Convention, Decision VII/4, 'Mechanism for Reviewing Compliance with the Alpine Convention and Its Implementation Protocols', 7th Alpine Conference (2002) and Decision XII, 'Mechanism for Reviewing Compliance with the Alpine Convention and Its Implementation Protocols', 12th Alpine Conference (2012) (Alpine Convention); Cartagena Protocol on Biosafety to the Convention on Biological Diversity (Cartagena Protocol), Article 34, and 'Establishment of procedures and mechanisms on compliance under the Cartagena Protocol on Biosafety', BS-I/7 (2004); Convention on International Trade in Endangered Species of Wild Fauna and Flora (CITES), 'CITES Compliance Procedures', Decision 14.3, Annex (2004); Protocol to the United Nations Framework Convention on Climate Change (Kyoto Protocol) Decision 27/CMP.1, 'Procedures and mechanisms relating to compliance under the Kyoto Protocol', First Session of the Conference of the Parties, FCCC/KP/CMP/2005/8/Add.3 (30 March 2006); Protocol to the Convention on the Prevention of Marine Pollution by Dumping of Wastes and Other Matter (Protocol to the Dumping Convention), Decision LC 29/17, Annex 7, 'Compliance Procedures and Mechanisms Pursuant to Article 11 of the 1996 Protocol to the London Convention 1972' (2007); Protocol on Water and Health to the 1992 Convention on the Protection and Use of Transboundary Watercourses and International Lakes (Protocol on Water and Health), Decision I/2 'Review of Compliance', ECE/MP.WH/2/Add.3 (3 July 2007); Barcelona Convention on the Protection of the Mediterranean (Barcelona Convention), Decision IG 17/2, 'Procedures and mechanisms on compliance under the Barcelona Convention and Its Protocols', UNEP(DEPI)/MED IG.17/10 Annex V (2008); Protocol on Pollutant Release and Transfer Registers, Decision I/2, Annex, 'Structure and Functions of the Compliance Committee and Procedures for the Review of Compliance', ECE/MP.PRTR/2010/2/Add.1 (March 2011); North American Agreement on Environmental Cooperation, 'Guidelines for Submissions on Enforcement Matters Under Article 14 and 15' (2012).

[90] Convention on Persistent Organic Pollutants (POPs Convention), Decision SC-6/24, 'Procedures and mechanisms on compliance with the Stockholm Convention', draft procedures adopted by the conference of the parties (2007); International Treaty on Plant Genetic Resources (ITPGR), Resolution 2/2011, 'Procedures and Operational Mechanisms to Promote Compliance and Address Issues of Non-Compliance (draft)', Fourth Session of the governing body (March 2011); Convention on the Prior Informed Consent Procedure for Certain Hazardous Chemicals and Pesticides in International Trade (PIC Convention), Decision

They occupy a function between conciliation and adjudication[91] and have the advantages of being faster, less costly and less confrontational than classical mechanisms of dispute settlement.

This section identifies compliance control as the outer frontiers of prevention or, in other words, as the maximum degree to which the preventive rationale can be extended before falling under a curative perspective. It shows that the preventive logic has conquered large portions of the traditional province of curative approaches in the context of compliance control mechanisms. The analysis explains how the principle of prevention drives compliance control methods by looking, based on selected examples, at the design and practice of NCPs. While the specificities intrinsic to each NCP ought to be acknowledged, their rationale (11.3.1), scope (11.3.2) and effects (11.3.3) are reflections of the principle of prevention.

11.3.1 *The Rationale: A Process Focusing on the Anticipation of Harm*

Non-compliance mechanisms do not adopt a traditional curative approach to an internationally wrongful act that concentrates on reparations but rather seek to induce the State to resume the performance of its obligation. The outcome of these mechanisms is, above all, to manage non-compliance, including through the provision of assistance. Compliance control takes the form of a 'process'[92] that uses reporting requirements to assess and monitor compliance[93] and, when necessary, 'advice and assistance'[94] to bring

RC-6/9, 'Procedures and mechanisms on compliance with the Rotterdam Convention', draft procedures adopted by the conference of the parties in application to Article 17 of the convention (2013); Minamata Convention on Mercury, Kumamoto, 10 October 2013, in force 16 August 2017 (Mercury Convention), Article 15; Paris Agreement to the United Nations Framework Convention on Climate Change, Paris, 12 December 2015, in force 4 November 2016, Doc. FCCC/CP/2015/10/Add.1, Article 15.

91 P Sands and J Peel, *Principles of International Environmental Law* (3rd edn, Cambridge University Press 2012) 163.

92 JE Viñuales, 'Managing Abidance by Standards for the Protection of the Environment', in A Cassese (ed), *Realizing Utopia* (Oxford University Press 2012) 326–39, at 327; A Chayes and AH Chayes, *The New Sovereignty: Compliance with International Regulatory Agreements* (Harvard University Press 1995) 123.

93 Methods differ and include reporting levels of emissions (e.g. Long-Range Transboundary Air Pollution Convention, Article 9(e)) and verification on the ground (e.g. CITES, Article XII(2)(d) and XIII(2)).

94 See e.g. Aarhus Convention, Decision I/7, para 37(a) and (b); Alpine Convention, Decision XII, para 4.2; Cartagena Protocol, Decision BS-I/7 (2004), para VI(1)(a); Kyoto Protocol, Decision 27/CMP.1, facilitation branch, section XIV(a); Protocol to the Dumping Convention, Decision LC 29/17, paras 5.1.1–5.1.2; Health and Water Protocol, Decision I/2, para 34(d).

the party back into compliance. This can take different forms, such as assistance for collecting and reporting data[95] or establishing a domestic regulatory regime[96] and providing technical,[97] legal[98] and financial[99] assistance, as well as by helping with technology[100] or information transfer[101] and capacity building (including training).[102] They accompany the party back to compliance with the elaboration of 'plans of action'[103] and submission of 'reports'[104] to follow progress. Non-compliance viewed from a preventive perspective is excused as long as the State attempts to go back into compliance. NCPs concentrate on the process instead of the result, on the reasons for the wrongful act, and not on the act per se, in order to provide means to avoid its repetition.

The anticipatory rationale that drives NCPs is evident. One significant example can be found in the approach taken by the Aarhus Compliance Committee in a case involving a proposal to establish an industrial and energy park north of the port of Vlora on the Adriatic coast.[105] The committee noted

95 Montreal Protocol, Decision UNEP/OzL.Pro.4/15 (1992), Annex V, para (a).

96 Basel Convention, Decision V/16, para 19 (a).

97 See, e.g., Montreal Protocol, Decision UNEP/OzL.Pro.4/15 (1992), Annex V, para (a); Cartagena Protocol, Decision BS-I/7 (2004), para VI(1)(b) and (2)(a); Kyoto Protocol, Decision 27/CMP.1, facilitation branch, section XIV (b) and (c); Health and Water Protocol, para 35(b) and (c).

98 ITPGR (draft), Resolution 2/2011, para 2(a).

99 See, e.g., Montreal Protocol, Decision UNEP/OzL.Pro.4/15 (1992), Annex V, para a; Basel Convention, Decision V/16, para 19(b); Cartagena Protocol, Decision BS-I/7 (2004), paras VI (1)(b) and (2)(a); Kyoto Protocol, Decision 27/CMP.1, facilitation branch, section XIV(b) and (c); Health and Water Protocol, Decision I/2, para 35(b) and (c).

100 See e.g. Montreal Protocol, Decision UNEP/OzL.Pro.4/15 (1992), Annex V, para a; Basel Convention, Decision V/16, para 19(b); Cartagena Protocol, Decision BS-I/7 (2004), para VI (1)(b) and (2)(a); Kyoto facilitation branch, section XIV(b) and (c).

101 Montreal Protocol, Decision UNEP/OzL.Pro.4/15 (1992), Annex V, para (a).

102 See e.g. Basel Convention, Decision V/16, para 19(b); Cartagena Protocol, Decision BS-I/7 (2004), para VI(1)(b) and (2)(a); Kyoto Protocol, Decision 27/CMP.1, facilitation branch, section XIV(b) and (c); CITES, Decision 14.3, para 29(d); Health and Water Protocol, Decision I/2, para 35(b) and (c); Barcelona Convention, Decision IG 17/2, para 33(a). Montreal Protocol, Decision UNEP/OzL.Pro.4/15 (1992), Annex V, para a; Cartagena Protocol, Decision BS-I/7 (2004), para VI(1)(b) and (2)(a); Health and Water Protocol, Decision I/2, para 35(b) and (c).

103 See e.g. Basel Convention, Decision V/16, para 19(c); Cartagena Protocol, Decision BS-I/7 (2004), para VI(1)(c); Kyoto Protocol, Decision 27/CMP.1, enforcement branch, section XV (1)(b); Protocol to the Dumping Convention, Decision LC 29/17, para 5.1.3; Health and Water Protocol, Decision I/2, para 34(b); CITES, Decision 14.3, para 29(h); Barcelona Convention, Decision IG 17/2, para 32(b); Aarhus Convention, Decision I/7, para 37(c); Alpine Convention, Decision XII, para 4.2.

104 Cartagena Protocol, Decision BS-I/7 (2004), para VI(1)(d) and (e); Health and Water Protocol, Decision I/2, para 35(g); Barcelona Convention, Decision IG 17/2, paras 32(c) and 33(c).

105 Aarhus Compliance Committee, 'Report of the Compliance Committee on Its Sixteenth Meeting (Addendum): Findings and Recommendations with Regard to Compliance by Albania' (2007) ECE/MP.PP/C.1/2007/4/Add.1.

with concern that it took more than two years to prepare findings and recommendations because the party failed to engage with it.[106] Aware that there might be other information relevant to the case, it decided nevertheless to publish its findings based on the following justification:

> [T]he process of compliance review is forward-looking and . . . the aim is to begin facilitating implementation and compliance at the national level once a need for such is established. It therefore prefers to put forward those conclusions and recommendations which it can make at this stage.[107]

The committee's comments are clear manifestations of the preventive rationale; they highlight the anticipatory ('forward-looking') focus of the mechanism and its process-like nature ('the aim is to begin'), which allows it to give recommendations even though not all the relevant information is available.

The main concern of the compliance mechanism is not to sanction a violation of the obligation per se but, as far as possible, to avoid the occurrence of harm. Such an approach is consequential because it has enabled some committees to issue warnings to a party even in the absence of evident breach. For instance, the Implementation Committee of the Espoo Convention regularly expresses concerns for a specific situation brought to its attention by third parties and provides recommendations,[108] even if it cannot start an initiative for lack of competence or evidence.

11.3.2 *The Scope: Adapting to the Specificities of* erga omnes *Obligations*

The principle of prevention, in its non-bilateralizable *erga omnes* character, manifests, to a certain extent, in three innovative possibilities relative to the entity that can trigger the mechanism. Firstly, NCPs can be triggered by

[106] Aarhus Compliance Committee, 'Report of the Compliance Committee on Its Sixteenth Meeting (Addendum): Findings and Recommendations with Regard to Compliance by Albania', para 88.

[107] Aarhus Compliance Committee, 'Report of the Compliance Committee on Its Sixteenth Meeting (Addendum): Findings and Recommendations with Regard to Compliance by Albania', para 89.

[108] Espoo Implementation Committee, Correspondence on specific compliance issues as a result of information provided to the Committee: EIA/IC/INFO/2 (Ukraine), 'Letter of 13 October 2009', paras 3 and 4 (on the fact that the convention cannot have retroactive effects but nevertheless expressing concern and making recommendations for future action); EIA/IC/INFO/4 (Belgium), 'Letter of 13 October 2009', para 3 (on the fact that there is not enough evidence to start an initiative but noting that the 'practical application of the Convention does not necessarily constitute good practice' and therefore making some observations); and EIA/IC/INFO/6 (Slovakia), 'Letter of 10 September 2010', para 3 (on the fact that there is not enough evidence to start an initiative but making nevertheless general recommendations).

a variety of entities that are not necessarily directly injured by the breach. Depending on the design of the NCP, this can be another State party,[109] the secretariat of the MEA,[110] the conference of the parties/meeting of the parties (COP/MOP),[111] the non-compliance procedure (NCP) itself[112] or the public.[113] Interestingly, not only States but also individuals and communities can bring a state of non-compliance to the scrutiny of a NCP. Their role as trustees of the environment, operating irrespective of territorial boundaries, is particularly well evidenced in a referral made to the Espoo Implementation Committee by Romanian NGOs regarding the transboundary effects of a nuclear waste repository in Romania, close to the Bulgarian border.[114] In this case, Romanian NGOs are effectively seeking to protect the rights of Bulgarian citizens (or, arguably, strategically using the convention to oppose an environmentally risky project in their territory), hence representing a situation in which an entity seeks to protect the environment irrespective of the location of harm.

Secondly, compliance mechanisms can, depending on their mandate, allow multiple States to bring a case of non-compliance to their attention. Given that a case of environmental degradation would, in effect, harm the international community as a whole, it only makes sense that several States would find that they have an interest in compliance. The advantage of NCPs in this context is that they ensure that the measures taken against non-complying States are proportional to the breach committed and provide an alternative to the disproportionate burden that multiple States taking counter-measures pursuant to the law of State responsibility[115] might put on the breaching State. It remains, however, that, in practice, this possibility has been sparsely used. One rare instance in which a collective referral was made can be found in the submission made to the Kyoto facilitative branch by South

109 See e.g. Espoo Convention, Decision III/2, para 5(a); Aarhus Convention, Decision I/7, paras 15 and 16.

110 E.g. Montreal Protocol, Decision UNEP/OzL.Pro.4/15 (1992), Annex IV, para 3; LRTAP Convention, para 5; Aarhus Convention, Decision I/7, para 17; and only in relation to reporting obligations: Basel Convention, Decision V/16, para 9(c).

111 Protocol to the Dumping Convention, Decision LC 29/17, para 4.1.1.

112 Espoo Convention, para 6; Aarhus Convention, Decision I/7, para 14.

113 See Aarhus Convention, Decision I/7, paras 18–24; Health and Water Protocol, Decision I/2, para 16.

114 Espoo Implementation Committee, Correspondence on specific compliance issues as a result of information provided to the Committee, EIA/IC/INFO/8 (Romania), 'Information provided by a Romanian NGO (17.05.2011) regarding the proposed construction of a low- and medium-level radioactive waste repository in Romania: Information form'.

115 ILC, 'Draft Articles on Responsibility of States for Internationally Wrongful Acts (with Commentaries)', Article 49.

Africa on behalf of the G77 and China group regarding the fact that several Annex I countries had not fulfilled their reporting obligations on time.[116] The referral, however, faced procedural difficulties. Indeed, while some NCPs explicitly provide for a referral by more than one party, no provision existed in this regard for the Kyoto facilitative branch. The branch was split on whether to proceed or not on the matter,[117] and no consensus was eventually found to proceed. The main point of contention related to the fact that the communication had not been submitted 'by a Party on its own behalf through a representative duly authorized for this purpose', hence highlighting the uneasiness of the committee towards collective referral, considered to be an unusual practice.[118]

Thirdly, the ultimate manifestation of the preventive rationale, in its non-reciprocal logic dictated by environmental protection, can be found in the possibility that States have to refer their own circumstances to the attention of the committee.[119] In practice, however, States very rarely use this possibility. Two examples illustrate how States are ill at ease with self-referral. One example is found in a self-referral made in the context of the Montreal Protocol; it is telling that the Russian Federation chose to notify its compliance difficulties to the meeting of the parties and not directly by addressing its submission to the secretariat, as requested by paragraph 4 of the procedure relative to self-referral.[120] Despite the lack of explicit referral, the Implementation Committee eventually decided to interpret the notification as a case of a self-trigger.[121] Another noticeable case relates to Albania's self-referral to the Aarhus Compliance Committee in 2016,[122] where the central government called on the committee to establish 'an independent international inquiry' on the basis of a violation of the convention with regards to a construction project at the Tirana Lake Park that was met with strong

116 Kyoto Facilitative Branch, 'Submission by South Africa, as Chairman of the Group of 77 and China, on behalf of the Group of 77 and China' (2006) CC-2006–1-1/FB to CC-2006–15-1/FB.

117 Kyoto Facilitative Branch, 'Report of the Compliance Committee on the Deliberations in the Facilitative Branch Relating to the Submission Entitled "Compliance with Article 3.1 of the Kyoto Protocol" (CC-2006–1-2/FB to CC-2006–15-2/FB)' (2006) CC-2006–1-2/FB, para 1.

118 Kyoto Facilitative Branch, 'Report of the Compliance Committee', para 4(a).

119 Montreal Protocol, Decision UNEP/OzL.Pro.4/15 (1992), Annex IV, para 4; LRTAP Convention, Decision 2012/25, para 4(b); Espoo Convention, Decision III/2, para 5(b); Aarhus Convention, Decision I/7, para 16; Basel Convention, Decision V/16, para 9(a); Cartagena Protocol, Decision BS-I/7 (2004), section IV(1)(a); Kyoto Protocol, Decision 27/CMP.1, section VI.I(a).

120 Montreal Protocol, Decision UNEP/OzL.Pro.4/15 (1992), Annex IV, para 4.

121 Montreal Protocol Committee, 'Decision VII/18: Compliance with the Montreal Protocol by the Russian Federation' (adopted at the Seventh Meeting of the Parties), para 1.

122 Aarhus Compliance Committee, case ACCC/S/2016/3 (Albania).

public opposition.[123] It took three letters from the secretariat, each asking the State party to clarify that its request for a 'fact-finding mission' was falling under paragraph 16 of decision I/7 on self-referral, to get confirmation that the State was actually proceeding to a self-referral.[124] To summarize, although the principle of prevention manifests clearly in the different solutions relative to trigger that some compliance mechanisms have integrated, States have not made full use, in practice, of these possibilities and remain rather reluctant to use tools that operate outside the traditional dogma of international law.

11.3.3 *The Effects: Declarations of Non-Compliance and Sanctions*

The boundaries of the principle of prevention extend to their maximum, and even trespass the curative realm, in the context of the few NCPs that sanction non-compliance. Techniques commonly found in the traditional curative realm are brought under a preventive rationale. Two forms of sanctions are generally available: a 'soft' version in the form of a declaration of non-compliance and a 'harder' version in the form of trade sanctions.

Compliance mechanisms can sometimes be mandated to make a declaration of non-compliance.[125] This can be assimilated to a declaration of breach in a dispute-settlement context, but framed under a preventive rationale, it does not concentrate on the injury. As a result, NCPs do not grant remedies, even in non-compliance cases more closely related to an inter-State dispute because they are brought by another State party, often directly injured by the breach.[126] The purely anticipatory outlook of the declarations of

[123] Aarhus Compliance Committee, case ACCC/S/2016/3 (Albania), 'Letter to the Chair of the Compliance Committee' (5 May 2016).

[124] Aarhus Compliance Committee, case ACCC/S/2016/3 (Albania), 'Letter to the Party concerned from the Chair of the Compliance Committee' (14 June 2016); 'Letter to the Party concerned from the Chair of the Compliance Committee' (5 July 2016); 'Letter to the Party concerned from the secretariat' (17 August 2016).

[125] Kyoto Protocol, Decision 27/CMP.1, enforcement branch, section XV(1)(a); Aarhus Convention, Decision I/7, para 37(e); Cartagena Protocol, decision BS-I/7 (2004), para VI (2)(3838c); Health and Water Protocol, Decision I/2, para 35(b) and (c); Barcelona Convention, Decision IG 17/2, para 33(d); Montreal Protocol, Decision UNEP/OzL.Pro.4/15 (1992), Annex V, para b; Basel Convention, Decision V/16, para 20(b); Cartagena Protocol, decision BS-I/7 (2004), para VI(2)(b); Aarhus Convention, Decision I/7, para 37(f); Health and Water Protocol, Decision I/2, para 34 (d); CITES, Decision 14.3, para 29(g); Barcelona Convention, Decision IG 17/2, para 34(a).

[126] Aarhus Compliance Committee, 'Findings and Recommendations with regard to compliance by Ukraine with the obligations under the Aarhus Convention in the case of Bystre deep-water navigation canal construction (submission ACCC/S/2004/01 by Romania and communication ACCC/C/2004/03 by Ecopravo-Lviv (Ukraine)', ECE/MP.PP/C.1/2005/2/Add.3 (18 February 2005).

non-compliance can sometimes be very striking in the eyes of the lawyer used to traditional dispute-settlement mechanisms. The declaration of breach made by the Espoo Implementation Committee in the context of the United Kingdom's non-compliance with its obligation to notify in the case of the construction of the Hinkley Point nuclear plant provides such illustration.[127] While the committee found that the United Kingdom had breached its obligation to notify other States that might be affected by the activity of the nuclear power plant,[128] it made two recommendations of limited reach. Firstly, it recommended that the United Kingdom enter 'into discussions with possibly affected Parties . . . in order to agree on whether notification is useful at the current stage for this proposed activity',[129] and secondly, it asked that the United Kingdom comply with its obligation to notify 'in the context of any future decision-making regarding the planned construction of a NPP'.[130] In sum, the consequences of non-compliance were very limited for the United Kingdom, the committee being more concerned about the United Kingdom's future behaviour than about the present effects of its breach. This initial position was, however, tempered by the fact that the committee became subsequently aware that the continuation of the construction of the NPP might render the discussions with possibly affected parties on notification irrelevant. As a result, its chair asked the United Kingdom to 'consider refraining from carrying out works at the proposed activity until it established whether notification was useful'.[131] This additional recommendation is telling

[127] Convention on Environmental Impact Assessment in a Transboundary Context, Implementation Committee, 'Findings and recommendations further to a Committee initiative concerning the United Kingdom of Great Britain and Northern Ireland (EIA/IC/CI/5)', in 'Report of the Implementation Committee on Its Thirty-Fifth Session' (2016) UN Doc. ECE/MP.EIA/IC/2016/2.

[128] Convention on Environmental Impact Assessment in a Transboundary Context, Implementation Committee, 'Findings and recommendations further to a Committee initiative concerning the United Kingdom of Great Britain and Northern Ireland (EIA/IC/CI/5)', para 67(a).

[129] Convention on Environmental Impact Assessment in a Transboundary Context, Implementation Committee, 'Findings and recommendations further to a Committee initiative concerning the United Kingdom of Great Britain and Northern Ireland (EIA/IC/CI/5)', para 67(b).

[130] Convention on Environmental Impact Assessment in a Transboundary Context, Implementation Committee, 'Findings and recommendations further to a Committee initiative concerning the United Kingdom of Great Britain and Northern Ireland (EIA/IC/CI/5)', para 67(d).

[131] Convention on Environmental Impact Assessment in a Transboundary Context, Meeting of the Parties, 'Report of the Implementation Committee on Its Thirty-Eighth Session' (March 2017), ECE/MP.EIA/IC/2017/2 UNECE, unedited advance version, para 61. The committee also recommended to the Meeting of the Parties that if a potentially affected

of the anticipatory rationale that generally drives the committee: its initial concern was to avoid a future repetition of the procedural violation, which meant that it paid limited attention to the actual consequences of the violation in the *cas d'espèce* – something it only subsequently sought to correct.

In effect, the addressee of a declaration of non-compliance is different from that of a declaration of breach in a judicial decision: when the declaration of breach is primarily aimed at bringing satisfaction to the injured State, an NCP hopes that the spotlight put on the non-complying State will force it change its behaviour. Closely related to the practice of 'naming and shaming' used in relation to human rights violations,[132] the rationale relies on the premise that the international community (including public opinion), united around shared values, can force a State to adhere to certain norms. One typical example of the 'bad publicity' brought by a declaration of non-compliance can be found in the work undertaken by the World Heritage Committee under the UNESCO Convention for the Protection of the World Cultural and Natural Heritage. The committee has the power to inscribe properties on the List of World Heritage in danger (i.e. properties for which the obligation of protection has not been respected) in order to raise awareness of the international community regarding the degradation of a site. States in which these sites lay often object strongly to their inscription on the list and generally take rapid measures to ensure that their heritage site is removed from a list that tarnishes the public image of the country.[133] The declaration of non-compliance is therefore an instrument commonly found in the curative realm that has been re-invented under the preventive rationale, with a stronger focus put on the non-compliant State instead of the injured State.

Compliance mechanisms also sometimes have the power to take more 'extreme' sanctions,[134] as a last-resort response to repeat non-compliance. While this is a rare scenario, it is the closest the principle of prevention gets to the traditional curative rationale. However, again, the instruments of the curative approach are brought under the preventive umbrella and are tweaked to fit better its anticipatory rationale. These sanctions suspend or limit the rights and

party requests to be notified, the United Kingdom should 'suspend works related to the proposed activity until the transboundary EIA procedure is finalized'.

132 EM Hafner-Burton, 'Sticks and Stones: Naming and Shaming the Human Rights Enforcement Problem' (2008) 62 *International Organization* 689.

133 N Affolder, 'Mining and the World Heritage Convention: Democratic Legitimacy and Treaty Compliance' (2007) 24 *Pace Environmental Law Review* 35, especially at 55.

134 CITES, Decision 14.3, paras 29 and 30; Montreal Protocol, Decision UNEP/OzL.Pro.4/15 (1992), Annex V, para c; Kyoto Protocol, Decision 27/CMP.1, enforcement branch, section XV.5; Aarhus Convention, Decision I/7, para 37(g) (by the meeting of the parties); Health and Water Protocol, Decision I/2, para 35(f).

privileges of the non-compliant State under a multilateral environmental treaty. These generally take the form of trade sanctions, driven by the fact if the economic interests of a State are hurt as a result of its non-compliance, the State will be incentivized to comply with its environmental obligations. In a way, it reproduces the reparation approach in the case of wrongful acts, which also uses economic loss as a means of sanction for the violation of an obligation, but pushes this strategy further as the economic impact of sanctions under a non-compliance mechanism is potentially higher than the economic burden of reparation for a wrongful act. As it turns out, these economic sanctions are very successful in forcing States back into compliance and undeniably have a strong deterrent effect.

The most successful example of a treaty using trade measures to force a State back into compliance is found in the Convention on International Trade in Endangered Species of Wild Fauna and Flora (CITES).[135] Under CITES, the conference of the parties has the power to recommend the suspension of commercial or all trade in specimens of one or more CITES-listed species when the party is persistently in non-compliance and shows no intention to achieve compliance.[136] This prerogative is being used extensively,[137] and the effects of the sanctions have been widely successful, often bringing the party quickly back into compliance. Indeed, sanctions can suspend trade only in relation to one CITES-listed species, which can have limited economic effects, but, most importantly, can also be country specific, excluding a non-complying State from legitimate international trade in some 30,000 species of commercially tradable wildlife and wildlife products.[138] While participation in the sanctions are not mandatory for the other parties because CITES suspensions are recommendations, the involvement of key players is often sufficient to exercise enough pressure on the non-complying State: sanctions, or even the mere threat thereof, have been said to produce 'near-instant compliance' by targeted countries.[139]

Similarly, the Kyoto Protocol can also sanction non-compliance with trade measures,[140] in particular, by declaring a non-complying party ineligible to

135 Convention on International Trade in Endangered Species of Wild Fauna and Flora, Washington, DC, 3 March 1973, in force 1 July 1975, 993 UNTS 243.

136 CITES, Decision 14.3, para 30.

137 The current list of trade suspensions is available at www.cites.org/eng/resources/ref/suspend.php (last accessed 14 August 2017).

138 PH Sand, 'Enforcing CITES: The Rise and Fall of Trade Sanctions' (2013) 22 *Review of European, Comparative & International Environmental Law* 251, at 263. See also R Reeve, 'Wildlife Trade, Sanctions and Compliance: Lessons from the CITES Regime' (2006) 82 *International Affairs* 881.

139 PH Sand, 'Enforcing CITES', 254.

140 Kyoto Protocol, Decision 27/CMP.1, enforcement branch, section XV, para 5.

participate in the market mechanisms set up by the protocol under Articles 6, 12 and 17.[141] The potential economic loss from these sanctions can be important and was arguably a factor in Canada's decision to withdraw from the Kyoto Protocol in 2008. Practice has shown that States return to compliance very quickly after such sanctions have been decided.[142] While the logic underpinning these sanctions is very close to the punitive rationale found in the law of State responsibility, they cannot be said to be purely curative. Indeed, they ultimately do not seek to repair the damage but rather force the State back into compliance. In effect, sanctions against non-compliance are indicative of the redrawn boundary between prevention and reparation. They are representative of the extent to which the principle of prevention has spread, leading to situations in which mechanisms that would normally fall under a curative perspective are brought under its scope.

11.4 CONCLUSION

As curative approaches are making a 'comeback' in the field of international environmental law, the frontiers of prevention are being redrawn. Undoubtedly, the 'prevention is better than cure' motto remains relevant, as reparation cannot be the ultimate approach to environmental protection. At the same time, given the continuing degradation of our planet, it has become clear that the principle of prevention cannot regulate environmental harm on its own. The law of State responsibility therefore has an important role to play to ensure that violations of the obligation of prevention are prosecuted. Despite inherent divergences between prevention and reparation, the two rationales tend to operate in a complementary manner. The exact boundaries between prevention and reparation are difficult to ascertain as they are becoming increasingly blurred. In particular, the multiplication of compliance control mechanisms is evidence of the extension of the preventive rationale in the curative realm, which leads to the redesign of the prevention/reparation boundary.

141 Kyoto Protocol, Decision 27/CMP.1, section XV, para 4.

142 There have been until now six cases in which a party has been found in non-compliance and declared ineligible to participate in the market mechanisms of the Protocol (under para c). In each case the party has rapidly returned to compliance, generally within one year. Greece, CC 2007/1/Greece/EB; Croatia, CC-2009–1-8/Croatia/EB; Bulgaria, CC-2010–1-8/Bulgaria/EB; Romania, CC-2011–1-8/Romania/EB; Ukraine, CC-2011–2-9/Ukraine/EB; Lithuania, CC-2011–3-8/Lithuania/EB; Slovakia, CC-2012–1-9/Slovakia/EB.

CONCLUSION TO PART IV

REVISITING THE CURATIVE RATIONALE

Part IV built on the initial finding of this study, that is, that the prevention principle emerged partly in opposition to the reparation approach. While the affirmation remains true, Chapter 11 has shown that as prevention has evolved, so has its relationship with the curative rationale. However, prevention, in its anticipatory approach and non-bilateralizable concerns, challenges the traditional dogma of international law. As Tractman put it, the Westphalian paradigm is today unable to explain the international legal system in its current form and does not provide the tools necessary to solve present problems.[1] In this context, the concept of 'responsibility', understood in its restrictive meaning found in the law of State responsibility, is ill suited to respond to the specificity of prevention. It fails to fully take into consideration the other participants of the international legal order, including international organizations and corporations, which play a major role in the protection or degradation of the environment. Alternative responses therefore have emerged, including the term 'accountability', which underlines how the international community increasingly expects corporations to follow a preventive approach despite inherent legal difficulties relative to making them direct duty holders. Similarly, 'responsibility' cannot be understood in a purely ex post perspective: prevention endows States with an 'active responsibility',[2] one that requires them to act proactively as trustees of the environment[3] and that relegates the law of State responsibility for wrongful

[1] J Tractman, 'The Crisis of International Law' (2011) 44(1) *Case Western Reserve Journal of International Law* 407, at 408.

[2] W Werner, 'Responding to the Undesired: State Responsibility, Risk Management and Precaution' (2005) 36 *Netherlands Yearbook of International Law* 57, at 68.

[3] *Maritime Delimitation in the Area between Greenland and Jan Mayen (Denmark v. Norway)* (1993) ICJ Rep 38, separate opinion of Judge Weeremantry, para 24, on the 'standard of due diligence expected of a trustee' protecting Earth resources.

acts as a last-resort option. Non-compliance mechanisms are therefore best equipped to deal with breaches in preventive obligations in a context of 'softer responsibility'[4] that sees sanctions not as a means of punishment[5] but as an incentive for compliance. In sum, prevention calls for a renewed understanding of the classical concepts of international law in order to ensure that the traditional structure of the legal order does not limit its implementation and enforcement.

[4] A Kiss, 'Present Limits to the Enforcement of State Responsibility for Environmental Damage', in F Francioni and T Scovazzi (eds), *International Responsibility for Environmental Harm* (Graham & Trotman 1991) 12; J-M Sorel, 'The Concept of "Soft Responsibility"?', in J Crawford, A Pellet and S Olleson (eds), *The Law of International Responsibility* (Oxford University Press 2010) 165–71.

[5] NCPs can be seen as an alternative to what Prosper Weil called the 'diabolical obligation/sanction couple'. P Weil, 'Le droit international en quête de son identité: cours général de droit international public' (1992) 237 *Collected Courses of the Hague Academy of International Law* 9–370, at 53.

Conclusion

This study has offered a dynamic vision of the ultimate norm that drives international law in the field of environmental protection. It insisted on the trajectory of the prevention principle in response to ecological crises, societal demands, political progress and setbacks. It sought to clarify the specific legal content of the prevention principle while, at the same time, placing it in its wider legal context. It did so by looking at the dialectic between reparation and prevention, from which the specificity of the principle of prevention could best be extracted because it emerged as a specialized response constructed in opposition to the general curative approach that international law adopts to harm. By contrasting prevention to reparation, the analysis culminated in the identification of three traits that define prevention: (1) its anticipatory rationale, (2) its due diligence content, and (3) its wide spatial scope protecting the environment as a whole. At the same time, and although prevention has developed in clear opposition to reparation, the complexity of the reparation/prevention dialectic was brought to light: in particular, an analysis of current trends showed that the two logics are progressively becoming complementary but also that the boundaries between the two are increasingly blurred, as best evidenced in the context of compliance control mechanisms.

FUTURE CHALLENGES FOR PREVENTION

The analysis offered by this study, concentrating on the evolution of the preventive norm, would not be complete without finishing on the three major challenges that lie ahead for prevention. The first challenge is one of specificity. The broad formulation of the prevention principle under customary international law still leaves significant doubts and uncertainties regarding its implementation. In addition, prevention depends on the large margin of manoeuvring left to the adjudicator in deciding whether the degree of diligence required has been met or not. Prevention is a salient example of the 'extreme elasticity and generality'[1] that characterize environmental norms. While such flexibility is essential to make sure that prevention responds best to a variety of circumstances, it also lends its way to criticisms that prevention is a vague norm without concrete legal effects. And, surely, in light of the ever-increasing environmental degradation that our planet is facing, the role of prevention could appear minimal, if at all useful. However, the preventive rationale remains a driving force internationally by guiding environmental negotiations and locally by shaping decisions relating to projects that might have negative impacts on the environment. The normative flexibility of the prevention principle ensures that it plays different roles in the protection of the environment. In addition, the normative impacts of prevention are constantly evolving, in particular, as its customary base broadens and as the wealth of international conventional norms is used for interpretation purposes.

The second challenge relates to the international legal system within which prevention operates and, more specifically, the extent to which a system initially designed to protect sovereignties is able to integrate a-territorial considerations. This study put in evidence how different dynamics coexist within international law related to its traditional objectives to facilitate inter-State relations and more progressive aspirations to protect international values. As a result, prevention does not necessarily follow a linear progression (i.e. from a traditional concept of no-harm to an advanced norm of environmental protection) but rather evolves concomitantly, sometimes in symbiosis, other times in conflict, with more basic norms. Prevention is recognized as an anticipatory principle of due diligence to protect the environment, but some of its definitional traits disrupt the international legal framework, which means that they have not yet deployed their full legal effects. As a result, their 'fuller implications ... have yet to be woven into the fabric of international law'.[2] This study highlighted a general discrepancy between the aspirations of international law to protect the Earth, 'our home',[3] and its traditional structure, relying on core concepts such as State responsibility and reparation that make

[1] *Pulp Mills on the River Uruguay (Argentina v. Uruguay)* (Judgment) (2010) ICJ Rep 14, joint dissenting opinion by Judges Al-Khasawneh and Simma, para 26.

[2] *Maritime Delimitation in the Area between Greenland and Jan Mayen (Denmark v. Norway)* (1993) ICJ Rep 38, separate opinion of Judge Weeremantry, para 240 (in relation to environmental principles).

[3] Rio de Janeiro Declaration on Environment and Development (Rio de Janeiro, 3 to 14 June 1992), (1992) 31 ILM 876. See also P-M Dupuy, 'The Philosophy of the Rio Declaration', in JE Viñuales (ed), *The Rio Declaration on Environment and Development: A Commentary* (Oxford University Press 2015) 65–75.

their concretization more difficult. The ability to think outside the 'Westphalian box' by relying on innovative techniques such as non-compliance procedures is instrumental to ensuring that prevention can fully express its legal effects.

The final challenge relates to the distributive objectives of international environmental law and how prevention fits in the balancing act that international environmental law constantly maintains between different interests and stakeholders. Finding an equilibrium between environmental and economic objectives is a difficult task that often results in detrimental consequences for prevention. Additionally, opening prevention to intra- and inter-generational considerations is necessary to guarantee the effectiveness of international environmental law but meets significant legal and policy hurdles. It also carries with it the risk that other norms might prevail over prevention, thereby diluting the preventive objective. For each of the three challenges, the role of international courts and tribunals in assessing how the principle of prevention plays out under specific circumstances will be central to consolidating, and clarifying, the legal effects of its most advanced traits.

PREVENTION BEYOND INTERNATIONAL ENVIRONMENTAL LAW

This study concludes with a final few words on prevention beyond international environmental law. Prevention not only plays a fundamental role in relation to the avoidance of harm in the context of environmental protection but also applies in a multiplicity of other contexts, including in relation to genocide,[4] terrorism[5] and cybercrime.[6] Yet, considerable disagreements exist regarding whether preventive norms are based on common denominators[7] and, as a result, whether prevention should be considered to be a general

[4] See e.g. E Ruvebana and M Brus, 'Before It's Too Late: Preventing Genocide by Holding the Territorial State Responsible for Not Taking Preventive Action' (2015) 62 *Netherlands International Law Review* 25; R Reike, S Sharma and J Welsh, 'Conceptualizing the Responsibility to Prevent', in S Sharma and J Welsh, *The Responsibility to Prevent: Overcoming the Challenges of Atrocity Prevention* (Oxford University Press 2015) 20–37.

[5] P-M Dupuy and C Hoss, '*Trail Smelter* and Terrorism: International Mechanisms to Combat Transboundary Harm', in R Bratspies and R Miller (eds), *Transboundary Harm in International Law: Lessons from the 'Trail Smelter' Arbitration* (Cambridge University Press 2006) 225–40.

[6] See E Jensen, 'State Obligations in Cyber Operations' (2014) 14 *Baltic Yearbook of International Law* 71.

[7] This is further complicated by the fact that even within a branch of international law, such as environmental law, but also human rights, it is uncertain whether the duty to prevent is a single or plural obligation. See E Decaux and S Touzé, *La prévention des violations des droits de l'homme. Actes du colloque des 13 et 14 juin 2013* (Pedone 2015) 12.

principle of international law.[8] Overall, a diffuse feeling exists in the scholarship that preventive obligations tend to be understudied and neglected.[9] In this context, there is a need to further clarify how preventive norms operate and to understand the extent to which they share common grounds. The cartography offered in this study can serve as a preliminary analytical framework: while it sought to bring the specificity of prevention in international environmental law into light, it could also contribute, more generally, to clarifying the rationale, content and scope of other preventive norms. The first trait is necessarily a core element of any obligation to prevent, with anticipation defining the *ratio legis* of preventive duties. The second trait will apply principally to obligations to prevent of a due-diligence character: it opens the door to further investigate the level of care required from a State in the face of risks, building on recent inquiries into whether there is a common standard of due diligence applicable across different branches.[10] The final trait, relative to the spatial scope of prevention, is specifically linked to the objective of environmental protection and might not be replicable per se. Yet, it brings to light the fact that preventive duties operate beyond a territorial anchorage to regulate transnational threats and represent the aspirations of international law to protect common universal values. Overall, it is hoped that this study not only offers a perspective on the main principle driving international environmental law but also is read as a contribution to advance the understanding of prevention under general international law.

8 See e.g. ILC, 'Summary Record of the 3178th Meeting', (2013) UN Doc. A/CN.4/SR.3178, where ILC member Murphy considers that to suggest that prevention is a general principle of international law is an 'unduly broad assertion'.

9 C Strohal, 'La prévention: orpheline du système international? L'exemple des droits de l'homme', in Decaux and Touzé, *La prévention des violations des droits de l'homme*, 221–28, noting that prevention tends to be neglected in the scholarship; I Renzulli, 'A Critical Reflection on the Conceptual and Legal Foundations of the Duty to Prevent Torture' (2016) 20(8) *International Journal of Human Rights* 1244, on how the duty to prevent torture has been under-conceptualized.

10 ILA, Study Group on Due Diligence in International Law, 'Due Diligence in International Law: First Report', Washington, DC, 76th Session, 2014.

Select Bibliography

BOOKS

Akhtarkhavari A, *Global Governance of the Environment: Environmental Principles and Change in International Law and Politics* (Edward Elgar 2010)

Alam S et al., (ed), *Routledge Handbook of International Environmental Law* (Routledge 2013)

Anderson M and Galizzi P (eds), *International Environmental Law in National Courts* (British Institute of International and Comparative Law 2002)

Andrassy J, 'Les relations internationales de voisinage' (1951) 79 *Collected Courses of the Hague Academy of International Law* 73–182

Arbour J-M and Lavallée S, *Droit international de l'environnement* (Bruylant 2006)

Atapattu S, *Emerging Principles of International Environmental Law* (Transnational Publishers 2006)

Aydinli E and Rosenau J, *Globalization, Security, and the Nation State: Paradigms in Transition* (State University of New York Press 2005)

Badie B, *La fin des territoires* (Fayard 1995)

Barboza J, 'International Liability for the Injurious Consequences of Acts Not Prohibited by International Law and Protection of the Environment' (1994) 247 *Collected Courses of the Hague Academy of International Law* 291–406

The Environment, Risk and Liability in International Law (Martinus Nijhoff 2011)

Barral V, *Le développement durable en droit international: Essai sur les incidences juridiques d'une norme évolutive* (Bruylant 2016)

Baxter R, 'Treaties and Custom' (1970) *Collected Courses of the Hague Academy of International Law* 25–104

Beyerlin U and Marauhn T, *International Environmental Law* (Hart 2011)

Birnie P, Boyle A and Redgwell C, *International Law and the Environment* (3rd edn, Oxford University Press 2009)

Bjorge E, *The Evolutionary Interpretation of Treaties* (Oxford University Press 2014)

Bodansky D, *The Art and Craft of International Environmental Law* (Harvard University Press 2010)

Bodansky D, Brunnée J and Hey E (eds), *The Oxford Handbook of International Environmental Law* (Oxford University Press 2007)

Boisson de Chazournes L, Leb C and Tignino M (eds), *International Law and Freshwater: The Multiple Challenges* (Edward Elgar 2013)
Bonnel G, 'Le principe juridique écrit et le droit de l'environnement', PhD dissertation, Université de Limoges 2005
Borges LE, *Les obligations de prévention dans le droit international de l'environnement et ses conséquences dans la responsabilité internationale des Etats* (L'Harmattan 2016)
Bowman M and Boyle A (eds), *Environmental Damage in International and Comparative Law: Problems of Definition and Valuation* (Oxford University Press 2002)
Boyle A and Freestone D (eds), *International Law and Sustainable Development: Past Achievements and Future Challenges* (Oxford University Press 1999)
Brans E, *Liability for Damage to Public Natural Resources: Standing, Damage and Damage Assessment* (Kluwer Law International 2001)
Bratspies R and Miller R (eds), *Transboundary Harm in International Law: Lessons from the 'Trail Smelter' Arbitration* (Cambridge University Press 2006)
Brown Weiss E, *In Fairness to Future Generations: International Law, Common Patrimony, and Intergenerational Equity* (Transnational Publishers 1989)
Brownlie I, 'Legal Status of Natural Resources in International Law (Some Aspects)' (1979) 162 *Collected Courses of the Hague Academy of International Law* 245–318
Bungenberg M and Hobe S (eds), *Permanent Sovereignty over Natural Resources* (Springer 2015)
Byers M (ed), *The Role of Law in International Politics: Essays in International Relations and International Law* (Oxford University Press 2000)
Caballero F, *Essai sur la notion juridique de nuisance* (Librairie générale de droit et de jurisprudence 1981)
Caflisch L, 'Règles générales du droit des cours d'eau internationaux' (1989) 219 *Collected Courses of the Hague Academy of International Law* 9–226
Caldwell L, *International Environmental Policy: Emergence and Dimensions* (2nd edn, Duke University Press 1990)
International Environmental Policy: From the Twentieth to the Twenty-First Century (3rd edn, Duke University Press 1996)
Cans C and Abrassart E (eds), *La responsabilité environnementale: prévention, imputation, réparation* (Dalloz 2009)
Caron D and Leben C (eds), *The International Aspects of Natural and Industrial Catastrophes* (Martinus Nijhoff 2001)
Cassese A, *International Law* (2nd edn, Oxford University Press 2004)
Chayes A and Chayes AH (eds), *The New Sovereignty: Compliance with International Regulatory Agreements* (Harvard University Press 1995)
Cheng B, *General Principles of Law as Applied by International Courts and Tribunals* (Stevens and Sons 1953)
Cordini G and Postiglione A (eds), *Prevention and Remedying of Environmental Damage: Proceedings of the Workshop on Environmental Law, Ostia Antica, 27 and 28 May 2005* (Bruylant 2005)
Craik N, *The International Law of Environmental Impact Assessment: Process, Substance and Integration* (Cambridge University Press 2008)

Crawford J, 'Multilateral Rights and Obligations in International Law' (2006) 319 *Collected Courses of the Hague Academy of International Law* 325–482
Brownlie's Principles of Public International Law (8th edn, Oxford University Press 2012)
State Responsibility: The General Part (Cambridge University Press 2013)
Crawford J, Pellet A and Olleson S (eds), *The Law of International Responsibility* (Oxford University Press 2010)
Cullet P, *Differential Treatment in International Environmental Law* (Ashgate 2003)
Davies P, Redgwell C and Bowman M, *Lyster's International Wildlife Law* (2nd edn, Cambridge University Press 2010)
Decaux E and Touzé S, *La prévention des violations des droits de l'homme. Actes du colloque des 13 et 14 juin 2013* (Pedone 2015)
De Sadeleer N, *Les principes du pollueur-payeur, de prévention et de précaution: Essai sur la genèse et la portée juridique de quelques principes du droit de l'environnement* (Bruylant 1999)
Environmental Principles: From Political Slogans to Legal Rules (Oxford University Press 2002)
Dinstein Y, 'The Interaction between Customary International Law and Treaties' (2007) *Collected Courses of the Hague Academy of International Law* 259–407
Di Turi C, 'Responsabilité pour risque et due diligence en droit de l'environnement', PhD dissertation, Graduate Institute of International and Development Studies 1991
Dupuy P-M, *La Responsabilité internationale des Etats pour les dommages d'origine technologique et industrielle* (Pedone 1977)
'L'unité de l'ordre juridique international. Cours général de droit international public' (2002) *Collected Courses of the Hague Academy of International Law* 9–496
Dupuy P-M and Viñuales JE (eds), *Harnessing Foreign Investment to Promote Environmental Protection: Incentives and Safeguards* (Cambridge University Press 2013)
International Environmental Law (Cambridge University Press 2015)
Dworkin R, *Taking Rights Seriously* (Duckworth 1977)
Ebbesson J and Okowa P (eds), *Environmental Law and Justice in Context* (Cambridge University Press 2009)
Elian G, 'Le principe de la souveraineté sur les ressources nationales et ses incidences juridiques sur le commerce international' (1976) 149 *Collected Courses of the Hague Academy of International Law* 1–85
The Principle of Sovereignty Over Natural Resources (Martinus Nijhoff 1979)
Fassbender B and Peters A, *The Oxford Handbook of the History of International Law* (Oxford University Press 2012)
Fisher E (ed), *Implementing the Precautionary Principle: Perspectives and Prospects* (Edward Elgar 2006)
Risk Regulation and Administrative Constitutionalism (Hart 2010)
Fisher E, Lange B and Scotford E, *Environmental Law: Text, Cases, and Materials* (Oxford University Press 2013)

Fitzmaurice G, 'The General Principles of International Considered from the Standpoint of the Rule of Law' (1957) 92 *Collected Courses of the Hague Academy of International Law* 1–228

Fitzmaurice M, 'International Protection of the Environment' (2001) 293 *Collected Courses of the Hague Academy of International Law* 9–488

Fitzmaurice M et al. (eds), *Research Handbook on International Environmental Law* (Edward Elgar 2010)

Foster C, *Science and the Precautionary Principle in International Courts and Tribunals: Expert Evidence, Burden of Proof and Finality* (Cambridge University Press 2011)

Francioni F and Scovazzi T (eds), *International Responsibility for Environmental Harm* (Graham & Trotman 1991)

Freestone D and Hey E (eds), *The Precautionary Principle and International Law: The Challenge of Implementation* (Kluwer Law International 1996)

Friedmann W, *The Changing Structure of International Law* (Stevens & Sons 1964)

Fuller LL, *The Morality of Law* (5th edn, Universal Law Publishing 2009)

Grinevald J, *La biosphère de l'anthropocène: climat et pétrole, la double menace. Repères transdisciplinaires (1824–2007)* (Georg 2007)

Guéhenno M, *The End of the Nation-State* (University of Minnesota Press 2000)

Handl G, Zekoll J and Zumbansen P, *Beyond Territoriality: Transnational Legal Authority in an Age of Globalization* (Martinus Nijhoff 2012)

Hardman Reis T, *Compensation for Environmental Damages under International Law: The Role of the International Judge* (Kluwer Law International 2011)

Haritz M, *An Inconvenient Deliberation: The Precautionary Principle's Contribution to the Uncertainties Surrounding Climate Change Liability* (Kluwer Law International 2011)

Hart H, *The Concept of Law* (3rd edn, Oxford University Press, 2012)

Henckaerts J-M and Doswald-Beck L, *Customary International Humanitarian Law: Rules* (vol I, Cambridge University Press, 2005)

Hey E, *Advanced Introduction to International Environmental Law* (Edward Elgar 2016)

Higgins R, *Problems and Process: International and How We Use It* (Oxford University Press 1993)

Hinteregger M (ed), *Environmental Liability and Ecological Damage in European Law* (Cambridge University Press 2008)

Holdgate M, *A Perspective of Environmental Pollution* (Cambridge University Press 1979)

Hunter D, Salzman J and Zaelke D, *International Environmental Law and Policy* (4th edn, Foundation Press, Thomson/West 2011)

Jayakumar S, Koh T et al. (eds), *Transboundary Pollution: Evolving Issues of International Law and Policy* (Edward Elgar 2015)

Jenks CW, 'Liability for Ultra-hazardous Activities in International Law' (1966) 117 *Collected Courses of the Hague Academy of International Law* 99–200

Jessup B and Rubenstein K (eds), *Environmental Discourses in Public and International Law* (Cambridge University Press 2012)

Karavias M, *Corporate Obligations under International Law* (Oxford University Press 2013)

Kerbrat Y and Maljean-Dubois S (eds), *The Transformation of International Environmental Law* (Hart 2011)

Kiss A, *L'abus de droit en droit international* (Librairie générale de droit et de jurisprudence 1953)

(ed), *La protection de l'environnement et le droit international: Colloque de l'Académie du droit de La Haye* (Martinus Nijhoff 1975)

Kiss A and Shelton D, *Guide to International Environmental Law* (Martinus Nijhoff 2007)

Kläger R, *'Fair and Equitable Treatment' in International Investment Law* (Cambridge University Press 2011)

Koivurova T, *Introduction to International Environmental Law* (Routledge 2014)

Koskenniemi M, *International Pollution in the System of International Law* (Suomalainen Lakimiesyhdistys 1984)

Kotuby, ChT and Sobota LA, *General Principles of Law and International Due Process: Principles and Norms Applicable in Transnational Disputes* (Oxford University Press 2017)

Kulesza J, *Due Diligence in International Law* (Brill/Martinus Nijhoff 2016)

Kummer K, *International Management of Hazardous Wastes: The Basel Convention and Related Legal Rules* (Oxford University Press 1995)

Kuokkanen T, *International Law and the Environment: Variations on a Theme* (Kluwer Law International 2002)

Lammers J, *Pollution of International Watercourses: A Search for Substantive Rules and Principles of Law* (Martinus Nijhoff 1984)

Lang W (ed), *Sustainable Development and International Law* (Graham & Trotman, Martinus Nijhoff 1995)

Langer MJ, 'Sovereignty in Trust: Territorial Sovereignty at the Crossroads in International Environmental Law', PhD dissertation, Graduate Institute of International and Development Studies 2016

Larsson M-L, *The Law of Environmental Damage: Liability and Reparation* (Martinus Nijhoff 1999)

Lauterpacht H, *The Function of Law in the International Community* (Clarendon Press 1933)

Leb C, *Cooperation in the Law of Transboundary Water Resources* (Cambridge University Press 2013)

Lefeber RJM, *Transboundary Environmental Interference and the Origin of State Liability* (Kluwer Law International 1996)

Louka E, *International Environmental Law: Fairness, Effectiveness, and World Order* (Cambridge University Press 2006)

Lyster S, *International Wildlife Law: An Analysis of International Treaties Concerned with the Conservation of Wildlife* (Grotius 1985)

MacCormick N, *Rhetoric and the Rule of Law: A Theory of Legal Reasoning* (Oxford University Press 2005)

Macrory R (ed), *Reflections on 30 Years of EU Environmental Law: A High Level of Protections?* (Europa Law Publishing 2006)

Macrory R and Havercroft I (eds), *Principles of European Environmental Law* (Europa Law Publishing 2004)

Maljean-Dubois S and Rajamani L, *La mise en oeuvre du droit de l'environnement: Implementation of International Environmental Law* (Martinus Nijhoff 2011)
Mbengue MM, *Essai sur une théorie du risque en droit international public: l'anticipation du risque environnemental et sanitaire* (Pedone 2009)
McCaffrey SC, *The Law of International Watercourses* (2nd edn, Oxford University Press 2007)
McIntyre O, *Environmental Protection of International Watercourses under International Law* (Ashgate 2007)
Milanovic M, *Extraterritorial Application of Human Rights Treaties. Law, Principles and Policy* (Oxford University Press 2011)
Minnerop P, Langenfeld C and Wolfrum R (eds), *Environmental Liability in International Law: Towards a Coherent Conception* (Schmidt 2005)
Moeckli D et al. (eds), *International Human Rights Law* (Oxford University Press 2014)
Morgera E, *Corporate Accountability in International Environmental Law* (Oxford University Press 2009)
Morin J-F and Orsini A (eds), *Essential Concepts of Global Environmental Governance* (Routledge 2014)
Morrison F and Wolfrum R, *International, Regional and National Environmental Law* (Kluwer Law International 2000)
Nijman J and Nollkaemper A (eds), *New Perspectives on the Divide between National and International Law* (Oxford University Press 2007)
Nollkaemper A, *The Legal Regime for Transboundary Water Pollution: Between Discretion and Constraint* (Martinus Nijhoff/Graham & Trotman 1993)
Nollkaemper A and Plakokefalos I (eds), *Principles of Shared Responsibility in International Law: An Appraisal of the State of the Art* (Cambridge University Press 2014)
Nordquist M (ed), *United Nations Convention on the Law of the Sea 1982: A Commentary* (Martinus Nijhoff 1985)
Okowa P, *State Responsibility for Transboundary Air Pollution in International Law* (Oxford University Press 2000)
Osborn F, *Our Plundered Planet* (Little, Brown 1948)
Ost F and Gutwirth S (eds), *Quel avenir pour le droit de l'environnement?* (Publications des Facultés universitaires Saint-Louis 1996)
Ouedraogo A, 'La diligence en droit international: contribution à l'étude d'une notion au contour imprécis', PhD dissertation, Graduate Institute of International and Development Studies 2011
Payne C and Sand P (eds), *Gulf War Reparations and the UN Compensation Commission: Environmental Liability* (Oxford University Press 2011)
Peel J, *Science and Risk Regulation in International Law* (Cambridge University Press 2010)
Perrez FX, *Cooperative Sovereignty: From Independence to Interdependence in the Structure of International Environmental Law* (Kluwer Law International 2000)
Pisillo Mazzeschi R, *Due Diligence e responsabilità internazionale degli Stati* (Giuffré 1989)
Politis NS, 'Le problème des limitations de la souveraineté et la théorie de l'abus des droits dans les rapports internationaux' (1925) 5 *Collected Courses of the Hague Academy of International Law* 1–122

Pop I, *Voisinage et bon voisinage en droit international* (Pedone 1980)
Ragazzi M, *The Concept of International Obligations Erga Omnes* (Oxford University Press 1997)
Rajamani L, *Differential Treatment in International Environmental Law* (Oxford University Press 2006)
Rao PK, *Climate Change Loss and Damage: Economic and Legal Foundations* (Springer-Verlag 2013)
Redgwell C, *Intergenerational Trusts and Environmental Protection* (Manchester University Press 1999)
Robb C and Palmer A (eds), *International Environmental Law in National Courts* (vol 4, Cambridge University Press 2004)
Rosenberg D, *Le principe de souveraineté des États sur leurs ressources naturelles* (Librairie générale de droit et de jurisprudence 1983)
Rosenne S, *Provisional Measures in International Law: The International Court of Justice and the International Tribunal for the Law of the Sea* (Oxford University Press 2005)
Roujou de Boubée M-E, *Essai sur la notion de réparation* (Librairie générale de droit et de jurisprudence 1974)
Sands P and Peel J, *Principles of International Environmental Law* (3rd edn, Cambridge University Press 2012)
Saunier R and Meganck R, *Dictionary and Introduction to Global Environmental Governance* (Earthscan 2009)
Schachter O, *Sharing the World's Resources* (Columbia University Press 1977)
International Law in Theory and Practice (Martinus Nijhoff 1991)
Schrijver N, *Sovereignty over Natural Resources: Balancing Rights and Duties* (Cambridge University Press 1997)
'The Evolution of Sustainable Development in International Law: Inception, Meaning and Status' (2008) 329 *Collected Courses of the Hague Academy of International Law* 215–370
Scotford E, *Environmental Principles and the Evolution of Environmental Law* (Bloomsbury 2017)
Sette-Camara J, 'Pollution of International Rivers' (1984) 186 *Collected Courses of the Hague Academy of International Law* 117–217
Seymour M, *Fate of the Nation State* (McGill-Queen's University Press 2004)
Sharma S and Welsh J, *The Responsibility to Prevent: Overcoming the Challenges of Atrocity Prevention* (Oxford University Press 2015)
Sheridan M and Lavrysen L (eds), *Environmental Law Principles in Practice* (Bruylant 2002)
Simma B, 'From Bilateralism to Community Interest in International Law' (1994) 250 *Collected Courses of the Hague Academy of International Law* 217–384
Smith B, *State Responsibility and the Marine Environment: The Rules of Decision* (Clarendon Press 1988)
Stephens T, *International Courts and Environmental Protection* (Cambridge University Press 2009)
Sunstein C, *Laws of Fear: Beyond the Precautionary Principle* (Cambridge University Press 2005)

Tams CJ, *Enforcing Obligations Erga Omnes in International Law* (Cambridge University Press 2010)
Tanaka Y, *The International Law of the Sea* (2nd edn, Cambridge University Press 2015)
Tanzi A and Arcari M, *The United Nations Convention on the Law of International Watercourses: A Framework for Sharing* (Kluwer Law International 2001)
Tanzi A et al., *The UNECE Convention on the Protection and Use of Transboundary Watercourses and International Lakes: Its Contribution to International Water Cooperation* (Brill/Martinus Nijhoff 2015)
Thirlway H, *The Sources of International Law* (Oxford University Press 2014)
Trachtman J, *The Future of International Law* (Cambridge University Press 2013)
Treves T et al. (eds), *Non-Compliance Procedures and Mechanisms and the Effectiveness of International Environmental Agreements* (Asser Press 2009)
Trouwborst A, *Evolution and Status of the Precautionary Principle in International Law* (Kluwer Law International 2002)
Tudor I, *The Fair and Equitable Treatment Standard in the International Law of Foreign Investment* (Oxford University Press 2008)
Urbinati S, *Les mécanismes de contrôle et de suivi des conventions internationales de protection de l'environnement* (Giuffrè 2009)
Veillard I, 'Prévenir les nouveaux risques: essai d'une approche globale pour la protection des personnes et de l'environnement', PhD dissertation (Université Paris I Panthéon-Sorbonne 2010)
Verheyen R, *Climate Change Damage and International Law: Prevention Duties and State Responsibility* (Martinus Nijhoff 2005)
Verschuuren J, *Principles of Environmental Law: The Ideal of Sustainable Development and the Role of Principles of International, European, and National Environmental Law* (Nomos 2003)
Victor DG, Raustiala K and Skolnikoff E (eds), *The Implementation and Effectiveness of International Environmental Commitments: Theory and Practice* (MIT Press 1998)
Viñuales JE, *Foreign Investment and the Environment in International Law* (Cambridge University Press 2012)
(ed), *The Rio Declaration on Environment and Development: A Commentary* (Oxford University Press 2015)
Weil P, 'Le droit international en quête de son identité: cours général de droit international public' (1992) 237 *Collected Courses of the Hague Academy of International Law* 9–370
Wetterstein P and Rosas A (eds), *Harm to the Environment: The Right to Compensation and the Assessment of Damages* (Clarendon Press 1997)
Winiarski B, 'Principes généraux du droit fluvial international' (1933) 45 *Collected Courses of the Hague Academy of International Law* 75–218
Wirth J, *Smelter Smoke in North America: The Politics of Transborder Pollution* (University Press of Kansas 2000)
Wolfrum R, 'Means of Ensuring Compliance with and Enforcement of International Environmental Law' (1998) 272 *Collected Courses of the Hague Academy of International Law* 155–410
Xue H, *Transboundary Damage in International Law* (Cambridge University Press 2009)
Yamin F and Depledge J, *The International Climate Change Regime: A Guide to Rules, Institutions and Procedures* (Cambridge University Press 2005)

ARTICLES AND CHAPTERS

Abi-Saab G, 'La souveraineté permanente sur les ressources naturelles', in M Bedjaoui (ed), *Droit international: bilan et perspectives* (vol 2, Pedone 1991) 639–61

Affolder N, 'Mining and the World Heritage Convention: Democratic Legitimacy and Treaty Compliance' (2007) 24 *Pace Environmental Law Review* 35

Alvarez J, 'Are Corporations "Subjects of International Law"?' (2011) 9 *Santa Clara Journal of International Law*

Angelet N, 'Fair and Equitable Treatment', in *Max Planck Encyclopedia of Public International Law* (Oxford University Press 2011)

Anton D, 'Case concerning Pulp Mills on the River Uruguay (*Argentina v. Uruguay*)' (2010) 13 *Australian International Law Journal* 213

Arajärvi NJ, 'The Lines Begin to Blur? Opinio Juris and the Moralisation of Customary International Law' (2011) Available at SSRN: https://papers.ssrn.com/sol3/papers.cfm?abstract_id=1823288

Barboza J, 'La Responsabilité "causale" à la Commission du Droit International' (1988) *Annuaire français de droit international* 513

Barnidge RP, 'The Due Diligence Principle Under International Law' (2006) 8 *International Community Law Review* 81

Barral V, 'Sustainable Development in International Law: Nature and Operation of an Evolutive Legal Norm' (2012) 23 *European Journal of International Law* 377

Bassiouni MC, 'A Functional Approach to General Principles of International Law' (1989) 11 *Michigan Journal of International Law* 768

Beckett J, 'Behind Relative Normativity: Rules and Process as Prerequisites of Law' (2001) 12 *European Journal of International Law* 627

Bell M, Devra D, Fletcher T, 'A Retrospective Assessment of Mortality from the London Smog Episode of 1952: The Role of Influenza and Pollution' (2004) 112 *Environmental Health Perspectives* 6

Bendel J and Harrison J, 'Determining the Legal Nature and Content of EIAs in International Environmental Law: What Does the ICJ Decision in the Joined *Costa Rica v. Nicaragua/Nicaragua v. Costa Rica* Cases Tell Us?' (2017) 42 *Questions of International Law Zoom-in* 13

Benvenisti E, 'Legislating for Humanity: May States Compel Foreigners to Promote Global Welfare?', in R Liivoja and J Petnam (eds), *International Law-making: Essays in Honour of Jan Klabbers* (Routledge 2014) 3–16

Berwick T, 'Responsibility and Liability for Environmental Damage: A Roadmap for International Environmental Regimes' (1997) 10 *Georgetown International Environmental Law Review* 257

Biddulph M and Newman D, 'A Contextualized Account General Principles of International Law' (2014) 26 *Pace International Law Review* 286

Bodansky D, 'Scientific Uncertainty and the Precautionary Principle' (1991) 33 *Environment* 4

'Customary (and Not So Customary) International Environmental Law' (1995) 3 *Indiana Journal of Global Legal Studies* 105

'What's So Bad about Unilateral Action to Protect the Environment?' (2000) 11 *European Journal of International Law* 339

'Rules vs Standards in International Environmental Law' (2004) 98 *Proceedings of the Annual Meeting of the American Society of International Law* 275
Bogdan M, 'General Principles of Law and the Problem of Lacunae in the Law of Nations' (1977) 46 *Nordisk Tidsskrift for International Ret* 37
Boisson de Chazournes L, 'La mise en oeuvre du droit international dans le domaine de la protection de l'environnement: enjeux et défis' (1995) *Revue générale de droit international public* 37
'Unilateralism and Environmental Protection: Issues of Perception and Reality of Issues' (2000) 11 *European Journal of International Law* 315
'Precaution in International Law: Reflection on its Composite Nature' in T Ndiaye et al. (eds), *Law of the Sea, Environmental Law and Settlement of Disputes: Liber Amicorum Judge Thomas A. Mensah* (Martinus Nijhoff 2007) 21–34
'Environmental Treaties in Time' (2009) 6 *Environmental Policy and Law* 293
'The Notion of Environmental Flows and the Law Applicable to International Watercourses' (2014) 108 *Proceedings of the One Hundred Eighth Annual Meeting of the American Society of International Law* 293
Boisson de Chazournes L and Campanelli D, 'Neighbour States' in *Max Planck Encyclopedia of Public International Law* (Oxford University Press 2006)
Boisson de Chazournes L and Maljean-Dubois S, 'Principes du droit international de l'environnement' (2011) *Jurisclasseur Environnement et Développement Durable* (LexisNexis)
Boon K, 'International Organizations and the Duty to Prevent' (2013) *Opinio Juris* post, available at http://opiniojuris.org/2013/06/18/international-organizations-and-the-duty-to-prevent/
Boos-Hersberger A, 'Transboundary Water Pollution and State Responsibility: The Sandoz Spill' (2010) 4 *Annual Survey of International & Comparative Law* 113
Bordin FL 'Reflections of Customary International Law: The Authority of Codification Conventions and ILC Draft Articles in International Law' (2014) 63 *International and Comparative Law Quarterly* 535
Bourne C, 'The International Law Commission's Draft Articles on the Law of International Watercourses: Principles and Planned Measures' (1992) 3 *Colorado Journal of International Environmental Law* 176
Boyle A, 'State Responsibility and International Liability for Injurious Consequences of Acts Not Prohibited by International Law: A Necessary Distinction?' (1990) 39 *International and Comparative Law Quarterly* 1
'Human Rights and the Environment: Where Next?' (2012) 23 *European Journal of International Law* 613
Bragdon S, 'National Sovereignty and Global Environmental Responsibility: Can the Tension Be Reconciled for the Conservation of Biological Diversity?' (1992) 33 *Harvard International Law Journal* 381
Bramsen C, 'Transnational Pollution and International Law' (1972) 42 *Nordisk Tidsskrift for International Ret* 153
Braz Jardim Oliveira T, 'La diligence due dans la prévention des dommages à l'environnement' (2012) 2 *Brazilian Yearbook of International Law* 205
Bremer N, 'Post-environmental Impact Assessment Monitoring of Measures or Activities with Significant Transboundary Impact: An Assessment of Customary

International Law' (2017) 26(1) *Review of European, Comparative & International Environmental Law* 80

Brent K, 'The *Certain Activities* Case: What Implications of the No-harm Rule?' (2017) 20 *Asia Pacific Journal of Environmental Law* 28

Brown Weiss E, 'The Planetary Trust: Conservation and Intergenerational Equity' (1984) 11 *Ecology Law Quarterly* 495

'The Evolution of International Environmental Law' (2011) 54 *Japanese Yearbook of International Law* 1

Brunnée J, 'The Responsibility of States for Environmental Harm in a Multinational Context: Problems and Trends' (1993) 34 *Cahiers de droit* 827

'Of Sense and Sensibility: Reflections on International Liability Regimes as Tools for Environmental Protection' (2004) 53 *International and Comparative Law Quarterly* 351

'Sic utere tuo ut alienum non laedas', in *Max Planck Encyclopedia of Public International Law* (Oxford University Press 2010)

'International Environmental Law and Community Interests: Procedural Aspects', in E Benvenisti and G Nolte (eds), *Community Interests Across International Law* (Oxford University Press, forthcoming, available on SSRN: https://papers.ssrn.com/sol3/papers.cfm?abstract_id=2784701)

'Procedure and Substance in International Environmental Law: Confused at a Higher Level?' (2016) 5(6) *ESIL Reflections*

Byers M, 'Abuse of Rights: An Old Principle, A New Age' (2002) 47 *McGill Law Journal* 389

Caldwell L, 'Concepts in Development of International Environmental Policies' (1973) 13 *Natural Resources Journal* 190

Christie G, 'The Model of Principles' (1968) 17 *Duke Law Journal* 649

Churchill R, 'Facilitating (Transnational) Civil Liability Litigation for Environmental Damage by Means of Treaties: Progress, Problems, and Prospects' (2002) 12 *Yearbook of International Environmental Law* 3

Combacau J, 'Obligations de résultat et obligations de comportement : Quelques questions et pas de réponse', in *Mélanges offerts à Paul Reuter, Le droit international: unité et diversité* (Pedone 1981) 181–204

Coppoc W, 'The Environment: No Respecter of National Boundaries' (1978) 43 *Albany Law Review* 520

Crawford J, 'Responsibility to the International Community as a Whole' (2001) 8 *Indiana Journal of Global Legal Studies* 303

'Right of Self-determination in International Law', in P Alston (ed), *Peoples Rights* (Oxford University Press 2001) 7–67

Croxton D, 'The Peace of Westphalia of 1648 and the Origins of Sovereignty' (1999) 21 *International History Review* 569

Cullet P, 'Differential Treatment in International Law: Towards a New Paradigm of Inter-State Relations' (1999) 10 *European Journal of International Law* 549

'Liability and Redress for Human-Induced Global Warming: Towards an International Regime' (2007) 43 *Stanford Journal of International Law* 99

D'Amato A, 'Do We Owe a Duty to Future Generations to Preserve the Global Environment?' (1990) 84 *American Journal of International Law* 190

Daigle C, 'The Era of Détente', in A Kalinovsky and C Daigle (eds), *The Routledge Handbook of the Cold War* (Routledge 2014) 195–208

Daniel A, 'Civil Liability Regimes as a Complement to Multilateral Environmental Agreements: Sound International Policy or False Comfort?' (2003) 12 *Review of European Community & International Environmental Law* 225

De Brabandere E, 'Human Rights and Transnational Corporations: The Limits of Direct Corporate Responsibility' (2010) 4 *Human Rights and International Legal Discourse* 66

De Vilchez Moragues P, 'Broadening the Scope: The Urgenda Case, the Oslo Principles and the Role of National Courts in Advancing Environmental Protection concerning Climate Change' (2016) 20 *Spanish Yearbook of International Law* 71

Desierto D, 'Evidence but Not Empiricism? Environmental Impact Assessments at the International Court of Justice in *Certain Activities Carried out by Nicaragua in the Border Area (Costa Rica v. Nicaragua)* and *Construction of a Road in Costa Rica along the San Juan River (Nicaragua v. Costa Rica)*' (26 February 2016) *EJIL: Talk!* available at www.ejiltalk.org/evidence-but-not-empiricism-environmental-impact-assessments-at-the-international-court-of-justice-in-certain-activities-carried-out-by-nicaragua-in-the-border-area-costa-rica-v-nicaragua-and-con/

Dickstein HL, 'National Environmental Hazards and International Law' (1974) 23 *International and Comparative Law Quarterly* 426

Dinwoodie D, 'The Politics of International Pollution Control: The *Trail Smelter* Case' (1972) 27 *International Journal* 219

Doeker G and Gehring T, 'Private or International Liability for Transnational Environmental Damage: The Precedent of Conventional Liability Regimes' (1990) 2 *Journal of Environmental Law* 1

Dominicé C, 'Obligation de prévention et droit international de l'environnement', in P Borba Casella (ed), *Dimensão internacional do direito: estudos em homenagem a G.E. do Nascimento e Silva* (LTr 2000) 187–99

Doumbe-Bille S and Kiss A, 'Conférence des Nations Unies sur l'environnement et le développement (Rio de Janeiro-Juin 1992)' (1992) 38 *Annuaire français de droit international* 823

Dupuy P-M, 'Sur des tendances récentes dans le droit international de l'environnement' (1974) 20 *Annuaire français de droit international* 815

'Soft Law and the International Law of the Environment' (1990–91) 12 *Michigan Journal of International Law* 420

'Où en est le droit international de l'environnement à la fin du siècle ?' (1997) 28 *Revue générale de droit international public* 886

'International Law: Torn between Coexistence, Cooperation and Globalization. General Conclusions' (1998) 9 *European Journal of International Law* 278

'Reviewing the Difficulties of Codification: On Ago's Classification of Obligations of Means and Obligations of Result in Relation to State Responsibility' (1999) 10 *European Journal of International Law* 371–85

'International Law and Domestic (Municipal) Law', in *Max Planck Encyclopedia of Public International Law* (Oxford University Press 2011)

Dupuy R-J, 'Coutume Sage, Coutume Sauvage', in *La communauté internationale: mélanges offerts à Charles Rousseau* (Pedone 1974) 75–87

Duvic-Paoli L-A, 'The Status of the Right to Public Participation in International Environmental Law: An Analysis of the Jurisprudence' (2012) 23 *Yearbook of International Environmental Law* 80

'Prevention and the Anticipation of Risk(s) in International Environmental Law: A Multifaceted Norm', in M Ambrus, R Rayfuse and W Werner (eds), *Conceptions of Risk and the Regulation of Uncertainty in International Law* (Oxford University Press 2017) 141–60

'The Prevention Principle', in L Krämer and E Orlando (eds), *Principles of Environmental Law* (Elgar Encyclopedia of Environmental Law Series, IUCN/ Elgar forthcoming)

'Vigilance and Prevention', in S Forlati and M Mbengue (eds), *The Gabčíkovo-Nagymaros Judgment and its Contribution to the Development of International Law* (Cambridge University Press forthcoming)

Duvic-Paoli L-A and Dupuy P-M, 'The Polluter-Pays Principle', in A Tanzi et al. (eds), *The UNECE Convention on the Protection and Use of Transboundary Watercourses and International Lakes* (Brill/Martinus Nijhoff 2015) 176–95

Dzidzornu D, 'Four Principles in Marine Environment Protection: A Comparative Analysis' (1998) 29 *Ocean Development & International Law* 91

Elias O and Lim C, '"General Principles of Law", "Soft Law" and the Identification of International Law' (1997) 28 *Netherlands Yearbook of International Law* 3

Elferink A, 'Environmental Impact Assessment in Areas beyond National Jurisdiction' (2012) 27 *International Journal of Marine and Coastal Law* 449

Elkind J, 'Footnote to the Nuclear Test Cases: Abuse of Right – A Blind Alley for Environmentalists' (1976) 9 *Vanderbilt Journal of Transnational Law* 57

Epiney A, 'Environmental Impact Assessment', in *Max Planck Encyclopedia of Public International Law* (Oxford University Press 2009)

Epstein RA, 'The Harm Principle: And How It Grew' (1995) 45 *University of Toronto Law Journal* 369

Esposito R, 'The ICJ and the Future of Transboundary Harm Disputes: A Preliminary Analysis of the Case concerning Aerial Herbicide Spraying (*Ecuador v. Colombia*)' (2010) 1 *Pace International Law Review Online Companion* 1

Faure MG and Nollkaemper A, 'International Liability as an Instrument to Prevent and Compensate for Climate Change' (2007) 26 *Stanford Environmental Law Journal* 123

Fitzmaurice M, 'Liability for Environmental Damage Caused to the Global Commons' (1996) 5 *Review of European Community & International Environmental Law* 305

'Responsibility and Climate Change' (2010) 53 *German Yearbook of International Law* 89

Fitzmaurice M and Redgwell C, 'Environmental Non-Compliance Procedures and International Law' (2000) 31 *Netherlands Yearbook of International Law* 35

Foster C, 'The ILC Draft Articles on the Allocation of Loss in the Case of Transboundary Harm Arising Out of Hazardous Activities: Privatizing Risk?' (2005) 14 *Review of European Community & International Environmental Law* 265

Francioni F, 'International Human Rights in an Environmental Horizon' (2010) 21 *European Journal of International Law* 41

French D, 'A Reappraisal of Sovereignty in the Light of Global Environmental Concerns' (2001) 21 *Legal Studies* 376

'Environmental Dispute Settlement: The First (Hesitant) Signs of Spring?' (2006) 19 *Hague Yearbook of International Law* 3

'From the Depths: Rich Pickings of Principles of Sustainable Development and General International Law on the Ocean Floor – The Seabed Disputes Chambers 2011 Advisory Opinion' (2011) 26 *International Journal of Marine and Coastal Law* 525

'*Trail Smelter*', in C Miles and E Bjorge (eds), *Landmark Cases in Public International Law* (Hart 2018) 153–88

French D and Rajamani L, 'Climate Change and International Environmental Law: Musings on a Journey to Somewhere' (2013) 25 *Journal of Environmental Law* 437

Fuentes X, 'The Criteria for the Equitable Utilization of International Rivers' (1996) 67 *British Yearbook of International Law* 337

Gaines S, 'Taking Responsibility for Transboundary Environmental Effects' (1990) 14 *Hastings International and Comparative Law Review* 781

Gaja G, 'The Relations between the European Union and Its Member States from the Perspective of the ILC Articles on Responsibility of International Organizations' (2013) *SHARES Research Paper* 25, available at www.sharesproject.nl

Garth B, 'The Stockholm Conference: A Synopsis and Analysis' (1973) 8 *Stanford Journal of International Studies* 31

Gess K, 'Permanent Sovereignty over Natural Resources' (1964) 13 *International and Comparative Law Quarterly* 398

Gjerde K, 'Challenges to Protecting the Marine Environment beyond National Jurisdiction' (2012) 27 *International Journal of Marine and Coastal Law* 839

Goldie LFE, 'Liability for Damage and the Progressive Development of International Law' (1965) 14 *International and Comparative Law Quarterly* 1189

'International Principles of Responsibility for Pollution' (1970) 9 *Columbia Journal of Transnational Law* 283

Goldmann M, 'Principles in International Law as Rational Reconstructions. A Taxonomy' *SSRN Scholarly Paper*, available at http://papers.ssrn.com/abstract=2442027

Goodrich C, 'The United Nations Conference on Resources' (1951) 5 *International Organization* 48

Gourgourinis A, 'General/Particular International Law and Primary/Secondary Rules: Unitary Terminology of a Fragmented System' (2011) 22 *European Journal of International Law* 993

Gupta J and Sanchez N, 'The Common But Different Responsibility (CBDR) Principle Elaborated in Relation to Other Principles of Law', in MC Bassiouni et al. (eds), *The Global Community Yearbook of International Law and Jurisprudence, Global Trends: Law, Policy and Justice. Essays in Honour of Professor Giuliana Ziccardi Capaldo* (Oxford University Press 2013) 23–39

Hafner-Burton EM, 'Sticks and Stones: Naming and Shaming the Human Rights Enforcement Problem' (2008) 62 *International Organization* 689

Hafner G and Pearson H, 'Environmental Issues in the Work of the International Law Commission' (2001) 11 *Yearbook of International Environmental Law* 3

Hahn R and Richards K, 'The Internationalization of Environmental Regulation' (1989) 30 *Harvard International Law Journal* 421

Handl G, 'Balancing of Interests and International Liability for the Pollution of International Watercourses: Customary Principles of Law Revisited' (1975) 13 *Canadian Yearbook of International Law* 156

'Territorial Sovereignty and the Problem of Transnational Pollution' (1975) 69 *American Journal of International Law* 50

'The Environment: International Rights and Responsibilities' (1980) 74 *Proceedings of the Annual Meeting of the American Society of International Law* 223

'Liability as an Obligation Established by a Primary Rule of International Law: Some Basic Reflections on the International Law Commission's Work' (1985) 16 *Netherlands Yearbook of International Law* 49

Hardin G, 'The Tragedy of the Commons' (1968) 162 *Science* 1243

Harrison J, 'Reflections on the Role of International Courts and Tribunals in the Settlement of Environmental Disputes and the Development of International Environmental Law' (2013) 25 *Journal of Environmental Law* 501

Heinzerling L, 'Environmental Law and the Present Future' (1998) 87 *Georgetown Law Journal* 2025

Henley K, 'Abstract Principles, Mid-Level Principles, and the Rule of Law' (1993) 12 *Law and Philosophy* 121

Hey E, 'The Precautionary Concept in Environmental Policy and Law: Institutionalizing Caution' (1991) 4 *Georgetown International Environmental Law Review* 303

Hinteregger M, 'Tort Law as an Instrument for the Prevention and Remediation of Catastrophic Harm', in A Herwig and M Simoncini (eds), *Law and the Management of Disasters: The Challenge of Resilience* (Routledge 2017) 208–23

Hoffman K, 'State Responsibility in International Law and Transboundary Pollution Injuries' (1976) 25 *International and Comparative Law Quarterly* 509

Humphreys S and Otomo Y, 'Theorising International Environmental Law', in A Orford and F Hoffman (eds), *The Oxford Handbook of International Legal Theory* (Oxford University Press 2016) 797–819

Hünemörder K, 'Environmental Crisis and Soft Politics: Détente and the Global Environment, 1968-1975', in JR McNeill and C Unger (eds), *Environmental Histories of the Cold War* (Cambridge University Press 2010) 257–76

Hyde JN, 'Permanent Sovereignty over Natural Wealth and Resources' (1956) 50 *American Journal of International Law* 854

Iluyomade BO, 'Scope and Content of a Complaint of Abuse of Right in International Law' (1975) 16 *Harvard International Law Journal* 47

Jacqmotte B, 'Definition and Assessment of the Concept of Harm in a Regime of Transboundary Harm Prevention' (1998) 3 *Austrian Review of International and European Law* 233

Jégouzo Y, 'Les principes généraux du droit de l'environnement' (1996) 12 *Revue française de droit administratif* 209

Jensen ET, 'State Obligations in Cyber Operations' (2014) 14 *Baltic Yearbook of International Law* 71

Johnson M, 'Liability for Environmental Damage in Antarctica: The Adoption of Annex VI to the Antarctic Environmental Protocol' (2006) 19 *Georgetown International Environmental Law Review* 33

Karimova T, 'Sustainable Development and Disasters', in S Breau and K Samuel (eds), *Research Handbook on Disasters and International Law* (Edward Elgar 2016) 177–203

Kelson J, 'State Responsibility and the Abnormally Dangerous Activity' (1972) 13 *Harvard International Law Journal* 197

Kennet W, 'The Stockholm Conference on the Human Environment' (1972) 48 *International Affairs* 33

Kindall MPA, 'UNCED and the Evolution of Principles of International Environmental Law' (1991) 25 *John Marshall Law Review* 19

Kiss A, 'La protection du Rhin contre la pollution : Etat actuel de la question' (1977) 23 *Annuaire français de droit international* 861

'La pollution du milieu marin' (1978) 38 *Heidelberg Journal of International Law* 902

'Dix ans après Stockholm – une décennie de droit international de l'environnement' (1982) 28 *Annuaire français de droit international* 784

'Emergence des principes généraux du droit international et d'une politique internationale de l'environnement', in I Rens (ed), *Le droit international face à l'éthique et à la politique de l'environnement* (Georg 1996) 19–35

'Abuse of Rights', in *Max Planck Encyclopedia of Public International Law* (Oxford University Press 2006)

Knox J, 'Myth and Reality of Transboundary Environmental Impact Assessment' (2002) 96 *American Journal of International Law* 291

'Diagonal Environmental Rights', in M Gibney and SI Skogly (eds), *Universal Human Rights and Extraterritorial Obligations* (University of Pennsylvania Press 2010) 82–103

Koivurova T, 'Due Diligence', in *Max Planck Encyclopedia of Public International Law* (Oxford University Press 2007)

Kornicker Uhlmann E, 'State Community Interests, *Jus Cogens* and Protection of the Global Environment' (1998) 11 *Georgetown International Environmental Law Review* 101

Koskenniemi M, 'Breach of Treaty or Non-Compliance? Reflections on the Enforcement of the Montreal Protocol' (1992) 3 *Yearbook of International Environmental Law* 123

Koyano M, 'The Significance of Procedural Obligations in International Environmental Law: Sovereignty and International Co-operation' (2011) 54 *Japanese Yearbook of International Law* 97

Kuhn A, 'The *Trail Smelter* Arbitration: United States and Canada' (1941) 35 *American Journal of International Law* 665

Kulovesi K, '"Make Your Own Special Song, Even If Nobody Else Sings Along": International Aviation Emissions and the EU Emissions Trading Scheme' (2011) 2 *Climate Law* 535

Lang W, 'UN Principles and International Environmental Law', (1999) 3 *Max Planck Yearbook of United Nations Law* 157

Lawson G, 'A Farewell to Principles' (1997) 82 *Iowa Law Review* 893

Leigh K, 'Liability for Damage to the Global Commons' (1992) 14 *Australian Yearbook of International Law* 129

Lester A, 'River Pollution in International Law' (1963) 57 *American Journal of International Law* 828

Lucchini L, 'Le principe de précaution en droit international de l'environnement: ombres plus que lumières' (1999) 45 *Annuaire français de droit international* 710

Lynham G, 'The *Sic Utere* Principle as Customary International Law: A Case of Wishful Thinking?' (1995) 2 *James Cook University Law Review* 172

Malone L, 'The Chernobyl Accident: A Case Study in International Law Regulating State Responsibility for Transboundary Nuclear Pollution' (1987) 12 *Columbia Journal of Environmental Law* 203

Marong A, 'From Rio to Johannesburg: Reflections on the Role of International Legal Norms in Sustainable Development' (2003) 16 *Georgetown International Environmental Law Review* 21

Marsden S, 'Determining Significance for EIA in International Environmental Law' (2017) 42 *Questions of International Law Zoom-in* 5

Mayer B, 'The Applicability of the Principle of Prevention to Climate Change: A Response to Zahar' (2015) 5 *Climate Law* 1

'The Relevance of the No-Harm Principle to Climate Change Law and Politics' (2016) 19 *Asia Pacific Journal of Environmental Law* 79

Mazzeschi RP, 'The Due Diligence Rule and the Nature of the International Responsibility of States' (1992) 35 *German Yearbook of International Law* 9

Mbengue MM, 'The South China Sea Arbitration: Innovations in Marine Environmental Fact-Finding and Due Diligence Obligations' (2016) *AJIL Unbound* 285

McCaffrey SC, 'The Harmon Doctrine One Hundred Years Later: Buried, Not Praised' (1996) 36 *Natural Resources Journal* 549

McIntyre O, 'The Emergence of an 'Ecosystem Approach' to the Protection of International Watercourses under International Law' (2004) 13 *Review of European, Comparative & International Environmental Law* 1

'The Protection of Freshwater Ecosystems Revisited: Towards a Common Understanding of the "Ecosystems Approach" to the Protection of Transboundary Water Resources' (2014) 23 *Review of European, Comparative & International Environmental Law* 88

Merrill T, 'Golden Rules for Transboundary Pollution' (1997) 46 *Duke Law Journal* 931

Michelson K, 'Rereading Trail Smelter' (1993) 31 *Canadian Yearbook of International Law* 219

Milkoreit M, 'Hot Deontology and Cold Consequentialism: An Empirical Exploration of Ethical Reasoning among Climate Change Negotiators' (2015) 30 *Climatic Change* 397

Miller R, 'Trail Smelter Arbitration', in *Max Planck Encyclopedia of Public International Law* (Oxford University Press 2007)

Misonne D, 'The Importance of Setting a Target: The EU Ambition of a High Level of Protection' (2015) 4 *Transnational Environmental Law* 11

Morgera E and Savaresi A, 'A Conceptual and Legal Perspective on the Green Economy' (2013) 22 *Review of European Community & International Environmental Law* 14

Nicoletti B, 'The Prevention of Natural and Man-Made Disasters: What Duties for States?', in A de Guttry, M Gestri and G Venturini (eds), *International Disaster Response Law* (Asser Press 2012)

Okowa P, 'Procedural Obligations in International Environmental Agreements' (1996) 67 *British Yearbook of International Law* 275

Orrego Vicuña F, 'Responsibility and Liability for Environmental Damage under International Law: Issues and Trends' (1997) 10 *Georgetown International Environmental Law Review* 279

Osiander A, 'Sovereignty, International Relations, and the Westphalian Myth' (2001) 55 *International Organization* 251

Ouedraogo A, 'La due diligence en droit international: de la règle de la neutralité au principe général' (2012) 42(2) *Revue générale de droit* 641

Palassis S, 'Beyond the Global Summits: Reflecting on the Environmental Principles of Sustainable Developments' (2011) 22 *Colorado Journal of International Environmental Law and Policy* 41

Pallemaerts M, 'International Environmental Law from Stockholm to Rio: Back to the Future?' (1992) 1 *Review of European Community & International Environmental Law* 254

Panjabi R, 'From Stockholm to Rio: A Comparison of the Declaratory Principles of International Environmental Law' (1992) 21 *Denver Journal of International Law and Policy* 215

Paradell-Trius L, 'Principles of International Environmental Law: An Overview' (2000) 9 *Review of European Community & International Environmental Law* 93

Parrish A, '*Trail Smelter* Deja Vu: Extraterritoriality, International Environmental Law, and the Search for Solutions to Canadian–US Transboundary Water Pollution Disputes' (2005) 85 *Boston University Law Review* 363

Pantazopoulos SE, 'Towards a Coherent Framework of Transnational Corporations' Responsibility in International Environmental Law' (2014) 24(1) *Yearbook of International Environmental Law* 131

Pauwelyn J, 'The End of Differential Treatment for Developing Countries? Lessons from the Trade and Climate Change Regimes' (2013) 22 *Review of European, Comparative & International Environmental Law* 29

Pavoni R, 'Mutual Supportiveness as a Principle of Interpretation and Law-Making: A Watershed for the "WTO-and-Competing Regimes" Debate?' (2010) 21 *European Journal of International Law* 649

Pedersen O, 'From Abundance to Indeterminacy: The Precautionary Principle and Its Two Camps of Custom' (2014) 3 *Transnational Environmental Law* 323

Peel J, 'Precaution: A Matter of Principle, Approach or Process?' (2004) 5 *Melbourne Journal of International Law* 483

Peiry K, 'Prior Informed Consent', in *Max Planck Encyclopedia of Public International Law* (Oxford University Press 2011)

Pellet A, 'Les Articles de la CDI sur la responsabilité de l'État pour fait internationalement illicite. Suite – et fin?' (2002) 48 *Annuaire français de droit international* 1

Perrez F, 'The Relationship between "Permanent Sovereignty" and the Obligation Not to Cause Transboundary Environmental Damage' (1996) 26 *Environmental Law* 1187

'The Efficiency of Cooperation: A Functional Analysis of Sovereignty' (1998) 15 *Arizona Journal of International and Comparative Law* 515

Perry S, 'Two Models of Legal Principles' (1997) 82 *Iowa Law Review* 787

Petaccio V, 'Water Pollution and the Future Law of the Sea' (1972) 21 *International and Comparative Law Quarterly* 15

Petersen N, 'The International Court of Justice and the Judicial Politics of Identifying Customary International Law' (2017) 28(2) *European Journal of International Law* 357

Picone P, 'Obblighi reciproci ed obblighi erga omnes' degli Stati nel campo della protezione internazionale dell'ambiente marino dall'inquinamento', in V Starace (ed), *Diritto internazionale e protezione dell'ambiente marino* (Giuffré 1983) 15, reproduced in P Picone, *Comunità internazionale e obblighi 'erga omnes': Studi critici di diritto internazionale* (3rd edn, Jovene Editore 2013) 1–127

'The Distinction between Jus Cogens and Obligations Erga Omnes', in E Cannizzaro (ed), *The Law of Treaties beyond the Vienna Convention* (Oxford University Press 2011) 411–24

Pisillo Mazzeschi R, 'The Due Diligence Rule and the Nature of the International Responsibility of States' (1992) 35 *German Yearbook of International Law* 9

'Closing Keynote Lecture: Coordination of Different Values in International Law', ESIL Annual Conference, 9 September 2017 (on file with the author)

Plakokefalos I, 'Prevention Obligations in International Environmental Law' (2012) 23 *Yearbook of International Environmental Law* 3

Quéneudec J-P, 'L'incidence de l'affaire du Torrey Canyon sur le droit de la mer' (1968) 14 *Annuaire français de droit international* 701

Rajamani L, 'The Changing Fortune of Differential Treatment in the Evolution of International Environmental Law' (2012) 88 *International Affairs* 605

Rayfuse R, 'Precaution and the Protection of Marine Biodiversity in Areas Beyond National Jurisdictions' (2012) 27 *International Journal of Marine and Coastal Law* 773

Raz J, 'Legal Principles and the Limits of Law' (1972) 81 *Yale Law Journal* 823

Read JE, 'The Trail Smelter Dispute' (1963) 1 *Canadian Yearbook of International Law* 213

Redgwell C, 'The Wrong Trousers: State Responsibility and International Environmental Law', in M Evans and P Koutrakos (eds), *The International Responsibility of the European Union. European and International Perspectives* (Hart 2013) 257–74

Reeve R, 'Wildlife Trade, Sanctions and Compliance: Lessons from the CITES Regime' (2006) 82 *International Affairs* 881

Renzulli I, 'A Critical Reflection on the Conceptual and Legal Foundations of the Duty to Prevent Torture' (2016) 20(8) *International Journal of Human Rights* 1244

Rieu-Clarke A, 'Notification and Consultation on Planned Measures concerning International Watercourses: Learning Lessons from the Pulp Mills and Kishenganga Cases' (2014) 24(1) *Yearbook of International Environmental Law* 102

Rubin A, 'Pollution by Analogy: The Trail Smelter Arbitration' (1970) 50 *Oregon Law Review* 259

Ruvebana E and Brus M, 'Before It's Too Late: Preventing Genocide by Holding the Territorial State Responsible for Not Taking Preventive Action' (2015) 62 *Netherlands International Law Review* 25

Sachariew K, 'The Definition of Thresholds of Tolerance for Transboundary Environmental Injury under International Law: Development and Present Status' (1990) 37 *Netherlands International Law Review* 193

'Promoting Compliance with International Environmental Legal Standards: Reflections on Monitoring and Reporting Mechanisms' (1991) 2 *Yearbook of International Environmental Law* 31

Sand PH, 'UNCED and the Development of International Environmental Law' (1992) 8 *Journal of Natural Resources & Environmental Law* 209

'International Environmental Law after Rio' (1993) 4 *European Journal of International Law* 377

'The Evolution of Transnational Environmental Law: Four Cases in Historical Perspective' (2012) 1 *Transnational Environmental Law* 183

'Enforcing CITES: The Rise and Fall of Trade Sanctions' (2013) 22 *Review of European, Comparative & International Environmental Law* 251

Sands P, 'The Environment, Community and International Law' (1989) 30 *Harvard International Law Journal* 393

'The Greening of International Law: Emerging Principles and Rules' (1993) 1 *Indiana Journal of Global Legal Studies* 293

'International Law in the Field of Sustainable Development' (1994) 65 *British Yearbook of International Law* 303

Schachter O, 'The Emergence of International Environmental Law' (1991) 44 *Journal of International Affairs* 457

Schlesinger RB, 'Research on the General Principles of Law Recognized by Civilized Nations' (1957) 51 *American Journal of International Law* 734

Schneider J, 'State Responsibility for Environmental Protection and Preservation: Ecological Unities and a Fragmented World Public Order' (1975) 2 *Yale Studies in World Public Order* 32

Schrijver N, 'The Changing Nature of State Sovereignty' (2000) 70 *British Yearbook of International Law* 65

'The New Delhi Declaration of Principles of International Law Relating to Sustainable Development: Commentary', in M-C Cordonier Segger and C Weeramantry (eds), *Sustainable Justice: Reconciling Economic, Social and Environmental Law* (Martinus Nijhoff 2005) 549–60

'Natural Resources, Permanent Sovereignty Over', in *Max Planck Encyclopedia of Public International Law* (Oxford University Press 2008)

Schwarte C, 'Environmental Concerns in the Adjudication of the International Tribunal for the Law of the Sea' (2003) 16 *Georgetown International Environmental Law Review* 421

Schwarte C and Frank W, 'The International Law Association's Legal Principles on Climate Change and Climate Liability under Public International Law' (2014) 4 *Climate Law* 201

Schwabach A, 'The Sandoz Spill: The Failure of International Law to Protect the Rhine from Pollution' (1989) 16 *Ecology Law Quarterly* 443

Scotford E, 'Mapping the Article 174(2) Case Law: A First Step to Analysing Community Environmental Principles' (2008) 8 *Yearbook of European Environmental Law* 1
Scott J and Rajamani L, 'EU Climate Change Unilateralism' (2012) 23 *European Journal of International Law* 469
Scovazzi T, 'State Responsibility for Environmental Harm' (2002) 12 *Yearbook of International Environmental Law* 43
Shuppert F, 'Beyond the National Resource Privilege: Towards an International Court of the Environment' (2014) 6 *International Theory* 68
Sohn L, 'The Stockholm Declaration on the Human Environment' (1973) 14 *Harvard International Law Journal* 423
Soljan L, 'The General Obligation to Prevent Transboundary Harm and Its Relation to Four Key Environmental Principles' (1998) 3 *Austrian Review of International and European Law* 209
Springer AL, 'Towards a Meaningful Concept of Pollution in International Law' (1977) 26 *International and Comparative Law Quarterly* 531
Strasser J, 'Preventing Pollution' (1997) 8 *Fordham Environmental Law Review* 1
Sunstein C, 'Two Conceptions of Irreversible Environmental Harm' (2008) *University of Chicago Public Law Working Paper No 218*, available at http://papers.ssrn.com/sol3/papers.cfm?abstract_id=1133164
Talmon S, 'Determining Customary International Law: The ICJ's Methodology between Induction, Deduction and Assertion' (2015) 26(2) *European Journal of International Law* 417
Tapper C, 'A Note on Principles' (1971) 34 *Modern Law Review* 628
Taylor GDS, 'The Content of the Rule against Abuse of Rights in International Law' (1972) 46 *British Yearbook of International Law* 323
Timoshenko A, 'The Problem of Preventing Damage to the Environment in National and International Law' (1988) 5 *Pace International Law Review* 475
Tomka P, 'Custom and the International Court of Justice' (2013) 12(2) *The Law & Practice of International Courts and Tribunals* 195
Tractman J, 'The Crisis of International Law' (2011) 44(1) *Case Western Reserve Journal of International Law* 407
Treves T, 'Customary International Law', in *Max Planck Encyclopedia of Public International Law* (Oxford University Press 2006)
Trouwborst A, 'Prevention, Precaution, Logic and Law: The Relationship between the Precautionary Principle and the Preventative Principle in International Law and Associated Questions' (2009) 2 *Erasmus Law Review* 105
Tunk G, 'Is General International Law Customary Law Only?' (1993) 4 *European Journal of International Law* 534
Urs P, 'Are States Injured by Whaling in the Antarctic?' (2014) *Opinio Juris* Post, available at http://opiniojuris.org/2014/08/14/guest-post-states-injured-whaling-antarctic/
Utton A, 'Which Rule Should Prevail in International Water Disputes: That of Reasonableness or That of No Harm' (1996) 36 *Natural Resources Journal* 635
Valencia-Ospina E, 'The International Court of Justice and International Environmental Law' (1994) 2 *Asian Yearbook of International Law* 1
Van der Burg W, 'The Importance of Ideals' (1997) 31 *Journal of Value Inquiry* 23

Vessey J, 'The Principle of Prevention in International Law' (1998) 3 *Austrian Review of International and European Law* 181

Viñuales JE, 'The Contribution of the International Court of Justice to the Development of International Environmental Law: A Contemporary Assessment' (2008) 32 *Fordham International Law Journal* 232

'Legal Techniques for Dealing with Scientific Uncertainty: The Contribution of International Environmental Law' (2010) 43 *Vanderbilt Journal of Transnational Law* 437

'Managing Abidance by Standards for the Protection of the Environment', in A Cassese (ed), *Realizing Utopia* (Oxford University Press 2012) 326–39

'The Rise and Fall of Sustainable Development' (2013) 23 *Review of European, Comparative & International Environmental Law*

'A Human Rights Approach to Extraterritorial Environmental Protection? An Assessment', in N Bhuta (ed), *The Frontiers of Human Rights* (Oxford University Press 2016) 177–222

'La Protección Ambiental en el Derecho Consuetudinario Internacional' (2017) 69 *Revista Española de Derecho Internacional* 71

Virally M, 'Vers un droit international du développement' (1965) *Annuaire français de droit international* 3

'Le rôle des "principes" dans le développement du droit international', in M Virally (ed), *Le droit international en devenir: essais écrits au fil des ans* (Presses universitaires de France 1990) 195–212

Voigt C, 'Equity in the 2015 Climate Agreement. Lessons from Differential Treatment in Multilateral Environmental Agreements' (2014) 4 *Climate Law* 50

Waldron J, 'The Need for Legal Principles' (1996) 82 *Iowa Law Review* 857

Weil P, 'Towards Relative Normativity in International Law?' (1983) 77 *American Journal of International Law* 413

Werner W, 'Responding to the Undesired: State Responsibility, Risk Management and Precaution' (2005) 36 *Netherlands Yearbook of International Law* 57

Williams S, 'Public International Law Governing Transboundary Pollution' (1983) 13 *University of Queensland Law Journal* 112

Wirth D, 'The Rio Declaration on Environment and Development: Two Steps Forward and One Back, or Vice Versa' (1994) 29 *Georgia Law Review* 599

Wöbse A-K, 'Oil on Troubled Waters? Environmental Diplomacy in the League of Nations' (2008) 32 *Diplomatic History* 519

'"The World after All Was One": The International Environmental Network of UNESCO and IUPN, 1945–1950' (2011) 20 *Contemporary European History* 331

Wolfrum R, 'Purposes and Principles of International Environmental Law' (1990) 33 *German Yearbook of International Law* 308

'General International Law (Principles, Rules and Standards)', in *Max Planck Encyclopedia of Public International Law* (Oxford University Press 2010)

Wouters P, 'An Assessment of Recent Developments in International Watercourse Law Through the Prism of the Substantive Rules Governing Use Allocation' (1996) 36 *Natural Resources Journal* 417

Wouters J, Chané A-L, 'Multinational Corporations in International Law', *Working Paper No.* 129 (Leuven Centre for Global Governance Studies December 2013), available at https://ghum.kuleuven.be/ggs/publications/working_papers.html

Wróblewski J, 'Principles, Values, and Rules in Legal Decision-Making and the Dimensions of Legal Rationality' (1990) 3 *Ratio Juris* 100
Wynne B, 'Uncertainty and Environmental Learning: Reconceiving Science and Policy in the Preventive Paradigm' (1992) 2 *Global Environmental Change* 111
Young M and Rioseco Sullivan S, 'Evolution Through the Duty to Cooperate: Implications of the Whaling Case at the International Court of Justice' (2015) 16 *Melbourne Journal of International Law* 311
Zahar A, 'Mediated versus Cumulative Environmental Damage and the International Law Association's Legal Principles on Climate Change' (2014) 4 *Climate Law* 217
'Methodological Issues in Climate Law' (2015) 5 *Climate Law* 25
Zeidan S, 'The Procedural Rules and Obligations Under International Law for Construction of a Nuclear Installation: Prevention and Reduction of Environmental Damage' (2011) 23 *Georgetown International Environmental Law Review* 263

Index